Liberty AND Order

Liberty AND Order

THE FIRST AMERICAN
PARTY STRUGGLE

Edited and with a Preface
by Lance Banning

LIBERTY FUND
Indianapolis

This book is published by Liberty Fund, Inc., a foundation established to encourage study of the ideal of a society of free and responsible individuals.

𒈬𒉺𒄄

The cuneiform inscription that serves as our logo and as the design motif for our endpapers is the earliest-known written appearance of the word "freedom" (*amagi*), or "liberty." It is taken from a clay document written about 2300 B.C. in the Sumerian city-state of Lagash.

Cover photo: Statuary Hall in the U.S. Capitol. ©Michael Freeman/CORBIS

Printed in the United States of America
08 07 06 05 04 C 5 4 3 2 I
08 07 06 05 04 P 5 4 3 2 I

Library of Congress Cataloging-in-Publication Data
Liberty and order: the first American party struggle/edited and with a preface by Lance Banning.
    p.   cm.
Includes bibliographical references (p.) and index.
ISBN 0-86597-417-9 (alk. paper)—ISBN 0-86597-418-7 (pbk.: alk. paper)
1. United States—Politics and government—1783–1865—Sources. 2. Political science—United States—History.
3. Federal Party (U.S.) 4. Republican Party (U.S.: 1792–1828)
I. Banning, Lance, 1942–
JK116.L53   2004
324.2732′2—dc21
2003054571

Liberty Fund, Inc.
8335 Allison Pointe Trail, Suite 300
Indianapolis, Indiana 46250-1684

To David, Paul, and the others

Contents

III   The French Revolution and the People   *139*

Preface

Within three years of the inauguration of the new federal Constitution, America's revolutionary leaders divided bitterly over the policies most appropriate for the infant nation. Within five years, two clashing groups were winning thousands of ordinary voters to their side. Within a decade, the collision had resulted in a full-blown party war.

There has never been another struggle like it. These were the first true parties in the history of the world—the first, that is, to mobilize and organize a large proportion of a mass electorate for a national competition. More than that, these parties argued at a depth and fought with a ferocity that has never been repeated. The Federalists and the Jeffersonian Republicans—the friends of order and the friends of liberty as they sometimes called themselves—were both convinced that more than office, more than clashing interests, and more, indeed, than even national policy in the ordinary sense were fundamentally at stake in their quarrel. Their struggle, they believed, was over nothing less profound than the sort of future the United States would have, the sort of nation America was to be. Each regarded the other as a serious threat to what was not yet called the American way. And from their own perspectives, both were right.

This first great party battle is, of course, completely fascinating for its own sake. Between the framing of the Constitution and the War of 1812, the generation that had made the world's first democratic revolution set about to put its revolutionary vision into practice on a national stage. This generation was a set of public men whose like has never been seen again. Without significant exception, they believed that the American experiment might well determine whether liberty would spread throughout the world or prove that men were too imperfect to be trusted with a government based wholly on elections. In an age of monarchies and aristocracies, they were experimenting with a governmental system—both republican and federal—unprecedented in the world. They had a never-tested and, in several respects, a quite unfinished Constitution to complete. They represented vastly differ-

ent regions, and they had profoundly different visions of the nature of a sound republic. To understand why they divided and how they created the first modern parties is a captivating object in itself. It is the more worthwhile because not even in the years preceding Independence or during the debate about adoption of the Constitution have better democratic statesmen argued more profoundly over concepts that are at the core of the American political tradition: popular self-governance, federalism, constitutionalism, liberty, and the rest. Perhaps they still have much to teach about the system they bequeathed us, along with entertaining stories of our roots.

No single volume could pretend to be a comprehensive sourcebook on the first party struggle. This one does, however, aim to make it possible to understand the grounds and development of the dispute. For this reason, it is fuller on the earlier years of the struggle, when positions were being defined, than on the later years, when the arguments had become more repetitive and routine. It focuses tightly on the dispute between the parties, not on national questions such as slavery, which seldom entered directly into the first party conflict, or on the development of constitutional jurisprudence in the courts. Although it tries, at several points, to capture something of the flavor of the grassroots conflict, it is weighted, more than some might like, with the writings of major national leaders. But this was very much a conflict that descended from the top, as major national figures developed their disagreements, took them to the public, and reached out for links with local politicians. Debates in Congress were probably the most widely read political publications of these years.

This is not primarily a work for scholars, who will find more-authoritative versions of the texts in sources such as those identified in the bibliography. Rather, to make the materials as accessible as possible, spelling and punctuation have been modernized, obvious printing errors or slips of the pen have been silently corrected, and abbreviations have been spelled out when that seemed useful.

So far as seemed possible, nevertheless, the documents are left to speak for themselves. Every volume of this sort must start with an editor's decisions, the most important of which are those excluding valuable materials because they would not fit between two covers. This, however, is as much or more of an intrusion than I have wanted to make. Editorial introductions are limited to providing identifications or essential context. Elisions are clearly indicated and seldom extensive. In every case, as with the light modernization, they have been done with conscientious concern for the author's thought and intent.

Several graduate students, two family members, one secretary, and a few undergraduates at the University of Kentucky provided materials for the collection or carried out the tedious job of typing the transcripts. Thanks are due to Todd Estes, Matt Schoenbachler, Colleen Murphy, Todd Hall, Jennifer Durben, Cheris Linebaugh, Lynn Hiler, JoAnne Shepler, and Clint and Lana Banning. A superb group of fifteen scholars from several disciplines devoted two days to a delightful discussion of a preliminary version of the volume at a Liberty Fund colloquium in Lexington in May 1998. In the process, they corrected some mistakes and made some valuable suggestions for additions. John Kaminski, Kenneth Bowling, and Norman Risjord reviewed the manuscript again. Finally, two of my students, Paul Douglas Newman and David Nichols, acted at different times as coresearchers and contributed essentially to making the project a quicker, fuller, and better one. Special thanks are due to them, and the volume is dedicated to them and their peers.

Lance Banning

PART I

Apprehensions

In his first address to the first session of the first federal Congress (contemporaries were sharply conscious of that litany of firsts) George Washington remarked that "The preservation of the sacred fire of liberty and the destiny of the republican model of government are justly considered as *deeply,* perhaps as *finally* staked on the experiment entrusted to the hands of the American people." Some eighteen months before, in the first number of *The Federalist,* Alexander Hamilton had said, "It seems to have been reserved to the people of this country . . . to decide the important question whether societies of men are really capable or not of establishing good government from reflection and choice, or whether they are forever destined to depend, for their political constitutions, on accident and force." By April 1789, when Washington delivered his inaugural address, supporters of the infant Constitution could be hopeful that the recent reconstruction of the federal system would permit the nation to fulfill its revolutionary aspirations. Washington was the unanimous selection of the first electoral college, and Washington's extraordinary reputation was sufficient by itself to assure the new government a fair trial by the people. Only two of twenty-two new senators had opposed the Constitution. Only ten of the newly chosen members of the House of Representatives had disapproved.

Nevertheless, as we are in the habit of forgetting, the victory of 1788 had been quite narrow. In Massachusetts and New York, majorities of voters had initially opposed the Constitution. Virginia had elected a convention that informed observers judged too close to call. In all these states, the Constitution would have been defeated, as it was in any case in North Carolina and Rhode Island, if its friends had not agreed that it might quickly be amended. Thus, when Washington addressed the first new Congress, no one could take anything for granted. The new regime, as one of its most able advocates observed, was utterly without example in the history of man; the members of the infant federal government were in a wilderness without a single precedent to guide them. The Constitution barely sketched the outlines of a working federal system. The problems that had wrecked the old Confederation remained to be resolved. Two of thirteen states were still outside the reconstructed Union. The apprehensions generated by that reconstruction had by no means disappeared. Indeed, those apprehensions, along with the fragility and novelty of the new federal system, would form the background and prepare the groundwork for the most profound political collision in our annals.

The Anti-Federalists

Letters from the Federal Farmer, No. 7

31 December 1787

Among the hundreds of pamphlets, newspaper articles, and published speeches opposing the new Constitution, a few were judged especially outstanding and have earned enduring fame. Among these, certainly, are the *Letters from the Federal Farmer,* which were widely read in pamphlet form after appearing initially in the Poughkeepsie *Country Journal* between November 1787 and January 1788. The seventh number developed one of the deepest concerns of many opponents of the Constitution: that the people could not be adequately represented in a single national legislature and, as power gravitated increasingly into federal hands, would end up being ruled by a few great men.

Most recent authorities reject the traditional identification of the "Federal Farmer" as Virginia's Richard Henry Lee. Several suspect that the author may have been Melancton Smith, some of whose speeches in the New York ratifying convention contain close parallels to passages in the letters. But, whoever the author, his concern with an inadequate representation and the creation of a unitary or "consolidated" central government is necessary background for an understanding of the arguments that would divide the first American parties.

Dear Sir,

In viewing the various governments instituted by mankind, we see their whole force reducible to two principles— . . . force and persuasion. By the former men are compelled, by the latter they are drawn. We denominate a government despotic or free as the one or other principle prevails in it. Perhaps it is not possible for a government to be so despotic as not to operate persuasively on some of its subjects; nor is it in the nature of things, I conceive, for a government to be so free, or so supported by voluntary consent, as never to want force to compel obedience to the laws. In despotic governments one man, or a few men, independent of the people, generally make the laws, command obedience, and enforce it by the sword: one-fourth part of the people are armed and obliged to endure the fatigues of soldiers to oppress the others and keep them subject to the laws. In free governments the people, or their representatives, make the laws; their execution is principally the effect of voluntary consent and aid; the people respect the magistrate, follow their private pursuits, and enjoy the fruits of their labor with very small deductions for the public use. The body of the people must evidently prefer the latter species of government; and it can be only those few who may be well paid for the part they take in enforcing despotism that can, for a moment, prefer the former. Our true object is to give full efficacy to one principle, to arm persuasion on every side, and to render force as little necessary as possible. Persuasion is never dangerous, not even in despotic governments; but military force, if often applied internally, can never fail to destroy the love and confidence, and break the spirits, of the people, and to render it totally impracticable and unnatural for him or them who govern . . . to hold their places by the peoples' elections. . . .

The plan proposed will have a doubtful operation between the two principles; and whether it will preponderate towards persuasion or force is uncertain.

Government must exist—If the persuasive principle be feeble, force is infallibly the next resort. The moment the laws of Congress shall be disregarded they must languish, and the whole system be convulsed—that moment we must have recourse to this next resort, and all freedom vanish.

It being impracticable for the people to assemble to make laws, they must elect legislators and assign men to the different departments of the government. In the representative branch we must expect chiefly to collect the confidence of the people, and in it to find almost entirely the force of persuasion. In forming this branch, therefore, several important considerations must be attended to. It must possess abilities to discern the situation of the people and of public affairs, a disposition to sympathize with the people, and a capacity and inclination to make laws congenial to their circumstances and condition; it must possess the confidence and have the voluntary support of the people. . . .

A fair and equal representation is that in which the interests, feelings, opinions and views of the people are collected in such manner as they would be were the people all assembled. . . . [But] there is no substantial representation of the people provided for in [the new] government, in which the most essential powers, even as to the internal police of the country, are proposed to be lodged. . . . There ought to be *an increase of the numbers of representatives:* And . . . the elections of them ought to be better secured.

The representation is insubstantial and ought to be increased. In matters where there is much room for opinion, you will not expect me to establish my positions with mathematical certainty; you must only expect my observations to be candid and such as are well founded in the mind of the writer. I am in a field where doctors disagree; and as to genuine representation, though no feature in government can be more important, perhaps no one has been less understood, and no one has received so imperfect a consideration by political writers. The ephori in Sparta and the tribunes in Rome were but the shadow [of representation]; the representation in Great Britain is unequal and insecure. In America we have done more in establishing this important branch on its true principles than, perhaps, all the world besides; yet even here, I conceive, that very great improvements in representation may be made. In fixing this branch, the situation of the people must be surveyed and the number of representatives and forms of election apportioned to that situation. When we find a numerous people settled in a fertile and extensive country, possessing equality, and few or none of them oppressed with riches or wants, it ought to be the anxious care of the constitution and laws to arrest them from national depravity and to preserve them in their happy condition. A virtuous people make just laws, and good laws tend to preserve unchanged a virtuous people. A virtuous and happy people, by laws uncongenial to their characters, may easily be gradually changed into servile and depraved creatures. Where the people, or their representatives, make the laws, it is probable they will generally be fitted to the national character and circumstances, unless the representation be partial and the imperfect substitute of the people. [Although] the people may be electors, if the representation be so formed as to give one or more of the natural classes of men in the society an undue ascendancy over the others, it is imperfect; the former will gradually become masters and the latter slaves. It is the first of all among the political balances to preserve in its proper station each of these classes. We talk of balances in the legislature and among the departments of government; we ought to carry them to the body of the people. . . . I have been sensibly struck with a sentence in the Marquis Beccaria's treatise: this sentence was quoted by Congress in 1774, and is as follows:—"In every society there is an effort continually tending to confer on one part the height of power and happiness and to reduce the others to the extreme of weakness and misery; the intent of good laws is to oppose this effort and to diffuse their influence universally and equally." Add to this Montesquieu's opinion that "in a free state every man who is supposed to be a free agent ought to be concerned in his own government; therefore, the legislative should reside in the whole body of the people, or their representatives." It is extremely clear that these writers had in view the several orders of men in society, which we call aristocratical, democratical, mercantile, mechanic, etc., and perceived the efforts they are constantly, from interested and ambitious views, disposed to make to elevate themselves and oppress others. Each order must have a share in the business of legislation actually and efficiently. It is deceiving a people to tell them they are electors and can choose their legislators if they cannot, in the nature of things, choose men from among themselves and genuinely like themselves. . . . To set this matter in a proper point of view, we must form some general ideas and descriptions of the different classes of men, as they may be divided by occupations and politically. The first class is the aristocratical. There are three kinds of aristocracy spoken of in this country. The first is a constitutional one, which does not exist in the United States in our common acceptation of the word. Montesquieu, it is true, observes, that where a part of the persons in a society, for want of property, age, or moral character, are excluded any share in the government, the others, who alone are the constitutional electors and elected, form this aristocracy; this, according to him, exists in each of the United States, where a considerable number of persons, as all convicted of crimes, under age, or not possessed of certain property, are excluded any share in the government. The second is an aristocratic faction: a junto of unprincipled men, often distinguished for their wealth or abilities, who combine together and make their object their private interests and aggrandizement. . . . The third is the natural aristocracy; this term we use to designate a respectable order of men, the line between whom and the natural democracy is in some degree arbitrary; we may place men on one side of this line which others may place on the other, and in all disputes between the few and the many, a considerable number are wavering and uncertain themselves on which side they are or ought to be. In my idea of our natural aristocracy in the United States, I include about four or five thousand men; and among these I reckon those who have been placed in the offices of governors, of members of Congress, and state senators generally, in the principal officers of Congress, of the army and militia, the superior judges, the most eminent professional men, etc., and men of large property. The other persons and orders in the community form the natural democracy; this includes in general the yeomanry, the subordinate officers, civil and military, the fishermen, mechanics and traders, many of the merchants and professional men. It is easy to perceive that men of these two classes, the aristocratical and democratical, with views equally honest, have sentiments widely different, especially respecting public and private expenses, salaries, taxes, etc. Men of the first class associate more extensively, have a high sense of honor, possess abilities, ambition, and general knowledge; men of the second class are not so much used to combining great objects; they possess less ambition and a larger share of honesty; their dependence is principally on middling and small estates, industrious pursuits, and hard labor, while that of the former is principally on the emoluments of large estates and of the chief offices of government. Not only the efforts of these two great parties are to be balanced, but other interests and parties also, which do not always oppress each other merely for want of power and for fear of the consequences. Though they, in fact, mutually depend on each other, yet such are their general views that the merchants alone would never fail to make laws favorable to themselves and oppressive to the farmers, etc. The farmers alone would act on like principles. The former would tax the land, the latter the trade. The manufacturers are often disposed to contend for monopolies, buyers make every exertion to lower prices, and sellers to raise them; men who live by fees and salaries endeavor to raise them, and the part of the people who pay them endeavor to lower them; the public creditors to augment taxes and the people at large to lessen them. Thus, in

every period of society, and in all the transactions of men, we see parties verifying the observation made by the Marquis; and those classes which have not their sentinels in the government, in proportion to what they have to gain or lose, most infallibly [will] be ruined.

Efforts among parties are not merely confined to property; they contend for rank and distinctions; all their passions in turn are enlisted in political controversies. Men, elevated in society, are often disgusted with the changeableness of the democracy, and the latter are often agitated with the passions of jealousy and envy. The yeomanry possess a large share of property and strength, are nervous and firm in their opinions and habits. The mechanics of towns are ardent and changeable, honest and credulous; they are inconsiderable for numbers, weight and strength, not always sufficiently stable for the supporting free governments. The fishing interest partakes partly of the strength and stability of the landed and partly of the changeableness of the mechanic interest. As to merchants and traders, they are our agents in almost all money transactions, give activity to government, and possess a considerable share of influence in it. It has been observed by an able writer that frugal industrious merchants are generally advocates for liberty. It is an observation, I believe, well founded, that the schools produce but few advocates for republican forms of government; gentlemen of the law, divinity, physic, etc. probably form about a fourth part of the people; yet their political influence, perhaps, is equal to that of all other descriptions of men; if we may judge from the appointments to Congress, the legal characters will often, in a small representation, be the majority; but the more representatives are increased, the more of the farmers, merchants, etc. will be found to be brought into the government.

These general observations will enable you to discern what I intend by different classes and the general scope of my ideas when I contend for uniting and balancing their interests, feelings, opinions, and views in the legislature; we may not only so unite and balance these as to prevent a change in the government by the gradual exaltation of one part to the depression of others, but we may derive many other advantages from the combination and full representation. A small representation can never be well informed as to the circumstances of the people; the members of it must be too far removed from the people, in general, to sympathize with them, and too few to communicate with them. A representation must be extremely imperfect where the representatives are not circumstanced to make the proper communications to their constituents, and where the constituents in turn cannot, with tolerable convenience, make known their wants, circumstances, and opinions to their representatives. Where there is but one representative to 30,000 or 40,000 inhabitants, it appears to me, he can only mix and be acquainted with a few respectable characters among his constituents; even double the federal representation, and then there must be a very great distance between the representatives and the people in general represented. On the proposed plan, the state of Delaware, the city of Philadelphia, the state of Rhode Island, the province of Maine, the county of Suffolk in Massachusetts will have one representative each; there can be but little personal knowledge, or but few communications, between him and the people at large of either of those districts. It has been observed that mixing only with the respectable men, he will get the best information and ideas from them; he will also receive impressions favorable to their purposes particularly. Many plausible shifts have been made to divert the mind from dwelling on this defective representation. . . .

Could we get over all our difficulties respecting a balance of interests and party efforts to raise some and oppress others, the want of sympathy, information, and intercourse between the representatives and the people, an insuperable difficulty will still remain. I mean the constant liability of a small number of representatives to private combinations. The tyranny of the one or the licentiousness of the multitude are, in my mind, but small evils, compared with the factions of the few. It is a consideration well worth pursuing how far this house of representatives will be liable to be formed into private juntos, how far influenced by expectations of appointments and offices, how far liable to be managed by the president and senate, and how far the people will have confidence in them. . . .

"Brutus," Essay II

1 November 1787

Addressed to "The People of the State of New York," the essays of "Brutus" appeared in Thomas Greenleaf's *New York Journal* between October 1787 and April 1788, contemporaneously with

the appearance of *The Federalist,* whose authors sometimes engaged "Brutus" in direct debates. As is true of the "Federal Farmer," the authorship remains in doubt, although the candidate most often mentioned is Robert Yates, one of New York's three delegates to the Constitutional Convention. The second number was among the most able explanations of the most common anti-Federalist fear of all.

. . . When a building is to be erected which is intended to stand for ages, the foundation should be firmly laid. The constitution proposed to your acceptance is designed not for yourselves alone, but for generations yet unborn. The principles, therefore, upon which the social compact is founded, ought to have been clearly and precisely stated, and the most express and full declaration of rights to have been made—But on this subject there is almost an entire silence.

If we may collect the sentiments of the people of America from their own most solemn declarations, they hold this truth as self evident, that all men are by nature free. No one man, therefore, or any class of men, have a right, by the law of nature, or of God, to assume or exercise authority over their fellows. The origin of society then is to be sought, not in any natural right which one man has to exercise authority over another, but in the united consent of those who associate. The mutual wants of men at first dictated the propriety of forming societies; and when they were established, protection and defense pointed out the necessity of instituting government. In a state of nature every individual pursues his own interest; in this pursuit it frequently happened that the possessions or enjoyments of one were sacrificed to the views and designs of another; thus the weak were a prey to the strong, the simple and unwary were subject to impositions from those who were more crafty and designing. In this state of things, every individual was insecure; common interest therefore directed that government should be established, in which the force of the whole community should be collected, and under such directions as to protect and defend everyone who composed it. The common good, therefore, is the end of civil government, and common consent the foundation on which it is established. To effect this end, it was necessary that a certain portion of natural liberty should be surrendered, in order that what remained should be preserved. How great a proportion of natural freedom is necessary to be yielded by individuals, when they submit to government, I shall not now inquire. So much, however, must be given up as will be sufficient to enable those to whom the administration of the government is committed to establish laws for the promoting the happiness of the community, and to carry those laws into effect. But it is not necessary, for this purpose, that individuals should relinquish all their natural rights. Some are of such a nature that they cannot be surrendered. Of this kind are the rights of conscience, the right of enjoying and defending life, etc. Others are not necessary to be resigned in order to attain the end for which government is instituted. These, therefore, ought not to be given up. To surrender them would counteract the very end of government, to wit, the common good. From these observations it appears that, in forming a government on its true principles, the foundation should be laid in the manner I before stated, by expressly reserving to the people such of their essential natural rights as are not necessary to be parted with. The same reasons which at first induced mankind to associate and institute government will operate to influence them to observe this precaution. If they had been disposed to conform themselves to the rule of immutable righteousness, government would not have been requisite. It was because one part exercised fraud, oppression, and violence on the other that men came together and agreed that certain rules should be formed to regulate the conduct of all and the power of the whole community lodged in the hands of rulers to enforce an obedience to them. But rulers have the same propensities as other men; they are as likely to use the power with which they are vested for private purposes and to the injury and oppression of those over whom they are placed, as individuals in a state of nature are to injure and oppress one another. It is therefore as proper that bounds should be set to their authority as that government should have at first been instituted to restrain private injuries.

This principle, which seems so evidently founded in the reason and nature of things, is confirmed by universal experience. Those who have governed have been found in all ages ever active to enlarge their powers and abridge the public liberty. This has induced the people in all countries, where any sense of freedom remained, to fix barriers against the encroachments of their rulers. The country from which we have derived our origin is an eminent example of this. Their magna charta and bill of rights have long been the boast, as well as the security, of that nation. I need say no

more, I presume, to an American, than that this principle is a fundamental one in all the constitutions of our own states; there is not one of them but what is either founded on a declaration or bill of rights or has certain express reservation of rights interwoven in the body of them. From this it appears that, at a time when the pulse of liberty beat high and when an appeal was made to the people to form constitutions for the government of themselves, it was their universal sense that such declarations should make a part of their frames of government. It is therefore the more astonishing that this grand security to the rights of the people is not to be found in this constitution.

It has been said, in answer to this objection, that such declaration of rights, however requisite they might be in the constitutions of the states, are not necessary in the general constitution, because, "in the former case, everything which is not reserved is given, but in the latter the reverse of the proposition prevails, and everything which is not given is reserved." It requires but little attention to discover that this mode of reasoning is rather specious than solid. The powers, rights, and authority granted to the general government by this constitution are as complete, with respect to every object to which they extend, as that of any state government—It reaches to everything which concerns human happiness—Life, liberty, and property are under its control. There is the same reason, therefore, that the exercise of power in this case should be restrained within proper limits as in that of the state governments. To set this matter in a clear light, permit me to instance some of the articles of the bills of rights of the individual states, and apply them to the case in question.

For the security of life, in criminal prosecutions, the bills of rights of most of the states have declared that no man shall be held to answer for a crime until he is made fully acquainted with the charge brought against him; he shall not be compelled to accuse or furnish evidence against himself—The witnesses against him shall be brought face to face, and he shall be fully heard by himself or counsel. That it is essential to the security of life and liberty that trial of facts be in the vicinity where they happen. Are not provisions of this kind as necessary in the general government as in that of a particular state? The powers vested in the new Congress extend in many cases to life; they are authorized to provide for the punishment of a variety of capital crimes, and no restraint is laid upon them in its exercise, save only that "the trial of all crimes, except in cases of impeachment, shall be by jury; and such trial shall be in the state where the said crimes shall have been committed." No man is secure of a trial in the county where he is charged to have committed a crime; he may be brought from Niagara to New York or carried from Kentucky to Richmond for trial for an offense supposed to be committed. What security is there that a man shall be furnished with a full and plain description of the charges against him? That he shall be allowed to produce all proof he can in his favor? That he shall see the witnesses against him face to face, or that he shall be fully heard in his own defense by himself or counsel?

For the security of liberty it has been declared, "that excessive bail should not be required, nor excessive fines imposed, nor cruel or unusual punishments inflicted— That all warrants, without oath or affirmation, to search suspected places or seize any person, his papers or property, are grievous and oppressive."

These provisions are as necessary under the general government as under that of the individual states; for the power of the former is as complete to the purpose of requiring bail, imposing fines, inflicting punishments, granting search warrants, and seizing persons, papers, or property, in certain cases, as the other.

For the purpose of securing the property of the citizens, it is declared by all the states, "that in all controversies at law, respecting property, the ancient mode of trial by jury is one of the best securities of the rights of the people, and ought to remain sacred and inviolable."

Does not the same necessity exist of reserving this right, under this national compact, as in that of this state? Yet nothing is said respecting it. In the bills of rights of the states it is declared that a well regulated militia is the proper and natural defense of a free government— That as standing armies in time of peace are dangerous, they are not to be kept up, and that the military should be kept under strict subordination to and controlled by the civil power.

The same security is as necessary in this constitution, and much more so; for the general government will have the sole power to raise and to pay armies, and are under no control in the exercise of it; yet nothing of this is to be found in this new system.

I might proceed to instance a number of other rights which were as necessary to be reserved, such as, that elections should be free, that the liberty of the press should be held sacred; but the instances adduced are sufficient to prove that this argument is without foundation.—Besides, it is evident that the reason here assigned was not the true one why the framers of this constitution omitted a bill of rights; if it had been, they would not have made certain reservations while they totally omitted others of more importance. We find they have, in the 9th section of the 1st article, declared that the writ of habeas corpus shall not be suspended, unless in cases of rebellion—that no bill of attainder, or ex post facto law, shall be passed—that no title of nobility shall be granted by the United States, etc. If everything which is not given is reserved, what propriety is there in these exceptions? Does this constitution anywhere grant the power of suspending the habeas corpus, to make ex post facto laws, pass bills of attainder, or grant titles of nobility? It certainly does not in express terms. The only answer that can be given is that these are implied in the general powers granted. With equal truth it may be said that all the powers which the bills of right guard against the abuse of are contained or implied in the general ones granted by this constitution.

So far it is from being true that a bill of rights is less necessary in the general constitution than in those of the states, the contrary is evidently the fact.—This system, if it is possible for the people of America to accede to it, will be an original compact; and being the last, will, in the nature of things, vacate every former agreement inconsistent with it. For it being a plan of government received and ratified by the whole people, all other forms which are in existence at the time of its adoption must yield to it. This is expressed in positive and unequivocal terms in the 6th article, "That this constitution and the laws of the United States, which shall be made in pursuance thereof, and all treaties made, or which shall be made, under the authority of the United States, shall be the supreme law of the land; and the judges in every state shall be bound thereby, anything in the *constitution,* or laws of any state, *to the contrary* notwithstanding.

"The senators and representatives before-mentioned, and the members of the several state legislatures, and all executive and judicial officers, both of the United States, and of the several states, shall be bound, by oath or affirmation, to support this constitution."

It is therefore not only necessarily implied thereby, but positively expressed, that the different state constitutions are repealed and entirely done away so far as they are inconsistent with this, with the laws which shall be made in pursuance thereof, or with treaties made, or which shall be made, under the authority of the United States. Of what avail will the constitutions of the respective states be to preserve the rights of its citizens? Should they be pleaded, the answer would be, the Constitution of the United States, and the laws made in pursuance thereof, is the supreme law, and all legislatures and judicial officers, whether of the general or state governments, are bound by oath to support it. No privilege reserved by the bills of rights or secured by the state government can limit the power granted by this, or restrain any laws made in pursuance of it. It stands therefore on its own bottom, and must receive a construction by itself without any reference to any other— And hence it was of the highest importance that the most precise and express declarations and reservations of rights should have been made.

This will appear the more necessary when it is considered that not only the constitution and laws made in pursuance thereof, but all treaties made, or which shall be made, under the authority of the United States, are the supreme law of the land, and supersede the constitutions of all the states. The power to make treaties is vested in the president, by and with the advice and consent of two thirds of the senate. I do not find any limitation, or restriction, to the exercise of this power. The most important article in any constitution may therefore be repealed, even without a legislative act. Ought not a government vested with such extensive and indefinite authority to have been restricted by a declaration of rights? It certainly ought.

So clear a point is this that I cannot help suspecting that persons who attempt to persuade people that such reservations were less necessary under this constitution than under those of the states are willfully endeavoring to deceive, and to lead you into an absolute state of vassalage.

Amendments Recommended by the Several State Conventions

In several of the largest states, the Federalists were able to secure approval of the Constitution only by accepting a procedure pioneered in Massachusetts, where a majority of delegates elected to the state convention initially opposed the plan. Working with Governor John Hancock, supporters of the document insisted that it must be ratified without condition, but agreed that subsequent amendments might be recommended to the first new Congress or the other states, two-thirds of which could constitutionally demand another Constitutional Convention.

Amendments Proposed by the Virginia Convention

27 June 1788

That there be a Declaration or Bill of Rights asserting and securing from encroachment the essential and unalienable Rights of the People in some such manner as the following:

FIRST, That there are certain natural rights of which men, when they form a social compact, cannot deprive or divest their posterity, among which are the enjoyment of life and liberty, with the means of acquiring, possessing and protecting property, and pursuing and obtaining happiness and safety. SECOND, That all power is naturally vested in and consequently derived from the people; that magistrates, therefore, are their trustees and agents and at all times amenable to them. THIRD, That government ought to be instituted for the common benefit, protection and security of the people; and that the doctrine of non-resistance against arbitrary power and oppression is absurd, slavish, and destructive of the good and happiness of mankind. FOURTH, That no man or set of men are entitled to exclusive or separate public emoluments or privileges from the community but in consideration of public services; which, not being descendible, neither ought the offices of magistrate, legislator or judge, or any other public office to be hereditary. FIFTH, That the legislative, executive, and judiciary powers of government should be separate and distinct, and that the members of the two first may be restrained from oppression by feeling and participating the public burdens, they should, at fixed periods be reduced to a private station, return into the mass of the people, and the vacancies be supplied by certain and regular elections; in which all or any part of the former members to be eligible or ineligible as the rules of the Constitution of Government and the laws shall direct. SIXTH, That elections of representatives in the legislature ought to be free and frequent, and all men having sufficient evidence of permanent common interest with and attachment to the community ought to have the right of suffrage; and no aid, charge, tax or fee can be set, rated, or levied upon the people without their own consent, or that of their representatives so elected, nor can they be bound by any law to which they have not in like manner assented for the public good. SEVENTH, That all power of suspending laws or the execution of laws by any authority without the consent of the representatives of the people in the legislature is injurious to their rights, and ought not to be exercised. EIGHTH, That in all capital and criminal prosecutions, a man hath a right to demand the cause and nature of his accusation, to be confronted with the accusers and witnesses, to call for evidence and be allowed counsel in his favor, and to a fair and speedy trial by an impartial jury of his vicinage, without whose unanimous consent he cannot be found guilty (except in the government of the land and naval forces) nor can he be compelled to give evidence against himself. NINTH, That no freeman ought to be taken, imprisoned, or disseised of his freehold, liberties, privileges or franchises, or outlawed or exiled, or in any manner destroyed or deprived of his life, liberty or property but by the law of the land. TENTH, That every freeman restrained of his liberty is entitled to a remedy, to inquire into the lawfulness thereof, and to remove the same, if unlawful, and that such remedy ought not to be denied nor delayed. ELEVENTH, That in controversies respecting property, and in suits between man and man, the ancient trial by jury is one of the greatest securities to the rights of the people, and ought to remain sacred and inviolable. TWELFTH, That every freeman ought to find a certain remedy by recourse to the laws for all injuries and wrongs he may receive in his person, property or character. He ought to obtain right and justice freely without sale, completely and without denial, promptly and without delay, and that all establishments or regulations contravening these rights, are oppressive and unjust.

THIRTEENTH, That excessive bail ought not to be required, nor excessive fines imposed, nor cruel and unusual punishments inflicted. FOURTEENTH, That every freeman has a right to be secure from all unreasonable searches and seizures of his person, his papers, and his property; all warrants, therefore, to search suspected places or seize any freeman, his papers or property, without information upon oath (or affirmation of a person religiously scrupulous of taking an oath) of legal and sufficient cause, are grievous and oppressive; and all general warrants to search suspected places, or to apprehend any suspected person, without specially naming or describing the place or person, are dangerous and ought not to be granted. FIFTEENTH, That the people have a right peaceably to assemble together to consult for the common good, or to instruct their representatives; and that every freeman has a right to petition or apply to the legislature for redress of grievances. SIXTEENTH, That the people have a right to freedom of speech, and of writing and publishing their sentiments; but the freedom of the press is one of the greatest bulwarks of liberty and ought not to be violated. SEVENTEENTH, That the people have a right to keep and bear arms; that a well regulated militia composed of the body of the people trained to arms is the proper, natural, and safe defense of a free state. That standing armies in time of peace are dangerous to liberty, and therefore ought to be avoided, as far as circumstances and protection of the community will admit; and that in all cases the military should be under strict subordination to and governed by the civil power. EIGHTEENTH, That no Soldier in time of peace ought to be quartered in any house without the consent of the owner, and in time of war in such manner only as the laws direct. NINETEENTH, That any person religiously scrupulous of bearing arms ought to be exempted upon payment of an equivalent to employ another to bear arms in his stead. TWENTIETH, That religion or the duty which we owe to our Creator, and the manner of discharging it, can be directed only by reason and conviction, not by force or violence, and therefore all men have an equal, natural and unalienable

right to the free exercise of religion according to the dictates of conscience, and that no particular religious sect or society ought to be favored or established by law in preference to others.

AMENDMENTS TO THE BODY OF THE CONSTITUTION

FIRST, That each State in the Union shall respectively retain every power, jurisdiction and right which is not by this Constitution delegated to the Congress of the United States or to the departments of the Federal Government.

SECOND, That there shall be one representative for every thirty thousand, according to the enumeration or Census mentioned in the Constitution, until the whole number of representatives amounts to two hundred; after which that number shall be continued or increased as the Congress shall direct, upon the principles fixed by the Constitution, by apportioning the representatives of each state to some greater number of people from time to time as population increases. THIRD, When Congress shall lay direct taxes or excises, they shall immediately inform the executive power of each state of the quota of such state according to the Census herein directed, which is proposed to be thereby raised; And if the legislature of any state shall pass a law which shall be effectual for raising such quota at the time required by Congress, the taxes and excises laid by Congress shall not be collected, in such state. FOURTH, That the members of the Senate and House of Representatives shall be ineligible to, and incapable of holding, any civil office under the authority of the United States, during the time for which they shall respectively be elected. FIFTH, That the journals of the proceedings of the Senate and House of Representatives shall be published at least once in every year, except such parts thereof relating to treaties, alliances or military operations, as in their judgment require secrecy.

SIXTH, That a regular statement and account of the receipts and expenditures of all public money shall be published at least once in every year. SEVENTH, That no commercial treaty shall be ratified without the concurrence of two thirds of the whole number of the members of the Senate; and no treaty ceding, contracting, restraining or suspending the territorial rights or claims of the United States or any of them, or any of their rights or claims to fishing in the American Seas or navigating the American rivers shall be but in cases of the most urgent and extreme necessity, nor shall any such treaty be ratified without the concurrence of three fourths of the whole number of the members of both houses respectively.

EIGHTH, That no navigation law or law regulating commerce shall be passed without the consent of two thirds of the members present in both houses. NINTH, That no standing army or regular troops shall be raised or kept up in time of peace without the consent of two thirds of the members present in both houses. TENTH, That no soldier shall be enlisted for any longer term than four years, except in time of war, and then for no longer term than the continuance of the war. ELEVENTH, That each state respectively shall have the power to provide for organizing, arming and disciplining its own militia, whensoever Congress shall omit or neglect to provide for the same. That the militia shall not be subject to martial law except when in actual service in time of war, invasion, or rebellion; and when not in the actual service of the United States, shall be subject only to such fines, penalties, and punishments as shall be directed or inflicted by the laws of its own state. TWELFTH, That the exclusive power of legislation given to Congress over the Federal Town and its adjacent District and other places purchased or to be purchased by Congress of any of the states shall extend only to such regulations as respect the police and good government thereof. THIRTEENTH, That no person shall be capable of being President of the United States for more than eight years in any term of sixteen years. FOURTEENTH, That the judicial power of the United States shall be vested in one Supreme Court, and in such courts of Admiralty as Congress may from time to time ordain and establish in any of the different states: The judicial power shall extend to all cases in Law and Equity arising under treaties made, or which shall be made, under the authority of the United States; to all cases affecting ambassadors, other foreign ministers and consuls; to all cases of admiralty and maritime jurisdiction; to controversies to which the United States shall be a party; to controversies between two or more states, and between parties claiming lands under the grants of different states. In all cases affecting ambassadors, other foreign ministers and consuls, and those in which a state shall be a party, the Supreme Court shall have original jurisdiction; in all other cases before mentioned the Supreme Court shall have appellate jurisdiction as to matters of law only; except in

cases of equity, and of admiralty and maritime jurisdiction, in which the Supreme Court shall have appellate jurisdiction both as to law and fact, with such exceptions and under such regulations as the Congress shall make. But the judicial power of the United States shall extend to no case where the cause of action shall have originated before the ratification of this Constitution; except in disputes between states about their territory, disputes between persons claiming lands under the grants of different states, and suits for debts due to the United States. FIFTEENTH, That in criminal prosecutions no man shall be restrained in the exercise of the usual and accustomed right of challenging or excepting to the Jury. SIXTEENTH, That Congress shall not alter, modify or interfere in the times, places, or manner of holding elections for Senators and Representatives or either of them, except when the legislature of any state shall neglect, refuse or be disabled by invasion or rebellion to prescribe the same. SEVENTEENTH, That those clauses which declare that Congress shall not exercise certain powers be not interpreted in any manner whatsoever to extend the powers of Congress. But that they may be construed either as making exceptions to the specified powers where this shall be the case, or otherwise as inserted merely for greater caution. EIGHTEENTH, That the laws ascertaining the compensation to Senators and Representatives for their services be postponed in their operation until after the election of Representatives immediately succeeding the passing thereof; that excepted, which shall first be passed on the subject. NINETEENTH, That some tribunal other than the Senate be provided for trying impeachments of Senators. TWENTIETH, That the salary of a judge shall not be increased or diminished during his continuance in office otherwise than by general regulations of salary which may take place on a revision of the subject at stated periods of not less than seven years to commence from the time such salaries shall be first ascertained by Congress.

Ratification of the State of New York
26 July 1788

We, the delegates of the people of the state of New York, duly elected and met in Convention, having maturely considered the Constitution for the United States of America, agreed to on the 17th day of September, in the year 1787, by the Convention then assembled at Philadelphia, in the Commonwealth of Pennsylvania (a copy whereof preceded these presents), and having also seriously and deliberately considered the present situation of the United States,—Do declare and make known,—

That all power is originally vested in, and consequently derived from, the people, and that government is instituted by them for their common interest, protection, and security.

That the enjoyment of life, liberty, and the pursuit of happiness are essential rights, which every government ought to respect and preserve.

That the powers of government may be reassumed by the people whensoever it shall become necessary to their happiness; that every power, jurisdiction, and right which is not by the said Constitution clearly delegated to the Congress of the United States, to the departments of the government thereof, remains to the people of the several states, or to their respective state governments, to whom they may have granted the same; and that those clauses in the said Constitution which declare that Congress shall not have or exercise certain powers do not imply that Congress is entitled to any powers not given by the said Constitution; but such clauses are to be construed either as exceptions to certain specified powers, or as inserted merely for greater caution.

That the people have an equal, natural, and unalienable right freely and peaceably to exercise their religion, according to the dictates of conscience; and that no religious sect or society ought to be favored or established by law in preference to others.

That the people have a right to keep and bear arms; that a well-regulated militia, including the body of the people *capable of bearing arms,* is the proper, natural, and safe defense of a free state.

That the militia should not be subject to martial law, except in time of war, rebellion, or insurrection.

That standing armies, in time of peace, are dangerous to liberty, and ought not to be kept up, except in cases of necessity; and that at all times the military should be under strict subordination to the civil power.

That, in time of peace, no soldier ought to be quartered in any house without the consent of the owner, and in time of war only by the civil magistrate, in such manner as the laws may direct.

That no person ought to be taken, imprisoned, or disseized of his freehold, or be exiled, or deprived of his privileges, franchises, life, liberty, or property, but by due process of law.

That no person ought to be put twice in jeopardy of life or limb for one and the same offense; nor, unless in case of impeachment, be punished more than once for the same offense.

That every person restrained of his liberty is entitled to an inquiry into the lawfulness of such restraint, and to a removal thereof if unlawful; and that such inquiry or removal ought not to be denied or delayed, except when, on account of public danger, the Congress shall suspend the privilege of the writ of *habeas corpus.*

That excessive bail ought not to be required, nor excessive fines imposed, nor cruel or unusual punishments inflicted.

That (except in the government of the land and naval forces, and of the militia when in actual service, and in cases of impeachment) a presentment or indictment by a grand jury ought to be observed as a necessary preliminary to the trial of all crimes cognizable by the judiciary of the United States; and such trial should be speedy, public, and by an impartial jury of the county where the crime was committed; and that no person can be found guilty without the unanimous consent of such jury. But in cases of crimes not committed within any county of any of the United States, and in cases of crimes committed within any county in which a general insurrection may prevail or which may be in the possession of a foreign enemy, the inquiry and trial may be in such county as the Congress shall by law direct; which county, in the two cases last mentioned, should be as near as conveniently may be to that county in which the crime may have been committed;—and that, in all criminal prosecutions, the accused ought to be informed of the cause and nature of his accusation, to be confronted with his accusers and the witnesses against him, to have the means of producing his witnesses, and the assistance of counsel for his defense; and should not be compelled to give evidence against himself.

That the trial by jury, in the extent that it obtains by the common law of England, is one of the greatest securities to the rights of a free people, and ought to remain inviolate.

That every freeman has a right to be secure from all unreasonable searches and seizures of his person, his papers, or his property; and therefore, that all warrants to search suspected places, or seize any freeman, his papers, or property, without information, upon oath or affirmation, or sufficient cause, are grievous and oppressive; and that all general warrants (or such in which the place or person suspected are not particularly designated) are dangerous, and ought not to be granted.

That the people have a right peaceably to assemble together to consult for their common good, or to instruct their representatives, and that every person has a right to petition or apply to the legislature for redress of grievances.

That the freedom of the press ought not to be violated or restrained.

That there should be, once in four years, an election of the President and Vice-President, so that no officer who may be appointed by the Congress to act as President, in case of the removal, death, resignation, or inability of the President and Vice-President, can in any case continue to act beyond the termination of the period for which the last President and Vice-President were elected.

That nothing contained in the said Constitution is to be construed to prevent the legislature of any state from passing laws at its discretion, from time to time, to divide such state into convenient districts, and to apportion its representatives to and amongst such districts.

That the prohibition contained in the said Constitution against *ex post facto* laws extends only to laws concerning crimes.

That all appeals in causes determinable according to the course of the common law ought to be by writ of error, and not otherwise.

That the judicial power of the United States, in cases in which a state may be a party, does not extend to criminal prosecutions, or to authorize any suit by any person against a state.

That the judicial power of the United States, as to controversies between citizens of the same state, claiming lands under grants from different states, is not to be construed to extend to any other controversies between them, except those which relate to such lands, so claimed, under grants of different states.

That the jurisdiction of the Supreme Court of the United States, or of any other court to be instituted by the Congress, is not in any case to be increased, enlarged, or extended by any faction, collusion, or mere suggestion; and that no treaty is to be construed so to operate as to alter the Constitution of any state.

Under these impressions, and declaring that the rights aforesaid cannot be abridged or violated, and that the expla-

nations aforesaid are consistent with the said Constitution, and in confidence that the amendments which shall have been proposed to the said Constitution will receive an early and mature consideration,—We, the said delegates, in the name and in the behalf of the people of the state of New York, do, by these presents, assent to and ratify the said Constitution. In full confidence, nevertheless, that until a convention shall be called and convened for proposing amendments to the said Constitution, the militia of this state will not be continued in service out of this state for a longer term than six weeks, without the consent of the legislature thereof; that the Congress will not make or alter any regulation in this state respecting the times, places, and manner of holding elections for senators or representatives, unless the legislature of this state shall neglect or refuse to make laws or regulations for the purpose, or from any circumstance be incapable of making the same; and that, in those cases, such power will only be exercised until the legislature of this state shall make provision in the premises; that no excise will be imposed on any article of the growth, production, or manufacture of the United States, or any of them, within this state, ardent spirits excepted; and when the Congress will not lay direct taxes within this state, but when the moneys arising from the impost and excise shall be insufficient for the public exigencies, nor then, until Congress shall first have made a requisition upon this state to assess, levy, and pay the amount of such requisition, made agreeably to the census fixed in the said Constitution, in such way and manner as the legislature of this state shall judge best; but that in such case, if the state shall neglect or refuse to pay its proportion, pursuant to such requisition, then the Congress may assess and levy this state's proportion, together with interest, at the rate of six per centum per annum, from the time at which the same was required to be paid.

And the Convention do, in the name and behalf of the people of the state of New York, enjoin it upon their representatives in Congress to exert all their influence, and use all reasonable means, to obtain a ratification of the following amendments to the said Constitution, in the manner prescribed therein; and in all laws to be passed by the Congress in the meantime, to conform to the spirit of the said amendments, as far as the Constitution will admit.

That there shall be one representative for every thirty thousand inhabitants, according to the enumeration or census mentioned in the Constitution, until the whole number of representatives amounts to two hundred, after which that number shall be continued or increased, but not diminished, as the Congress shall direct, and according to such ratio as the Congress shall fix, in conformity to the rule prescribed for the apportionment of representatives and direct taxes.

That the Congress do not impose any excise on any article (ardent spirits excepted) of the growth, production, or manufacture of the United States, or any of them.

That Congress do not lay direct taxes but when the moneys arising from the impost and excise shall be insufficient for the public exigencies, nor then, until Congress shall first have made a requisition upon the states to assess, levy, and pay their respective proportions of such requisition, agreeably to the census fixed in the said Constitution, in such way and manner as the legislatures of the respective states shall judge best; and in such case, if any state shall neglect or refuse to pay its proportion, pursuant to such requisition, then Congress may assess and levy such state's proportion, together with interest at the rate of six per centum per annum, from the time of payment prescribed in such requisition.

That the Congress shall not make or alter any regulation, in any state, respecting the times, places, and manner of holding elections for senators and representatives, unless the legislature of such state shall neglect or refuse to make laws or regulations for the purpose, or from any circumstance be incapable of making the same, and then only until the legislature of such state shall make provision in the premises; provided that Congress may prescribe the time for the election of representatives.

That no persons, except natural-born citizens, or such as were citizens on or before the 4th day of July 1776, or such as held commissions under the United States during the war, and have at any time since the 4th day of July 1776, become citizens of one or other of the United States, and who shall be freeholders, shall be eligible to the places of President, Vice-President, or members of either House of the Congress of the United States.

That the Congress do not grant monopolies, or erect any company with exclusive advantages of commerce.

That no standing army or regular troops shall be raised, or kept up, in time of peace, without the consent of two thirds of the senators and representatives present in each house.

That no money be borrowed on the credit of the United States without the assent of two thirds of the senators and representatives present in each house.

That the Congress shall not declare war without the concurrence of two thirds of the senators and representatives present in each house.

That the privilege of the *habeas corpus* shall not, by any law, be suspended for a longer term than six months, or until twenty days after the meeting of the Congress next following the passing the act for such suspension.

That the right of Congress to exercise exclusive legislation over such district, not exceeding ten miles square, as may, by cession of a particular state and the acceptance of Congress, become the seat of government of the United States, shall not be so exercised as to exempt the inhabitants of such district from paying the like taxes, imposts, duties, and excises as shall be imposed on the other inhabitants of the state in which such district may be; and that no person shall be privileged within the said district from arrest for crimes committed, or debts contracted, out of the said district.

That the right of exclusive legislation with respect to such places as may be purchased for the erection of forts, magazines, arsenals, dock-yards, and other needful buildings shall not authorize the Congress to make any law to prevent the laws of the states, respectively, in which they may be, from extending to such places in all civil and criminal matters, except as to such persons as shall be in the service of the United States; nor to them with respect to crimes committed without such places.

That the compensation for the senators and representatives be ascertained by standing laws; and that no alteration of the existing rate of compensation shall operate for the benefit of the representatives until after a subsequent election shall have been had.

That the Journals of the Congress shall be published at least once a year, with the exception of such parts, relating to treaties or military operations, as, in the judgment of either house, shall require secrecy; and that both houses of Congress shall always keep their doors open during their sessions, unless the business may, in their opinion, require secrecy. That the yeas and nays shall be entered on the Journals whenever two members in either house may require it.

That no capitation tax shall ever be laid by Congress.

That no person be eligible as a senator for more than six years in any term of twelve years; and that the legislatures of the respective states may recall their senators, or either of them, and elect others in their stead, to serve the remainder of the time for which the senators so recalled were appointed.

That no senator or representative shall, during the time for which he was elected, be appointed to any office under the authority of the United States.

That the authority given to the executives of the states to fill up the vacancies of senators be abolished, and that such vacancies be filled by the respective legislatures.

That the power of Congress to pass uniform laws concerning bankruptcy shall only extend to merchants and other traders; and the states respectively may pass laws for the relief of other insolvent debtors.

That no person shall be eligible to the office of President of the United States a third time.

That the executive shall not grant pardons for treason, unless with the consent of the Congress; but may, at his discretion, grant reprieves to persons convicted of treason, until their cases can be laid before the Congress.

That the President, or person exercising his powers for the time being, shall not command an army in the field in person without the previous desire of the Congress.

That all letters patent, commissions, pardons, writs, and processes of the United States shall run in the name of *the people of the United States,* and be tested in the name of the President of the United States, or the person exercising his powers for the time being, or the first judge of the court out of which the same shall issue, as the case may be.

That the Congress shall not constitute, ordain, or establish, any tribunals or inferior courts with any other than appellate jurisdiction, except such as may be necessary for the trial of cases of admiralty and maritime jurisdiction, and for the trial of piracies and felonies committed on the high seas; and in all other cases to which the judicial power of the United States extends, and in which the Supreme Court of the United States has not original jurisdiction, the causes shall be heard, tried, and determined in some one of the state courts, with the right of appeal to the Supreme Court of the United States, or other proper tribunal, to be established for that purpose by the Congress, with such exceptions, and under such regulations, as the Congress shall make.

That the court for the trial of impeachments shall consist of the Senate, the judges of the Supreme Court of the United States, and the first or senior judge, of the time being, of the highest court of general and ordinary common-law jurisdiction in each state; that the Congress shall, by standing laws, designate the courts in the respective states answering this description, and, in states having no courts exactly answering this description, shall designate some other court, preferring such, if any there be, whose judge or judges may hold their places during good behavior; provided, that no more than one judge, other than judges of the Supreme Court of the United States, shall come from one state.

That the Congress be authorized to pass laws for compensating the judges for such services, and for compelling their attendance; and that a majority, at least, of the said judges shall be requisite to constitute the said court. That no person impeached shall sit as a member thereof; that each member shall, previous to the entering upon any trial, take an oath or affirmation honestly and impartially to hear and determine the cause; and that a majority of the members present shall be necessary to a conviction.

That persons aggrieved by any judgment, sentence, or decree of the Supreme Court of the United States, in any cause in which that court has original jurisdiction, with such exceptions, and under such regulations, as the Congress shall make concerning the same, shall, upon application, have a commission, to be issued by the President of the United States to such men learned in the law as he shall nominate, and by and with the advice and consent of the Senate appoint, not less than seven, authorizing such commissioners, or any seven or more of them, to correct the errors in such judgment, or to review such sentence and decree, as the case may be, and to do justice to the parties in the premises.

That no judge of the Supreme Court of the United States shall hold any other office under the United States, or any of them.

That the judicial power of the United States shall extend to no controversies respecting land, unless it relate to claims of territory or jurisdiction between states, and individuals under the grants of different states.

That the militia of any state shall not be compelled to serve without the limits of the state, for a longer term than six weeks without the consent of the legislature thereof.

That the words *without the consent of the Congress* in the seventh clause of the ninth section of the first article of the Constitution be expunged.

That the senators and representatives, and all executive and judicial officers of the United States, shall be bound by oath or affirmation not to infringe or violate the constitutions or rights of the respective states.

That the legislatures of the respective states may make provision, by law, that the electors of the election districts, to be by them appointed, shall choose a citizen of the United States, who shall have been an inhabitant of such district for the term of one year immediately preceding the time of his election, for one of the representatives of such state.

The Circular Letter from the Ratification Convention of the State of New York to the Governors of the Several States in the Union

28 July 1788

Sir:

We, the members of the Convention of this state, have deliberately and maturely considered the Constitution proposed for the United States. Several articles in it appear so exceptionable to a majority of us that nothing but the fullest confidence of obtaining a revision of them by a general convention, and an invincible reluctance to separating from our sister states, could have prevailed upon a sufficient number to ratify it, without stipulating for previous amendments. We all unite in opinion that such a revision will be necessary to recommend it to the approbation and support of a numerous body of our constituents.

We observe that amendments have been proposed, and are anxiously desired, by several of the states, as well as by this; and we think it of great importance that effectual measures be immediately taken for calling a convention to meet at a period not far remote; for we are convinced that the apprehensions and discontents which those articles occasion cannot be removed or allayed unless an act to provide for it be among the first that shall be passed by the new Congress.

As it is essential that an application for the purpose should be made to them by two thirds of the states, we earnestly exhort and request the legislature of your state to take the earliest opportunity of making it. We are persuaded that a similar one will be made by our legislature at their next session; and we ardently wish and desire that the other states may concur in adopting and promoting the measure.

It cannot be necessary to observe that no government, however constructed, can operate well unless it possesses the confidence and good will of the body of the people; and as we desire nothing more than that the amendments proposed by this or other states be submitted to the consideration and decision of a general convention, we flatter ourselves that motives of mutual affection and conciliation will conspire with the obvious dictates of sound policy to induce even such of the states as may be content with every article in the Constitution to gratify the reasonable desires of that numerous class of American citizens who are anxious to obtain amendments of some of them.

Our amendments will manifest that none of them originated in local views, as they are such as, if acceded to, must equally affect every state in the Union. Our attachment to our sister states, and the confidence we repose in them, cannot be more forcibly demonstrated than by acceding to a government which many of us think very imperfect, and devolving the power of determining whether that government shall be rendered perpetual in its present form or altered agreeably to our wishes and a minority of the states with whom we unite.

We request the favor of your excellency to lay this letter before the legislature of your state; and we are persuaded that your regard for our national harmony and good government will induce you to promote a measure which we are unanimous in thinking very conducive to those interesting objects.

We have the honor to be, with the highest respect, your excellency's most obedient servants.

By the unanimous order of the Convention,

George Clinton, *President*

Federalist Concerns

James Madison to George Washington

New York, 11 August 1788

You will have seen the circular letter from the convention of this state. It has a most pestilent tendency. If an early General Convention cannot be parried, it is seriously to be feared that the system which has resisted so many direct attacks may be at last successfully undermined by its enemies. It is now perhaps to be wished that Rhode Island may not accede till this new crisis of danger be over. Some think it would have been better if even N. York had held out till the operation of the government could have dissipated the fears which artifice had created and the attempts resulting from those fears & artifices. We hear nothing yet from N. Carolina more than comes by the way of Petersburg.

Madison to Washington

New York, 24 August 1788

. . . The circular letter from this state is certainly a matter of as much regret as the *unanimity* with which it passed is matter of surprise. I find it is everywhere, and particularly in Virginia, laid hold of as the signal for united exertions in pursuit of *early* amendments. In Pennsylva. the antifederal leaders are, I understand, soon to have a meeting at Harrisburg in order to concert proper arrangements on the part of that state. I begin now to accede to the opinion, which has been avowed for some time by many, that the circumstances involved in the ratification of New York will prove more injurious than a rejection would have done. The latter would have rather alarmed the well meaning Antifederalists elsewhere, would have had no ill effect on the other party, and would have been necessarily followed by a speedy reconsideration of the subject. I am not able to account for the concurrence of the federal part of the Convention in the circular address on any other principle than the determination to purchase an immediate ratification in any form and at any price rather than disappoint this City of a chance for the new Congress. This solution is sufficiently justified by the eagerness displayed on this point, and the evident disposition to risk and sacrifice everything to it. Unfortunately, the disagreeable question continues to be undecided, and is now in a state more perplexing than ever. By the last vote taken, the whole arrangement was thrown out, and the departure of Rho. Island & the refusal of N. Carolina to participate further in the business has left eleven states only to take it up anew. In this number there are not seven states for any place, and the disposition to relax, as usually happens, decreases with the progress of the contest. What and when the issue is to be is really more than I can foresee. It is truly mortifying that the outset of the new government should be immediately preceded by such a display of locality as portends the continuance of an evil which has dishonored the old, and gives countenance to some of the most popular arguments which have been inculcated by the Southern Antifederalists.

New York has appeared to me extremely objectionable on the following grounds. It violates too palpably the simple and obvious principle that the seat of public business should be made as equally convenient to every part of the public as the requisite accommodations for executing the business will permit. This consideration has the more weight as well on account of the catholic spirit professed by the Constitution as of the increased resort which it will require from every quarter of the continent. It seems to be particularly essential that an eye should be had in all our public arrangements to the accommodation of the Western Country, which perhaps cannot be sufficiently gratified at any rate, but which might be furnished with new fuel to its jealousy by being summoned to the sea-shore & almost at one end of the continent. There are reasons, but of too confidential a nature for any other than verbal communication, which make it of critical importance that neither cause nor pretext should be given for distrusts in that quarter of the policy towards it in this. I have apprehended also that a preference so favorable to the Eastern States would be represented in the Southern as a decisive proof of the preponderance of that scale, and a justification of all the antifederal arguments drawn from that danger. Adding to all this the recollection that the first year or two will produce all the great arrangements under the new system, and which may fix its tone for a long time to come, it seems of real importance that the temporary residence of the new Congress, apart from its relation to the final residence, should not be thrown too much towards one extremity of the Union. It may perhaps be the more necessary to guard against suspicions of partiality in this case as the early measures of the new government, including a navigation act, will of course be more favorable to this extremity.

James Madison to Thomas Jefferson

21 September 1788

. . . The Circular Letter from the New York Convention has rekindled an ardor among the opponents of the Federal Constitution for an *immediate* revision of it by another General Convention. You will find in one of the papers enclosed the result of the consultations in Pennsylvania on that subject. Mr. Henry and his friends in Virginia enter with great zeal into the scheme. Governor Randolph also espouses it; but with a wish to prevent if possible danger to the article which extends the power of the government to internal as well as external taxation. It is observable that the views of the Pennsylva. meeting do not rhyme very well with those of the Southern advocates for a Convention; the objects most eagerly pursued by the latter being unnoticed in the Harrisburg proceedings. The effect of the circular letter on other states is less known. I conclude that it will be the same everywhere among those who opposed the Constitution or contended for a conditional ratification of it. Whether an early Convention will be the result of this united effort is more than can at this moment be foretold. The measure will certainly be industriously opposed in some parts of the Union, not only by those who wish for no alterations, but by others who would prefer the other mode provided in the Constitution as most expedient at present for introducing those supplemental safeguards to liberty against which no objections can be raised, and who would moreover approve of a Convention for amending the frame of the government itself, as soon as time shall have somewhat corrected the feverish state of the public mind and trial have pointed its attention to the true defects of the system.

You will find also by one of the papers enclosed that the arrangements have been completed for bringing the new government into action. The dispute concerning the place of its meeting was the principal cause of delay, the Eastern States with N. Jersey and S. Carolina being attached to N. York, and the others strenuous for a more central position. Philadelphia, Wilmington, Lancaster and Baltimore were successively tendered without effect by the latter before they finally yielded to the superiority of [numbers?] in favor of this City. I am afraid the decision will give a great handle to the Southern Antifederalists who have inculcated a jealousy of this end of the continent. It is to be regretted also as entailing this pernicious question on the new Congress who will have enough to do in adjusting the other delicate matters submitted to them. Another consideration of great weight with me is that the temporary residence here will probably end in a permanent one at Trenton, or at the farthest on the Susquehannah. A removal in the first instance beyond the Delaware would have removed the alternative to the Susquehannah and the Potomac. The best chance of the latter depends on a delay of the permanent establishment for a few years, until the Western and South Western population comes more into view. This delay cannot take place if so eccentric a place as N. York is to be the intermediate seat of business.

Madison to Jefferson

8 December 1788

. . . Notwithstanding the formidable opposition made to the new federal government, first in order to prevent its adoption, and since in order to place its administration in the hands of disaffected men, there is now both a certainty of its peaceable commencement in March next and a flattering prospect that it will be administered by men who will give it a fair trial. General Washington will certainly be called to the executive department. Mr. Adams who is *pledged to support him* will probably be the vice president. The enemies to the government, at the head and the most inveterate of whom is Mr. Henry, are laying a train for the election of Governor Clinton, but it cannot succeed unless the federal votes be more dispersed than can well happen. Of the seven states which have appointed their Senators, Virginia alone will have antifederal members in that branch. Those of N. Hampshire are President Langdon and Judge Bartlett, of Massachusetts Mr. Strong and Mr. Dalton, of Connecticut Dr. Johnson and Mr. Ellsworth, of N. Jersey Mr. Patterson and Mr. Elmer, of Penna. Mr. R. Morris and Mr. McClay, of Delaware Mr. Geo. Reed and Mr. Bassett, of Virginia Mr. R. H. Lee and Col. Grayson. Here is already a majority of the ratifying states on the side of the Constitution. And it is not doubted that it will be reinforced by the appointments of Maryland, S. Carolina and Georgia. As one branch of the Legislature of N. York is attached to the Constitution, it is not improbable that one of the Senators from that state also will be added to the majority.

In the House of Representatives the proportion of antifederal members will of course be greater, but cannot if present appearances are to be trusted amount to a majority or even a very formidable minority. The election for this branch has taken place as yet nowhere except in Penna. and here the returns are not yet come in from all the counties. It is certain however that seven out of the eight, and probable that the whole eight representatives will bear the federal stamp. Even in Virginia where the enemies to the government form 2/3 of the *legislature* it is computed that more than half the number of Representatives, who will be elected by the *people,* formed into districts for the purpose, will be of the same stamp. By some it is computed that 7 out of the 10 allotted to that state will be opposed to the politics of the present legislature.

The questions which divide the public at present relate 1. to the extent of the amendments that ought to be made to the Constitution, 2. to the mode in which they ought to be made. The friends of the Constitution, some from an approbation of particular amendments, others from a spirit of conciliation, are generally agreed that the system should be revised. But they wish the revisal to be carried no farther than to supply additional guards for liberty, without abridging the sum of power transferred from the states to the general government or altering previous to trial the particular structure of the latter and are fixed in opposition to the risk of another Convention whilst the purpose can be as well answered by the other mode provided for introducing amendments. Those who have opposed the Constitution are, on the other hand, zealous for a second Convention, and for a revisal which may either not be restrained at all or extend at least as far as alterations have been proposed by any state. Some of this class are, no doubt, friends to an effective government, and even to the substance of the particular government in question. It is equally certain that there are others who urge a second Convention with the insidious hope of throwing all things into confusion, and of subverting the fabric just established, if not the Union itself. If the first Congress embrace the policy which circumstances mark out, they will not fail to propose of themselves every desirable safeguard for popular rights; and by thus separating the well meaning from the designing opponents fix on the latter their true character, and give to the government its due popularity and stability.

The Bill of Rights

Although he was a staunch opponent of the anti-Federalist demand for a second federal convention—and of any amendments that would substantially reduce the powers of the new regime—Madison had said at the Virginia Ratifying Convention that he would not oppose amendments that might provide additional securities for liberty. During the first federal elections, in which he overcame a formidable challenge for a seat in the House, he announced that he was positively committed to such amendments, though still convinced that these could be secured most speedily, with the greatest security against damaging alterations in the substance of the Constitution, and with the greatest likelihood of general acceptance, if they were prepared by Congress rather than another general convention. Over the succeeding months, he took it on himself to lead this effort, combing through the many amendments recommended by the states, together with the states' declarations of rights, for such additions and changes as he considered advisable and safe. Public assurances of speedy action on the subject were inserted in Washington's inaugural address and in the House of Representatives' reply, both of which Madison drafted. On 4 May 1789, he announced to the House that he would introduce amendments on 25 May. The press of other business forced him to accept a postponement on that date. But on 8 June he interrupted other business to introduce some nineteen propositions.

Madison faced considerable resistance in his drive for these amendments—from anti-Federalists who wanted more-substantial alterations than he proposed, from Federalists who resisted any changes, and from general impatience to get on with other business. The propositions of 8 June were referred to a select committee on 26 July and did not come before the House until the middle of August. At that point, Madison insisted on action and persevered until Congress agreed to submit twelve amendments to the states. Ten were ratified by 1791. One was finally adopted, as the twenty-seventh amendment, after a lapse of two hundred years. The twelfth, providing for an enlargement of the House of Representatives, was quickly rendered obsolete.

Proceedings in the House of Representatives
8 June 1789

Madison moved that the House resolve itself into a committee of the whole to consider amendments to the Constitution.

William Loughton Smith (S.C.)

was not inclined to interrupt the measures which the public were so anxiously expecting by going into a committee of the whole at this time. He observed there were two modes of introducing this business to the house: one by appointing a select committee to take into consideration the several amendments proposed by the state conventions; this he thought the most likely way to shorten the business. The other was that the gentleman should lay his propositions on the table for the consideration of the members; that they should be printed and taken up for discussion at a future day. Either of these modes would enable the house to enter upon the business better prepared than could be the case by a sudden transition from other important concerns to which their minds were strongly bent. He therefore hoped the honorable gentleman would consent to bring the subject forward in one of those ways, in preference to going into a committee of the whole. For, he said, it must appear extremely impolitic to go into the consideration of amending the government before it is organized, before it has begun to operate; certainly, upon reflection, it must appear to be premature. . . .

James Jackson (Ga.)

I am of opinion we ought not to be in a hurry with respect to altering the Constitution. For my part I have no idea of speculating in this serious matter on theory; if I agree to alterations in the mode of administering this government, I shall like to stand on the sure ground of experience, and not be treading air. What experience have we had of the good or bad qualities of this Constitution? Can any gentleman affirm to me one proposition that is a certain and absolute amendment? I deny that he can. Our Constitution, sir, is like a vessel just launched and lying at the wharf, she is untried, you can hardly discover any one of her properties; it is not known how she will answer her helm or lay her course; whether she will bear in safety the precious freight to be deposited in her hold. But, in this state, will the prudent merchant attempt alterations? Will he employ two thousand workmen to tear off the planking and take asunder the frame? He certainly will not. Let us gentlemen, fit out our vessel, set up her masts, and expand her sails, and be guided by the experiment in our alterations. If she sails upon an uneven keel, let us right her by adding weight where it is wanting. In this way, we may remedy her defects to the satisfaction of all concerned; but if we proceed now to make alterations, we may deface a beauty or deform a well proportioned piece of workmanship. In short, Mr. Speaker, I am not for amendments at this time, but if gentlemen should think it a subject deserving of attention, they will surely not neglect the more important business which is now unfinished before them. Without we pass the collection bill, we can get no revenue, and without revenue the wheels of government cannot move. I am against taking up the subject at present and shall therefore be totally against the amendments if the government is not organized, that I may see whether it is grievous or not.

When the propriety of making amendments shall be obvious from experience, I trust there will be virtue enough in my country to make them. . . .

Let the Constitution have a fair trial, let it be examined by experience, discover by that test what its errors are, and then talk of amending; but to attempt it now is doing it at risk, which is certainly imprudent. I have the honor of coming from a state that ratified the Constitution by the unanimous vote of a numerous convention: the people of Georgia have manifested their attachment to it, by adopting a state constitution framed upon the same plan as this. But although they are thus satisfied, I shall not be against such amendments as will gratify the inhabitants of other states, provided they are judged of by experience and not theory. For this reason I wish the consideration of the subject postponed until the first of March, 1790.

Benjamin Goodhue (Mass.)

I believe it would be perfectly right in the gentleman who spoke last to move a postponement to the time he has mentioned, because he is opposed to the consideration of amendments altogether. But I believe it will be proper to attend to the subject earlier, because it is the wish of many of our constituents that something should be added to the Constitution to secure in a stronger manner their liberties from the inroads of power. Yet I think the present time premature, inasmuch as we have other business before us, which is incomplete, but essential to the public interest; when that is finished, I shall concur in taking up the subject of amendments.

Aedenus Burke (S.C.)

thought amendments to the Constitution necessary, but this was not the proper time to bring them forward; he wished the government completely organized before they entered upon the ground. The law for collecting the revenue was immediately necessary, the treasury department must be established; till these and other important subjects were determined, he was against taking this up. He said it might interrupt the harmony of the house, which was necessary to be preserved to dispatch the great objects of legislation. He hoped it would be postponed for the present, and pledged himself to bring it forward again, if nobody else would.

James Madison (Va.)

The gentleman from Georgia (Mr. Jackson) is certainly right in his opposition to my motion for going into a committee of the whole, because he is unfriendly to the object I have in contemplation; but I cannot see that the gentlemen who wish for amendments being proposed at the present session stand on good ground when they object to the house going into committee on this business.

When I first hinted to the house my intention of calling their deliberations to this object, I mentioned the pressure of other important subjects and submitted the propriety of postponing this till the more urgent business was dispatched; but finding that business not dispatched, when the order of the day for considering amendments arrived, I thought it a good reason for a farther delay. I moved the postponement accordingly. I am sorry the same reason still exists in some degree; but operates with less force when it is considered that it is not now proposed to enter into a full and minute discussion of every part of the subject, but merely to bring it before the house, that our constituents may see we pay a proper attention to a subject they have much at heart; and if it does not give that full gratification which is to be wished, they will discover that it proceeds from the urgency of business of a very important nature. But if we continue to postpone from time to time, and refuse to let the subject come into view, it may occasion suspicions which, though not well founded, may tend to inflame or prejudice the public mind against our decisions: they may think we are not sincere in our desire to incorporate such amendments in the Constitution as will secure those rights which they consider as not sufficiently guarded. The applications for amendments come from a very respectable number of our constituents, and it is certainly proper for Congress to consider the subject, in order to quiet that anxiety which prevails in the public mind: Indeed I think it would have been of advantage to the government, if it had been practicable, to have made some propositions for amendments the first business we entered upon; it would stifle the voice of complaint and make friends of many who doubted its merits. Our future measures would then have been more universally agreeable and better supported; but the justifiable anxiety to put the government in operation prevented that; it therefore remains for us to take it up as soon as possible. I wish then to commence the consideration at the present moment; I hold it to be my duty to unfold my ideas and explain myself to the house in some form or other without delay. I only wish to introduce the great work, and as I said before, I do not expect it will be decided immediately; but if some step is taken in the business it will give reason to believe that we may come at a final result. This will inspire a reasonable hope in the advocates for amendments that full justice will be done to the important subject; and I have reason to believe their expectation will not be defeated. I hope the house will not decline my motion for going into a committee.

Roger Sherman (Conn.)

I am willing that this matter should be brought before the house at a proper time. I suppose a number of gentlemen think it their duty to bring it forward; so that there is no apprehension it will be passed over in silence. Other gentlemen may be disposed to let the subject rest

until the more important objects of government are attended to; and I should conclude from the nature of the case that the people expect the latter of us in preference of altering the Constitution, because they have ratified that instrument in order that the government may begin to operate. If this was not their wish, they might well have rejected the Constitution, as North Carolina has done, until the amendments took place. The state I have the honor to come from adopted this system by a very great majority, because they wished for the government; but they desired no amendments. I suppose this was the case in other states; it will therefore be imprudent to neglect much more important concerns for this. The executive part of the government wants organization; the business of the revenue is incomplete, to say nothing of the judiciary business. Now, will gentlemen give up these points to go into a discussion of amendments when no advantage can arise from them? For my part, I question if any alteration which can be now proposed would be an amendment in the true sense of the word; but nevertheless I am willing to let the subject be introduced; if the gentleman only desires to go into committee for the purpose of receiving his propositions, I shall consent; but I have strong objections to being interrupted in completing the more important business, because I am well satisfied it will alarm the fears of twenty of our constituents where it will please one.

Alexander White (Va.)

I hope the house will not spend much time on this subject till the more pressing business is dispatched, but, at the same time, I hope we shall not dismiss it altogether, because I think a majority of the people who have ratified the Constitution did it under an expectation that Congress would, at some convenient time, examine its texture and point out where it is defective, in order that it might be judiciously amended. Whether, while we are without experience, amendments can be digested in such a manner as to give satisfaction to a constitutional majority of this house, I will not pretend to say, but I hope the subject may be considered with all convenient speed. I think it would tend to tranquilize the public mind; therefore I shall vote in favor of going into a committee of the whole, and after receiving the subject shall be content to refer it to a special committee to arrange and report. . . .

Mr. Smith

thought the gentleman who brought forward the subject had done his duty: He had supported his motion with ability and candor, and if he did not succeed he was not to blame. On considering what had been urged for going into a committee, he was induced to join the gentleman; but it would be merely to receive his propositions; after which he would move something to this effect: That however desirous this house may be to go into the consideration of amendments to the Constitution, in order to establish the liberties of the people of America on the securest foundation, yet the important and pressing business of the government prevents their entering upon that subject at present.

John Page (Va.)

My colleague tells you he is ready to submit to the committee of the whole his ideas on this subject; if no objection had been made to his motion, the whole business might have been finished before this. He has done me the honor of showing me certain propositions which he has drawn up. They are very important, and I sincerely wish the house may receive them. After they are published, I think the people will wait with patience till we are at leisure to resume them; but it must be very disagreeable to them to have it postponed from time to time, in the manner it has been, for six weeks past; they will be tired out by a fruitless expectation. Putting myself into the place of those who favor amendments, I should suspect Congress did not mean seriously to enter upon the subject; that it was vain to expect redress from them; I should begin to turn my attention to the alternative contained in the fifth article, and think of joining the legislatures of those states which have applied for calling a new convention. How dangerous such an expedient would be, I need not mention, but I venture to affirm that unless you take early notice of this subject, you will not have power to deliberate. The people will clamor for a new convention, they will not trust the house any longer; those, therefore, who dread the assembling of a convention will do well to acquiesce in the present motion and lay the foundation of a most important work. I do not think we need consume more than half an hour in the committee of the whole; this is not so much time but we may conveniently spare it, considering the nature of the business. I do not wish to divert the attention of Congress from the organization of the government, nor do I think it need be done, if we comply with the present motion. . . .

Mr. Madison

I am sorry to be accessory to the loss of a single moment of time by the house. If I had been indulged in my motion, and we had gone into a committee of the whole, I think we might have rose and resumed the consideration of other business before this time. . . . As that mode seems not to give satisfaction, I will withdraw the motion and move you, sir, that a select committee be appointed to consider and report such amendments as are proper for Congress to propose to the legislatures of the several states, conformably to the Fifth Article of the Constitution. I will state my reasons why I think it proper to propose amendments; and state the amendments themselves, so far as I think they ought to be proposed. If I thought I could fulfill the duty which I owe to myself and my constituents, to let the subject pass over in silence, I most certainly should not trespass upon the indulgence of this house. But I cannot do this; and am therefore compelled to beg a patient hearing to what I have to lay before you. And I do most sincerely believe that if Congress will devote but one day to this subject, so far as to satisfy the public that we do not disregard their wishes, it will have a salutary influence on the public councils and prepare the way for a favorable reception of our future measures. It appears to me that this house is bound by every motive of prudence not to let the first session pass over without proposing to the state legislatures some things to be incorporated into the Constitution as will render it as acceptable to the whole people of the United States as it has been found acceptable to a majority of them. I wish, among other reasons why something should be done, that those who have been friendly to the adoption of this Constitution may have the opportunity of proving to those who were opposed to it that they were as sincerely devoted to liberty and a republican government as those who charged them with wishing the adoption of this Constitution in order to lay the foundation of an aristocracy or despotism. It will be a desirable thing to extinguish from the bosom of every member of the community any apprehensions that there are those among his countrymen who wish to deprive them of the liberty for which they valiantly fought and honorably bled. And if there are amendments desired of such a nature as will not injure the Constitution, and they can be engrafted so as to give satisfaction to the doubting part of our fellow citizens, the friends of the federal government will evince that spirit of deference and concession for which they have hitherto been distinguished.

It cannot be a secret to the gentlemen in this house that, notwithstanding the ratification of this system of government by eleven of the thirteen United States, in some cases unanimously, in others by large majorities; yet still there is a great number of our constituents who are dissatisfied with it; among whom are many respectable for their talents, their patriotism, and respectable for the jealousy they have for their liberty, which, though mistaken in its object, is laudable in its motive. There is a great body of the people falling under this description who, at present, feel much inclined to join their support to the cause of federalism, if they were satisfied in this one point: We ought not to disregard their inclination, but, on principles of amity and moderation, conform to their wishes, and expressly declare the great rights of mankind secured under this Constitution. The acquiescence which our fellow citizens show under the government calls upon us for a like return of moderation. But perhaps there is a stronger motive than this for our going into a consideration of the subject; it is to provide those securities for liberty which are required by a part of the community. I allude in a particular manner to those two states who have not thought fit to throw themselves into the bosom of the confederacy; it is a desirable thing, on our part as well as theirs, that a reunion should take place as soon as possible. I have no doubt, if we proceed to take those steps which would be prudent and requisite at this juncture, that in a short time we should see that disposition prevailing in those states that are not come in that we have seen prevailing in those states which are.

But I will candidly acknowledge that, over and above all these considerations, I do conceive that the Constitution may be amended; that is to say, if all power is subject to abuse, that then it is possible the abuse of the powers of the general government may be guarded against in a more secure manner than is now done, while no one advantage arising from the exercise of that power shall be damaged or endangered by it. We have in this way something to gain and, if we proceed with caution, nothing to lose; and in this case it is necessary to proceed with caution; for while we feel all these inducements to go into a revisal of the Constitution, we must feel for the Constitution itself, and make that revisal a moderate one. I should be unwilling to see a door opened for a reconsideration of the whole structure of the government, for a reconsideration of the principles and the substance of the powers given; because

I doubt, if such a door was opened, if we should be very likely to stop at that point which would be safe to the government itself: But I do wish to see a door opened to consider, so far as to incorporate those provisions for the security of rights, against which I believe no serious objection has been made by any class of our constituents. Such as would be likely to meet with the concurrence of two-thirds of both houses and the approbation of three-fourths of the state legislatures. I will not propose a single alteration which I do not wish to see take place, as intrinsically proper in itself, or proper because it is wished for by a respectable number of my fellow citizens; and therefore I shall not propose a single alteration but is likely to meet the concurrence required by the Constitution.

There have been objections of various kinds made against the Constitution: Some were leveled against its structure, because the president was without a council; because the senate, which is a legislative body, had judicial powers in trials on impeachments; and because the powers of that body were compounded in other respects in a manner that did not correspond with a particular theory; because it grants more power than is supposed to be necessary for every good purpose; and controls the ordinary powers of the state governments. I know some respectable characters who opposed this government on these grounds; but I believe that the great mass of the people who opposed it disliked it because it did not contain effectual provision against encroachments on particular rights, and those safeguards which they have been long accustomed to have interposed between them and the magistrate who exercised the sovereign power: nor ought we to consider them safe, while a great number of our fellow citizens think these securities necessary.

It has been a fortunate thing that the objection to the government has been made on the ground I stated; because it will be practicable on that ground to obviate the objection, so far as to satisfy the public mind that their liberties will be perpetual, and this without endangering any part of the Constitution which is considered as essential to the existence of the government by those who promoted its adoption.

The amendments which have occurred to me, proper to be recommended by Congress to the state legislatures, are these:

The first of these amendments relates to what may be called a bill of rights; I will own that I never considered this provision so essential to the federal constitution as to make it improper to ratify it until such an amendment was added; at the same time, I always conceived that, in a certain form and to a certain extent, such a provision was neither improper nor altogether useless. I am aware that a great number of the most respectable friends to the government and champions for republican liberty have thought such a provision not only unnecessary, but even improper, nay, I believe some have gone so far as to think it even dangerous. Some policy has been made use of perhaps by gentlemen on both sides of the question: I acknowledge the ingenuity of those arguments which were drawn against the Constitution by a comparison with the policy of Great Britain, in establishing a declaration of rights; but there is too great a difference in the case to warrant the comparison; therefore the arguments drawn from that source were in a great measure inapplicable. In the declaration of rights which that country has established, the truth is, they have gone no farther than to raise a barrier against the power of the crown; the power of the legislature is left altogether indefinite. Altho' I know whenever the great rights, the trial by jury, freedom of the press, or liberty of conscience, came in question in that body, the invasion of them is resisted by able advocates, yet their Magna Charta does not contain any one provision for the security of those rights respecting which the people of America are most alarmed. The freedom of the press and rights of conscience, those choicest privileges of the people, are unguarded in the British constitution.

But altho' the case may be widely different, and it may not be thought necessary to provide limits for the legislative power in that country, yet a different opinion prevails in the United States. The people of many states have thought it necessary to raise barriers against power in all forms and departments of government, and I am inclined to believe, if once bills of rights are established in all the states as well as the federal constitution, we shall find that altho' some of them are rather unimportant, yet, upon the whole, they will have a salutary tendency.

It may be said, in some instances they do no more than state the perfect equality of mankind; this to be sure is an absolute truth, yet it is not absolutely necessary to be inserted at the head of a constitution.

In some instances they assert those rights which are exercised by the people in forming and establishing a plan of government. In other instances, they specify those rights which are retained when particular powers are given up to be exercised by the legislature. In other instances, they specify positive rights which may seem to result from the nature of the compact. Trial by jury cannot be considered as a natural right, but a right resulting from the social compact which regulates the action of the community, but is as essential to secure the liberty of the people as any one of the pre-existent rights of nature. In other instances they lay down dogmatic maxims with respect to the construction of the government: declaring that the legislative, executive, and judicial branches shall be kept separate and distinct: Perhaps the best way of securing this in practice is to provide such checks as will prevent the encroachment of the one upon the other.

But whatever may be the form which the several states have adopted in making declarations in favor of particular rights, the great object in view is to limit and qualify the powers of government, by excepting out of the grant of power those cases in which the government ought not to act, or to act only in a particular mode. They point these exceptions sometimes against the abuse of the executive power, sometimes against the legislative, and, in some cases, against the community itself; or, in other words, against the majority in favor of the minority.

In our government it is, perhaps, less necessary to guard against the abuse in the executive department than any other; because it is not the stronger branch of the system, but the weaker: It therefore must be leveled against the legislative, for it is the most powerful, and most likely to be abused, because it is under the least control; hence, so far as a declaration of rights can tend to prevent the exercise of undue power, it cannot be doubted but such declaration is proper. But I confess that I do conceive that, in a government modified like this of the United States, the great danger lies rather in the abuse of the community than in the legislative body. The prescriptions in favor of liberty ought to be leveled against that quarter where the greatest danger lies, namely, that which possesses the highest prerogative of power: But this is not found in either the executive or legislative departments of government, but in the body of the people, operating by the majority against the minority.

It may be thought all paper barriers against the power of the community are too weak to be worthy of attention. I am sensible they are not so strong as to satisfy gentlemen of every description who have seen and examined thoroughly the texture of such a defense; yet as they have a tendency to impress some degree of respect for them, to establish the public opinion in their favor, and rouse the attention of the whole community, it may be one mean to control the majority from those acts to which they might be otherwise inclined.

It has been said by way of objection to a bill of rights, by many respectable gentlemen out of doors, and I find opposition on the same principles likely to be made by gentlemen on this floor, that they are unnecessary articles of a republican government, upon the presumption that the people have those rights in their own hands, and that is the proper place for them to rest. It would be a sufficient answer to say that this objection lies against such provisions under the state governments as well as under the general government; and there are, I believe, but few gentlemen who are inclined to push their theory so far as to say that a declaration of rights in those cases is either ineffectual or improper. It has been said that in the federal government they are unnecessary because the powers are enumerated, and it follows that all that are not granted by the Constitution are retained: that the Constitution is a bill of powers, the great residuum being the rights of the people; and therefore a bill of rights cannot be so necessary as if the residuum was thrown into the hands of the government. I admit that these arguments are not entirely without foundation; but they are not conclusive to the extent which has been supposed. It is true the powers of the general government are circumscribed, they are directed to particular objects; but even if government keeps within those limits, it has certain extraordinary powers with respect to the means, which may admit of abuse to a certain extent, in the same manner as the powers of the state governments under their constitutions may to an indefinite extent; because in the Constitution of the United States there is a clause granting to Congress the power to make all laws which shall be necessary and proper for carrying into execution all the powers vested in the government of the United States, or in any department or officer thereof; this enables them to fulfill every purpose for which the government was established. Now, may not laws be considered necessary and proper by Congress, for it is them who are to judge of the necessity and propriety to accomplish those special purposes which they may have in contemplation, which laws in themselves are neither necessary or proper; as well as improper laws could be enacted by the state legislatures for fulfilling the more extended objects of those

governments. I will state an instance which I think in point, and proves that this might be the case. The general government has a right to pass all laws which shall be necessary to collect its revenue; the means for enforcing the collection are within the direction of the legislature: may not general warrants be considered necessary for this purpose, as well as for some purposes which it was supposed at the framing of their constitutions the state governments had in view? If there was reason for restraining the state governments from exercising this power, there is like reason for restraining the federal government.

It may be said, because it has been said, that a bill of rights is not necessary because the establishment of this government has not repealed those declarations of rights which are added to the several state constitutions: that those rights of the people, which had been established by the most solemn act, could not be annihilated by a subsequent act of that people, who meant, and declared at the head of the instrument, that they ordained and established a new system for the express purpose of securing to themselves and posterity the liberties they had gained by an arduous conflict.

I admit the force of this observation, but I do not look upon it to be conclusive. In the first place, it is too uncertain ground to leave this provision upon, if a provision is at all necessary to secure rights so important as many of those I have mentioned are conceived to be, by the public in general, as well as those in particular who opposed the adoption of this Constitution. Beside some states have no bills of rights, there are others provided with very defective ones, and there are others whose bills of rights are not only defective, but absolutely improper; instead of securing some in the full extent which republican principles would require, they limit them too much to agree with the common ideas of liberty.

It has been objected also against a bill of rights that, by enumerating particular exceptions to the grant of power, it would disparage those rights which were not placed in that enumeration, and it might follow by implication that those rights which were not singled out were intended to be assigned into the hands of the general government, and were consequently insecure. This is one of the most plausible arguments I have ever heard urged against the admission of a bill of rights into this system; but, I conceive, that may be guarded against. I have attempted it, as gentlemen may see by turning to the last clause of the 4th resolution.

It has been said that it is unnecessary to load the Constitution with this provision, because it was not found effectual in the constitutions of the particular states. It is true, there are a few particular states in which some of the most valuable articles have not, at one time or other, been violated; but it does not follow but they may have, to a certain degree, a salutary effect against the abuse of power. If they are incorporated into the Constitution, independent tribunals of justice will consider themselves in a peculiar manner the guardians of those rights; they will be an impenetrable bulwark against every assumption of power in the legislative or executive; they will be naturally led to resist every encroachment upon rights expressly stipulated for in the Constitution by the declaration of rights. Beside this security, there is a great probability that such a declaration in the federal system would be enforced; because the state legislatures will jealously and closely watch the operations of this government and be able to resist with more effect every assumption of power than any other power on earth can do; and the greatest opponents to a federal government admit the state legislatures to be sure guardians of the people's liberty. I conclude from this view of the subject that it will be proper in itself, and highly politic, for the tranquility of the public mind, and the stability of the government, that we should offer something in the form I have proposed, to be incorporated in the system of government as a declaration of the rights of the people.

In the next place I wish to see that part of the constitution revised which declares that the number of representatives shall not exceed the proportion of one for every thirty thousand persons, and allows one representative to every state which rates below that proportion. If we attend to the discussion of this subject which has taken place in the state conventions, and even in the opinion of the friends to the Constitution, an alteration here is proper. It is the sense of the people of America that the number of representatives ought to be increased, but particularly that it should not be left in the discretion of the government to diminish them below that proportion which certainly is in the power of the legislature as the Constitution now stands; and they may, as the population of the country increases, increase the House of Representatives to a very unwieldy degree. I confess I always thought this part of the Constitution defective, though not dangerous; and that it ought to be particularly attended to whenever Congress should go into the consideration of amendments.

There are several lesser cases enumerated in my proposition in which I wish also to see some alteration take place. That article which leaves it in the power of the legislature to ascertain its own emolument is one to which I allude. I do not believe this is a power which, in the ordinary course of government, is likely to be abused, perhaps of all the powers granted it is least likely to abuse; but there is a seeming impropriety in leaving any set of men without control to put their hand into the public coffers, to take out money to put in their pockets; there is a seeming indecorum in such power, which leads me to propose a change. We have a guide to this alteration in several of the amendments which the different conventions have proposed. I have gone therefore so far as to fix it that no law varying the compensation shall operate until there is a change in the legislature; in which case it cannot be for the particular benefit of those who are concerned in determining the value of the service.

I wish also, in revising the Constitution, we may throw into that section which interdicts the abuse of certain powers in the state legislatures some other provisions of equal if not greater importance than those already made. The words, "No state shall pass any bill of attainder, ex post facto law, etc." were wise and proper restrictions in the Constitution. I think there is more danger of those powers being abused by the state governments than by the government of the United States. The same may be said of other powers which they possess, if not controlled by the general principle that laws are unconstitutional which infringe the rights of the community. I should therefore wish to extend this interdiction, and add, as I have stated in the 5th resolution, that no state shall violate the equal right of conscience, freedom of the press, or trial by jury in criminal cases; because it is proper that every government should be disarmed of powers which trench upon those particular rights. I know in some of the state constitutions the power of the government is controlled by such a declaration, but others are not. I cannot see any reason against obtaining even a double security on those points; and nothing can give a more sincere proof of the attachment of those who opposed this constitution to these great and important rights, than to see them join in obtaining the security I have now proposed; because it must be admitted on all hands that the state governments are as liable to attack these invaluable privileges as the general government is, and therefore ought to be as cautiously guarded against.

I think it will be proper, with respect to the judiciary powers, to satisfy the public mind on those points which I have mentioned. Great inconvenience has been apprehended to suitors from the distance they would be dragged to obtain justice in the Supreme Court of the United States upon an appeal on an action for a small debt. To remedy this, declare that no appeal shall be made unless the matter in controversy amounts to a particular sum: This, with the regulations respecting jury trials in criminal cases and suits at common law, it is to be hoped will quiet and reconcile the minds of the people to that part of the Constitution.

I find, from looking into the amendments proposed by the state conventions, that several are particularly anxious that it should be declared in the Constitution that the powers not therein delegated should be reserved to the several states. Perhaps words which may define this more precisely than the whole of the instrument now does may be considered as superfluous. I admit they may be deemed unnecessary; but there can be no harm in making such a declaration, if gentlemen will allow that the fact is as stated; I am sure I understand it so, and do therefore propose it.

These are the points on which I wish to see a revision of the Constitution take place. How far they will accord with the sense of this body, I cannot take upon me absolutely to determine; but I believe every gentleman will readily admit that nothing is in contemplation, so far as I have mentioned, that can endanger the beauty of the government in any one important feature, even in the eyes of its most sanguine admirers. I have proposed nothing that does not appear to me as proper in itself, or eligible as patronized by a respectable number of our fellow citizens; and if we can make the Constitution better in the opinion of those who are opposed to it, without weakening its frame, or abridging its usefulness, in the judgment of those who are attached to it, we act the part of wise and liberal men to make such alterations as shall produce that effect.

Having done what I conceived was my duty in bringing before this house the subject of amendments, and also stated such as I wish for and approve, and offered the reasons which occurred to me in their support; I shall content myself for the present with moving that a committee be appointed to consider of and report such amendments as ought to be proposed by Congress to the legislatures of the states, to become, if ratified by three-fourths thereof, part of the Constitution of the United States. By agreeing to this motion, the subject may be going on in the committee while other important business is proceeding to a conclusion in the house. I should advocate greater dispatch in the business of amendments if I was not convinced of the absolute necessity there is of pursuing the organization of the government; because I think we should obtain the confidence of our fellow citizens in proportion as we fortify the rights of the people against the encroachments of the government.

Mr. Jackson

The more I consider the subject of amendments, the more, Mr. Speaker, I am convinced it is improper. I revere the rights of my constituents as much as any gentleman in Congress, yet I am against inserting a declaration of rights in the Constitution, and that upon some of the reasons referred to by the gentleman last up. If such an addition is not dangerous or improper, it is at least unnecessary; that is a sufficient reason for not entering into the subject at a time when there are urgent calls for our attention to important business. . . .

Elbridge Gerry (Mass.)

I do not rise to go into the merits or demerits of the subject of amendments, nor shall I make any other observations on the motion for going into a committee of the whole, . . . which is now withdrawn, than merely to say that referring the subject to that committee is treating it with the dignity its importance requires. But I consider it improper to take up this business at this time, when our attention is occupied by other important objects. We should dispatch the subjects now on the table and let this lie over until a period of more leisure for discussion and attention. . . . I would not have it understood that I am against entering upon amendments when the proper time arrives. I shall be glad to set about it as soon as possible, but I would not stay the operation of the government on this account. . . .

I say, sir, I wish as early a day as possible may be assigned for taking up this business in order to prevent the necessity which the states may think themselves under of calling a new convention. . . . I think, if it is referred to a new convention, we run the risk of losing some of its best properties; this is a case I never wish to see. Whatever might have been my sentiments of the ratification of the Constitution without amendments, my sense now is that the salvation of America depends upon the establishment of this government, whether amended or not. If the Constitution which is now ratified should not be supported, I despair of ever having a government of these United States.

I wish the subject to be considered early for another reason: There are two states not in the union; it would be a very desirable circumstance to gain them. I should therefore be in favor of such amendments as might tend to invite them and gain their confidence; good policy will dictate to us to expedite that event. . . .

I have another reason for going early into this business: It is necessary to establish an energetic government. But . . . we appear afraid to exercise the constitutional powers of the government, which the welfare of the state requires, lest a jealousy of our power be the consequence. What is the reason of this timidity? Why, because we see a great body of our constituents opposed to the Constitution as it now stands, who are apprehensive of the enormous powers of governments. But if this business is taken up and it is thought proper to make amendments, it will remove this difficulty. Let us deal fairly and candidly with our constituents, and give the subject a full discussion; after that I have no doubt but the decision will be such as, upon examination, we shall discover to be right. . . .

I am against referring the subject to a select committee, because I conceive it would be disrespectful to those states which have proposed amendments. The conventions of the states consisted of the most wise and virtuous men of the community; they have ratified this Constitution in full confidence that their objections would at least be considered; and shall we, sir, preclude them by the appointment of a special committee to consider of a few propositions brought forward by an individual gentleman. . . . The ratification of the Constitution in several states would never have taken place had they not been assured that the objections would have been duly attended to by Congress. . . .

Mr. Sherman

I do not suppose the Constitution to be perfect, nor do I imagine if Congress and all the legislatures on the continent were to revise it, that their united labors would make it perfect. I do not expect any perfection on this side the grave in the works of man; but my opinion is that we are not at present in circumstances to make it better. It is a wonder that there has been such unanimity in adopting it, considering the ordeal it had to undergo; and the unanimity which prevailed at its formation is equally astonishing; amidst all the members from the twelve states present at the federal convention, there were only three who did not sign the instrument to attest their opinion of its goodness. Of the eleven states who have received it, the majority have ratified it without proposing a single amendment; this circumstance leads me to suppose that we shall not be able to propose any alterations that are likely to be adopted by nine states; and gentlemen know before the alterations take effect, they must be agreed to by the legislatures of three-fourths of the states in the union. Those states that have not recommended alterations will hardly adopt them, unless it is clear that they tend to make the Constitution better; now how this can be made out to their satisfaction I am yet to learn; they know of no defect from experience. It seems to be the opinion of gentlemen generally that this is not the time for entering upon the discussion of amendments; our only question, therefore, is how to get rid of the subject; now for my own part I would prefer to have it referred to a committee of the whole rather than a special committee, and therefore shall not agree to the motion now before the house.

Proceedings in the House of Representatives
13 August 1789

Madison's propositions of 8 June were referred to a select committee of eleven, which reported them out without substantial change. After further debate about delaying the subject, the House finally went into committee of the whole to consider the amendments. The debates on the Bill of Rights were too extensive to be presented here in full, but Congress added nothing that Madison had not initially proposed and defeated him, in substance, on only two important points. The House approved, but (in debates that were not recorded) the Senate defeated Madison's proposal to guarantee the freedoms of religion and the press against infringements by the states as well as against infringements by the federal government. And, led by Roger Sherman, a stubborn minority compelled Madison to forgo his original idea that the changes ought to be interwoven into the body of the Constitution, not tacked onto the end.

Mr. Sherman

I believe, Mr. Chairman, this is not the proper mode of amending the Constitution. We ought not to interweave our propositions into the work itself, because it will be destructive of the whole fabric. We might as well endeavor to mix brass, iron, and clay as to incorporate such heterogeneous articles, the one contradictory to the other. Its absurdity will be discovered by comparing it with a law: would any legislature endeavor to introduce into a former act a subsequent amendment, and let them stand so connected. When an alteration is made in an act, it is done by way of supplement; the latter act always repealing the former in every specified case of difference.

Beside this, sir, it is questionable whether we have the right to propose amendments in this way. The Constitution is the act of the people, and ought to remain entire. But the amendments will be the act of the state governments; again, all the authority we possess is derived from that instrument; if we mean to destroy the whole and establish a new Constitution, we remove the basis on which we mean to build. For these reasons I will move to strike out that paragraph and substitute another.

The paragraph proposed was to the following effect: Resolved by the Senate and House of Representatives of the United States in Congress assembled, That the following articles be proposed as amendments to the Constitution; and when ratified by three-fourths of the state legislatures shall become valid to all intents and purposes as part of the same.

Under this title, the amendments might come in nearly as stated in the report, only varying the phraseology so as to accommodate them to a supplementary form.

Mr. Madison

Form, sir, is always of less importance than the substance; but on this occasion, I admit that form is of some consequence, and it will be well for the house to pursue that which, upon reflection, shall appear to the most eligible. Now it appears to me that there is a neatness and propriety in incorporating the amendments into the Constitution itself; in that case the system will remain uniform and entire; it will certainly be more simple when the amendments are interwoven into those parts to which they naturally belong than it will if they consist of separate and distinct parts; we shall then be able to determine its meaning without references or comparison; whereas, if they are supplementary, its meaning can only be ascertained by a comparison of the two instruments, which will be a very considerable embarrassment; it will be difficult to ascertain to what parts of the instrument the amendments particularly refer; they will create unfavorable comparisons, whereas, if they are placed upon the footing here proposed, they will stand upon as good foundation as the original work.

Nor is it so uncommon a thing as gentlemen suppose; systematic men frequently take up the whole law and, with its amendments and alterations, reduce it into one act. I am not, however, very solicitous about the form, provided the business is but well completed.

Mr. Smith [S.C.]

did not think the amendment proposed by the honorable gentleman from Connecticut was compatible with the Constitution, which declared that the amendments recommended by Congress and ratified by the legislatures of three-fourths of the several states should be part of this Constitution; in which case it would form one complete system; but according to the idea of the amendment, the instrument is to have five or six suits of improvements. Such a mode seems more calculated to embarrass the people than anything else, while nothing in his opinion was a juster cause of complaint than the difficulties of knowing the law, arising from legislative obscurities that might easily be avoided. He said that it had certainly been the custom in several of the state governments to amend their laws by way of supplement; but South Carolina has been an instance of the contrary practice, in revising the old code; instead of making acts in addition to acts, which is always attended with perplexity, she has incorporated them, and brought them forward as a complete system, repealing the old. This is what he understood was intended to be done by the committee: the present copy of the Constitution was to be done away and a new one substituted in its stead.

Samuel Livermore (N.H.)

was clearly of opinion that whatever amendments were made to the Constitution, that they ought to stand separate from the original instrument. We have no right, said he, to alter a clause any otherwise than by a new proposition. We have well-established precedents for such a mode of procedure in the practice of the British Parliament and the state legislatures throughout America. I do not mean, however, to assert that there has been no instance of a repeal of a whole law on enacting another; but this has generally taken place on account of the complexity of the original, with its supplements. Were we a mere legislative body, no doubt it might be warrantable in us to pursue a similar method, but it is questionable whether it is possible for us, consistent with the oath we have taken, to attempt a repeal of the Constitution of the United States, by making a new one to substitute in its place. The reason of this is grounded on a very simple consideration. It is by virtue of the present Constitution, I presume, that we attempt to make another; now, if we proceed to the repeal of this, I cannot see upon what authority we shall erect another; if we destroy the base, the superstructure falls of course. At some future day it may be asked upon what authority we proceeded to raise and appropriate public monies. We suppose we do it in virtue of the present Constitution; but it may be doubted whether we have a right to exercise any of its authorities while it is suspended, as it will certainly be, from the time that two-thirds of both houses have agreed to submit it to the state legislatures; so that unless we mean to destroy the whole Constitution, we ought to be careful how we attempt to amend it in the way proposed by the committee. From hence I presume it will be more prudent to adopt the mode proposed by the gentleman from Connecticut, than it will be to risk the destruction of the whole by proposing amendments in the manner recommended by the committee. . . .

Mr. Jackson

I do not like to differ with gentlemen about form, but as so much has been said, I wish to give my opinion . . . that the original Constitution ought to remain inviolate, and not be patched up from time to time with various stuffs resembling Joseph's coat of many colors. . . .

The Constitution of the Union has been ratified and established by the people, let their act remain inviolable; if anything we can do has a tendency to improve it, let it be done, but without mutilating and defacing the original.

Mr. Sherman

If I had looked upon this question as mere matter of form, I should not have brought it forward or troubled the committee with such a lengthy discussion. But, sir, I contend that amendments made in the way proposed by the committee are void: No gentleman ever knew an addition

and alteration introduced into an existing law, and that any part of such law was left in force; but if it was improved or altered by a supplemental act, the original retained all its validity and importance in every case where the two were not incompatible. But if these observations alone should be thought insufficient to support my motion, I would desire gentlemen to consider the authorities upon which the two constitutions are to stand. The original was established by the people at large by conventions chosen by them for the express purpose. The preamble to the Constitution declares the act: But will it be a truth in ratifying the next constitution, which is to be done perhaps by the state legislatures and not conventions chosen for the purpose? Will gentlemen say it is "We the people" in this case; certainly they cannot, for by the present constitution, we nor all the legislatures in the union together do not possess the power of repealing it: All that is granted us by the 5th article is that, whenever we shall think it necessary, we may propose *amendments to the Constitution;* not that we may propose to repeal the old and substitute a new one.

Gentlemen say it would be convenient to have it in one instrument that people might see the whole at once; for my part I view no difficulty on this point. The amendments reported are a declaration of rights; the people are secure in them whether we declare them or not; the last amendment but one provides that the three branches of government shall each exercise its own rights, this is well secured already; and in short, I do not see that they lessen the force of any article in the Constitution; if so, there can be little more difficulty in comprehending them whether they are combined in one or stand distinct instruments.

Mr. Gerry

The honorable gentleman from Connecticut, if I understand him right, says that the words "We the people" cannot be retained if Congress should propose amendments, and they be ratified by the state legislatures: Now if this is a fact, we ought most undoubtedly adopt his motion; because if we do not, we cannot obtain any amendment whatever. But upon what ground does the gentleman's position stand? The Constitution of the United States was proposed by a convention met at Philadelphia, but with all its importance it did not possess as high authority as the President, Senate, and House of Representatives of the union: For that convention was not convened in consequence of any express will of the people, but an implied one, through their members in the state legislatures. The Constitution derived no authority from the first convention; it was concurred in by conventions of the people, and that concurrence armed it with power and invested it with dignity. Now the Congress of the United States are expressly authorized by the sovereign and uncontrollable voice of the people to propose amendments whenever two-thirds of both houses shall think fit: Now if this is the fact, the propositions of amendment will be found to originate with a higher authority than the original system. The conventions of the states respectively have agreed for the people that the state legislatures shall be authorized to decide upon these amendments in the manner of a convention. If these acts of the state legislatures are not good because they are not specifically instructed by their constituents, neither were the acts calling the first and subsequent conventions.

Does he mean to put amendments on this ground, that after they have been ratified by the state legislatures they are not to have the same authority as the original instrument; if this is his meaning, let him avow it, and if it is well founded, we may save ourselves the trouble of proceeding in the business. But for my part I have no doubt but a ratification of the amendments, in any form, would be as valid as any part of the Constitution. The legislatures are elected by the people; I know no difference between them and conventions, unless it be that the former will generally be composed of men of higher characters than may be expected in conventions; and in this case, the ratification by the legislatures would have the preference.

Now if it is clear that the effect will be the same in either mode, will gentlemen hesitate to approve the most simple and clear? It will undoubtedly be more agreeable to have it all brought into one instrument than have to refer to five or six different acts.

Apprehensions Unallayed

Much of the resistance to Madison's insistence on amendments came from Federalists who sharply disapproved of any action that would tend to reopen the debate about the Constitution. Anti-Federalists in Congress did attempt, without success, to add substantive amendments to the ones the Virginian introduced. Federalist resentment was well expressed in an essay signed by "Pacificus," who was, in fact, Noah Webster. On the other side, Virginia's anti-Federalist senators complained that none of the amendments actually approved truly addressed the substantive concerns of the opponents of the Constitution. One further episode from the congressional debates about amendments, the argument about popular instruction of representatives, helps us grasp the depth of feeling on both sides; and few incidents during the first session of the First Congress were more suggestive of the members' consciousness that they were making precedents for ages to come—or of the sharpness of persistent fears about the new regime—than the debate on titles for executive officials.

On the Constitutional Amendments

"Pacificus" to James Madison

New York Daily Advertiser

14 August 1789

In a debate upon the Impost Bill, you declared yourself an enemy to local attachments and said you considered yourself not merely the representative of *Virginia,* but of the *United States.* This declaration was liberal, and the sentiment just. But Sir, does this accord with the interest you take in amending the Constitution? You now hold out in justification of the part you take in forwarding amendments that you have pledged yourself in some measure to your *constituents.* But, Sir, who are your *constituents?* Are they the electors of a small district in Virginia? These indeed gave you a place in the federal legislature; but the moment you were declared to be elected, you became the representative of three millions of people, and you are bound, by the principles of representation and by your own declaration, to

promote the general good of the United States. You had no right to declare that you would act upon the sentiments and wishes of your immediate constituents, unless you should be convinced that the measures you advocate coincide with the wishes and interest of the whole Union. If I have any just ideas of legislation, this doctrine is incontrovertible; and if I know your opinions, you believe it to be so.

Permit me, then, with great respect to ask, Sir, how you can justify yourself in the eyes of the world for espousing the cause of amendments with so much earnestness? Do you, Sir, believe, that the people you represent generally wish for amendments? If you do Sir, you are more egregiously mistaken than you ever were before. I know from the unanimous declaration of men in several states, through which I have lately traveled, that amendments are not generally wished for; on the other hand, amendments are not mentioned but with the most pointed disapprobation.

The people, Sir, admit what the advocates of amendments in Congress generally allow, that the alterations proposed can do very little good or hurt as to the merits of the Constitution; but for this very reason they reprobate any attempt to introduce them. They say, and with great justice, that, at the moment when an excellent government is going into operation; when the hopes of millions are revived, and their minds disposed to acquiesce peaceably in the federal laws; when the demagogues of faction have ceased to clamor and their adherents are reconciled to the Constitution—Congress are taking a step which will revive the spirit of party, spread the causes of contention through all the states, call up jealousies which have no real foundation, and weaken the operations of government, when the people themselves are wishing to give it energy. We see, in the debates, it is frequently asserted that some amendments will satisfy the opposition and give stability to the government.

The people, Sir, in the northern and middle states do not believe a word of this—they do not see any opposition—they find information and experience everywhere operating to remove objections, and they believe that these causes will, though slowly, produce a change of conduct in North Carolina and Rhode Island. Is it not better to wait for this event than risk the tumults that must grow out of another debate upon the Constitution in every one of the United States.

It seems to be agreed on all hands that paper declarations of rights are trifling things and no real security to liberty. In general they are a subject of ridicule. In England, it has been necessary for parliament to ascertain and declare what rights the nation possesses in order to limit the powers and claims of the crown; but for a sovereign free people, whose power is always equal, to declare, with the solemnity of a constitutional act, *We are all born free, and have a few particular rights which are dear to us, and of which we will not deprive ourselves, altho' we leave ourselves at full liberty to abridge any of our other rights,* is a farce in government as novel as it is ludicrous.

I am not disposed to treat you, Sir, with disrespect; many years acquaintance has taught me to esteem your virtues and respect your abilities. No man stands higher in my opinion, and people are everywhere willing to place you among the most able, active and useful representatives of the United States. But they regret that Congress should spend their time in throwing out an empty tub to catch people, either factious or uninformed, who might be taken more honorably by reason and equitable laws. They regret particularly that Mr. Madison's talents should be employed to bring forward amendments which, at best can have little effect upon the merits of the Constitution, and may sow the seeds of discord from New Hampshire to Georgia.

Richard Henry Lee and William Grayson to the Speaker of the Virginia House of Delegates
28 September 1789

We have now the honor of enclosing the propositions of Amendments to the Constitution of the United States that has been finally agreed upon by Congress. We can assure you Sir that nothing on our part has been omitted to procure the success of those radical amendments proposed by the convention and approved by the legislature of our country, which as our constituent, we shall always deem it our duty with respect and reverence to obey. The Journal of the Senate herewith transmitted will at once show how exact and how unfortunate we have been in this business. It is impossible for us not to see the necessary tendency to consolidate empire in the natural operation of the Constitution if no further amended than now proposed. And it is equally impossible for us not to be apprehensive for civil liberty when we know no instance in the records of history that show a people ruled in freedom when subject to an undivided government and inhabiting a territory so extensive as that of the United States, and when, as it seems to us, the nature of man and things join to prevent it. The impracticability in such case of carrying representation sufficiently near to the people for procuring their confidence and consequent obedience compels a resort to fear resulting from great force and excessive power in government. Confederated republics, when the federal hand is not possessed of absorbing power, may permit the existence of freedom, whilst it preserves union, strength, and safety. Such amendments therefore as may secure against the annihilation of the state government we devoutly wish to see adopted.

If a persevering application to Congress from the states that have desired such amendments should fail of its object, we are disposed to think, reasoning from causes to effects, that unless a dangerous apathy should invade the public mind it will not be many years before a constitutional number of legislatures will be found to demand a Convention for the purpose.

William Grayson to Patrick Henry
29 September 1789

With respect to amendments matters have turned out exactly as I apprehended from the extraordinary doctrine of playing the after game: the lower house sent up amendments which held out a safeguard to personal liberty in a great many instances, but this disgusted the Senate, and though we made every exertion to save them, they are so mutilated & gutted that in fact they are good for nothing, & I believe as many others do, that they will do more harm than benefit: The Virginia amendments were all brought into view, and regularly rejected. Perhaps they may think differently on the subject the next session, as Rhode Island has refused for the present acceding to the Constitution. . . .

Popular Instruction of Representatives

15 August 1789

During the House discussion of the first amendments, Thomas Tudor Tucker, a South Carolina anti-Federalist, moved to insert a declaration of the people's right "to instruct their representatives." This led to a longer discussion than the House devoted to freedom of the press or freedom of religious conscience. Only snippets are presented here, but they include a sharp exchange between Madison and Aedanus Burke over whether Madison's amendments would allay the public's fears.

Thomas Hartley (Pa.)

. . . Representation is the principle of our government; the people ought to have confidence in the honor and integrity of those they send forward to transact their business; their right to instruct them is a problematical subject. We have seen it attended with bad consequences both in England and America. When the passions of the people were excited, instructions have been resorted to and obtained to answer party purposes; and although the public opinion is generally respectable, yet at such moments it has been known to be often wrong; and happy is that government composed of men of firmness and wisdom to discover and resist the popular error. . . .

John Page (Va.)

. . . The people have a right to consult for the common good; but to what end will this be done if they have not the power of instructing their representatives? Instruction and representation in a republic appear to me to be inseparably connected. . . . Every friend of mankind, every well-wisher of his country will be desirous of obtaining the sense of the people on every occasion of magnitude; but how can this be so well expressed as in instructions to their representatives? . . .

George Clymer (Pa.)

. . . If they have a constitutional right to instruct us, it infers that we are bound by those instructions. . . ; this is a most dangerous principle, utterly destructive of all ideas of an independent and deliberative body. . . .

Roger Sherman

. . . When the people have chosen a representative, it is his duty to meet others from the different parts of the union, and consult, and agree with them to such acts as are for the general benefit of the whole community; if they were to be guided by instructions, there would be no use in deliberation. . . . From hence I think it may be fairly inferred that the right of the people to consult for the common good can go no further than to petition to legislature or apply for a redress of grievances.

James Jackson

. . . Let the people consult and give their opinion, let the representative judge of it, and if it is just, let him govern himself by it as a good member ought to do; but if it is otherwise, let him have it in his power to reject their advice.

Elbridge Gerry

. . . I think the representative, notwithstanding the insertion of these words, would be at liberty to act as he pleased; . . . yet I think the people have a right both to instruct and bind them. . . . The sovereignty resides in the people, and . . . they do not part with it on any occasion. . . . But much good may result from a declaration in the Constitution that they possess this privilege; the people will be encouraged to come forward with their instructions, which will form a fund of useful information for the legislature. . . . I hope we shall never shut our ears against that information which is to be derived from the petitions and instructions of our constituents. . . .

James Madison

. . . If we confine ourselves to an enumeration of simple acknowledged principles, the ratification will meet with but little difficulty. Amendments of a doubtful nature will have a tendency to prejudice the whole system; the proposition now suggested partakes highly of this nature. . . . In one sense this declaration is true, in many others it is certainly not true; . . . if we mean nothing more than this, that the people have a right to express and communicate their sentiments and wishes, we have provided for it already. . . . If gentlemen mean to go further and to say that the people have a right to instruct their representatives in such a sense as that the delegates were obliged to conform to those instructions, the declaration is not true. Suppose they instruct a representative by his vote to violate the Constitution, is he at liberty to obey such instructions? Suppose he is instructed to patronize certain measures, and from circumstances known to him but not to his constituents, he is convinced that they will endanger the public good, is he obliged to sacrifice his own judgment to them? Suppose he refuses, will his vote be the less valid. . . . What sort of a right is this in the Constitution to instruct a representative who has a right to disregard the order if he pleases? . . .

Michael Jenifer Stone (Md.)

I think the clause would change the government entirely; instead of being a government founded upon representation, it would be a democracy of singular properties.

I differ from the gentleman from Virginia (Mr. Madison) if he thinks this clause would not bind the representative; in my opinion it would bind him effectually, and I venture to assert without diffidence that any law passed by the legislature would be of no force if a majority of the members of this house were instructed to the contrary, provided the amendment become part of the Constitution . . .

Aedanus Burke (S.C.)

I am not positive with respect to the particular expression in the declaration of rights of the people of Maryland, but the constitutions of Massachusetts, Pennsylvania, and North Carolina all of them recognize, in express terms, the right of the people to give instructions to their representatives. I do not mean to insist particularly upon this amendment, but I am very well satisfied that those that are reported and likely to be adopted by this house are very far from giving satisfaction to our constituents; they are not those solid and substantial amendments which the people expect; they are little better than whip-syllabub, frothy and full of wind, formed only to please the palate, or they are like a tub thrown out to a whale to secure the freight of the ship and its peaceable voyage. . . . I think it will be found that we have done nothing but lose our time, and that it will be better to drop the subject now and proceed to the organization of the government.

James Madison

was unwilling to take up any more of the time of the committee, but on the other hand, he was not willing to be silent after the charges that had been brought against the committee and the gentleman who introduced the amendments by the honorable members on each side of him (Mr. Sumter and Mr. Burke). Those gentlemen say that we are precipitating the business and insinuate that we are not acting with candor; I appeal to the gentlemen who have heard the voice of their country, to those who have attended the debates of the state conventions, whether the amendments now proposed are not those most strenuously required by the opponents to the constitution? It was wished that some security should be given for those great and essential rights which they had been taught to believe were in danger. I concurred, in the convention of Virginia, with those gentlemen, so far as to agree to a declaration of those rights which corresponded with my own judgment, and [to] the other alterations which I had the honor to bring forward before the present Congress. I appeal to the gentlemen on this floor who are desirous of amending the Constitution whether these proposed are not compatible with what are required by our constituents. Have not the people been told that the rights of conscience, the freedom of speech, the liberty of the press, and trial by jury were in jeopardy; that they ought not to adopt the Constitution until those important rights were secured to them?

But while I approve of these amendments, I should oppose the consideration at this time of such as are likely to change the principles of the government, or that are of a doubtful nature; because I apprehend there is little prospect of obtaining the consent of two-thirds of both houses of Congress, and three-fourths of the state legislatures, to ratify propositions of this kind; therefore, as a friend to what is attainable, I would limit it to the plain, simple, and important security that has been required. If I was inclined to make no alteration in the constitution I would bring forward such amendments as were of a dubious cast, in order to have the whole rejected.

Aedanus Burke

never entertained an idea of charging gentlemen with the want of candor, but he would appeal to any man of sense and candor whether the amendments contained in the report were anything like the amendments required by the states of New York, Virginia, New Hampshire and Carolina, and having these amendments in his hand, he turned to them to show the difference, concluding that all the important amendments were omitted in the report. . . .

The question was now called for from several parts of the house, but a desultory conversation took place before the question was put; at length the call becoming very general, it was stated from the chair and determined in the negative, 10 rising in favor of it and 41 against it.

Titles

As Madison remarked in a letter to his father, the members of the First Federal Congress were "in a wilderness without a single footstep to guide us." Everything was new, and every action likely to establish precedents for all the Congresses to come. Hardly had its serious business begun before the legislature had to pause to settle the first disagreement between its two houses. As Madison reported to Jefferson, the House of Representatives, in its reply to Washington's inaugural address, had included no "degrading appendages of Excellency, Esquire," or the like. But on 9 May, a committee of the Senate, where the matter had preoccupied the members for a week, recommended that the president should be addressed as His Highness the President of the United States and Protector of their Liberties. The reaction in the House, together with letters by Madison and Massachusetts congressman Fisher Ames, are among the finest sources for an understanding of the temperament in which much of the session's business was conducted.

Proceedings in the House of Representatives
11 May 1789

Josiah Parker (Va.) moved to disagree with the Senate and insist, as the House had already done implicitly in its reply to the inaugural address, "That it is not proper to annex any style or title" to the constitutional titles of federal officials.

John Page (Va.)
seconded the motion, observing that in his opinion the House had no right to interfere in the business; the Constitution expressly prescribed the power of Congress as to bestowing titles. He did not conceive the real honor or dignity of either of those situations to consist in high sounding titles. The House had, on a former occasion, expressed their disapprobation of any title being annexed to their own members, and very justly too. After having soulfully and explicitly declared their sentiments against such measures, he thought it behooved them to be explicit with the Senate. Indeed, he felt himself a good deal hurt that gentlemen on this floor, after having refused their permission to the clerk to enter any more than their plain names on the journal, should be standing up and addressing one another by the title of "the honorable gentleman." He wished the practice could be got over, because it added neither to the honor nor dignity of the House.

Richard Bland Lee (Va.)
approved of the appointment of a committee to confer with a committee of the Senate, as the mode due to the occasion, but he was against adding any title.

Thomas Tudor Tucker (S.C.)
When this business was first brought before the House, I objected to the appointment of a committee to confer with a committee of the Senate; because I thought it a subject which this House had no right to take into consideration. I then stood single and unsupported in my opinion, but have had the pleasure to find since that some gentlemen on this floor agree that I was right. If I was then right, I shall, from stronger reasoning, be right now in opposing the appointment of another committee on the same subject. The joint committee reported that no titles ought to be given; we agreed to the report, and I was in hopes we should have heard no more of the matter. The Senate rejected the report and have now sent us a resolution expressive of a determination to give a title, to which they desire our concurrence. I am still of opinion, that we were wrong in appointing the first committee and think that we shall be guilty of greater impropriety if we now appoint another. What, sir, is the intention of this business? will it not alarm our fellow-citizens? will it not give them just cause of alarm? will they not say that they have been deceived by the Convention that framed the Constitution? that it has been contrived with a view to lead them on by degrees to that kind of government which they have thrown off with abhorrence? Shall we not justify the fears of those who were opposed to the Constitution, because they considered it as insidious and hostile to the liberties of the people? One of its warmest advocates, one of the framers of it (Mr. Wilson of Pennsylvania), has recommended it by calling it a pure democracy. Does this look like a democracy, when one of the first acts of the two

branches of the Legislature is to confer titles? surely not. To give dignity to our government we must give a lofty title to our chief magistrate. Does the dignity of a nation consist in the distance betwixt the first magistrate and his citizens? does it consist in the exaltation of one man and the humiliation of the rest? if so, the most despotic government is the most dignified; and to make our dignity complete we must give a high title, an embroidered robe, a princely equipage, and finally a crown and hereditary succession. Let us, Sir, establish tranquility and good order at home and wealth, strength, and national dignity will be the infallible result. The aggregate of dignity will be the same, whether it be divided amongst all or centered in one. And whom, Sir, do we mean to gratify? Is it our present President? Certainly, if we expect to please him we shall be greatly disappointed. He has a real dignity of character and is above such little vanities. We shall give him infinite pain; we shall do him an essential injury; we shall place him in a most delicate and disagreeable situation; we shall reduce him to the necessity of evincing to the world his disapprobation of our measures or of risking some diminution of that high reputation for disinterested patriotism which he has so justly acquired. If it is not for his gratification, for whose then are we to do this? Where is the man amongst us who has the presumption and vanity to expect it? Who is it that shall say: for my aggrandizement three millions of people have entered into a calamitous war, they have persevered in it for eight long years, they have sacrificed their property, they have spilt their blood, they have rendered thousands of families wretched by the loss of their only protectors and means of support? This spirit of imitation, Sir, this spirit of mimicry and apery will be the ruin of our country. Instead of giving us dignity in the eyes of foreigners, it will expose us to be laughed at as apes. They gave us credit for our exertions in effecting the Revolution, but they will say that we want independence of spirit to render it a blessing to us. I hope, sir, that we shall not appoint a committee. I thought it improper before, and I still think that we cannot be justified in doing it.

Jonathan Trumbell, Jr. (Conn.)
moved for the appointment of a committee of conference to consider on the difference which appeared in the votes of the two houses upon the report of the joint committee.

Aedanus Burke (S.C.)
hoped the House would express their decided disapprobation of bestowing titles in any shape whatever; it would be an indignity in the House to countenance any measures of this nature. Perhaps some gentlemen might think the subject was a matter of indifference, but it did not appear to him in that light; the introduction of two words which he could mention into the title of these officers would alter the Constitution itself; but he would forbear to say anything farther, as he had a well grounded expectation that the House would take no further notice of the business. . . .

James Madison
I may be well disposed to concur in opinion with gentlemen that we ought not to recede from our former vote on this subject, yet at the same time I may wish to proceed with due respect to the Senate, and give dignity and weight to our own opinion so far as it contradicts theirs by the deliberate and decent manner in which we decide. For my part, Mr. Speaker, I do not conceive titles to be so pregnant with danger as some gentlemen apprehend. I believe a President of the United States clothed with all the powers given in the Constitution would not be a dangerous person to the liberties of America if you were to load him with all the titles of Europe or Asia. We have seen superb and august titles given without conferring power and influence or without even obtaining respect; one of the most impotent sovereigns in Europe has assumed a title as high as human invention can devise; for example, what words can imply a greater magnitude of power and strength than that of high mightiness; this title seems to border almost upon impiety; it is assuming the pre-eminence and omnipotency of the deity; yet this title and many others cast in the same mold have obtained a long time in Europe, but have they conferred power? Does experience sanctify such opinion? Look at the republic I have alluded to and say if their present state warrants the idea.

I am not afraid of titles because I fear the danger of any power they could confer, but I am against them because they are not very reconcilable with the nature of our government or the genius of the people; even if they were proper in themselves, they are not so at this juncture of time. But my strongest objection is founded in principle; instead of increasing they diminish the true dignity and importance of a republic, and would in particular, on this occasion, diminish the true dignity of the first magistrate himself. If we give titles, we must either borrow or invent them—if we have recourse to the fertile fields of luxuriant fancy and deck out an airy being of our own creation, it is a great chance but its fantastic properties renders the empty fanthom ridiculous and absurd. If we borrow, the servile imitation will be odious, not to say ridiculous also—we must copy from the pompous sovereigns of the East or follow the inferior potentates of Europe; in either case, the splendid tinsel or gorgeous robe would disgrace the manly shoulders of our Chief. The more truly honorable shall we be, by showing a total neglect and disregard to things of this nature; the more simple, the more republican we are in our manners, the more rational dignity we acquire; therefore I am better pleased with the report adopted by the House, than I should have been with any other whatsoever.

The Senate, no doubt, entertain different sentiments on this subject. I would wish therefore to treat their opinion with respect and attention, I would desire to justify the reasonable and republican decision of this house to the other branch of Congress, in order to prevent a misunderstanding. But that the motion of my worthy colleague (Mr. Parker) has possession of the house, I would move a more temperate proposition, and I think it deserves some pains to bring about that good will and urbanity which, for the dispatch of public business, ought to be kept up between the two houses. I do not think it would be a sacrifice of dignity to appoint a committee of conference, but imagine it would tend to cement that harmony which has hitherto been preserved between the Senate and this House—therefore, while I concur with the gentlemen who express in such decided terms their disapprobation of bestowing titles, I concur also with those who are for the appointment of a committee of conference, not apprehending they will depart from the principles adopted and acted upon by the House. . . .

Josiah Parker (Va.)

wanted to know what was the object of gentlemen in the appointment of a committee of conference. The committee could only say that the House had refused their consent to annexing any titles whatever to the President and Vice President; for certainly the committee would not descend into the merits of a question already established by the House. For his part he could not see what purpose was to be answered by the appointment of such a committee.

He wished to have done with the subject, because while it remained a question in the House, the people's minds would be much agitated; it was impossible that a true republican spirit could remain unconcerned when a principle was under consideration so repugnant to the principles of equal liberty.

Roger Sherman

thought it was pretty plain that the House could not comply with the proposition of the Senate. The appointment of a committee on the part of the House to consider and determine what stile or titles will be proper to annex to the President and Vice-President would imply that the House meant that some stile or title should be given; now this, they never could intend, because they have decided that no stile or title ought to be given—it will be sufficient to adduce this reason for not complying with the request of the Senate.

James Jackson

wondered what title the Senate had in contemplation to add dignity or luster to the person that filled the presidential Chair. For his part he could conceive none. Would it add to his fame to be called after the petty and insignificant princes of Europe? Would styling him his Serene Highness, His Grace, or Mightiness add one tittle to the solid properties he possessed? He thought it would not; and therefore conceived the proposition to be trifling with the dignity of the government. As a difference had taken place between the two Houses, he had no objection to a conference taking place, he hoped it might be productive of good consequences and the Senate be induced to follow the laudable example of the House.

James Madison

was of opinion that the House might appoint a committee of conference without being supposed to countenance the measure. The standing rule of the House declared that, in case of disagreeing votes, a committee of conference should be appointed; now, the case provided for in the rule had actually happened, he inferred that it was proper to proceed in the manner directed by the rules of the House; the subject was still open to discussion, but there was little probability that the House would rescind their adoption of the report. I presume gentlemen do not intend to compel the Senate into their measures; they should recollect that the Senate stand upon independent ground and will do nothing but what they are convinced of the propriety of; it would be better, therefore, to treat them with delicacy and offer some reasons to induce them to come into our measure. He expected this would be the result of a conference and therefore was in favor of such a motion. . . .

George Clymer (Pa.)

thought there was little occasion to add any title to either the President or Vice-President. He was very well convinced by experience that titles did not confer power; on the contrary, they frequently made their possessors ridiculous. The most impotent potentates, the most insignificant powers, generally assumed the highest and most lofty titles. That they do not indicate power and prerogative is very observable in the English history; for when the chief magistrate of that nation wore the simple stile of his Grace or Highness, his prerogatives were much more extensive than since he has become His Most Sacred Majesty.

Titular distinctions are said to be unpopular in the United States, yet a person would be led to think otherwise from the vast number of honorable gentlemen we have in America. As soon as a man is selected for the public service, his fellow citizens with liberal hand shower down titles on him — either excellency or honorable. He would venture to affirm there were more honorable esquires in the United States than all the world beside. He wished to check a propensity so notoriously evidenced in favor of distinctions, and hoped the example of the House might prevail to extinguish what predilection that appeared in favor of titles.

John Page

. . . I must tell gentlemen I differ from them when they think titles can do no harm. Titles I say, Sir, may do harm and have done harm. If we contend now for a right to confer titles, I apprehend the time will come when we shall form a reservoir for honor and make our President the fountain of it; in such case, may not titles do an injury to the union? They have been the occasion of an eternal faction in the kingdom we were formerly connected with, and may beget like inquietude in America; for, I contend, if you give the title, you must follow it with the robe and the diadem, and then the principles of your government are subverted.

Richard Bland Lee (Va.)

moved the previous question, as the best mode of getting rid of the motion before the House. He was supported by

a sufficient number. And on the question, Shall the main question be now put? it passed in the negative; and so the motion was lost.

On motion, it was resolved, that a committee be appointed to join with such committee as the Senate may appoint to confer on the disagreeing votes of the two Houses upon the report of their joint committee, appointed to consider what titles shall be given to the President and Vice President of the United States, if any other than those given in the Constitution. Messrs. Madison, Page, Benson, Trumbull, and Sherman were the committee elected.

Fisher Ames to George Richards Minot
14 May 1789

. . . It is not easy to write the transactions of the House, because I forget the topics which do not reach you by the newspaper. A committee of both Houses had reported that it is not proper to address the President by any other title than that in the Constitution. The House agreed to the report without debate. But the Senate rejected it and notified the House that they had nonconcurred. The House was soon in a ferment. The antispeakers edified all aristocratic hearts by their zeal against titles. They were not warranted by the Constitution; repugnant to republican principles; dangerous, vain, ridiculous, arrogant, and damnable. Not a soul said a word *for* titles. But the zeal of these folks could not have risen higher in case of contradiction. Whether the arguments were addressed to the galleries or intended to hurry the House to a resolve censuring the Senate, so as to set the two Houses at odds, and to nettle the Senate to bestow a title in *their* address, is not clear. The latter was supposed, and a great majority agreed to appoint a committee of conference. The business will end here. Prudence will restrain the Senate from doing anything at present, and they will call him President, etc., simply.

James Madison to Thomas Jefferson
23 May 1789

. . . My last enclosed copies of the President's inauguration speech and the answer of the House of Representatives. I now add the answer of the Senate. It will not have escaped you that the former was addressed with a truly republican simplicity to G. W., President of the U.S. The latter follows the example, with the omission of the personal name but without any other than the constitutional title. The proceeding on this point was in the House of Representatives spontaneous. The imitation by the Senate was extorted. The question became a serious one between the two houses. J. Adams espoused the cause of titles with great earnestness. His friend R. H. Lee, altho elected as a republican enemy to an aristocratic constitution, was a most zealous second. The projected title was—His Highness the President of the U.S. and protector of their liberties. Had the project succeeded it would have subjected the President to a severe dilemma and given a deep wound to our infant government.

PART 2

The Leadership Divides

In all of American history, no Congress has accomplished quite so much, so very well, as the first one did in 1789. It framed the Bill of Rights. It passed an impost act, assuring the new government a steady source of revenues from duties on imports of foreign goods. It filled the Constitution's parchment outline of a working federal government with the Judiciary Act of 1789, establishing a system of federal courts, and legislation creating four executive departments. It confirmed the president's superb appointments to the new executive positions: Thomas Jefferson at State, Alexander Hamilton at the Treasury, Henry Knox at the War Department, and Edmund Randolph as Attorney General.

When Congress reassembled for its second session, in December 1789, the largest problem unaddressed by the preceding session was the heavy burden of remaining revolutionary debt. Including the arrears of interest (since the portion owed to American citizens had gone unserviced for years), the nation owed about $55 million: a fifth of it to foreign governments and bankers; the rest to citizens who had purchased bonds during the war or accepted payment for goods and services in promissory notes. The individual states, which had made quite different degrees of progress in retiring their own debts, owed another $25 million. The Secretary of the Treasury, who had been ordered to report a plan for managing the debt, presented his proposals on 14 January 1790.

For Hamilton, the reestablishment of public credit, narrowly conceived, was only the first of several steps required to put the national finances on a firm foundation and begin addressing larger economic needs. Accordingly, his first Report on Public Credit recommended measures cleverly designed to underpin a larger program, although the secretary's full design would only be unveiled as he delivered a succession of additional reports proposing the creation of a national bank, creation of an adequate supply of circulating money, and encouragement of rapid economic growth. Simply put, the secretary recommended that the old certificates of public debt should be exchanged for new ones paying a smaller rate of interest. In exchange, the government would pledge most of the revenues deriving from the impost to payment of that interest, and, from time to time, federal commissioners would purchase bonds on private money markets, which would gradually retire the obligations. To rationalize the national finances, the federal government would also assume responsibility for the unpaid debts of the states, paying for this assumption with an excise tax on spirits, coffee, and tea. If state and federal creditors could be assured of steady payment of the interest due them on their notes, the government's certificates of debt, which had been trading for a fraction of their value, would quickly rise toward par and could be passed from one investor to another almost as readily as cash; indeed, they could be used, like coin, to underpin a range of further investments, beginning with a national bank. Meanwhile, public credit (or the government's ability to borrow) would be instantly restored. With its finances placed on this foundation, the United States might even refinance the smaller sums still owed to foreign governments and bankers at a lower rate of interest.

The funding plan did work, in practice, much as Hamilton envisioned. But congressmen were quick to notice that the secretary's plan made slight provision for actually paying off the debt, proposing to dedicate to this purpose only the surplus revenues of the post office. Indeed, in order to protect the market value of the bonds, the plan deliberately limited the amount of debt that could be retired in any single year. For this and other reasons, the funding and assumption plans sparked the sharpest disagreements since the approval of the Constitution, and Hamilton's larger plan would split the men who had secured the Constitution into the contending groups from which the first American parties would emerge.

Funding and Assumption

ALEXANDER HAMILTON

The First Report on Public Credit

14 January 1790

Already thinking far beyond the reestablishment of public credit, Hamilton took pains in the report to counter alternative suggestions that were already circulating in the country. He particularly objected to the ideas of funding the debt at its depreciated value, discriminating between original and current holders of the notes, or forgoing an assumption of the debts of the states.

. . . While the observance of that good faith which is the basis of public credit is recommended by the strongest inducements of political expediency, it is enforced by considerations of still greater authority. There are arguments for it which rest on the immutable principles of moral obligation. And in proportion as the mind is disposed to contemplate, in the order of Providence, an intimate connection between public virtue and public happiness, will be its repugnancy to a violation of those principles.

This reflection derives additional strength from the nature of the debt of the United States. It was the price of liberty. The faith of America has been repeatedly pledged for it, and with solemnities that give peculiar force to the obligation. There is indeed reason to regret that it has not hitherto been kept; that the necessities of the war, conspiring with inexperience in the subjects of finance, produced direct infractions; and that the subsequent period has been a continued scene of negative violation, or non-compliance. But a diminution of this regret arises from the reflection that the last seven years have exhibited an earnest and uniform effort, on the part of the government of the union, to retrieve the national credit, by doing justice to the creditors of the nation; and that the embarrassments of a defective constitution, which defeated this laudable effort, have ceased. . . .

It cannot but merit particular attention that among ourselves the most enlightened friends of good government are those whose expectations are the highest.

To justify and preserve their confidence; to promote the increasing respectability of the American name; to answer the calls of justice; to restore landed property to its due value; to furnish new resources both to agriculture and commerce; to cement more closely the union of the states; to add to their security against foreign attack; to establish public order on the basis of an upright and liberal policy. These are the great and invaluable ends to be secured by a proper and adequate provision, at the present period, for the support of public credit.

To this provision we are invited, not only by the general considerations which have been noticed, but by others of a more particular nature. It will procure to every class of the community some important advantages and remove some no less important disadvantages.

The advantage to the public creditors from the increased value of that part of their property which constitutes the public debt needs no explanation.

But there is a consequence of this, less obvious, though not less true, in which every other citizen is interested. It is a well known fact that in countries in which the national debt is properly funded and an object of established confidence, it answers most of the purposes of money. Transfers of stock or public debt are there equivalent to payments in specie; or in other words, stock, in the principal transactions of business, passes current as specie. The same thing would in all probability happen here, under the like circumstances.

The benefits of this are various and obvious.

First. Trade is extended by it; because there is a larger capital to carry it on, and the merchant can at the same time afford to trade for smaller profits as his stock, which, when unemployed, brings him in an interest from the government, serves him also as money, when he has a call for it in his commercial operations.

Secondly. Agriculture and manufactures are also promoted by it: For the like reason, that more capital can be commanded to be employed in both; and because the merchant, whose enterprize in foreign trade gives to them activity and extension, has greater means for enterprize.

Thirdly. The interest of money will be lowered by it, for this is always in a ratio to the quantity of money and to the quickness of circulation. This circumstance will enable both the public and individuals to borrow on easier and cheaper terms.

And from the combination of these effects, additional aids will be furnished to labour, to industry, and to arts of every kind.

But these good effects of a public debt are only to be looked for when, by being well funded, it has acquired an *adequate* and *stable* value. Till then, it has rather a contrary tendency. The fluctuation and insecurity incident to it in an unfunded state render it a mere commodity, and a precarious one. As such, being only an object of occasional and particular speculation, all the money applied to it is so much diverted from the more useful channels of circulation, for which the thing itself affords no substitute: So that, in fact, one serious inconvenience of an unfunded debt is that it contributes to the scarcity of money.

This distinction, which has been little if at all attended to, is of the greatest moment. It involves a question immediately interesting to every part of the community; which is no other than this —Whether the public debt, by a provision for it on true principles, shall be rendered a *substitute* for money; or whether, by being left as it is, or by being provided for in such a manner as will wound those principles and destroy confidence, it shall be suffered to continue, as it is, a pernicious drain of our cash from the channels of productive industry.

The effect which the funding of the public debt, on right principles, would have upon landed property, is one of the circumstances attending such an arrangement which has been least adverted to, though it deserves the most particular attention. The present depreciated state of that species of property is a serious calamity. The value of cultivated lands, in most of the states, has fallen since the revolution from 25 to 50 per cent. In those farthest south, the decrease is still more considerable. Indeed, if the representations continually received from that quarter may be credited, lands there will command no price which may not be deemed an almost total sacrifice.

This decrease in the value of lands ought, in a great measure, to be attributed to the scarcity of money. Consequently, whatever produces an augmentation of the monied capital of the country must have a proportional effect in raising that value. The beneficial tendency of a funded debt, in this respect, has been manifested by the most decisive experience in Great-Britain.

The proprietors of lands would not only feel the benefit of this increase in the value of their property, and of a more prompt and better sale when they had occasion to sell; but the necessity of selling would be, itself, greatly diminished. As the same cause would contribute to the facility of loans, there is reason to believe that such of them as are indebted would be able, through that resource, to satisfy their more urgent creditors.

It ought not however to be expected that the advantages described as likely to result from funding the public debt would be instantaneous. It might require some time to bring the value of stock to its natural level, and to attach to it that fixed confidence which is necessary to its quality as money. Yet the late rapid rise of the public securities encourages an expectation that the progress of stock to the desirable point will be much more expeditious than could have been foreseen. And as in the mean time it will be increasing in value, there is room to conclude that it will, from the outset, answer many of the purposes in contemplation. Particularly it seems to be probable that from creditors who are not themselves necessitous it will early meet with a ready reception in payment of debts, at its current price.

Having now taken a concise view of the inducements to a proper provision for the public debt, the next enquiry which presents itself is, what ought to be the nature of such a provision? This requires some preliminary discussions.

It is agreed on all hands that that part of the debt which has been contracted abroad, and is denominated the foreign debt, ought to be provided for according to the precise terms of the contracts relating to it. The discussions which can arise, therefore, will have reference essentially to the domestic part of it, or to that which has been contracted at home. It is to be regretted that there is not the same unanimity of sentiment on this part as on the other.

The Secretary has too much deference for the opinions of every part of the community not to have observed one which has, more than once, made its appearance in the public prints, and which is occasionally to be met with in conversation. It involves this question, whether a discrimination ought not to be made between original holders of the public securities and present possessors by purchase. Those who advocate a discrimination are for making a full provision for the securities of the former, at their nominal value, but contend that the latter ought to receive no more than the cost to them and the interest: And the idea is sometimes suggested of making good the difference to the primitive possessor.

In favor of this scheme, it is alledged that it would be unreasonable to pay twenty shillings in the pound to one who had not given more for it than three or four. And it is added, that it would be hard to aggravate the misfortune of the first owner, who, probably through necessity, parted with his property at so great a loss, by obliging him to contribute to the profit of the person who had speculated on his distresses.

The Secretary, after the most mature reflection on the force of this argument, is induced to reject the doctrine it contains, as equally unjust and impolitic, as highly injurious even to the original holders of public securities; as ruinous to public credit.

It is inconsistent with justice, because in the first place, it is a breach of contract; in violation of the rights of a fair purchaser.

The nature of the contract in its origin is that the public will pay the sum expressed in the security to the first holder, or his *assignee*. The *intent*, in making the security assignable, is that the proprietor may be able to make use of his property by selling it for as much as it *may be worth in the market*, and that the buyer may be *safe* in the purchase.

Every buyer therefore stands exactly in the place of the seller, has the same right with him to the identical sum expressed in the security, and having acquired that right, by fair purchase and in conformity to the original *agreement* and *intention* of the government, his claim cannot be disputed, without manifest injustice.

That he is to be considered as a fair purchaser results from this: Whatever necessity the seller may have been under was occasioned by the government, in not making a proper provision for its debts. The buyer had no agency in it, and therefore ought not to suffer. He is not even chargeable with having taken an undue advantage. He paid what the commodity was worth in the market, and took the risks of reimbursement upon himself. He of course gave a fair equivalent, and ought to reap the benefit of his hazard; a hazard which was far from inconsiderable and which, perhaps, turned on little less than a revolution in government.

That the case of those who parted with their securities from necessity is a hard one, cannot be denied. But whatever complaint of injury or claim of redress they may have respects the government solely. They have not only nothing to object to the persons who relieved their necessities, by giving them the current price of their property, but they are even under an implied condition to contribute to the reimbursement of those persons. They knew that by the terms of the contract with themselves, the public were bound to pay to those to whom they should convey their title the sums stipulated to be paid to them; and, that as citizens of the United States, they were to bear their proportion of the contribution for that purpose. This, by the act of assignment, they tacitly engage to do; and if they had an option, they could not, with integrity or good faith, refuse to do it, without the consent of those to whom they sold.

But though many of the original holders sold from necessity, it does not follow that this was the case with all of them. It may well be supposed that some of them did it either through want of confidence in an eventual provision or from the allurements of some profitable speculation. How shall these different classes be discriminated from each other? How shall it be ascertained, in any case, that the money which the original holder obtained for his security was not more beneficial to him than if he had held it to the present time, to avail himself of the provision which shall be made? How shall it be known whether, if the purchaser had employed his money in some other way, he would not be in a better situation than by having applied it in the purchase of securities, though he should now receive their full amount? And if neither of these things can be known, how shall it be determined whether a discrimination, independent of the breach of contract, would not do a real injury to purchasers; and if it included a compensation to the primitive proprietors, would not give them an advantage to which they had no equitable pretension.

It may well be imagined, also, that there are not wanting instances in which individuals, urged by a present necessity, parted with the securities received by them from the public and shortly after replaced them with others, as an indemnity for their first loss. Shall they be deprived of the indemnity which they have endeavoured to secure by so provident an arrangement?

Questions of this sort, on a close inspection, multiply themselves without end, and demonstrate the injustice of a discrimination even on the most subtle calculations of equity, abstracted from the obligation of contract.

The difficulties too of regulating the details of a plan for that purpose, which would have even the semblance of equity, would be found immense. It may well be doubted whether they would not be insurmountable and replete with such absurd, as well as inequitable consequences, as to disgust even the proposers of the measure. . . .

But there is still a point in view in which it will appear perhaps even more exceptionable than in either of the former. It would be repugnant to an express provision of the Constitution of the United States. This provision is that "all debts contracted and engagements entered into before the adoption of that Constitution shall be as valid against the United States under it, as under the confederation," which amounts to a constitutional ratification of the contracts respecting the debt, in the state in which they existed under the confederation. And resorting to that standard, there can be no doubt that the rights of assignees and original holders must be considered as equal.

In exploding thus fully the principle of discrimination, the Secretary is happy in reflecting that he is only the advocate of what has been already sanctioned by the formal and express authority of the government of the Union, in these emphatic terms—"The remaining class of creditors (say Congress in their circular address to the states of the 26th of April 1783) is composed partly of such of our fellow-citizens as originally lent to the public the use of their funds or have since manifested *most confidence* in their country by receiving transfers from the lenders; and partly of those whose property has been either advanced or assumed for the public service. To *discriminate* the merits of these several descriptions of creditors would be a task equally unnecessary and invidious. If the voice of humanity plead more loudly in favor of some than of others, the voice of policy, no less than of justice, pleads in favor of all. A WISE NATION will never permit those who relieve the wants of their country, or who *rely most* on its *faith,* its *firmness,* and its *resources,* when either of them is distrusted, to suffer by the event."

The Secretary, concluding that a discrimination between the different classes of creditors of the United States cannot with propriety be *made,* proceeds to examine whether a difference ought to be permitted to *remain* between them and another description of public creditors—Those of the states individually.

The Secretary, after mature reflection on this point, entertains a full conviction that an assumption of the debts of the particular states by the Union, and a like provision for them as for those of the Union, will be a measure of sound policy and substantial justice.

It would, in the opinion of the Secretary, contribute, in an eminent degree, to an orderly, stable and satisfactory arrangement of the national finances.

Admitting, as ought to be the case, that a provision must be made in some way or other for the entire debt, it will follow that no greater revenues will be required whether that provision be made wholly by the United States or partly by them and partly by the states separately.

The principal question then must be whether such a provision cannot be more conveniently and effectually made by one general plan issuing from one authority than by different plans originating in different authorities.

In the first case there can be no competition for resources; in the last, there must be such a competition. The consequences of this, without the greatest caution on both sides, might be interfering regulations, and thence collision and confusion. Particular branches of industry might also be oppressed by it. The most productive objects of revenue are not numerous. Either these must be wholly engrossed by one side, which might occasion an accumulation upon them beyond what they could properly bear. If this should not happen, the caution requisite to avoiding it would prevent the revenue's deriving the full benefit of each object. The danger of interference and of excess would be apt to impose restraints very unfriendly to the complete command of those resources which are the most convenient; and to compel the having recourse to others, less eligible in themselves, and less agreeable to the community. . . .

If all the public creditors receive their dues from one source, distributed with an equal hand, their interest will be the same. And having the same interests, they will unite in the support of the fiscal arrangements of the government: As these, too, can be made with more convenience where there is no competition, these circumstances combined will insure to the revenue laws a more ready and more satisfactory execution.

If on the contrary there are distinct provisions, there will be distinct interests, drawing different ways. That union and concert of views among the creditors, which in every government is of great importance to their security and to that of public credit, will not only not exist, but will be likely to give place to mutual jealousy and opposition. And from this cause, the operation of the systems which may be adopted, both by the particular states and by the Union, with relation to their respective debts, will be in danger of being counteracted.

There are several reasons which render it probable that the situation of the state creditors would be worse than that of the creditors of the Union if there be not a national assumption of the state debts. Of these it will be sufficient to mention two; one, that a principal branch of revenue is exclusively vested in the Union; the other, that a state must always be checked in the imposition of taxes on articles of consumption from the want of power to extend the same regulation to the other states and from the tendency of partial duties to injure its industry and commerce. Should the state creditors stand upon a less eligible footing than the others, it is unnatural to expect they would see with pleasure a provision for them. The influence which their dissatisfaction might have could not but operate injuriously, both for the creditors and the credit of the United States.

Hence it is even the interest of the creditors of the Union that those of the individual states should be comprehended in a general provision. Any attempt to secure to the former either exclusive or peculiar advantages would materially hazard their interests.

Neither would it be just that one class of the public creditors should be more favoured than the other. The objects for which both descriptions of the debt were contracted are in the main the same. Indeed a great part of the particular debts of the states has arisen from assumptions by them on account of the Union. And it is most equitable that there should be the same measure of retribution for all.

There is an objection, however, to an assumption of the state debts which deserves particular notice. It may be supposed that it would increase the difficulty of an equitable settlement between them and the United States.

The principles of that settlement, whenever they shall be discussed, will require all the moderation and wisdom of the government. In the opinion of the Secretary, that discussion, till further lights are obtained, would be premature.

All therefore which he would now think adviseable on the point in question would be that the amount of the debts assumed and provided for should be charged to the respective states, to abide an eventual arrangement. This, the United States, as assignees to the creditors, would have an indisputable right to do. . . .

Persuaded as the Secretary is that the proper funding of the present debt will render it a national blessing, yet he is so far from acceding to the position, in the latitude in which it is sometimes laid down, that "public debts are public benefits," a position inviting to prodigality and liable to dangerous abuse, that he ardently wishes to see it incorporated as a fundamental maxim in the system of public credit of the United States, that the creation of debt should always be accompanied with the means of extinguishment. This he regards as the true secret for rendering public credit immortal. And he presumes that it is difficult to conceive a situation in which there may not be an adherence to the maxim. At least he feels an unfeigned solicitude that this may be attempted by the United States, and that they may commence their measures for the establishment of credit with the observance of it.

Under this impression, the Secretary proposes that the net product of the post-office, to a sum not exceeding one million of dollars, be vested in commissioners to consist of the Vice-President of the United States or President of the Senate, the Speaker of the House of Representatives, the Chief Justice, Secretary of the Treasury and Attorney-General of the United States, for the time being, in trust, to be applied by them, or any three of them, to the discharge of the existing public debt, either by purchases of stock in the market or by payments on account of the principal, as shall appear to them most adviseable, in conformity to the public engagements; to continue so vested until the whole of the debt shall be discharged. . . .

Debates in the House of Representatives on the First Report on Public Credit

9–18 February 1790

Deliberations on Hamilton's report opened on 9 February with a resolution "that permanent funds ought to be appropriated for the payment of interest on and the gradual discharge of the domestic debt of the United States." The proceedings could be followed closely by the public, since newspapers at the seat of government published the House of Representatives' debates and papers around the country copied them from these sources.

James Jackson (Ga.)

Believe me, Mr. Chairman, I have as high a sense of the obligation we are under to the public creditors, and feel as much gratitude toward them, as any man on this floor. I shall ever cheerfully acknowledge the duty we owe to our benefactors and, in a peculiar manner, to those brave soldiers who, at the risk of their lives and fortunes, secured the independency of America. I have also the most sincere wishes for the re-establishment of public credit, and that upon firm and solid ground, and on principles which cannot be called in question. But there appears to me a previous question, which has not yet been brought forward; it is this, whether there exists an immediate necessity of funding the national debts, or not, in the permanent manner proposed?

The high regard I have for the nature and circumstances of the foreign debt induced me to let the first proposition pass without any animadversion. The vote which has been taken on that point will serve to show foreigners that we are concerned to preserve our credit with them, by a rigid performance of our stipulations; trusting, at the same time, that our fellow citizens cannot object to a distinction so just and proper in itself; for, notwithstanding what the domestic creditors may say, it is the money of foreigners that has, in a great measure, established our independence.

But it is doubted with me whether a permanent funded debt is beneficial or not to any country. Some of the first writers in the world, and who are most admired on account of the clearness of their perceptions, have thought otherwise; and declared that wherever funding systems have been adopted in a government, they tend more to injure posterity than they would injure the inhabitants to pay the whole debt at the time it was contracted. This principle, I apprehend, is demonstrated by experience. The first system of the kind that we have an account of originated in the state of Florence, in the year 1334; that government then owed about 60,000 sterling, and being unable to pay it, formed the principal into a funded debt, transferable, with interest, at 5 per cent. What is the situation of Florence in consequence of this event? Her ancient importance is annihilated. . . . Spain seems to have learned the practice from the Italian republics, and she, by the anticipation of her immense revenue, has sunk her consequence beneath that level which her natural situation might have maintained. France is considerably enfeebled and languishes under a heavy load of debt. England is a melancholy instance of the ruin attending such engagements. In the reign of King William, 1706, the policy of the English parliament laid the foundation of what is called the national debt; but the sum was inconsiderable; it little exceeded 5,000,000 sterling. The example then set has been closely followed. In 1711, it amounted to 9,177,769 sterling, during the wars in the reign of Queen Anne. Since that, the capital of the debt of Great Britain amounted, in 1777, to about 136,000,000 sterling; and to such a pitch has the spirit of funding and borrowing been carried in that country that, in 1786, the national debt there had increased to 230,000,000 sterling; a burthen the most sanguine mind can never contemplate they will ever be relieved from. If future difficulties should involve that nation still further, what must be the consequence? The same effect must be produced that has taken place in other nations; it must either bring on a national bankruptcy or annihilate her existence as an independent empire. Hence I contend, sir, that a funding system, in this country, will be highly dangerous to the welfare of the republic; it may, for a moment, raise our credit and increase the circulation, by multiplying a new species of currency; but it must, in times afterward, settle upon our posterity a burthen which they can neither bear nor relieve themselves from. It will establish a precedent in America that may, and in all probability will, be pursued by the sovereign authority until it brings upon us that ruin which it has never failed to bring, or is inevitably bringing, upon all the nations of the earth who have had the temerity to make the experiment. Let us take warning by the errors of Europe and guard against the introduction of a system followed by calamities so universal. Though our present debt be but a few millions, in the course of a single century, they may be multiplied to an extent we dare not think of; for my part, I would rather have direct taxes imposed at once, which, in the course of a few years, should annihilate the principal of our debt. A few years exertion, in this way, will prevent our posterity from a load of annual interest amounting to the fifth, or perhaps the half, of the sum we are now under engagements to pay.

But why, Mr. Chairman, should we hasten on this business of funding? Are our debts ascertained? The report of the secretary of the treasury proposes that we should not only fund the debts that are ascertained, but the unliquidated and unsettled debts due from the continent; nor does the plan stop here, it proposes that we should assume the payment of the state debts, debts, to us, totally unknown. Many of the states, sir, have not yet ascertained what they owe, and if we do not know the amount of what we are, or are to be, indebted, shall we establish funds? Shall we put our hands into the pockets of our constituents, and appropriate monies for uses we are undetermined of? But more especially shall we do this when, in doing it, it is indisputably certain that the incumbrance will more than exceed all the benefits and conveniencies? Gentlemen may come forward, perhaps, and tell me that funding of the public debt will increase the circulating medium of the country, by means of its transferable quality; but this is denied by the best informed men. They occasion enormous taxes for the payment of the interest. These taxes hurt both agriculture and commerce. It is charging the active and industrious citizen, who pays his share of the taxes, to pay the indolent and idle creditor who receives them, to be spent and wasted in the course of the year without any hope of a future reproduction; for the new capital which they acquire must have existed in the country before, and must have been employed, as all capitals are, in maintaining productive labor. Thus the honest, hard working part of the community are adding to the ease and luxury of men of wealth. Such a system may benefit large cities, like Philadelphia or New-York, but the remote parts of the continent may not feel the invigorating warmth of the American treasury; in the proportion that it benefits one, it depresses another. . . .

Under these impressions, sir, I am led to conclude that it is becoming the wisdom of congress to postpone the consideration of the remaining propositions; let us endeavor to discover whether there is an absolute necessity for adopting a funding system or not. If there is no such necessity, a short time will make it apparent, and let it be remembered what funds the United States possess in their Western Territory. The disposal of those lands may, perhaps, supercede the necessity of establishing a permanent system of taxation. The secretary of the treasury is directed to report on this head to the House, and perhaps that report may show us that this property is likely to be more productive than we at present apprehend. These considerations induced me to wish that the further consideration be postponed for the present.

Roger Sherman (Conn.)

. . . I think, whatever doubts there may be with respect to the advantage or disadvantage of a public debt, we can none of us hesitate to decide that provision of some kind ought to be made for what we have already incurred. It is true, if we were now about to borrow money, it would be highly prudent to consider whether the anticipation should not be repaid by a speedy collection of taxes or duties to the amount; but when a debt is acquired beyond our present ability to discharge, we ought to make some provision for its gradual extinction, but, in the interim, we ought to pay punctually the interest. Now, this resolution goes no further.

Some of the propositions which follow go further than this; they propose perpetual annuities and talk of irredeemable stock. Now, this is more than I am willing to agree to, because I think it prudent for us to get out of debt as soon as we can. But then I do not suppose we can raise money enough to pay off the whole principal and interest in two, three, or ten years. If I am right in this, we ought to agree to some mode of paying the interest in the interim.

William Loughton Smith (S.C.)

The report of the secretary of the treasury contains a proposition for the establishment of a sinking fund. I wish the gentleman who brought forward the resolutions under consideration had included that part of the system in his propositions, as it might have had a tendency to ease the mind of the honorable gentleman from Georgia and to have shown him that the public debt was not intended to acquire the permanency which he dreads. If our present debt cannot be paid off at once, all that can be done is to provide such funds for its gradual extinction as will morally ensure the object.

The gentleman has contended that public funding is a public injury. I agree with him that funding a debt to a very great amount may be very injurious; yet, funding a small debt is beneficial. But whether this is or is not a fact is not the object of our present enquiry. We are not in a situation to determine whether we will, or will not, have a public debt. 'Tis already acquired, and it appears to me to be a matter of necessity that we should appropriate some funds for the payment of the interest thereon. When we consider the nature of the contract, for what it is we owe the money, and our ability to comply, it follows, of consequence, that we must pay; it follows as close as the shadow follows its substance, or as close as the night does the day. The only question that can come before us is the mode of doing it. . . .

James Jackson

begged the committee would not understand him that he was against paying the debts of the United States; he had no such object in view. The sinking fund alluded to by the gentleman from South-Carolina had not escaped his attention; but he very much doubted whether it ought to be relied on to effect the purpose he had in view. He believed sinking funds were generally considered as a kind of stand-by or subsidiary fund, always at hand to be mortgaged when money was proposed to be raised on any exigency of the state. . . .

Samuel Livermore (N.H.)

I do not clearly understand the import of the resolution before the committee; it seems worded rather in a doubtful manner. If it means that funds ought to be appropriated for the payment of the interest and principal of the domestic debt as the amount appears on the face of the certificates, I shall be totally against it; whether it pointedly carries that meaning or not I cannot say.

For my part, I consider the foreign and domestic debt to carry with them very material distinctions. The one is not like a debt, while the other has all the true qualities of one. However gentlemen may think on this subject, there is a great difference between the merits of that debt which was lent the United States in real money, in solid coin, by disinterested persons, not concerned or benefited by the revolution, and at a low rate of interest; and in those debts which have been accumulating upon the United States at the rate of 6 per cent interest and which were not incurred for efficient money lent, but for depreciated paper or services done at exorbitant rates, or for goods or provisions supplied for more than their real worth, by those who received all the benefits arising from our change of condition. It is within the notice and knowledge of every gentleman that a very considerable part of our domestic loan-office debt arose in this manner; it is well known that loan-office certificates were issued as a kind of circulating medium when the United States were in such straits for cash that they could not raise the necessary supplies in any other way; and it is very well known that those who sold goods or provisions for this circulating medium raised their prices from six shillings to ten shillings at least.

There is another observation I would beg leave to make. The prices at which our supplies were procured were such, even in hard money, that it might be said specie had

depreciated, or what amounted to the same thing, the commodities were sold for more than they ought to have fetched; in many cases, half the price would now purchase the same thing. If so, there is as much reason that we should now consider these public securities in a depreciated state as every holder of them has considered them from that [time forward] . . .

Thomas Scott of Pennsylvania then moved for a discrimination between current and original holders of the government's obligations.

Thomas Scott

. . . All I contend for is this, that the present government pay the debts of the United States, but as the domestic part of the debt has been contracted, in depreciated notes; [and] that less interest should be paid upon it than 6 per cent. Six per cent was the usual interest upon the certificates when they were issued by Congress; but if the possessor has received no part of his 6 per cent until this time, that now the principal and interest be consolidated into one sum, hereafter to bear an interest of three or four per cent; then those citizens who now stand as creditors of the union will find that [that] part of their property has been the most productive of any, much more productive than the property of the citizens of the United States has generally been. Those who lent their money to individuals before and during the late war generally lost, or suffered by the depreciation, some three-quarters of the capital, nay some 39/40ths. But is this the case of the domestic creditor of the United States? No, Mr. Chairman, he will preserve his property through the chaos of the revolution and be put now in a more eligible situation than he was at the time he loaned his money. The capital sum which he lent is now encreased, and very rapidly encreased, for 6 per cent is a very large interest. He will now receive 160 dollars for his 100, and putting that into the funds, at three or four per cent, he will find more productive than any other method in which he could employ his money; for I contend that neither improved nor unimproved lands will give an interest of near half of what the public creditor will have. People who have held real property have sunk, with the taxes and other losses, the greatest part of it; but the public creditor has let his run through the confusion of the revolution and nevertheless gets it returned to him safe and, so far from being impaired, that it has prodigiously accumulated, not only in a manner superior to the property of his fellow-citizens, but superior to the foreigner who lent his money at 4 per cent. Justice and equity require, on the behalf of the community, that these people be content with reasonable profit. They ought not, therefore, to receive, on a funded debt, so much as six per cent; whether three or four, or something between three and four, would be a proper sum, I shall not pretend to determine. But I consider it a proper question for this committee to consider, in justice to those who are to pay, as to those who are to receive; nor do I believe the domestic creditors would be dissatisfied with it, provided they were sure of receiving this annual interest; for their debts, on such a footing, would be better to them than if they were established on an extravagant plan that could never be effected, but which would be likely to throw the nation into confusion. Every body has suffered more or less by the depreciation, but the public creditors very little in regard to that part of their property which they had deposited in the hands of government. It is true that it has slept; but it is now waked up to some purpose.

Roger Sherman

I do not differ much in principle from the gentleman who spoke last, from Pennsylvania (Mr. Scott) but I do not extend my views so far as he extends his in the exercise of the power which he contends is vested in this body. I look upon it that every legislature acts in a threefold capacity: They have a power to make laws for the good government of the people and a right to repeal and alter those laws as public good requires. In another capacity, they have a right to make contracts. But here I must contend that they have no right to violate, alter or abolish [those contracts]. . . . When bills of credit were first emitted, it was declared that they should be redeemed with specie; indeed, they passed as such at first, but the opinion of their real value was changed by common consent. . . . I don't see but what the public are bound by that contract, as much as an individual, and that they cannot reduce it down in either principal or interest unless by an arbitrary power, and in that case there never will be any security in the public promises. If we should now agree to reduce the domestic debt to 4 per cent, the world may justly fear that we may, on some future occasion, reduce it to two; if this government once establishes such a principle, our credit is inevitably gone for ever. . . .

James Jackson

. . . Gentlemen . . . contend that no sort of discrimination ought to take place, yet from what they have let fall on this occasion, I am led to believe that they favor that part of the report of the secretary which makes a discrimination, in fact, equal to one-third loss of the principal. What will hold good in one case ought to hold good in another, and a discrimination might take place upon the same principles between those to whom the government were originally indebted and who have never received satisfaction therefor and those who had nothing to do with the government in the first transaction but have merely speculated and purchased up the evidence of an original debt. Some gentlemen think that this latter class merit that greater degree of attention should be paid to their claims because, by their actions, they seem to have evinced a greater degree of confidence in the government than those who sold them. But, sir, these men have had more information; they have been at the seat of government and knew what was in contemplation before the other parts of the union could be acquainted with it. There has been no kind of proportion of knowledge between the two classes. To use the expression of a British minister, the reciprocity has been all on one side. The people in this city are, sir, informed of all the motions of government; they have sent out their money, in swift sailing vessels, to purchase up the property of uninformed citizens in the remote parts of the union; but were those citizens acquainted with our present deliberations and assured of the good intent of congress to provide for their just demands, they would be on an equal footing; they would not incline to throw away their property for considerations totally inadequate. Such attempts at fraud, Mr. Chairman, would justify the government in interfering in the transactions between individuals, without a breach of the public faith. . . .

11 February 1790
James Madison (Va.)

. . . It has been said by some gentlemen that the debt itself does not exist in the extent and form which is generally supposed. I confess, sir, I differ altogether from the gentleman who takes that ground. Let us consider, first, by whom the debt was contracted, and then let us consider, sir, to whom it is due. The debt was contracted by the United States, who, with respect to that particular transaction, were in a national capacity. The government was nothing more than the agent, or organ, by which the whole body of the people acted. The change in the government which has taken place has enlarged its national capacity, but it has not varied the national obligation with respect to the engagements entered into by that transaction. For, in like manner, the present government is nothing more than the organ, or agent, of the public. The obligation which they are under is precisely the same with that under which the debt was contracted; although the government has been changed, the nation remains the same. There is no change in our political duty, nor in the moral or political obligation. The language I now use, sir, is the language of the constitution itself; it declares that all debts shall have the same validity against the United States, under the new, as under their old form of government. The obligation remains the same, though I hope experience will prove that the ability has been favorably varied.

The next question is, to what amount the public are at present engaged? I conceive the question may be answered in a few words. The United States owe the value they received, which they acknowledge, and which they have promised to pay. What is that value? It is a certain sum in principal, bearing an interest of six per cent. No logic, no magic, in my opinion, can diminish the force of the obligation.

The only point on which we can deliberate is, to whom the payment is really due. For this purpose, it will be proper to take notice of the several descriptions of people who are creditors of the union and lay down some principles respecting them, which may lead us to a just and equitable decision. . . . It may here be proper to notice four classes into which they may be divided.

First. Original creditors, who have never alienated their securities.

Second. Original creditors, who have alienated.

Third. Present holders of alienated securities.

Fourth. Intermediate holders, through whose hands securities have circulated.

The only principles that can govern the decision on their respective pretensions I take to be 1. public justice; 2. public faith; 3. public credit; 4. public opinion.

With respect to the first class, there can be no difficulty. Justice is in their favor, for they have advanced the value which they claim; public faith is in their favor, for the written promise is in their hands; respect for public credit is in their favor, for if claims so sacred are violated, all

confidence must be at an end; public opinion is in their favor, for every honest citizen cannot but be their advocate.

With respect to the last class, the intermediate holders, their pretensions, if they have any, will lead us into a labyrinth for which it is impossible to find a clue. This will be the less complained of because this class were perfectly free, both in becoming and ceasing to be creditors; and because, in general, they must have gained by their speculations.

The only rival pretensions, then, are those of the original creditors who have assigned, and of the present holders of the assignments.

The former may appeal to justice, because the value of the money, the service, or the property advanced by them, has never been really paid to them.

They may appeal to good faith, because the value stipulated and expected is not satisfied by the steps taken by the government. The certificates put into the hands of the creditors, on closing their settlements with the public, were of less real value than was acknowledged to be due; they may be considered as having been forced, in fact, on the receivers. They cannot, therefore, be fairly adjudged an extinguishment of the debt. They may appeal to the motives for establishing public credit, for which justice and faith form the natural foundation. They may appeal to the precedent furnished by the compensation allowed to the army during the late war, for the depreciation of bills, which nominally discharged the debts. They may appeal to humanity, for the sufferings of the military part of the creditors can never be forgotten while sympathy is an American virtue. To say nothing of the singular hardship, in so many mouths, of requiring those who have lost four-fifths or seven-eighths of their due to contribute the remainder in favor of those who have gained in the contrary proportion.

On the other hand, the holders by assignment, have claims, which I by no means wish to depreciate. They will say that whatever pretensions others may have against the public, these cannot affect the validity of theirs: That if they gain by the risk taken upon themselves, it is but the just reward of that risk. That as they hold the public promise, they have an undeniable demand on the public faith. That the best foundation of public credit is that adherence to literal engagements on which it has been erected by the most flourishing nations. That if the new government should swerve from so essential a principle, it will be regarded by all the world as inheriting the infirmities of the old. Such being the interfering claims on the public, one of three things must be done; either pay both, reject wholly one or the other, or make a *composition* between them on some principle of equity. To pay both is perhaps beyond the public faculties; and as it would far exceed the value received by the public, it will not be expected by the world, nor even by the creditors themselves; to reject wholly the claims of either is equally inadmissible; such a sacrifice of those who possess the written engagements would be fatal to the proposed establishment of public credit; it would moreover punish those who had put their trust in the public promises and resources. To make the other class the sole victims was an idea at which human nature recoiled.

A composition, then, is the only expedient that remains. Let it be a liberal one in favor of the present holders; let them have the highest price which has prevailed in the market; and let the residue belong to the original sufferers. This will not do perfect justice; but it will do more real justice and perform more of the public faith than any other expedient proposed. The present holders, where they have purchased at the lowest price of the securities, will have a profit that cannot reasonably be complained of; where they have purchased at a higher price, the profit will be considerable; and even the few who have purchased at the highest price cannot well be losers, with a well funded interest of 6 per cent. The original sufferers will not be fully indemnified; but they will receive from their country a tribute due to their merits, which, if it does not entirely heal their wounds, will assuage the pain of them. I am aware that many plausible objections will lie against what I have suggested, some of which, I foresee, will be taken some notice of. It will be said that the plan is impracticable. Should this be demonstrated, I am ready to renounce it; but it does not appear to me in that light. . . .

The discrimination proposed by me requires nothing more than a knowledge of the present holders, which will be shown by the certificates; and of the original holders, which the office documents will show. It may be objected that if the government is to go beyond the literal into the equitable claims against the United States, it ought to go back to every case where injustice has been done. To this the answer is obvious: The case in question is not only different from others in point of magnitude and of practicability, but forces itself on the attention of the committee, as necessarily involved in the business before them. It may be objected that public credit will suffer, especially abroad: I think this danger will be effectually obviated by the honesty and disinterestedness of the government displayed in the measure, by a continuance of the punctual discharge of foreign interest, by the full provision to be made for the whole foreign debt, and the equal punctuality I hope to see in the future payments on the domestic debts. I trust also that all future loans will be founded on a previous establishment of adequate funds and that a situation like the present will be thereby rendered impossible.

I cannot but regard the present case as so extraordinary, in many respects, that the ordinary maxims are not strictly applicable to it. The fluctuations of stock in Europe, so often referred to, have no comparison with those in the United States. The former never exceeded 50, 60, or 70 per cent. Can it be said that because a government thought this evil insufficient to justify an interference, it would view in the same light a fluctuation amounting to seven or 800 per cent?

I am of opinion that were Great Britain, Holland, or any other country to fund its debts precisely in the same situation as the American debt, some equitable interference of the government would take place. The South-Sea scheme, in which a change amounting to 1000 per cent happened in the value of stock, is well known to have produced an interference, and without any injury whatever to the subsequent credit of the nation. It is true that, in many respects, the case differed from that of the United States; but, in other respects, there is a degree of similitude which warrants the conjecture. It may be objected that such a provision as I propose, will exceed the public ability. I do not think the public unable to discharge honorably all its engagements, or that it will be unwilling, if the appropriations shall be satisfactory. I regret, as much as any member, the unavoidable weight and duration of the burdens to be imposed, having never been a proselyte to the doctrine that public debts are public benefits. I consider them, on the contrary, as evils which ought to be removed as fast as honor and justice will permit, and shall heartily join in the means necessary for that purpose. I conclude with declaring, as my opinion, that if any case were to happen among individuals bearing an analogy to that of the public, a court of equity would interpose its redress; or that if a tribunal existed on earth by which nations could be compelled to do right, the United States would be compelled to do something not dissimilar in its principles to what I have contended for. . . .

Elias Boudinot (Mass.)

said, he had long been in the habit of paying great respect to the sentiments of the gentleman from Virginia, but he feared, on this occasion, he had not viewed the subject with his usual accuracy. But he was not surprised that the gentleman was led away by the dictates of his heart, for he believed he really felt for the misfortunes of his fellow-citizens who had been the prey of avaricious men. Indeed, it is matter of less surprise, on another account, said he, for heretofore I contemplated the subject in nearly the same point of view. Influenced by a desire to do justice to every person connected with the public, I wished for the means of compensating the original holders who had sold their certificates at a great loss; but I found the thing, upon long and careful examination, to be both unjust and impracticable.

The honorable gentleman tells us that the debt was contracted for meritorious services and enquires whether the creditor received an adequate compensation in full discharge? I say, sir, the debt is still due and that the person to whom it is due has received nothing but a certificate as evidence of his claim; but then, if any of our first creditors have put another person in their shoes, the question will arise, are we to disown the act of the party himself? Are we to say, we will not be bound by your transfer, we will not treat with your representative, but insist upon a resettlement with you alone? But the same reasoning will oblige us to go farther and investigate all the claims of those who received of the government continental money, which they afterwards parted with for ten, forty, or one hundred for one.

But, putting all this out of the question and supposing the motion to be founded on principles of justice, I would ask how it is to be carried into execution? The nature of the public debt will demonstrate its impracticability. A great part of this was contracted by the clerks in office, who, when the continental money was stopped, were supplied with some millions of dollars in loan-office certificates; they were given out in their names and afterwards distributed among the farmers, mechanics, and others who had furnished supplies or performed services. Now, how is it possible that you can ever trace a certificate, under these circumstances, up to the man who was the original *bona fide* creditor? Not from the name on the face of the paper, because it is the name of the clerk in office, the mere agent of the public. Other certificates were taken out of the loan-office by persons who were not concerned in making the loan; many neighbors sent money by one hand, who went and took out certificates in his own name, which he afterward returned to the real lender. I have been entrusted myself with numerous commissions of this kind, when I have been going to the capital where the loan-office was kept. Now, suppose, as has been the case, that I took 10,000 dollars from ten of my neighbors, each 1000 dollars, and that I placed the whole in the continental loan-office at Philadelphia, taking out therefor ten loan-office certificates of 1000 dollars each, which, on my return, I gave to those who had sent their money by me; all these certificates had my name in them, and here I should appear to be the original holder of 10,000 dollars without any right whatever, and the men, who deserve much of their country, for the aid they furnished her in the hour of distress, are stripped, in a moment, of the greatest part of their property. I believe, if we adopt this motion, we shall give room for such scenes of enormity as humanity will be shocked at the bare prospect of. I am, therefore, clearly of opinion, that, if the principles be ever so just, we ought to reject it on account of its impracticability. . . .

15 February 1790

Mr. Madison's motion for a discrimination being under consideration,

Theodore Sedgwick (Mass.)

The proposition, Mr. Chairman, contains a question of the utmost importance. And the committee must be obliged to the gentleman who brought it forward for his very ingenious discussion of the subject of the domestic debt. With respect to the question now before the committee, so much has been said that I think it will not be necessary to consume much of their time in the investigation. On the subject of contracts I have to observe that whenever a voluntary engagement is made for a valuable consideration for property advanced or services rendered, and the terms of the contract are understood, if no fraud or imposition is practiced, the party engaging is bound to the performance according to the literal meaning of the words in which it is expressed. Such contract, whether of a Government or an individual, may be either transferable or not transferable. The latter species of contract receives an additional value from its capacity of being transferred, if the circumstances of the possessor should render the sale of it necessary or convenient to him. To render the transferable quality of such evidences of contract in any degree advantageous to the possessor, it is necessary to consider, in case of sale, the alienee possessed of all the property of the original holder; and indeed it is highly absurd and even contradictory to say that such evidences of debt are transferable and at the same time to say that there is in them a kind of property that the holder could not convey by *bona fide* contract.

This is the construction which has invariably been given to these contracts, whether formed by Government or by individuals. To deprive the citizen of the power of binding himself by his own voluntary contract, or to prevent a disposition of property in its nature alienable, would be a violent and unjustifiable invasion of one of those rights of which man, as a citizen, is the most tenacious, and would indeed break one of the strongest bonds by which society is holden together.

In the transfers which have been made, the contracts were fairly made; the whole rights have been transferred. It is not pretended any fraud or imposition has been practiced. The risk was calculated by the parties, and it was observed that the risk contemplated a revolution in the Government.

From the foregoing deduction of particulars, it is presumed to be proved that a property is vested in the transferees. That if this property is divested by the Government, the law for that purpose would have a retrospective operation, and that no *ex post facto* law could be more alarming than that by which the right of private property is violently invaded. . . .

With regard, more particularly, to the proposition before the committee, I have to observe, that with regard to these contracts, there has existed a depreciation in consequence of the failure of Government regularly to pay the interest. That in this depreciated state, the securities have been alienated; that of course the original holders have sustained a loss; that if the loss resulted from the fault and not the misfortune of Government, the creditors have, undeniably, a demand against the Government for compensation; that this demand, however well founded, can never authorize the Government to invade the honestly acquired property of the present possessors, a property warranted by the terms of the contract itself and sanctioned by the act of Congress of April, 1783, and the validity of it recognized by the Constitution we have sworn to support.

With regard to the claims of the original holders, it is, however, observable, that the domestic creditor, at the time the contract was formed, well knew the nature of the Constitution of the Government administered by Congress, the other contracting party; that its power of performance depended on the ability and good-will of the States; that Congress had always performed its duty, had made the necessary requisitions; that this was its utmost power; and that the failure had arisen wholly from the neglect of the States. I therefore submit it to the committee, whether, if the original holder has a just or equitable demand, he should not resort to the State of which he is a member?

I admit that the case of an original holder is indeed a hard one; that I have a respect for his misfortunes and for his pretensions; that if satisfaction is discovered to be just and practicable, I would not hesitate to go to the utmost ability of the Government for that purpose. But let me ask, what merit will the Government possess if we strip one class of citizens, who have acquired property by the known and established rules of the law, under the specious pretence of doing justice to another class of citizens?

It was implicitly agreed, that eighty per cent depreciation would not authorize the interference proposed by the motion. I ask, then, for some point of depreciation to be pointed out which will authorize such interference.

The question for which I contend has received the universal approbation of mankind, there are no instances of the interference contended for, and this general sense of mankind affords me some evidence of truth. . . .

. . . By reason of the circumstances which have taken place, the honorable gentleman (Mr. Madison) supposes that if the whole amount of security shall be paid to the present possessor he will have a sum of money to which the original holder is equitably entitled. If this is true, then no interposition is necessary, it being a well-known rule of law that an action will always lie to recover money out of the hands of another to which the plaintiff, from the principles of equity and good conscience, is entitled.

With regard to the effects which will probably result from this measure, I have to observe that they will be destructive to our national character. That the world is now willing, charitably, to impute our former miscarriages to events we could not control; but should our first measures in regard to public faith be a violent infraction of our contracts, it will sanction all our bitterest enemies have said to our disadvantage. With regard to its effects on credit, little dependence will be placed on the plighted faith of a Government which, under the pretence of doing equity, has exercised a power of dispensing with its contracts and has thereby formed for itself a precedent of future violations, both with respect to its funds and contracts. With regard to discovering who was the original holder, except so far as respects the army debt, I am certain there are no documents by which the necessary facts can be discovered. . . .

I have only to add, that the proposed system will lay a foundation for infinite frauds and perjuries, and that it will, beyond all powers of calculation, multiply the evils of speculation.

John Laurence (N.Y.)
observed that the proposition of the gentleman from Virginia (Mr. Madison) derived force from the talents and knowledge of that gentleman in public transactions; but that, on examination, it would be found to contain doctrines very repugnant to the interest and prosperity of the Union.

He then stated that the debts contracted by the United States were for loans of money, supplies of articles necessary for the public wants, and for actual services rendered in different employments. That these debts were ultimately adjusted and reduced to their present transferable form. That every part of the contract was essential to it. The negotiability was a material part. That the nature of the contract was frequently recognized by the late Government. That, in 1783, Congress recommended certain funds to be established to pay the interest and put the principal in a course of discharge. That this recommendation was unequivocal, as to the nature of it, and made no discrimination between the possessor and original holder. That the subsequent conduct of that body was conformable to this recommendation. That they had annually called on the States to furnish money to pay the interest without discriminating between the original holder and present possessor. That they had paid interest on the securities without making any discrimination. That provision had been made for holders of loan-office certificates that were subject to liquidation to have them cancelled and others issued for the specie value. That the holders of certificates were enabled to have them registered to guard against accidents; and that no distinction was made between the original holder and the alienee. That the transferable nature of the claim was for the benefit of the creditor, because it gave it an active value. That he consented to take it, and consulted his own advantage. That the conduct of the late Congress, since the war, had been uniform in the support of this contract, and they had done no act to impair its obligation according to the terms of it. That this contract was valid against the Government; for, notwithstanding the truth of the gentleman's observations that the nation is the same, though the bodies that administered the Government were different, there was yet far greater security; and to remove all doubt, a clause that made all debts and engagements valid against the United States under the late General Government valid against the present was inserted in the Constitution.

He further observed that this contract having descended upon the Government, there was no right in the Legislature to impair the force of it. That the particular Governments are restrained from passing laws impairing the obligations of contracts. That this interference would be a violation of the contract between individuals when the certificate was transferred; and it would not be presumed, the States being prohibited, that the General Government had the power to do it.

He then adverted to the principles of the gentleman, to wrest the obligation of the public to the original holder, and observed that the same principles were in favor of the present possessor. That public justice required a performance of contracts when there was no fraud on the part of the holder. That the possessor had been guilty of no fraud, no deception. That the contract between him and the original holder was fair, and that a hazard and risk attended the purchase adequate to the advantage. That nothing short of a revolution in Government could have produced payment. That if there was an imposition, the public occasioned it; and between the original holder and the public, there might be a claim for retribution. That public faith was as sacredly pledged to the bearer, or present possessor, as to the original creditor. That public credit results from fair and upright conduct. That the Government, to support it, must perform its contract. That this was a contract recognized by them, and as such should be discharged. That the condition we have been in made it proper for us to be cautious on this subject; and even at present, people doubted our disposition to establish our credit. That this would give a fatal blow to it, and when we should recover, if ever, was doubtful. That the public opinion was difficult to be ascertained; gentlemen had different modes to determine it. He supposed it was better ascertained by the acts of public bodies than by squibs in the newspapers or by pamphlets written by individuals. That the uniform conduct of men deputed by the particular States to represent them in the late General Government was the best standard; and their opinion, from the year 1783, was in favor of the present possessor. That the conduct of the particular States was another circumstance; that he did not know of any discrimination made by them, though it had been attempted. That the general opinion of men of property was in favor of it; and that these sources of public opinion were more certain than those he had before mentioned.

He further observed, that although he believed gentlemen supposed no advantage would be derived to the United States from this discrimination, yet much would arise. That part of the army was composed of foreigners; many had left the country, others were dead. All their part would be unclaimed. That certificates were issued to public officers to a great amount and were paid by them to persons from whom they purchased. The difficulty of making proof of the original creditor would be great; and, from this circumstance, great sums would be gained to the public. That there were persons enough who would have sagacity to discern this; and they would doubt the purity of the public motive, should the gentleman's plan be adopted.

He then adverted to the circumstance of the new creditor receiving paper. That this paper might be subject to another liquidation on the same principle as the present. That it would introduce doubt and distrust of public engagements; and there would be no greater security, although a fund was pledged, than there is at present, for whenever the public pleased, they might destroy the obligation. Arguments were improperly addressed to their feelings; but that, however hard it may be for the original creditor who had parted with his certificates to contribute to pay the debt, yet it would be equally hard on him who had been injured by the Continental money, who had been plundered by the enemy, who had had his property burned by them in the course of the war; and that instances of these kinds were numerous.

He then adverted to the doctrine of the Court of Equity and urged that this Court must be governed by principle.

That were the Committee this high Court and the United States, the original creditor, and the present possessor before them, and if there appeared no fraud on the part of the possessor, the original creditor would have no just claim on him. That between the United States and original creditors, the United States were in fault, and the claim, if good, would be against them. . . .

He concluded with saying that he was still open to conviction; but that he was, at the time of speaking, against the gentleman's propositions.

William Loughton Smith (S.C.)
remarked that it was necessary and proper the House should give the subject the most ample discussion. The question had long agitated the public mind, and the people should know that it had occupied the serious attention of their Representatives and be made acquainted with the principles of their decision. For his part, having bestowed on it the most attentive consideration, he could assert that the more he contemplated it, the more he was impressed with a conviction that the proposition was unjust, impolitic, and impracticable. It consisted of two parts: The one was to take away the property of one person; the other was to give that property to another; and this by a voluntary interposition of the House, by a mere act of power, without the assent of the former or without even the application of the latter. For it was remarkable that the original holders who had alienated their certificates had not come forward with this demand; and it is presumable that, had they applied for redress, they would reject any indemnification which was the result of such manifest injustice. To prove that this was taking away the property of a citizen by force, he observed that the purchaser had, by a fair purchase, acquired a right to the full amount of the sum expressed in the certificate, which it was not within the power of the House to divest him of. No tribunal on earth could lawfully deprive a man of his property fairly obtained. The purchaser bought under the act of Congress making the securities transferable; and having given the market price, without fraud or imposition, he was, by virtue of such purchase, vested with the complete and absolute ownership of the certificate, as fully as the original holder; and had as much right to demand full payment as the original holder would have had, had the security been still in his hands. Even should the House refuse, by an act

of power, to pay him more than half his demand, the other half would still remain against the public; it could not be extinguished. The debt would continually haunt them; the creditors would loudly clamor for justice, and sooner or later the balance would be paid. Then would they incur all the odium of a violation of private rights, without deriving to the public any advantage whatever. He considered the measure as doing a certain evil, that a possible good might result from it. This was not, in his opinion, the proper mode of doing good. Justice cannot be founded on injustice; and to take money out of the pocket of one man to put it into that of another is a precedent which may justify future interferences. This step would lead the House to others: for, if the principle be a just one, then the Government should look into all the transactions and speculations of individuals in order to correct them and make retribution to every individual according to his losses. He was persuaded that the true policy of a Legislative body was, to pursue the broad road of justice, clearly marked out before them; for it was an undeniable truth, that whenever they deviated into by-roads and trackless paths, without any other guide than their own imagination, they would get bewildered in a labyrinth of difficulties, and rejoice to trace back their steps, and regain the plain road. Now, the plain line of conduct is to do strict justice, such as is enforced in judicial tribunals, between man and man, in a similar case. The debtor is bound to pay the debt to the holder of the security; the contract between the giver of the bond and the person to whom it was given is done away the moment the latter assigns it to another person. If A gives a bond to B, who parts with it to C, there is no longer any obligation on the part of A to pay B, but he must pay it to C. A has nothing to do with the private negotiations between B and C, nor to inquire what consideration was given for the security. All that he has to inquire is whether he really signed it and had value received for it, and the amount of it. He cannot say to the holder, you gave but fifty dollars for this security of one hundred dollars, and I will pay you only fifty; for the law will compel him to pay the hundred. This is a point of justice between man and man. Is there another point of law and justice for the Government? By what rule is the Government to square its conduct if not by those sacred rules which form the basis of civil society and are the safeguard of private property? . . .

18 February 1790
James Madison

next rose and observed that the opponents of his proposition had imposed on its friends not only a heavy task, by the number of their objections, but a delicate one by the nature of some of them. . . .

It could not have escaped the committee that the gentleman to whom he was opposed had reasoned on this momentous question as on an ordinary case in a court of law; that they had equally strained all the maxims that could favor the purchasing or be adverse to the original holder; and that they had dwelt with equal pleasure on every circumstance which could brighten the pretensions of the former or discredit those of the latter. He had not himself attempted, nor did he mean, to undervalue the pretensions of the actual holders: in stating them he had even used as strong terms as they themselves could have dictated; but beyond a certain point he could not go. He must renounce every sentiment which he had hitherto cherished before his complaisance could admit that America ought to erect the monuments of her gratitude, not to those who saved her liberties, but to those who had enriched themselves in her funds.

All that he wished was that the claims of the original holders, not less than those of the actual holders, should be fairly examined and justly decided. They had been invalidated by nothing yet urged. A debt was fairly contracted. According to justice and good faith, it ought to have been paid in gold or silver. A piece of paper only was substituted. Was this paper equal in value to gold or silver? No: it was worth in the market, which the argument for the purchasing holders makes the criterion, no more than one-eighth or one-seventh of that value. Was this depreciated paper freely accepted? No: the government offered that or nothing. The relation of the individual to the government and circumstances of the offer rendered the acceptance a forced, not a free one. The same degree of constraint would vitiate a transaction between man and man before any court of equity on the face of the earth. There are even cases where consent cannot be pretended, where the property of the planter or farmer has been taken at the point of the bayonet and a certificate presented in the same manner. But why did the creditors part with their acknowledgment of the debt? In some instances from necessity; in others, from a well-founded distrust of the public.

Whether from the one or the other, they had been injured: they had suffered loss through the default of the debtor, and the debtor cannot, in justice or honor, take advantage of the default.

Here then was a debt acknowledged to have been once due and which was never discharged, because the payment was forced and defective. The balance consequently is still due, and is of as sacred a nature as the claims of the purchasing holder can be; and if both are not to be paid in the whole, is equally entitled to payment in part.

He begged gentlemen would not yield too readily to the artificial niceties of forensic reasoning; that they would consider not the form, but the substance—not the letter, but the equity—not the bark, but the pith of the business. It was a great and an extraordinary case. It ought to be decided on the great and fundamental principles of justice. He had been animadverted upon for appealing to the heart as well as the head: he would be bold, nevertheless, to repeat, that in great and unusual questions of morality, the heart is the best casuist.

It had been said, by a member from Massachusetts, that the proposition was founded on a new principle in Congress. If the present Congress be meant, that is not strange, for Congress itself is new; if the former Congress be meant, it is not true, for the principle is found in an act which had been already cited. After the pay of the army had, during the war, been nominally and legally discharged in depreciated paper, the loss was made up to the sufferers.

It had been said by a member from New York that the case was not parallel, there being no third party like the present holder of certificates. This objection could not be valid. The government paid ten dollars, worth in fact but one, to a soldier: the soldier was then the original holder. The soldier assigned it to a citizen; the citizen then became the actual holder. What was the event? The loss of the original holder was repaired, after the actual holder had been settled with according to the highest market value of his paper. . . .

It had been said by another member, from Massachusetts, that the old government did every thing in its power. It made requisitions, used exhortations, and in every respect discharged its duty; but it was to be remembered that the debt was not due from the government, but the United States. An attorney with full powers to form without the means to fulfill engagements could

never by his ineffectual, though honest efforts, exonerate his principal.

He had been repeatedly reminded of the address of Congress in 1783, which rejected a discrimination between original and purchasing holders. At that period, the certificates to the army and citizens at large had not been issued. The transfers were confined to loan-office certificates, were not numerous, and had been in great part made with little loss to the original creditor. At present the transfers extend to a vast proportion of the whole debt, and the loss to the original holders has been immense. The injustice which has taken place has been enormous and flagrant, and makes redress a great national object. This change of circumstances destroys the argument from the act of Congress referred to; but if implicit regard is to be paid to the doctrines of that act, any modification of the interest of the debt will be as inadmissible as a modification of the principal.

It had been said that if the losses of the original creditors are entitled to reparation, Congress ought to repair those suffered from paper money, from the ravages of the war, and from the act barring claims not produced within a limited time. As to the paper money, either the case is applicable or it is not: if not applicable, the argument falls; if applicable, either the depreciated certificates ought to be liquidated by a like scale as was applied to the depreciated money or the money, even if the whole mass of it was still in circulation, ought now to be literally redeemed like the certificates. Leaving the gentleman to make his own choice out of these dilemmas, he would only add, himself, that if there were no other difference between the cases, the manifest impossibility of redressing the one and the practicability of redressing the other was a sufficient answer to the objection. With respect to the towns burnt and other devastations of war, it was taught by the writers on the law of nations that they were to be numbered among the inevitable calamities of mankind. Still, however, a government owed them every alleviation which it could conveniently afford; but no authority could be found that puts on the same footing with those calamities such as proceed from a failure to fulfil the direct and express obligations of the public. The just claims barred by the act of limitation were, in his opinion, clearly entitled to redress. That act was highly objectionable. The public which was interested in shortening the term, undertook to decide that no claim, however just, should be admitted if not presented within nine months. The act made none of the exceptions usual in such acts, not even in favor of the most distant parts of the union. In many instances it had been absolutely impossible for the persons injured to know of the regulation. Some of these instances were within his own knowledge. To limit the duration of a law to a period within which it could not possibly be promulged, and then taking advantage of the impossibility, would be imitating the Roman tyrant, who posted up his edicts so high that they could not be read and then punished the people for not obeying them.

It had been said that if the purchased certificates were funded at the rate proposed, they would fall in the market and the holders be injured. It was pretty certain that the greater part, at least, would be gainers. He believed that the highest market rate, especially with the arrears of interest incorporated, well funded at 6 per cent would prevent every loss that could justify complaint.

But foreigners had become purchasers, and ought to be particularly respected. Foreigners, he remarked, had themselves made a difference between the value of the foreign and domestic debt; they would therefore the less complain of a difference made by the government here. It was his opinion that the terms stated in the proposition would yield a greater profit to the foreign purchasers than they could have got for their money advanced by them in any of the funds in Europe.

The proposition had been charged with robbing one set of men to pay another. If there were robbery in the case, it had been committed on the original creditors. But, to speak more accurately, as well as more moderately, the proposition would do no more than withhold a part from each of two creditors, where both were not to be paid the whole.

A member from New York had asked whether an original creditor, who had assigned his certificate, could in conscience accept a reimbursement in the manner proposed? He would not deny that assignments might have been made with such explanations, or under such circumstances, as would have that effect. But in general the assignments had been made with reference merely to the market value and the uncertainty of the steps that might be taken by the government. The bulk of the creditors had assigned under circumstances from which no scruple could arise. In all cases where a scruple existed, the benefit of the provision might be renounced. He would in turn ask the gentleman whether there was not more room to apprehend that the present holder, who had got his certificate of a distressed and meritorious fellow-citizen for one-eighth or one-tenth of its ultimate value, might not feel some remorse in retaining so unconscionable an advantage?

Similar propositions, it was said, had been made and rejected in the state legislatures. This was not fact. The propositions made in the state legislatures were not intended to do justice to the injured, but to seize a profit to the public.

But no petitions for redress had come from the sufferers. Was merit then to be the less regarded because it was modest? Perhaps, however, another explanation ought to be given. Many of the sufferers were poor and uninformed. Those of another description were so dispersed that their interests and efforts could not be brought together. The case of the purchasing holders was very different.

The constitutionality of the proposition had been drawn into question. He asked whether words could be devised that would place the new government more precisely in the same relation to the real creditors with the old? The power was the same; the obligation was the same: the means only were varied.

An objection had been drawn from the article prohibiting *ex post facto* laws. But *ex post facto* laws relate to criminal, not civil cases. The constitution itself requires this definition, by adding to a like restriction on the states, an express one against retrospective laws of a civil nature.

It had been said that foreigners had been led to purchase by their faith in the article of the constitution relating to the public debts. He would answer this objection by a single fact: foreigners had shewn by the market price in Europe that they trusted the nature of the foreign debt more under the old government than the nature of the domestic debt under the new government.

Objections to the measure had been drawn from its supposed tendency to impede public credit. He thought it, on the contrary, perfectly consistent with the establishment of public credit. It was in vain to say that government ought never to revise measures once decided. Great caution on this head ought, no doubt, to be observed; but there were situations in which, without some legislative interposition, the first principles of justice and the very ends of civil society would be frustrated. The gentlemen themselves had been compelled to make exceptions to the general doctrine. They would probably make more before the business was at an end.

It had been urged that if government should interpose in the present case, an interposition would be authorized in any case whatever where the stock might fluctuate; the principle would apply as well to a fall of 60 or 70 per cent as to a fall of 600 or 700 per cent. He could not admit this inference. A distinction was essential between an extreme case and a case short of it. The line was difficult to be drawn; but it was no more incumbent on him than on his opponents to draw it. They themselves could not deny that a certain extremity of the evil would have justified the interposition. Suppose that the distress of the alienating creditors had been ten times as great as it was; that instead of 2, 3, or 4s. in the pound, they had received a farthing only in the pound; and that the certificates lay now in the hands of the purchasers in that state or even at a less value: was there a member who would rise up and say that the purchasers ought to be paid the entire nominal sum and the original sufferer be entitled to no indemnification whatever?

Gentlemen had triumphed in the want of a precedent to the measure. No government, it was said, had interposed to redress fluctuations in its public paper. But where was the government that had funded its debts under the circumstances of the American debt? If no government had done so, there could be no precedent either for or against the measure, because the occasion itself was unprecedented. And if no similar occasion had before existed in any country, the precedent to be set would at least be harmless, because no similar occasion would be likely to happen in this. . . .

The best source of confidence in a government was the apparent honesty of its views. The proposition on the table could not possibly be ascribed to any other motive than this, because the public was not to gain a farthing by it. The next source was an experienced punctuality in the payments due from the government. For this support to public credit, he relied on what had been experienced by a part of the foreign creditors; on the provision to be made for the residue; and on the punctuality which he flattered himself would be observed in all future payments of the domestic creditors. He was more apprehensive of injury to public credit from such modifications of the interest of the public debt as some gentlemen seemed

to have in view. In these the public would be the gainer, and the plea of inability the more alarming; because it was so easy to be set up, so difficult to be disproved, and consequently for which the temptations would be so alluring.

The impracticability of the measure was the remaining ground on which it had been attacked. He did not deny that it would be attended with difficulties and that perfect justice would not be done: but these were not the questions. It was sufficient that a grievous injustice would be lessened, and that the difficulties might be surmounted. What he had in view was that, for the conveniency of claimants, some authority should be provided and properly distributed thro' the union in order to investigate and ascertain the claims; and that for the security of the public the burden of proof should be thrown on the claimants. A scrutiny on this plan, aided by original settlements in the books of the army department, and the state commissioners, and other office-documents, would be a remedy at once for all the difficulties started with regard to fictitious names, certificates issued as money by commissaries and quarter-masters, due-bills, etc.

For some particular cases special provisions might be requisite. The case of loan-office certificates alienated at early periods, before they were much depreciated, fell under this description. Legacies might be another. He should have no objection to some special regulation as to the payments of debts in certificates to persons within the British lines, said to have been authorized by the laws of New York though he presumed few such payments had been made, and that of these few the greater part had by this time passed from the creditors into other hands. There might be a few other cases equally entitled to some particular attention in the details of the provision. As to the merchants who had compounded for their debts in certificates or persons who had exchanged bonds for them, it could not be doubted that the transactions had reference to the market value of the paper, and therefore had nothing peculiar in them.

The expense incident to such a plan of investigation ought to form no difficulty. It bears no proportion to the expense already incurred by commissioners, etc. for effecting a less proportion of justice. Rather than justice should not be done, the expense might be taken out of the portion to the original sufferers. . . .

THOMAS JEFFERSON

Memorandum on the Compromise of 1790

Madison's proposal to discriminate between original and secondary holders was overwhelmingly defeated and the funding of the federal debt approved on much the terms that Hamilton had recommended. But, against a background of maneuvers in both branches of Congress over a permanent location for the seat of the federal government, the House then deadlocked on the question of federal assumption of the debts of the states, which was repeatedly defeated. Writing probably in 1792, Jefferson left the only first-person account of the bargain that apparently ensued. He surely misremembered some of the details, but no one doubts the main lines of his story.

The assumption of the state debts in 1790 was a supplementary measure in Hamilton's fiscal system. When attempted in the House of Representatives it failed. This threw Hamilton himself and a number of members into deep dismay. Going to the President's one day I met Hamilton as I approached the door. His look was sombre, haggard, and dejected beyond description. Even his dress uncouth and neglected. He asked to speak with me. We stood in the street near the door. He opened the subject of the assumption of the state debts, the necessity of it in the general fiscal arrangement and its indispensible necessity towards a preservation of the Union: and particularly of the New England states, who had made great expenditures during the war, on expeditions which tho' of their own undertaking were for the common cause: that they considered the assumption of these by the Union so just, and its denial so palpably injurious, that they would make it a sine qua non of a continuance of the Union. That as to his own part, if he had not credit enough to carry such a measure as that, he could be of no use, and was determined to resign. He observed at the same time, that tho' our particular business laid in separate departments, yet the administration and its success was a common concern, and that we should make common cause in supporting one another. He added his wish that I would interest my friends from the South, who were those most opposed to it. I answered that I had been so long absent from my country that I had lost a familiarity with its affairs, and being but lately returned had not yet got into the train of them, that the fiscal system being out of my department, I had not yet undertaken to consider and understand it, that the assumption had struck me in an unfavorable light, but still not having considered it sufficiently I had not concerned in it, but that I would revolve what he had urged in my mind. It was a real fact that the Eastern and Southern members (S. Carolina, however, was with the former) had got into the most extreme ill humor with one another. This broke out on every question with the most alarming heat, the bitterest animosities seemed to be engendered, and tho' they met every day, little or nothing could be done from mutual distrust and antipathy. On considering the situation of things I thought the first step towards some conciliation of views would be to bring Mr. Madison and Colo. Hamilton to a friendly discussion of the subject. I immediately wrote to each to come and dine with me the next day, mentioning that we should be alone, that the object was to find some temperament for the present fever, and that I was persuaded that men of sound heads and honest views needed nothing more than explanation and mutual understanding to enable them to unite in some measures which might enable us to get along. They came. I opened the subject to them, acknowledged that my situation had not permitted me to understand it sufficiently, but encouraged them to consider the thing together. They did so. It ended in Mr. Madison's acquiescence in a proposition that the question should be again brought before the House by way of amendment from the Senate, that tho' he would not vote for it, nor entirely withdraw his opposition, yet he should not be strenuous, but leave it to its fate. It was observed, I forget by which of them, that as the pill would be a bitter one to the Southern states, something should be done to soothe them; that the removal of the seat of government to the Potomac was a just measure, and would probably be a popular one with them, and would be a proper one to follow the assumption. It was agreed to speak to Mr. White and Mr. Lee, whose districts lay on the Potomac and to refer to them to consider how far the interests of their particular districts might be a sufficient inducement to them to yield to the assumption. This was done. Lee came into it without hesitation. Mr. White had some qualms, but finally agreed. The measure came down by way of amendment from the Senate and was finally carried by the change of White's and Lee's votes. But the removal to Potomac could not be carried unless Pennsylvania could be engaged in it. This Hamilton took on himself, and chiefly, as I understood, through the agency of Robert Morris, obtained the vote of that state, on agreeing to an intermediate residence at Philadelphia. This is the real history of the assumption, about which many erroneous conjectures have been published. It was unjust, in itself oppressive to the states, and was acquiesced in merely from a fear of disunion, while our government was still in its most infant state. It enabled Hamilton so to strengthen himself by corrupt services to many that he could afterwards carry his bank scheme and every measure he proposed in defiance of all opposition; in fact it was a principal ground whereon was reared up that Speculating phalanx, in and out of Congress which has since been able to give laws and to change the political complexion of the government of the U.S.

Opposition Out of Doors

As Congress debated Hamilton's proposals, Madison's incoming correspondence suggested sharp and mounting opposition to the funding plan—from Virginia especially, but also from friends such as the Philadelphia physician Benjamin Rush. An occasional newspaper squib also publicly condemned the funding plan or the expense of the tedious debates in Congress.

Benjamin Rush to Madison

27 February 1790

. . . In reviewing the decision upon your motion, I feel disposed to wish that my name was blotted out from having contributed a single mite towards the American Revolution. We have effected a deliverance from the national injustice of Great Britain to be *subjugated* by a mighty Act of national injustice by the United States.

It is amusing to hear Gentlemen talk of the "public blessing" of a debt contracted to foreigners & a few American speculators of four or five millions of dollars a year. Nothing fundamentally *unjust* can ever produce happiness in its issue. It will lay the foundation of an aristocracy in our country. It will change the property of nine tenths of the freeholders of the States, and it will be a lasting monument of the efficacy of idleness, speculation, & fraud above

industry, economy, & integrity in obtaining wealth & independence. Nor is this all. It will be a beacon to deter other nations & future generations from attempting to better their situations, for it clearly establishes this proposition, that revolutions, like party spirit, are the rage of *many* for the benefit of a *few*.

Walter Jones to Madison

25 March 1790

. . . [The complexion of public affairs] appears not quite satisfactory to the few of us here who think on public affairs; but whether we think justly or not is another question. I freely confess, for myself, no small abatement of ardor in the expectations I had formed of the New Government, because I apprehend that a certain description of men in power have vicious views of government; that they, with strong auxiliary numbers, have views equally vicious in finance; and that both are in combination with a predominating interest in a certain quarter of the union, which is in opposition to the great agricultural interest of the states at large. . . .

In Great Britain the interest of money is low; the commerce, wealth, & resources of the country astonishingly great—the infinite quantity & variety of art & labour that are hourly & momentarily at market invigorates circulation and probably makes a Guinea perform more uses in a week than it does here in six months. Yet the ruinous tendency of her national debt & its consequences has ever been maintained by the most impartial & enlightened writers & speakers on the subject. In these states every thing is proportionally unfavorable to the sustaining national debt. . . . With the balance of trade against us on the east, the drain of emigration on the west, the immense load of private and public debt due (and as the Secretary of the Treasury will have it) to be due to foreigners, together with the shock which between £20 and 30,000,000 of property has received by premature & impracticable steps towards the emancipation of slaves, I know not how the landed interest of the states will answer the additional demands of the systemmongers & fund jobbers who have become such fashionable subjects of newspaper panegyric. Indeed, Sir, unless I am deluded in the extreme, there are men & measures blended in the composition of the Government of the union that should put us much on our guard. I earnestly hope that every attempt to undermine the respectability of the State Governments may be defeated; for if experience should evince that the component parts of the union are too heterogeneous to be kept together, but by the artificial force & *Influence* of Government, those of the States would be potent instruments in effecting such a modification and reunion of parts, as would cure the mischiefs. . . .

I have ever considered the condition of society in these states to be sui generis. As the characteristic feature of the Scythians is termed pastoral, may we not call ours agricultural? And from the vast extent of territory, this characteristic promises to be of long duration. The general uniformity & simplicity of our interests, makes government, comparatively, an easy art; and the equality of our rights and rank is naturally allied to a republican form; if, therefore, some maritime parts of the union are calculated for the more complicated conditions of society (and to a great degree it is impossible they should be) they merit due attention but should never be held in competition with the great republican, agricultural interest of the continent at large. I should, therefore, ever oppose the introduction of those artificial modes of administration & influence in the executive departments of Government which are engendered in the inveterate corruption and complex interests & relations, internal & external, of the old European governments. . . .

Henry Lee to Madison

3 April 1790

. . . Every day adds new testimony of the growing ill will of the people here to the government. . . . [Patrick] Henry already is considered as a prophet; his predictions are daily verifying. His declaration with respect to the division of interest which would exist under the constitution & predominate in all the doings of the govt. already has been undeniably proved.

But we are committed & we cannot be relieved I fear only by disunion. To disunite is dreadful to my mind, but dreadful as it is, I consider it a lesser evil than union on the present conditions.

I had rather myself submit to all the hazards of war & risk the loss of everything dear to me in life than to live under the rule of a fixed insolent northern majority. At present this is the case, nor do I see any prospect of alteration or alleviation.

Change of the seat of govt. to the territorial center, direct taxation, & the abolition of gambling systems of finance might & would effect a material change. But these suggestions are vain & idle. No policy will be adopted by Congress which does not more or less tend to depress the south & exalt the north. I have heard it asserted that your vice president should say the southern people were formed by nature to subserve the convenience & interests of the north—or in plain words to be slaves to the north. Very soon will his assertion be thoroughly exemplified. How do you feel, what do you think, is your love for the constitution so ardent as to induce you to adhere to it tho it should produce ruin to your native country. I hope not, I believe not. However, I will be done, for it is disagreeable to utter unpleasant opinions. Yours always—

Edward Carrington to Madison

7 April 1790

I have seen the decision of the House of Representatives upon the Quaker Memorial [on the slave trade]. . . . The very circumstances of such a subject being taken up in Congress has given some alarm, and it might have been better that a debate of such a nature, which could not possibly be productive of any kind of effect, had never been entered into at all. . . . Notwithstanding the long debates there was little or no difference of opinion as to what must be the issue of the business. Why then were the people of the interested states to be alarmed in consequence of a fruitless discussion? . . . The Assumption of the State Debts remains now a subject of discontent. Upon two principles it creates serious complaint. It is by all Anti's and many Fed's considered as leading to the dreaded consolidation—and by all discriptions of men who think at all it is considered as iniquitous from the unequal situations of the states respecting their debts. Of the latter I am one. Having already written you pretty fully I will not add more here. Whether the constitution is yet so firmly on its legs that it cannot be shocked I will not undertake to decide. I am not apt to croak. Of this, however, I am certain; the adoption of this measure without giving to the states the benefit of their respective redeemed debts will [have] considerable effect in abridging the confidence of the people in it.

George Lee Turberville to Madison

7 April 1790

. . . I am not unacquainted personally with [the] *Gentleman* at the head of [the] Department of the Revenue & still less so with the powers of *his* mind—his acquirements, disposition, & character. I tremble at the thoughts of his being at the head of such an immense sum as 86 millions of dollars—and the annual revenue of the Union. The number of dependents on him necessary to manage the great Department of Revenue, the multitude who will be interested in the funds (in opposition too to the landed interest of the U.S.), all of whom will in some measure be dependent or at any rate attached to the principal officer of the revenue, I profess creates with me apprehensions that from the complicated nature of the subject I am at a loss to determine whether I ought to foster or to discourage.

I am nevertheless persuaded that the funding business founded upon loans will never answer in America. The example set by Great Britain can never be followed here until our country becomes as thickly populated, as commercial and as highly cultivated as G. Britain is. . . .

The idea of consolidating the debt of the states with that of the union is a very unpopular one & for that reason only ought to be laid aside. But I do not think it even political. The debts of Virga. are sinking fast. Every creditor appears satisfied—and the monied men are very fond of becoming adventurers & purchasing the state paper. Many have made their fortunes by it. Why in heaven then should Congress interfere with us? I hope and trust that part of the plan will at least be negatived.

Benjamin Rush to Madison

10 April 1790

I congratulate you upon the prospect of the funding system being delayed 'till the next session of Congress. I hope an election will intervene before you meet again. Should this be the case, I think it probable that no one of our members who has voted against your motion & in favor of the leading principles of Mr. Hamilton's report will be reelected.

I have long deplored the temporary residence of Congress in New York. . . . I question whether more dishonorable influence has ever been used by a British minister (bribery excepted) to carry a measure than has [been] used to carry the report of the Secretary. This influence is not confined to nightly visits, promises, compromises, sacrifices, & threats in New York. It has extended one or two of its polluted streams to this city, the particulars of which you shall hear when I have the pleasure of seeing you on your way to Virginia. . . .

I have just committed to the press a small pamphlet entitled "Information to Europeans disposed to migrate to the United States" in which I have dwelt with peculiar pleasure upon the safety and agreeable prospects of our country under her present government. The establishment of the Secretary's report can alone contradict the information I have given upon that subject. It will in seven years introduce among us all the corruptions of the British funding system. The principal part of the information is addressed to cultivators of the earth, mechanics, laborers, servants, & [the?] members of the learned professions. I shall b[eg] your acceptance of a copy of it as soon as it [is] published. It is addressed to a friend in Great Britain.

Boston *Independent Chronicle*

12 August 1790

Wanted

A number of Stock-Jobbers, Speculators, and Negotiators for the purpose of aiding and assisting certain members of the Robin-Hood Society in accomplishing their foreign contracts. As this fraternity are about to receive the reward of their seven-months' services, many of them wish to dispose of their exhorbitant wages in such manner as will augment their property twofold during recess. As they began their speculations during session, they mean to continue them for the short time they adjourn to attend to their reelection; when this is accomplished it is expected they will return to Philadelphia and there spend the remainder of the year in promoting their own interest to the impoverishing of their constituents.

Virginia's Remonstrance Against the Assumption of State Debts

16 December 1790

Though Madison and Jefferson believed that they had struck a necessary bargain, and one which rendered the details of the assumption fairer to Virginia, the alterations in the plan—even when combined with the decision that the seat of government would move to the Potomac—were not enough to reconcile other Virginia politicians. Issuing from a committee that included Henry Lee and Patrick Henry, the remonstrance of the state legislature provoked Alexander Hamilton to his earliest surviving denunciation of opposition to his plans.

The General Assembly of the Commonwealth of Virginia to the United States in Congress assembled, represent:

That it is with great concern they find themselves compelled, from a sense of duty, to call the attention of Congress to an act of their last session, entitled "An act making provision for the debt of the United States," which the General Assembly conceives neither policy, justice, nor the Constitution warrants. Republican policy, in the opinion of your memorialists, could scarcely have suggested those clauses in the aforesaid act which limit the right of the United States in their redemption of the public debt. On the contrary, they discern a striking resemblance between this system and that which was introduced into England at the Revolution—a system which has perpetuated upon that nation an enormous debt, and has, moreover, insinuated into the hands of the Executive an unbounded influence, which, pervading every branch of the Government, bears down all opposition, and daily threatens the destruction of every thing that appertains to English liberty. The same causes produce the same effects.

In an agricultural country like this, therefore, to erect and concentrate and perpetuate a large moneyed interest is a measure which your memorialists apprehend must, in the course of human events, produce one or other of two evils: the prostration of agriculture at the feet of commerce, or a change in the present form of Federal Government fatal to the existence of American liberty.

The General Assembly pass by various other parts of the said act which they apprehend will have a dangerous and impolitic tendency and proceed to show the injustice of it as it applies to this Commonwealth. It pledges the faith of the United States for the payment of certain debts due by the several states in the Union, contracted by them during the late war.

A large proportion of the debt thus contracted by this state has been already redeemed by the collection of heavy taxes levied on its citizens, and measures have been taken for the gradual payment of the balance, so as to afford the most certain prospect of extinguishing the whole at a period not very distant. But, by the operation of the aforesaid act, a heavy debt, and consequently heavy taxes, will be entailed on the citizens of this Commonwealth, from which they never can be relieved by all the efforts of the General Assembly whilst any part of the debts contracted by any state in the American Union, and so assumed, shall remain unpaid; for it is with great anxiety your memorialists perceive that the said act, without the smallest necessity, is calculated to extort from the General Assembly the power of taxing their own constituents for the payment of their own debts in such a manner as would be best suited to their own ease and convenience.

Your memorialists cannot suppress their uneasiness at the discriminating preference which is given to the holders of the principal of the Continental debt over the holders of the principal of the state debts, in those instances where states have made ample provision for the annual payment of the interest and where, of course, there can be no interest to compound with the principal, which happens to be the situation of this Commonwealth.

The continental creditors have preferences in other respects which the General Assembly forbear to mention, satisfied that Congress must allow that policy, justice, and the principles of public credit abhor discrimination between fair creditors.

Your memorialists turn away from the impolicy and injustice of the said act and view it in another light, in which, to them, it appears still more odious and deformed.

During the whole discussion of the federal constitution by the convention of Virginia, your memorialists were taught to believe "that every power not granted, was retained;" under this impression, and upon this positive condition, declared in the instrument of ratification, the said Government was adopted by the people of this Commonwealth; but your memorialists can find no clause in the constitution authorizing Congress to assume debts of the states! As the guardians, then, of the rights and interests of their constituents; as sentinels placed by them over the ministers of the Federal Government, to shield it from their encroachments, or at least to sound the alarm when it is threatened with invasion; they can never reconcile it to their consciences silently to acquiesce in a measure which violates that hallowed maxim—a maxim, on the truth and sacredness of which, the Federal Government depended for its adoption in this Commonwealth. But this injudicious act not only deserves the censure of the General Assembly, because it is not warranted by the constitution of the United States, but because it is repugnant to an express provision of that constitution. This provision is "that all debts contracted, and engagements entered into, before the adoption of this constitution, shall be as valid against the United States, under this constitution, as under the Confederation;" which amounts to a constitutional ratification of the contracts respecting the state debts in the situation in which they existed under the Confederation; and, resorting to that standard, there can be no doubt that, in the present question, the rights of states, as contracting parties with the United States, must be considered as sacred.

The General Assembly of the Commonwealth of Virginia confide so fully in the justice and wisdom of Congress, upon the present occasion, as to hope that they will revise and amend the aforesaid act generally and repeal, in particular, so much of it as relates to the assumption of the State debts.

1790, December 23.
Agreed to by the Senate

The Constitution and the National Bank

Hamilton's Second Report on Public Credit, delivered to the third session of the First Congress, recommended the creation of a national bank. A semipublic institution, modeled on the Bank of England (one-fifth of its stock would be held by the federal government, which would appoint a minority of its directors), the Bank of the United States would hold an exclusive charter from Congress and act as an adjunct to the Treasury in several respects. It would hold the government's funds, shift them around the country on request, and serve as a ready source of short-term loans. In exchange for these services, it would be authorized, as well, to make private loans in notes that were to be receivable for taxes and payable in specie on demand. With an initial fund of $10 million—four times the capital of America's three existing banks, a sum exceeding all the country's coin, and an amount sufficient to permit some regulation of the country's other lenders—the bank would concentrate the capital required for major commercial ventures. Circulating through the country, its notes would be a valuable resource for merchants, providing the nation, for the first time in its history, with an ample, stable substitute for cash. Starting with only $500,000 in specie, it would be capable quite safely of extending its commitments to the limits of its capitalization. The private holders of the bank stock were to pay in four installments: one-fourth in specie, three-fourths in government certificates of debt. They would be nearly guaranteed a good return on their investment, both from private loans and from the interest payments on the government's bonds. This proposal, though, provoked an even fiercer resistance than had funding and assumption, since opponents saw it not only as objectionable in itself, but as a violation of the new Constitution.

ALEXANDER HAMILTON

Notes on the Advantages of a National Bank

27 March 1791

Hamilton's Report on a National Bank is inconveniently long and too detailed to be offered here. A memorandum to President Washington, however, nicely summarized the secretary's objects and thinking.

The report to the House of Representatives proposing the plan of a Bank enters fully into the advantages attending institutions of this nature. They are summarily these:

1. They tend to increase the active or productive capital of a country by keeping it in more constant employment and by adding to the real an artificial capital in the credit of the Bank which answers equally with specie the purpose of money.

2. They increase and quicken circulation from the foregoing cause from the introduction of bank notes as money, from the greater facility of remittances in notes than in money, from their obviating the necessity in a great number of cases of transporting specie backwards and forwards, from their rendering it unnecessary to lock up specie for the periodical payments of interest, etc., whence a greater plenty of specie is left in circulation and an additional medium is furnished. And thence

3. They assist industry and trade. This they also do by facilitating loans to individuals within the spheres of their immediate operation. Accordingly, wherever they have been established they have given a new spring to agriculture, manufactures, & commerce. This has been most remarkably exemplified of late years in Scotland & Ireland and has been confirmed by the experience of the United States.

4. They facilitate the payment of taxes by keeping the circulation more full and active everywhere and by direct loans to the merchants to pay their duties.

5. They aid the Government *in ordinary* [cases] by facilitating the collection of taxes, by rendering remittances to and from the Treasury more easy, safe, and free from expence, and lastly, in extraordinary cases, by being an instrument of loans in sudden emergencies. The drawing a large capital to a point and the vast credit annexed to it enable banks to come at once to the aid of the Government in a manner that no individual resources are equal to. This was felt during the latter periods of the late war in the most

important operations; and even at this moment it is the only resort for whatever pecuniary aids may be found necessary for carrying into execution the measures taken for the defence of the frontier.

But it is said, admitting the utility of banks in general, why establish a new one, since there are such institutions already in being? The answers to this are:

1. That all these institutions now rest on state foundations and may cease to exist if the state legislatures should not be inclined to continue. That of Pennsylvania has virtually surrendered its old charter by accepting a new one incompatible with it. It is therefore neither compatible with the dignity nor interest of the United States to suffer so important an engine of its administration to depend on so precarious a tenure & one so foreign from itself.

2. By being mere local institutions they cannot serve as engines of a general circulation. For this they have neither sufficient capital nor have they enough of the confidence of all parts of the Union. As *local* institutions they are rather objects of jealousy.

3. They would be improper foundations on which to rest the security of the public revenue by suffering their paper to be receivable in all payments to the public.

1. Because they have not adequate capital.

2. Because their continuance or discontinuance does not depend on the will of the U. States.

3. Because the Government of the Union can have no *inspection* of their proceedings, consequently no security for their prudent administration of their affairs.

4. They are too limited in their capital to afford such extensive aid to the United States as they may require in future emergencies. They may answer well enough for an Indian war; but in a war with a European power they could do nothing adequate to the public necessities.

5. Their constitutions have not those precautions which are calculated to guard against the abuses to which such institutions are subject. They are therefore in this light also insecure reliances for national circulation.

But admitting a National Bank ought to be instituted, the duration is said to be too long and contrary to precedent; too long because the affairs of this country from its peculiar situation must change so rapidly as to render it questionable whether a good thing now will continue to be

a good thing for twenty years. With regard to precedent it is presumed that the matter is mistaken. The Banks of Venice, Genoa, Hamburgh & Amsterdam are understood to be indefinite in point of duration. The Bank of England indeed has been limited to different periods under different circumstances [but] the assertion that it was in its first creation limited to 11 years is not founded. It was incorporated for an indefinite period; but there was a right reserved to the government at the end of eleven years to *pay off* the debt which constituted its capital and *thereby* to dissolve the corporation. But it could not be dissolved nor was it to cease in any other way.

With regard to the argument drawn from the changing situation of the country, the answer is that banks are not novel institutions. They have been long tried, and in different countries. They had eleven years experience in their favour in this country. Their *effects* therefore can *now* be perfectly judged of and pronounced upon with certainty. They are *necessary* in countries little advanced in wealth; they have been found very *useful* in countries greatly advanced in wealth.

In a country like this, which having vast tracts of vacant land and few manufactures, can have no great abundance of specie, the auxiliary circulation of banks must be peculiarly useful. Though the country may advance in manufactures & in wealth considerably in the course of twenty years, yet very obvious causes must leave it during all that period in a condition to stand in need of the same auxiliary. Besides, as has been remarked, banks are at this day found useful in the wealthiest countries—Holland, England, France.

If the nature of the institution is attended to, it must be perceived that its relations to the future are as easy to be comprehended and pronounced upon as its relations to the present. Its operation must be always of the same tendency, and there is no more difficulty in pronouncing that it will be good for twenty years to come as easily as that it is good at the present moment.

How far one place or another may be the proper seat of it may be a thing variable by time; but the time which can vary this must evidently be more than twenty years. It is manifest that a *large commercial city* with a great deal of *capital* and *business* must be the fittest seat of the Bank. It is morally certain that for twenty years to come Philadelphia will continue to have as good pretensions as any of the principal trading cities now established. And with regard to the future seat of the Government, it is morally impossible that it can become in less than twenty years a place of sufficient trade and capital to be the principal scene of the operations of the National Bank. Governments must always act upon reasonable probabilities and, in doing so, they can hardly fail to do right.

The motives to a considerable duration to the charter of the Bank were these—to strengthen the inducement to men of property throughout the United States to embark in it, and to enhance the value of the public stock by a prospect of greater advantage.

This last idea is of great moment. All those acquainted with the operation of the thing will admit that the institution in question has been a main cause of the rise [in value] of the public debt. It operated upon it like a charm. Now it is evident that its effect in this way must have been greater or less in proportion to the prospect of advantage which a long or short duration afforded.

The raising of the public debt is a circumstance of immense importance in the affairs of the country. It is tantamount to the establishment of public credit. No man can be in credit whose bonds are selling for one third or one half their value: the same thing in respect to a Government. Besides, while the debt is low, foreigners become possessed of the property of the citizens of this country greatly below its true value. And every shilling which they pay less for the debt than its true value is so much loss to the country. The distress to this country would have been prodigious in time to come if it had had to pay millions to foreigners for which they had given little or no value. And the existence of a public debt would have been truly a curse.

As far as this essential object might have been made to give way to the speculative possibility of a better arrangement of the Bank in reference to future changes in the situation of the country, it would have been to sacrifice substance to shadow, reality to supposition.

Objection. The advantages of the Bank will not be *equal* in all the States.

This is hardly even an objection to a measure of Government, because there is scarcely one to which it may not be objected. Is there a law for the advancement of navigation? It will benefit *most* those states which have *most* aptitudes for navigation. Is there a law for the encouragement of manufactures? The same thing may be observed—Is there *one* for the encouragement of particular objects of agriculture? The same observation applies. What is the

duty upon foreign cotton? As far as its operation may correspond with its intention it will be a direct bounty upon the industry of a few of the states. For there are only particular states adapted to the raising of cotton.

In short such is the state of human affairs that public measures unavoidably benefit or injure some part more than others. Consequently, that must be a good public measure which *benefits* all the *parts* of a country, though some more than others. If *all* gain, the general mass of public prosperity is promoted, though some gain more than others.

It is certain the operations of the proposed Bank will be most directly useful to the spot upon which they are carried on; but by aiding general circulation, and establishing a convenient medium of remittance & exchange between the states, all will be benefitted in different degrees.

If branches are established the immediate benefit will be diffused still more extensively.

Objection. It will interfere with the several state banks. This cannot happen, unless branches are established in the same states. If this is done no inconvenience to the community can accrue. Either the State Bank and the branch of the National Bank can go on together, and then trade & industry will be promoted by larger supplies, or the one will subvert the other. If the state bank subverts the branch, the injury is at least temporary. If the branch subverts the state bank, it furnishes to the commerce & industry of the place a better substitute; one which, to all the common advantages, will add this peculiar one, the affording a medium of circulation which is useful in all the states and not merely on the spot, and can of course be employed in the intercourse with other states.

But in fact all this is exaggerated supposition. It is not probable, except at the immediate seat of the Bank, where the competition will be compensated by obvious advantages, that there will be any interference. It can never be the interest of the National Bank to quarrel with the local institutions. The local institutions will in all likelihood either be adopted by the National Bank or establishments where they exist will be foreborne.

Lastly an attentive consideration of the tendency of an institution immediately connected with the national government which will interweave itself into the *monied* interest of every state, which will by its notes insinuate itself into every branch of industry and will affect the interests of all classes of the community, ought to produce strong prepossessions in its favor in all who consider the firm establishment of the national government as necessary to the safety & happiness of the country, and who at the same time believe that it stands in need of additional props.

James Madison's Speech on the Bank Bill

2 February 1791

Mr. Madison began with a general review of the advantages and disadvantages of banks. The former he stated to consist in, first, the aids they afford to merchants who can thereby push their mercantile operations farther with the same capital.   2d.   The aids to merchants in paying punctually the customs.   3d.   Aids to the government in complying punctually with its engagements, when deficiencies or delays happen in the revenue.   4th. In diminishing usury.   5th. In saving the wear of the gold and silver kept in the vaults and represented by notes.   6th.   In facilitating occasional remittances from different places where notes happen to circulate. The effect of the proposed bank, in raising the value of stock, he thought, had been greatly overrated. It would no doubt raise that of the stock subscribed into the bank; but could have little effect on stock in general, as the interest on it would remain the same, and the quantity taken out of the market would be replaced by bank stock.

The principal disadvantages consisted in,   1st. banishing the precious metals, by substituting another medium to perform their office: This effect was inevitable. It was admitted by the most enlightened patrons of banks, particularly by Smith on *The Wealth of Nations.* The common answer to the objection was, that the money banished was only an exchange for something equally valuable that would be imported in return. He admitted the weight of this observation in general, but doubted whether, in the present habits of this country, the returns would not be in articles of no permanent use to it.   2d. Exposing the public and individuals to all the evils of a run on the bank, which would be particularly calamitous in so great a country as this, and might happen from various causes, as false rumours, bad management of the institution, an unfavorable balance of trade from short crops, etc.

It was proper to be considered also that the most important of the advantages would be better obtained by several banks properly distributed than by a single one. The aids to commerce could only be afforded at or very near the seat of the bank. The same was true of aids to merchants in the payment of customs. Anticipations of the government would also be most convenient at the different places where the interest of the debt was to be paid. The case in America was different from that in England: the interest there was all due at one place, and the genius of the monarchy favored the concentration of wealth and influence at the metropolis.

He thought the plan liable to other objections: It did not make so good a bargain for the public as was due to its interests. The charter to the bank of England had been granted for 11 years only, and was paid for by a loan to the government on terms better than could be elsewhere got. Every renewal of the charter had in like manner been purchased; in some instances at a very high price. The same had been done by the banks of Genoa, Naples, and other like banks of circulation. The plan was unequal to the public creditors—it gave an undue preference to the holders of a particular denomination of the public debt and to those at and within reach of the seat of government. If the subscriptions should be rapid, the distant holders of paper would be excluded altogether.

In making these remarks on the merits of the bill, he had reserved to himself, he said, the right to deny the authority of Congress to pass it. He had entertained this opinion from the date of the Constitution. His impression might perhaps be the stronger because he well recollected that a power to grant charters of incorporation had been proposed in the general convention and rejected.

Is the power of establishing an *incorporated bank* among the powers vested by the Constitution in the legislature of the United States? This is the question to be examined.

After some general remarks on the limitations of all political power, he took notice of the peculiar manner in which the federal government is limited. It is not a general grant, out of which particular powers are excepted—it is a grant of particular powers only, leaving the general mass in other hands. So it had been understood by its friends and its foes, and so it was to be interpreted.

As preliminaries to a right interpretation, he laid down the following rules:

An interpretation that destroys the very characteristic of the government cannot be just.

Where a meaning is clear, the consequences, whatever they may be, are to be admitted—where doubtful, it is fairly triable by its consequences.

In controverted cases, the meaning of the parties to the instrument, if to be collected by reasonable evidence, is a proper guide.

Cotemporary and concurrent expositions are reasonable evidence of the meaning of the parties.

In admitting or rejecting a constructive authority, not only the degree of its incidentality to an express authority is to be regarded, but the degree of its importance also, since on this will depend the probability or improbability of its being left to construction.

Reviewing the Constitution with an eye to these positions, it was not possible to discover in it the power to incorporate a Bank. The only clauses under which such a power could be pretended, are either—

1. The power to lay and collect taxes to pay the debts and provide for the common defence and general welfare; Or,

2. The power to borrow money on the credit of the United States; Or,

3. The power to pass all laws necessary and proper to carry into execution those powers.

The bill did not come within the first power. It laid no tax to pay the debts, or provide for the general welfare. It laid no tax whatever. It was altogether foreign to the subject.

No argument could be drawn from the terms "common defence and general welfare." The power as to these general purposes was limited to acts laying taxes for them; and the general purposes themselves were limited and explained by the particular enumeration subjoined. To understand these terms in any sense that would justify the power in question would give to Congress an unlimited power; would render nugatory the enumeration of particular powers; would supercede all the powers reserved to the state governments. These terms are copied from the Articles of Confederation; had it ever been pretended that they were to be understood otherwise than as here explained?

It had been said that "general welfare" meant cases in which a general power might be exercised by Congress without interfering with the powers of the States; and that the establishment of a National Bank was of this sort. There were, he said, several answers to this novel doctrine.

1. The proposed Bank would interfere so as indirectly to defeat a State Bank at the same place.   2. It would directly interfere with the rights of the states *to prohibit* as well as to establish banks and the circulation of bank notes. He mentioned a law of Virginia, actually prohibiting the circulation of notes payable to bearer.   3. Interference with the power of the states was no constitutional criterion of the power of Congress. If the power was not given, Congress could not exercise it; if given, they might exercise it, altho it should interfere with the laws or even the constitution of the states.   4. If Congress could incorporate a Bank, merely because the act would leave the states free to establish banks also, any other incorporations might be made by Congress. They could incorporate companies of manufacturers, or companies for cutting canals, or even religious societies, leaving similar incorporations by the states, like state banks, to themselves. Congress might even establish religious teachers in every parish and pay them out of the Treasury of the United States, leaving other teachers unmolested in their functions. These inadmissible consequences condemned the controverted principle.

The case of the Bank established by the former Congress had been cited as a precedent. This was known, he said, to have been the child of necessity. It never could be justified by the regular powers of the Articles of Confederation. Congress betrayed a consciousness of this in recommending to the states to incorporate the Bank also. They did not attempt to protect the Bank Notes by penalties against counterfeiters. These were reserved wholly to the authority of the states.

The second clause to be examined is that which empowers Congress to borrow money.

Is this a bill to borrow money? It does not borrow a shilling. Is there any fair construction by which the bill can be deemed an exercise of the power to borrow money? The obvious meaning of the power to borrow money is that of accepting it from and stipulating payments to those who are *able* and *willing* to lend.

To say that the power to borrow involves a power of creating the ability, where there may be the will, to lend is not only establishing a dangerous principle, as will be immediately shewn, but is as forced a construction as to say that it involves the power of compelling the will, where there may be the ability, to lend.

The third clause is that which gives the power to pass all laws necessary and proper to execute the specified powers.

Whatever meaning this clause may have, none can be admitted that would give an unlimited discretion to Congress.

Its meaning must, according to the natural and obvious force of the terms and the context, be limited to means *necessary* to the *end* and *incident* to the *nature* of the specified powers.

The clause is in fact merely declaratory of what would have resulted by unavoidable implication, as the appropriate, and as it were, technical means of executing those powers. In this sense it had been explained by the friends of the Constitution and ratified by the state conventions.

The essential characteristic of the government, as composed of limited and enumerated powers, would be destroyed: If instead of direct and incidental means, any means could be used which, in the language of the preamble to the bill, "might be conceived to be conducive to the successful conducting of the finances; or might be *conceived* to *tend* to give *facility* to the obtaining of loans." He urged an attention to the diffuse and ductile terms which had been found requisite to cover the stretch of power contained in the bill. He compared them with the terms *necessary* and *proper,* used in the Constitution, and asked whether it was possible to view the two descriptions as synonimous, or the one as a fair and safe commentary on the other.

If, proceeded he, Congress, by virtue of the power to borrow, can create the means of lending, and in pursuance of these means, can incorporate a Bank, they may do any thing whatever creative of like means.

The East-India Company has been a lender to the British government, as well as the Bank, and the South-Sea Company is a greater creditor than either. Congress then may incorporate similar companies in the United States, and that too not under the idea of regulating trade, but under that of borrowing money.

Private capitals are the chief resources for loans to the British government. Whatever then may be conceived to favor the accumulation of capitals may be done by Congress. They may incorporate manufactures. They may give monopolies in every branch of domestic industry.

If, again, Congress by virtue of the power to borrow money can create the ability to lend, they may by virtue of the power to levy money create the ability to pay it. The ability to pay taxes depends on the general wealth of the society, and this on the general prosperity of agriculture,

manufactures and commerce. Congress then may give bounties and make regulations on all of these objects.

The states have, it is allowed on all hands, a concurrent right to lay and collect taxes. This power is secured to them not by its being expressly reserved, but by its not being ceded by the Constitution. The reasons for the bill cannot be admitted because they would invalidate that right; why may it not be *conceived* by Congress that a uniform and exclusive imposition of taxes would, not less than the proposed Banks, be *conducive* to the successful conducting of the national finances, and *tend* to *give facility* to the obtaining of revenue, for the use of the government?

The doctrine of implication is always a tender one. The danger of it has been felt in other governments. The delicacy was felt in the adoption of our own; the danger may also be felt, if we do not keep close to our chartered authorities.

Mark the reasoning on which the validity of the bill depends. To borrow money is made the *end* and the accumulation of capitals *implied* as the *means.* The accumulation of capitals is then the *end* and a bank *implied* as the *means.* The bank is then the *end* and a charter of incorporation, a monopoly, capital punishments, etc. *implied* as the *means.*

If implications thus remote and thus multiplied can be linked together, a chain may be formed that will reach every object of legislation, every object within the whole compass of political economy.

The latitude of interpretation required by the bill is condemned by the rule furnished by the constitution itself.

Congress have power "to regulate the value of money"; yet it is expressly added, not left to be implied, that counterfeitors may be punished.

They have the power "to declare war," to which armies are more incident than incorporated Banks to borrowing; yet is expressly added, the power "to raise and support armies"; and to this again, the express power "to make rules and regulations for the government of armies"; a like remark is applicable to the powers as to a navy.

The regulation and calling out of the militia are more appurtenant to war than the proposed bank to borrowing; yet the former is not left to construction.

The very power to borrow money is a less remote implication from the power of war than an incorporated monopoly bank from the power of borrowing—yet the power to borrow is not left to implication.

It is not pretended that every insertion or omission in the constitution is the effect of systematic attention. This is not the character of any human work, particularly the work of a body of men. The examples cited, with others that might be added, sufficiently inculcate nevertheless a rule of interpretation very different from that on which the bill rests. They condemn the exercise of any power, particularly a great and important power, which is not evidently and necessarily involved in an express power.

It cannot be denied that the power proposed to be exercised is an important power.

As a charter of incorporation the bill creates an artificial person previously not existing in law. It confers important civil rights and attributes which could not otherwise be claimed. It is, though not precisely similar, at least equivalent to the naturalization of an alien, by which certain new civil characters are acquired by him. Would Congress have had the power to naturalize if it had not been expressly given?

In the power to make bylaws, the bill delegated a sort of legislative power, which is unquestionably an act of a high and important nature. He took notice of the only restraint on the bylaws, that they were not to be contrary to the law and the constitution of the bank; and asked what law was intended; if the law of the United States, the scantiness of their code would give a power never before given to a corporation—and obnoxious to the states, whose laws would then be superceded not only by the laws of Congress, but by the bylaws of a corporation within their own jurisdiction. If the law intended was the law of the state, then the state might make laws that would destroy an institution of the United States.

The bill gives a power to purchase and hold lands; Congress themselves could not purchase lands within a state "without the consent of its legislature." How could they delegate a power to others which they did not possess themselves?

It takes from our successors, who have equal rights with ourselves, and with the aid of experience will be more capable of deciding on the subject, an opportunity of exercising that right for an immoderate term.

It takes from our constituents the opportunity of deliberating on the untried measure, although their hands are also to be tied by it for the same term.

It involves a monopoly, which affects the equal rights of every citizen.

It leads to a penal regulation, perhaps capital punishments, one of the most solemn acts of sovereign authority.

From this view of the power of incorporation exercised in the bill, it could never be deemed an accessary or subaltern power, to be deduced by implication, as a means of executing another power; it was in its nature a distinct, an independent and substantive prerogative, which not being enumerated in the Constitution could never have been meant to be included in it, and not being included could never be rightfully exercised.

He here adverted to a distinction which he said had not been sufficiently kept in view, between a power necessary and proper for the government or union and a power necessary and proper for executing the enumerated powers. In the latter case, the powers included in each of the enumerated powers were not expressed, but to be drawn from the nature of each. In the former, the powers composing the government were expressly enumerated. This constituted the peculiar nature of the government; no power therefore not enumerated could be inferred from the general nature of government. Had the power of making treaties, for example, been omitted, however necessary it might have been, the defect could only have been lamented or supplied by an amendment of the Constitution.

But the proposed bank could not even be called necessary to the government; at most it could be but convenient. Its uses to the government could be supplied by keeping the taxes a little in advance—by loans from individuals—by the other banks over which the government would have equal command, nay greater, as it may grant or refuse to these the privilege, made a free and irrevocable gift to the proposed bank, of using their notes in the federal revenue.

He proceeded next to the cotemporary expositions given to the Constitution.

The defence against the charge founded on the want of a bill of rights presupposed, he said, that the powers not given were retained and that those given were not to be extended by remote implications. On any other supposition, the power of Congress to abridge the freedom of the press, or the rights of conscience, etc. could not have been disproved.

The explanations in the state conventions all turned on the same fundamental principle, and on the principle that the terms necessary and proper gave no additional powers to those enumerated. (Here he read sundry passages from the debates of the Pennsylvania, Virginia and North-Carolina conventions, shewing the grounds on which the Constitution had been vindicated by its principal advocates against a dangerous latitude of its powers, charged on it by its opponents.) He did not undertake to vouch for the accuracy or authenticity of the publications which he quoted—he thought it probable that the sentiments delivered might in many instances have been mistaken or imperfectly noted; but the complexion of the whole, with what he himself and many others must recollect, fully justified the use he had made of them.

The explanatory declarations and amendments accompanying the ratifications of the several states formed a striking evidence wearing the same complexion. He referred those who might doubt on the subject to the several acts of ratification.

The explanatory amendments proposed by Congress themselves, at least, would be good authority with them; all these renunciations of power proceeded on a rule of construction excluding the latitude now contended for. These explanations were the more to be respected, as they had not only been proposed by Congress, but ratified by nearly three-fourths of the states. He read several of the articles proposed, remarking particularly on the 11th and 12th: the former, as guarding against a latitude of interpretation—the latter, as excluding every source of power not within the constitution itself.

With all this evidence of the sense in which the Constitution was understood and adopted, will it not be said, if the bill should pass, that its adoption was brought about by one set of arguments and that it is now administered under the influence of another set; and this reproach will have the keener sting, because it is applicable to so many individuals concerned in both the adoption and administration.

In fine, if the power were in the Constitution, the immediate exercise of it cannot be essential—if not there, the exercise of it involves the guilt of usurpation, and establishes a precedent of interpretation leveling all the barriers which limit the powers of the general government and protect those of the state governments. If the point be doubtful only, respect for ourselves, who ought to shun the appearance of precipitancy and ambition; respect for our successors, who ought not lightly to be deprived of the opportunity of exercising the rights of legislation; respect for our constituents who have had no opportunity

of making known their sentiments and who are themselves to be bound down to the measure for so long a period: all these considerations require that the irrevocable decision should at least be suspended until another session.

It appeared on the whole, he concluded, that the power exercised by the bill was condemned by the silence of the Constitution; was condemned by the rule of interpretation arising out of the Constitution; was condemned by its tendency to destroy the main characteristic of the Constitution; was condemned by the expositions of the friends of the Constitution whilst depending before the public; was condemned by the apparent intention of the parties which ratified the Constitution; was condemned by the explanatory amendments proposed by Congress themselves to the Constitution; and he hoped it would receive its final condemnation, by the vote of this house.

THOMAS JEFFERSON

Opinion on the Constitutionality of a National Bank
15 February 1791

At the outset of the new administration, Madison, the most important architect of constitutional reform, had been the president's most regular advisor and the draftsman of his most important messages to Congress. Believing that the presidential veto should be used to guard the Constitution, Washington asked Madison to draft a veto message and called on his cabinet for their opinions on Madison's views. Jefferson's and Hamilton's responses are among the most famous of the early expositions of strict and broad constructions of the Constitution, although neither was publicized at the time. In the end, of course, Washington accepted Hamilton's opinion, which would also be adopted by the Marshall court in its decision in the celebrated case of *M'Culloch* v. *Maryland* (1819).

The bill for establishing a National Bank undertakes among other things:

1. To form the subscribers into a corporation.

2. To enable them in their corporate capacities to receive grants of land; and so far is against the laws of *Mortmain*.

3. To make alien subscribers capable of holding lands; and so far is against the laws of *Alienage*.

4. To transmit these lands, on the death of a proprietor, to a certain line of successors; and so far changes the course of *Descents.*

5. To put the lands out of the reach of forfeiture or escheat; and so far is against the laws of *Forfeiture* and *Escheat.*

6. To transmit personal chattels to successors in a certain line; and so far is against the laws of *Distribution.*

7. To give them the sole and exclusive right of banking under the national authority; and so far is against the laws of Monopoly.

8. To communicate to them a power to make laws paramount to the laws of the States: for so they must be construed, to protect the institution from the control of the State legislatures; and so, probably, they will be construed.

I consider the foundation of the Constitution as laid on this ground: That "all powers not delegated to the United States by the Constitution, nor prohibited by it to the States, are reserved to the States or to the people." [XIIth amendment.] To take a single step beyond the boundaries thus specially drawn around the powers of Congress, is to take possession of a boundless field of power, no longer susceptible of any definition.

The incorporation of a bank, and the powers assumed by this bill, have not, in my opinion, been delegated to the United States by the Constitution.

I. They are not among the powers specially enumerated: for these are: 1st. A power to lay taxes for the purpose of paying the debts of the United States; but no debt is paid by this bill, nor any tax laid. Were it a bill to raise money, its origination in the Senate would condemn it by the Constitution.

2d. "To borrow money." But this bill neither borrows money nor ensures the borrowing it. The proprietors of the bank will be just as free as any other money holders to lend or not to lend their money to the public. The operation proposed in the bill, first to lend them two millions, and then to borrow them back again, cannot change the nature of the latter act, which will still be a payment, and not a loan, call it by what name you please.

3. To "regulate commerce with foreign nations, and among the States, and with the Indian tribes." To erect a bank, and to regulate commerce, are very different acts. He who erects a bank, creates a subject of commerce in its bills; so does he who makes a bushel of wheat, or digs a dollar out of the mines; yet neither of these persons regulates commerce thereby. To make a thing which may be bought and sold, is not to prescribe regulations for buying and selling. Besides, if this was an exercise of the power of regulating commerce, it would be void, as extending as much to the internal commerce of every State as to its external. For the power given to Congress by the Constitution does not extend to the internal regulation of the commerce of a state (that is to say of the commerce between citizen and citizen), which remain exclusively with its own legislature; but to its external commerce only, that is to say, its commerce with another state, or with foreign nations, or with the Indian tribes. Accordingly the bill does not propose the measure as a regulation of trade, but as "productive of considerable advantages to trade." Still less are these powers covered by any other of the special enumerations.

II. Nor are they within either of the general phrases, which are the two following:—

1. To lay taxes to provide for the general welfare of the United States, that is to say, "to lay taxes for *the purpose* of providing for the general welfare." For the laying of taxes is the *power* and the general welfare the *purpose* for which the power is to be exercised. They are not to lay taxes *ad libitum for any purpose they please;* but only *to pay the debts or provide for the welfare of the Union.* In like manner, they are not *to do anything they please* to provide for the general welfare, but only to *lay taxes* for that purpose. To consider the latter phrase, not as describing the purpose of the first, but as giving a distinct and independent power to do any act they please, which might be for the good of the Union, would render all the preceding and subsequent enumerations of power completely useless.

It would reduce the whole instrument to a single phrase, that of instituting a Congress with power to do whatever would be for the good of the United States; and, as they would be the sole judges of the good or evil, it would be also a power to do whatever evil they please.

It is an established rule of construction where a phrase will bear either of two meanings, to give it that which will allow some meaning to the other parts of the instrument, and not that which would render all the others useless. Certainly no such universal power was meant to be given them. It was intended to lace them up straitly within the enumerated powers, and those without which, as means, these powers could not be carried into effect. It is known that the very power now proposed *as a means* was rejected as *an end* by the Convention which formed the Constitution. A proposition was made to them to authorize Congress to open canals, and an amendatory one to empower them to incorporate. But the whole was rejected, and one of the reasons for rejection urged in debate was, that then they would have a power to erect a bank, which would render the great cities, where there were prejudices and jealousies on the subject, adverse to the reception of the Constitution.

2. The second general phrase is "to make all laws *necessary* and proper for carrying into execution the enumerated powers." But they can all be carried into execution without a bank. A bank therefore is not *necessary,* and consequently not authorized by this phrase.

It has been urged that a bank will give great facility or convenience in the collection of taxes. Suppose this were true: yet the Constitution allows only the means which are "*necessary,*" not those which are merely "convenient" for effecting the enumerated powers. If such a latitude of construction be allowed to this phrase as to give any non-enumerated power, it will go to every one, for there is not one which ingenuity may not torture into a *convenience* in some instance *or other* to *some one* of so long a list of enumerated powers. It would swallow up all the delegated powers, and reduce the whole to one power, as before observed. Therefore it was that the Constitution restrained them to the *necessary* means, that is to say, to those means without which the grant of power would be nugatory.

But let us examine this convenience and see what it is. The report on this subject, page 3, states the only *general* convenience to be the preventing the transportation and re-transportation of money between the states and the treasury (for I pass over the increase of circulating medium, ascribed to it as a want, and which, according to my ideas of paper money, is clearly a demerit). Every state will have to pay a sum of tax money into the treasury; and the treasury will have to pay, in every state, a part of the interest on the public debt and salaries to the officers of government resident in that state. In most of the states there will still be a surplus of tax money to come up to the seat of government for the officers residing there. The payments of interest and salary in each state may be made by treasury orders on the state collector. This will take up the greater part of the money he has collected in his state, and consequently prevent the great mass of it from being drawn out of the state. If there be a balance of commerce in favor of that state against the one in which the government resides, the surplus of taxes will be remitted by the bills of exchange drawn for that commercial balance. And so it must be if there was a bank. But if there be no balance of commerce, either direct or circuitous, all the banks in the world could not bring up the surplus of taxes but in the form of money. Treasury orders then, and bills of exchange may prevent the displacement of the main mass of the money collected without the aid of any bank; and where these fail, it cannot be prevented even with that aid.

Perhaps, indeed, bank bills may be a more *convenient* vehicle than treasury orders. But a little *difference* in the degree of *convenience,* cannot constitute the necessity which the constitution makes the ground for assuming any non-enumerated power.

Besides, the existing banks will, without a doubt, enter into arrangements for lending their agency, and the more favorable, as there will be a competition among them for it; whereas the bill delivers us up bound to the national bank, who are free to refuse all arrangement, but on their own terms, and the public not free, on such refusal, to employ any other bank. That of Philadelphia, I believe, now does this business, by their post-notes, which, by an arrangement with the treasury, are paid by any state collector to whom they are presented. This expedient alone suffices to prevent the existence of that *necessity* which may justify the assumption of a non-enumerated power as a means for carrying into effect an enumerated one. The thing may be done, and has been done, and well done, without this assumption; therefore, it does not stand on that degree of *necessity* which can honestly justify it.

It may be said that a bank whose bills would have a currency all over the states, would be more convenient than one whose currency is limited to a single State. So it would be still more convenient that there should be a bank, whose bills should have a currency all over the world. But it does not follow from this superior conveniency, that there exists anywhere a power to establish such a bank; or that the world may not go on very well without it.

Can it be thought that the Constitution intended that for a shade or two of *convenience,* more or less, Congress should be authorized to break down the most ancient and fundamental laws of the several states, such as those against Mortmain, the laws of Alienage, the rules of descent, the acts of distribution, the laws of escheat and forfeiture, the laws of monopoly? Nothing but a necessity invincible by any other means, can justify such a prostitution of laws which constitute the pillars of our whole system of jurisprudence. Will Congress be too straight-laced to carry the Constitution into honest effect, unless they may pass over the foundation-laws of the state government for the slightest convenience of theirs?

The negative of the President is the shield provided by the Constitution to protect against the invasions of the legislature: 1. The right of the Executive. 2. Of the Judiciary. 3. Of the States and state legislatures. The present is the case of a right remaining exclusively with the states, and consequently one of those intended by the Constitution to be placed under its protection.

It must be added, however, that unless the President's mind on a view of everything which is urged for and against this bill is tolerably clear that it is unauthorized by the Constitution; if the pro and the con hang so even as to balance his judgment, a just respect for the wisdom of the legislature would naturally decide the balance in favor of their opinion. It is chiefly for cases where they are clearly misled by error, ambition, or interest, that the Constitution has placed a check in the negative of the President.

ALEXANDER HAMILTON

Opinion on the Constitutionality of a National Bank

15 February 1791

The Secretary of the Treasury having perused with attention the papers containing the opinions of the Secretary of State and Attorney General concerning the constitutionality of the bill for establishing a National Bank proceeds according to the order of the President to submit the reasons which have induced him to entertain a different opinion.

It will naturally have been anticipated that, in performing this task, he would feel uncommon solicitude. Personal considerations alone arising from the reflection that the measure originated with him would be sufficient to produce it. The sense which he has manifested of the great importance of such an institution to the successful administration of the department under his particular care, and an expectation of serious ill consequences to result from

a failure of the measure, do not permit him to be without anxiety on public accounts. But the chief solicitude arises from a firm persuasion that principles of construction like those espoused by the Secretary of State and the Attorney General would be fatal to the just & indispensable authority of the United States.

In entering upon the argument it ought to be premised that the objections of the Secretary of State and Attorney General are founded on a general denial of the authority of the United States to erect corporations. The latter indeed expressly admits that if there be anything in the bill which is not warranted by the Constitution, it is the clause of incorporation.

Now it appears to the Secretary of the Treasury that this *general principle* is *inherent* in the very *definition* of *Government* and *essential* to every step of the progress to be made by that of the United States: namely—that every power vested in a Government is in its nature *sovereign* and includes by *force* of the *term* a right to employ all the *means* requisite and fairly *applicable* to the attainment of the *ends* of such power; and which are not precluded by restrictions & exceptions specified in the Constitution, or not immoral, or not contrary to the essential ends of political society.

This principle in its application to Government in general would be admitted as an axiom. And it will be incumbent upon those who may incline to deny it to *prove* a distinction; and to shew that a rule which in the general system of things is essential to the preservation of the social order is inapplicable to the United States.

The circumstances that the powers of sovereignty are in this country divided between the national and state governments does not afford the distinction required. It does not follow from this that each of the *portions* of powers delegated to the one or to the other is not sovereign *with regard to its proper objects*. It will only *follow* from it that each has sovereign power as to *certain things,* and not as to *other things.* To deny that the Government of the United States has sovereign power as to its declared purposes & trusts, because its power does not extend to all cases, would be equally to deny that the state governments have sovereign power in any case, because their power does not extend to every case. The tenth section of the first article of the Constitution exhibits a long list of very important things which they may not do. And thus the United States would furnish the singular spectacle of a *political society* without *sovereignty,* or of a people *governed* without *government.*

If it would be necessary to bring proof to a proposition so clear as that which affirms that the powers of the federal government, *as to its objects,* are sovereign, there is a clause of its Constitution which would be decisive. It is that which declares that the Constitution and the laws of the United States made in pursuance of it, and all treaties made or which shall be made under their authority shall be the supreme law of the land. The power which can create the *Supreme law* of the land, in any case, is doubtless sovereign *as to such case.*

This general & indisputable principle puts at once an end to the *abstract* question—Whether the United States have power to *erect a corporation?* that is to say, to give a *legal* or *artificial capacity* to one or more persons, distinct from the natural. For it is unquestionably incident to *sovereign power* to erect corporations, and consequently to *that* of the United States, in *relation to the objects* intrusted to the management of the government. The difference is this—where the authority of the government is general, it can create corporations in *all cases;* where it is confined to certain branches of legislation, it can create corporations only in those cases.

Here then as far as concerns the reasoning of the Secretary of State & the Attorney General, the affirmative of the constitutionality of the bill might be permitted to rest. It will occur to the President that the principle here advanced has been untouched by either of them.

For a more complete elucidation of the point nevertheless, the arguments which they have used against the power of the government to erect corporations, however foreign they are to the great & fundamental rule which has been stated, shall be particularly examined. And after shewing that they do not tend to impair its force, it shall also be shewn that the power of incorporation incident to the government in certain cases does fairly extend to the particular case which is the object of the bill.

The first of these arguments is that the foundation of the Constitution is laid on this ground "that all powers not delegated to the United States by the Constitution nor prohibited to it by the States are reserved to the States or to the people," whence it is meant to be inferred that Congress can in no case exercise any power not included in those enumerated in the Constitution. And it is affirmed that the power of erecting a corporation is not included in any of the enumerated powers.

The main proposition here laid down, in its true signification, is not to be questioned. It is nothing more than a consequence of this republican maxim, that all government is a delegation of power. But how much is delegated in each case is a question of fact to be made out by fair reasoning & construction upon the particular provisions of the Constitution—taking as guides the general principles & general ends of government.

It is not denied that there are *implied* as well as *express* powers, and that the former are as effectually delegated as the latter. And for the sake of accuracy it shall be mentioned that there is another class of powers which may be properly denominated *resulting* powers. It will not be doubted that if the United States should make a conquest of any of the territories of its neighbors, they would possess sovereign jurisdiction over the conquered territory. This would rather be a result from the whole mass of the powers of the government & from the nature of political society, than a consequence of either of the powers specially enumerated.

But be this as it may, it furnishes a striking illustration of the general doctrine contended for. It shews an extensive case in which a power of erecting corporations is either implied in or would result from some or all of the powers vested in the National Government. The jurisdiction acquired over such conquered territory would certainly be competent to every species of legislation.

To return—It is conceded, that implied powers are to be considered as delegated equally with express ones.

Then it follows that as a power of erecting a corporation may as well be *implied* as any other thing; it may as well be employed as an *instrument* or *mean* of carrying into execution any of the specified powers as any other instrument or mean whatever. The only question must be, in this as in every other case, whether the mean to be employed, or in this instance the corporation to be erected, has a natural relation to any of the acknowledged objects or lawful ends of the government. Thus a corporation may not be erected by Congress for superintending the police of the city of Philadelphia because they are not authorized to *regulate* the *police* of that city; but one may be erected in relation to the collection of the taxes, or to the trade with foreign countries, or to the trade between the states, or with the Indian Tribes, because it is the province of the federal government to regulate those objects & because it is incident to a general *sovereign* or *legislative power* to *regulate* a thing to employ all the means which relate to its regulation to the *best & greatest advantage.*

A strange fallacy seems to have crept into the manner of thinking & reasoning upon the subject. Imagination appears to have been unusually busy concerning it. An incorporation seems to have been regarded as some great, independent, substantive thing—as a political end of peculiar magnitude & moment; whereas it is truly to be considered as a *quality, capacity,* or *mean* to an end. Thus a mercantile company is formed with a certain capital for the purpose of carrying on a particular branch of business. Here the business to be prosecuted is the *end;* the association in order to form the requisite capital is the primary mean. Suppose that an incorporation were added to this; it would only be to add a new *quality* to that association; to give it an artificial capacity by which it would be enabled to prosecute the business with more safety & convenience.

That the importance of the power of incorporation has been exaggerated, leading to erroneous conclusions, will further appear from tracing it to its origin. The Roman law is the source of it, according to which a *voluntary* association of individuals at *any time* or *for any purpose* was capable of producing it. In England, whence our notions of it are immediately borrowed, it forms a part of the executive authority, & the exercise of it has been often *delegated* by that authority. Whence, therefore, the ground of the supposition that it lies beyond the reach of all those very important portions of sovereign power, legislative as well as executive, which belong to the government of the United States?

To this mode of reasoning respecting the right of employing all the means requisite to the execution of the specified powers of the government, it is objected that none but *necessary* & proper means are to be employed, & the Secretary of State maintains that no means are to be considered as *necessary* but those without which the grant of the power would be *nugatory.* Nay so far does he go in his restrictive interpretation of the word as even to make the case of *necessity* which shall warrant the constitutional exercise of the power to depend on *casual & temporary* circumstances, an idea which alone refutes the construction. The *expediency* of exercising a particular power, at a particular time, must indeed depend on *circumstances;* but the constitutional right of exercising it must be uniform & invariable—the same today as tomorrow.

All the arguments therefore against the constitutionality of the bill derived from the accidental existence of certain state-banks, institutions which *happen* to exist today, & for ought that concerns the government of the United States, may disappear tomorrow, must not only be rejected as fallacious, but must be viewed as demonstrative that there is a *radical* source of error in the reasoning.

It is essential to the being of the national government that so erroneous a conception of the meaning of the word *necessary* should be exploded.

It is certain that neither the grammatical nor popular sense of the term requires that construction. According to both, *necessary* often means no more than *needful, requisite, incidental, useful,* or *conducive* to. It is a common mode of expression to say that it is *necessary* for a government or a person to do this or that thing when nothing more is intended or understood than that the interests of the government or person require, or will be promoted, by the doing of this or that thing. The imagination can be at no loss for exemplification of the use of the word in this sense.

And it is the true one in which it is to be understood as used in the Constitution. The whole turn of the clause containing it indicates that it was the intent of the convention by that clause to give a liberal latitude to the exercise of the specified powers. The expressions have peculiar comprehensiveness. They are—"to make *all laws,* necessary and proper for *carrying into execution* the foregoing powers & all *other powers* vested by the constitution in the *government* of the United States, or in any *department* or *officer* thereof." To understand the word as the Secretary of State does would be to depart from its obvious & popular sense, and to give it a *restrictive* operation; an idea never before entertained. It would be to give it the same force as if the word *absolutely* or *indispensably* had been prefixed to it.

Such a construction would beget endless uncertainty & embarassment. The cases must be palpable & extreme in which it could be pronounced with certainty that a measure was absolutely necessary, or one without which the exercise of a given power would be nugatory. There are few measures of any government which would stand so severe a test. To insist upon it would be to make the criterion of the exercise of any implied power a *case of extreme necessity;* which is rather a rule to justify the overleaping of the bounds of constitutional authority than to govern the ordinary exercise of it.

It may be truly said of every government, as well as of that of the United States, that it has only a right to pass such laws as are necessary & proper to accomplish the objects intrusted to it. For no government has a right to do *merely what it pleases.* Hence by a process of reasoning similar to that of the Secretary of State, it might be proved that neither of the state governments has a right to incorporate a bank. It might be shewn that all the public business of the state could be performed without a bank, and inferring thence that it was unnecessary it might be argued that it could not be done, because it is against the rule which has been just mentioned. A like mode of reasoning would prove that there was no power to incorporate the inhabitants of a town, with a view to a more perfect police: For it is certain that an incorporation may be dispensed with, though it is better to have one. It is to be remembered that there is no *express* power in any state constitution to erect corporations.

The *degree* in which a measure is necessary can never be a test of the *legal* right to adopt it. That must ever be a matter of opinion; and can only be a test of expediency. The *relation* between the *measure* and the *end,* between the *nature* of *the mean* employed towards the execution of a power and the object of that power, must be the criterion of constitutionality, not the more or less of *necessity* or *utility*.

The practice of the government is against the rule of construction advocated by the Secretary of State. Of this the act concerning light houses, beacons, buoys & public piers is a decisive example. This doubtless must be referred to the power of regulating trade, and is fairly relative to it. But it cannot be affirmed that the exercise of that power, in this instance, was strictly necessary; or that the power itself would be *nugatory* without that of regulating establishments of this nature.

This restrictive interpretation of the word *necessary* is also contrary to this sound maxim of construction: namely, that the powers contained in a constitution of government, especially those which concern the general administration of the affairs of a country, its finances, trade, defence, etc. ought to be construed liberally in advancement of the public good. This rule does not depend on the particular form of a government or on the particular demarkation of the boundaries of its powers, but on the nature and objects of government itself. The means by which national exigencies are to be provided for, national inconveniencies obviated, national prosperity promoted, are of such infinite variety, extent and complexity, that there must, of necessity, be great latitude of discretion in the selection & application of those means. Hence, consequently, the necessity & propriety of exercising the authorities intrusted to a government on principles of liberal construction. . . .

But while, on the one hand, the construction of the Secretary of State is deemed inadmissible, it will not be contended on the other that the clause in question gives any *new* or *independent* power. But it gives an explicit sanction to the doctrine of *implied* powers, and is equivalent to an admission of the proposition that the government, *as to its specified powers* and *objects,* has plenary & sovereign authority, in some cases paramount to that of the states, in others coordinate with it. For such is the plain import of the declaration that it may pass *all laws* necessary & proper to carry into execution those powers.

It is no valid objection to the doctrine to say that it is calculated to extend the powers of the general government throughout the entire sphere of state legislation. The same thing has been said and may be said with regard to every exercise of power by *implication* or *construction.* The moment the literal meaning is departed from, there is a chance of error and abuse. And yet an adherence to the letter of its powers would at once arrest the motions of the government. It is not only agreed, on all hands, that the exercise of constructive powers is indispensable, but every act which has been passed is more or less an exemplification of it. One has been already mentioned, that relating to light houses, etc. That which declares the power of the President to remove officers at pleasure acknowledges the same truth in another and a signal instance.

The truth is that difficulties on this point are inherent in the nature of the federal constitution. They result inevitably from a division of the legislative power. The consequence of this division is that there will be cases clearly within the power of the National Government; others clearly without its power; and a third class, which will leave room for controversy & difference of opinion, & concerning which a reasonable latitude of judgment must be allowed.

But this doctrine which is contended for is not chargeable with the consequence imputed to it. It does not affirm that the national government is sovereign in all respects, but that it is sovereign to a certain extent: that is, to the extent of the objects of its specified powers.

It leaves therefore a criterion of what is constitutional and of what is not so. This criterion is the *end* to which the measure relates as a *mean*. If the end be clearly comprehended within any of the specified powers, & if the measure have an obvious relation to that end, and is not forbidden by any particular provision of the constitution—it may safely be deemed to come within the compass of the national authority. There is also this further criterion which may materially assist the decision. Does the proposed measure abridge a preexisting right of any state, or of any individual? If it does not, there is a strong presumption in favour of its constitutionality; & slighter relations to any declared object of the Constitution may be permitted to turn the scale. . . .

There are two points in the suggestions of the Secretary of State which have been noted that are peculiarly incorrect. One is that the proposed incorporation is against the laws of monopoly, because it stipulates an exclusive right of banking under the national authority. The other that it gives power to the institution to make laws paramount to those of the states.

But with regard to the first point, the bill neither prohibits any state from erecting as many banks as they please, nor any number of individuals from associating to carry on the business, & consequently is free from the charge of establishing a monopoly: for monopoly implies a *legal impediment* to the carrying on of the trade by others than those to whom it is granted.

And with regard to the second point, there is still less foundation. The bylaws of such an institution as a bank can operate only upon its own members; can only concern the disposition of its own property; and must essentially resemble the rules of a private mercantile partnership. They are expressly not to be contrary to law; and law must here mean the law of a state as well as of the United States. There never can be a doubt that a law of the corporation, if contrary to a law of a state, must be overruled as void; unless the law of the state is contrary to that of the United States; and then the question will not be between the law of the state and that of the corporation, but between the law of the state and that of the United States.

Another argument made use of by the Secretary of State is the rejection of a proposition by the convention to empower Congress to make corporations, either generally, or for some special purpose.

What was the precise nature or extent of this proposition, or what the reasons for refusing it, is not ascertained by any authentic document, or even by accurate recollection. As far as any such document exists, it specifies only canals. If this was the amount of it, it would at most only prove that it was thought inexpedient to give a power to incorporate for the purpose of opening canals, for which purpose a special power would have been necessary; except with regard to the Western Territory, there being nothing in any part of the Constitution respecting the regulation of canals. It must be confessed, however, that very different accounts are given of the import of the proposition and of the motives for rejecting it. Some affirm that it was confined to the opening of canals and obstructions in rivers; others, that it embraced banks; and others, that it extended to the power of incorporating generally. Some again alledge that it was disagreed to because it was thought improper to vest in Congress a power of erecting corporations—others, because it was thought unnecessary to *specify* the power, and inexpedient to furnish an additional topic of objection to the Constitution. In this state of the matter, no inference whatever can be drawn from it.

But whatever may have been the nature of the proposition or the reasons for rejecting it concludes nothing in respect to the real merits of the question. The Secretary of State will not deny that whatever may have been the intention of the framers of a constitution, or of a law, that intention is to be sought for in the instrument itself, according to the usual & established rules of construction. Nothing is more common than for laws to *express* and *effect* more or less than was intended. If then a power to erect a corporation, in any case, be deducible by fair inference from the whole or any part of the numerous provisions of the Constitution of the United States, arguments drawn from extrinsic circumstances, regarding the intention of the convention, must be rejected. . . .

It is presumed to have been satisfactorily shewn in the course of the preceding observations

1. That the power of the government *as to* the objects intrusted to its management is in its nature sovereign.

2. That the right of erecting corporations is one inherent in & inseparable from the idea of sovereign power.

3. That the position that the government of the United States can exercise no power but such as is delegated to it by its constitution does not militate against this principle.

4. That the word *necessary* in the general clause can have no *restrictive* operation, derogating from the force of this principle, indeed, that the degree in which a measure is or is not necessary cannot be a *test* of *constitutional* right, but of expediency only.

5. That the power to erect corporations is not to be considered as an *independent* & *substantive* power but as an *incidental* & *auxiliary* one; and was therefore more properly left to implication than expressly granted.

6. That the principle in question does not extend the power of the government beyond the prescribed limits, because it only affirms a power to *incorporate* for *purposes within the sphere of the specified powers.*

And lastly that the right to exercise such a power, in certain cases, is unequivocally granted in the most *positive* & *comprehensive* terms.

To all which it only remains to be added that such a power has actually been exercised in two very eminent instances: namely in the erection of two governments, One, northwest of the river Ohio, and the other southwest—*the last, independent of any antecedent compact.*

And there results a full & complete demonstration that the Secretary of State & Attorney General are mistaken when they deny generally the power of the national government to erect corporations.

It shall now be endeavored to be shewn that there is a power to erect one of the kind proposed by the bill. This will be done by tracing a natural & obvious relation between the institution of a bank and the objects of several of the enumerated powers of the government; and by shewing that, *politically* speaking, it is necessary to the effectual execution of one or more of those powers. In the course of this investigation, various instances will be stated by way of illustration of a right to erect corporations under those powers.

Some preliminary observations may be proper.

The proposed bank is to consist of an association of persons for the purpose of creating a joint capital to be employed, chiefly and essentially, in loans. So far the object is not only lawful, but it is the mere exercise of a right which the law allows to every individual. The Bank of New York, which is not incorporated, is an example of such an association. The bill proposes in addition that the government shall become a joint proprietor in this undertaking, and that it shall permit the bills of the company payable on demand to be receivable in its revenues, & stipulates that it shall not grant privileges similar to those which are to be allowed to this company to any others. All this is incontrovertibly within the compass of the discretion of the government. The only question is, whether it has a right to incorporate this company in order to enable it the more effectually to accomplish *ends* which are in themselves lawful.

To establish such a right, it remains to shew the relation of such an institution to one or more of the specified powers of the government.

Accordingly it is affirmed that it has a relation more or less direct to the power of collecting taxes; to that of borrowing money; to that of regulating trade between the states; and to those of raising, supporting & maintaining fleets & armies. To the two former, the relation may be said to be *immediate.*

And, in the last place, it will be argued that it is, *clearly,* within the provision which authorizes the making of all *needful* rules & *regulations* concerning the *property* of the United States, as the same has been practiced upon by the government.

A Bank relates to the collection of taxes in two ways; *indirectly,* by increasing the quantity of circulating medium & quickening circulation, which facilitates the means of paying—*directly,* by creating a *convenient species* of *medium* in which they are to be paid. . . .

A Bank has a direct relation to the power of borrowing money, because it is a usual and in sudden emergencies an essential instrument in the obtaining of loans to government.

A nation is threatened with a war. Large sums are wanted, on a sudden, to make the requisite preparations. Taxes are laid for the purpose, but it requires time to obtain the benefit of them. Anticipation is indispensable. If there be a bank, the supply can at once be had; if there be none loans from individuals must be sought. The progress of these is often too slow for the exigency; in some situations they are not practicable at all. Frequently, when they are, it is of great consequence to be able to anticipate the product of them by advances from a bank. . . .

The institution of a bank has also a natural relation to the regulation of trade between the states: in so far as it is conducive to the creation of a convenient medium of *exchange* between them, and to the keeping up a full circulation by preventing the frequent displacement of the metals in reciprocal remittances. Money is the very hinge on which commerce turns. And this does not mean merely gold & silver; many other things have served the purpose with different degrees of utility. Paper has been extensively employed. . . .

Illustrations of this kind might be multiplied without end. They shall, however, be pursued no further.

There is a sort of evidence on this point arising from an aggregate view of the Constitution, which is of no inconsiderable weight. The very general power of laying & collecting taxes & appropriating their proceeds—that of borrowing money indefinitely—that of coining money & regulating foreign coins—that of making all needful rules and regulations respecting the property of the United States—these powers combined, as well as the reason & nature of the thing speak strongly this language: That it is the manifest design and scope of the Constitution to vest in Congress all the powers requisite to the effectual administration of the finances of the United States. As far as concerns this object, there appears to be no parsimony of power.

To suppose, then, that the government is precluded from the employment of so usual as well as so important an instrument for the administration of its finances as that of a bank, is to suppose what does not coincide with the general tenor & complexion of the Constitution, and what is not agreeable to impressions that any mere spectator would entertain concerning it. Little less than a prohibitory clause can destroy the strong presumptions which result from the general aspect of the government. Nothing but demonstration should exclude the idea that the power exists.

In all questions of this nature the practice of mankind ought to have great weight against the theories of individuals.

The fact, for instance, that all the principal commercial nations have made use of trading corporations or companies for the purposes of *external commerce* is a satisfactory proof that the establishment of them is an incident to the regulation of that commerce.

This other fact, that banks are an usual engine in the administration of national finances, & an ordinary & the most effectual instrument of loans, & one which in this country has been found essential, pleads strongly against the supposition that a government clothed with most of the most important prerogatives of sovereignty in relation to the revenues, its debts, its credit, its defense, its trade, its intercourse with foreign nations—is forbidden to make use of that instrument as an appendage to its own authority. . . .

It is presumed, that nothing of consequence in the observations of the Secretary of State and Attorney General has been left unnoticed.

There are indeed a variety of observations of the Secretary of State designed to shew that the utilities ascribed to a bank in relation to the collection of taxes and to trade could be obtained without it, to analyse which would prolong the discussion beyond all bounds. It shall be forborne for two reasons—first because the report concerning the Bank may speak for itself in this respect; and secondly, because all those observations are grounded on the erroneous idea that the *quantum* of necessity or utility is the test of a constitutional exercise of power. . . .

JAMES MADISON TO THOMAS JEFFERSON

On Speculative Excess
Summer 1791

Soon after the adjournment of the third session of Congress and Washington's approval of the national bank, Jefferson joined Madison in New York City for a pleasure tour through upper New York and part of New England, taking time before departing from the city for a breakfast with the revolutionary poet and journalist Philip Freneau, whom they were seeking to persuade to launch a national newspaper. Upon their return to the city, Jefferson traveled on to Philadelphia to catch up on business. Madison remained in New York, where he witnessed the opening of subscriptions for stock in the new national bank.

10 July

. . . The Bank-Shares have risen as much in the market here as at Philadelphia. It seems admitted on all hands now that the plan of the institution gives a moral certainty of gain to the subscribers with scarce a physical possibility of loss. The subscriptions are consequently a mere scramble for so much public plunder which will be engrossed by those already loaded with the spoils of indi[vi]duals. The event shews what would have been the operation of the plan if, *as originally proposed,* subscriptions had been limited to the 1st of April and to the favorite species of stock which the Bank-Jobbers had monopolized. It pretty clearly appears also in what proportions the public debt lies in the country—What sort of hands hold it, and by whom the people of the U.S. are to be governed. Of all the shameful circumstances of this business, it is among the greatest to see the members of the Legislature who were most active in pushing this job, openly grasping its emoluments. [Philip] Schuyler is to be put at the head of the Directors, if the weight of the N.Y. subscribers can effect it. Nothing new is talked of here. In fact stockjobbing drowns every other subject. The Coffee House is in an eternal buzz with the gamblers. . . .

8 August

. . . It is said that packet boats & expresses are again sent from this place to the southern states to buy up the paper of all sorts which has risen in the market here. These & other abuses make it a problem whether the system of the old paper under a bad government, or of the new under a good one, be chargeable with the greater substantial injustice. The true difference seems to be that by the former the few were the victims to the many; by the latter the many to the few. It seems agreed on all hands now that the bank is a certain & gratuitous augmentation of the capitals subscribed in a proportion of not less than 40 or 50 percent. And if the deferred debt should be immediately provided for in favor of the purchasers of it in the deferred shape, & since the unanimous vote that no change shd. be made in the funding system, my imagination will not attempt to set bounds to the daring depravity of the times. The stockjobbers will become the praetorian band of the government—at once its tool & its tyrant; bribed by its largesses, & overawing it by clamours and combinations. . . .

Commerce and Manufactures

When the War for Independence was succeeded by a sharp, postwar depression, numerous Americans began to think again about the economic and commercial policies appropriate for the new republic. Early in the Revolution, few had doubted that an American doctrine of free trade would revolutionize the world and bring unprecedented prosperity at home. By 1784, it was clear that it had actually done neither. Many blamed the economic troubles, in no small part, on European policies that favored their own merchants and excluded American ships or products from some of the best potential markets. Britain's navigation laws—and, most especially, the closure of the British West Indies to American ships—were widely seen as the most objectionable of all. The best response, however, was a matter for intense dispute. During the Confederation years, various states attempted individually, without success, to retaliate against the British regulations. Some Americans began to advocate encouragement of native manufactures and the development of a larger domestic market for American goods. Jefferson and Madison were more reluctant to promote intensive economic change or to accept the inequalities that urbanization and industrialization seemed to entail. But men of both persuasions were convinced that it was critical to grant the central government authority to regulate the nation's commerce, to negotiate commercial treaties, and to retaliate against the European regulations if required. None of the nation's needs was more responsible for the demand for federal reform. The Constitution was barely ratified, however, before the underlying differences among its advocates erupted in ferocious disagreements.

THOMAS JEFFERSON

Notes on the State of Virginia
1785

Jefferson's only book, originating as a response to a set of inquiries by the secretary of the French legation to the United States and initially published in France when Jefferson succeeded Benjamin Franklin as minister to that court, included a classic statement of the agrarianism characteristic of the views of both of the Virginia leaders of the emerging opposition.

Query XIX: The Present State of Manufactures, Commerce, Interior and Exterior Trade?

We never had an interior trade of any importance. Our exterior commerce has suffered very much from the beginning of the present contest. During this time we have manufactured within our families the most necessary articles of cloathing. Those of cotton will bear some comparison with the same kinds of manufacture in Europe; but those of wool, flax, and hemp are very coarse, unsightly, and unpleasant; and such is our attachment to agriculture, and such our preference for foreign manufactures, that be it wise or unwise, our people will certainly return as soon as they can to the raising raw materials and exchanging them for finer manufactures than they are able to execute themselves.

The political economists of Europe have established it as a principle that every state should endeavour to manufacture for itself; and this principle, like many others, we transfer to America without calculating the difference of circumstance which should often produce a difference of result. In Europe the lands are either cultivated or locked up against the cultivator. Manufacture must therefore be resorted to of necessity, not of choice, to support the surplus of their people. But we have an immensity of land courting the industry of the husbandman. Is it best then that all our citizens should be employed in its improvement or that one half should be called off from that to exercise manufactures and handicraft arts for the other? Those who labor in the earth are the chosen people of God, if ever he had a chosen people, whose breasts he has made his peculiar deposit for substantial and genuine virtue. It is the focus in which he keeps alive that sacred fire which otherwise might escape from the face of the earth. Corruption of morals in the mass of cultivators is a phenomenon of which no age nor nation has furnished an example. It is the mark set on those who not looking up to heaven, to their own soil and industry, as does the husbandman, for their subsistance, depend for it on the casualties and caprice of customers. Dependence begets subservience and venality, suffocates the germ of virtue, and prepares fit tools for the designs of ambition. This, the natural progress and consequence of the arts, has sometimes perhaps been retarded by accidental circumstances; but, generally speaking, the proportion which the aggregate of the other classes of citizens bears in any state to that of its husbandmen is the proportion of its unsound to its healthy parts, and is a good-enough barometer whereby to measure its degree of corruption. While we have land to labor then, let us never wish to see our citizens occupied at a work-bench, or twirling a distaff. Carpenters, masons, smiths, are wanting in husbandry; but, for the general operations of manufacture, let our work-shops remain in Europe. It is better to carry provisions and materials to workmen there than bring them to the provisions and materials, and with them their manners and principles. The loss by the transportation of commodities across the Atlantic will be made up in happiness and permanence of government. The mobs of great cities add just so much to the support of pure government as sores do to the strength of the human body. It is the manners and spirit of a people which preserve a republic in vigour. A degeneracy in these is a canker which soon eats to the heart of its laws and constitution.

Jefferson and Madison on Republican Political Economy

Thomas Jefferson to G. K. van Hogendorp
13 October 1785

. . . You ask what I think on the expediency of encouraging our states to be commercial? Were I to indulge my own theory, I should wish them to practice neither commerce nor navigation, but to stand with respect to

Europe precisely on the footing of China. We should thus avoid wars, and all our citizens should be husbandmen. Whenever indeed our numbers should so increase as that our produce would overstock the markets of those nations who should come to seek it, the farmers must either employ the surplus of their time in manufactures or the surplus of our hands must be employed in manufactures or in navigation. But that day would, I think be distant, and we should long keep our workmen in Europe, while Europe should be drawing rough materials & even subsistence from America. But this is theory only, & a theory which the servants of America are not at liberty to follow. Our people have a decided taste for navigation & commerce. They take this from their mother country; & their servants are in duty bound to calculate all their measures on this datum: we wish to do it by throwing open all the doors of commerce & knocking off its shackles. But as this cannot be done for others, unless they will do it for us, & there is no great probability that Europe will do this, I suppose we shall be obliged to adopt a system which may shackle them in our ports as they do us in theirs.

James Madison to Thomas Jefferson
19 June 1786

. . . Your reflections on the idle poor of Europe form a valuable lesson to the legislators of every country, and particularly of a new one. I hope you will enable yourself before you return to America to compare with this description of people in France the condition of the indigent part of other communities in Europe where the like causes of wretchedness exist in a less degree. I have no doubt that the misery of the lower classes will be found to abate wherever the government assumes a freer aspect & the laws favor a subdivision of property. Yet I suspect that the difference will not fully account for the comparative comfort of the mass of people in the United States. Our limited population has probably as large a share in producing this effect as the political advantages which distinguish us. A certain degree of misery seems inseparable from a high degree of populousness. If the lands in Europe which are now dedicated to the amusement of the idle rich were parcelled out among the idle poor, I readily conceive the happy revolution which would be experienced by a certain proportion of the latter. But still would there not remain a great proportion unrelieved? No problem in political economy has appeared to me more puzzling than that which relates to the most proper distribution of the inhabitants of a country fully peopled. Let the lands be shared among them ever so wisely, & let them be supplied with laborers ever so plentifully, as there must be a great surplus of subsistence, there will also remain a great surplus of inhabitants, a greater by far than will be employed in clothing both themselves & those who feed them and in administering to both every other necessary & even comfort of life. What is to be done with this surplus? Hitherto we have seen them distributed into manufacturers of superfluities, idle proprietors of productive funds, domestics, soldiers, merchants, mariners, and a few other less numerous classes. All these classes notwithstanding have been found insufficient to absorb the redundant members of a populous society; and yet a reduction of most of those classes enters into the very reform which appears so necessary & desireable. From a more equal partition of property, must result a greater simplicity of manners, consequently a less consumption of manufactured superfluities, and a less proportion of idle proprietors & domestics. From a juster government must result less need of soldiers either for defense agst. dangers from without or disturbances from within. The number of merchants must be inconsiderable under any modification of society; and that of mariners will depend more on geographical position than on the plan of legislation. But I forget that I am writing a letter not a dissertation. . . .

James Madison to James Monroe

7 August 1785

. . . Viewing in the abstract the question whether the power of regulating trade, to a certain degree at least, ought to be vested in Congress, it appears to me not to admit of a doubt but that it should be decided in the affirmative. If it be necessary to regulate trade at all, it surely is necessary to lodge the power where trade can be regulated with effect, and experience has confirmed what reason foresaw, that it can never be so regulated by the states acting in their separate capacities. They can no more exercise this power separately than they could separately carry on war or separately form treaties of alliance or commerce. The nature of the thing therefore proves the former power, no less than the latter, to be within the reason of the federal Constitution. Much indeed is it to be wished, as I conceive, that no regulations of trade, that is to say no restrictions or imposts whatever, were necessary. A perfect freedom is the system which would be my choice. But before such a system will be eligible perhaps for the U.S., they must be out of debt; before it will be attainable, all other nations must concur in it. Whilst any one of these imposes on our vessels, seamen, &c in their ports, clogs from which they exempt their own, we must either retort the distinction or renounce not merely a just profit, but our only defence against the danger which may most easily beset us. Are we not at this moment under this very alternative? The policy of G.B. (to say nothing of other nations) has shut against us the channels without which our trade with her must be a losing one, and she has consequently the triumph, as we have the chagrin, of seeing accomplished her prophetic threats that our independence should forfeit commercial advantages for which it would not recompence us with any new channels of trade. What is to be done? Must we remain passive victims to foreign politics; or shall we exert the lawful means which our independence has put into our hands of extorting redress? The very question would be an affront to every citizen who loves his country. What then are those means? Retaliating regulations of trade only. How are these to be effectuated? Only by harmony in the measures of the states. How is this harmony to be obtained? Only by an acquiescence of all the states in the opinion of a reasonable majority. If Congress as they are now constituted can not be trusted with the power of digesting and enforcing this opinion, let them be otherwise constituted: let their numbers be encreased, let them be chosen oftener, and let their period of service be shortened; or if any better medium than Congress can be proposed by which the wills of the states may be concentered, let it be substituted, or lastly let no regulation of trade adopted by Congress be in force untill it shall have been ratified by a certain proportion of the states. But let us not sacrifice the end to the means: let us not rush on certain ruin in order to avoid a possible danger. I conceive it to be of great importance that the defects of the federal system should be amended, not only because such amendments will make it better answer the purpose for which it was instituted, but because I apprehend danger to its very existence from a continuance of defects which expose a part if not the whole of the empire to severe distress. The suffering part, even when the minor part, can not long respect a government which is too feeble to protect their interest; but when the suffering part came to be the major part, and they despair of seeing a protecting energy given to the general government, from what motives is their allegiance to be any longer expected. Should G.B. persist in the machinations which distress us, and seven or eight of the states be hindered by the others from obtaining relief by federal means, I own, I tremble at the anti-federal expedients into which the former may be tempted. As to the objection against intrusting Congress with a power over trade, drawn from the diversity of interests in the states, it may be answered 1. that if this objection had been listened to, no confederation could have ever taken place among the states. 2. that if it ought now to be listened to, the power held by Congress of forming commercial treaties, by which 9 states may indirectly dispose of the commerce of the residue, ought to be immediately revoked. 3. that the fact is that a case can scarcely be imagined in which it would be the interest of any 2/3ds of the states to oppress the remaining 1/3d. 4. that the true question is whether the commercial interests of the states do not meet in more points than they differ. To me it is clear that they do; and if they do there are so many more reasons for, than against, submitting the commercial interest of each state to the direction and care of the majority. Put the West India trade alone, in which the interest of every state is involved, into the scale against all the inequalities which may result from any probable regulation by nine states, and who will say that the latter ought to preponderate? I have heard the different interest which the Eastern States have as carriers pointed out as a ground of caution to the Southern States who have no bottoms of their own agst their concurring hastily in retaliations on G.B. But will the present system of G.B. ever give the Southern States bottoms; and if they are not their own carriers I should suppose it no mark either of folly or incivility to give our custom to our brethren rather than to those who have not yet entitled themselves to the name of friends. . . .

JAMES MADISON

Speech in the House of Representatives on Commercial Retaliation and Discrimination
25 April 1789

On 8 April 1789, the first day of business for the First Federal Congress, Madison introduced a set of resolutions looking toward the imposition of import and tonnage duties, which would provide the new government with a steady source of independent revenues. In addition to favoring native shippers, these would have levied higher duties on the merchants of nations that did not have commercial treaties with the United States than on those of nations that did—a proposition clearly aimed to discriminate against the English and in favor of America's French allies. Madison defended this proposition in a speech of 9 April and again in this speech of 25 April.

. . . Let us review the policy of Great Britain toward us; has she ever shown any disposition to enter into reciprocal regulations? Has she not by a temporising policy plainly declared that until we are able and willing to do justice to ourselves, she will shut us out from her ports and make us tributary to her? Have we not seen her taking one legislative step after another to destroy our commerce? Has not her legislature given discretionary powers to the executive, that so she might be ever on the watch and ready to seize every advantage the weakness of our situation might expose? Have we not reason to believe she will continue a policy void of regard to us, whilst she can continue to gather into her lap the benefits we feebly endeavor to withhold, and for which she ought rather to court us by an open and liberal participation of the commerce we desire? Will she not, if she finds us indecisive in counteracting her machinations, continue to consult her own interest as heretofore? If we remain in a state of apathy, we do not fulfill the object of our appointment; most of the states in the union have, in some shape or other, shown symptoms of disapprobation of British policy; those states have now relinquished the power of continuing their systems, but under an impression that a more efficient government would effectually support their views. If we are timid and inactive we disappoint the just expectations of our constituents, and I venture to say, we disappoint the very nation against whom the measure is principally directed.

It has been said that Great Britain receives all the produce of this country in our own bottoms. I believe that in some ports of that kingdom our vessels are admitted, but those in the West Indies, into which we want admission most, are closely barred against us; but the reason that she admits us is because it is necessary to repay herself for her exports to this country and to constitute herself a market for this and the European nations. Adventitious causes have drawn within the commercial vortex of her policy almost all the trade of America, and the productions of the most distant clime, consumed among us, are tributary to her revenue; as long therefore as we do not protect ourselves and endeavor to restore the stream of commerce to its natural channel, we shall find no relaxation on the part of Britain, the same obnoxious policy will be pursued while we submissively bear the oppression. This is a copious subject, and leads to serious and important reflections. After what has passed, I am certain that there is a disposition to make a discrimination, to teach the nations that are not in alliance with us that there is an advantage to be gained by the connection. To give some early symptom of the power and will of the new government to redress our national wrongs must be productive of benefit. We soon shall be in a condition, we now are in a condition, we now are in a condition, to wage a commercial warfare with that nation. The produce of this country is more necessary to the rest of the world than that of other countries is to America. If we were disposed to hazard the experiment of interdicting the intercourse between us and the powers not in alliance, we should have overtures of the most advantageous kind tendered by those nations. If we have the disposition, we have abundantly the power to vindicate our cause; let us but show the world that we know justly how to consider our commercial friends and commercial adversaries. Let us show that if a war breaks out in Europe, and is extended and carried on in the West Indies, that we can treat with friendship and succour the one, while we can shut the other out of our ports. By these favors, without entering into the contest, or violating the law of nations, or even the privilege of neutrals, we can give the most decided advantage.

I will not enlarge on this subject; but it must be apparent to every gentleman that we possess natural advantages which no other nation does; we can therefore with justice stipulate for a reciprocity in commerce. The way to obtain this is by discrimination; and therefore, though the proposed measure may not be very favorable to the nations in alliance,

yet I hope it will be adopted for the sake of the principle it contains. I should rather be in favor of a small discrimination than a large one, on purpose to avoid the loss of revenue which anyhow in this article will be but trifling.

Congressional Proceedings on Commercial Discrimination
1789

Madison's proposals passed the House of Representatives in 1789, but were rejected in the Senate by a combination of southern members who feared higher duties, northerners who opposed the concept of discrimination in principle, and a few who favored even stronger retaliation than Madison had proposed. He summarized the congressional debates for Jefferson, who was still in France but sympathized entirely with his friend's position. Madison would press the matter again in 1790 and 1791, but was again defeated. Fortified by Jefferson's powerful report on American commerce, he would revive it once again in 1794.

James Madison to Thomas Jefferson
30 June 1789

The Senate has [rejected the House of Representatives' proposal for commercial discrimination]. It had been proposed by the H. of Reps. that, besides a discrimination in the tonnage, a small reduction should be made in the duty on distilled spirits imported from countries in treaty with the U. States. The Senate were opposed to any discrimination whatsoever, contending that even G. Britain should stand on the same footing with the most favored nations. The arguments on that side of the question were that the U.S. were not bound by treaty to give any commercial preferences to particular nations—that they were not bound by gratitude, since our allies had been actuated by their own interest and had obtained their compensation in the dismemberment of a rival empire—that in national and particularly in commercial measures, gratitude was, moreover, no proper motive, interest alone being the statesman's guide—that G.B. made no discrimination against the U.S. compared with other nations; but on the contrary distinguished them by a number of advantages—that if G.B. possessed almost the whole of our trade it proceeded from causes which proved that she could carry it on for us on better terms than the other nations of Europe—that we were too dependent on her trade to risk her displeasure by irritating measures which might induce her to put us on a worse footing than at present—that a small discrimination could only irritate without operating on her interests or fears—that if any thing were done it would be best to make a bolder stroke at once and that in fact the Senate had appointed a committee to consider the subject in that point of view.

On the other side it was contended that it would be absurd to *give* away every thing that could *purchase* the stipulation wanted by us, that the motives in which the new government originated, the known sentiments of the people at large, and the laws of most of the states subsequent to the peace showed clearly that a distinction between nations in treaty and nations not in treaty would coincide with the public opinion, and that it would be offensive to a great number of citizens to see G.B. in particular put on the footing of the most favored nations by the first act of a government instituted for the purpose of uniting the states in the vindication of their commercial interests against her monopolizing regulations—that this respect to the sentiments of the people was the more necessary in the present critical state of the government—that our trade at present entirely contradicted the advantages expected from the Revolution, no new channels being opened with other European nations, and the British channels being narrowed by a refusal of the most natural and valuable one to the U.S.—that this evil proceeded from the deep hold the British monopoly had taken of our country, and the difficulty experienced by France, Holland, etc. in entering into competition with her—that in order to break this monopoly, those nations ought to be aided till they could contend on equal terms—that the market of France was particularly desireable to us—that her disposition to open it would depend on the disposition manifested on our part, etc., etc.—that our trade would not be in its proper channels until it should flow *directly* to the countries making the exchange, in which case, too, American vessels would have a due share in the transaction, whereas at present the whole carriage of our bulky produce is confined to British bottoms—that with respect to G.B. we had good reason to suppose that her conduct would be regulated by the apparent temper of the new government—that a passiveness under her restrictions would confirm her in them, whilst an evidence of intention as well as ability to face them would ensure a reconsideration of her policy—that it would be sufficient to begin with a moderate discrimination, exhibiting a readiness to invigorate our measures as circumstances might require—that we had no reason to apprehend a disposition in G.B. to resort to a commercial contest, or the consequences of such an experiment, her dependence on us being greater than ours on her. The supplies of the United States are necessary to the existence, and their market to the value, of her islands. The returns are either superfluities or poisons. In time of famine, the cry of which is heard every three or four years, the bread of the United States is essential. In time of war, which is generally decided in the West Indies, friendly offices, not violating the duties of neutrality, might effectually turn the scale in favor of an adversary. In the direct trade with Great Britain, the consequences ought to be equally dreaded by her. The raw and bulky exports of the United States employ her shipping, contribute to her revenue, enter into her manufactures, and enrich her merchants, who stand between the United States and the consuming nations of Europe. A suspension of the intercourse would suspend all these advantages, force the trade into rival channels from which it might not return, and besides a temporary loss of a market for 1/4 of her exports, hasten the establishment of manufactures here, which would so far cut off the market forever. On the other side, the United States would suffer but little. The manufactures of Great Britain, as far as desirable, would find their way through other channels, and if the price were a little augmented it would only diminish an excessive consumption. They could do almost wholly without such supplies, and better without than with many of them. In one important view the contest would be particularly in their favor. The articles of luxury, a privation of which would be salutary to them, being the work of the indigent, may be regarded as necessaries to the manufacturing party: . . .

Thomas Jefferson to James Madison

28 August 1789

It is impossible to desire better dispositions towards us than prevail in [the French] assembly. Our proceedings have been viewed as a model for them on every occasion; and tho in the heat of debate men are generally disposed to contradict every authority urged by their opponents, ours has been treated like that of the Bible, open to explanation but not to question. I am sorry that in the moment of such a disposition anything should come from us to check it. The placing them on a mere footing with the English will have this effect. When of two nations, the one has engaged herself in a ruinous war for us, has spent her blood and money to save us, has opened her bosom to us in peace, and receive us almost on the footing of her own citizens, while the other has moved heaven, earth and hell to exterminate us in war, has insulted us in all her councils in peace, shut her doors to us in every part where her interests would admit it, libelled us in foreign nations, endeavored to poison them against the reception of our most precious commodities, to place these two nations on a footing is to give a great deal more to one than to the other if the maxim be true that to make unequal quantities equal you must add more to the one than the other. To say in excuse that gratitude is never to enter into the motives of national conduct is to revive a principle which has been buried for centuries with its kindred principles of the lawfulness of assassination, poison, perjury, etc. All of these were legitimate principles in the dark ages which intervened between ancient and modern civilization, but exploded and held in just horror in the 18th century. I know but one code of morality for man whether acting singly or collectively. . . . Let us hope that our new government will take some other occasion to show that they mean to proscribe no virtue from the canons of their conduct with other nations. In every other instance the new government has ushered itself to the world as honest, masculine and dignified. It has shown genuine dignity in my opinion in exploding adulatory titles; they are the offerings of abject baseness, and nourish that degrading vice in the people. . . .

ALEXANDER HAMILTON

Report on the Subject of Manufactures

5 December 1791

Hamilton's economic program culminated in the great Report on Manufactures, which has rightly been described as his response to the Virginians' program of commercial discrimination. Most of the recommendations of the report were never enacted by Congress, but the constitutional assumptions on which it rested and the vision of the American future that it advanced would both become major subjects for future disputes.

The Secretary of the Treasury, in obedience to the order of the House of Representatives of the 15th day of January, 1790, has applied his attention at as early a period as his other duties would permit to the subject of Manufactures; and particularly to the means of promoting such as will tend to render the United States independent on foreign nations for military and other essential supplies. And he there[upon] respectfully submits the following Report.

The expediency of encouraging manufactures in the United States, which was not long since deemed very questionable, appears at this time to be pretty generally admitted. The embarrassments which have obstructed the progress of our external trade have led to serious reflections on the necessity of enlarging the sphere of our domestic commerce: the restrictive regulations which in foreign markets abrige the vent of the increasing surplus of our agricultural produce serve to beget an earnest desire that a more extensive demand for that surplus may be created at home; and the complete success which has rewarded manufacturing enterprise in some valuable branches, conspiring with the promising symptoms which attend some less mature essays in others, justify a hope that the obstacles to the growth of this species of industry are less formidable than they were apprehended to be; and that it is not difficult to find, in its further extension, a full indemnification for any external disadvantages which are or may be experienced, as well as an accession of resources favorable to national independence and safety.

There still are, nevertheless, respectable patrons of opinions unfriendly to the encouragement of manufactures. The following are, substantially, the arguments by which these opinions are defended.

"In every country (say those who entertain them) agriculture is the most beneficial and *productive* object of human industry. This position, generally if not universally true, applies with peculiar emphasis to the United States on account of their immense tracts of fertile territory, uninhabited and unimproved. Nothing can afford so advantageous an employment for capital and labour as the conversion of this extensive wilderness into cultivated farms. Nothing, equally with this, can contribute to the population, strength and real riches of the country."

"To endeavor by the extraordinary patronage of Government to accelerate the growth of manufactures is, in fact, to endeavor by force and art to transfer the natural current of industry from a more to a less beneficial channel. Whatever has such a tendency must necessarily be unwise. Indeed it can hardly ever be wise in a government, to attempt to give a direction to the industry of its citizens. This, under the quicksighted guidance of private interest, will, if left to itself, infallibly find its own way to the most profitable employment; and 'tis by such employment that the public prosperity will be most effectually promoted. To leave industry to itself, therefore, is, in almost every case, the soundest as well as the simplest policy."

"This policy is not only recommended to the United States by considerations which affect all nations, it is, in a manner, dictated to them by the imperious force of a very peculiar situation. The smallness of their population compared with their territory—the constant allurements to emigration from the settled to the unsettled parts of the country—the facility with which the less independent condition of an artisan can be exchanged for the more independent condition of a farmer, these and similar causes conspire to produce, and for a length of time must continue to occasion, a scarcity of hands for manufacturing occupation, and dearness of labor generally. To these disadvantages for the prosecution of manufactures, a deficiency of pecuniary capital being added, the prospect of a successful competition with the manufactures of Europe must be regarded as little less than desperate. Extensive manufactures can only be the offspring of a redundant, at least of a full, population. Till the latter shall characterize the situation of this country, 'tis vain to hope for the former."

"If, contrary to the natural course of things, an unseasonable and premature spring can be given to certain fabrics by heavy duties, prohibitions, bounties, or by other forced expedients, this will only be to sacrifice the interests of the community to those of particular classes. Besides the misdirection of labor, a virtual monopoly will be given to the persons employed on such fabrics; and an enhancement of price, the inevitable consequence of every monopoly, must be defrayed at the expence of the other parts of the society. It is far preferable that those persons should be engaged in the cultivation of the earth and that we should procure, in exchange for its productions, the commodities with which foreigners are able to supply us in greater perfection and upon better terms."

This mode of reasoning is founded upon facts and principles which have certainly respectable pretensions. If it had governed the conduct of nations more generally than it has done, there is room to suppose that it might have carried them faster to prosperity and greatness than they have attained by the pursuit of maxims too widely opposite. Most general theories, however, admit of numerous exceptions, and there are few, if any, of the political kind which do not blend a considerable portion of error with the truths they inculcate.

In order to an accurate judgement how far that which has been just stated ought to be deemed liable to a similar imputation, it is necessary to advert carefully to the considerations which plead in favour of manufactures, and which appear to recommend the special and positive encouragement of them, in certain cases, and under certain reasonable limitations.

It ought readily to be conceded that the cultivation of the earth—as the primary and most certain source of national supply—as the immediate and chief source of subsistence of man—as the principal source of those materials which constitute the nutriment of other kinds of labor—as including a state most favorable to the freedom and independence of the human mind—one, perhaps, most conducive to the multiplication of the human species—has *intrinsically a strong claim to pre-eminence over every other kind of industry.*

But, that it has a title to anything like an exclusive predilection, in any country, ought to be admitted with great caution. That it is even more productive than every other branch of industry requires more evidence than has yet been given in support of the position. That its real interests, precious and important as without the help of exaggeration, they truly are, will be advanced, rather than injured, by the due encouragement of manufactures, may, it is believed, be satisfactorily demonstrated. And it is also believed that the expediency of such encouragement in a general view may be shown to be recommended by the most cogent and persuasive motives of national policy. . . .

. . . Manufacturing establishments not only occasion a positive augmentation of the produce and revenue of the society, . . . they contribute essentially to rendering them greater than they could possibly be, without such establishments. These circumstances are—

1. The division of labor.
2. An extension of the use of machinery.

3. Additional employment to classes of the community not ordinarily engaged in the business.

4. The promoting of emigration from foreign countries.

5. The furnishing greater scope for the diversity of talents and dispositions which discriminate men from each other.

6. The affording a more ample and various field for enterprise.

7. The creating in some instances a new, and securing in all, a more certain and steady demand for the surplus produce of the soil.

Each of these circumstances has a considerable influence upon the total mass of industrious effort in a community. Together, they add to it a degree of energy and effect which are not easily conceived. Some comments upon each of them, in the order in which they have been stated, may serve to explain their importance.

I. As to the Division of Labor.

It has justly been observed that there is scarcely anything of greater moment in the economy of a nation than the proper division of labor. The separation of occupations causes each to be carried to a much greater perfection than it could possibly acquire if they were blended. This arises principally from three circumstances.

1st—The greater skill and dexterity naturally resulting from a constant and undivided application to a single object. It is evident that these properties must increase in proportion to the separation and simplification of objects and the steadiness of the attention devoted to each, and must be less in proportion to the complication of objects and the number among which the attention is distracted.

2nd—The economy of time—by avoiding the loss of it incident to a frequent transition from one operation to another of a different nature. This depends on various circumstances—the transition itself—the orderly disposition of the impliments, machines and materials employed in the operation to be relinquished—the preparatory steps to the commencement of a new one—the interruption of the impulse which the mind of the workman acquires from being engaged in a particular operation—the distractions, hesitations and reluctances which attend the passage from one kind of business to another.

3rd—An extension of the use of machinery. A man occupied on a single object will have it more in his power and will be more naturally led to exert his imagination in devising methods to facilitate and abrige labor than if he were perplexed by a variety of independent and dissimilar operations. Besides this, the fabrication of machines, in numerous instances becoming itself a distinct trade, the artist who follows it has all the advantages which have been enumerated for improvement in his particular art; and in both ways the invention and application of machinery are extended.

And from these causes united, the mere separation of the occupation of the cultivator from that of the artificer has the effect of augmenting the *productive powers* of labor and, with them, the total mass of the produce or revenue of a country. In this single view of the subject, therefore, the utility of artificers or manufacturers towards promoting an increase of productive industry is apparent.

II. As to an extension of the use of machinery, a point which though partly anticipated requires to be placed in one or two additional lights.

The employment of machinery forms an item of great importance in the general mass of national industry. 'Tis an artificial force brought in aid of the natural force of man and, to all the purposes of labor, is an increase of hands; an accession of strength, *unencumbered too by the expense of maintaining the laborer.* May it not therefore be fairly inferred that those occupations which give greatest scope to the use of this auxiliary contribute most to the general stock of industrious effort, and, in consequence, to the general product of industry?

It shall be taken for granted, and the truth of the position referred to observation, that manufacturing pursuits are susceptible in a greater degree of the application of machinery than those of agriculture. If so, all the difference is lost to a community which, instead of manufacturing for itself, procures the fabrics requisite to its supply from other countries. The substitution of foreign for domestic manufactures is a transfer to foreign nations of the advantages accruing from the employment of machinery, in the modes in which it is capable of being employed, with most utility and to the greatest extent.

The cotton mill, invented in England within the last twenty years, is a signal illustration of the general proposition which has been just advanced. In consequence of it, all the different processes for spinning cotton are performed by means of machines, which are put in motion by water and attended chiefly by women and children; and by a smaller number of persons, in the whole, than are requisite in the ordinary mode of spinning. And it is an advantage of great moment that the operations of this mill continue with convenience during the night as well as through the day. The prodigious effect of such a machine is easily conceived. To this invention is to be attributed essentially the immense progress which has been so suddenly made in Great Britain in the various fabrics of cotton.

III. As to the additional employment of classes of the community not ordinarily engaged in the particular business.

This is not among the least valuable of the means by which manufacturing institutions contribute to augment the general stock of industry and production. In places where those institutions prevail, besides the persons regularly engaged in them, they afford occasional and extra employment to industrious individuals and families who are willing to devote the leisure resulting from the intermissions of their ordinary pursuits to collateral labors as a resource of multiplying their acquisitions or enjoyments. The husbandman himself experiences a new source of profit and support from the encreased industry of his wife and daughters, invited and stimulated by the demands of the neighboring manufactories.

Besides this advantage of occasional employment to classes having different occupations, there is another of a nature allied to it and of a similar tendency. This is—the employment of persons who would otherwise be idle (and in many cases a burthen on the community), either from the bias of temper, habit, infirmity or body, or some other cause, indisposing or disqualifying them for the toils of the country. It is worthy of particular remark that, in general, women and children are rendered more useful, and the latter more early useful, by manufacturing establishments than they would otherwise be. Of the number of persons employed in the cotton manufactories of Great Britain, it is computed that 4/7 nearly are women and children, of whom the greatest proportion are children and many of them of a very tender age.

And thus it appears to be one of the attributes of manufactures, and one of no small consequence, to give occasion to the exertion of a greater quantity of industry, even by the *same number* of persons, where they happen to prevail, than would exist if there were no such establishments.

IV. As to the promoting of emigration from foreign countries. Men reluctantly quit one course of occupation and livelihood for another, unless invited to it by very apparent and proximate advantages. Many who would go from one country to another, if they had a prospect of

continuing with more benefit the callings to which they have been educated, will often not be tempted to change their situation, by the hope of doing better, in some other way. Manufacturers who, listening to the powerful invitations of a better price for their fabrics, or their labor, of greater cheapness of provisions and raw materials, of an exemption from the chief part of the taxes, burthens and restraints which they endure in the old world, of greater personal independence and consequence under the operation of a more equal government, and of what is far more precious than mere religious toleration—a perfect equality of religious privileges—would probably flock from Europe to the United States to pursue their own trades or professions if they were once made sensible of the advantages they would enjoy, and were inspired with an assurance of encouragement and employment, will with difficulty be induced to transplant themselves with a view to becoming cultivators of land.

If it be true, then, that it is the interest of the United States to open every possible avenue to emigration from abroad, it affords a weighty argument for the encouragement of manufactures, which for the reasons just assigned, will have the strongest tendency to multiply the inducements to it.

Here is perceived an important resource, not only for extending the population and with it the useful and productive labor of the country, but likewise for the prosecution of manufactures without deducting from the number of hands which might otherwise be drawn to tillage; and even for the indemnification of agriculture for such as might happen to be diverted from it. Many whom manufacturing views would induce to emigrate would afterwards yield to the temptations which the particular situation of this country holds out to agricultural pursuits. And while agriculture would in other respects derive many signal and unmingled advantages from the growth of manufactures, it is a problem whether it would gain or lose as to the article of the number of persons employed in carrying it on.

V. As to the furnishing greater scope for the diversity of talents and dispositions which discriminate men from each other.

This is a much more powerful means of augmenting the fund of national industry than may at first sight appear. It is a just observation that minds of the strongest and most active powers for their proper objects fall below mediocrity and labor without effect if confined to uncongenial pursuits. And it is thence to be inferred that the results of human exertion may be immensely increased by diversifying its objects. When all the different kinds of industry obtain in a community, each individual can find his proper element and can call into activity the whole vigor of his nature. And the community is benefitted by the services of its respective members in the manner in which each can serve it with most effect.

If there be anything in a remark often to be met with— namely, that there is in the genius of the people of this country a peculiar aptitude for mechanic improvements, it would operate as a forcible reason for giving opportunities to the exercise of that species of talent by the propagation of manufactures.

VI. As to the affording a more ample and various field for enterprise.

This also is of greater consequence in the general scale of national exertion than might perhaps on a superficial view be supposed, and has effects not altogether dissimilar from those of the circumstance last noticed. To cherish and stimulate the activity of the human mind by multiplying the objects of enterprise is not among the least considerable of the expedients by which the wealth of a nation may be promoted. Even things in themselves not positively advantageous sometimes become so by their tendency to provoke exertion. Every new scene which is opened to the busy nature of man to rouse and exert itself is the addition of a new energy to the general stock of effort.

The spirit of enterprise, useful and prolific as it is, must necessarily be contracted or expanded in proportion to the simplicity or variety of the occupations and productions which are to be found in a society. It must be less in a nation of mere cultivators than in a nation of cultivators and merchants, less in a nation of cultivators and merchants than in a nation of cultivators, artificers and merchants.

VII. As to the creating, in some instances, a new, and securing in all, a more certain and steady demand for the surplus produce of the soil.

This is among the most important of the circumstances which have been indicated. It is a principal mean by which the establishment of manufactures contributes to an augmentation of the produce or revenue of a country, and has an immediate and direct relation to the prosperity of agriculture.

It is evident that the exertions of the husbandman will be steady or fluctuating, vigorous or feeble, in proportion

to the steadiness or fluctuation, adequateness, or inadequateness of the markets on which he must depend for the vent of the surplus which may be produced by his labor; and that such surplus in the ordinary course of things will be greater or less in the same proportion.

For the purpose of this vent, a domestic market is greatly to be preferred to a foreign one, because it is, in the nature of things, far more to be relied upon.

It is a primary object of the policy of nations to be able to supply themselves with subsistence from their own soils; and manufacturing nations, as far as circumstances permit, endeavor to procure from the same source the raw materials necessary for their own fabrics. This disposition, urged by the spirit of monopoly, is sometimes even carried to an injudicious extreme. It seems not always to be recollected that nations who have neither mines nor manufactures can only obtain the manufactured articles of which they stand in need by an exchange of the products of their soils; and that, if those who can best furnish them with such articles are unwilling to give a due course to this exchange, they must of necessity make every possible effort to manufacture for themselves, the effect of which is that the manufacturing nations abridge the natural advantages of their situation through an unwillingness to permit the agricultural countries to enjoy the advantages of theirs, and sacrifice the interests of a mutually beneficial intercourse to the vain project of *selling every thing* and *buying nothing*.

But it is also a consequence of the policy which has been noted that the foreign demand for the products of agricultural countries is, in a great degree, rather casual and occasional than certain or constant. To what extent injurious interruptions of the demand for some of the staple commodities of the United States may have been experienced from that cause must be referred to the judgement of those who are engaged in carrying on the commerce of the country, but it may be safely assumed that such interruptions are at times very inconveniently felt, and that cases not unfrequently occur in which markets are so confined and restricted as to render the demand very unequal to the supply.

Independently likewise of the artificial impediments which are created by the policy in question, there are natural causes tending to render the external demand for the surplus of agricultural nations a precarious reliance. The differences of seasons in the countries which are the consumers make immense differences in the produce of their own soils, in different years; and consequently in the degrees of their necessity for foreign supply. Plentiful harvests with them, especially if similar ones occur at the same time in the countries which are the furnishers, occasion of course a glut in the markets of the latter.

Considering how fast and how much the progress of new settlements in the United States must increase the surplus produce of the soil, and weighing seriously the tendency of the system which prevails among most of the commercial nations of Europe, whatever dependence may be placed on the force of natural circumstances to counteract the effects of an artificial policy, there appear strong reasons to regard the foreign demand for that surplus as too uncertain a reliance, and to desire a substitute for it in an extensive domestic market.

To secure such a market, there is no other expedient than to promote manufacturing establishments. Manufacturers, who constitute the most numerous class after the cultivators of land, are for that reason the principal consumers of the surplus of their labor.

This idea of an extensive domestic market for the surplus produce of the soil is of the first consequence. It is of all things that which most effectually conduces to a flourishing state of agriculture. If the effect of manufactories should be to detach a portion of the hands which would otherwise be engaged in tillage, it might possibly cause a smaller quantity of lands to be under cultivation, but by their tendency to procure a more certain demand for the surplus produce of the soil, they would, at the same time, cause the lands which were in cultivation to be better improved and more productive. And while, by their influence, the condition of each individual farmer would be meliorated, the total mass of agricultural production would probably be increased. For this must evidently depend as much, if not more, upon the degree of improvement than upon the number of acres under culture.

It merits particular observation that the multiplication of manufactories not only furnishes a market for those articles which have been accustomed to be produced in abundance in a country, but it likewise creates a demand for such as were either unknown or produced in inconsiderable quantities. The bowels as well as the surface of the earth are ransacked for articles which were before neglected. Animals, plants and minerals acquire a utility and value which were before unexplored.

The foregoing considerations seem sufficient to establish, as general propositions, that it is the interest of nations to diversify the industrious pursuits of the individuals who compose them — that the establishment of manufactures is calculated not only to increase the general stock of useful and productive labor, but even to improve the state of agriculture in particular; certainly to advance the interests of those who are engaged in it. There are other views that will be hereafter taken of the subject, which, it is conceived, will serve to confirm these inferences.

VIII. Previously to a further discussion of the objections to the encouragement of manufactures which have been stated, it will be of use to see what can be said in reference to the particular situation of the United States against the conclusions appearing to result from what has been already offered.

It may be observed, and the idea is of no inconsiderable weight, that however true it might be that a state which, possessing large tracts of vacant and fertile territory, was at the same time secluded from foreign commerce, would find its interest and the interest of agriculture in diverting a part of its population from tillage to manufactures; yet it will not follow that the same is true of a state which, having such vacant and fertile territory, has at the same time ample opportunity of procuring from abroad, on good terms, all the fabrics of which it stands in need for the supply of its inhabitants. The power of doing this at least secures the great advantage of a division of labor, leaving the farmer free to pursue exclusively the culture of his land and enabling him to procure with its products the manufactured supplies requisite either to his wants or to his enjoyments. And though it should be true that, in settled countries, the diversification of industry is conducive to an increase in the productive powers of labor, and to an augmentation of revenue and capital, yet it is scarcely conceivable that there can be anything of so solid and permanent advantage to an uncultivated and unpeopled country as to convert its wastes into cultivated and inhabited districts. If the revenue, in the mean time, should be less, the capital, in the event, must be greater.

To these observations, the following appears to be a satisfactory answer—

If the system of perfect liberty to industry and commerce were the prevailing system of nations — the arguments which dissuade a country in the predicament of the United States from the zealous pursuits of manufactures would doubtless have great force. It will not be affirmed that they might not be permitted, with few exceptions, to serve as a rule of national conduct. In such a state of things, each country would have the full benefit of its peculiar advantages to compensate for its deficiencies or disadvantages. If one nation were in condition to supply manufactured articles on better terms than another, that other might find an abundant indemnification in a superior capacity to furnish the produce of the soil. And a free exchange, mutually beneficial, of the commodities which each was able to supply on the best terms, might be carried on between them, supporting in full vigor the industry of each. And though the circumstances which have been mentioned and others which will be unfolded hereafter render it probable that nations merely agricultural would not enjoy the same degree of opulence, in proportion to their numbers, as those which united manufactures with agriculture, yet the progressive improvement of the lands of the former might, in the end, atone for an inferior degree of opulence in the mean time; and in a case in which opposite considerations are pretty equally balanced, the option ought perhaps always to be in favor of leaving industry to its own direction.

But the system which has been mentioned is far from characterizing the general policy of nations. The prevalent one has been regulated by an opposite spirit.

The consequence of it is that the United States are to a certain extent in the situation of a country precluded from foreign commerce. They can, indeed, without difficulty obtain from abroad the manufactured supplies of which they are in want; but they experience numerous and very injurious impediments to the emission and vent of their own commodities. Nor is this the case in reference to a single foreign nation only. The regulations of several countries with which we have the most extensive intercourse throw serious obstructions in the way of the principal staples of the United States.

In such a position of things, the United States cannot exchange with Europe on equal terms; and the want of reciprocity would render them the victim of a system which should induce them to confine their views to agriculture and refrain from manufactures. A constant and encreasing necessity on their part for the commodities of Europe, and only a partial and occasional demand for their own in return, could not but expose them to a state of impoverishment, compared with the opulence to which their political and natural advantages authorise them to aspire. . . .

Whatever room there may be for an expectation that the industry of a people, under the direction of private interest, will upon equal terms find out the most beneficial employment for itself, there is none for a reliance that it will struggle against the force of unequal terms, or will of itself surmount all the adventitious barriers to a successful competition which may have been erected either by the advantages naturally acquired from practice and previous possession of the ground, or by those which may have sprung from positive regulations and an artificial policy. This general reflection might alone suffice as an answer to the objection under examination, exclusively of the weighty considerations which have been particularly urged. . . .

One more point of view only remains in which to consider the expediency of encouraging manufactures in the United States.

It is not uncommon to meet with an opinion that though the promoting of manufactures may be the interest of a part of the Union, it is contrary to that of another part. The Northern & Southern regions are sometimes represented as having adverse interests in this respect. Those are called manufacturing, these agricultural states; and a species of opposition is imagined to subsist between the manufacturing and agricultural interests.

This idea of an opposition between those two interests is the common error of the early periods of every country, but experience gradually dissipates it. Indeed they are perceived so often to succor and to befriend each other that they come at length to be considered as one: a supposition which has been frequently abused and is not universally true. Particular encouragements of particular manufactures may be of a nature to sacrifice the interests of landholders to those of manufacturers, but it is nevertheless a maxim well established by experience, and generally acknowledged, where there has been sufficient experience, that the *aggregate* prosperity of manufactures and the *aggregate* prosperity of agriculture are intimately connected. In the course of the discussion which has [taken] place, various weighty considerations have been adduced operating in support of that maxim. Perhaps the superior steadiness of the demand of a domestic market for the surplus produce of the soil is alone a convincing argument of its truth.

Ideas of a contrariety of interest between the Northern and Southern regions of the Union are in the main as unfounded as they are mischievous. The diversity of circumstances on which such contrariety is usually predicated authorises a directly contrary conclusion. Mutual wants constitute one of the strongest links of political connection, and the extent of these bears a natural proportion to the diversity in the means of mutual supply.

Suggestions of an opposite complexion are ever to be deplored, as unfriendly to the steady pursuit of one great common cause, and to the perfect harmony of all the parts. . . .

A question has been made concerning the constitutional right of the Government of the United States to apply this species of encouragement, but there is certainly no good foundation for such a question. The national legislature has express authority "To lay and collect taxes, duties, imposts and excises, to pay the debts and provide for the *common defense* and *general welfare*" with no other qualifications than that "all duties, imposts and excises, shall be *uniform* throughout the United States," that no capitation or other direct tax shall be laid unless in proportion to numbers ascertained by a census or enumeration taken on the principles prescribed in the Constitution, and that "no tax or duty shall be laid on articles exported from any state." These three qualifications excepted, the power to *raise money* is *plenary* and *indefinite;* and the objects to which it may be *appropriated* are no less comprehensive than the payment of the public debts and the providing for the common defense and

"*general welfare.*" The terms "*general welfare*" were doubtless intended to signify more than was expressed or imported in those which preceded; otherwise numerous exigencies incident to the affairs of a nation would have been left without a provision. The phrase is as comprehensive as any that could have been used; because it was not fit that the constitutional authority of the Union to appropriate its revenues should have been restricted within narrower limits than the "general welfare" and because this necessarily embraces a vast variety of particulars, which are susceptible neither of specification nor of definition.

It is therefore, of necessity, left to the discretion of the national legislature to pronounce upon the objects which concern the general welfare and for which, under that description, an appropriation of money is requisite and proper. And there seems to be no room for a doubt that whatever concerns the general interests of *learning,* of *agriculture,* of *manufactures,* and of *commerce* are within the sphere of the national councils *as far as regards an application of money.*

The only qualification of the generality of the phrase in question which seems to be admissible is this—that the object to which an appropriation of money is to be made be *general* and not *local,* its operation extending in fact, or by possibility, throughout the Union, and not being confined to a particular spot. . . .

The Collision

Even as Jefferson and Madison grew more alarmed about Hamilton's economic policies and the constitutional constructions employed to justify them, Jefferson's private correspondence revealed equal concern with what he saw as the undemocratic tenor of comments in Philadelphia social circles, uncritical praise of the administration in John Fenno's *Gazette of the United States* (the only newspaper with something like a national audience), and publications he considered unfriendly to the French Revolution and even to republican government itself. He was especially disgusted by the "Discourses on Davila," a series published anonymously in Fenno's Philadelphia paper, but easily recognized as an effort by Vice President John Adams to carry on his long-standing argument with French proponents of a unicameral legislature. In consequence, Jefferson left Philadelphia after the adjournment of the First Congress and approval of the national bank in the midst of a furor provoked by the appearance of an American edition of Thomas Paine's *The Rights of Man.* The publisher had prefaced Paine's response to Edmund Burke's *Reflections on the Revolution in France* with a private note in which the secretary of state had remarked that he was "extremely pleased to find . . . that something is at length to be publicly said against the political heresies which have sprung up among us." In New York City, Jefferson joined with Madison for a tour up the Hudson River and Lake Champlain, through Vermont, and back to the city by way of Connecticut and Long Island. Before departing on the tour, the two of them had breakfast with the revolutionary poet and publicist Philip Freneau, a former classmate whom Madison was already urging to move to Philadelphia to launch the new newspaper that Freneau had been planning. With an aid of an offer of a position as a translator in Jefferson's Department of State, the two Virginians eventually succeeded in this negotiation. Freneau launched his *National Gazette,* a semiweekly intended to compete for a national audience with the proadministration *Gazette of the United States,* on 31 October 1791, concurrently with the first meeting of the Second Congress and shortly before the appearance of Hamilton's Report on Manufactures. The *National Gazette's* anonymous attacks on Hamilton and his allies, escalating gradually into the spring, were a landmark in the transformation of a quarrel among the members of the new government into a public and national dispute.

JAMES MADISON

Essays for the *National Gazette*
1792

Madison prepared at least seventeen anonymous essays for the *National Gazette* during the meeting of the first session of the Second Congress. He added two more before the meeting of the second session in the fall. Intermixed with essays by Freneau himself and by unidentified writers signing their pieces with pseudonyms such as "Caius," "Brutus," or "Sidney," Madison's essays were part of a gradually escalating campaign against Hamiltonian political economy, broad construction of the Constitution, and growing criticism of the revolutionary experiment in France. The examples offered below provide a sound introduction to the breadth and depth of this attack.

"Consolidation"
3 December 1791

Much has been said, and not without reason, against a consolidation of the states into one government. Omitting lesser objections, two consequences would probably flow from such a change in our political system, which would justify the cautions used against it. *First,* it would be impossible to avoid the dilemma of either relinquishing the present energy and responsibility of a *single* executive magistrate for some *plural* substitute, which by dividing so great a trust might lessen the danger of it, or suffering so great an accumulation of powers in the hands of that officer as might by degrees transform him into a monarch. The incompetency of one legislature to regulate all the various objects belonging to the local governments would evidently force a transfer of many of them to the executive department, whilst the increasing splendor and number of its prerogatives supplied by this source might prove excitements to ambition too powerful for a sober execution of the elective plan, and consequently strengthen the pretexts for a hereditary designation of the magistrate. *Second*, were the state governments abolished, the same space of country that would produce an undue growth of the executive power would prevent that control on the legislative body which is essential to a faithful discharge of its trust; neither the voice nor the sense of ten or twenty millions of people, spread through so many latitudes as are comprehended within the United States, could ever be combined or called into effect if deprived of those local organs through which both can now be conveyed. In such a state of things, the impossibility of acting together might be succeeded by the inefficacy of partial expressions of the public mind and this, at length, by a universal silence and insensibility, leaving the whole government to that *self-directed course* which, it must be owned, is the natural propensity of every government.

But if a consolidation of the states into one government be an event so justly to be avoided, it is not less to be desired, on the other hand, that a consolidation should prevail in their interests and affections. . . . In proportion as uniformity is found to prevail in the interests and sentiments of the several states, will be the practicability of accommodating legislative regulations to them, and thereby of withholding new and dangerous prerogatives from the executive. Again, the greater the mutual confidence and affection of all parts of the Union, the more likely they will be to concur amicably or to differ with moderation in the elective designation of the chief magistrate, and by such examples to guard and adorn the vital principle of our republican constitution. Lastly, the less the supposed difference of interests and the greater the concord and confidence throughout the great body of the people, the more readily must they sympathize with each other, the more seasonably can they interpose a common manifestation of their sentiments, the more certainly will they take the alarm at usurpation or oppression, and the more effectually will they *consolidate* their defense of the public liberty.

Here, then, is a proper object presented, both to those who are most jealously attached to the separate authority reserved to the states and to those who may be more inclined to contemplate the people of America in the light of one nation. Let the former continue to watch against every encroachment which might lead to a gradual consolidation of the states into one government. Let the latter employ their utmost zeal, by eradicating local prejudices and mistaken rivalships, to consolidate the affairs of the states into one harmonious interest; and let it be the patriotic study of all to maintain the various authorities established by our complicated system, each in its respective constitutional sphere, and to erect over the whole one paramount empire of reason, benevolence, and brotherly affection.

"Charters"

18 January 1792

In Europe, charters of liberty have been granted by power. America has set the example and France has followed it of charters of power granted by liberty. This revolution in the practice of the world may, with an honest praise, be pronounced the most triumphant epoch of its history, and the most consoling presage of its happiness. We look back, already, with astonishment, at the daring outrages committed by despotism on the reason and the rights of man; We look forward with joy to the period when it shall be despoiled of all its usurpations and bound for ever in the chains with which it had loaded its miserable victims.

In proportion to the value of this revolution, in proportion to the importance of instruments every word of which decides a question between power and liberty, in proportion to the solemnity of acts proclaiming the will and authenticated by the seal of the people, the only earthly source of authority, ought to be the vigilance with which they are guarded by every citizen in private life and the circumspection with which they are executed by every citizen in public trust.

As compacts, charters of government are superior in obligation to all others, because they give effect to all others. As trusts, none can be more sacred, because they are bound on the conscience by the religious sanctions of an oath. As metes and bounds of government, they transcend all other landmarks, because every public usurpation is an encroachment on the private right, not of one, but of all.

The citizens of the United States have peculiar motives to support the energy of their constitutional charters.

Having originated the experiment, their merit will be estimated by its success.

The complicated form of their political system, arising from the partition of government between the states and the union, and from the separations and subdivisions of the several departments in each, requires a more than common reverence for the authority which is to preserve order thro' the whole.

Being republicans, they must be anxious to establish the efficacy of popular charters in defending liberty against power and power against licentiousness; and in keeping every portion of power within its proper limits, by this means discomfiting the partizans of anti-republican contrivances for the purpose.

All power has been traced up to opinion. The stability of all governments and security of all rights may be traced to the same source. The most arbitrary government is controlled where the public opinion is fixed. The despot of Constantinople dares not lay a new tax, because every slave thinks he ought not. The most systematic governments are turned by the slightest impulse from their regular path, when the public opinion no longer holds them in it. We see at this moment the *executive* magistrate of Great-Britain exercising under the authority of the representatives of the *people* a *legislative* power over the West-India commerce.

How devoutly is it to be wished, then, that the public opinion of the United States should be enlightened, that it should attach itself to their governments as delineated in the *great charters*, derived not from the usurped power of kings, but from the legitimate authority of the people; and that it should guarantee, with a holy zeal, these political scriptures from every attempt to add to or diminish from them. Liberty and order will never be *perfectly* safe until a trespass on the constitutional provisions for either, shall be felt with the same keenness that resents an invasion of the dearest rights; until every citizen shall be an Argus to espy, and an Aegeon to avenge, the unhallowed deed.

"Parties"

23 January 1792

In every political society, parties are unavoidable. A difference of interests, real or supposed, is the most natural and fruitful source of them. The great object should be to combat the evil: 1. By establishing a political equality among all; 2. By witholding *unnecessary* opportunities from a few to increase the inequality of property by an immoderate, and especially an unmerited, accumulation of riches; 3. By the silent operation of laws which, without violating the rights of property, reduce extreme wealth towards a state of

mediocrity and raise extreme indigence towards a state of comfort; 4. By abstaining from measures which operate differently on different interests, and particularly such as favor one interest at the expense of another; 5. By making one party a check on the other so far as the existence of parties cannot be prevented nor their views accommodated. If this is not the language of reason, it is that of republicanism.

In all political societies, different interests and parties arise out of the nature of things, and the great art of politicians lies in making them checks and balances to each other. Let us then increase these *natural distinctions* by favoring an inequality of property; and let us add to them *artificial distinctions,* by establishing *kings* and *nobles* and *plebians*. We shall then have the more checks to oppose to each other: we shall then have the more scales and the more weights to perfect and maintain the equilibrium. This is as little the voice of reason as it is that of republicanism.

From the expediency, in politics, of making natural parties mutual checks on each other, to infer the propriety of creating artificial parties, in order to form them into mutual checks, is not less absurd than it would be, in ethics, to say that new vices ought to be promoted, where they would counteract each other, because this use may be made of existing vices.

"Government of the United States"

4 February 1792

Power being found by universal experience liable to abuses, a distribution of it into separate departments has become a first principle of free governments. By this contrivance, the portion entrusted to the same hands being less, there is less room to abuse what is granted; and the different hands being interested, each in maintaining its own, there is less opportunity to usurp what is not granted. Hence the merited praise of governments modelled on a partition of their powers into legislative, executive, and judiciary, and a repartition of the legislative into different houses.

The political system of the United States claims still higher praise. The power delegated by the people is first divided between the general government and the state governments, each of which is then subdivided into legislative, executive, and judiciary departments. And as in a single government these departments are to be kept separate and safe, by a defensive armour for each; so, it is to be hoped, do the two governments possess each the means of preventing or correcting unconstitutional encroachments of the other.

Should this improvement on the theory of free government not be marred in the execution, it may prove the best legacy ever left by lawgivers to their country, and the best lesson ever given to the world by its benefactors. If a security against power lies in the division of it into parts mutually controlling each other, the security must increase with the increase of the parts into which the whole can be conveniently formed.

It must not be denied that the task of forming and maintaining a division of power between different governments is greater than among different departments of the same government, because it may be more easy (though sufficiently difficult) to separate, by proper definitions, the legislative, executive, and judiciary powers, which are more distinct in their nature, than to discriminate by precise enumerations one class of legislative powers from another class, one class of executive from another class, and one class of judiciary from another class, where the powers being of a more kindred nature, their boundaries are more obscure and run more into each other.

If the task be difficult, however, it must by no means be abandoned. Those who would pronounce it impossible offer no alternative to their country but schism or consolidation, both of them bad, but the latter the worst, since it is the high road to monarchy, than which nothing worse, in the eye of republicans, could result from the anarchy implied in the former.

Those who love their country, its repose, and its republicanism, will therefore study to avoid the alternative, by elucidating and guarding the limits which define the two governments, by inculcating moderation in the exercise of the powers of both, and particularly a mutual abstinence from such as might nurse present jealousies or engender greater.

In bestowing the eulogies due to the partitions and internal checks of power, it ought not the less to be remembered that they are neither the sole nor the chief palladium of constitutional liberty. The people, who are the authors of this blessing, must also be its guardians.

Their eyes must be ever ready to mark, their voice to pronounce, and their arm to repel or repair aggressions on the authority of their constitutions, the highest authority next to their own, because the immediate work of their own, and the most sacred part of their property, as recognizing and recording the title to every other.

"Republican Distribution of Citizens"
3 March 1792

A perfect theory on this subject would be useful, not because it could be reduced to practice by any plan of legislation, or ought to be attempted by violence on the will or property of individuals, but because it would be a monition against empirical experiments by power, and a model to which the free choice of occupations by the people might gradually approximate the order of society.

The best distribution is that which would most favor *health, virtue, intelligence* and *competency* in the *greatest number* of citizens. It is needless to add to these objects *liberty* and *safety*. The first is presupposed by them. The last must result from them.

The life of the husbandman is pre-eminently suited to the comfort and happiness of the individual. *Health,* the first of blessings, is an appurtenance of his property and his employment. *Virtue,* the health of the soul, is another part of his patrimony, and no less favored by his situation. *Intelligence* may be cultivated in this as well as in any other walk of life. If the mind be less susceptible of polish in retirement than in a crowd, it is more capable of profound and comprehensive efforts. Is it more ignorant of some things? It has a compensation in its ignorance of others. *Competency* is more universally the lot of those who dwell in the country, when liberty is at the same time their lot. The extremes both of want and of waste have other abodes. 'Tis not the country that peoples either the Bridewells or the Bedlams. These mansions of wretchedness are tenanted from the distresses and vices of overgrown cities.

The condition to which the blessings of life are most denied is that of the sailor. His health is continually assailed and his span shortened by the stormy element to which he belongs. His virtue, at no time aided, is occasionally exposed to every scene that can poison it. His mind, like his body, is imprisoned within the bark that transports him. Though traversing and circumnavigating the globe, he sees nothing but the same vague objects of nature, the same monotonous occurrences in ports and docks; and at home in his vessel, what new ideas can shoot from the unvaried use of the ropes and the rudder, or from the society of comrades as ignorant as himself. In the supply of his wants he often feels a scarcity, seldom more than a bare sustenance; and if his ultimate prospects do not embitter the present moment, it is because he never looks beyond it. How unfortunate that in the intercourse by which nations are enlightened and refined, and their means of safety extended, the immediate agents should be distinguished by the hardest condition of humanity.

The great interval between the two extremes is, with a few exceptions, filled by those who work the materials furnished by the earth in its natural or cultivated state.

It is fortunate in general, and particularly for this country, that so much of the ordinary and most essential consumption takes place in fabrics which can be prepared in every family, and which constitute indeed the natural ally of agriculture. The former is the work within doors, as the latter is without; and each being done by hands or at times that can be spared from the other, the most is made of every thing.

The class of citizens who provide at once their own food and their own raiment may be viewed as the most truly independent and happy. They are more: they are the best basis of public liberty, and the strongest bulwark of public safety. It follows that the greater the proportion of this class to the whole society, the more free, the more independent, and the more happy must be the society itself.

In appreciating the regular branches of manufacturing and mechanical industry, their tendency must be compared with the principles laid down, and their merits graduated accordingly. Whatever is least favorable to vigor of body, to the faculties of the mind, or to the virtues or the utilities of life, instead of being forced or fostered by public authority, ought to be seen with regret as long as occupations more friendly to human happiness lie vacant.

The several professions of more elevated pretensions, the merchant, the lawyer, the physician, the philosopher, the divine, form a certain proportion of every civilized society, and readily adjust their numbers to its demands and its circumstances.

"Fashion"
20 March 1792

A humble address has been lately presented to the Prince of Wales by the BUCKLE MANUFACTURERS of Birmingham, Wassal, Wolverhampton, and their environs, stating that the BUCKLE TRADE gives employment to more than TWENTY THOUSAND persons, numbers of whom, in consequence of the prevailing fashion of SHOESTRINGS & SLIPPERS, are at present without employ, almost destitute of bread, and exposed to the horrors of want at the most inclement season; that to the manufactures of BUCKLES and BUTTONS, Birmingham owes its important figure on the map of England, that it is to no purpose to address FASHION herself, she being void of feeling and deaf to argument, but fortunately accustomed to listen to his voice, and to obey his commands: and finally, IMPLORING his Royal Highness to consider the deplorable condition of their trade, which is in danger of being ruined by the *mutability of fashion,* and to give that direction to the *public taste,* which will insure the lasting gratitude of the petitioners.

Several important reflections are suggested by this address.

I. The most precarious of all occupations which give bread to the industrious are those depending on mere fashion, which generally changes so suddenly, and often so considerably, as to throw whole bodies of people out of employment.

II. Of all occupations those are the least desirable in a free state which produce the most servile dependence of one class of citizens on another class. This dependence must increase as the *mutuality* of wants is diminished. Where the wants on one side are the absolute necessaries and on the other are neither absolute necessaries, nor result from the habitual economy of life, but are the mere caprices of fancy, the evil is in its extreme; or if not,

III. The extremity of the evil must be in the case before us, where the absolute necessaries depend on the caprices of fancy and the caprice of a single fancy directs the fashion of the community. Here the dependence sinks to the lowest point of servility. We see a proof of it in the *spirit* of the address. *Twenty thousand* persons are to get or go without their bread as a wanton youth may fancy to wear his shoes with or without straps, or to fasten his straps with strings or with buckles. Can any despotism be more cruel than a situation in which the existence of thousands depends on one will, and that will on the most slight and fickle of all motives, a mere whim of the imagination.

IV. What a contrast is here to the independent situation and manly sentiments of American citizens, who live on their own soil, or whose labour is necessary to its cultivation, or who were occupied in supplying wants which, being founded in solid utility, in comfortable accommodation, or in settled habits, produce a reciprocity of dependence, at once ensuring subsistence and inspiring a dignified sense of social rights.

V. The condition of those who receive employment and bread from the precarious source of fashion and superfluity is a lesson to nations, as well as to individuals. In proportion as a nation consists of that description of citizens, and depends on external commerce, it is dependent on the consumption and caprice of other nations. If the laws of propriety did not forbid, the manufacturers of Birmingham, Wassal, and Wolverhampton had as real an interest in supplicating the arbiters of fashion in America as the patron they have addressed. The dependence in the case of nations is even greater than among individuals of the same nation: for besides the *mutability of fashion* which is the same in both, the *mutability of policy* is another source of danger in the former.

"Property"

27 March 1792

This term in its particular application means "that dominion which one man claims and exercises over the external things of the world, in exclusion of every other individual."

In its larger and juster meaning, it embraces every thing to which a man may attach a value and have a right; and *which leaves to every one else the like advantage.*

In the former sense, a man's land, or merchandize, or money is called his property.

In the latter sense, a man has a property in his opinions and the free communication of them.

He has a property of peculiar value in his religious opinions, and in the profession and practice dictated by them.

He has a property very dear to him in the safety and liberty of his person.

He has an equal property in the free use of his faculties and free choice of the objects on which to employ them.

In a word, as a man is said to have a right to his property, he may be equally said to have a property in his rights.

Where an excess of power prevails, property of no sort is duly respected. No man is safe in his opinions, his person, his faculties, or his possessions.

Where there is an excess of liberty, the effect is the same, tho' from an opposite cause.

Government is instituted to protect property of every sort, as well that which lies in the various rights of individuals as that which the term particularly expresses. This being the end of government, that alone is a *just* government which *impartially* secures to every man whatever is his *own*.

According to this standard of merit, the praise of affording a just security to property should be sparingly bestowed on a government which, however scrupulously guarding the possessions of individuals, does not protect them in the enjoyment and communication of their opinions, in which they have an equal, and in the estimation of some, a more valuable property.

More sparingly should this praise be allowed to a government where a man's religious rights are violated by penalties, or fettered by tests, or taxed by a hierarchy. Conscience is the most sacred of all property, other property depending in part on positive law [but] the exercise of that being a natural and unalienable right. To guard a man's house as his castle, to pay public and enforce private debts with the most exact faith, can give no title to invade a man's conscience, which is more sacred than his castle, or to withhold from it that debt of protection for which the public faith is pledged by the very nature and original conditions of the social pact.

That is not a just government, nor is property secure under it, where the property which a man has in his personal safety and personal liberty is violated by arbitrary seizures of one class of citizens for the service of the rest. A magistrate issuing his warrants to a press gang would be in his proper functions in Turkey or Indostan, under appellations proverbial of the most compleat despotism.

That is not a just government, nor is property secure under it, where arbitrary restrictions, exemptions, and monopolies deny to part of its citizens that free use of their faculties and free choice of their occupations which not only constitute their property in the general sense of the word, but are the means of acquiring property strictly so called. What must be the spirit of legislation where a manufacturer of linen cloth is forbidden to bury his own child in a linen shroud, in order to favor his neighbor who manufactures woolen cloth; where the manufacturer and wearer of woolen cloth are again forbidden the economical use of buttons of that material, in favor of the manufacturer of buttons of other materials!

A just security to property is not afforded by that government under which unequal taxes oppress one species of property and reward another species; where arbitrary taxes invade the domestic sanctuaries of the rich and excessive taxes grind the faces of the poor; where the keenness and competitions of want are deemed an insufficient spur to labor and taxes are again applied by an unfeeling policy as another spur; in violation of that sacred property, which Heaven, in decreeing man to earn his bread by the sweat of his brow, kindly reserved to him in the small repose that could be spared from the supply of his necessities.

If there be a government then which prides itself in maintaining the inviolability of property, which provides that none shall be taken *directly* even for public use without indemnification to the owner, and yet *directly* violates the property which individuals have in their opinions, their religion, their persons, and their faculties; nay more, which *indirectly* violates their property, in their actual possessions, in the labor that acquires their daily subsistence, and in the hallowed remnant of time which ought to relieve their fatigues and soothe their cares, the in[ference] will have been anticipated that such a government is not a pattern for the United States.

If the United States mean to obtain or deserve the full praise due to wise and just governments, they will equally respect the rights of property and the property in rights: they will rival the government that most sacredly guards the former; and by repelling its example in violating the latter, will make themselves a pattern to that and all other governments.

WILLIAM BRANCH GILES

Speech in the House of Representatives on the Apportionment Bill

9 April 1792

As public controversy mounted, the House of Representatives increasingly divided across a broad range of issues between Madison's allies and supporters of administration programs. Among the most vocal of the Madisonians was a young, new congressman from Virginia, who would remain active in national politics for many years to come. Giles's speech on reapportioning (and enlarging) the House in accord with the Census of 1790 was perhaps the earliest to accuse Hamilton and his supporters of a deliberate design to subvert American liberty.

. . . He observed that all representative governments appeared to possess a natural tendency from republicanism to monarchy; that great inequalities in the distribution of wealth among individuals, consequent upon the progress of all governments, appeared to be the cause of their political evolutions; that no competent remedy against this evil had been heretofore discovered, or at least practically applied by any government; that perhaps this great political light may first shine forth through the medium of the American constitutions, and serve, as some others have previously done, to illumine not only the American, but the European world.

The peculiar circumstances of the United States, however, since the late Revolution, and in the infancy of the American governments, favored extremely this natural principle of the growing inequality in the distribution of wealth amongst individuals. An extensive, unexhausted, fertile country furnished full scope for agriculture, the plenty and cheapness of provisions and rude materials for manufactures, and an unshackled commerce for the merchant; and to these were added the blessings of peace and laws securing to the individual the exclusive possession of the fruits of his own industry, however abundant. There were intrinsic circumstances; there was a contingent one. A public debt—the price of the Revolution itself and its consequent blessings—had been incurred and, from the imbecility of the then existing Confederacy and other causes, was depreciated considerably below its nominal value; but it was then in small masses and not very unequally spread amongst the individuals throughout the whole United States. The Government of the United States, instead of managing this contingent circumstance with caution, and declaring so in its ministration, seized upon it with its fiscal arrangements and applied it as the most powerful machine to stimulate this growing inequality in the distribution of wealth—a principle perhaps too much favored by other existing causes. The Government, not satisfied with the debts contracted by the former Confederacy, assumed the payment of a great proportion of the debts contracted by the respective state governments and established funds for paying the interest of the whole. This measure produced two effects, not very desirable amongst individuals. It gathered these scattered debts, at a very inferior price, from the hands of the many and placed them into the hands of the few; and it stimulates the value of them. Thus collected into greater masses, beyond all calculation, by the artificial application of fiscal mechanism, it produced a variety of serious effects with respect to the Government. In opposition to the agricultural or republican, it enlisted a great moneyed interest in the United States, who, having embarked their fortunes with the Government, would go all lengths with its Administration, whether right or wrong, virtuous or vicious, by rendering the debt but partially redeemable, passing perpetual tax laws, and mortgaging their products to the payment of the interest of this perpetually existing debt. It gave the Executive a qualified control over the best moneyed resources of the United States, not contemplated by the Constitution, nor founded in wisdom. It gave rise to an unauthorized incorporation of the moneyed interest, and placed it as far as possible from the reach of future Legislative influence. It established the doctrine that one systematic financier was better able to originate money bills and tax the people of the United States than the whole collected wisdom of their Representatives, with the aid of a reciprocity of feeling. It gave rise to the idea of a Sinking Fund, without limitation as to amount, to be placed in the hands of a few trustees and there to be protected from Legislative control by all the sanctions and securities annexed to private property. In short, it established the doctrine that all authority could be more safely intrusted to, and better executed by a few, than by many; and, in pursuance of this idea, made more continual drafts of authority from the Representative branch of the Government and placed it in the hands of the Executive; lessening, by this mechanism of adminis- tration, the constitutional influence of the people in the Government and fundamentally changing its native genius and original principle. He (Mr. G) knew of no competent remedy against the abominable evils to be apprehended from the future operation of these unhal- lowed principles but a permanent establishment of the candid or Republican interest in this House; and the best chance of effecting this great object he conceived to be a full representation of the people. His alarms respect- ing these fashionable, energetic principles were greatly increased by a perspective view of some of the proposed measures of Government. He saw systems introduced to carve out of the common rights of one part of the community privileges, monopolies, exclusive rights, &c., for the benefit of another, with no other view, in his opinion, but to create nurseries of immediate dependants upon the Government, whose interest will always stimu- late them to support its measures, however iniquitous and tyrannical, and, indeed, the very emoluments which will compose the price of their attachment to the Government will grow out of a tyrannical violation of the rights of others. He would forbear to mention a variety of other circumstances to prove that principle[s] having a ten- dency to change the very nature of the Government have pervaded even the minutest ramifications of its fiscal arrangements, nor would he dwell upon the undue influ- ence to be apprehended from moneyed foreigners, who had become adventurers in the funds, nor the various avenues opened to facilitate the operation of corruption. He would merely remark that, acting under impressions produced by these considerations and strengthened by others not less pertinent and important, suggested by a number of gentlemen, in the course of the discussion of this subject, and believing that a full representation of the people will furnish the only chance of remedy for the existing and a competent protection against future evils, he should feel himself criminal if by his vote he should give up a single representative authorized by the Con- stitution. . . . The Government of America was now in a state of puberty, that is, at this time. She is to assume a fixed character, and he thought it in some degree rested upon the vote now to be given whether she would preserve the simplicity, chastity, and purity of her native representation and Republicanism, in which alone the true dignity and greatness of her character must consist; or whether she will, so early in youth, prostitute herself to the venal and borrowed artifices and corruptions of a stale and pampered monarchy? Whatever his own opin- ions or suspicions may be respecting the tendency of the present Administration, and whatever may be the discussion of today, he should still preserve a hope that the increased representation, supported by the enlightened spirit of the people at large, will form an effectual resis- tance to the pressure of the whole vices of the Adminis- tration and may yet establish the Government upon a broad, permanent, and republican basis. . . .

Letters of Fisher Ames to George Richards Minot

1791–1792

On the other side of the House, the letters of Fisher Ames, the acerbic congressman from Massachusetts who would be a leading Federalist speaker and writer well into the Jeffersonian ascendancy, were another indicator of sharpening feelings.

30 November 1791

. . . The remark so often made on the difference of opinion between the members [of Congress] from the two ends of the continent appears to me not only true, but founded on causes which are equally unpleasant and lasting. To the northward, we see how necessary it is to defend property by steady laws. Shays confirmed our habits and opinions. The men of sense and property, even a little above the multitude, wish to keep the government in force enough to govern. We have trade, money, credit, and industry, which is at once cause and effect of the others.

At the southward, a few gentlemen govern; the law is their coat of mail; it keeps off the weapons of the foreigners, their creditors, and at the same time it governs the multitude, secures negroes, etc., which is of double use to them. It is both government and anarchy, and in each case is better than any possible change, especially in favor of an exterior (or federal) government of any strength. . . . Therefore, and for other causes, the men of weight in the four southern states (Charleston city excepted) were more generally *antis* and are now far more turbulent than they are with us. Many were federal among them at first, because they needed some remedy to evils which they saw and felt, but mistook, in their view of it, the remedy. A debt-compelling government is no remedy to men who have lands and negroes, and debts and luxury, but neither trade nor credit, nor cash, nor the habits of industry, or of submission to a rigid execution of law. My friend, you will agree with me that, ultimately, the same system of strict law which has done wonders for us would promote their advantage. But that relief is speculative and remote. Enormous debts required something better and speedier. I am told that, to this day, no British debt is recovered in North Carolina. . . . You will agree that our immediate wants were different—we to enforce, they to relax, law. . . .

Patrick Henry and some others of eminent talents and influence have continued *antis*, and have assiduously nursed the embryos of faction, which the adoption of the Constitution did not destroy. It soon gave popularity to the *antis* with a grumbling multitude. It made two parties.

Most of the measures of Congress have been opposed by the southern members. I speak not merely of their members, but their gentlemen, etc. at home. As men, they are mostly enlightened, clever fellows. I speak of the tendency of things upon their politics, not their morals. This has sharpened discontent at home. The funding system, they say, is in favor of the moneyed interest, oppressive to the land; that is, favorable to us, hard on them. They pay tribute, they say, and the middle and eastern people, holders of seven eighths of the debt, receive it. And here is the burden of the song: almost all the little that they had, and which cost them twenty shillings for supplies or services, has been bought up at a low rate, and now they pay more tax towards the interest than they received for the paper. This *tribute,* they say, is aggravating, for all the reasons before given; they add, had the state debts not been assumed, they would have wiped it off among themselves very speedily and easily. Being assumed, it has become a great debt; and now an excise, that abhorrence of free states, must pay it. This they have never adopted in their states. The states of Virginia, North Carolina, and Georgia are large territories. Being strong and expecting by increase to be stronger, the government of Congress over them seems mortifying to their state pride. The pride of the strong is not soothed by yielding to a stronger. How much there is, and how much more can be made of all these themes of grief and anger by men who are inclined and qualified to make the most of them, need not be pointed out to a man who has seen so much and written so well upon the principles which disturb and endanger government.

I confess I have recited these causes rather more at length than I had intended. But you are an observer, and I hope will be a writer of our history. The picture I have drawn, though just, is not noticed. Public happiness is in our power as a nation. Tranquillity has smoothed the surface. But (what I have said of southern parties is so true that I may affirm) faction glows within like a coal-pit. The President lives—is a southern man, is venerated as a demi-god, he is chosen by unanimous vote, etc., etc. Change the key and . . . You can fill up the blank. But while he lives, a steady prudent system by Congress may guard against the danger. Peace will enrich our southern friends. Good laws will establish more industry and economy. The peculiar causes of discontent will have lost their force with time. Yet, circumstanced as they are, I think other subjects of uneasiness will be found. For it is impossible to administer the government according to their ideas. We must have a revenue; of course an excise. The debt must be kept sacred; the rights of property must be held inviolate. We must, to be safe, have some regular force and an efficient militia. All these, except the last, and that except in a form not worth having, are obnoxious to them. I have not noticed what they call their republicanism, because having observed what their situation is, you will see what their theory must be, in seeing what it is drawn from. I have not exhausted, but I quit this part of the subject. In fine, those three states are circumstanced not unlike our state in 1786.

I think these deductions flow from the premises: That the strength as well as hopes of the Union reside with the middle and eastern states. That our good men must watch and pray on all proper occasions for the preservation of federal measures and principles. That so far from being in a condition to swallow up the state governments, Congress cannot be presumed to possess too much force to preserve its constitutional authority, whenever the crisis to which these discontents are hastening shall have brought its power to the test. And, above all, that in the supposed crisis, the state partisans who seem to wish to clip the wings of the Union would be not the least zealous to support the Union. For, zealous as they may be to extend the power of the General Court of Massachusetts, they would not wish to be controlled by that of Virginia. I will not tire you with more speculation; but I will confess my belief that if, now, a vote was to be taken, "Shall the Constitution be adopted," and the people of Virginia and the other more southern states (the city of Charleston excepted) should answer instantly, according to their present feelings and opinions, it would be in the negative. . . .

8 March 1792

My Dear Friend,—Congress moves slowly, too slowly. The spirit of debate is a vice that grows by indulgence. It is a sort of captiousness that delights in nothing but contradiction. Add to this, we have near twenty *antis*, dragons watching

the tree of liberty, and who consider every strong measure, and almost every ordinary one, as an attempt to rob the tree of its fair fruit. We hear, incessantly, from the old foes of the Constitution, "this is unconstitutional, and that is"; and indeed, what is not? I scarce know a point which has not produced this cry, not excepting a motion for adjourning. If the Constitution is what they affect to think it, their former opposition to such a nonentity was improper. I wish they would administer it a little more in conformity to their first creed. The men who would hinder all that is done, and almost all that ought to be done, hang heavy on the debates. The fishery bill was unconstitutional; it is unconstitutional to receive plans of finance from the Secretary; to give bounties; to make the militia worth having; order is unconstitutional; credit is tenfold worse. . . .

3 May 1792

I am tired of the session. Attending Congress is very like going to school. Every day renews the round of yesterday; and if I stay a day or two after the adjournment, I shall be apt to go to Congress from habit, as some old horses are said to go to the meeting-house on Sunday without a rider, by force of their long habit of going on that day. . . .

Causes which I have in a former letter explained to you have generated a regular, well-disciplined opposition party, whose leaders cry "liberty," but mean, as all party leaders do, "power," who will write and talk and caress weak and vain men till they displace their rivals. The poor Vice will be baited before the election. All the arts of intrigue will be practiced—but more of this when we meet. . . .

PHILIP FRENEAU

"Rules for Changing a Limited Republican Government into an Unlimited Hereditary One"

4 and 7 July 1792

By midsummer 1792, the *National Gazette* was in full cry against the Hamiltonian program and the critics of the French. The following satire encapsulated nearly all of the opposition's charges.

I. It being necessary, in order to effect the change, to get rid of constitutional shackles and popular prejudices, all possible means and occasions are to be used for both these purposes.

II. Nothing being more likely to prepare the vulgar mind for aristocratical ranks and hereditary powers than TITLES, endeavor in the offset of the government to confer those on its most dignified officers. If the principal magistrate should happen to be particularly venerable in the eyes of the people, take advantage of that fortunate circumstance in setting the example.

III. Should the attempt fail, thro' his republican aversion to it, or from the danger of alarming the people, do not abandon the enterprise altogether, but lay up the proposition in record. Time may gain it respect, and it will be there always ready cut and dried for any favourable conjuncture that may offer.

IV. In drawing all bills, resolutions, and reports, keep constantly in view that the limitations in the constitution are ultimately to be explained away. Precedents and phrases may thus be shuffled in, without being adverted to by candid or weak people, of which good use may afterwards be made.

V. As the novelty and bustle of inaugurating the government will for some time keep the public mind in a heedless and unsettled state, let the *Press* during this period be busy in propagating the doctrines of monarchy and aristocracy. For this purpose it will be particularly useful to confound a mobbish democracy with a representative republic, that by exhibiting all the turbulent examples and enormities of the former, an odium may be thrown on the character of the latter. Review all the civil contests, convulsions, factions, broils, squabbles, bickerings, black eyes and bloody noses of ancient, middle and modern ages, caricature them into the most frightful forms and colors that can be imagined, and unfold one scene of the horrible tragedy after another 'till the people be made, if possible, to tremble at their own shadows.—*Let the Discourses on [Davila]*—then contrast with these pictures of terror the quiet of hereditary succession, the reverence claimed by birth and nobility, and the fascinating influence of stars, ribbands, and garters, cautiously suppressing all the bloody tragedies and unceasing oppressions which form the history of this species of government. No pains should be spared in this part of the undertaking, for the greatest will be wanted, it being extremely difficult, especially when a people have been taught to reason and feel their rights, to convince them that a king who is always an enemy to the people, and a nobility who are perhaps still more so, will take better care of the people than the people will take care of themselves.

VI. But the grand *nostrum* will be a PUBLIC DEBT, provided enough of it can be got, and it be medicated with the proper ingredients. If by good fortune a debt be ready at hand, the most is to be made of it. Stretch it and swell it to the utmost the items will bear. Allow as many extra claims as decency will permit. Assume all the debts of your neighbours: In a word, get as much debt as can be raked and scraped together, and when you have got all you can, "advertise" for more, and have the debt made *as big as possible*. This object being accomplished, the next will be to make it *as perpetual as possible,* and the next to that, to get it into *as few hands as possible.* The more effectually to bring this about, modify the debt, complicate it, divide it, subdivide it, subtract it, postpone it, let there be one third of two thirds: let there be three per cents, and four per cents, and six per cents, and present six per cents, and future six per cents. To be brief, let the whole be such a mystery that a *few only* can understand it; and let all possible opportunities and informations fall in the way of *these few,* to clinch their advantage over the many.

VII. It must not be forgotten that the members of the legislative body are to have a deep stake in the game. This is an essential point, and happily is attended with no difficulty. A sufficient number, properly disposed, can alternately legislate and speculate, and speculate and legislate, and buy and sell, and sell and buy, until a due portion of the property of their constituents has passed into their hands to give them an interest against their constituents, and to ensure the part they are to act. All this however must be carried on under cover of the closest secrecy; and it is particularly lucky that dealings in paper admit of more secrecy than any other. Should a discovery take place, the whole plan may be blown up.

VIII. The ways in which a great debt, so constituted and applied, will contribute to the ultimate end in view are both numerous and obvious. 1. The *favorite few,* thus possessed of it, whether within or without the government, will feel the staunchest fealty to it, and will go through thick and thin to support it in all its oppressions and usurpations. 2. Their money will give them consequence and influence, even among those who have been tricked out of it.

3. They will be the readiest materials that can be found for an hereditary aristocratic order, and whenever matters are ripe for one.   4. A great debt will require great taxes, great taxes many taxgatherers & other officers; & all officers are auxiliaries of power.   5. Heavy taxes may produce discontents; these may threaten resistance; and in proportion to this danger will be the pretence of a *standing army* to repel it.   6. A standing army in its turn will increase the moral force of the government by means of its appointments, and give it physical force by means of the sword, thus doubly forwarding the main object.

IX. The management of a great funded debt and an extensive system of taxes will afford a plea not to be neglected for establishing a great incorporated bank. The use of such a machine is well understood. If the constitution, according to its fair meaning, should not authorize it, so much the better. Push it through by a forced meaning, and you will get in the bargain an admirable precedent for future misconstructions. In fashioning the bank remember that it is to be made particularly instrumental in enriching and aggrandizing the elect few, who are to be called in due season to the honors and felicities of the *kingdom* preparing for them, and who are the pillars that must support it. It will be easy to throw the benefit entirely into their hands, and to make it a solid addition of 50, or 60, or 70 per cent to their former capitals of 800 per cent or 900 per cent without costing them a shilling, whilst it will be so difficult to explain to the people that this gain of the few is at the cost of the many, that the *contrary* may be boldly and safely pretended. The bank will be pregnant with other important advantages. It will admit the same men to be, at the same time, members of the bank and members of the government. The two institutions will thus be soldered together, and each made the stronger. Money will be put under the direction of the government, and the government under the direction of money. To crown the whole, the bank will have a proper interest in *swelling and perpetuating the public debt and public taxes,* with all the blessings of both, because its agency and its profits will be extended in exact proportion.

X. "Divide and govern" is a maxim consecrated by the experience of ages, and should be as familiar in its use to every politician as the knife he carries in his pocket. In the work here to be executed the best effects may be produced by this maxim, and with peculiar facility. An extensive republic made up of lesser republics necessarily contains various sorts of people, distinguished by local and other interests and prejudices. Let the whole group be well examined in all its parts and relations, geographical and political, metaphysical and metaphorical; let there be first a northern and a southern section by a line running east and west, and then an eastern and western section by a line running north and south. By a suitable nomenclature, the landholders cultivating different articles can be discriminated from one another, all from the class of merchants, and both from that of manufacturers. One of the subordinate republics may be represented as a commercial state, another as a navigation state, another as a manufacturing state, others as agricultural states; and although the great body of the people in each be really agricultural, and the other characters be more or less common to all, still it will be politic to take advantage of such an arrangement. Should the members of the great republic be of different sizes, and subject to little jealousies on that account, another important division will be ready formed to your hand. Add again the divisions that may be carved out of *personal interests,* political opinions, and local parties.— With so convenient an assortment of votes, especially with the help of the *marked ones,* a majority may be packed for any question with as much ease as the odd trick by an adroit gamester, and any measure whatever be carried or defeated, as the great revolution to be brought about may require. It is only necessary therefore to recommend that full use be made of the resource: and to remark that, besides the direct benefit to be drawn from these artificial divisions, they will tend to smother the true and natural one, existing in all societies between the few who are always impatient of political equality, and the many who can never rise above it; between those who are to mount to the prerogatives, and those who are to be saddled with the burthens of the hereditary government to be introduced; in one word, between the general mass of the people, attached to their republican government and republican interests, and the chosen band devoted to monarchy and mammon.

XI. As soon as sufficient progress in the intended change shall have been made, and the public mind duly prepared according to the rules already laid down, it will be proper to venture on another and a bolder step towards a removal of the constitutional land-marks. Here the aid of former encroachments, and all the other precedents and way-paving manoeuvres, will be called in of course. But, in order to render success the more certain, it will be of special moment to give the most plausible and popular name that can be found to the power that is to be usurped. It may be called, for example, a power for the common safety or the public good, or "the general welfare." If the people should not be too much enlightened, the name will have a most imposing effect. It will escape attention that it means, in fact, the same thing with a power to do anything the government pleases "in all cases whatsoever." To oppose the power may consequently seem to the ignorant, and be called by the artful, opposing the "general welfare," and may be cried down under that deception. As the people, however, may not run so readily into the snare as might be wished, it will be prudent to bait it well with some specious popular interest, such as the encouragement of manufactures, or even of agriculture, taking care not even to mention any unpopular object to which the power is equally applicable, such as religion, &c. &c. &c. By this contrivance, particular classes of people may possibly be taken in who will be a valuable reinforcement. With respect to the patronage of agriculture, there is not indeed much to be expected from it. It will be too quickly seen through by the owners and tillers of the soil that to tax them with one hand and pay back a part only with the other is a losing game on their side. From the power over manufactures more is to be hoped. It will not be so easily perceived that the premium bestowed may not be equal to the circuitous tax on consumption, which pays it. There are particular reasons, too, for pushing the experiment on this class of citizens.   1. As they live in towns and can act together, it is of vast consequence to gain them over to the interest of monarchy.   2. If the power over them be once established, the government can grant favors or monopolies as it pleases; can raise or depress this or that place, as it pleases; can gratify this or that individual, as it pleases; in a word, by creating a dependence in so numerous and important a class of citizens, it will increase its own independence of every class, and be more free to pursue the grand object in contemplation.   3. The expense of this operation will not in the end cost the government a shilling, for the moment any branch of manufacture has been brought to a state of tolerable maturity, *the exciseman will be ready* with his constable and his search-warrant to demand a reimbursement and as much more as can be squeezed out of the article. All this, it is to be remembered,

supposes that the manufacturers will be weak enough to be cheated, in some respects, out of their *interests,* and wicked enough, in others, to betray those of their fellow citizens, a supposition that, if known, would totally mar the experiment. Great care, therefore, must be taken to prevent it from leaking out.

XII. The expediency of seizing every occasion of external danger for augmenting and perpetuating the standing military force is too obvious to escape. So important is this matter that for any loss or disaster whatever attending the national arms, there will be ample consolation and compensation in the opportunity for enlarging the establishment. A military defeat will become a political victory, and the loss of a little vulgar blood contributes to ennoble that which flows in the veins of our future dukes and marquisses.

XIII. The same prudence will improve the opportunity afforded by an increase of the military expenditures, for perpetuating the taxes required for them. If the inconsistency and absurdity of establishing a *perpetual* tax for a temporary service should produce any difficulty in the business, *Rule* 10 must be resorted to. Throw in as many extraneous motives as will make up a majority, and the thing is effected in an instant. What was before evil will become good as easily as black could be made white by the same magical operation.

XIV. Throughout this great undertaking it will be wise to have some particular model constantly in view. The work can then be carried on more systematically, and every measure be fortified, in the progress, by apt illustrations and authorities. Should there exist a particular monarchy against which there are fewer prejudices than against any other; should it contain a mixture of the representative principle so as to present on one side the semblance of a republican aspect; should it moreover have a great, funded, complicated, irredeemable debt, with all the apparatus and appurtenances of excises, banks, &c. &c. &c. upon that a steady eye is to be kept. In all cases it will assist, and in most its statute-book will furnish a precise pattern by which there may be cut out any monied or monarchical project that may be wanted.

XV. As it is not to be expected that the change of a republic into a monarchy, with the rapidity desired, can be carried through without occasional suspicions and alarms, it will be necessary to be prepared for such events. The best general rule on the subject is to be taken from the example of crying "Stop thief" first.—Neither lungs nor pens must be spared in charging every man who whispers, or even thinks, that the revolution on foot is meditated, with being himself an enemy to the established government and meaning to overturn it. Let the charge be reiterated and reverberated, till at last such confusion and uncertainty be produced that the people, being not able to find out where the truth lies, withdraw their attention from the contest.

Many other rules of great wisdom and efficacy ought to be added: but it is conceived that the above will be abundantly enough for the purpose. This will certainly be the case if the people can be either kept asleep so as not to discover, or be thrown into artificial divisions, so as not to resist, what is silently going forward.—Should it be found impossible, however, to prevent the people from awaking and uniting; should all artificial distinctions give way to the natural division between the lordly minded few and the well-disposed many; should all who have common interest make a common cause and shew an inflexible attachment to republicanism in opposition to a government of monarchy and of money, why then ****--

Alexander Hamilton to Edward Carrington

26 May 1792

Goaded by the mounting attacks in Congress and even more concerned about the campaign in the *National Gazette,* by means of which the opposition to his programs threatened to spread quite widely among the public, Hamilton decided to open a counteroffensive. The first step was a letter to Edward Carrington, a Virginia collector of customs, former Confederation congressman, and ally of Hamilton and Madison in the quest for federal reform. The second step would be a public attack on Jefferson's connection with Freneau and his gazette.

The analysis advanced in Hamilton's letter was, of course, a private communication, but later in 1792 a very similar attack on Jefferson and Madison appeared in the form of a 36-page pamphlet by William Loughton Smith, "The Politicks and Views of a Certain Party Displayed." The representative from South Carolina often spoke for Hamilton in Congress, and it is natural to suspect that there was also some collaboration here.

Believing that I possess a share of your personal friendship and confidence and yielding to that which I feel towards you—persuaded also that our political creed is the same on *two essential points,* 1st the necessity of *Union* to the respectability and happiness of this Country and 2. the necessity of an *efficient* general government to maintain that Union—I have concluded to unbosom myself to you on the present state of political parties and views. I ask no reply to what I shall say. I only ask that you will be persuaded the representations I shall make are agreeable to the real and sincere impressions of my mind. You will make the due allowances for the influence of circumstances upon it—you will consult your own observations and you will draw such a conclusion as shall appear to you proper.

When I accepted the office I now hold, it was under a full persuasion that from similarity of thinking, conspiring with personal goodwill, I should have the firm support of Mr. Madison in the *general course* of my administration. Aware of the intrinsic difficulties of the situation and of the powers of Mr. Madison, I do not believe I should have accepted under a different supposition.

I have mentioned the similarity of thinking between that gentleman and myself. This was relative not merely to the general principles of national policy and government but to the leading points which were likely to constitute questions in the administration of the finances. I mean 1. the expediency of *funding* the debt 2. the inexpediency of *discrimination* between original and present holders 3. the expediency of *assuming* the state debts.

As to the first point, the evidence of Mr. Madison's sentiments at one period is to be found in the address of Congress of April 26, 1783, which was planned by him in conformity to his own ideas and without any previous suggestions from the committee and with his hearty cooperation in every part of the business. His conversations upon various occasions since have been expressive of a continuance in the same sentiment, nor indeed has he yet contradicted it by any part of his official conduct. How far there is reason to apprehend a change in this particular will be stated hereafter.

As to the second part, the same address is an evidence of Mr. Madison's sentiments at the same period. And I had been informed that at a later period he had been in the Legislature of Virginia a strenuous and successful opponent of the principle of discrimination. Add to this that a variety of conversations had taken place between him and myself respecting the public debt down to the commencement of the new government in none of which had he glanced at the idea of a change of opinion. I wrote him a letter after my appointment in the recess of Congress to obtain his sentiments on the subject of the finances. In his answer there is not a lisp of his new system.

As to the third point, the question of an assumption of the state debts by the United States was in discussion when the convention that framed the present government was sitting at Philadelphia; and in a long conversation, which I had with Mr. Madison in an afternoon's walk, I well remember that we were perfectly agreed in the expediency and propriety of such a measure, though we were both of opinion that it would be more advisable to make it a measure of administration than an article of constitution; from the impolicy of multiplying obstacles to its reception on collateral details.

Under these circumstances, you will naturally imagine that it must have been a matter of surprise to me when I was apprised that it was Mr. Madison's intention to oppose my plan on both the last mentioned points.

Before the debate commenced, I had a conversation with him on my report, in the course of which I alluded to the calculation I had made of his sentiments and the grounds of that calculation. He did not deny them, but alledged in his justification that the very considerable alienation of the debt, subsequent to the periods at which he had opposed a discrimination, had essentially changed the state of the question—and that as to the assumption, he had contemplated it to take place *as matters stood at the peace.*

While the change of opinion avowed on the point of discrimination diminished my respect for the force of Mr. Madison's mind and the soundness of his judgment— and while the idea of reserving and setting afloat a vast mass of already extinguished debt as the condition of a measure the leading objects of which were an accession of strength to the national government and an assurance of order and vigour in the national finances by doing away the necessity of thirteen complicated and conflicting systems of finance—appeared to me somewhat extraordinary: Yet my previous impressions of the fairness of Mr. Madison's character and my reliance on his good will towards me disposed me to believe that his suggestions were sincere; and even, on the point of an assumption of the debts of the states as they stood at the peace, to lean towards a cooperation in his view; 'till on feeling the

ground I found the thing impracticable, and on further reflection I thought it liable to immense difficulties. It was tried and failed with little countenance.

At this time and afterwards repeated intimations were given to me that Mr. Madison, from a spirit of rivalship or some other cause, had become personally unfriendly to me; and one gentleman in particular, whose honor I have no reason to doubt, assured me that Mr. Madison in a conversation with him had made a pretty direct attempt to insinuate unfavorable impressions of me.

Still I suspended my opinion on the subject. I knew the malevolent officiousness of mankind too well to yield a very ready acquiescience to the suggestions which were made, and resolved to wait 'till time and more experience should afford a solution.

It was not 'till the last session that I became unequivocally convinced of the following truth—"*That Mr. Madison cooperating with Mr. Jefferson is at the head of a faction decidedly hostile to me and my administration, and actuated by views in my judgment subversive of the principles of good government and dangerous to the union, peace and happiness of the Country.*"

These are strong expressions; they may pain your friendship for one or both of the gentlemen whom I have named. I have not lightly resolved to hazard them. They are the result of a *Serious alarm* in my mind for the public welfare, and of a full conviction that what I have alledged is a truth, and a truth which ought to be told and well attended to by all the friends of Union and efficient National Government. The suggestion will, I hope, at least awaken attention, free from the bias of former prepossessions.

This conviction in my mind is the result of a long train of circumstances; many of them minute. To attempt to detail them all would fill a volume. I shall therefore confine myself to the mention of a few.

First—As to the point of opposition to me and my administration.

Mr. Jefferson with very little reserve manifests his dislike of the funding system generally, calling in question the expediency of funding a debt at all. Some expressions which he has dropped in my own presence (sometimes without sufficient attention to delicacy) will not permit me to doubt on this point representations which I have had from various respectable quarters. I do not mean that he advocates directly the undoing of what has been done, but he censures the whole on principles which, if they should become general, could not but end in the subversion of the system.

In various conversations with *foreigners* as well as citizens, he has thrown censure on my *principles* of government and on my measures of administration. He has predicted that the people would not long tolerate my proceedings & that I should not long maintain my ground. Some of those, whom he *immediately* and *notoriously* moves, have even whispered suspicions of the rectitude of my motives and conduct. In the question concerning the Bank he not only delivered an opinion in writing against its constitutionality & expediency; but he did it *in a style and manner* which I felt as partaking of asperity and ill humour towards me. As one of the trustees of the sinking fund, I have experienced in almost every leading question opposition from him. When any turn of things in the community has threatened either odium or embarrassment to me, he has not been able to suppress the satisfaction which it gave him.

A part of this is of course information, and might be misrepresentation. But it comes through so many channels and so well accords with what falls under my own observation that I can entertain no doubt.

I find a strong confirmation in the following circumstances. *Freneau,* the present printer of the *National Gazette,* who was a journeyman with Childs & Swain at New York, was a known anti-federalist. It is reduced to a certainty that he was brought to Philadelphia by Mr. Jefferson to be the conductor of a newspaper. It is notorious that cotemporarily with the commencement of his paper he was a clerk in the department of state for foreign languages. Hence a clear inference that his paper has been set on foot and is conducted under the patronage & not against the views of Mr. Jefferson. What then is the complexion of this paper? Let any impartial man peruse all the numbers down to the present day; and I never was more mistaken, if he does not pronounce that it is a paper devoted to the subversion of me & the measures in which I have had an agency; and I am little less mistaken if he do not pronounce that it is a paper of a tendency *generally unfriendly* to the Government of the U States. . . .

With regard to Mr. Madison—the matter stands thus. I have not heard, but in the one instance to which I have alluded, of his having held language unfriendly to me in private conversation. But in his public conduct there has been a more uniform & persevering opposition than I have been able to resolve into a sincere difference of opinion.

I cannot persuade myself that Mr. Madison and I, whose politics had formerly so much the *same point of departure,* should now diverge so widely in our opinions of the measures which are proper to be pursued. The opinion I once entertained of the candor and simplicity and fairness of Mr. Madison's character has, I acknowledge, given way to a decided opinion that *it is one of a peculiarly artificial and complicated kind.*

For a considerable part of the last session, Mr. Madison lay in a great measure *perdu.* But it was evident from his votes & a variety of little movements and appearances that he was the prompter of Mr. Giles & others, who were the open instruments of opposition. . . .

Mr. Jefferson is an avowed enemy to a funded debt. Mr. Madison disavows in public any intention to *undo* what has been done; but in a private conversation with Mr. Charles Carroll (Senator)—this gentleman's name I mention confidentially though he mentioned the matter to Mr. King & several other gentlemen as well as myself, & if any chance should bring you together you would easily bring him to repeat it to you—he favored the sentiment in Mr. Mercer's speech that a legislature had no right to *fund* the debt by mortgaging permanently the public revenues because they had no right to bind posterity. The inference is that what has been unlawfully done may be undone. . . .

The discourse of partisans in the Legislature & the publications in the party newspapers direct their main battery against the *principle* of a funded debt, & represent it in the most odious light as a perfect *Pandora's box.* . . .

Whatever were the original merits of the funding system, after having been so solemnly adopted, & after so great a transfer of property under it, what would become of the Government should it be reversed? What of the national reputation? Upon what system of morality can so atrocious a doctrine be maintained? In me, I confess it excites *indignation & horror!*

What are we to think of those maxims of government by which the power of a legislature is denied to bind the nation by a *Contract* in an affair of *property* for twenty-four years? For this is precisely the case of the debt. What are to become of all the legal rights of property, of all charters to corporations, nay, of all grants to a man his heirs & assigns forever, if this doctrine be true? What is the term for which a government is in capacity to *contract?* Questions might be multiplied without end to demonstrate the perniciousness & absurdity of such a doctrine.

In almost all the questions great & small which have arisen since the first session of Congress, Mr. Jefferson & Mr. Madison have been found among those who were disposed to narrow the Federal authority. The question of a National Bank is one example. The question of bounties to the fisheries is another. Mr. Madison resisted it on the ground of constitutionality 'till it was evident, by the intermediate questions taken, that the bill would pass & he then under the wretched subterfuge of a change of a single word "bounty" for "allowance" went over to the majority & voted for the bill. In the Militia bill & in a variety of minor cases he has leaned to abridging the exercise of federal authority, & leaving as much as possible to the states, & he has lost no opportunity of *sounding the alarm* with great affected solemnity at encroachments meditated on the rights of the states, & of holding up the bugbear of a faction in the government having designs unfriendly to liberty.

This kind of conduct has appeared to me the more extraordinary on the part of Mr. Madison as I know for a certainty it was a primary article in his creed that the real danger in our system was the subversion of the national authority by the preponderancy of the state governments. All his measures have proceeded on an opposite supposition.

I recur again to the instance of Freneau's paper. In matters of this kind one cannot have direct proof of man's latent views; they must be inferred from circumstances. As the coadjutor of Mr. Jefferson in the establishment of this paper, I include Mr. Madison in the consequences imputable to it.

In respect to our foreign politics the views of these gentlemen are in my judgment equally unsound & dangerous. *They have a womanish attachment to France and a womanish resentment against Great Britain.* They would draw us into the closest embrace of the former & involve us in all the consequences of her politics, & they would risk the peace of the country in their endeavors to keep us at the greatest possible distance from the latter. This disposition goes to a length particularly in Mr. Jefferson of which, till lately, I had no adequate idea. Various circumstances prove to me that if these gentlemen were left to pursue their own course there would be in less than six months *an open War between the U States* & *Great Britain.*

I trust I have a due sense of the conduct of France towards this country in the late Revolution, & that I shall always be among the foremost in making her every suitable return; but there is a wide difference between this & implicating ourselves in all her politics; between bearing good will to her, & hating and wrangling with all those whom she hates. The neutral & the pacific policy appear to me to mark the true path to the U States.

Having now delineated to you what I conceive to be the true complexion of the politics of these gentlemen, I will now attempt a solution of these strange appearances.

Mr. Jefferson, it is known, did not in the first instance cordially acquiesce in the new constitution for the U States; he had many doubts and reserves. He left this country before we had experienced the imbecilities of the former.

In France he saw government only on the side of its abuses. He drank deeply of the French Philosophy, in religion, in science, in politics. He came from France in the moment of a fermentation which he had had a share in exciting, & in the passion and feelings of which he shared both from temperament and situation.

He came here probably with a too partial idea of his own powers, and with the expectation of a greater share in the direction of our councils than he has in reality enjoyed. I am not sure that he had not peculiarly marked out for himself the department of the Finances.

He came electrified *plus* with attachment to France and with the project of knitting together the two countries in the closest political bonds.

Mr. Madison had always entertained an exalted opinion of the talents, knowledge and virtues of Mr. Jefferson. The sentiment was probably reciprocal. A close correspondence subsisted between them during the time of Mr. Jefferson's absence from this country. A close intimacy arose upon his return.

Whether any peculiar opinions of Mr. Jefferson concerning the public debt wrought a change in the sentiments of Mr. Madison (for it is certain that the former is more radically wrong than the latter) or whether Mr. Madison seduced by the expectation of popularity and possibly by the calculation of advantage to the state of Virginia was led to change his own opinion—certain it is, that a very material *change* took place, & that the two gentlemen were united in the new ideas. Mr. Jefferson was indiscreetly open in his approbation of Mr. Madison's principles, upon his first coming to the seat of government. I say indiscreetly, because a gentleman in the administration in one department ought not to have taken sides against another, in another department.

The course of this business & a variety of circumstances which took place left Mr. Madison a very discontented & chagrined man and begot some degree of ill humour in Mr. Jefferson.

Attempts were made by these gentlemen in different ways to produce a commercial warfare with Great Britain. In this too they were disappointed. And as they had the liveliest wishes on the subject their dissatisfaction has been proportionally great; and as I had not favored the project, I was comprehended in their displeasure.

These causes and perhaps some others created, much sooner than I was aware of it, a systematic opposition to me on the part of those gentlemen. My subversion, I am now satisfied, has been long an object with them.

Subsequent events have encreased the spirit of opposition and the feelings of personal mortification on the part of these Gentlemen.

A mighty stand was made on the affair of the Bank. There was much *commitment* in that case. I prevailed.

On the Mint business I was opposed from the same quarter, & with still less success. In the affair of ways & means for the Western expedition—on the supplementary arrangements concerning the debt except as to the additional assumption, my views have been equally prevalent in opposition to theirs. This current of success on one side & defeat on the other have rendered the opposition furious, & have produced a disposition to subvert their competitors even at the expence of the Government.

Another circumstance has contributed to widening the breach. 'Tis evident beyond a question, from every movement, that Mr. Jefferson aims with ardent desire at the Presidential Chair. This too is an important object of the party-politics. It is supposed, from the nature of my former personal & political connexions, that I may favor some other candidate more than Mr. Jefferson when the question shall occur by the retreat of the present gentleman. My influence therefore with the community becomes a thing, on ambitious & personal grounds, to be resisted & destroyed.

You know how much it was a point to establish the Secretary of State as the officer who was to administer the Government in defect of the President & Vice President. Here I acknowledge, though I took far less part than was supposed, I ran counter to Mr. Jefferson's wishes; but if I had had no other reason for it, I had already *experienced opposition* from him which rendered it a measure of *self defense.*

It is possible too (for men easily heat their imaginations when their passions are heated) that they have by degrees persuaded themselves of what they may have at first only sported to influence others—namely that there is some dreadful combination against state government & republicanism; which according to them, are convertible terms. But there is so much absurdity in this supposition that the admission of it tends to apologize for their hearts, at the expense of their heads.

Under the influence of all these circumstances, the attachment to the Government of the U States, originally weak in Mr. Jefferson's mind, has given way to something very like dislike; in Mr. Madison's, it is so counteracted by personal feelings as to be more an affair of the head than of the heart—more the result of a conviction of the necessity of Union than of cordiality to the thing itself. I hope it does not stand worse than this with him.

In such a state of mind, both these gentlemen are prepared to hazard a great deal to effect a change. Most of the important measures of every government are connected with the Treasury. To subvert the present head of it they deem it expedient to risk rendering the Government itself odious; perhaps foolishly thinking that they can easily recover the lost affections & confidence of the people, and not appreciating as they ought to do the natural resistance to Government which in every community results from the human passions, the degree to which this is strengthened by the *organized rivality* of state governments, & the infinite danger that the national government once rendered odious will be kept so by these powerful & indefatigable enemies.

They forget an old but a very just, though a coarse, saying—That it is much easier to raise the Devil than to lay him.

Poor *Knox* has come in for a share of their persecution as a man who generally thinks with me & who has a portion of the President's good will & confidence.

In giving you this picture of political parties, my design is, I confess, to awaken your attention, if it has not yet been awakened to the conduct of the gentlemen in question. If my opinion of them is founded, it is certainly of great moment to the public weal that they should be understood. I rely on the strength of your mind to appreciate men as they merit—when you have a clue to their real views.

A word on another point. I am told that serious apprehensions are disseminated in your state as to the existence of a monarchical party mediating the destruction of state & republican government. If it is possible that so absurd an idea can gain ground it is necessary that it should be combatted. I assure you on my *private faith* and *honor* as a man that there is not in my judgment a shadow of foundation of it. A very small number of men indeed may entertain theories less republican than Mr. Jefferson & Mr. Madison; but I am persuaded there is not a man among them who would not regard as both *criminal* & *visionary* any attempt to subvert the republican system of the country. Most of these men rather *fear* that it may not justify itself by its fruits than feel a predilection for a different form; and their fears are not diminished by the factions & fanatical politics which they find prevailing among a certain set of gentlemen and threatening to disturb the tranquillity and order of the government.

As to the destruction of state governments, the *great* and *real* anxiety is to be able to preserve the national from the too potent and counteracting influence of those governments. As to my own political creed, I give it to you with the utmost sincerity. I am *affectionately* attached to the republican theory. I desire *above all things* to see the *equality* of political rights exclusive of all *hereditary* distinction firmly established by a practical demonstration of its being consistent with the order and happiness of society.

As to state governments, the prevailing bias of my judgment is that if they can be circumscribed within bounds consistent with the preservation of the national government they will prove useful and salutary. If the states were all of the size of Connecticut, Maryland or New Jersey, I should decidedly regard the local governments as both safe & useful. As the thing now is, however, I acknowledge the most serious apprehensions that the Government of the U States will not be able to maintain itself against their influence. I see that influence already penetrating into the national councils & perverting their direction.

Hence a disposition on my part towards a liberal construction of the powers of the national government and to erect every fence to guard it from depredations, which is, in my opinion, consistent with constitutional propriety.

As to the combination to prostrate the state governments, I disavow and deny it. From an apprehension lest the judiciary should not work efficiently or harmoniously I have been desirous of seeing some rational scheme of connection adopted as an amendment to the Constitution; otherwise I am for maintaining things as they are, though I doubt much the possibility of it, from a tendency in the nature of things towards the preponderancy of the state governments.

I said that I was *affectionately* attached to the republican theory. This is the real language of my heart which I open to you in the sincerity of friendship; & I add that I have strong hopes of the success of that theory; but in candor I ought also to add that I am far from being without doubts. I consider its success as yet a problem.

It is yet to be determined by experience whether it be consistent with that *stability* and *order* in government which are essential to public strength & private security and happiness. On the whole, the only enemy which republicanism has to fear in this country is in the spirit of faction and anarchy. If this will not permit the ends of government to be attained under it—if it engenders disorders in the community, all regular & orderly minds will wish for a change—and the demagogues who have produced the disorder will make it for their own aggrandizement. This is the old story.

If I were disposed to promote monarchy & overthrow state governments, I would mount the hobby horse of popularity—I would cry out usurpation—danger to liberty etc., etc.—I would endeavor to prostrate the national government—raise a ferment—and then "ride in the Whirlwind and direct the Storm." That there are men acting with Jefferson & Madison who have this in view I verily believe. I could lay my finger on some of them. That Madison does *not* mean it I also verily believe, and I rather believe the same of Jefferson; but I read him upon the whole thus—"A man of profound ambition & violent passions."

You must be by this time tired of my epistle. Perhaps I have treated certain characters with too much severity. I have however not meant to do them injustice—and from the bottom of my soul believe I have drawn them truly and that it is of the utmost consequence to the public weal they should be viewed in their true colors. . . .

An Administration Divided

On 25 July 1792, the following paragraph appeared in John Fenno's *Gazette of the United States* over the signature "T.L.":

The editor of the *National Gazette* receives a salary from government. Query—Whether this salary is paid him for translations, or for publications, the design of which is to vilify those to whom the voice of the people has committed the administration of public affairs.

In this, in two more notes over the same signature, and in a series of longer essays signed by "An American," all of them printed in the *Gazette of the United States* in July and August 1792, Hamilton went to war with his tormenters, accusing Jefferson of initially opposing the Constitution, identifying him as the leader of a determined opposition, and calling on him to resign his office if he could not support administration policies. Jefferson's friends, led by Madison and Monroe, jumped publicly (though anonymously) to his defense, and the rival editors of the two national newspapers were soon involved in a public argument over their relative independence from the political leaders. As the argument spread by way of reprintings into New England and the South, the whole country was treated to the spectacle of a full-blown newspaper war between the great executive officials.

Though Jefferson did not himself contribute to the public quarrel, he had long been warning Washington about Hamilton's character and designs. In July, Washington asked Hamilton to respond to the opposition's accusations (as these had been communicated to him by Jefferson). Then, in the middle of August, the president intervened with similar letters to the two principals, pleading for an end to public disputes. Both were chastened. Both were eager to persuade the president to serve another term. But neither would recede.

THOMAS JEFFERSON

Memorandum of a Conversation with the President

29 February 1792

. . . After breakfast we retired to his room & I unfolded my plan for the post-office, and after such an approbation of it as he usually permitted himself on the first presentment of any idea, and desiring me to commit it to writing, he, during that pause of conversation which follows a business closed, said in an affectionate tone that he had felt much concern at an expression which dropt from me yesterday & which marked my intention of retiring when he should. That as to himself, many motives obliged him to it. He had through the whole course of the war and most particularly at the close of it, uniformly declared his resolution to retire from public affairs & never to act in any public office; that he had retired under that firm resolution, that the government however which had been formed being found evidently too inefficacious, and it being supposed that his aid was of some consequence towards bringing the people to consent to one of sufficient efficacy for their own good, he consented to come into the [Constitutional] Convention & on the same motive, after much pressing, to take a part in the new government and get it under way. That were he to continue longer, it might give room to say that having tasted the sweets of office he could not do without them; that he really felt himself growing old, his bodily health less firm, his memory, always bad, becoming worse, and perhaps the other faculties of his mind showing a decay to others of which he was insensible himself, that this apprehension particularly oppressed him, that he found moreover his activity lessened, business therefore more irksome, and tranquility & retirement become an irresistible passion. That however he felt himself obliged for these reasons to retire from the government, yet he should consider it as unfortunate if that should bring on the retirement of the great officers of the government, and that this might produce a shock on the public mind of dangerous consequence. I told him that no man had ever had less desire of entering into public offices than myself; that the circumstance of a perilous war, which brought everything into danger & called for all the services which every citizen could render, had induced me to undertake the administration of the government of Virginia, that I had both before & after refused repeated appointments of Congress to go abroad in that sort of office, which if I had consulted my own gratification, would always have been the most agreeable to me, that at the end of two years, I resigned the government of Virginia & retired with a firm resolution never more to appear in public life, that a domestic loss however happened and made me fancy that absence & a change of scene for a time might be expedient for me, that I therefore accepted a foreign appointment limited to two years, that at the close of that, Dr. Franklin having left France, I was appointed to supply his place, which I had accepted, & tho' I continued in it three or four years, it was under the constant idea of remaining only a year or two longer; that the revolution in France coming on, I had so interested myself in the event of that, that when obliged to bring my family home, I had still an idea of returning & awaiting the close of that to fix the era of my final retirement; that on my arrival here I found he had appointed me to my present office, that he knew I had not come into it without some reluctance, that it was on my part a sacrifice of inclination to the opinion that I might be more serviceable here than in France, & with a firm resolution in my mind to indulge my constant wish for retirement at no very distant day: that when, therefore, I received his letter written from Mount Vernon on his way to Carolina & Georgia (April 1791) and discovered from an expression in that that he meant to retire from the government ere long, & as to the precise epoch there could be no doubt, my mind was immediately made up to make that the epoch of my own retirement from those labors of which I was heartily tired. That, however, I did not believe there was any idea in either of my brethren in the administration of retiring, that on the contrary I had perceived at a late meeting of the trustees of the sinking fund that the Secretary of the Treasury had developed the plan he intended to pursue, & that it embraced years in its view.— He said that he considered the Treasury Department as a much more limited one, going only to the single object of revenue, while that of the Secretary of State, embracing nearly all the objects of administration, was much more important, & the retirement of the officer therefore would be more noticed: that tho' the government had set out with a pretty general good will of the public, yet that symptoms of dissatisfaction had lately shown themselves far beyond what he could have expected, and to what height these might arise in case of too great a change in the administration, could not be foreseen.—

I told him that in my opinion there was only a single source of these discontents. Tho' they had indeed appeared to spread themselves over the War Department also, yet I considered that as an overflowing only from their real channel, which would never have taken place if they had not first been generated in another department, to wit that of the treasury. That a system had there been contrived for deluging the states with paper money instead of gold & silver, for withdrawing our citizens from the pursuits of commerce, manufactures, buildings, & other branches of useful industry, to occupy themselves & their capitals in a species of gambling destructive of morality & which had introduced its poison into the government itself. That it was a fact, as certainly known as that he & I were then conversing, that particular members of the legislature, while those laws were on the carpet, had feathered their nests with paper, had then voted for the laws, and

constantly since lent all the energy of their talents & instrumentality of their offices to the establishment & enlargement of this system: that they had chained it about our necks for a great length of time, & in order to keep the game in their hands had from time to time aided in making such legislative constructions of the Constitution as made it a very different thing from what the people thought they had submitted to; that they had now brought forward a proposition far beyond every one ever yet advanced, & to which the eyes of many were turned as the decision was to let us know whether we live under a limited or an unlimited government.—He asked me to what proposition I alluded? I answered to that in the Report on Manufactures which, under color of giving *bounties* for the encouragement of particular manufactures, meant to establish the doctrine that the power given by the Constitution to collect taxes to provide for the *general welfare* of the U.S. permitted Congress to take everything under their management which *they* should deem for the *public welfare* & which is susceptible of the application of money: consequently that the subsequent enumeration of their powers was not the description to which resort must be had, & did not at all constitute the limits of their authority: that this was a very different question from that of the bank, which was thought an incident to an enumerated power: that therefore this decision was expected with great anxiety: that indeed I hoped the proposition would be rejected, believing there was a majority in both houses against it, and that if it should be, it would be considered as a proof that things were returning into their true channel; & that at any rate I looked forward to the broad representation which would shortly take place for keeping the general constitution on its true ground, & that this would remove a great deal of the discontent which had shown itself. The conversation ended with this last topic. It is here stated nearly as much at length as it really was, the expressions preserved where I could recollect them, and their substance always faithfully stated.

Thomas Jefferson to George Washington

23 May 1792

I have determined to make the subject of a letter what for some time past has been a subject of inquietude to my mind without having found a good occasion of disburthening itself to you in conversation during the busy scenes which occupied you here. Perhaps too you may be able, in your present situation, or on the road, to give it more time & reflection than you could do here at any moment.

When you first mentioned to me your purpose of retiring from the government, tho' I felt all the magnitude of the event, I was in a considerable degree silent. I knew that to such a mind as yours, persuasion was idle & impertinent: that before forming your decision, you had weighed all the reasons for & against the measure, had made up your mind on full view of them, & that there could be little hope of changing the result. Pursuing my reflections too I knew we were some day to try to walk alone; and if the essay should be made while you should be alive & looking on, we should derive confidence from that circumstance & resource if it failed. The public mind too was calm & confident, and therefore in a favorable state for making the experiment. Had no change of circumstances intervened, I should not, with any hope of success, have now ventured to propose to you a change of purpose. But the public mind is no longer confident and serene; and that from causes in which you are in no ways personally mixed. Tho these causes have been hackneyed in the public papers in detail, it may not be amiss, in order to calculate the effect they are capable of producing, to take a view of them in the mass, giving to each the form, real or imaginary, under which they have been presented.

It has been urged then that a public debt, greater than we can possibly pay before other causes of adding new debt to it will occur, has been artificially created, by adding together the whole amount of the debtor & creditor sides of accounts instead of taking only their balances, which could have been paid off in a short time: That this accumulation of debt has taken forever out of our power those easy sources of revenue which, applied to the ordinary necessities and exigencies of government, would have answered them habitually and covered us from habitual murmurings against taxes & tax-gatherers, reserving extraordinary calls for those extraordinary occasions which would animate the people to meet them. That though the calls for money have been no greater than we must generally expect for the same or equivalent exigencies, yet we are already obliged to strain the impost till it produces clamor and will produce evasion & war on our own citizens to collect it: and even to resort to an *Excise* law, of odious character with the people, partial in its operation, unproductive unless enforced by arbitrary & vexatious means, and committing the authority of the government in parts where resistance is most probable & coercion least practicable. They cite propositions in Congress and suspect other projects on foot still to increase the mass of debt. They say that by borrowing at 2/3 of the interest, we might have paid off the principal in 2/3 of the time: but that from this we are precluded by its being made irredeemable but in small portions & long terms: That this irredeemable quality was given it for the avowed purpose of inviting its transfer to foreign countries. They predict that this transfer of the principal, when completed, will occasion an exportation of 3 millions of dollars annually for the interest, a drain of coin of which as there has been no example, no calculation can be made of its consequences: That the banishment of our coin will be completed by the creation of 10 millions of paper money in the form of bank bills, now issuing into circulation. They think the 10 or 12 percent annual profit paid to the lenders of this paper medium taken out of the pockets of the people, who would have had without interest the coin it is banishing. That all the capital employed in paper speculation is barren & useless, producing, like that on a gaming table, no accession to itself, and is withdrawn from commerce & agriculture where it would have produced addition to the common mass: That it nourishes in our citizens habits of vice and idleness instead of industry & morality: That it has furnished effectual means of corrupting such a portion of the legislature as turns the balance between the honest voters whichever way it is directed: That this corrupt squadron, deciding the voice of the legislature, have manifested their dispositions to get rid of the limitations imposed by the Constitution on the general legislature, limitations on the faith of which the states acceded to that instrument: That the ultimate object of all this is to prepare the way for a change from the present republican form of government to that of a monarchy, of which the English constitution is to be the model. That this was contemplated in the Convention is no secret, because its partisans have made none of it. To effect it then was impracticable, but they are still eager after their object, and are predisposing everything for its ultimate attainment. So many of them have got into the legislature that, aided by the corrupt squadron of paper dealers, who are at their devotion, they make a majority in both houses. The republican party, who wish to preserve the government in its present form, are fewer in number. They are fewer even when joined by the two, three, or half dozen anti-federalists, who, tho they dare not avow it, are still opposed to any general government: but being less so to a republican than a monarchical one, they naturally join those whom they think pursuing the lesser evil.

Of all the mischiefs objected to the system of measures before mentioned, none is so afflicting and fatal to every honest hope as the corruption of the legislature. As it was the earliest of these measures, it became the instrument for producing the rest, & will be the instrument for producing in future a king, lords & commons, or whatever else those who direct it may choose. Withdrawn such a distance from the eye of their constituents, and these so dispersed as to be inaccessible to public information, & particularly to that of the conduct of their own representatives, they will form the most corrupt government on earth, if the means of their corruption be not prevented. The only hope of safety hangs now on the numerous representation which is to come forward the ensuing year. Some of the new members will probably be, either in principle or interest, with the present majority, but it is expected that the great mass will form an accession to the republican party. They will not be able to undo all which the two preceding legislatures, & especially the first, have done. Public faith & right will oppose this. But some parts of the system may be rightfully reformed; a liberation from the rest unremittingly pursued as fast as right will permit, & the door shut in future against similar commitments of the nation. Should the next legislature take this course, it will draw upon them the whole monarchical & paper interest. But the latter I think will not go all lengths with the former, because creditors will never, of their own accord, fly off entirely from their debtors. Therefore this is the alternative least likely to produce convulsion. But should the majority of the new members be still in the same principles with the present, & show that we have nothing to expect but a continuance of the same practices, it is not easy to conjecture what would be the result, nor what means would be resorted to for correction of the evil. True wisdom would direct that they should be temperate & peaceable, but the division of sentiment & interest happens unfortunately to be so geographical that no mortal can say that what is most wise & temperate would prevail against what is most easy & obvious. I can scarcely contemplate a more incalculable evil than the breaking of the union into two or more parts. Yet when we review the mass which opposed the original coalescence, when we consider that it lay chiefly in the Southern quarter, that the

legislature have availed themselves of no occasion of allaying it, but on the contrary whenever Northern & Southern prejudices have come into conflict, the latter have been sacrificed & the former soothed; that the owners of the debt are in the Southern & the holders of it in the Northern division; that the Antifederal champions are now strengthened in argument by the fulfilment of their predictions; that this has been brought about by the Monarchical federalists themselves, who, having been for the new government merely as a stepping stone to monarchy, have themselves adopted the very constructions of the Constitution of which, when advocating its acceptance before the tribunal of the people, they declared it insusceptible; that the republican federalists, who espoused the same government for its intrinsic merits, are disarmed of their weapons, that which they denied as prophecy being now become true history: who can be sure that these things may not proselyte the small number which was wanting to place the majority on the other side? And this is the event at which I tremble, & to prevent which I consider your continuance at the head of affairs as of the last importance. The confidence of the whole union is centered in you. Your being at the helm will be more than an answer to every argument which can be used to alarm & lead the people in any quarter into violence or secession. North & South will hang together if they have you to hang on; and, if the first correction of a numerous representation should fail in its effect, your presence will give time for trying others not inconsistent with the union & peace of the states.

I am perfectly aware of the oppression under which your present office lays your mind & of the ardor with which you pant for retirement to domestic life. But there is sometimes an eminence of character on which society have such peculiar claims as to control the predilection of the individual for a particular walk of happiness, & restrain him to that alone arising from the present & future benedictions of mankind. This seems to be your condition & the law imposed on you by providence in forming your character & fashioning the events on which it was to operate; and it is to motives like these, & not to personal anxieties of mine or others who have no right to call on you for sacrifices, that I appeal from your former determination & urge a revisal of it, on the ground of change in the aspect of things. Should an honest majority result from the new & enlarged representation; should those acquiesce whose principles or interest they may control, your wishes for retirement would be gratified with less danger as soon as that shall be manifest, without awaiting the completion of the second period of four years. One or two sessions will determine the crisis; and I cannot but hope that you can resolve to add one or two more to the many years you have already sacrificed to the good of mankind. . . .

THOMAS JEFFERSON

Memorandum of a Conversation with Washington

10 July 1792

My letter of [May 23] to the President, directed to him at Mt. Vernon, had not found him there, but came to him here. He told me of this & that he would take an occasion of speaking with me on the subject. He did so this day. He began by observing that he had put it off from day to day because the subject was painful, to wit his remaining in office which that letter solicited. He said that the declaration he had made when he quitted his military command of never again acting in public was sincere. That however when he was called on to come forward to set the present government in motion, it appeared to him that circumstances were so changed as to justify a change in his resolution: he was made to believe that in 2 years all would be well in motion & he might retire. At the end of two years he found some things still to be done. At the end of the 3d year he thought it was not worthwhile to disturb the course of things as in one year more his office would expire & he was decided then to retire. Now he was told there would still be danger in it. Certainly, if he thought so, he would conquer his longing for retirement. But he feared it would be said his former professions of retirement had been mere affectation, & that he was like other men, when once in office he could not quit it. He was sensible too of a decay of his hearing; perhaps his other faculties might fall off & he not be sensible of it. That with respect to the existing causes of uneasiness, he thought there were suspicions against a particular party which had been carried a great deal too far, there might be *desires,* but he did not believe there were *designs* to change the form of government into a monarchy. That there might be a few who wished it in the higher walks of life, particularly in the

great cities, but that the main body of the people in the Eastern states were as steadily for republicanism as in the Southern. That the pieces lately published, & particularly in Freneau's paper, seemed to have in view the exciting opposition to the government. That this had taken place in Pennsylvania as to the excise law, according to information he had received from General Hand, that they tended to produce a separation of the Union, the most dreadful of all calamities, and that whatever tended to produce anarchy, tended of course to produce a resort to monarchical government. He considered those papers as attacking him directly, for he must be a fool indeed to swallow the little sugar plumbs here & there thrown out to him. That in condemning the administration of the government they condemned him, for if they thought there were measures pursued contrary to his sentiment, they must conceive him too careless to attend to them or too stupid to understand them. That tho indeed he had signed many acts which he did not approve in all their parts, yet he had never put his name to one which he did not think on the whole was eligible. That as to the bank, which had been an act of so much complaint, until there was some infallible criterion of reason, a difference of opinion must be tolerated. He did not believe the discontents extended far from the seat of government. He had seen & spoken with many people in Maryland & Virginia in his late journey. He found the people contented & happy. He wished however to be better informed on this head. If the discontent were more extensive than he supposed, it might be that the desire that he should remain in the government was not general.

My observations to him tended principally to enforce the topics of my letter. I will not therefore repeat them except where they produced observations from him. I said that the two great complaints were that the national debt was unnecessarily increased, & that it had furnished the means of corrupting both branches of the legislature. That he must know & everybody knew there was a considerable squadron in both whose votes were devoted to the paper & stock-jobbing interest, that the names of a weighty number were known & several others suspected on good grounds. That on examining the votes of these men they would be found uniformly for every treasury measure, & that as most of these measures had been carried by small majorities they were carried by these very votes. That therefore it was a cause of just uneasiness when we saw a legislature legislating for their own interests in opposition to those of the people. He said not a word on the corruption of the legislature, but took up the other point, defended the assumption, & argued that it had not increased the debt, for that all of it was honest debt. He justified the excise law, as one of the best laws which could be past, as nobody would pay the tax who did not choose to do it. With respect to the increase of the debt by the assumption, I observed to him that what was meant & objected to was that it increased the debt of the general government and carried it beyond the possibility of payment. That if the balances had been settled & the debtor states directed to pay their deficiencies to the creditor states, they would have done it easily and by resources of taxation in their power and acceptable to the people, by a direct tax in the South & an excise in the North. Still he said it would be paid by the people. Finding him really approving the treasury system I avoided entering into argument with him on those points.

Alexander Hamilton to George Washington, Objections and Answers Respecting the Administration of the Government

August 1792

I. Object. The public debt is greater than we can possibly pay before other causes of adding to it will occur; and this has been artificially created by adding together the *whole amount* of the debtor and creditor sides of the account.

Answer. The public debt was produced by the late war. It is not the fault of the present government that it exists, unless it can be proved that public morality and policy do not require of a government an honest provision for its debts. Whether it is greater than can be paid before new causes of adding to it will occur is a problem incapable of being solved but by experience; and this would be the case if it were not one fourth as much as it is. If the policy of the country be prudent, cautious and *neutral* towards foreign nations, . . . there is a rational probability that war may be avoided long enough to wipe off the debt. The Dutch, in a situation not near so favorable for it as that of the U States, have enjoyed intervals of peace longer than with proper exertions would suffice for the purpose. The debt of the U States compared with its present and

growing abilities is really a very light one. It is little more than 15,000,000 of pounds sterling, about the annual expenditure of Great Britain.

But whether the public debt shall be extinguished or not within a moderate period depends on the temper of the people. If they are rendered dissatisfied by misrepresentation of the measures of the government, the government will be deprived of an efficient command of the resources of the community towards extinguishing the debt. And thus, those who clamor are likely to be the principal causes of protracting the existence of the debt.

As to having been artificially increased, this is denied; perhaps indeed the true reproach of the system which has been adopted is that it has artificially diminished the debt as will be explained by and by.

The assertion that the debt has been increased by adding together the whole amount of the debtor and creditor sides of the account, not being very easy to be understood, is not easy to be answered. . . .

The general inducements to a provision for the public debt are—I. To preserve the public faith and integrity by fulfilling as far as was practicable the public engagements. II. To manifest a due respect for property by satisfying the public obligations in the hands of the public creditors and which were as much their property as their houses or their lands, their hats or their coats. III. To revive and establish public credit, the palladium of public safety. IV. To preserve the government itself by showing it worthy of the confidence which was placed in it, to procure to the community the blessings which in innumerable ways attend confidence in the government, and to avoid the evils which in as many ways attend the want of confidence in it.

The particular inducements to an assumption of the state debts were—I. To consolidate the finances of the country and give an assurance of permanent order in them, avoiding the collisions of thirteen different and independent systems of finance under concurrent and coequal authorities and the scramblings for revenue which would have been incident to so many different systems. II. To secure to the Government of the Union, by avoiding those entanglements, an effectual command of the resources of the Union for present and future exigencies. III. To *equalize the condition* of the *citizens* of the several states in the important article of taxation, rescuing a part of them from being oppressed with burthens beyond their strength, on account of extraordinary exertions in the war and through the want of certain adventitious resources, which it was the good fortune of others to possess.

A mind naturally attached to order and system and capable of appreciating their immense value, unless misled by particular feelings, is struck at once with the prodigious advantages which in the course of time must attend such a simplification of the financial affairs of the country as results from placing all the parts of the public debt upon one footing—under one direction—regulated by one provision. The want of this sound policy has been a continual source of disorder and embarrassment in the affairs of the United Netherlands.

The true justice of the case of the public debt consists in that equalization of the condition of the citizens of all the states which must arise from a consolidation of the debt and common contributions towards its extinguishment. Little inequalities, as to the past, can bear no comparison with the more lasting inequalities which, without the assumption, would have characterized the future condition of the people of the U States, leaving upon those who had done most or suffered most a great additional weight of burthen.

If the foregoing inducements to a provision for the public debt (including an assumption of the state debts) were sufficiently cogent—then the justification of the excise law lies within a narrow compass. Some further source of revenue, besides the duties on imports, was indispensable, and none equally productive would have been so little exceptionable to the mass of the people.

Other reasons cooperated in the minds of some able men to render an excise at an early period desirable. They thought it well to lay hold of so valuable a resource of revenue before it was generally preoccupied by the state governments. They supposed it not amiss that the authority of the national government should be visible in some branch of internal revenue, lest a total non-exercise of it should beget an impression that it was never to be exercised & next that it ought not to be exercised. It was supposed too that a thing of the kind could not be introduced with a greater prospect of easy success than at a period when the government enjoyed the advantage of first impressions—when state-factions to resist its authority were not yet matured—when so much aid was to be derived from the popularity and firmness of the actual Chief Magistrate.

Facts hitherto do not indicate the measure to have been rash or ill advised. The law is in operation with perfect acquiescence in all the states north of New York, though they contribute most largely. In New York and New Jersey it is in full operation, with some very partial complainings fast wearing away. In the greatest part of Pennsylvania it is in operation and with increasing good humor towards it. The four western counties continue exceptions. In Delaware it has had some struggle, which by the last accounts was surmounted. In Maryland and Virginia, it is in operation and without material conflict. In South Carolina it is now in pretty full operation, though in the interior parts it has had some serious opposition to overcome. In Georgia, no material difficulty has been experienced. North Carolina, Kentucky, & the four western counties of Pennsylvania present the only remaining impediments of any consequence to the full execution of the law. The latest advices from NC & Kentucky were more favorable than the former. . . .

The debt existed. It was to be provided for. In whatever shape the provision was made the object of speculation and the speculation would have existed. Nothing but abolishing the debt could have obviated it. It is therefore the fault of the Revolution not of the government that paper speculation exists.

An unsound or precarious provision would have increased this species of speculation in its most odious forms. The defects & casualties of the system would have been as much subjects of speculation as the debt itself.

The difference is that under a bad system the public stock would have been too uncertain an article to be a substitute for money & all the money employed in it would have been diverted from useful employment without anything to compensate for it. Under a good system the stock becomes more than a substitute for the money employed in negotiating it. . . .

Objection 11. Paper Speculation nourishes in our citizens &c.

Answer. This proposition within certain limits is true. Jobbing in the funds has some bad effects among those engaged in it. It fosters a spirit of gambling and diverts a certain number of individuals from other pursuits. But if the proposition be true that stock operates as capital, the effect upon the citizens at large is different. It promotes among them industry by furnishing a larger field of employment. Though this effect of a funded debt has been called in question in England by some theorists, yet most theorists & all practical men allow its existence. And there is no doubt, as already intimated, that if we look into those scenes among ourselves where the largest portions of the debt are accumulated we shall perceive that a new spring has been given to industry in various branches.

But be all this as it may, the observation made under the last head applies here. The debt was the creature of the Revolution. It was to be provided for. Being so, in whatever form, it must have become an object of speculation and jobbing.

Objection 12.   The funding of the debt has furnished effectual means of corrupting &c.

Answer.   This is one of those assertions which can only be denied and pronounced to be malignant and false. No facts exist to support it, and being a mere matter of fact, no *argument* can be brought to repel it.

The assertors beg the question. They assume to themselves and to those who think with them infallibility. Take their words for it, they are the only honest men in the community. But compare the tenor of men's lives and *at least* as large a proportion of virtuous and independent characters will be found among those whom they malign as among themselves.

A member of a majority of the legislature would say to these defamers—

"In your vocabulary, Gentlemen, *creditor* and *enemy* appear to be synonymous terms—the *support of public credit* and *corruption* of similar import—an *enlarged* and *liberal* construction of the Constitution for the public good and for the maintenance of the due energy of the national authority of the same meaning with usurpation and a conspiracy to overturn the republican government of the country—every man of a different opinion from your own an ambitious despot or a corrupt knave. You bring everything to the standard of your narrow and depraved ideas, and you condemn without mercy or even decency whatever does not accord with it. Every man who is either too long or too short for your political couch must be stretched or lopped to suit it. But your pretensions must be rejected. Your insinuations despised. Your politics originate in immorality, in a disregard of the maxims of good faith and the rights of property, and if they could prevail must end in national disgrace and confusion. Your rules of construction for the authorities vested in the Government of the Union would arrest all its essential movements and

bring it back in practice to the same state of imbecility which rendered the old confederation contemptible. Your principles of liberty are principles of licentiousness incompatible with all government. You sacrifice everything that is venerable and substantial in society to the vain reveries of a false and new fangled philosophy. As to the motives by which I have been influenced, I leave my general conduct in private and public life to speak for them. Go and learn among my *fellow citizens* whether I have not uniformly maintained the character of an honest man. As to the love of liberty and country, you have given no stronger proofs of being actuated by it than I have done. Cease then to arrogate to yourself and to your party all the patriotism and virtue of the country. Renounce if you can the intolerant spirit by which you are governed—and begin to reform yourself instead of reprobating others, by beginning to doubt of your own infallibility."

Such is the answer which would naturally be given by a member of the majority in the legislature to such an objector. And it is the only one that could be given, until some evidence of the supposed corruption should be produced.

As far as I know, there is not a member of the legislature who can properly be called a stock-jobber or a paper dealer. There are several of them who were proprietors of public debt in various ways. Some for money lent & property furnished for the use of the public during the war, others for sums received in payment of debts—and it is supposeable enough that some of them had been purchasers of the public debt with intention to hold it as a valuable & convenient property, considering an honorable provision for it as matter of course.

It is a strange perversion of ideas, and as novel as it is extraordinary, that men should be deemed corrupt & criminal for becoming proprietors in the funds of their country. Yet I believe the number of members of Congress is very small who have ever been considerably proprietors in the funds.

And as to improper speculations on measures depending before Congress, I believe never was any *body* of men freer from them.

There are indeed several members of Congress who have become proprietors in the Bank of the United States, and a *few* of them to a pretty large amount, say 50 or 60 shares; but all operations of this kind were necessarily subsequent to the determination upon the measure. The subscriptions were of course subsequent & purchases still more so. Can there be anything really blameable in this? Can it be culpable to invest property in an institution which has been established for the most important national purposes? Can that property be supposed to corrupt the holder? It would indeed tend to render him friendly to the preservation of the Bank; but in this there would be no collision between duty & interest, and it could give him no improper bias in other questions.

To uphold public credit and to be friendly to the Bank must be presupposed to be *corrupt things* before the being a proprietor in the funds or of bank stock can be supposed to have a *corrupting influence*. The being a proprietor in either case is a very different thing from being, in a proper sense of the term, a stock jobber. On this point of the corruption of the legislature one more observation of great weight remains. Those who oppose a *funded* debt and mean any provision for it contemplate an *annual* one. Now, it is impossible to conceive a more fruitful source of legislative corruption than this. All the members of it who should incline to speculate would have an annual opportunity of speculating upon their influence in the legislature to promote or retard or put off a provision. Every session the question whether the annual provision should be continued would be an occasion of pernicious caballing and corrupt bargaining. In this very view when the subject was in deliberation, it was impossible not to wish it declared upon once for all & out of the way.

Objection the 13. The Corrupt Squadron &c.

Here again the objectors beg the question. They take it for granted that their constructions of the Constitution are right and that the opposite ones are wrong, and with great good nature and candor ascribe the effect of a difference of opinion to a disposition to get rid of the limitations on the government.

Those who have advocated the constructions which have obtained have met their opponents on the ground of fair argument and they think have refuted them. How shall it be determined which side is right?

There are some things which the general government has clearly a right to do—there are others which it has clearly no right to meddle with, and there is a good deal of middle ground, about which honest & well disposed men may differ. The most that can be said is that some of this middle ground may have been occupied by the national legislature; and this surely is no evidence of a disposition to get rid of the limitations in the Constitution, nor can it be viewed in that light by men of candor.

The truth is one description of men is disposed to do the essential business of the nation by a liberal construction of the powers of the government; another from disaffection would fritter away those powers—a third from an over-weening jealousy would do the same thing—a fourth from party & personal opposition are torturing the Constitution into objections to everything they do not like.

The Bank is one of the measures which is deemed by some the greatest stretch of power; and yet its constitutionality has been established in the most satisfactory manner.

And the most incorrigible theorist among its opponents would in one month's experience as head of the Department of the Treasury be compelled to acknowledge that it is an absolutely indispensable engine in the management of the finances and would quickly become a convert to its perfect constitutionality.

Objection XIV. The ultimate object of all.

To this there is no other answer than a flat denial—except this, that the project from its absurdity refutes itself.

The idea of introducing a monarchy or aristocracy into this country by employing the influence and force of a government continually changing hands towards it is one of those visionary things that none but madmen could meditate and that no wise men will believe.

If it could be done at all, which is utterly incredible, it would require a long series of time, certainly beyond the life of any individual to effect it. Who then would enter into such plot? For what purpose of interest or ambition?

To hope that the people may be cajoled into giving their sanctions to such institutions is still more chimerical. A people so enlightened and so diversified as the people of this country can surely never be brought to it but from convulsions and disorders, in consequence of the acts of popular demagogues.

The truth unquestionably is that the only path to a subversion of the republican system of the country is by flattering the prejudices of the people and exciting their jealousies and apprehensions, to throw affairs into confusion and bring on civil commotion. Tired at length of anarchy, or want of government, they may take shelter in the arms of monarchy for repose and security.

Those, then, who resist a confirmation of public order are the true artificers of monarchy—not that this is the intention of the generality of them. Yet it would not be difficult to lay the finger upon some of their party who may justly be suspected. When a man unprincipled in private life, desperate in his fortune, bold in his temper, possessed of considerable talents, having the advantage of military habits—despotic in his ordinary demeanour—known to have scoffed in private at the principles of liberty—when such a man [Aaron Burr?] is seen to mount the hobby horse of popularity—to join in the cry of danger to liberty—to take every opportunity of embarrassing the general government & bringing it under suspicion—to flatter and fall in with all the nonsense of the zealots of the day—It may justly be suspected that his object is to throw things into confusion that he may "ride the storm and direct the whirlwind."

It has aptly been observed that *Cato* was the Tory—*Caesar* the Whig of his day. The former frequently resisted—the latter always flattered—the follies of the people. Yet the former perished with the Republic; the latter destroyed it.

No popular government was ever without its Catalines & its Caesars. These are its true enemies.

As far as I am informed, the anxiety of those who are calumniated is to keep the government in the state in which it is, which they fear will be no easy task, from a natural tendency in the state of things to exalt the local on the ruins of the national government. Some of them appear to wish, in a constitutional way, a change in the judiciary department of the government, from an apprehension that an orderly and effectual administration of justice cannot be obtained without a more intimate connection between the state and national tribunals. But even this is not an object of any set of men as a party. There is a difference of opinion about it on various grounds among those who have generally acted together. As to any other change of consequence, I believe nobody dreams of it.

Tis curious to observe the anticipations of the different parties. One side appears to believe that there is a serious plot to overturn the state governments and substitute monarchy to the present republican system. The other side firmly believes that there is a serious plot to overturn the general government & elevate the separate power of the states upon its ruins. Both sides may be equally wrong, & their mutual jealousies may be materially causes of the appearances which mutually disturb them and sharpen them against each other. . . .

No man, that I know of, contemplated the introducing into this country of a monarchy. A very small number (not more than three or four) manifested theoretical opinions favorable in the abstract to a constitution like that of Great Britain, but everyone agreed that such a constitution except as to the general distribution of departments and powers was out of the question in reference to this country. The member who was most explicit on this point (a member from New York) declared in strong terms that the republican theory ought to be adhered to in this country as long as there was any chance of its success—that the idea of a perfect equality of political rights among the citizens, exclusive of all permanent or hereditary distinctions, was of a nature to engage the good wishes of every good man, whatever might be his theoretic doubts—that it merited his best efforts to give success to it in practice—that hitherto from an incompetent structure of the government it had not had a fair trial, and that the endeavor ought then to be to secure to it a better chance of success by a government more capable of energy and order.

Alexander Hamilton to George Washington
9 September 1792

I have the pleasure of your private letter of the 26th of August.

The feelings and views which are manifested in that letter are such as I expected would exist. And I most sincerely regret the causes of the uneasy sensations you experience. It is my most anxious wish, as far as may depend upon me, to smooth the path of your administration, and to render it prosperous and happy. And if any prospect shall open of healing or terminating the differences which exist, I shall most cheerfully embrace it, though I consider myself as the deeply injured party. The recommendation of such a spirit is worthy of the moderation and wisdom which dictated it; and if your endeavors should prove unsuccessful, I do not hesitate to say that in my opinion the period is not remote when the public good will require *substitutes* for the *differing members* of your administration. The continuance of a division there must destroy the energy of government, which will be little enough with the strictest Union. On my part there will be a most cheerful acquiescence in such a result.

I trust, Sir, that the greatest frankness has always marked and will always mark every step of my conduct towards you. In this disposition, I cannot conceal from you that

I have had some instrumentality of late in the retaliations which have fallen upon certain public characters and that I find myself placed in a situation not to be able to recede *for the present.*

I considered myself as compelled to this conduct by reasons public as well as personal of the most cogent nature. I *know* that I have been an object of uniform opposition from Mr. Jefferson, from the first moment of his coming to the City of New York to enter upon his present office. I *know,* from the most authentic sources, that I have been the frequent subject of the most unkind whispers and insinuations from the same quarter. I have long seen a formed party in the legislature, under his auspices, bent upon my subversion. I cannot doubt, from the evidence I possess, that the *National Gazette* was instituted by him for political purposes and that one leading object of it has been to render me and all the measures connected with my department as odious as possible.

Nevertheless I can truly say that, except explanations to confidential friends, I never directly or indirectly retaliated or countenanced retaliation till very lately. I can even assure you that I was instrumental in preventing a very severe and systematic attack upon Mr. Jefferson by an association of two or three individuals, in consequence of the persecution which he brought upon the Vice President by his indiscreet and light letter to the printer, transmitting *Paine's* pamphlet.

As long as I saw no danger to the government from the machinations which were going on, I resolved to be a silent sufferer of the injuries which were done me. I determined to avoid giving occasion to anything which could manifest to the world dissentions among the principal characters of the government, a thing which can never happen without weakening its hands and in some degree throwing a stigma upon it.

But when I no longer doubted that there was a formed party deliberately bent upon the subversion of measures which in its consequences would subvert the government—when I saw that the undoing of the funding system in particular (which, whatever may be the original merits of that system, would prostrate the credit and the honor of the nation and bring the government into contempt with that description of men who are in every society the only firm supporters of government) was an avowed object of the party; and that all possible pains were taking to produce that effect by rendering it odious to the body of the people—I considered it as a duty to endeavour to resist the torrent, and as an essential mean to this end, to draw aside the veil from the principal actors. To this strong impulse, to this decided conviction, I have yielded. And I think events will prove that I have judged rightly.

Nevertheless I pledge my honor to you, Sir, that if you shall hereafter form a plan to reunite the members of your administration upon some steady principle of cooperation, I will faithfully concur in executing it during my continuance in office. And I will not directly or indirectly say or do a thing that shall endanger a feud. . . .

Thomas Jefferson to George Washington, Monticello

9 September 1792

. . . When I embarked in the government, it was with a determination to intermeddle not at all with the legislature, & as little as possible with my co-departments. The first and only instance of variance from the former part of my resolution, I was duped into by the Secretary of the Treasury and made a tool for forwarding his schemes, not then sufficiently understood by me; and of all the errors of my political life, this has occasioned me the deepest regret. It has ever been my purpose to explain this to you when, from being actors on the scene, we shall have become uninterested spectators only. The second part of my resolution has been religiously observed with the War Department &, as to that of the Treasury, has never been farther swerved from than by the mere enunciation of my sentiments in conversation, and chiefly among those who, expressing the same sentiments, drew mine from me. If it has been supposed that I have ever intrigued among the members of the legislatures to defeat the plans of the Secretary of the Treasury, it is contrary to all truth. As I never had the desire to influence the members, so neither had I any other means than my friendships, which I valued too highly to risk by usurpations on their freedom of judgment & the conscientious pursuit of their own sense of duty. That I have utterly, in my private conversations, disapproved of the system of the Secretary of the Treasury, I acknowledge & avow: and this was not merely a speculative difference. His system flowed from principles adverse to liberty, & was calculated to undermine and demolish the republic, by creating an influence of his department over the members of the legislature. I saw this influence actually produced, & its first fruits to be the establishment of the great outlines of his project by the votes of the very persons who, having swallowed his bait, were laying themselves out to profit by his plans: & that had these persons withdrawn, as those interested in a question ever should, the vote of the disinterested majority was clearly the reverse of what they made it. These were no longer the votes then of the representatives of the people, but of deserters from the rights & interests of the people: & it was impossible to consider their decisions, which had nothing in view but to enrich themselves, as the measures of the fair majority, which ought always to be respected.—If what was actually doing begat uneasiness in those who wished for virtuous government, what was further proposed was not less threatening to the friends of the Constitution. For, in a Report on the subject of manufactures (still to be acted on) it was expressly assumed that the general government has a right to exercise all powers which may be for the *general welfare,* that is to say all the legitimate powers of government: since no government has a legitimate right to do what is not for the welfare of the governed. There was indeed a sham-limitation of the universality of this power *to cases where money is to be employed.* But about what is it that money cannot be employed? Thus the object of these plans taken together is to draw all the powers of government into the hands of the general legislature, to establish means for corrupting a sufficient corps in that legislature to divide the honest votes & preponderate, by their own, the scale which suited, & to have that corps under the command of the Secretary of the Treasury for the purpose of subverting step by step the principles of the Constitution, which he has so often declared to be a thing of nothing which must be changed. Such views might have justified something more than mere expressions of dissent, beyond which, nevertheless, I never went.—Has abstinence from the department committed to me been equally observed by him? To say nothing of other interferences equally known, in the case of the two nations with which we have the most intimate connections, France & England, my system was to give some satisfactory distinctions to the former, of little cost to us, in return for the solid advantages yielded us by them; & to have met the English with some restrictions which might induce them to abate their severities against our commerce. I have always supposed this coincided with your sentiments. Yet the Secretary of the Treasury, by his cabals with members of the legislature, & by high-toned declamation on other occasions, has forced down his own system, which was exactly the reverse. He undertook, of his own authority, the conferences with the ministers of those two nations, & was, on every consultation, provided with some report of a conversation with the one or the other of them, adapted to his views. These views, thus made to prevail, their execution fell of course to me; & I can safely appeal to you, who have seen all my letters & proceedings, whether I have not carried them into execution as sincerely as if they had been my own, tho' I ever considered them as inconsistent with the honor & interest of our country. That they have been inconsistent with our interest is but too fatally proved by the stab to our navigation given by the French.—So that if the question be By whose fault is it that Colo. Hamilton & myself have not drawn together? the answer will depend on that to two other questions; whose principles of administration best justify, by their purity, conscientious adherence? and which of us has, notwithstanding, stepped farthest into the control of the department of the other?

To this justification of opinions, expressed in the way of conversation, against the views of Colo. Hamilton, I beg leave to add some notice of his late charges against me in Fenno's gazette; for neither the style, matter, nor venom of the pieces alluded to can leave a doubt of their author. Spelling my name & character at full length to the public, while he conceals his own under the signature of "An American," he charges me 1. With having written letters from Europe to my friends to oppose the present constitution while depending. 2. With a desire of not paying the public debt. 3. With setting up a paper to decry & slander the government. 1. The first charge is most false. No man in the U.S. I suppose, approved of every title in the Constitution; no one, I believe approved more of it than I did: and more of it was certainly disapproved by my accuser than by me, and of its parts most vitally republican. Of this the few letters I wrote on the subject (not half a dozen I believe) will be a proof: & for my own satisfaction & justification, I must tax you with the reading of them when I return to where they are. You will there see that my objection to the Constitution was that it wanted a bill of rights securing freedom of religion, freedom of the press, freedom from standing armies, trial by jury, & a constant Habeas Corpus act. Colo. Hamilton's was that it wanted a king and house of lords. The sense of America has approved my objection & added the bill of rights, not the king and lords. I also thought a longer term of service, insusceptible of renewal, would have made a President more independent. My country has thought otherwise, & I have acquiesced implicitly. He wishes the general government should have power to make laws binding the states in all cases whatsoever. Our country has thought otherwise: has he acquiesced? Notwithstanding my wish for a bill of rights, my letters strongly urged the adoption of the constitution, by nine states at least, to secure the good it contained. I at first thought that the best method of securing the bill of rights would be for four states to hold off till such a bill should be agreed to. But the moment I saw Mr. Hancock's proposition to pass the constitution as it stood and give perpetual instructions to the representatives of every state to insist on a bill of rights, I acknowledged the superiority of his plan, & advocated universal adoption. 2. The second charge is equally untrue. My whole correspondence while in France, & every word, letter, & act on the subject since my return, prove that no man is more ardently intent to see the public debt soon & sacredly paid off than I am. This exactly marks the difference between Colo. Hamilton's views & mine, that I would wish the debt paid tomorrow; he wishes it never to be paid, but always to be a thing wherewith to corrupt & manage the legislature. 3. I have never enquired what number of sons, relations, & friends of senators, representatives, printers or other useful partisans Colo. Hamilton has provided for among the hundred clerks of his department, the thousand excisemen, custom-house officers, loan officers, &c. &c. &c. appointed by him, or at his nod, and spread over the Union; nor could ever have imagined that the man who has the shuffling of millions backwards & forwards from paper into money & money into paper, from Europe to America, & America to Europe, the dealing out of Treasury-secrets among his friends in what time & measure he pleases, and who never slips an occasion for making friends with his means, that such a one I say would have brought forward a charge against me for having appointed the poet Freneau translating clerk to my office, with a salary of 250 dollars a year. That fact stands thus. While the government was at New York I was applied to

on behalf of Freneau to know if there was any place within my department to which he could be appointed. I answered there were but four clerkships, all of which I found full, and continued without any change. When we removed to Philadelphia, Mr. Pintard, the translating clerk, did not choose to remove with us. His office then became vacant. I was again applied to there for Freneau, & had no hesitation to promise the clerkship for him. I cannot recollect whether it was at the same time, or afterwards, that I was told he had a thought of setting up a newspaper there. But whether then, or afterwards, I considered it as a circumstance of some value, as it might enable me to do, what I had long wished to have done, that is, to have the material parts of the Leyden Gazette brought under your eye & that of the public, in order to possess yourself & them of a juster view of the affairs of Europe than could be obtained from any other public source. This I had ineffectually attempted through the press of Mr. Fenno while in New York, selecting & translating passages myself at first then having it done by Mr. Pintard the translating clerk, but they found their way too slowly into Mr. Fenno's papers. Mr. Bache essayed it for me in Philadelphia, but his being a daily paper, did not circulate sufficiently in the other states. He even tried, at my request, the plan of a weekly paper of recapitulation from his daily paper, in hopes that that might go into the other states, but in this too we failed. Freneau, as translating clerk & the printer of a periodical paper likely to circulate thro' the states (uniting in one person the parts of Pintard & Fenno) revived my hopes that the thing could at length be effected. On the establishment of his paper, therefore, I furnished him with the Leyden Gazettes, with an expression of my wish that he could always translate & publish the material intelligence they contained; & have continued to furnish them from time to time, as regularly as I received them. But as to any other direction or indication of my wish how his press should be conducted, what sort of intelligence he should give, what essays encourage, I can protest in the presence of heaven, that I never did by myself or any other, directly or indirectly, say a syllable, nor attempt any kind of influence. I can further protest, in the same awful presence, that I never did by myself or any other, directly or indirectly, write, dictate or procure any one sentence or sentiment to be inserted *in his, or any other, gazette* to which my name was not affixed or that of my office.—I surely need not except here a thing so foreign to the present subject as a little paragraph about our Algerine captives, which I put once into Fenno's paper.—Freneau's proposition to publish a paper, having been about the time that the writings of Publicola & the Discourses on Davila had a good deal excited the public attention, I took for granted from Freneau's character, which had been marked as that of a good whig, that he would give free place to pieces written against the aristocratical & monarchical principles these papers had inculcated. This having been in my mind, it is likely enough I may have expressed it in conversation with others; tho' I do not recollect that I did. To Freneau I think I could not, because I had still seen him but once, & that was at a public table, at breakfast, at Mrs. Elsworth's, as I passed thro' New York the last year. And I can safely declare that my expectations looked only to the chastisement of the aristocratical & monarchical writers, & not to any criticisms on the proceedings of government. Colo. Hamilton can see no motive for any appointment but that of making a convenient partizan. But you Sir, who have received from me recommendations of a Rittenhouse, Barlow, Paine, will believe that talents & science are sufficient motives with me in appointments to which they are fitted: & that Freneau, as a man of genius, might find a preference in my eye to be a translating clerk, & make good title to the little aids I could give him as the editor of a gazette, by procuring subscriptions to his paper, as I did some, before it appeared, & as I have with pleasure done for the labors of other men of genius. I hold it to be one of the distinguishing excellencies of elective over hereditary successions that the talents which nature has provided in sufficient proportion should be selected by the society for the government of their affairs, rather than that this should be transmitted through the loins of knaves & fools passing from the debauches of the table to those of the bed. . . . He & Fenno are rivals for the public favor. The one courts them by flattery, the other by censure, & I believe it will be admitted that the one has been as servile as the other severe. But is not the dignity, & even decency of government committed, when one of its principal ministers enlists himself as an anonymous writer or paragraphist for either the one or the other of them?—No government ought to be without censors; & where the press is free, no one ever will. If virtuous, it need not fear the fair operation of attack & defense. Nature has given

to man no other means of sifting out the truth either in religion, law, or politics. I think it as honorable to the government neither to know nor notice its sycophants or censors as it would be undignified & criminal to pamper the former & persecute the latter.—So much for the past. A word now of the future.

When I came into this office, it was with a resolution to retire from it as soon as I could with decency. It pretty early appeared to me that the proper moment would be the first of those epochs at which the constitution seems to have contemplated a periodical change or renewal of the public servants. In this I was confirmed by your resolution respecting the same period; from which however I am happy in hoping you have departed. I look to that period with the longing of a wave-worn mariner, who has at length the land in view, & shall count the days & hours which still lie between me & it. In the meanwhile my main object will be to wind up the business of my office, avoiding as much as possible all new enterprise. With the affairs of the legislature, as I never did intermeddle, so I certainly shall not now begin. I am more desirous to predispose everything for the repose to which I am withdrawing than expose it to be disturbed by newspaper contests. If these however cannot be avoided altogether, yet a regard for your quiet will be a sufficient motive for my deferring it till I become merely a private citizen, when the propriety or impropriety of what I may say or do may fall on myself alone. I may then too avoid the charge of misapplying that time which now belonging to those who employ me, should be wholly devoted to their service. If my own justification or the interests of the republic shall require it, I reserve to myself the right of then appealing to my country, subscribing my name to whatever I write, & using with freedom & truth the facts & names necessary to place the cause in its just form before that tribunal. To a thorough disregard of the honors & emoluments of office I join as great a value for the esteem of my countrymen, & conscious of having merited it by an integrity which cannot be reproached, & by an enthusiastic devotion to their rights & liberty, I will not suffer my retirement to be clouded by the slanders of a man whose history, from the moment at which history can stoop to notice him, is a tissue of machinations against the liberty of the country which has not only received and given him bread, but heaped its honors on his head.—Still however I repeat the hope that it will not be necessary to make such an appeal. Though little known to the people of America, I believe that, as far as I am known, it is not as an enemy to the republic, nor an intriguer against it, nor a waster of its revenue, nor prostitutor of it to the purposes of corruption, as the American represents me; and I confide that yourself are satisfied that, as to dissensions in the newspapers, not a syllable of them has ever proceeded from me; & that no cabals or intrigues of mine have produced those in the legislature, & I hope I may promise, both to you & myself, that none will receive aliment from me during the short space I have to remain in office, which will find ample employment in closing the present business of the department. . . .

THOMAS JEFFERSON

Memorandum of a Conversation with the President

1 October 1792

. . . [Washington] expressed his concern at the difference which he found to subsist between the Sec. of the Treasury & myself, of which he said he had not been aware. He knew indeed that there was a marked difference in our political sentiments, but he had never suspected it had gone so far in producing a personal difference, and he wished he could be the mediator to put an end to it. That he thought it important to preserve the check of my opinions in the administration in order to keep things in their proper channel & prevent them from going too far. That as to the idea of transforming this government into a monarchy he did not believe there were ten men in the U.S. whose opinions were worth attention who entertained such a thought. I told him there were many more than he imagined. I recalled to his memory a dispute at his own table a little before we left Philadelphia, between General Schuyler on one side & Pinckney & myself on the other, wherein the former maintained the position that hereditary descent was as likely to produce good magistrates as election. I told him that tho' the people were sound, there were a numerous sect who had monarchy in contemplation. That the Secretary of the Treasury was one of these. That I had heard him say that this constitution was a shilly shally thing of mere milk & water, which could not last, & was only good as a step to something better. That when we reflected that he had

endeavored in the convention to make an English constitution of it, and when failing in that we saw all his measures tending to bring it to the same thing, it was natural for us to be jealous: and particularly when we saw that these measures had established corruption in the legislature, where there was a squadron devoted to the nod of the treasury, doing whatever he had directed & ready to do what he should direct. That if the equilibrium of the three great bodies legislative, executive, & judiciary could be preserved, if the legislative could be kept independent, I should never fear the result of such a government but that I could not but be uneasy when I saw that the executive had swallowed up the legislative branch. He said that as to that interested spirit in the legislature, it was what could not be avoided in any government, unless we were to exclude particular descriptions of men, such as the holders of the funds from all office. I told him there was great difference between the little accidental schemes of self interest which would take place in every body of men & influence their votes, and a regular system for forming a corps of interested persons who should be steadily at the orders of the Treasury. He touched on the merits of the funding system, observed that there was a difference of opinion about it, some thinking it very bad, others very good. That experience was the only criterion of right which he knew & this alone would decide which opinion was right. That for himself he had seen our affairs desperate & our credit lost, and that this was in a sudden & extraordinary degree raised to the highest pitch. I told him all that was ever necessary to establish our credit was an efficient government & an honest one declaring it would sacredly pay our debts, laying taxes for this purpose & applying them to it. I avoided going further into the subject. He finished by another exhortation to me not to decide too positively on retirement, & here we were called to breakfast.

THOMAS JEFFERSON

Memorandum of a Conversation with the President

7 February 1793

. . . [Washington expressed] his earnest wish that Hamilton & myself could coalesce in the measures of the government, and urged here the general reasons for it which he had done to me on two former conversations. He said he had proposed the same thing to Hamilton, who expressed his readiness, and he thought our coalition would secure the general acquiescence of the public. I told him my concurrence was of much less importance than he seemed to imagine; that I kept myself aloof from all cabal & correspondence on the subject of the government & saw & spoke with as few as I could. That as to a coalition with Mr. Hamilton, if by that was meant that either was to sacrifice his general system to the other, it was impossible. We had both no doubt formed our conclusions after the most mature consideration, and principles conscientiously adopted could not be given up on either side. My wish was to see both houses of Congress cleansed of all persons interested in the bank or public stocks; & that a pure legislature being given us, I should always be ready to acquiesce under their determinations even if contrary to my own opinions, for that I subscribe to the principle that the will of the majority honestly expressed should give law. I confirmed him in the fact of the great discontents to the South, that they were grounded on seeing that their judgments & interests were sacrificed to those of the Eastern states on every occasion & their belief that it was the effect of a corrupt squadron of voters in Congress at the command of the Treasury, & they see that if the votes of those members who had an interest distinct from & contrary to the general interest of their constituents had been withdrawn, as in decency & honesty they should have been, the laws would have been the reverse of what they are in all the great questions. I instanced the new assumption carried in the House of Representatives by the Speaker's votes. On this subject he made no reply. . . .

JAMES MADISON

Further Essays for the *National Gazette*

"Spirit of Governments"

18 February 1792

No government is perhaps reducible to a sole principle of operation. Where the theory approaches nearest to this character, different and often heterogeneous principles mingle their influence in the administration. It is useful nevertheless to analyze the several kinds of government, and to characterize them by the spirit which predominates in each.

Montesquieu has resolved the great operative principles of government into fear, honor, and virtue, applying the first to pure despotisms, the second to regular monarchies, and the third to republics. The portion of truth blended with the ingenuity of this system sufficiently justifies the admiration bestowed on its author. Its accuracy however can never be defended against the criticisms which it has encountered. Montesquieu was in politics not a Newton or a Locke, who established immortal systems, the one in matter, the other in mind. He was in his particular science what Bacon was in universal science: He lifted the veil from the venerable errors which enslaved opinion and pointed the way to those luminous truths of which he had but a glimpse himself.

May not governments be properly divided, according to their predominant spirit and principles, into three species of which the following are examples?

First. A government operating by a permanent military force, which at once maintains the government and is maintained by it; which is at once the cause of burdens on the people and of submission in the people to their burdens. Such have been the governments under which human nature has groaned through every age. Such are the governments which still oppress it in almost every country of Europe, the quarter of the globe which calls itself the pattern of civilization and the pride of humanity.

Secondly. A government operating by corrupt influence; substituting the motive of private interest in place of public duty; converting its pecuniary dispensations into bounties to favorites or bribes to opponents; accommodating its measures to the avidity of a part of the nation instead of the benefit of the whole: in a word, enlisting an army of interested partizans, whose tongues, whose pens, whose intrigues, and whose active combinations, by supplying the terror of the sword, may support a real domination of the few under an apparent liberty of the many. Such a government, wherever to be found, is an imposter. It is happy for the new world that it is not on the west side of the Atlantic. It will be both happy and honorable for the United States if they never descend to mimic the costly pageantry of its form, nor betray themselves into the venal spirit of its administration.

Thirdly. A government deriving its energy from the will of the society, and operating by the reason of its measures on the understanding and interest of the society. Such is the government for which philosophy has been searching, and humanity been sighing, from the most remote ages. Such are the republican governments which it is the glory of America to have invented, and her unrivalled happiness to possess. May her glory be completed by every improvement on the theory which experience may teach; and her happiness be perpetuated by a system of administration corresponding with the purity of the theory.

"A Candid State of Parties"

22 September 1792

As it is the business of the contemplative statesman to trace the history of parties in a free country, so it is the duty of the citizen at all times to understand the actual state of them. Whenever this duty is omitted, an opportunity is given to designing men, by the use of artificial or nominal distinctions, to oppose and balance against each other those who never differed as to the end to be pursued, and may no longer differ as to the means of attaining it. The most interesting state of parties in the United States may be referred to three periods. Those who espoused the cause of independence and those who adhered to the British claims formed the parties of the first period, if, indeed, the disaffected class were considerable enough to deserve the name of a party. This state of things was superseded by the treaty of peace in 1783. From 1783 to 1787 there were parties in abundance, but being rather local than general, they are not within the present review.

The Federal Constitution, proposed in the latter year, gave birth to a second and most interesting division of the people. Everyone remembers it, because everyone was involved in it.

Among those who embraced the Constitution, the great body were unquestionably friends to republican liberty, tho' there were, no doubt, some who were openly or secretly attached to monarchy and aristocracy, and hoped to make the Constitution a cradle for these hereditary establishments.

Among those who opposed the Constitution, the great body were certainly well affected to the union and to good government, tho' there might be a few who had a leaning

unfavorable to both. This state of parties was terminated by the regular and effectual establishment of the federal government in 1788; out of the administration of which, however, has arisen a third division, which being natural to most political societies, is likely to be of some duration in ours.

One of the divisions consists of those who, from particular interest, from natural temper, or from the habits of life, are more partial to the opulent than to the other classes of society; and having debauched themselves into a persuasion that mankind are incapable of governing themselves, it follows with them, of course, that government can be carried on only by the pageantry of rank, the influence of money and emoluments, and the terror of military force. Men of those sentiments must naturally wish to point the measures of government less to the interest of the many than of a few, and less to the reason of the many than to their weaknesses; hoping perhaps in proportion to the ardor of their zeal, that by giving such a turn to the administration, the government itself may by degrees be narrowed into fewer hands and approximated to a hereditary form.

The other division consists of those who, believing in the doctrine that mankind are capable of governing themselves and hating hereditary power as an insult to the reason and an outrage to the rights of man, are naturally offended at every public measure that does not appeal to the understanding and to the general interests of the community, or that is not strictly conformable to the principles and conducive to the preservation of republican government.

This being the real state of parties among us, an experienced and dispassionate observer will be at no loss to decide on the probable conduct of each.

The antirepublican party, as it may be called, being the weaker in point of numbers, will be induced by the most obvious motives to strengthen themselves with the men of influence, particularly of moneyed, which is the most active and insinuating influence. It will be equally their true policy to weaken their opponents by reviving exploded parties and taking advantage of all prejudices, local, political, and occupational, that may prevent or disturb a general coalition of sentiments.

The Republican party, as it may be termed, conscious that the mass of people in every part of the union, in every state, and of every occupation must at bottom be with them, both in interest and sentiment, will naturally find their account in burying all antecedent questions, in banishing every other distinction than that between enemies and friends to republican government, and in promoting a general harmony among the latter, wherever residing or however employed.

Whether the republican or the rival party will ultimately establish its ascendance is a problem which may be contemplated now; but which time alone can solve. On one hand experience shows that in politics as in war, stratagem is often an overmatch for numbers: and among more happy characteristics of our political situation, it is now well understood that there are peculiarities, some temporary, others more durable, which may favor that side in the contest. On the republican side, again, the superiority of numbers is so great, their sentiments are so decided, and the practice of making a common cause, where there is a common sentiment and common interest, in spight of circumstantial and artificial distinctions, is so well understood, that no temperate observer of human affairs will be surprised if the issue in the present instance should be reversed, and the government be administered in the spirit and form approved by the great body of the people.

PART 3

The French Revolution and the People

Neutrality

On 1 February 1793, eleven days after the execution of Louis XVI, the infant French Republic, already at war with Austria and Prussia, declared war also on Great Britain. By April, as the Republic's first ambassador, "Citizen" Edmond Genet, made his way triumphantly from Charleston to Philadelphia, Washington's cabinet was meeting repeatedly to deliberate the proper policy for the country in what was now a worldwide war pitting the former mother country (and much the most important trading partner of the new United States) against the revolutionary nation with which America still had a treaty of alliance. Although the treaty of 1778 obliged the United States to defend the French West Indies only in the event of a defensive war, and all of Washington's secretaries agreed that the United States was not obliged to fulfill this guarantee, other clauses gave France superior advantages as a belligerent in American ports. It was difficult to define a policy that would not, in practice, favor one or the other of the warring powers and risk entanglement in the conflict. The president's decision incorporated some of both Hamilton's and Jefferson's advice. Genet would be received as the representative of the legitimate government of France. The treaty would not be abrogated. But on 22 April 1793, Washington proclaimed that the United States would pursue a "friendly and impartial" conduct toward the belligerent powers.

Neutrality (a word the proclamation avoided) was not a popular decision at first. Though few if any Americans wanted to become involved in the war, many did identify the revolution overseas as a product of the American example and hoped at least to lean in the French direction. Some objected, too, that the executive, in issuing the proclamation, was encroaching on the legislative power over war and peace. From this point forward, foreign policy assumed a growing role in what was rapidly becoming a full-fledged party conflict, and the conflicting sympathies of the two emerging parties drew swelling numbers of Americans into the party war.

"An Old French Soldier"
(Philadelphia) *General Advertiser*
27 August 1793

The period so earnestly wished for by your enemies and by ours is at length at hand. Who would have thought, when the blood of Frenchmen drenched the foundation of the temple of your liberty, that a day would come when the interests of your former tyrants and those of your allies should be weighed in the same balance, and that those of the first should preponderate? Who . . . would have imagined that efforts tending to break off the bonds that unite us would ever have obtained the approbation of the American people? I surely had no thoughts of this kind when, at Yorktown, I saw a whole army of your tyrants render homage to your rights to independence and bend under the united standards of America and France. Let those brave soldiers who witnessed that memorable day, let your illustrious general whose labors it crowned with victory, ask themselves, and let them tell me, whether a Frenchman will not ever be to them as a brother and a friend? Whether our interests, our perils, and our glory can be indifferent to them?

Who, then, has been able to effect the sudden change I am so unfortunate as to witness? Do you, also, wish to punish us for being free; and generous Americans, if it is a crime, recollect that you set the example. What; because we are free, rights are disputed which would have been acknowledged if the tyrant were yet alive; because we are free our friendship is disregarded when the good will of our last master was courted with so much care and attention. It is because we are free that our advances are despised and that advantages which were solicited so earnestly of our former government are now, when granted, disregarded—Americans: the whole world, posterity will judge you. What can you answer? Your public prints overflow with learned discussions. All the rubbish of low writers is brought forward, authorities are scraped up, all to prove to you that ingratitude is a virtue in certain cases. But do you not feel something within you that spurns at such a decline? My friends! the honest and upright man has no need to consult voluminous works to determine what is right; his heart and his conscience are sufficient guides. What is right cannot cease to be so, and virtue is out of the reach of elaborate calculations.

I am not deep in political knowledge, but I have been forcibly impressed with this truth—*that the present war in Europe is a war of principle; it is a war between liberty and despotism.* Your situation does not permit you to take a part in this war; well, then, we will fight alone in the common cause; but at least give us the consolation to see that on every occasion your wishes are with us, as you have sworn it. Let your own interest prevent your throwing yourselves in the arms of your bitterest enemies.—Do not furnish them with weapons against you by abandoning your only friends.

ALEXANDER HAMILTON

"Pacificus," No. 1

29 June 1793

Despite a sharp initial reaction, public opinion shifted steadily in support of the administration's course. Among the reasons were the increasingly outrageous conduct of Citizen Genet, who eventually threatened to appeal his disagreements with the administration to the public, and the seven essays of "Pacificus," which appeared initially in the *Gazette of the United States* between 29 June and 30 July 1793. The pseudonym, as usual, did not disguise the author's pen.

. . . What is the nature and design of a proclamation of neutrality?

The true nature & design of such an act is—to *make known* to the powers at war and to the citizens of the country whose government does the act that such country is in the condition of a nation at peace with the belligerent

parties and under no obligations of treaty to become an *associate in the war* with either of them; that this being its situation its intention is to observe a conduct conformable with it and to perform towards each the duties of neutrality; and as a consequence of this state of things, to give warning to all within its jurisdiction to abstain from acts that shall contravene those duties, under the penalties which the laws of the land (of which the law of nations is a part) annexes to acts of contravention. . . .

. . . If this be a just view of the true force and import of the Proclamation, it will remain to see whether the President in issuing it acted within his proper sphere or stepped beyond the bounds of his constitutional authority and duty.

It will not be disputed that the management of the affairs of this country with foreign nations is confided to the Government of the U States.

It can as little be disputed that a Proclamation of Neutrality, when a nation is at liberty to keep out of a war in which other nations are engaged and means so to do, is a *usual* and *a proper measure. Its main object and effect are to prevent the nation being immediately responsible for acts done by its citizens, without the privity or connivance of the Government, in contravention of the principles of neutrality.*

An object this of the greatest importance to a country whose true interest lies in the preservation of peace.

The inquiry then is—what department of the Government of the U States is the proper one to make a declaration of neutrality in the cases in which the engagements of the nation permit and its interests require such a declaration.

A correct and well informed mind will discern at once that it can belong neither to the Legislative nor Judicial Department and of course must belong to the Executive.

The Legislative Department is not the *organ* of intercourse between the U States and foreign nations. It is charged neither with *making* nor *interpreting* treaties. It is therefore not naturally that organ of the Government which is to pronounce the existing condition of the nation with regard to foreign powers, or to admonish the citizens of their obligations and duties as founded upon that condition of things. Still less is it charged with enforcing the execution and observance of these obligations and those duties.

It is equally obvious that the act in question is foreign to the Judiciary Department of the Government. The province of that Department is to decide litigations in particular cases. It is indeed charged with the interpretation of treaties; but it exercises this function only in the litigated cases; that is where contending parties bring before it a specific controversy. It has no concern with pronouncing upon the external political relations of treaties between government and government. This position is too plain to need being insisted upon.

It must then of necessity belong to the Executive Department to exercise the function in question—when a proper case for the exercise of it occurs.

It appears to be connected with that department in various capacities, as the *organ* of intercourse between the nation and foreign nations—as the interpreter of the national treaties in those cases in which the Judiciary is not competent, that is in the cases between government and government—as that power which is charged with the execution of the laws, of which treaties form a part—as that power which is charged with the command and application of the public force.

This view of the subject is so natural and obvious—so analogous to general theory and practice—that no doubt can be entertained of its justness, unless such doubt can be deduced from particular provisions of the Constitution of the U States.

Let us see then if cause for such doubt is to be found in that constitution.

The second Article of the Constitution of the U States, section 1st, establishes this general proposition, That "The EXECUTIVE POWER shall be vested in a President of the United States of America."

The same article in a succeeding section proceeds to designate particular cases of executive power. It declares among other things that the President shall be Commander in Chief of the army and navy of the U States and of the militia of the several states when called into the actual service of the U States, that he shall have power by and with the advice of the senate to make treaties; that it shall be his duty to receive ambassadors and other public ministers and to take care that the laws be faithfully executed.

It would not consist with the rules of sound construction to consider this enumeration of particular authorities as derogating from the more comprehensive grant contained in the general clause, further than as it may be coupled with express restrictions or qualifications, as in regard to the cooperation of the Senate in the appointment of officers and the making of treaties, which are qualifications of the

general executive powers of appointing officers and making treaties: Because the difficulty of a complete and perfect specification of all the cases of executive authority would naturally dictate the use of general terms—and would render it improbable that a specification of certain particulars was designed as a substitute for those terms, when antecedently used. The different mode of expression employed in the constitution in regard to the two powers the Legislative and the Executive serves to confirm this inference. In the article which grants the legislative powers of the government the expressions are—"*All Legislative powers herein granted shall be vested in a Congress of the U States;*" in that which grants the Executive Power the expressions are, as already quoted, "The Executive Power shall be vested in a President of the U States of America."

The enumeration ought rather therefore to be considered as intended by way of greater caution, to specify and regulate the principal articles implied in the definition of executive power, leaving the rest to flow from the general grant of that power, interpreted in conformity to other parts of the constitution and to the principles of free government.

The general doctrine then of our Constitution is that the EXECUTIVE POWER of the Nation is vested in the President, subject only to the *exceptions* and *qualifications* which are expressed in the instrument.

Two of these have been already noticed—the participation of the Senate in the appointment of officers and the making of treaties. A third remains to be mentioned: the right of the Legislature "to declare war and grant letters of marque and reprisal."

With these exceptions the EXECUTIVE POWER of the Union is completely lodged in the President. This mode of construing the Constitution has indeed been recognized by Congress in formal acts, upon full consideration and debate. The power of removal from office is an important instance.

And since upon general principles for reasons already given, the issuing of a proclamation of neutrality is merely an executive act, since also the general Executive Power of the Union is vested in the President, the conclusion is that the step which has been taken by him is liable to no just exception on the score of authority.

It may be observed that this inference would be just if the power of declaring war had not been vested in the Legislature, but that this power naturally includes the right of judging whether the nation is under obligations to make war or not.

The answer to this is that however true it may be that the right of the Legislature to declare war includes the right of judging whether the nation be under obligations to make war or not—it will not follow that the Executive is in any case excluded from a similar right of judgment in the execution of its own functions.

If the Legislature have a right to make war on the one hand—it is on the other the duty of the Executive to preserve peace till war is declared; and in fulfilling that duty, it must necessarily possess a right of judging what is the nature of the obligations which the treaties of the country impose on the government; and when in pursuance of this right it has concluded that there is nothing in them inconsistent with a *state* of neutrality, it becomes both its province and its duty to enforce the laws incident to that state of the nation. The Executive is charged with the execution of all laws, the laws of nations as well as the municipal law, which recognizes and adopts those laws. It is consequently bound, by faithfully executing the laws of neutrality, when that is the state of the nation, to avoid giving a cause of war to foreign powers.

This is the direct and proper end of the proclamation of neutrality. It declares to the U States their situation with regard to the powers at war and makes known to the community that the laws incident to that situation will be enforced. In doing this, it conforms to an established usage of nations, the operation of which as before remarked is to obviate a responsibility on the part of the whole society for secret and unknown violations of the rights of any of the warring parties by its citizens.

Those who object to the proclamation will readily admit that it is the right and duty of the Executive to judge of, or to interpret, those articles of our treaties which give to France particular privileges, in order to the enforcement of those privileges; but the necessary consequence of this is that the Executive must judge what are the proper bounds of those privileges—what rights are given to other nations by our treaties with them—what rights the law of nature and nations gives and our treaties permit in respect to those nations with whom we have no treaties; in fine what are the reciprocal rights and obligations of the United States & of all & each of the powers at war.

The right of the Executive to receive ambassadors and other public ministers may serve to illustrate the relative duties of the Executive and Legislative Departments. This right includes that of judging, in the case of a revolution of government in a foreign country, whether the new rulers are competent organs of the national will and ought to be recognized or not: And where a treaty antecedently exists between the U States and such nation that right involves the power of giving operation or not to such treaty. For until the new government is *acknowledged,* the treaties between the nations, as far at least as regards *public* rights, are of course suspended.

This power of determining virtually in the case supposed upon the operation of national treaties as a consequence of the power to receive ambassadors and other public ministers is an important instance of the right of the Executive to decide the obligations of the nation with regard to foreign nations. To apply it to the case of France, if there had been a treaty of alliance *offensive* and defensive between the U States and that country, the unqualified acknowledgment of the new government would have put the U States in a condition to become an associate in the war in which France was engaged—and would have laid the Legislature under an obligation, if required, and there was otherwise no valid excuse, of exercising its power of declaring war.

This serves as an example of the right of the Executive, in certain cases, to determine the condition of the nation, though it may consequentially affect the proper or improper exercise of the power of the Legislature to declare war. The Executive indeed cannot control the exercise of that power—further than by the exercise of its general right of objecting to all acts of the Legislature; liable to being overruled by two thirds of both houses of Congress. The Legislature is free to perform its own duties according to its own sense of them—though the Executive in the exercise of its constitutional powers may establish an antecedent state of things which ought to weigh in the legislative decisions. From the division of the Executive Power there results, in reference to it, a *concurrent* authority in the distributed cases.

Hence in the case stated, though treaties can only be made by the President and Senate, their activity may be continued or suspended by the President alone.

No objection has been made to the Presidents having acknowledged the Republic of France by the reception of its minister, without having consulted the Senate, though that body is connected with him in the making of treaties, and though the consequence of his act of reception is to give operation to the treaties heretofore made with that country: But he is censured for having declared the U States to be in a state of peace & neutrality with regard to the Powers at War, because the right of *changing* that state & *declaring war* belongs to the Legislature.

It deserves to be remarked that as the participation of the Senate in the making of treaties and the power of the Legislature to declare war are exceptions out of the general "Executive Power" vested in the President, they are to be construed strictly—and ought to be extended no further than is essential to their execution.

While therefore the Legislature can alone declare war, can alone actually transfer the nation from a state of peace to a state of war—it belongs to the "Executive Power" to do whatever else the laws of nations cooperating with the treaties of the country enjoin in the intercourse of the U States with foreign powers.

In this distribution of powers the wisdom of our constitution is manifested. It is the province and duty of the Executive to preserve to the nation the blessings of peace. The Legislature alone can interrupt those blessings, by placing the nation in a state of war.

But though it has been thought advisable to vindicate the authority of the Executive on this broad and comprehensive ground—it was not absolutely necessary to do so. That clause of the Constitution which makes it his duty to "take care that the laws be faithfully executed" might alone have been relied upon, and this simple process of argument pursued.

The President is the constitutional executor of the laws. Our treaties and the laws of nations form a part of the law of the land. He who is to execute the laws must first judge for himself of their meaning. In order to the observance of that conduct which the laws of nations combined with our treaties prescribed to this country in reference to the present war in Europe, it was necessary for the President to judge for himself whether there was any thing in our treaties incompatible with an adherence to neutrality. Having judged that there was not, he had a right, and if in his opinion the interests of the nation required it, it was his duty, as executor of the laws, to proclaim the neutrality of the nation, to exhort all persons to observe it, and to warn them of the penalties which would attend its non-observance.

The Proclamation has been represented as enacting some new law. This is a view of it entirely erroneous. It only proclaims a *fact* with regard to the *existing state* of the nation, informs the citizens of what the laws previously established require of them in that state, & warns them that these laws will be put in execution against the infractors of them.

JAMES MADISON

"Helvidius," No. 1

24 August 1793

Though Jefferson seemed satisfied, at first, with the administration's actions, Madison was quick to write him from Virginia of their countrymen's dismay over a policy of strict neutrality and of his own concern that the executive's initiative had usurped the legislature's power to decide on war and peace. Quickly, Jefferson retreated, and as popular opinion moved behind the proclamation, he increasingly expressed his own concern, not least about the constitutional interpretations Hamilton was using to defend the proclamation. "Nobody answers him," he wailed, "and his doctrines will therefore be taken for confessed. For God's sake, my dear Sir, take up your pen, select the most striking heresies, and cut him to pieces in the face of the public. There is nobody else who can and will enter the lists with him." Madison's response appeared in the *Gazette of the United States* between 24 August and 18 September 1793.

Several pieces with the signature of Pacificus were lately published, which have been read with singular pleasure and applause by the foreigners and degenerate citizens among us, who hate our republican government and the French Revolution; whilst the publication seems to have been too little regarded or too much despised by the steady friends to both.

Had the doctrines inculcated by the writer, with the natural consequences from them, been nakedly presented to the public, this treatment might have been proper. Their true character would then have struck every eye and been rejected by the feelings of every heart. But they offer themselves to the reader in the dress of an elaborate dissertation; they are mingled with a few truths that may serve them as a passport to credulity; and they are introduced with professions of anxiety for the preservation of peace, for the welfare of the government, and for the respect due to the present head of the executive, that may prove a snare to patriotism.

In these disguises they have appeared to claim the attention I propose to bestow on them; with a view to show, from the publication itself, that under color of vindicating an important public act of a chief magistrate who enjoys the confidence and love of his country, principles are advanced which strike at the vitals of its constitution, as well as at its honor and true interest.

As it is not improbable that attempts may be made to apply insinuations which are seldom spared when particular purposes are to be answered to the author of the ensuing observations, it may not be improper to premise that he is a friend to the constitution, that he wishes for the preservation of peace, and that the present chief magistrate has not a fellow-citizen who is penetrated with deeper respect for his merits or feels a purer solicitude for his glory.

This declaration is made with no view of courting a more favorable ear to what may be said than it deserves. The sole purpose of it is to obviate imputations which might weaken the impressions of truth; and which are the more likely to be resorted to in proportion as solid and fair arguments may be wanting.

The substance of the first piece, sifted from its inconsistencies and its vague expressions, may be thrown into the following propositions:

That the powers of declaring war and making treaties are, in their nature, executive powers:

That being particularly vested by the constitution in other departments, they are to be considered as exceptions out of the general grant to the executive department:

That being, as exceptions, to be construed strictly, the powers not strictly within them remain with the executive:

That the executive consequently, as the organ of intercourse with foreign nations and the interpreter and executor of treaties and the law of nations, is authorized to expound all articles of treaties, those involving questions of war and peace, as well as others; to judge of the obligations of the United States to make war or not, under any casus federis or eventual operation of the contract relating to war; and to pronounce the state of things resulting from the obligations of the United States as understood by the executive:

That in particular the executive had authority to judge whether in the case of the mutual guaranty between the United States and France, the former were bound by it to engage in the war:

That the executive has, in pursuance of that authority, decided that the United States are not bound: And,

That its proclamation of the 22nd of April last is to be taken as the effect and expression of that decision.

The basis of the reasoning is, we perceive, the extraordinary doctrine that the powers of making war and treaties are in their nature executive; and therefore comprehended in the general grant of executive power, where not specially and strictly excepted out of the grant.

Let us examine this doctrine; and that we may avoid the possibility of mistaking the writer, it shall be laid down in his own words: a precaution the more necessary, as scarce any thing else could outweigh the improbability that so extravagant a tenet should be hazarded, at so early a day, in the face of the public.

His words are—"Two of these (exceptions and qualifications to the executive powers) have been already noticed—the participation of the Senate in the *appointment of officers* and the *making of treaties*. A *third* remains to be mentioned—the right of the legislature to *declare war; and grant letters of marque and reprisal.*"

Again—"It deserves to be remarked, that as the participation of the Senate in the *making of treaties* and the power of the legislature to *declare war* are *exceptions* out of the general *executive power* vested in the President, they are to be construed *strictly,* and ought to be extended no farther than is essential to their execution."

If there be any countenance to these positions, it must be found either 1st, in the writers of authority on public law; or 2nd, in the quality and operation of the powers to make war and treaties; or 3rd, in the Constitution of the United States.

It would be of little use to enter far into the first source of information, not only because our own reason and our own constitution are the best guides but because a just analysis and discrimination of the powers of government according to their executive, legislative and judiciary qualities are not to be expected in the works of the most received jurists, who wrote before a critical attention was paid to those objects and with their eyes too much on monarchical governments, where all powers are confounded in the sovereignty of the prince. It will be found however, I believe, that all of them, particularly Wolfius, Burlamaqui and Vattel, speak of the powers to declare war, to conclude peace, and to form alliances as among the highest acts of the sovereignty, of which the legislative power must at least be an integral and preeminent part.

Writers such as Locke and Montesquieu, who have discussed more particularly the principles of liberty and the structure of government, lie under the same disadvantage, of having written before these subjects were illuminated by the events and discussions which distinguish a very recent period. Both of them too are evidently warped by a regard to the particular government of England, to which one of them owed allegiance* and the other professed an admiration bordering on idolatry. Montesquieu, however, has rather distinguished himself by enforcing the reasons and the importance of avoiding a confusion of the several powers of government than by enumerating and defining the powers which belong to each particular class. And Locke, notwithstanding the early date of his work on civil government and the example of his own government before his eyes, admits that the particular powers in question, which, after some of the writers on public law, he calls *federative,* are really *distinct* from the *executive,* though almost always united with it and *hardly to be separated into distinct hands.* Had he not lived under a monarchy, in which these powers were united; or had he written by the lamp which truth now presents to lawgivers, the last observation would probably never have dropt from his pen. But let us quit a field of research which is more likely to perplex than to decide and bring the question to other tests of which it will be more easy to judge.

2. If we consult for a moment the nature and operation of the two powers to declare war and make treaties, it will be impossible not to see that they can never fall within a proper definition of executive powers. The natural province of the executive magistrate is to execute laws, as that of the legislature is to make laws. All his acts therefore, properly executive, must pre-suppose the existence of the laws to be executed. A treaty is not an execution of laws: it does not pre-suppose the existence of laws. It is, on the contrary, to have itself the force of a *law* and to be carried into *execution,* like all *other laws,* by the *executive magistrate.* To say then that the power of making treaties, which

* The chapter on prerogative shows how much the reason of the philosopher was clouded by the royalism of the Englishman.

are confessedly laws, belongs naturally to the department which is to execute laws, is to say that the executive department naturally includes a legislative power. In theory, this is an absurdity—in practice a tyranny.

The power to declare war is subject to similar reasoning. A declaration that there shall be war is not an execution of laws: it does not suppose pre-existing laws to be executed: it is not in any respect an act merely executive. It is, on the contrary, one of the most deliberative acts that can be performed; and when performed, has the effect of *repealing* all the *laws* operating in a state of peace, so far as they are inconsistent with a state of war; and of *enacting* as *a rule for the executive* a *new code* adapted to the relation between the society and its foreign enemy. In like manner a conclusion of peace *annuls* all the *laws* peculiar to a state of war and *revives* the general *laws* incident to a state of peace.

These remarks will be strengthened by adding that treaties, particularly treaties of peace, have sometimes the effect of changing not only the external laws of the society, but operate also on the internal code, which is purely municipal, and to which the legislative authority of the country is of itself competent and compleat.

From this view of the subject it must be evident that, although the executive may be a convenient organ of preliminary communications with foreign governments on the subjects of treaty or war, and the proper agent for carrying into execution the final determinations of the competent authority, yet it can have no pretensions from the nature of the powers in question compared with the nature of the executive trust, to that essential agency which gives validity to such determinations.

It must be further evident that, if these powers be not in their nature purely legislative, they partake so much more of that than of any other quality, that under a constitution leaving them to result to their most natural department, the legislature would be without a rival in its claim.

Another important inference to be noted is, that the powers of making war and treaty being substantially of a legislative, not an executive nature, the rule of interpreting exceptions strictly must narrow instead of enlarging executive pretensions on those subjects.

3. It remains to be enquired whether there be any thing in the constitution itself which shows that the powers of making war and peace are considered as of an executive nature and as comprehended within a general grant of executive power.

It will not be pretended that this appears from any *direct* position to be found in the instrument.

If it were *deducible* from any particular expressions it may be presumed that the publication would have saved us the trouble of the research.

Does the doctrine then result from the actual distribution of powers among the several branches of the government? Or from any fair analogy between the powers of war and treaty and the enumerated powers vested in the executive alone?

Let us examine.

In the general distribution of powers, we find that of declaring war expressly vested in the Congress, where every other legislative power is declared to be vested, and without any other qualification than what is common to every other legislative act. The constitutional idea of this power would seem then clearly to be that it is of a legislative and not an executive nature.

This conclusion becomes irresistible when it is recollected that the constitution cannot be supposed to have placed either any power legislative in its nature entirely among executive powers or any power executive in its nature entirely among legislative powers, without charging the constitution with that kind of intermixture and consolidation of different powers which would violate a fundamental principle in the organization of free governments. If it were not unnecessary to enlarge on this topic here, it could be shown that the constitution was originally vindicated, and has been constantly expounded, with a disavowal of any such intermixture.

The power of treaties is vested jointly in the President and in the Senate, which is a branch of the legislature. From this arrangement merely, there can be no inference that would necessarily exclude the power from the executive class: since the Senate is joined with the President in another power, that of appointing to offices, which as far as relate to executive offices at least, is considered as of an executive nature. Yet on the other hand, there are sufficient indications that the power of treaties is regarded by the constitution as materially different from mere executive power and as having more affinity to the legislative than to the executive character.

One circumstance indicating this is the constitutional regulation under which the Senate give their consent in the case of treaties. In all other cases the consent of the body is expressed by a majority of voices. In this particular case, a concurrence of two thirds at least is made necessary, as a substitute or compensation for the other branch of the legislature, which on certain occasions could not be conveniently a party to the transaction.

But the conclusive circumstance is that treaties, when formed according to the constitutional mode, are confessedly to have the force and operation of *laws,* and are to be a rule for the courts in controversies between man and man, as much as any *other laws.* They are even emphatically declared by the constitution to be "the supreme law of the land."

So far the argument from the constitution is precisely in opposition to the doctrine. As little will be gained in its favor from a comparison of the two powers with those particularly vested in the President alone.

As there are but few it will be most satisfactory to review them one by one.

"The President shall be commander in chief of the army and navy of the United States, and of the militia when called into the actual service of the United States."

There can be no relation worth examining between this power and the general power of making treaties. And instead of being analogous to the power of declaring war, it affords a striking illustration of the incompatibility of the two powers in the same hands. Those who are to *conduct a war* cannot in the nature of things be proper or safe judges whether *a war ought to be commenced, continued,* or *concluded.* They are barred from the latter functions by a great principle in free government analogous to that which separates the sword from the purse, or the power of executing from the power of enacting laws.

"He may require the opinion in writing of the principal officers in each of the executive departments upon any subject relating to the duties of their respective offices; and he shall have power to grant reprieves and pardons for offences against the United States, except in case of impeachment." These powers can have nothing to do with the subject.

"The President shall have power to fill up vacancies that may happen during the recess of the senate, by granting commissions which shall expire at the end of the next session." The same remark is applicable to this power, as also to that of "receiving ambassadors, other public ministers and consuls." The particular use attempted to be made of this last power will be considered in another place.

"He shall take care that the laws shall be faithfully executed and shall commission all officers of the United States." To see the laws faithfully executed constitutes the essence of the executive authority. But what relation has it to the power of making treaties and war, that is, of determining what the *laws shall be* with regard to other nations? No other certainly than what subsists between the powers of executing and enacting laws; no other consequently, than what forbids a coalition of the powers in the same department.

I pass over the few other specified functions assigned to the President, such as that of convening of the legislature, &c. &c., which cannot be drawn into the present question.

It may be proper however to take notice of the power of removal from office, which appears to have been adjudged to the President by the laws establishing the executive departments; and which the writer has endeavoured to press into his service. To justify any favorable inference from this case, it must be shown that the powers of war and treaties are of a kindred nature to the power of removal, or at least are equally within a grant of executive power. Nothing of this sort has been attempted, nor probably will be attempted. Nothing can in truth be clearer than that no analogy, or shade of analogy, can be traced between a power in the supreme officer responsible for the faithful execution of the laws to displace a subaltern officer employed in the execution of the laws; and a power to make treaties, and to declare war, such as these have been found to be in their nature, their operation, and their consequences.

Thus it appears that by whatever standard we try this doctrine, it must be condemned as no less vicious in theory than it would be dangerous in practice. It is countenanced neither by the writers on law, not by the nature of the powers themselves, not by any general arrangements or particular expressions, or plausible analogies, to be found in the constitution.

Whence then can the writer have borrowed it?

There is but one answer to this question.

The power of making treaties and the power of declaring war are *royal prerogatives* in the *British government,* and are accordingly treated as Executive prerogatives by *British commentators.*

We shall be the more confirmed in the necessity of this solution of the problem by looking back to the era of the constitution and satisfying ourselves that the writer could not have been misled by the doctrines maintained by our own commentators on our own government. That I may not ramble beyond prescribed limits, I shall content myself with an extract from a work which entered into a systematic explanation and defence of the constitution, and to which there has frequently been ascribed some influence in conciliating the public assent to the government in the form proposed. Three circumstances conspire in giving weight to this cotemporary exposition. It was made at a time when no application to *persons or measures* could bias; the opinion given was not transiently mentioned, but formally and critically elucidated; it related to a point in the constitution which must consequently have been viewed as of importance in the public mind. The passage relates to the power of making treaties, that of declaring war being arranged with such obvious propriety among the legislative powers as to be passed over without particular discussion.

"Tho' several writers on the subject of government place that power (*of making treaties*) in the class of *Executive authorities,* yet this is *evidently* an *arbitrary disposition.* For if we attend *carefully* to its operation, it will be found to partake *more* of the *legislative* than of the *executive* character, though it does not seem strictly to fall within the definition of either of them. The essence of the legislative authority is to enact laws; or in other words, to prescribe rules for the regulation of the society. While the execution of the laws and the employment of the common strength, either for this purpose, or for the common defence, seem to comprize *all* the functions of the *Executive magistrate.* The power of making treaties is *plainly* neither the one nor the other. It relates neither to the execution of the subsisting laws, nor to the enaction of new ones, and still less to an exertion of the common strength. Its objects are contracts with foreign nations, which have the *force of law,* but derive it from the obligations of good faith. They are not rules prescribed by the sovereign to the subject, but agreements between sovereign and sovereign. The power in question seems therefore to form a distinct department, and to belong properly neither to the legislative nor to the executive. The qualities elsewhere detailed as indispensable in the management of foreign *negotiations* point out the executive as the most fit agent in those transactions: whilst the vast importance of the trust, and the operation of treaties *as Laws,* plead strongly for the participation of the whole or a part of the *legislative body* in the office of making them." Federalist vol. 2. p. 273.

It will not fail to be remarked on this commentary that, whatever doubts may be started as to the correctness of its reasoning against the legislative nature of the power to make treaties, it is *clear, consistent* and *confident,* in deciding that the power is *plainly* and *evidently* not an *executive power.*

JAMES MADISON

"Helvidius," No. 4

14 September 1793

The last papers completed the view proposed to be taken of the arguments in support of the new and aspiring doctrine which ascribes to the executive the prerogative of judging and deciding whether there be causes of war or not in the obligations of treaties, notwithstanding the express provision in the constitution by which the legislature is made the organ of the national will on questions whether there be or be not a cause for declaring war. If the answer to these arguments has imparted the conviction which dictated it, the reader will have pronounced that they are generally superficial, abounding in contradictions, never in the least degree conclusive to the main point, and not unfrequently conclusive against the writer himself; whilst the doctrine—that the powers of treaty and war are in their nature executive powers—which forms the basis of those arguments, is as indefensible and as dangerous as the particular doctrine to which they are applied.

But it is not to be forgotten that these doctrines, though ever so clearly disproved, or ever so weakly defended, remain before the public a striking monument of the principles and views which are entertained and propagated in the community.

It is also to be remembered that, however the consequences flowing from such premises may be disavowed at this time or by this individual, we are to regard it as morally certain that in proportion as the doctrines make their way into the creed of the government and the acquiescence of the public, every power that can be deduced from them will be deduced and exercised sooner or later by those who may have an interest in so doing. The character of human nature gives this salutary warning to every sober and reflecting mind. And the history of government, in all its forms and in every period of time, ratifies the danger. A people, therefore, who are so happy as to possess the inestimable blessing of a free and defined constitution cannot be too watchful against the introduction, nor too critical in tracing the consequences, of new principles and new constructions that may remove the landmarks of power.

Should the prerogative which has been examined be allowed in its most limited sense to usurp the public countenance, the interval would probably be very short before it would be heard from some quarter or other that the prerogative either amounts to nothing, or means a right to judge and conclude that the obligations of treaty impose war, as well as that they permit peace. That it is fair reasoning to say that if the prerogative exists at all, an *operative* rather than an *inert* character ought to be given to it.

In support of this conclusion, there could be enough to echo "that the prerogative in this active sense, is connected with the executive in various capacities—as the organ of intercourse between the nation and foreign nations—as the interpreter of national treaties" (a violation of which may be a cause of war) "as that power which is charged with the execution of the laws of which treaties make a part—as that power which is charged with *the command and application of the public force.*"

With additional force, it might be said, that the executive is as much the *executor* as the *interpreter* of treaties: that if by virtue of the *first* character it is to judge of the *obligations* of treaties, it is by virtue of the *second* equally authorized to carry those obligations *into effect.* Should there occur, for example, a *casus federis* claiming a military co-operation of the United States, and a military force should happen to be under the command of the executive, it must have the same right as *executor of public treaties to employ* the public force as it has in quality of *interpreter of public treaties* to decide whether it ought to be *employed.*

The case of a treaty of peace would be an auxiliary to comments of this sort. It is a condition annexed to every treaty that an infraction even of an important article on one side extinguishes the obligations on the other: and the immediate consequence of a dissolution of a treaty of peace is a restoration of a state of war. If the executive is "to decide on the obligation of the nation with regard to foreign nations"—"to pronounce the *existing condition* (in the sense annexed by the writer) of the nation with regard to them; and to admonish the citizens of their obligations and duties as founded upon *that condition* of things"—"to judge what are the *reciprocal rights* and obligations of the United States, and of all and each of the powers at war":— add, that if the executive moreover possesses all powers relating to war *not strictly* within the power *to declare war,* which any pupil of political casuistry could distinguish from a mere *relapse* into a war that *had been declared:* With this store of materials and the example given of the use to be made of them, would it be difficult to fabricate a power in the executive to plunge the nation into war whenever a treaty of peace might happen to be infringed?

But if any difficulty should arise, there is another mode chalked out by which the end might clearly be brought about, even without the violation of the treaty of peace; especially if the other party should happen to change its government at the crisis. The executive, in the case, could *suspend* the treaty of peace *by refusing to receive an ambassador* from the *new* government, and the state of war *emerges of course.*

This is a sample of the use to which the extraordinary publications we are reviewing might be turned. Some of the inferences could not be repelled at all. And the least regular of them must go smoothly down with those who had swallowed the gross sophistry which wrapped up the original dose.

Every just view that can be taken of this subject admonishes the public of the necessity of a rigid adherence to the simple, the received and the fundamental doctrine of the constitution, that the power to declare war including the power of judging of the causes of war is *fully* and *exclusively* vested in the legislature: that the executive has no right in any case to decide the question whether there is or is not cause for declaring war: that the right of convening and informing Congress, whenever such a question seems to call for a decision, is all the right which the constitution has deemed requisite or proper: and that for such more than for any other contingency, this right was specially given to the executive.

In no part of the constitution is more wisdom to be found than in the clause which confides the question of war or peace to the legislature, and not to the executive department. Beside the objection to such a mixture of heterogeneous powers, the trust and the temptation would be too great for any one man: not such as nature may offer as the prodigy of many centuries, but such as may be expected in the ordinary successions of magistracy. War is in fact the true nurse of executive aggrandizement. In war a physical force is to be created, and it is the executive will which is to direct it. In war the public treasures are to be unlocked, and it is the executive hand which is to dispense them. In war the honors and emoluments of office are to be multiplied; and it is the executive patronage under which they are to be enjoyed. It is in war, finally, that laurels are to be gathered, and it is the executive brow they are to encircle. The strongest passions and most dangerous weaknesses of the human breast, ambition, avarice, vanity, the honorable or venial love of fame, are all in conspiracy against the desire and duty of peace.

Hence it has grown into an axiom that the executive is the department of power most distinguished by its propensity to war: hence it is the practice of all states, in proportion as they are free, to disarm this propensity of its influence.

As the best praise then that can be pronounced on an executive magistrate is that he is the friend of peace, a praise that rises in its value as there may be a known capacity to shine in war, so it must be one of the most sacred duties of a free people to mark the first omen in the society of principles that may stimulate the hopes of other magistrates of another propensity, to intrude into questions on which its gratification depends. If a free people be a wise people also, they will not forget that the danger of surprise can never be so great as when the advocates for the prerogative of war can sheathe it in a symbol of peace.

The constitution has manifested a similar prudence in refusing to the executive the *sole* power of making peace. The trust in this instance also would be too great for the wisdom, and the temptations too strong for the virtue, of a single citizen. The principal reasons on which the constitution proceeded in its regulation of the power of treaties, including treaties of peace, are so aptly furnished by the work already quoted more than once, that I shall borrow another comment from that source.

"However proper or safe it may be in a government where the executive magistrate is an hereditary monarch to commit to him the entire power of making treaties, it would be utterly unsafe and improper to entrust that power to an elective magistrate of four years duration. It has been remarked upon another occasion, and the remark is unquestionably just, that a hereditary monarch, though often the oppressor of his people, has personally too much at stake in the government to be in any material danger of being corrupted by foreign powers. But that a man raised from the station of a private citizen to the rank of chief magistrate, possessed of but a moderate or slender fortune, and looking forward to a period not very remote when he may probably be obliged to return to the station from which he was taken, might sometimes be under temptations to sacrifice his duty to his interest, which it would require superlative virtue to withstand. An avaricious man might be tempted to betray the interest of the state to the acquisition of wealth. An ambitious man might make his own aggrandizement, by the aid of a foreign power, the price of his treachery to his constituents. The history of human conduct does not warrant that exalted opinion of human virtue which would make it wise in a nation to commit interests of so delicate and momentous a kind as *those which concern its intercourse* with the rest of the world to the *sole* disposal of a magistrate, created and circmstanced, as would be a President of the United States."

I shall conclude this paper and this branch of the subject with two reflections which naturally arise from this view of the Constitution.

The first is that, as the personal interest of a hereditary monarch in the government is the *only* security against the temptation incident to a commitment of the delicate and momentous interests of the nation which concern its intercourse with the rest of the world to the disposal of a single magistrate, it is a plain consequence that every addition that may be made to the *sole* agency and influence of the Executive in the intercourse of the nation with foreign nations is an increase of the dangerous temptation to which an *elective and temporary* magistrate is exposed; and an *argument* and *advance* towards the security afforded by the personal interest of a *hereditary* magistrate.

Secondly, as the constitution has not permitted the Executive *singly* to conclude or judge that peace ought to be made, it might be inferred from that circumstance alone that it never meant to give it authority, *singly,* to judge and conclude that war ought not to be made. The trust would be precisely similar and equivalent in the two cases. The right to say that war ought not to go on would be no greater than the right to say that war ought to begin. Every danger of error or corruption incident to such a prerogative in one case, is incident to it in the other. If the Constitution therefore has deemed it unsafe or improper in the one case, it must be deemed equally so in the other case.

Commerce and Seizures

France and Britain both intended to deny the other the benefits of neutral commerce; and during 1793, seizures of American vessels posed an increasing problem, especially with Great Britain. Partly as a consequence of this and partly as a consequence of their continuing disgust with British commercial restrictions and British domination of the American import trade, Jefferson and Madison determined to renew the old campaign for commercial discrimination. On 16 December 1793, two weeks before retiring from his position as secretary of state, Jefferson delivered to the first session of the Third Congress a huge "Report on the Privileges and Restrictions on the Commerce of the United States with Foreign Countries," comparing British policies unfavorably with those of France. Madison followed up, in January 1794, by introducing seven resolutions to retaliate against Great Britain's mercantilistic regulations. Events defeated him again. By early March, the British had seized some 250 U.S. vessels trading with the French West Indies. The Republicans in Congress moved behind a bill to introduce nonintercourse with Britain and a measure to sequester British debts. The Federalists preferred a final effort to negotiate the crisis, accompanied by measures to bolster the national defenses. Madison's resolutions were dropped. John Adams cast a tie-breaking vote defeating nonintercourse in the Senate. On 16 April 1794, Washington nominated Chief Justice John Jay to make a final effort at a diplomatic resolution of the crisis.

WILLIAM LOUGHTON SMITH

Speech in the House of Representatives

13 January 1794

The most effective speech against Madison's resolutions was delivered by his old foe, William Loughton Smith of South Carolina. In his biography of Hamilton, however, John C. Hamilton reported that the speech was drafted by his father.

The House again resolved itself into a Committee of the Whole House on the Report of the Secretary of State on the Privileges and Restrictions on the Commerce of the United States in Foreign Countries. When

Mr. SMITH, of South Carolina, rose and addressed the Chair as follows:

Mr. Chairman:—Among the various duties which are assigned by the Constitution to the Legislature of the United States, there is, perhaps, none of a more important nature than the regulation of commerce, none more generally interesting to our fellow-citizens, none which more seriously claims our diligent and accurate investigation. . . .

It will not be denied that this country is at present in a very delicate crisis, and one requiring dispassionate reflection, cool and mature deliberation. It will be much to be regretted then, if passion should usurp the place of reason, if superficial, narrow, and prejudiced views should mislead the public councils from the true path of national interest.

The report of the Secretary of State . . . (whatever may have been the design of the reporter) appears . . . to induce a false estimate of the comparative condition of our commerce with certain foreign nations, and to urge the Legislature to adopt a scheme of retaliating regulations, restrictions, and exclusions.

The most striking contrast which the performance evidently aims at is between Great Britain and France. For this reason, and as these are the two powers with whom we have the most extensive relations in trade, I shall, by a particular investigation of the subject, endeavor to lay before the Committee an accurate and an impartial comparison of the commercial systems of the two countries in reference to the United States, as a test of the solidity of the inferences which are attempted to be established by the report. A fair comparison can only be made with an eye to what may be deemed the permanent system of the countries in question. The proper epoch for it, therefore, will precede the commencement of the pending French Revolution.

The commercial regulations of France during the period of the Revolution have been too fluctuating, too much influenced by momentary impulses, and, as far as they have looked towards this country with a favorable eye, too much manifesting an object of the moment . . . to consider them as a part of a system. But though the comparison will be made with principal reference to the condition of our trade with France and Great Britain antecedent to the existing revolution, the regulations of the subsequent period will perhaps not be passed over altogether unnoticed.

The table which I have before me comprises the principal features of the subject within a short compass. It is the work of a gentleman of considerable commercial knowledge, and I believe may be relied on for its correctness. . . .

Accustomed as our ears have been to a constant panegyric on the generous policy of France towards this country in commercial relations and to as constant a philippic on the unfriendly, illiberal, and persecuting policy of Great Britain towards us in the same relations, we naturally expect to find in a table which exhibits their respective systems numerous discriminations in that of France in our favor and many valuable privileges granted to us which are refused to other foreign countries, in that of Great Britain frequent discriminations to our prejudice and a variety of privileges refused to us which are granted to other foreign nations. But an inspection of the table will satisfy every candid mind that the reverse of what has been supposed is truly the case—that neither in France nor the French West Indies is there more than one solitary and important distinction in our favor (I mean the article of fish oil) either with regard to our exports thither, our imports from thence, or our shipping; that both in Great Britain and the British West Indies there are several material distinctions in our favor with regard both to our exports thither and to our imports from thence, and, as it respects Great Britain, with regard also to our shipping; that in the market of Great Britain, a preference is secured to six of our most valuable staples by considerably higher duties on the rival articles of other foreign countries; that our navigation thither is favored by our ships, when carrying our own productions, being put upon as good a footing as their own ships, and by the exemption of several of our productions, when carried in our ships, from duties which are paid on the like articles of other foreign countries carried in the ships of those countries; and that several of our productions may be carried from the United States to the British West Indies, while the like productions cannot be carried thither from any other foreign country; and that

several of the productions of those countries may be brought from thence to the United States, which cannot be carried from thence to any other foreign country. . . .

[Smith then proceeded, item by item, to compare French and British regulations affecting American exports (flour, tobacco, rice, wood, fish, salted meats, etc.), arguing that, in the great majority of cases, British regulations were more favorable to American products than were those of France. He next observed that three-fourths of America's imports came from Britain and its dominions— some seven and one-half times the dollar value as came from France. This, he said, was not a grievance but a natural consequence of Britain's ability to "supply us with the greatest number of the articles we want, on the best terms." It could not be changed except by an effective system of encouraging home manufactures or "by means violent and contrary to our interests": premiums for imports from other countries or higher duties on British goods "at the expense of the people of the United States." Turning finally to a comparison of French and British treatment of American shipping, he admitted that French regulations were generally more favorable than those of Britain: American ships carrying American products directly to Great Britain were treated more favorably than those of any other nation, which was not the case in France; but American ships were not permitted to carry the products of other nations to Britain, and Britain excluded American ships from the British West Indies, whereas France admitted American vessels of sixty tons or more. He insisted, nevertheless, that both nations "aimed at securing the greatest possible portion of benefit to themselves, with no greater concession to our interests than was supposed to coincide with their own," that there were no grounds for extolling the policies of one of them or denouncing those of the other.]

. . . The system of every country is selfish according to its circumstances and contains all those restrictions and exclusions which it deems useful to its own interest. Besides this, a desire to secure to the mother country a monopoly of the trade of its colonies is a predominant feature in the system of almost every country in Europe. Nor is it without foundation in reason. Colonies, especially small islands, are usually maintained and defended at the expense of the mother country, and it seems a natural recompense for that service that the mother country should enjoy, exclusively of other nations, the benefit of trade with its colonies. This was thought reasonable by the United States while colonies even after their disputes on the point of taxation had begun; and however the question may stand between the mother country and its colonies, between the former and foreign nations, it is not easy to see how the equity of the exclusion can be contested. At any rate, its being the most prevailing system of nations having colonies, there is no room for acrimony against a particular one that pursues it. This ought not to dissuade the United States from availing itself of every just and proper influence to gain admission into the colony trade of the nations concerned; but this object ought to be pursued with moderation, not under the instigation of a sense of injury, but on the ground of temperate negotiation and reasonable equivalent.

These observations ought to produce two effects: to moderate our resentments against particular nations and our partialities for others, and to evince the impracticability and Quixotism of an attempt by violence, on the part of this young country, to break through the fetters which the universal policy of nations imposes on their intercourse with each other. . . .

The Secretary of State, after pointing out the exclusions, restrictions, and burdens which prevent our enjoying all the advantages which we could desire in the trade with foreign countries, proceeds to indicate the remedies; these are counter-exclusions, restrictions, and burdens.

The reason of the thing and the general observations of the Secretary of State would extend the regulations to be adopted to all the nations with whom we have connexions in trade; but his conclusion would seem to confine them to Great Britain, on the suggestion that she alone has declined friendly arrangements by treaty, and that there is no reason to conclude that friendly arrangements would be declined by other nations. . . .

Why, then, is Great Britain selected, but that it is most in unison with our passions to enter into collisions with her?

If retaliations for restrictions, exclusions, and burdens are to take place, they ought to be dealt out, with a proportional hand, to all those from whom they are experienced. This, justice and an inoffensive conduct require. If, suffering equal impediments to our trade from one power as another, we retaliate on one and not on another, we manifest that we are governed by a spirit of hostility towards the power against whom our retaliation is directed, and we ought to count upon a reciprocation of that spirit. If, suffering fewer from one than from another, we retaliate only on that party from whom we suffer least, the spirit of enmity by which we were actuated becomes more unequivocal. If, receiving a positively better treatment from one than another, we deal most harshly towards that power which treats us best, will it be an evidence either of justice or moderation? Will it not be a proof either of caprice or of a hatred and aversion of a nature to overrule the considerations both of equity and prudence? . . .

Whatever may be the motive, the operation may clearly be pronounced to be a phenomenon in political history—a government attempting to aid commerce by throwing it into confusion; by obstructing the most precious channels in which it flows, under the pretence of making it flow more freely; by damming up the best outlet for the surplus commodities of the country and the best inlet for the supplies of which it stands in need; by disturbing, without temptation, a beneficial course of things, in an experiment precarious, if not desperate; by arresting the current of a prosperous and progressive navigation to transfer it to other countries, and by making all this wild work in the blameable, but feeble attempt to build up the manufactures and trade of another country at the expense of the United States. . . .

It is a project calculated to disturb the existing course of three-fourths of our import trade, two-fifths of our export trade, and the means on which depend two-thirds, at least, of our revenues.

To be politic, therefore, it ought to unite these different ingredients:

First. An object of adequate utility to the country.

Second. A moral certainty, at least, of success.

Third. An assurance that the advantage likely to be obtained is not overbalanced by the inconveniences likely to be incurred, and as an equivalent for the jeopardy to which advantages in our possession are exposed.

1st. The direct object professed to be aimed at is a freer trade with Great Britain and access to her West India Islands, in our own ships. A collateral one, the success of which seems most relied on, is to transfer a part of our too great trade with Great Britain to other nations, particularly France.

The first is no doubt an object of real magnitude, worthy of every reasonable and promising exertion.

The second, in the single light of obviating a too great dependence for supply on one nation, is not unworthy of attention, but, as before observed, it ought only to be aimed at by expedients neither embarrassing nor expensive; it is a very insufficient object to be pursued either at hazard or expense to the people of the United States. It has been already shown, that to pursue it, either by prohibitions or partial increase of duties, would be a costly undertaking to this country.

2nd. The second ingredient is, "a moral certainty of success." The argument used to prove the probability, nay, the certainty of success, is this: the United States are a most important customer to Great Britain; they now take off near three millions in her manufactures, and by the progress of their population, which is likely to exceed that of their manufactures, the probability is that their importance as a customer will increase every year; their importance to Great Britain, as a source of supply, is not less than as a customer for her manufactures; the articles with which they furnish her, are those of prime necessity, consisting of the means of subsistence and the materials for ship-building and manufactures, while the articles we derive from her are mostly those of convenience and luxury; her supplies to us are therefore less useful than ours to her; that it would be contrary to all good policy in Great Britain to hazard the turning of a commerce so beneficial into other channels; besides all this, Great Britain is immersed in debt and in a state of decrepitude; derangement of our commerce with her would endanger a shock to the whole fabric of her credit, and by affecting injuriously the interests of a great portion of her mercantile body, and by throwing out of employ a large number of her manufacturers, would raise a clamor against the Ministry too loud and too extensive to be resisted; and that they would consequently be compelled, by the weight of these considerations to yield to our wishes.

It is as great an error in the councils of a country to over-rate as to under-rate its importance. The foregoing argument does this, and it does it in defiance of experience. Similar arguments were formerly used in favor of a non-importation scheme; the same consequences now foretold were then predicted in the most sanguine manner; but the prediction was not fulfilled. This it would seem, ought to be a caution to us now, and ought to warn us against relying upon the like effects, promised from a measure of much less force, namely, an increase of duties.

If our calculations are made on the ordinary course of the human passions, or on a just estimate of relative advantages for the contest proposed, we shall not be sanguine in expecting that the victory will be readily yielded to us, or that it will be easily obtained.

The Navigation Act of Great Britain, the principles of which exclude us from the advantages we wish to enjoy, is deemed by English politicians as the palladium of her riches, greatness, and security.

After having cherished it for such a long succession of years, after having repeatedly hazarded much for the maintenance of it, with so strong a conviction of its immense importance, is it at all probable that she would surrender it to us without a struggle—that she would permit us to extort the abandonment of it from her without a serious trial of strength?

Prejudices riveted by time and habit, opinions fixed by long experience of advantages, a sense of interest, irritated pride, a spirit of resentment at the attempt, all these strong circumstances would undoubtedly prompt to resistance. It would be felt that if a concession were made to us upon the strength of endeavors to extort it, the whole system must be renounced; it would be perceived that the way having been once successfully pointed out to other nations, would not fail to be followed, and that a surrender to one would be a surrender to all.

Resistance, therefore, would certainly follow in one or other mode, a war of arms or of commercial regulations.

If the first should be determined upon, it would not be difficult for Great Britain to persuade the other powers with whom she is united that they ought to make common cause with her. She would represent that our regulations were in fact only a covert method of taking part in the war by embarrassing her, and that it was the interest of the cause in which they were combined to frustrate our attempts.

If war could be foreseen as the certain consequence of the experiment proposed to be made, no arguments would be necessary to dissuade from it. Everybody would be sensible that more was to be lost than gained, and that so great a hazard ought not to be run.

But we are assured that there is no danger of this consequence, that no nation would have a right to take umbrage at any regulations we should adopt with regard to our own trade, and that Great Britain would take care how she put to risk so much as she would hazard by a quarrel with us.

All this is far more plausible than solid. Experience has proved to us that the councils of that country are influenced by passion as well as our own. If we should seize the present moment to attack her in a point where she is peculiarly susceptible, she would be apt to regard it as a mark of determined hostility. This would naturally tend to kindle those sparks of enmity which are alleged to exist on her side. War is as often the result of resentment as of calculation. A direct and immediate war between us would not be surprising; but if this should not take place, mutual ill offices and irritations, which naturally grow out of such a state of things, would be apt quickly to lead to it. Insults and aggressions might become so multiplied and open as not to permit forbearance on either side. . . .

Let us, however, take it for granted that she would prefer the other course, that of retaliating regulations; how will the contest stand? The proportion of the whole exports of Great Britain which comes to the United States is about one-fifth; the proportion of our exports which goes to Great Britain is about one-eighth of the whole amount of her imports. Taking the mean of these proportions of imports and exports, the proportion which our trade with Great Britain bears to the totality of her trade is about one-sixth.

The proportion of imports from the dominions of Great Britain into the United States may be stated at three-fourths of our whole importation; the proportion which our exports to the same dominions bears to our total exportation may be stated at two-fifths; taking the mean of those two, the proportion which our trade with Great Britain bears to our whole trade is something more than one-half.

This much greater proportional derangement of our trade than of hers by a contest is a mathematical demonstration that the contest would be unequal on our part; that we should put more to hazard than Great Britain would do; should be likely to suffer greater inconvenience than her, and consequently (the resolution and perseverance of the two parties being supposed equal) would be soonest induced to abandon the contest. . . .

The main argument for the chance of success is that our supplies to Great Britain are more necessary to her than hers to us. But this is a position which our self-love gives more credit to than facts will altogether authorize. Well-informed men in other countries (whose opportunities of information are at least as good as ours) affirm that Great Britain can obtain a supply of most of the articles she obtains from us as cheap and of as good a quality elsewhere, with only two exceptions, namely, tobacco and grain, and the latter is only occasionally wanted; a considerable substitute for our tobacco, though not of equal quality, may be had elsewhere; and even admitting this position to be too strongly stated, yet there is no good reason to doubt that it is in a great degree true. The colonies of the different European powers on this continent, some countries on the Mediterranean, and the northern countries of Europe, are in situations adapted to becoming our competitors.

On the other hand, the manufactured articles which we do not make ourselves (the greatest part of which are, in civilized countries, necessaries) are as important to us as our materials for manufacture (the only articles for which her demand is constant) are to Great Britain. The position is as true that no other nation can supply us as well as that country with several essential articles which we want, as that no nation can supply her equally well with certain articles which she takes from us; and as to other articles of subsistence, it is certain that our demand for manufactured supplies is more constantly urgent than her demand for those articles. Where, indeed, shall we find a substitute for the vast supply of manufactures which we get from that country? No gentleman will say that we can suddenly replace them by our manufactures, or that this, if practicable, could be done without a violent distortion of the natural course of our industry. A substitute of our own being out of the question, where else shall we find one?

France was the power which could best have filled any chasm that might have been created. But this is no longer the case. It is undeniable that the money capitals of that country have been essentially destroyed; that manufacturing establishments, except those for war, have been essentially deranged. The destruction to which Lyons appears to be doomed is a severe blow to the manufactures of France; that city, second in importance, in all respects, was perhaps the first in manufacturing importance. It is more than probable that France, for years to come, will herself want a foreign supply of manufactured articles. . . .

JAMES MADISON

Speech in the House of Representatives

14 January 1794

The House again resolved itself into a Committee of the Whole House on the Report of the Secretary of State . . . when Mr. Madison rose in reply to Mr. Smith. . . . The propositions immediately before the committee turned on the question whether any thing ought to be done at this time, in the way of commercial regulations, towards vindicating and advancing our national interests. Perhaps it might be made a question with some whether, in any case, legislative regulations of commerce were consistent with its nature and prosperity.

He professed himself to be a friend to the theory which gives to industry a free course, under the impulse of individual interest and the guidance of individual sagacity. He was persuaded that it would be happy for all nations if the barriers erected by prejudice, by avarice, and by despotism were broken down and a free intercourse established among them. Yet to this, as to all other general rules, there might be exceptions. And the rule itself required, what did not exist, that it should be general. . . .

This subject, as had been remarked on a former occasion, was not a novel one. It was co-eval with our political birth and has at all times exercised the thoughts of reflecting citizens. As early as the year succeeding the peace, the effect of the foreign policy which began to be felt in our trade and navigation excited universal attention and inquietude. The first effort thought of was an application of Congress to the states for a grant of power for a limited time to regulate our foreign commerce, with a view to control the influence of unfavorable regulations in some cases and to conciliate an extension of favorable ones in others. From some circumstances then incident to our situation, and particularly from a radical vice in the then political system of the United States, the experiment did not take effect.

The states next endeavored to effect their purpose by separate but concurrent regulations. Massachusetts opened a correspondence with Virginia and other states in order to bring about the plan. Here again the effort was abortive. Out of this experience grew the measures which terminated in the establishment of a government competent to the regulation of our commercial interests and the vindication of our commercial rights.

As these were the first objects of the people in the steps taken for establishing the present government, they were universally expected to be among the first fruits of its operation. In this expectation the public were disappointed. An attempt was made in different forms and received the repeated sanction of this branch of the legislature, but they expired in the Senate. Not indeed, as was alledged, from a dislike to the attempt altogether, but the modifications given to it. It has not appeared, however, that it was ever renewed in a different form in that house; & for some time it has been allowed to sleep in both.

If the reasons which originally prevailed against measures such as those now proposed had weight in them, they can no longer furnish a pretext for opposition.

When the subject was discussed in the first Congress at New-York, it was said that we ought to try the effect of a generous policy towards Great-Britain; that we ought to give time for negotiating a treaty of commerce; that we ought to await the close of negotiations for explaining and executing the treaty of peace. We have now waited a term of more than four years. The treaty of peace remains unexecuted on her part, tho' all pretext for delay has been removed by the steps taken on ours. No treaty of commerce is either in train or in prospect. Instead of relaxations in former articles complained of, we suffer new and aggravated violations of our rights.

In the view which he took of the subject, he called the attention of the committee particularly to the subject of navigation, of manufactures, and of the discrimination proposed in the motion between some nations and others.

On the subject of navigation, he observed that we were prohibited by the British laws from carrying to Great-Britain the produce of other countries from their ports, or our own produce from the ports of other countries, or the produce of other countries from our own ports, or to send our own produce from our own or other ports in the vessels of other countries. This last restriction was, he observed, felt by the United States at the present moment. It was indeed the practice of Great-Britain sometimes to relax her navigation act so far in time of war as to permit to neutral vessels a circuitous carriage; but as yet the act was in full force against the use of them for transporting the produce of the United States.

On the other hand, the laws of the United States allowed Great-Britain to bring into their ports any thing she might please, from her own or from other ports, and in her own or in other vessels.

In the trade between the United States and the British West-Indies, the vessels of the former were under an absolute prohibition, whilst British vessels in that trade enjoyed all the privileges granted to other, even the most favored, nations in their trade with us. The inequality in this case was the more striking as it was evident that the West-Indies were dependent on the United States for the supplies essential to them, and that the circumstances which secured to the United States this advantage enabled their vessels to transport the supplies on far better terms than could be done by British vessels.

To illustrate the policy requisite in our commercial intercourse with other nations, he presented a comparative view of the American and foreign tonnage employed in the respective branches of it, from which it appeared that the foreign stood to the American as follows—

Spain	1 to 5
Portugal	1 to 6
The United Netherlands	1 to 15
Denmark	1 to 12
Russia	——
France	1 to 5
Great-Britain	5 to 1

It results from these facts that in proportion as the trade might be diminished with Great-Britain and increased with other nations, would be the probable increase of the American tonnage. It appeared, for example, that as the trade might pass from British channels into those of France it would augment our tonnage at the rate of ten to one. . . .

Such a disproportion, taking even the reduced one, in the navigation with Great-Britain was the more mortifying when the nature and amount of our exports are considered. Our exports are not only for the most part either immediately necessaries of life or . . . necessaries of employment and life to manufacturers, and must thence command a sure market wherever they are received at all. But the peculiar bulkiness of them furnishes an advantage over the exports of every other country, and particularly over those of Great-Britain. . . . The bulk of her exports to us compared with that of ours to her is as nothing. An inconsiderable quantity of shipping would suffice for hers, whilst ours can load about 222,000 tons. Including the articles she exports from the West-Indies to this country, they bear no proportion to ours. Yet in the entire trade between the United States and the British dominions, her tonnage is to that of the United States as 156,000, employing 9,360 seamen, to 66,000, employing 3,690 seamen. Were a rigid exertion of our right to take place, it would extend our tonnage to 222,000, and leave to G.B. employment for much less than the actual share now enjoyed by the United States. It could not be wished to push matters to this extremity. It showed, however, the very unequal and unfavorable footing on which the carrying trade, the great resource of our safety and respectability, was placed by foreign regulations, and the reasonableness of peaceable attempts to meliorate it. We might at least, in availing ourselves of the merit of our exports, contend for such regulations as would reverse the proportion and give the United States the 156,000 tonnage and 9,360 seamen, instead of the 66,000 tonnage and 3,690 seamen. . . .

It was not the *imports* but *exports* that regulated the quantity of tonnage. What was imported in American vessels, which would otherwise return empty, was no doubt a benefit to the American merchant, but could slightly only, if at all, increase the mass of our tonnage. The way to effect this was to secure *exportations* to American bottoms.

Proceeding to the subject of manufactures, he observed that it presented no compensations for the inequalities in the principles and effects of the navigation system.

We consume British manufactures to double the amount of what Britain takes from us; and *quadruple* the amount of what she actually *consumes*.

We take everything after it has undergone all the profitable labor that can be bestowed on it. She receives, in return, raw materials, the food of her industry.

We send necessaries to her. She sends superfluities to us.

We admit *every thing* she pleases to send us, whether of her own or alien production. She refuses not only our manufactures, but the articles we wish most to send her; our wheat and flour, our fish, and our salted provisions. These constitute our best staples for exportation, as her manufactures constitute hers.

It appeared by an authentic document he had examined that of the *manufactured* articles imported in 1790, amounting to 15,295,638 dollars 97 cents, we received from and *thro'* Great-Britain, 13,965,464 dollars 95 cents.

During the same year, the *manufactures* imported from France, the next great commercial country, and consuming more of our produce than Great-Britain, amounted to no more than 155,136 dollars and 63 cents.

To give a fuller view of our foreign commerce, he stated the balances with the several nations of Europe and their dominions as follow:

	Dollars	
Spain	1,670,797	in favor of U.S.
Portugal	1,687,699	ditto
U. Netherlands	791,118	ditto
Sweden	32,965	ditto
Denmark	126,949	against the U.S.
France	2,630,387	in favor of U.S.
G. Britain	5,922,012	against the U.S.

This enormous balance to G.B. is on the *exports* to her. On her *consumption* the balance is still greater, amounting to nine or ten millions, to which again is to be added her profits on the re-exports in a manufactured and raw state.

It might be said that an unfavorable balance was no proof of an unfavorable trade, that the only important balance was the ultimate one on our aggregate commerce.

That there was much truth in this general doctrine was admitted, at the same time it was equally certain that there were exceptions to it, some of which were conceived to be applicable to the situation of the United States.

But whether the doctrine were just or not, as applied to the United States, it was well known that the reasoning and practice of other countries were governed by a contrary doctrine. In all of them, an unfavorable balance to be paid in specie was considered as an evil. Great-Britain in particular had always studied to prevent it as much as she could. What then may be the effect on the policy of a nation with which we have the most friendly and beneficial relations when it sees the balance of trade with us not only so much against her, but all the specie that pays it flowing immediately into the lap of her greatest rival, if not her most inveterate enemy.

As to the discrimination proposed between nations having and not having commercial treaties with us, the principle was embraced by the laws of most, if not all the states, whilst the regulation of trade was in their hands.

It had the repeated sanction of votes in the House of Representatives during the session of the present government at New-York.

It has been practiced by other nations, and in a late instance against the United States.

It tends to procure beneficial treaties from those who refuse them, by making them the price of enjoying an equality with other nations in our commerce.

It tends, as a conciliatory preference, to procure better treaties from those who have not refused them.

It was a prudent consideration, in dispensing commercial advantages, to favor rather those whose friendship and support may be expected in case of necessity than those whose disposition wore a contrary aspect. He did not wish to enter at present, nor at all, if unnecessary, into a display of the unfriendly features which marked the policy of Great-Britain towards the United States. He should be content to lay aside, at least for the present, the subject of the Indians, the Algerines, the spoliations, &c. but he could not forbear remarking, generally, that if that or any other nation were known to bear us a settled ill-will, nothing could be more impolitic than to foster resources which would be more likely to be turned against us than exerted in our favor.

It had been admitted by the gentleman who spoke yesterday (Mr. Smith of South Carolina) to be a misfortune that our trade should be so far engrossed by any one nation as it is in the hands of Great-Britain. But the gentleman added nothing to alleviate the misfortune when he advised us to make no efforts for putting an end to it. The evils resulting from such a state of things were as serious as they were numerous. To say nothing of sudden derangements from the caprice with which sovereigns might be seized, there were casualties which might not be avoidable. A general bankruptcy, which was a possible event, in a nation with which we were so connected, would reverberate upon us with a most dreadful shock. A partial bankruptcy had actually and lately taken place; and was severely felt in our commerce. War is a common event particularly to G. Britain and involves us in the embarrassments it brings on her commerce whilst ours is so disproportionately interwoven with it. Add the influence that may be conveyed into the public councils by a nation directing the course of our trade by her capital, & holding so great a share in our pecuniary institutions, and the effect that may finally ensue on our taste, our manners, and our form of government itself.

If the question be asked, what might be the consequence of counter-efforts, and whether this attempt to vindicate our public interests would not produce them? His answer was that he did not in the least apprehend such a consequence, as well because the measure afforded no pretext, being short of what was already done by Great-Britain in her commercial system, as because she would be the greatest sufferer from a stagnation of the trade between the two countries if she should force on such a crisis.

Her merchants would feel it. Her navigation would feel it. Her manufacturers would feel it. Her West-Indies would be ruined by it. Her revenue would deeply feel it. And her government would feel it thro' every nerve of its operations. We too should suffer in some respects but in a less degree, and, if the virtue and temper of our fellow citizens were not mistaken, the experiment would find in them a far greater readiness to bear it. It was clear to him, therefore, that if Great-Britain should, contrary to all the rules of probability, stop the commerce between the two countries, the issue would be a complete triumph to the United States.

He dwelt particularly on the dependence of British manufactures on the market of the United States. He referred to a paper in Anderson's History of Commerce, which states the amount of British manufactures at £51,310,000 sterling, and the number of souls employed in, and supported by them, at 5,250,000. Supposing the United States to consume two and a half millions of British manufactures, which is a moderate estimate, the loss of their market would deprive of subsistence 250,000 souls. Add 50,000 who depend for employment on our raw materials. Here are 300,000 souls who live by our custom. Let them be driven to poverty and despair by acts of their own government, and what would be the consequence? Most probably an acquisition of so many useful citizens to the United States, which form the natural asylum against the distresses of Europe. But whether they should remain in discontent and wretchedness in their own country or seek their fortunes in another, the evil would be felt by the British government as equally great, and be avoided with equal caution.

It might be regarded, he observed, as a general rule, that where one nation consumed the necessaries of life produced by another, the consuming nation was dependent on the producing one. On the other hand, where the consumption consisted of superfluities, the producing nation was dependent on the consuming one. The United States were in the fortunate situation of enjoying both

these advantages over Great-Britain. They supply a part of her dominions with the necessaries of life. They consume superfluities which give bread to her people in another part. Great-Britain, therefore, is under a double dependence on the commerce of the United States. She depends on them for what she herself consumes; she depends on them for what they consume.

In proportion as a nation manufactures luxuries must be its disadvantage in contests of every sort with its customers. The reason is obvious. What is a luxury to the consumer is a necessary to the manufacturer. By changing a fashion, or disappointing a fancy only, bread may be taken from the mouths of thousands whose industry is devoted to the gratification of artificial wants.

He mentioned the case of a petition from a great body of buckle makers presented a few years ago to the Prince of Wales, complaining of the use of strings instead of buckles in the shoes and supplicating his royal highness, as giving the law to fashions, to save them from want and misery by discontinuing the new one. It was not, he observed, the prince who petitioned the manufacturers to continue to make the buckles, but the manufacturers who petitioned their customers to buy them. The relation was similar between the American customers and the British manufacturers. And if a law were to pass for putting a stop to the use of their superfluities, or a stop were otherwise to be put to it, it would quickly be seen from which the distress and supplications would flow.

Suppose that Great-Britain received from us alone the whole of the necessaries she consumes, and that our market alone took off the luxuries with which she paid for them. Here the dependence would be complete, and we might impose whatever terms we pleased on the exchange. This to be sure is not absolutely the case; but in proportion as it is the case, her dependence is on us.

The West-Indies, however, are an example of complete dependence. They cannot subsist without our food. They cannot flourish without our lumber and our use of their rum. On the other hand we depend on them for not a single necessary, and can supply ourselves with their luxuries from other sources. Sugar is the only article about which there was ever a question, and he was authorized to say that there was not at the most one sixth of our consumption supplied from the British islands.

In time of war or famine the dependence of the West-Indies is felt in all its energy. It is sometimes such as to appeal to our humanity as well as our interest for relief. At this moment, the governor of Jamaica is making proclamation of their distresses. If ever, therefore, there was a case where one country could dictate to another the regulations of trade between them, it is the case of the United States and the British West-Indies. And yet the gentleman from South Carolina (Mr. Smith) had considered it as a favor that we were allowed to send our provisions in British bottoms, & in these only, to the West-Indies. The favor reduced to plain language in the mouth of their planters would run thus: We will agree to buy your provisions rather than starve and let you have our rum, which we can sell nowhere else; but we reserve out of this indulgence a monopoly of the carriage to British vessels.

With regard to revenue, the British resources were extremely exhausted in comparison with those of the United States.

The people of Great-Britain were taxed at the rate of 4s a head; the people of the United States at not more than 6d a head, less than one-sixth of the British tax.

As the price of labor which pays the tax is double in the United States to what it is in Great-Britain, the burden on American citizens is less than one-twelfth of the burden on British subjects.

It is true, indeed, that Britain alone does not bear the whole burden. She levies indirect taxes on her West-Indies and on her East-Indies, and derives from an acquiescence in her monopolizing regulations an imperceptible tribute from the whole commercial world.

Still, however, the difference of burden in the two countries is immense.

Britain has moreover great arrears of unfunded debts. She is threatened with defects in her revenue even at this time. She is engaged in an expensive war. And she raises the supplies for it on the most expensive terms.

Add to the whole that her population is stationary if not diminishing, whilst that of the United States is in a course of increase beyond example.

Should it still be asked whether the impost might not be affected, and how a deficiency could be supplied? He thought sufficient answers might be given.

He took for granted that the articles subjected to the additional duties would continue to come according to the demand for them. And believed if the duties were prudently adjusted, the increase of the duties would balance the decrease of importation. . . .

JAMES MADISON
"Political Observations"
20 April 1795

After the Third Congress adjourned, Madison again defended his commercial propositions and Republican conduct in general in this anonymous pamphlet.

A variety of publications, in pamphlets and other forms, have appeared in different parts of the Union since the session of Congress which ended in June, 1794, endeavoring, by discolored representations of our public affairs, and particularly of certain occurrences of that session, to turn the tide of public opinion into a party channel. The immediate object of the writers was either avowedly or evidently to operate on the approaching elections of Federal Representatives. As that crisis will have entirely elapsed before the following observations will appear, they will, at least, be free from a charge of the same views; and will, consequently, have the stronger claim to that deliberate attention and reflection to which they are submitted.

The publications alluded to have passed slightly over the transactions of the First and Second Congress; and so far, their example will here be followed.

Whether, indeed, the funding system was modelled either on the principles of substantial justice or on the demands of public faith? Whether it did not contain ingredients friendly to the duration of the public debt and implying that it was regarded as a public good? Whether the assumption of the state debts was not enforced by overcharged representations; and Whether, if the burdens had been equalized only, instead of being assumed in the gross, the states could not have discharged their respective proportions by their local resources sooner and more conveniently than the general government will be able to discharge the whole debts by general resources? Whether the excise system be congenial with the spirit and conducive to the happiness of our country; or can even justify itself as a productive source of revenue? Whether, again, the bank was not established without authority from the Constitution? Whether it did not throw unnecessary and unreasonable advantages into the hands of men previously enriched beyond reason or necessity? And whether it can be allowed the praise of a salutary operation until its effects shall have been more accurately traced and its hidden transactions shall be fully unveiled to the public eye: These and others are questions which, though of great importance, it is not intended here to examine. Most of them have been finally decided by the competent authority; and the rest have, no doubt, already impressed themselves on the public attention.

Passing on then to the session of Congress preceding the last, we are met in the first place by the most serious charges against the southern members of Congress in general and particularly against the representatives of Virginia. They are charged with having supported a policy which would inevitably have involved the United States in the war of Europe, have reduced us from the rank of a free people to that of French colonies, and possibly have landed us in disunion, anarchy, and misery; and the policy from which these tremendous calamities was to flow is referred to certain commercial resolutions moved by a member from Virginia in the House of Representatives.

To place in its true light the fallacy which infers such consequences from such a cause, it will be proper to review the circumstances which preceded and attended the resolutions.

It is well known that at the peace between the United States and Great Britain, it became a question with the latter whether she should endeavor to regain the lost commerce of America by liberal and reciprocal arrangements or trust to a relapse of it into its former channels without the price of such arrangements on her part. Whilst she was fearful that our commerce would be conducted into new and rival channels, she leaned to the first side of the alternative, and a bill was actually carried in the House of Commons by the present Prime Minister corresponding with that sentiment. She soon, however, began to discover (or to hope) that the weakness of our Federal Government and the want of concurrence among the state governments would secure her against the danger at first apprehended. From that moment all ideas of conciliation and concession vanished. She determined to enjoy at once the full benefit of the freedom allowed by our regulations and of the monopolies established by her own.

In this state of things, the pride as well as the interest of America were everywhere aroused. The mercantile world in particular was all on fire; complaints flew from one end of the continent to the other; projects of retaliation and redress engrossed the public attention. At one time, the states endeavored by separate efforts to counteract the unequal laws of Great Britain. At another, correspondencies were opened for uniting their efforts. An attempt was also made to vest in the former Congress a limited power for a limited time, in order to give effect to the general will.

All these experiments, instead of answering the purpose in view, served only to confirm Great Britain in her first belief, that her restrictive plans were in no danger of retaliation.

It was at length determined by the Legislature of Virginia to go to work in a new way. It was proposed, and most of the states agreed, to send commissioners to digest some change in our general system that might prove an effectual remedy. The commissioners met; but finding their powers too circumscribed for the great object which expanded itself before them, they proposed a convention on a more enlarged plan for a general revision of the Federal Government.

From this convention proceeded the present Federal Constitution, which gives to the general will the means of providing in the several necessary cases for the general welfare; and particularly in the case of regulating our commerce in such manner as may be required by the regulations of other countries.

It was natural to expect that one of the first objects of deliberation under the new constitution would be that which had been first and most contemplated in forming it. Accordingly it was, at the first session, proposed that something should be done analogous to the wishes of the several states and expressive of the efficiency of the new government. A discrimination between nations in treaty and those not in treaty, the mode most generally embraced by the states, was agreed to in several forms, and adhered to in repeated votes, by a very great majority of the House of Representatives. The Senate, however, did not concur with the House of Representatives, and our commercial arrangements were made up without any provision on the subject.

From that date to the session of Congress ending in June, 1794, the interval passed without any effective appeal to the interest of Great Britain. A silent reliance was placed on her voluntary justice, or her enlightened interest.

The long and patient reliance being ascribed (as was foretold) to other causes than a generous forbearance on the part of the United States had, at the commencement of the Third Congress, left us with respect to a reciprocity of commercial regulations between the two countries precisely where the commencement of the First Congress had found us. This was not all, the western posts, which entailed an expensive Indian war on us, continued to be withheld, although all pretext for it had been removed on our part. Depredations as derogatory to our rights as grievous to our interests had been licenced by the British Government against our lawful commerce on the high seas. And it was believed, on the most probable grounds, that the measure by which the Algerine Pirates were let loose on the Atlantic had not taken place without the participation of the same unfriendly counsels. In a word, to say nothing of the American victims to savages and barbarians, it was estimated that our annual damages from Great Britain were not less than three or four millions of dollars.

This distressing situation spoke the more loudly to the patriotism of the representatives of the people as the nature and manner of the communications from the President seemed to make a formal and affecting appeal on the subject to their co-operation. The necessity of some effort was palpable. The only room for different opinions seemed to lie in the different modes of redress proposed. On one side nothing was proposed, beyond the eventual measures of defence, in which all concurred, except the building of six frigates, for the purpose of enforcing our rights against Algiers. The other side, considering this measure as pointed at one only of our evils, and as inadequate even to that, thought it best to seek for some safe but powerful remedy that might be applied to the root of them; and with this view the Commercial Propositions were introduced.

They were at first opposed on the ground that Great Britain was amicably disposed towards the United States, and that we ought to await the event of the depending negociation. To this it was replied that more than four years of appeal to that disposition had been tried in vain by the new government; that the negotiation had been abortive and was no longer depending; that the late letters from Mr. Pinckney, the minister at London, had not only cut off all remaining hope from that source, but had expressly pointed commercial regulations as the most eligible redress to be pursued.

Another ground of opposition was that the United States were more dependent on the trade of Great Britain than Great Britain was on the trade of the United States. This will appear scarcely credible to those who understand the commerce between the two countries, who recollect that it supplies us chiefly with superfluities whilst in return it employs the industry of one part of her people, sends to another part the very bread which keeps them from starving, and remits moreover, an annual balance in specie of ten or twelve millions of dollars. It is true, nevertheless, as the debate shows, that this was the language, however strange, of some who combated the propositions.

Nay, what is still more extraordinary, it was maintained that the United States had, on the whole, little or no reason to complain of the footing of their commerce with Great Britain; although such complaints had prevailed in every state, among every class of citizens, ever since the year 1783; and although the Federal Constitution had originated in those complaints, and had been established with the known view of redressing them.

As such objections could have little effect in convincing the judgement of the House of Representatives, and still less that of the public at large, a new mode of assailing the propositions has been substituted. The American People love peace; and the cry of war might alarm when no hope remained of convincing them. The cry of war has accordingly been echoed through the continent, with a loudness proportioned to the emptiness of the pretext; and to this cry has been added another still more absurd, that the propositions would in the end enslave the United States to their allies and plunge them into anarchy and misery.

It is truly mortifying to be obliged to tax the patience of the reader with an examination of such gross absurdities; but it may be of use to expose, where there may be no necessity to refute them.

What were the commercial propositions? They discriminated between nations in treaty and nations not in treaty by an additional duty on the manufactures and trade of the latter; and they reciprocated the navigation laws of all nations who excluded the vessels of the United States from a common right of being used in the trade between the United States and such nations.

Is there any thing here that could afford a cause or a pretext for war to Great Britain or any other nation? If we hold at present the rank of a free people, if we are no longer colonies of Great Britain, if we have not already relapsed into some dependence on that nation, we have the self-evident right to regulate our trade according to our own will and our own interest, not according to her will or her interest. This right can be denied to no independent nation. It has not been and will not be denied to ourselves by any opponent of the propositions.

If the propositions could give no right to Great Britain to make war, would they have given any color to her for such an outrage on us? No American citizen will affirm it. No British subject who is a man of candor will pretend it; because he must know that the commercial regulations of Great Britain herself have discriminated among foreign nations whenever it was thought convenient. They have discriminated against particular nations by name; they have discriminated with respect to particular articles by name, by the nations producing them, and by the places exporting them. And as to the navigation articles proposed, they were not only common to the other countries along with Great Britain; but reciprocal between Great Britain and the United States: Nay, it is notorious that they fell short of an immediate and exact reciprocity of her own Navigation Laws.

Would any nation be so barefaced as to quarrel with another for doing the same thing which she herself has done, for doing less than she herself has done, towards that particular nation? It is impossible that Great Britain would ever expose herself by so absurd as well as arrogant a proceeding. If she really meant to quarrel with this country, common prudence and common decency would prescribe some other less odious pretext for her hostility.

It is the more astonishing that such a charge against the propositions should have been hazarded when the opinion and the proceedings of America on the subject of our commercial policy is reviewed.

Whilst the power over trade remained with the several states, there were few of them that did not exercise it on the principle, if not in the mode, of the commercial propositions. The eastern states generally passed laws either discriminating between some foreign nations and others or levelled against Great Britain by name. Maryland and Virginia did the same. So did two, if not the three, of the more southern states. Was it ever, during that period, pretended at home or abroad that a cause or pretext for quarrel was given to Great Britain or any other nation? Or were our rights better understood at that time than at this or more likely then than now to command the respect due to them.

Let it not be said, Great Britain was then at peace, she is now at war. If she would not wantonly attempt to control the exercise of our sovereign rights when she had no other enemy on her hands, will she be mad enough to make the attempt when her hands are fully employed with the war already on

them? Would not those who say now, postpone the measures until Great Britain shall be at peace, be more ready, nay have more reason to say in time of peace, postpone them until she should be at war; there will then be no danger of her throwing new enemies into the scale against her.

Nor let it be said that the combined powers would aid and stimulate Great Britain to wage an unjust war on the United States. They are too fully occupied with their present enemy to wish for another on their hands; not to add that two of those powers, being in treaty with the United States, are favored by the propositions; and that all of them are well known to entertain an habitual jealousy of the monopolizing character and maritime ascendency of that nation.

One thing ought to be regarded as certain and conclusive on this head; whilst the war against France remains unsuccessful, the United States are in no danger from any of the powers engaged in it. In the event of a complete overthrow of that Republic, it is impossible to know what might follow. But if the hostile views of the combination should be turned towards this continent, it would clearly not be to vindicate the commercial interests of Great Britain against the commercial rivals of the United States. The object would be to root out Liberty from the face of the earth. No pretext would be wanted, or a better would be contrived than anything to be found in the commercial proposition.

On whatever other side we view the clamor against these propositions as inevitably productive of war, it presents neither evidence to justify it nor argument to color it.

The allegation necessarily supposes either that the friends of the propositions could discover no probability, where its opponents could see a certainty, or that the former were less averse to war than the latter.

The first supposition will not be discussed. A few observations on the other may throw new lights on the whole subject.

The members, in general, who espoused these propositions have been constantly in that part of the Congress who have professed with most zeal, and pursued with most scruple, the characteristics of republican government. They have adhered to these characteristics in defining the meaning of the Constitution, in adjusting the ceremonial of public proceedings, and in marking out the course of the Administration. They have manifested, particularly, a deep conviction of the danger to liberty and the Constitution from a gradual assumption or extension of discretionary powers in the executive departments; from successive augmentations of a standing army; and from the perpetuity and progression of public debts and taxes. They have been sometimes reprehended in debate for an excess of caution and jealousy on these points. And the newspapers of a certain stamp, by distorting and discolouring this part of their conduct, have painted it in all the deformity which the most industrious calumny could devise.

Those best acquainted with the individuals who more particularly supported the propositions will be foremost to testify that such are the principles which not only govern them in public life, but which are invariably maintained by them in every other situation. And it cannot be believed nor suspected that with such principles they could view war as less an evil than it appeared to their opponents.

Of all the enemies to public liberty, war is, perhaps, the most to be dreaded, because it comprises and develops the germ of every other. War is the parent of armies; from these proceed debts and taxes; and armies, and debts, and taxes are the known instruments for bringing the many under the domination of the few. In war, too, the discretionary power of the Executive is extended; its influence in dealing out offices, honors, and emoluments is multiplied; and all the means of seducing the minds are added to those of subduing the force of the people. The same malignant aspect in republicanism may be traced in the inequality of fortunes and the opportunities of fraud growing out of a state of war, and in the degeneracy of manners and of morals engendered by both. No nation could reserve its freedom in the midst of continual warfare.

Those truths are well established. They are read in every page which records the progression from a less arbitrary to a more arbitrary government, or the transition from a popular government to an aristocracy or a monarchy.

It must be evident, then, that in the same degree as the friends of the propositions were jealous of armies and debts and prerogative, as dangerous to a republican Constitution, they must have been averse to war, as favourable to armies and debts and prerogative.

The fact accordingly appears to be that they were particularly averse to war. They not only considered the propositions as having no tendency to war, but preferred them as the most likely means of obtaining our objects without war. They thought, and thought truly, that Great Britain was more vulnerable in her commerce than in her fleets and armies; that she valued our necessaries for her markets and our markets for her superfluities, more than

she feared our frigates or our militia; and that she would, consequently, be more ready to make proper concessions under the influence of the former than of the latter motive.

Great Britain is a commercial nation. Her power, as well as her wealth, is derived from commerce. The American commerce is the most valuable branch she enjoys. It is the more valuable, not only as being of vital importance to her in some respects, but of growing importance beyond estimate in its general character. She will not easily part with such a resource. She will not rashly hazard it. She would be particularly aware of forcing a perpetuity of regulations which not merely diminish her share, but may favour the rivalship of other nations. If anything, therefore, in the power of the United States could overcome her pride, her avidity, and her repugnancy to this country, it was justly concluded to be, not the fear of our arms, which, though invincible in defense, are little formidable in a war of offense, but the fear of suffering in the most fruitful branch of her trade and of seeing it distributed among her rivals.

If any doubt on this subject could exist, it would vanish on a recollection of the conduct of the British ministry at the close of the war in 1783. It is a fact which has been already touched, and it is as notorious as it is instructive, that during the apprehension of finding her commerce with the United States abridged or endangered by the consequences of the revolution, Great Britain was ready to purchase it, even at the expense of her West-Indies monopoly. It was not until after she began to perceive the weakness of the federal government, the discord in the counteracting plans of the state governments, and the interest she would be able to establish here, that she ventured on that system to which she has since inflexibly adhered. Had the present federal government, on its first establishment, done what it ought to have done, what it was instituted and expected to do, and what was actually proposed and intended it should do; had it revived and confirmed the belief in Great Britain that our trade and navigation would not be free to her without an equal and reciprocal freedom to us in her trade and navigation, we have her own authority for saying that she would long since have met us on proper ground; because the same motives which produced the bill brought into the British Parliament by Mr. Pitt, in order to prevent the evil apprehended, would have produced the same concession at least, in order to obtain a recall of the evil after it had taken place.

The aversion to war in the friends of the propositions

may be traced through the whole proceedings and debates of the session. After the depredations in the West-Indies, which seemed to fill up the measure of British aggressions, they adhered to their original policy of pursuing redress rather by commercial than by hostile operations; and with this view unanimously concurred in the bill for suspending importations from British ports, a bill that was carried through the House by a vote of fifty-eight against thirty-four. The friends of the propositions appeared, indeed, never to have admitted that Great Britain could seriously mean to force a war with the United States, unless in the event of prostrating the French Republic; and they did not believe that such an event was to be apprehended.

Confiding in this opinion, to which time has given its full sanction, they could not accede to those extraordinary measures which nothing short of the most obvious and imperious necessity could plead for. They were as ready as any to fortify our harbours and fill our magazines and arsenals; these were safe and requisite provisions for our permanent defense. They were ready and anxious for arming and preparing our militia; that was the true republican bulwark of our security. They joined also in the addition of a regiment of artillery to the military establishment, in order to complete the defensive arrangement on our eastern frontier. These facts are on record, and are the proper answer to those shameless calumnies which have asserted that the friends of the commercial propositions were enemies to every proposition for the national security.

But it was their opponents, not they, who continually maintained that on a failure of negotiation, it would be more eligible to seek redress by war than by commercial regulations; who talked of raising armies that might threaten the neighbouring possessions of foreign powers; who contended for delegating to the executive the prerogatives of deciding whether the country was at war or not, and of levying, organizing, and calling into the field a regular army of ten, fifteen, nay, of twenty-five thousand men.

It is of some importance that this part of the history of the session, which has found no place in the late reviews of it, should be well understood. They who are curious to learn the particulars must examine the debates and the votes. A full narrative would exceed the limits which are here prescribed. It must suffice to remark that the efforts were varied and repeated until the last moment of the session, even after the departure of a number of members

forbade new propositions, much more a renewal of rejected ones; and that the powers proposed to be surrendered to the executive were those which the Constitution has most jealously appropriated to the legislature.

The reader shall judge on this subject for himself.

The Constitution expressly and exclusively vests in the legislature the power of declaring a state of war; it was proposed that the executive might, in the recess of the legislature, declare the United States to be in a state of war.

The Constitution expressly and exclusively vests in the legislature the power of raising armies: it was proposed, that in the recess of the legislature, the executive might, at its pleasure, raise or not raise an army of ten, fifteen, or twenty-five thousand men.

The Constitution expressly and exclusively vests in the legislature the power of creating offices; it was proposed that the executive, in the recess of the legislature, might create offices, as well as appoint officers, for an army of ten, fifteen, or twenty-five thousand men.

A delegation of such powers would have struck, not only at the fabric of our Constitution, but at the foundation of all well organized and well checked governments.

The separation of the power of declaring war from that of conducting it is wisely contrived to exclude the danger of its being declared for the sake of its being conducted.

The separation of the power of raising armies from the power of commanding them is intended to prevent the raising of armies for the sake of commanding them.

The separation of the power of creating offices from that of filling them is an essential guard against the temptation to create offices for the sake of gratifying favorites or multiplying dependents.

Where would be the difference between the blending of these incompatible powers, by surrendering the legislative part of them into the hands of the executive, and by assuming the executive part of them into the hands of the legislature? In either case the principle would be equally destroyed, and the consequences equally dangerous.

An attempt to answer these observations by appealing to the virtues of the present chief magistrate and to the confidence justly placed in them will be little calculated either for his genuine patriotism or for the sound judgment of the American public.

The people of the United States would not merit the praise universally allowed to their intelligence if they did not distinguish between the respect due to the man and the functions belonging to the office. In expressing the former, there is no limit or guide but the feelings of their grateful hearts. In deciding the latter, they will consult the Constitution; they will consider human nature, and, looking beyond the character of the existing magistrate, fix their eyes on the precedent which must descend to his successors.

Will it be more than truth to say that this great and venerable name is too often assumed for what cannot recommend itself, and for what there is neither proof nor probability that its sanction can be claimed? Do arguments fail? Is the public mind to be encountered? There are not a few ever ready to invoke the name of Washington; to garnish their heretical doctrines with his virtues and season their unpallatable measures with his popularity. Those who take this liberty will not, however, be mistaken; his truest friends will be the last to sport with his influence, above all for electioneering purposes. And it is but a fair suspicion that they who draw most largely on that fund are hastening fastest to bankruptcy in their own.

As vain would be the attempt to explain away such alarming attacks on the Constitution by pleading the difficulty, in some cases, of drawing a line between the different departments of power; of recurring to the little precedents which may have crept in at urgent or unguarded moments.

It cannot be denied that there may, in certain cases, be a difficulty in distinguishing the exact boundary between legislative and executive powers; but the real friend of the Constitution and of liberty, by his endeavors to lessen or avoid the difficulty, will easily be known from him who labours to encrease the obscurity, in order to remove the constitutional landmarks without notice.

Nor will it be denied that precedents may be found where the line of separation between these powers has not been sufficiently regarded; where an improper latitude of discretion, particularly, has been given or allowed to the executive departments. But what does this prove? That the line ought to be considered as imaginary; that constitutional organizations of power ought to lose their effect? No—It proves with how much deliberation precedents ought to be established, and with how much caution arguments from them should be admitted. It may furnish another criterion, also, between the real and ostensible friend of constitutional liberty. The first will be as vigilant in resisting as the last will be in promoting the growth of inconsiderate or insidious precedents into established encroachments.

The next charge to be examined, is the tendency of the propositions to degrade the United States into French colonies.

As it is difficult to argue against suppositions made and multiplied at will, so it is happily impossible to impose on the good sense of this country by arguments which rest on suppositions only. In the present question it is first supposed that the exercise of the self-evident and sovereign right of regulating trade, after the example of all independent nations and that of the example of Great Britain towards the United States, would inevitably involve the United States in a war with Great Britain. It is then supposed that the other combined powers, though some of them be favored by the regulations proposed, and all of them be jealous of the maritime predominance of Great Britain, would support the wrongs of Great Britain against the rights of the United States. It is lastly supposed that our allies (the French) in the event of success in establishing their own liberties, which they owe to our example, would be willing, as well as able, to rob us of ours, which they assisted us in obtaining; and that so malignant is their disposition on this head that we should not be spared, even if embarked in a war against her own enemy. To finish the picture, it is intimated that in the character of allies, we are the more exposed to this danger, from the secret and hostile ambition of France.

It will not be expected, that any formal refutation should be wasted on absurdities which answer themselves. None but those who have surrendered their reasoning faculties to the violence of their prejudices will listen to suggestions implying that the freest nation in Europe is the basest people on the face of the earth; that instead of the friendly and festive sympathy indulged by the people of the United States, they ought to go into mourning at every triumph of the French arms; that instead of regarding the French Revolution as a blessing to mankind and a bulwark to their own, they ought to anticipate its success as of all events the most formidable to their liberty and sovereignty; and that, calculating on the political connection with that nation as the source of additional danger from its enmity and its usurpation, the first favorable moment ought to be seized for putting an end to it. . . .

The Popular Societies, the Excise, and the Whiskey Rebellion

Beginning in Philadelphia in the spring of 1793, concurrently with Citizen Genet's arrival in the country and inspired in part by the Jacobin societies in France, a score of popular societies sprang up in every portion of the country. Suspicion of the Federalists as well as friendship for France was one of their identifying features, and the excise tax on whiskey, which was provoking sharp resistance along the whole frontier, was one of their favorite targets.

By the summer of 1794, resistance to the excise had taken a violent turn in western Pennsylvania. On 7 August, President Washington issued a proclamation ordering the rebels to desist and mobilizing fifteen thousand militia from Virginia, Maryland, New Jersey, and Pennsylvania. When the trouble continued, the militia marched. Commanded by Virginia's governor, Henry ("Light Horse Harry") Lee, and with Hamilton along to act in place of the absent secretary at war, the militia suppressed the Whiskey Rebellion without an armed collision. Two captured insurgents were tried and convicted of treason. Washington pardoned them both.

Republicans very generally condemned the whiskey rebels' violent opposition to the laws, and it was said that the Pennsylvania Democratic Society (the "mother club") could have made a quorum in the army that suppressed them. The president, however, blamed the trouble partly on the agitation of the "self-created societies," which he condemned in his annual message when the Fourth Congress convened. Led by Madison, who considered Washington's message the worst mistake of his political career, Republicans in Congress jumped to the societies' defense. Most of the societies disintegrated fairly rapidly in the face of the president's condemnation, but they had played a notable part in popular political mobilization and in disputes about the proper role for ordinary people in political affairs.

The Democratic Society of Pennsylvania (Philadelphia) Principles, Articles, and Regulations
30 May 1793

The rights of man, the genuine objects of society, and the legitimate principles of government have been clearly developed by the successive Revolutions of America and France. Those events have withdrawn the veil which concealed the dignity and the happiness of the human race, and have taught us, no longer dazzled with adventitious splendor or awed by antiquated usurpation, to erect the Temple of LIBERTY on the ruins of *Palaces* and *Thrones.*

At this propitious period, when the nature of freedom and equality is thus practically displayed, and when their value (best understood by those who have paid the price of acquiring them) is universally acknowledged, the patriotic mind will naturally be solicitous, by every proper precaution, to preserve and perpetuate the blessings which Providence hath bestowed upon our country: For, in reviewing the history of nations, we find occasion to lament that the vigilance of the people has been too easily absorbed in victory; and that the prize which has been achieved by the wisdom and valor of one generation has too often been lost by the ignorance and supineness of another.

With a view, therefore, to cultivate the just knowledge of rational liberty, to facilitate the enjoyment and exercise of our civil rights, and to transmit, unimpaired, to posterity, the glorious inheritance of a *free Republican Government,* the DEMOCRATIC SOCIETY of Pennsylvania is constituted and established. Unfettered by *religious* or *national* distinctions, unbiased by party and unmoved by ambition, this institution embraces the interest and invites the support of every virtuous citizen. The public good is indeed its sole object, and we think that the best means are pursued for obtaining it when we recognize the following as the fundamental principles of our association.

I. That the people have the inherent and exclusive right and power of making and altering forms of government; and that for regulating and protecting our social interests, a REPUBLICAN GOVERNMENT is the most natural and beneficial form which the wisdom of man has devised.

II. That the Republican Constitutions of the UNITED STATES and of the STATE of PENNSYLVANIA, being framed and established by the people, it is our duty as good citizens to support them. And in order effectually to do so, it [is] likewise the duty of every freeman to regard with attention and to discuss without fear the conduct of the public servants in every department of government.

III. That in considering the administration of public affairs, men and measures should be estimated according to their intrinsic merits; and therefore, regardless of party spirit or political connection, it is the duty of every citizen, by making the general welfare the rule of his conduct, to aid and approve those men and measures which have an influence in promoting the prosperity of the Commonwealth.

IV. That in the choice of persons to fill the offices of government, it is essential to the existence of a free Republic that every citizen should act according to his own judgment, and, therefore, any attempt to corrupt or delude the people in exercising the rights of suffrage, either by promising the favor of one candidate or traducing the character of another, is an offence equally injurious to moral rectitude and civil liberty.

V. That the *People of Pennsylvania* form but one indivisible community, whose political rights and interest, whose national honor and prosperity, must in degree and duration be forever the same; and, therefore it is the duty of every freeman and shall be the endeavor of the Democratic Society to remove the prejudices, to conciliate the affections, to enlighten the understanding, and to promote the happiness of all our fellow-citizens. . . .

Condemnations, Defenses, and Society Attacks on the Excise

"A Friend to Good Government"

New York Daily Gazette

21 February 1794

Mr. M'Lean,

Upon reading the constitution of a society lately established in this city, entitled "The Democratic Society," published in your paper yesterday, the following Queries struck me:

Is liberty in danger, either from the form or administration of the general government?

Or, is the government in danger from the excess of liberty?

Is America in so critical a situation as to require the aid of new councils?

Is it necessary we should be in a revolutionary state, and try new projects?

Do the people require intermediary guides betwixt them and the constituted authorities?

Or, are they weak and uninformed, after having performed wonders in legislation and arms—Is a *restless* society necessary to their preserving it?

Are the members who compose this society more virtuous or less ambitious than others?

Have they long given proofs of piety, patriotism, morality, and various other duties that characterize good citizens?

Are these people organizers, or disorganizers; are they federalists or anti-federalists?

Do they associate to electioneer to effect, or to prevent others from doing it?

Above all, Mr. Printer, I ask, Are they chosen by the people? If not, as I know no other authority, I shall hereafter regard them as self-creators, as a branch, perhaps, of the Jacobin Society of Paris.

"A Friend to Rational Government"

New York Journal

22 February 1794

A member of the Democratic Society, in answer to the QUERIST in Mr. M'Lean's paper of yesterday, informs him, That the *old whigs* in this city, observing of late the warm attachment of the old tories (who deserted their country, and joined their enemies, during her conflict with the British Dey) who are now enemies of our good allies, the French—I say, we, observing their attachment for measures and men in government that no patriot can approve of, suspect all is not right, and it behooves us, who purchased Liberty at the risque of life and fortune, to be *on our watch*. I hope this explanation will satisfy the *Querist;* if not, by calling at No. 244, Cooper-street, he may be further informed of the designs of the Society.

A Member

Republican Society of the Town of Newark (New Jersey)

Newark Gazette

19 March 1794

Friends and Countrymen

It is not a strange matter to see the moneyed part of the people of America in general opposed to Republican Societies; the only reason is because a great many of them have crept into offices, and [are] jealous least too great a share of political knowledge should be diffused among the people and, of course, their conduct would be examined into, which they are doubtful will not stand the test, and of consequence they will be hurled from their easy situation; a change which they cannot think of undergoing while there is possibility of avoiding it. For this reason, they oppose the forming of Republican Societies, because it will have a tendency to enlighten the minds of the people.

The forming of Republican Societies has caused a great stir in many parts of America amongst the Tory part of the people; but in none more than it has in this place; the Tories and the nobility have joined their efforts to prevent the forming of a Republican Society in this town; but (to the praise of the Republicans be it spoken) they have not succeeded.

It must be the mechanics and farmers or the poorer class of people (as they are generally called) that must support the freedom of America; the freedom which they and their fathers purchased with their blood—the nobility will never do it—they will be always striving to get the reins of government into their own hands, and then they can ride the people at pleasure.

It stands the people in hand, who would keep up the spirit of freedom in America, to stir themselves up, lest while they are sleeping, the lamp of liberty goes out and they be left to grope in the dark land of despotism and oppression. Now is the time—every day you slumber gives strength to the enemies of freedom—they are waking while you are sleeping—trust not the enemies of the precious diadem—you have won in the field of battle, amidst blood and carnage to be the guardians of it.

It is said that we have a good constitution—let us know it well—let us see whether we have a good constitution or not; and if we have, let us see whether the administration is agreeable to it or not; if so let us endeavor to make each other as happy under such a constitution as possible, if it is a good constitution let us take care that neither ruler nor ruled infringe upon it!

A good constitution is like good wine, unless it is kept corked tight, it will degenerate. And it may be compared to a fountain, that if ever so pure, if the spouts are filthy, the streams will be corrupted. Let us therefore watch with attention and let us take great care that we do not pin our faith upon other men's sleeves.

Address of the Democratic Society in Wythe County, Virginia, to the People of the United States

Newark Gazette

18 June 1794

Fellow Citizens,

It is a right of the people peaceably to assemble and deliberate. It is a right of the people to publish their sentiments. These rights we exercise, and esteem invaluable.

A war raging in Europe, a war of tyrants against liberty, cannot be unfelt by the people of the United States—It has roused our feelings. We have rejoiced when victory followed the standard of liberty. When despots were successful, we have experienced the deepest anxiety.—We have lamented that our good wishes were the only aid we could give the French. . . .

While with anxious expectation we contemplate the affairs of Europe, it would be criminal to forget our own country. . . . A Session of Congress having just passed, the first in which the people were equally represented, it is a fit time to take a retrospective view of the proceedings of government. We have watched each motion of those in power, but are sorry we cannot exclaim, "well done thou good and faithful servant!" We have seen the nation insulted, our rights violated, our commerce ruined; and what has been the conduct of Government? Under the corrupt influence of the paper system, it has uniformly crouched to Britain, while on the contrary our allies the French, to whom we owe our political existence, have been treated unfriendly; denied any advantages from their treaties with us; their Minister abused; and those individuals among us who desired to aid their arms prosecuted as traitors. Blush Americans for the conduct of your government!!!

Citizens!

Shall we Americans, who have kindled the spark of liberty, stand aloof and see it extinguished when burning a bright flame in France, which hath caught it from us? Do you not see if despots prevail, you must have a despot like the rest of the nations? If all tyrants unite against free people, should not all free people unite against tyrants? Yes! Let us unite with France and stand or fall together.

We lament that a man who hath so long possessed the public confidence as the head of the Executive Department hath possessed it should put it to so severe a trial as he hath by a late appointment. The constitution hath been trampled on, and your rights have no security. Citizens! What is despotism? Is it not a union of executive, legislative, and judicial authorities to an executive office by the head of that branch of Government; in that capacity he is to make treaties: Those treaties are your supreme law?—and of this supreme law he is supreme Judge!!! What has become of your constitution & liberties?

Fellow Citizens,

We hope the misconduct of the executive may have proceeded from bad advice; but we can only look to the immediate cause of the mischief. To us, it seems a radical change of measures is necessary. How shall this be effected? Citizens it is to be effected by a change of men. Deny the continuance of our confidence to such members of the legislative body as have an interest distinct from that of the people. To trust yourselves to stock holders what is it but, like the Romans, to deliver the poor debtor to his creditor, as his absolute property. To trust yourselves to speculators, what is it, but to committ the lamb to the wolf to be devoured.

It was recommended by the conventions of some of the states so to amend the Constitution as to incapacitate any man to serve as President more than eight years successively. Consider well this experiment. 'Tis probably the most certain way to purge the different departments and produce a new state of things.

Believe us fellow citizens, the public welfare is our only motive.

William Neely, Chairman

Republican Society of Newark

9 June 1794

Resolved, as the opinion of this society that the raising a revenue by means of excise, except in cases of eminent necessity, is incompatible with the spirit of a free people. Insomuch as to make it productive, it would become necessary to throw open the sacred doors of domestic retirement and expose the persons of all ages and sex to the ferocious insolence of the lowest order of revenue officers, which would have a tendency either to debase the minds of the citizens and prepare them for slavery or excite disgust against the government and produce convulsions and the dissolution of society. Besides its being the most expensive mode of taxation is a sufficient reason for disapproving of it, experience having taught that the mode of raising a revenue by excise takes more money out of the pockets of the citizens and puts less into the public coffers than another—it having a tendency to corrupt the morals of the people, by opening another door to fraud and perjury, is in the opinion of this society an additional argument against the adoption of an excise system of revenue.

The Democratic Society of Philadelphia

Resolved, as the opinion of this society, that taxation by excise has ever been justly abhorred by free men; that it is a system attendant with numerous vexations, opens the door to manifold frauds, and is most expensive in its collection; It is also highly objectionable by the number of officers it renders necessary, ever ready to join in a firm phalanx to support government even in unwarrantable measures.

"For the *Columbian Centinel*," Boston

27 September 1794

Every part of the conduct of our *Genetines* affords proof of their inconsistency and deceit; their conduct and their professions are at open variance in every instance. We call them Genetines rather than Jacobins or Democrats; it is more precisely descriptive, and there is a marked propriety in deriving their name from their patron and founder.

Those who pretend to superior virtue and patriotism ought, at least, to equal their more modest neighbors, who make no such professions, in a disinterested, consistent display of regard for the happiness of others and a willingness to share equally with them the burdens as well as the benefits of society. But our Genetines are as conspicuous for their endeavors to secure to themselves every office of honor and profit as they are for encroaching upon the rights of others. They are professed advocates for equality, but in all cases they assume rights to themselves which they deny to others.

The leaders of our Genetine Club were among the first who clamored at the institution of the Cincinnati, because they were self-created and had taken the liberty of an appropriate badge, a peculiar mark of distinction to themselves and their descendents. A desire to set up and retain this idle gewgaw of a Ribbon and a Goose must have originated in aristocratic principles, it was urged, and was conclusive proof of a lust of domination. Upon this ground, the members of the Cincinnati were held up and denounced as Aristocrats, men who meant to lord it over others and who were dangerous to the state.

But the Genetines are as unfounded and unknown to our constitution and laws as were the Cincinnati, and the object of their institution and the views and principles of their leaders are much more alarming and dangerous to society. The former were chargeable only with a foolish pride for an empty distinction, at the worst; but the latter assume the right of a papal inquisition to arraign before the public the men and the measures of the people, and exclusively and definitively to pass sentence upon them. They even go so far in their *publications* in the *Chronicle* and in their *private* discussions and votes as to *style* themselves the people and to criminate the President and other servants of the public as if they had been created to office by the voice of *their Clubs* alone. As well might a band of midnight *robbers* style themselves the people and seize upon the *public* treasure, under pretence of its being the *people's* property. The band indeed would appear less criminal and dangerous before any tribunal than the Clubs; for the former will have robbed the community only of its wealth, but the latter destroy also its peace, its safety, and happiness. . . .

The Rebellion

Letter to General Lee from Alexander Addison

The excise tax of 1791 imposed significant hardships on farmers beyond the mountains. It was collectible in specie among a people who seldom saw much coin and who could export or barter their grain only by distilling it into a portable (and potable) form.

Resistance was common along the whole frontier from Pennsylvania to Kentucky to North Carolina, fed by the revolutionary tradition of opposition to internal taxes, traditional Anglo-American hostility to intrusive revenue collectors (who had to travel around the countryside to measure the output of presses and stills), rising condemnations of the motives of the Federalist administration, and increasing western resentment of the lack of federal action to control the Indians or open the Mississippi River to American trade. Nowhere, though, was the resistance quite so fierce as in the western parts of Pennsylvania. As early as 21 August 1792, a convention of the western counties condemned the tax and advocated legal measures to impede its collection, leading Washington to issue a proclamation warning against illegal combinations. The trouble culminated in the summer of 1794 with intimidation of complying distillers as well as excise officers, an armed attack on the home of Inspector John Neville, a menacing assembly of perhaps six thousand armed militia near the town of Pittsburgh, Washington's second proclamation, and the march across the mountains of the militia army under Hamilton and Henry Lee.

Contemporaries came to know the insurrection best from book-length histories by opponents of the excise: William Findley's *History of the Insurrection of the Four Western Counties of Pennsylvania* (1796), and Hugh Henry Brackenridge's *Incidents of the Insurrection in the Western Parts of Pennsylvania* (1795). A shorter, more immediate, less partisan account was prepared on 23 November 1794 by Alexander Addison, presiding judge of Pennsylvania's fifth judicial district, in the form of a letter to General Lee. Addison was a Federalist, though an opponent of the excise. Direct enforcement of the tax had not been within his province as state judge for the western counties.

Sir,

You desired me to state to you my opinion of the late insurrection, the measures taken by government for its suppression, and the effects to be expected from those measures on the people of this country. I undertook to do so, at the same time cautioning you that you were to consider what I should say not so much as facts, or a solid system, as a mere opinion, though certainly a sincere one.

It is not uncommon to trace the origin of this unfortunate business to speculations on the subject of the excise law and on the administration of government in general, and to meetings and resolutions at various and distant times on these subjects; and these have not only been considered as having prepared the minds of the people of this country for the outrages which they afterwards committed, but as evidence of a deep and long formed plot, contrived by men who kept themselves out of view in its execution, to resist the excise system and the government itself, by violence.

Without undertaking to examine or contradict this opinion, I shall content myself with observing that I think it may well be said of it that, at least, more stress has been laid on it than it will bear.

In all countries, the introduction of the excise has been odious and its officers have been held contemptible. . . . Many now in the country talk of their having seen the riots and resistance against the excise in Ireland. In Ireland, the ordinary power of government seems incompetent to suppress riots, which have perpetual existence, from successive and varying causes. This country is in a great measure settled from Ireland. Being but a new settlement, and a frontier settlement, harassed by the danger, distress, and ravage of an Indian war, [it] did not consider itself, and was not considered, as a proper [object] for even equal taxation. Every frontier settlement at a distance from the seat of government . . . and in some degree composed of fugitives from justice, civil or criminal, must be supposed to be but little accustomed to the subordination [to] regular government. This natural *untamedness* of temper was increased by the peculiar circumstances of this country. The clashing jurisdictions of Virginia and Pennsylvania excited animosities in the minds of the advocates of each state, hardly yet healed by the mutual concessions of both, and an opposition to the government of Pennsylvania hardly yet overcome by the experience of its authority. The idea of a new state on this side of the mountains became so prevalent that an act of the Assembly declared it high treason to propose it. Under all these circumstances, an attempt was made to carry into execution the excise law of Pennsylvania. The officer, in his progress through Washington County, was seized by a number of rioters, collected from different quarters. His hair was cut off from one-half of his head. His papers were taken from him, and he was made to tear his commission and tread it under his feet. They then in a body, gathering size as it proceeded, conducted him out of the county with every possible mark of contumely to him and the government and threats of death if he returned. The same object, the removal of an excise officer from the country, was accomplished here as in the [case] of General Neville. If the violence and

enormity was less, it was because more was not necessary to accomplish their object. If their madness had been excited by resistance, and if burning houses or even murder had then been necessary to suspend the operation of the law, I now believe they would have thought the crimes sanctioned by the cause. Yet there were then no men of great influence or passion for office or popularity who, for their selfish purposes, inflamed the minds of the people against the excise law; nor could the destruction of the federal government [have] been then in view; for the confederation was not interested in the law, and the Constitution of the United States did not then exist. The excise law of Pennsylvania continued, as to this county, to be a mere dead letter.

When the excise law of the United States came into operation, those people who, without reasoning and merely from prejudice, were its greatest enemies supposed that it possessed all the evils which they had ever heard ascribed to any excise law; and, without reflecting on the difference of circumstances, supposed its operation might be defeated by the same means by which they had defeated the operation of the excise law of Pennsylvania. Accordingly, they had recourse to riots, tarring and feathering, and carrying off papers. These things were done in Washington County and Fayette County. Unfortunately, the prosecutor for the state in Washington County was David Bradford, whose disposition inclined him to omit all prosecution of such offenses. In Fayette County, industry to collect testimony was wanting. The agents of the United States choose to bring all their complaints into the federal courts. The difficulties in the way of the marshall, a stranger in the country, were inevitably great. And there must have been an indisposition in the people of this country, hitherto accustomed to trials in all cases in their own counties, without evident necessity, to aid a jurisdiction which drew them for trial three hundred miles from home [in Philadelphia]. These circumstances contributed to impunity in delinquency and outrage; and impunity produced boldness and perseverance. Animated by their hatred to the law and their past experience of success, and wanting prudence to foresee the consequences, they imagined that they could compel the excise officer of the United States, as they had compelled the excise officer of Pennsylvania, to surrender his commission; and thus reduce the excise law of the United States, as they had reduced the excise law of Pennsylvania, as to them, to a dead letter. With this view they proceeded to General Neville's to call for a surrender of his commission and papers; and, that they might accomplish all their objects at once as to past and future, a surrender also of the papers of the marshall. Probably they presumed their numbers sufficient to extort by fear alone, without actual force, a ready compliance. Irritated by refusal, resistance, and repulse, and too deeply engaged to retreat, in their frenzy they drew into their guilt all within reach of their terror and proceeded to the extremity of burning the house.

Yet here perhaps they might have stopped, and the rioters in this case, like the rioters in the case of the excise law of Pennsylvania, might have been prosecuted and convicted. But they unhappily mistook in their objects and their means and blindly rushed into measures that involved the whole country. Those subsequent measures I consider as really the insurrection of this country, and the authors of them, whoever they may be, as really the authors of this insurrection. From the ancient aversion of some to the government of Pennsylvania, perhaps some remains of the idea of a new state, which had long ago existed, yet continued to exist, in this country. Perhaps the distinction between a separation from the state and from the United States was not attended to. Perhaps even this last, a seizure of the western lands, a union with Kentucky, the navigation of the Mississippi, and a connection with Great Britain were thought of. Perhaps they never extended their reflections to any system or distant object, but acted from the blind impulse of the moment. Whatever might have been their ideas, measures were determined on which aimed at resistance to government in all its parts and open war. The public post was robbed of the mail, the militia of the country was called out for the purpose of seizing the garrison of Pittsburgh and possessing themselves of the arms and ammunition there. To obey this call many were compelled by fear, many were induced by usefulness in preventing mischief, many were seduced by wanton curiosity, and many were instigated by love of plunder and destruction. The appearance of their strength added ferocity to the ruffians, and a total contempt of the powers of the government and a general anarchy and confusion pervaded the whole country.

I shall here remark that none of those men whom I have heard considered as the distant and secret authors of those acts of violence seem to have been at all consulted in their contrivance or execution, or to have possessed

any confidence of those who perpetrated them. All reprobated them, and one (I mean Mr. Gallatin) was the foremost at the public meetings to step forward to stem the torrent of popular rage, openly and at great peril to resist their mad delusions and, by arguments and eloquence the most ingenious and impressive, to expose to them the danger and effects of their conduct and the vanity and impracticability of their schemes. Whether any and what conclusion is to be drawn from this, I submit to you.

To quell the disturbances in this country and restore it to peace and government, the measures taken by the President were, in my opinion, the most prudent that could have been devised; and they seem to have been executed with a correspondent propriety and effect. The appointment of commissioners, by showing the awakened spirit of public exertion, gave a check to the spirit of revolution in this country and to the progress of disorder into other parts of the Union. A fair opportunity was given to men of sense and virtue here who, to guide the current, had seemed to run with it, to step out and change its course. And it gave a rallying point to all well-disposed men to flock to. The confidence arising from their supposed strength now began to abandon the violent; jealousy and distrust crept in among them; and the approach of an army far superior to all remaining ideas of resistance altogether broke their resolutions and, as it advanced, subdued their temper.

Previous to the advance of the army into the country, some attempts were made to stop its progress. At that time, the temper of the country was materially changed. The well disposed were recovering spirit and consistency; and they possessed the disposition, and they believed the strength, of gradually restoring energy to the laws and peace and subordination to the country. They knew the expense of maintaining the army was great, and, more than that, they regarded the labor and fatigue of their patriotic brethren, who, with the sacrifice of domestic interest and enjoyment, at the approach of an inclement season, had undertaken to traverse deep swamps and vast and rugged mountains to relieve them from anarchy and restore them to safety and peace. They blushed for an armed force entering their country to enforce submission to the laws. They feared also something for themselves; there were still among them disorderly men who talked wildly. These, without property to secure their attachment to the government or the country, unaccustomed to a regular industry, and trained to a rambling life, had the arms in their hands, were known and associated to each other, and could, without any sacrifice, remove to wherever they pleased. It was this kind of men that were the great terrors during all the troubles and now only remained to keep those troubles alive. The well disposed were more inclined to quiet, were not generally armed, and had as yet no complete system to bind them together. They believed that the turbulent would not then assemble, in any force, to oppose the army; but that, under the pretense of opposing the army, might plunder or destroy their fellow citizens and quit a country in which they could no longer remain. Some fears also existed, justly provoked as the army was, that it would not be possible to restrain all of them from some intemperate acts, which might provoke at least secret revenge and introduce general destruction. On all these grounds, representations were sent down to the President of the changed state of the country, and those who sent them were willing to give yet stronger assurances of sincerity and risk the peace of the country on its internal exertions. The propositions were honestly meant. Perhaps their rejection was wise. Consequences showed that it was. The army conducted itself with unexampled discipline and tenderness to an offending country and manifested a temper equaled only by the spirit which roused them in defense of the laws and constitution. The peace of the country and energy of the laws, which otherwise might have been the work of some time, were suddenly restored; and a precedent of the force of government and the danger of sedition has been set before the people of this country which, I trust, they will never forget and, I believe, will never need to be repeated.

Notwithstanding the settled malignity in the minds of several, perhaps many, individuals, considering the country in general, I believe there is a complete practical reformation produced among us.

Yet the plan of leaving part of the army for some months in this country appears to me a prudent one. Many of the turbulent spirits have fled from the settlement, thinking that their concealment would be but temporary and thinking that they might soon return without fear of punishment. But, as part of the army remains, they will be convinced that they must submit either to the laws or to permanent exile. And countenanced by this remainder of military force, not a hostile army, but a body of citizens armed to support the laws, the people of this country will acquire the habit of aiding and obeying public authority.

These are my sentiments. I may be mistaken, but I am sincere. This is a statement of opinions, not facts; and the opinions of different men on the same facts will vary from various circumstances. You will qualify my opinions by your own observations and the information of others.

"Self-Created Societies"

GEORGE WASHINGTON

Message to the Third Congress
19 November 1794

Fellow-citizens of the Senate, and of the House of Representatives:

When we call to mind the gracious indulgence of Heaven, by which the American people became a nation; when we survey the general prosperity of our country and look forward to the riches, power, and happiness to which it seems destined; with the deepest regret do I announce to you that, during your recess, some of the citizens of the United States have been found capable of an insurrection. It is due, however, to the character of our government, and to its stability, which cannot be shaken by the enemies of order, freely to unfold the course of this event.

During the session of the year one thousand seven hundred and ninety, it was expedient to exercise the legislative power granted by the Constitution of the United States "to lay and collect excises." In a majority of the states, scarcely an objection was heard to this mode of taxation. In some, indeed, alarms were at first conceived, until they were banished by reason and patriotism. In the four western counties of Pennsylvania, a prejudice, fostered and embittered by the artifice of men who labored for an ascendency over the will of others, by the guidance of their passions, produced symptoms of riot and violence. It is well known that Congress did not hesitate to examine the complaints which were presented; and to relieve them, as far as justice dictated or general convenience would permit. But the impression which this moderation made on the discontented did not correspond with what it deserved. The arts of delusion were no longer confined to the efforts of designing individuals. The very forbearance to press prosecutions was misinterpreted into a fear of urging the execution of the laws; and associations of men began to denounce threats against the officers employed. From a belief that, by a more formal concert, their operation might be defeated, certain self-created societies assumed the tone of condemnation. Hence, while the greater part of Pennsylvania itself were conforming themselves to the acts of excise, a few counties were resolved to frustrate them. It was now perceived that every expectation from the tenderness which had been hitherto pursued was unavailing, and that further delay could only create an opinion of impotency or irresolution in the Government. Legal process was therefore delivered to the marshal against the rioters and delinquent distillers.

No sooner was he understood to be engaged in this duty than the vengeance of armed men was aimed at *his* person, and the person and property of the Inspector of the Revenue. They fired upon the marshal, arrested him, and detained him, for some time, as a prisoner. He was obliged, by the jeopardy of his life, to renounce the service of other process on the west side of the Allegany mountain; and a deputation was afterwards sent to him to demand a surrender of that which he *had* served. A numerous body repeatedly attacked the house of the Inspector, seized his papers of office, and finally destroyed by fire his buildings and whatsoever they contained. Both of these officers, from a just regard to their safety, fled to the Seat of Government, it being avowed that the motives to such outrages were to compel the resignation of the Inspector, to withstand by force of arms the authority of the United States, and thereby to extort a repeal of the laws of excise and an alteration in the conduct of Government.

Upon the testimony of these facts, an Associate Justice of the Supreme Court of the United States notified to me that "in the counties of Washington and Allegany, in Pennsylvania, laws of the United States were opposed and the execution thereof obstructed by combinations too powerful to be suppressed by the ordinary course of judicial proceedings, or by the powers vested in the marshal of that district." On this call, momentous in the extreme, I sought and weighed what might best subdue the crisis. On the one hand, the judiciary was pronounced to be stripped of its capacity to enforce the laws; crimes which reached the very existence of social order were perpetuated without control; the friends of Government were insulted, abused, and overawed into silence, or an apparent acquiescence; and, to yield to the treasonable fury of so small a portion of the United States would be to violate the fundamental principle of our Constitution, which enjoins that the will of the majority shall prevail. On the other, to array citizen against citizen, to publish the dishonor of such excesses, to encounter the expense and other embarrassments of so distant an expedition, were steps too delicate, too closely interwoven with many affecting considerations, to be lightly adopted. I postponed, therefore, the summoning the militia immediately into the field; but I required them to be held in readiness, that, if my anxious endeavors to reclaim the deluded and to convince the malignant of their danger, should be fruitless, military force might be prepared to act before the season should be too far advanced.

My proclamation of the 7th of August last was accordingly issued, and accompanied by the appointment of commissioners, who were charged to repair to the scene of insurrection. They were authorized to confer with any bodies of men or individuals. They were instructed to be candid and explicit in stating the sensations which had been excited in the Executive and his earnest wish to avoid a resort to coercion; to represent, however, that, without submission, coercion *must* be the resort; but to invite them, at the same time, to return to the demeanor of faithful citizens by such accommodations as lay within the sphere of Executive power. Pardon, too, was tendered to them by the Government of the United States and that of Pennsylvania, upon no other condition than a satisfactory assurance of obedience to the laws.

Although the report of the commissioners marks their firmness and abilities, and must unite all virtuous men, by showing that the means of conciliation have been exhausted, all of those who had committed or abetted the tumults did not subscribe the mild form which was proposed as the atonement; and the indications of a peaceable temper were neither sufficiently general nor conclusive to recommend or warrant the further suspension of the march of the militia.

Thus, the painful alternative could not be discarded. I ordered the militia to march—after once more admonishing the insurgents, in my Proclamation of the 25th of September last.

It was a task too difficult to ascertain with precision the lowest degree of force competent to the quelling of the insurrection. From a respect, indeed, to economy and the case of my fellow-citizens belonging to the militia, it would have gratified me to accomplish such an estimate.

My very reluctance to ascribe too much importance to the opposition, had its extent been accurately seen, would have been a decided inducement to the smallest efficient numbers. In this uncertainty, therefore, I put into motion fifteen thousand men, as being an army which, according to all human calculation, would be prompt and adequate in every view and might, perhaps, by rendering resistance desperate, prevent the effusion of blood. Quotas had been assigned to the States of New Jersey, Pennsylvania, Maryland, and Virginia, the Governor of Pennsylvania having declared, on this occasion, an opinion which justified a requisition to the other States.

As Commander-in-Chief of the Militia, when called into the actual service of the United States, I have visited the places of general rendezvous, to obtain more exact information and to direct a plan for ulterior movements. Had there been room for a persuasion that the laws were secure from obstruction; that the civil magistrate was able to bring to justice such of the most culpable as have not embraced the proffered terms of amnesty, and may be deemed fit objects of example; that the friends to peace and good government were not in need of that aid and countenance which they ought always to receive and, I trust, ever will receive, against the vicious and turbulent; I should have caught with avidity the opportunity of restoring the militia to their families and home. But succeeding intelligence has tended to manifest the necessity of what has been done; it being now confessed by those who were not inclined to exaggerate the ill conduct of the insurgents that their malevolence was not pointed merely to a particular law; but that a spirit, inimical to all order, has actuated many of the offenders. If the state of things had afforded reason for the continuance of my presence with the army, it would not have been withholden. But every appearance assuring such an issue as will redound to the reputation and strength of the United States, I have judged it most proper to resume my duties at the Seat of Government, leaving the chief command with the Governor of Virginia.

Still, however, as it is probable that, in a commotion like the present, whatsoever may be the pretence, the purposes of mischief and revenge may not be laid aside, the stationing of a small force, for a certain period in the four western counties of Pennsylvania will be indispensable, whether we contemplate the situation of those who are connected with the execution of the laws or of others who may have exposed themselves by an honorable attachment to them. Thirty days from the commencement of this session being the legal limitation of the employment of the militia, Congress cannot be too early occupied with this subject. . . .

While there is cause to lament that occurrences of this nature should have disgraced the name or interrupted the tranquility of any part of our community, or should have diverted to a new application any portion of the public resources, there are not wanting in real and substantial consolations for the misfortune. It has demonstrated that our prosperity rests on solid foundations; by furnishing an additional proof that my fellow-citizens understand the true principles of government and liberty; that they feel their inseparable union; that, notwithstanding all the devices which have been used to sway them from their interest and duty, they are now as ready to maintain the authority of the laws against licentious invasions as they were to defend their rights against usurpation. It has been a spectacle displaying to the highest advantage the value of Republican government to behold the most and the least wealthy of our citizens standing in the same ranks, as private soldiers, pre-eminently distinguished by being the army of the Constitution; undeterred by a march of three hundred miles over rugged mountains, by the approach of an inclement season, or by any other discouragement. Nor ought I to omit to acknowledge the efficacious and patriotic co-operation which I have experienced from the Chief Magistrates of the States to which my requisitions have been addressed.

To every description of citizens, indeed, let praise be given. But let them persevere in their affectionate vigilance over that precious depository of American happiness, the Constitution of the United States. Let them cherish it, too, for the sake of those who, from every clime, are daily seeking a dwelling in our land. And when, in the calm moments of reflection, they shall have retraced the origin and progress of the insurrection, let them determine whether it has not been fomented by combinations of men who, careless of consequences and disregarding the unerring truth that those who rouse cannot always appease a civil convulsion, have disseminated, from an ignorance or perversion of facts, suspicions, jealousies, and accusations, of the whole Government.

Having thus fulfilled the engagement which I took when I entered into office, "to the best of my ability to preserve, protect, and defend, the Constitution of the United States," on you, gentlemen, and the people by whom you are deputed, I rely for support. . . .

Proceedings in the House of Representatives on the President's Speech

24–27 November 1794

Serving, as he usually did, on the House committee to prepare an answer to the president's address, Madison helped draft a reply which passed in silence over Washington's denunciation of the "self-created societies." Federalists quickly moved to insert an echo of the phrase.

Monday, 24 November

. . . Mr. FITZSIMONS then rose and said that it would seem somewhat incongruous for the House to present an Address to the President which omitted all notice of so very important an article in his speech as that referring to the self-created societies. Mr. F. then read an amendment, which gave rise to a very interesting debate. The amendment was in these words:

"As part of this subject, we cannot withhold our reprobation of the self-created societies, which have risen up in some parts of the Union, misrepresenting the conduct of the Government, and disturbing the operation of the laws, and which, by deceiving and inflaming the ignorant and the weak, may naturally be supposed to have stimulated and urged the insurrection."

These are "institutions, not strictly unlawful, yet not less fatal to good order and true liberty; and reprehensible in the degree that our system of government approaches to perfect political freedom." . . .

Mr. GILES . . . began by declaring that, when he saw, or thought he saw, the House of Representatives about to erect itself into an office of censorship, he could not sit silent. He did not rise with the hope of making proselytes, but he trusted that the fiat of no person in America should ever be taken for truth, implicitly and without evidence.

Mr. Giles next entered into an encomium of some length on the public services and personal character of the President. He vindicated himself from any want of respect or esteem towards him. He then entered into an examination of the propriety of the expression employed by the

President with regard to self-created societies. Mr. G. said that there was not an individual in America who might not come under the charge of being a member of some one or other self-created society. Associations of this kind, religious, political, and philosophical, were to be found in every quarter of the Continent. The Baptists and Methodists, for example, might be termed self-created societies. The people called the Friends were of the same kind. Every pulpit in the United States might be included in this vote of censure, since, from every one of them, upon occasion, instructions had been delivered, not only for the eternal welfare, but likewise for the temporal happiness of the people. There had been other societies in Pennsylvania for several purposes. The venerable Franklin had been at the head of one, entitled a society for political information. They had criminated the conduct of the Governor of this State and of the Governors of other States, yet they were not prosecuted or disturbed. There was, if he mistook not, once a society in this State for the purpose of opposing or subverting the existing Constitution. They also were unmolested. If the House are to censure the Democratic societies, they might do the same by the Cincinnati Society. It is out of the way of the legislature to attempt checking or restraining public opinion. If the self-created societies act contrary to law, they are unprotected, and let the law pursue them. That a man is a member of one of these societies will not protect him from an accusation for treason, if the charge is well founded. If the charge is not well founded, if the societies, in their proceedings, keep within the verge of the law, Mr. G. would be glad to learn what was to be the sequel? If the House undertake to censure particular classes of men, who can tell where they will stop? Perhaps it may be advisable to commence moral philosophers and compose a new system of ethics for the citizens of America. In that case, there would be many other subjects for censure, as well as the self-created societies. Land-jobbing, for example, has been in various instances brought to such a pass that it might be defined swindling on a broad scale. Paper money, also, would be a subject of very tolerable fertility for the censure of a moralist. Mr. G. proceeded to enumerate other particulars on this head, and again insisted on the sufficiency of the existing laws for the punishment of every existing abuse. He observed that gentlemen were sent to this House, not for the purpose of passing indiscriminate votes of censure, but to legislate only. By adopting the amendment of Mr. Fitzsimons, the House would only produce recrimination on the part of the societies and raise them into much more importance than they possibly could have acquired if they had not been distinguished by a vote of censure from that House. Gentlemen were interfering with a delicate right, and they would be much wiser to let the democratic societies alone. Did the House imagine that their censure, like the wand of a magician, would lay a spell on these people? It would be quite the contrary, and the recrimination of the societies would develop the propriety of having meddled with them at all. One thing ought never to be forgotten, that if these people acted wrong, the law was open to punish them; and if they did not, they would care very little for a vote of that House. Why all this particular deviation from the common line of business to pass random votes of censure? The American mind was too enlightened to bear the interposition of this House, to assist either in their contemplations or conclusions on this subject. Members are not sent here to deal out applauses or censures in this way. Mr. G. rejected all aiming at a restraint on the opinions of private persons. As to the societies themselves, Mr. G. personally had nothing to do with them, nor was he acquainted with any of the persons concerned in their original organization. . . .

Mr. W. Smith then rose and entered at large into the subject. He said that if the Committee withheld an expression of their sentiments in regard to the societies pointed out by the President, their silence would be an avowed desertion of the Executive. He had no scruple to declare that the conduct of these people had tended to blow up the insurrection. Adverting to Mr. Giles, he thought the assertion of that gentleman too broad, when he spoke of not meddling with the opinions of other than political societies.

He considered the dissemination of improper sentiments as a suitable object for the public reprobation of that House. Suppose an agricultural society were to establish itself, and under that title to disseminate opinions subversive of good order; the difference of a name should not make Mr. S. think them exempted from becoming objects of justice. Would any man say that the sole object of self-created societies has been the publication of political doctrines? The whole of their proceedings has been a chain of censures on the conduct of Government. If we do not support the President, the silence of the House will be interpreted into an implied disapprobation of that part of his speech. He will be left in a dilemma. It will be said that he has committed himself.

Mr. S. declared that he was a friend to the freedom of the press; but would any one compare a regular town meeting where deliberations were cool and unruffled to these societies, to the nocturnal meetings of individuals, after they have dined, where they shut their doors, pass votes in secret, and admit no members into their societies but those of their own choosing? . . . In objection to this amendment it had been stated that the self-created societies would acquire importance from a vote of censure passed on them. They were, for his part, welcome to the whole importance that such a vote could give them. He complained in strong terms of the calumnies and slanders which they had propagated against Government. Every gentleman who thought that these clubs had done mischief was by this amendment called upon to avow his opinion. This was the whole. Mr. S. begged the House to take notice, and he repeated his words once or twice, that he did not mean to go into the constitution of these societies or to say that they were illegal. The question before the House was not whether these societies were illegal or not, but whether they have been mischievous in their consequences. . . .

Mr. Tracy . . . declared that if the President had not spoke of the matter, he should have been willing to let it alone, because whenever a subject of that kind was touched, there were certain gentlemen in that House who shook their backs, like a sore-backed horse, and cried out The Liberties of the people! Mr. T. wished only that the House, if their opinion of these societies corresponded with that of the President, should declare that they had such an opinion. This was quite different from attempting to legislate on the subject. Has not the Legislature done so before? Is there any impropriety in paying this mark of respect to a man to whom all America owes such indelible obligations? He thought that this declaration from the House of Representatives would tend to discourage Democratic societies, by uniting all men of sense against them. . . .

Mr. Nicholas—When we see an attempt made in this House to reprobate whole societies, on account of the conduct of individuals, it may truly be suspected that some of the members of this House have sore backs. . . .

He had always thought them the very worst advocates for the cause which they espoused; but he had come two hundred miles to legislate, and not to reprobate private societies. He was not paid by his constituents for doing business of that sort. The President knew the business of the House better than to call for any such votes of censure. It was wrong to condemn societies for particular acts. That there never should be a Democratical society in America, said Mr. N., I would give my most hearty consent; but I cannot agree to persecution for the sake of opinions. With respect either to the propriety or the power of suppressing them. Mr. N. was in both cases equally of opinion that it was much better to let them alone. They must stand or fall by the general sentiments of the people of America. Is it possible that these societies can exist, for any length of time, when they are of no real use to the country? No. But this amendment will make the people at large imagine that they are of consequence. . . .

Tuesday, 25 November
. . . The House went again into Committee of the Whole on the Address of the President and the amendment of Mr. Fitzsimons. . . .

Mr. FITZSIMONS had no violent predilection for any performance of his own. He had, therefore, to prevent so much disputing, prepared to withdraw his motion, provided the Committee be willing that he should do so, and, in the room of this motion, he would read another, for which he was indebted to a gentleman at his right hand [Mr. B. Bourne].

The Committee consented. The former motion was withdrawn, and the other was read. This was an echo of that part of the Speech of the President which mentions self-created societies. . . .

Mr. NICHOLAS—Gentlemen have brought us into a discussion and then say we must decide as they please, in deference to the President. This is the real ground and foundation of their arguments. But who started this question? If the gentlemen have brought themselves into a difficulty with regard to the President by their participation in proposing votes of censure which they cannot carry through, they have only to blame themselves. Is it expected, said Mr. N., that I am to abandon my independence for the sake of the President? He never intended that we should take any such notice of his reference to these societies; but if the popularity of the President has, in the present case, been committed, let those who have hatched this thing, and who have brought it forward, answer for the consequences. . . .

Mr. SEDGWICK thought that the President would have been defective in his duty had he omitted to mention what he religiously believed to be true, viz: that the Democratic societies had in a great measure originated the late disturbances. It was the indispensable duty of the President to speak as he had spoken. The present amendment [of Mr. Fitzsimons] would have a tendency to plunge these societies into contempt and to sink them still farther into abhorrence and detestation. He pronounced them to be illicit combinations. One gentleman [Mr. Nicholas] tells you that he despises them most heartily. Another [Mr. Lyman] says that they begin to repent. Will the American people perversely propose to shoulder and bolster up these despised and repenting societies, which are now tumbling into dust and contempt? Their conduct differed as far from a fair and honorable investigation, as Christ and Belial. They were men prowling in the dark. God is my judge, said Mr. S., that I would not wish to check a fair discussion.

One gentleman [Mr. McDowell] had told the Committee, that the assumption and Funding transactions were a cause of public discontent. It has been the trick of these people to make this assertion. They have said that the Funding System is mass of favoritism, for the purpose of erecting an oppressive aristocracy and a paper nobility. There is not a man among them who is able to write and who does not know that these assertions are false. As to the assumption of the debts of individual States, it has been said that this measure was undertaken for the purpose of making up a large debt. There was no such thing. Before the adoption of the new Constitution, of which Mr. S., considered the Funding and Assumption Systems to be essential preliminaries, the credit and commerce of America were declining or gone. The States were disagreeing at home, and the American name was disgraced abroad. It was not to be supposed that every one of the measures of the new Government could please every body. Among the rest, excise was objected to in both Houses of Congress; but at last the good sense of the people acquiesced. At this crisis, a foreign agent (*Genet*) landed at Charleston. On his way to this city he was attended by the hosannahs of all the disaffected. He did the utmost mischief that was in his power; and in consequence of his efforts, Democratic societies sprung up. . . .

He said that it was to be noticed, and he proclaimed it here, that antecedent to the Democratic societies making their appearance, the flame of discontent seemed smothered. But these men told the people that they would be slaves. Was not this wrong? They should have told what was well done as well as ill done. From Portland, in Maine, to the other end of the Continent, have they ever approved of one single act? They have scrutinized with eagle eyes into every fault. Whom are we to trust them or the man that more than any other human man ever did, possesses the affection of a whole people? The question is, shall we support the Constitution or not? . . .

Wednesday, 26 November
. . . Mr. AMES stated that it was the duty of the President, by the Constitution, to inform Congress of the state of the Union. That he had accordingly in his speech stated the insurrection and the causes which (he thought) had brought it on. Among them, he explicitly reckons the self-created societies and combinations of men to be one. . . . He said further that an amendment was now offered to the House, expressed, as nearly as may be in the very words of the President; an objection is urged against this amendment that the proposition contained in it is not true in fact. It is also said that although it were true, it would be dangerous to liberty to assent to it in our Answer to the Speech. It is moreover, say they, improper, unnecessary, and indecent to mention the self-created societies. The amendment now urged upon the House has been put to vote in the Committee of the Whole House, and rejected. What will the world say, and that too from the evidence of our own records, if we reject it again in the House? . . .

The right to form political clubs has been urged as if it had been denied. It is not, however, the right to meet, it is the abuse of the right after they have met, that is charged upon them. Town meetings are authorized by law, yet they may be called for seditious or treasonable purposes. The legal right of the voters in that case would be an aggravation, not an excuse, for the offence. But if persons meet in a club with an intent to obstruct the laws, their meeting is no longer innocent or legal; it is a crime.

The necessity for forming clubs has been alleged with some plausibility in favor of all the states except New England, because town meetings are little known and not practicable in a thinly settled country. But if people have grievances are they to be brought to a knowledge of them

only by clubs? Clubs may find out more complaints against the laws than the sufferers themselves had dreamed of. The number of those which a man will learn from his own and his neighbor's experience will be quite sufficient for every salutary purpose of reform in the laws or of relief to the citizens. He may petition Congress, his own Representatives will not fail to advocate or, at least, to present and explain his memorial. As a juror, he applies the law; as an elector, he effectually controls the legislators. A really aggrieved man will be sure of sympathy and assistance within this body and with the public. The most zealous advocate of clubs may think them useful, but he will not insist on their being indispensably so.

The plea for their usefulness seems to rest on their advantage of meeting for political information. The absurdity of this pretence could be exposed in a variety of views. I shall decline (said Mr. A.) a detailed consideration of the topic. I would just ask, however, whether the most inflamed party men, who usually lead the clubs, are the best organs of authentic information? Whether they meet in darkness; whether they hide their names, their numbers, and their doings; whether they shut their doors to admit information?

A laudable zeal for inquiry need not shun those who could satisfy it; it need not blush in the daylight. With open doors and an unlimited freedom of debate, political knowledge might be introduced even among the intruders.

But, instead of exposing their affected pursuit of information, it will be enough to show hereafter what they actually spread among the people—whether it is information or, in the words of the President, "jealousies, suspicions and accusations of the Government;" whether, disregarding the truth, they have not fomented the daring outrages against the social order and the authority of the laws. (*Vide* the President's speech.)

They have arrogantly pretended sometimes to be the people and sometimes the guardians, the champions of the people. They affect to feel more zeal for a popular government, and to enforce more respect for republican principles, than the real Representatives are admitted to entertain. Let us see whether they are set up for the people or in opposition to them and their institutions.

Will any reflecting person suppose, for a moment, that this great people, so widely extended, so actively employed, could form a common will and make that will law in their individual capacity, and without representation? They could not. Will clubs avail them as a substitute for representation? A few hundred persons only are members of clubs, and if they should act for the others, it would be an usurpation, and the power of the few over the many, in every view infinitely worse than sedition itself, will represent this Government. . . .

We are asked, with some pathos, will you punish clubs with your censure, unheard, untried, confounding the innocent with the guilty? Censure is not punishment, unless it is merited, for we merely allude to certain self-created societies, which have disregarded the truth and fomented the outrages against the laws. Those which have been innocent will remain uncensured. It is said, worthy men belong to those clubs. They may be as men not wanting in merit, but when they join societies which are employed to foment outrages against the laws, they are no longer innocent. They become bad citizens. If innocence happens to stray into such company, it is lost. The men really good will quit such connexions, and it is a fact that the most respected of those who were said to belong to them have long ago renounced them. Honest, credulous men may be drawn in to favor very bad designs, but so far as they do it, they deserve the reproach which this vote contains, that of being unworthy citizens.

If the worst men in society have led the most credulous and inconsiderate astray, the latter will undoubtedly come to reflection the sooner for an appeal to their sense of duty. This appeal is made in terms which truth justifies and which apply only to those who have been criminal. . . .

In the course of his remarks, Mr. A. strongly insisted that the vote was not indefinite in its terms. Societies were not reprobated because they were self-made, nor because they were political societies. Everybody has readily admitted that they might be innocent as they have been generally imprudent. It is such societies as have been regardless of the truth and have fomented the outrages against the law, &c.

Nor is the intention of this amendment to flatter the President, as it has been intimated. He surely has little need of our praise on any personal account. This late signal act of duty is already with his grateful country, with faithful history: nor is it in our power, or in those of any offended self-created societies, to impair that tribute which will be offered to him. As little ground is there for saying that it is intended to stifle the freedom of speech and of the press. The question is, simply, will you support your Chief Magistrate? Our vote does not go merely to one man and to his feelings, it goes to the trust. When clubs are arrayed against your Government, and your Chief Magistrate decidedly arrays the militia to suppress their insurrection, will you countenance or discountenance the officer? Will you ever suffer this House, the country, or even one seditious man in it, to question for an instant whether your approbation and co-operation will be less prompt and cordial than his efforts to support the laws? Is it safe, is it honorable, to make a precedent, and that no less solemn than humiliating, which will authorize, which will compel every future President to doubt whether you will approve him or the clubs? The President now in office would doubtless do his duty promptly and with decision in such a case. But can you expect it of human nature? and if you could, would you put it at risk whether in future a President shall balance between his duty and his fear of your censure. The danger is that a Chief Magistrate, elective as ours is, will temporize, will delay, will put the laws into treaty with offenders, and will even insure a civil war, perhaps the loss of our free Government, by the want of proper energy to quench the first sparks. You ought, therefore, on every occasion, to show the most cordial support to the Executive in support of the laws.

This is the occasion. If it is dangerous to liberty, against right and justice, against truth and decency, to adopt the amendment, as it has been argued, then the President and Senate have done all this. . . .

Thursday, 27 November

Mr. MADISON—said he entirely agreed with those gentlemen who had observed that the house should not have advanced into this discussion, if it could have been avoided—but having proceeded thus far it was indispensably necessary to finish it.

Much delicacy had been thrown into the discussion in consequence of the chief magistrate; he always regretted the circumstance when this was the case.

This, he observed, was not the first instance of difference in opinion between the President and this House. It may be recollected that the President dissented both from the Senate and this House on a particular law (he referred to that apportioning the representatives)—on that occasion he thought the President right. On the present question, supposing the President really to entertain the opinion ascribed to him, it affords no conclusive reason for the House to sacrifice its own judgment. . . .

Members seem to think that in cases not cognizable by law there is room for the interposition of the House. He conceived it to be a sound principle that an action innocent in the eye of the law could not be the object of censure to a legislative body. When the people have formed a constitution, they retain those rights which they have not expressly delegated. It is a question whether what is thus retained can be legislated upon. Opinions are not the objects of legislation. You animadvert on the *abuse* of reserved rights—how far will this go? It may extend to the liberty of speech and of the press.

It is in vain to say that this indiscriminate censure is no punishment. If it falls on classes or individuals it will be a severe punishment. He wished it to be considered how extremely guarded the Constitution was in respect to cases not within its limits. Murder or treason cannot be noticed by the legislature. Is not this proposition, if voted, a vote of attainder? To consider a principle, we must try its nature and see how far it will go; in the present case he considered the effects of the principle contended for would be pernicious. If we advert to the nature of republican government, we shall find that the censorial power is in the people over the government, and not in the government over the people.

As he had confidence in the good sense and patriotism of the people, he did not anticipate any lasting evil to result from the publications of these societies; they will stand or fall by the public opinion; no line can be drawn in this case. The law is the only rule of right; what is consistent with that is not punishable; what is not contrary to that, is innocent, or at least not censurable by the legislative body.

With respect to the body of the people, (whether the outrages have proceeded from weakness or wickedness) what has been done and will be done by the Legislature will have a due effect. If the *proceedings* of the government should not have an effect, will this declaration produce it? The people at large are possessed of proper sentiments on the subject of the insurrection—the whole continent reprobates the conduct of the insurgents, it is not therefore necessary to take the extra step. The press he believed would not be able to shake the confidence of the people in the government. In a republic, light will prevail over darkness, truth over error—he had undoubted confidence in this principle. If it be admitted that the law cannot animadvert on a particular case, neither can we do it. Governments are administered by men—the same degree

of purity does not always exist. Honesty of motives may at present prevail—but this affords no assurance that it will always be the case—at a future period a Legislature may exist of a very different complexion from the present; in this view, we ought not by any vote of ours to give support to measures which now we do not hesitate to reprobate. The gentleman from Georgia had anticipated him in several remarks—no such inference can fairly be drawn as that we abandon the President should we pass over the whole business. The vote passed this morning for raising a force to complete the good work of peace, order, and tranquility begun by the executive, speaks quite a different language from that which has been used to induce an adoption of the principle contended for.

Mr. Madison adverted to precedents—none parallel to the subject before us existed. The inquiry into the failure of the expedition under St. Clair was not in point. In that case the house appointed a committee of enquiry into the conduct of an individual in the public service—the democratic societies are not. He knew of nothing in the proceedings of the Legislature which warrants the house in saying that institutions confessedly not illegal were subjects of legislative censure. . . .

The question was then put, Shall the words "self-created societies, and" be replaced in the amendment of Mr. Fitzsimons? This was carried by a majority of forty-seven against forty-five. . . .

Friday, 28 November
The Address, as amended, was then read throughout at the Clerk's table, as follows:

Sir: The House of Representatives, calling to mind the blessings enjoyed by the people of the United States, and especially the happiness of living under constitutions and laws which rest on their authority alone, could not learn with other emotions than those you have expressed that any part of our fellow citizens should have shown themselves capable of an insurrection. And we learn, with the greatest concern, that any misrepresentations whatever of the Government and its proceedings, either by individuals or combinations of men, should have been made and so far credited as to foment the flagrant outrage which has been committed on the laws. We feel, with you, the deepest regret at so painful an occurrence in the annals of our country. As men regardful of the tender interests of humanity, we look with grief at scenes which might have stained our land with civil blood. As lovers of public order, we lament that it has suffered so flagrant a violation: as zealous friends of Republican Government, we deplore every occasion which, in the hands of its enemies, may be turned into a calumny against it.

This aspect of the crisis, however, is happily not the only one which it presents. There is another, which yields all the consolations which you have drawn from it. It has demonstrated to the candid world, as well as to the American People themselves, that the great body of them, everywhere, are equally attached to the luminous and vital principle of our Constitution which enjoins that the will of the majority shall prevail; that they understand the indissoluble union between true liberty and regular government; that they feel their duties no less than they are watchful over their rights; that they will be as ready, at all times, to crush licentiousness as they have been to defeat usurpation: in a word, that they are capable of carrying into execution that noble plan of self-government which they have chosen as the guarantee of their own happiness and the asylum for that of all, from every clime, who may wish to unite their destiny with ours. . . .

James Madison to James Monroe

4 December 1794

. . . You will learn from the newspapers and official communications the unfortunate scene in the Western parts of Pennsylvania which unfolded itself during the recess. The history of its remote & immediate causes, the measures produced by it, and the manner in which it has been closed, does not fall within the compass of a letter. It is probable also that many explanatory circumstances are yet but imperfectly known. I can only refer to the printed accounts which you will receive from the Department of State and the comments which your memory will assist you in making on them. The event was in several respects a critical one for the cause of liberty, and the real authors of it, if not in the service, were in the most effectual manner, doing the business of despotism. You well know the general tendency of insurrections to increase the momentum of power. You will recollect the particular effect of what happened some years ago in Massachusetts. Precisely the same calamity was to be dreaded on a larger scale in this case. There were

enough as you may well suppose ready to give the same turn to the crisis, and to propagate the same impressions from it. It happened most auspiciously, however, that with a spirit truly republican, the people everywhere and of every description condemned the resistance to the will of the majority and obeyed with alacrity the call to vindicate the authority of the laws. You will see in the answer of the House of Representatives to the President's speech that the most was made of this circumstance as an antidote to the poisonous influence to which Republicanism was exposed. If the insurrection had not been crushed in the manner it was I have no doubt that a formidable attempt would have been made to establish the principle that a standing army was necessary for *enforcing the laws*. When I first came to this City about the middle of October, this was the fashionable language. Nor am I sure that the attempt would not have been made if the President could have been embarked in it, and particularly if the temper of N. England had not been dreaded on this point. I hope we are over that danger for the present. You will readily understand the business detailed in the newspapers relating to the denunciation of the "self created societies." The introduction of it by the President was perhaps the greatest error of his political life. For his sake, as well as for a variety of obvious reasons, I wish'd it might be passed over in silence by the House of Representatives. The answer was penned with that view; and so reported. This moderate course would not satisfy those who hoped to draw a party-advantage out of the President's popularity. The game was to connect the democratic societies with the odium of the insurrection—to connect the Republicans in Congress with those Societies—to put the President ostensibly at the head of the other party, in opposition to both, and by these means prolong the illusions in the North—& try a new experiment on the South. To favor the project, the answer of the Senate was accelerated & so framed as to draw the President into the most pointed reply on the subject of the Societies. At the same time, the answer of the House of Representatives was procrastinated till the example of the Senate & the commitment of the President could have their full operation. You will see how nicely the House was divided, and how the matter went off. As yet the discussion has not been revived by the newspaper combatants. If it should and equal talents be opposed, the result can not fail to wound the President's popularity more than anything that has yet happened. It must be seen that no two principles can be either more indefensible in reason or more dangerous in practice—than that 1. arbitrary denunciations may punish what the law permits & what the Legislature has no right, by law, to prohibit—and that 2. the Government may stifle all censures whatever on its misdoings; for if it be itself the judge it will never allow any censures to be just, and if it can suppress censures flowing from one lawful source it may those flowing from any other—from the press and from individuals as well as from Societies, &c. . . .

Democratic Society of Pennsylvania

9 October 1794

Fellow-Citizens,

Sensations of the most unpleasant kind must have been experienced by every reflecting person who is not leagued against the liberties of this country on hearing and reading the various charges and invectives fabricated for the destruction of the Patriotic Societies in America. So indefatigable are the aristocratical faction among us in disseminating principles unfriendly to the rights of man—at the same time so artful as to envelop their machinations with the garb of patriotism, that it is much feared, unless vigilence, union and firmness mark the conduct of all real friends to equal liberty, their combinations and schemes will have their desired effect.

The enemies of liberty and equality have never ceased to traduce us—even certain influential and public characters have ventured to publicly condemn all political societies. When denunciations of this kind are presented to the world supported by the influence of character and great names, they too frequently obtain a currency which they are by no means entitled to either on the score of justice, propriety, or even common sense. Sometimes by a nice stroke of policy, or by a combination of some favorable circumstance, which the address of the Liberticide turns to his advantage, the imposition gains ground even with the best informed men. As the history of other countries as well as our own has taught us that this influence has too frequently given a death wound to freedom, it is the indispensable duty of every man who is desirous of enjoying and transmitting to posterity equal liberty to guard against its pernicious effects.

Our society with others established upon similar principles in this and the different states were early viewed with a jealous eye by those who were hostile to the rights of man. It has ever been a favorite and important pursuit with

aristocracy to stifle free enquiry, to envelop its proceedings in mystery, and as much as possible, to impede the progress of political knowledge. No wonder therefore that societies whose objects were to cultivate a just knowledge of rational liberty—to inquire into the public conduct of men in every department of government, and to exercise those constitutional rights which as freemen they possess, should become obnoxious to designing men. Accordingly, their shafts have been darted from many quarters. We have been accused of an intention to destroy the government. The old cry of anarchy and anti-federalism have been played off. The inconsistency of our adversaries is remarkable. At one time we were described as too insignificant to merit attention—too contemptible to be dangerous; again—so numerous and so wicked as to endanger the administration—so formidable as to be no longer tolerated.

Unfortunately, a favorable circumstance for the designs of aristocracy lately took place—we mean an insurrection in the western counties of this state. A number of people, dreading the oppressive effects of the Excise Law, were carried to pursue redress by means unwarrantable and unconstitutional. Passion instead of reason having assumed the direction of their affairs, disorder and disunion were the consequences. The executive, however, by marching an army into that country, *many of whom were members of this and* other political societies, soon obliged those people to acknowledge obedience to the laws. Now to the astonishment and indignation of every good citizen, there are not wanting some in administration who are attempting to persuade the people in a belief that the insurrection was encouraged and abetted by the wicked designs *of certain self-created societies*—that no cause of discontent with respect to the laws or administration could reasonably exist. Strange that such palpable absurdities are offered in the face of day. Is it not an indisputable fact that the complaints of the western people against the excise law have sounded in the ears of Congress for some time before the existence of the present Patriotic Societies? Is it not equally true that the general voice of America have considered their complaints as well founded? [If] the public opinion was ever undubitably manifested on any occasion, it was at the late election in this city, where the citizens exhibited a decided proof of their abhorrence of excise systems, even at the fountain head of aristocracy, by depriving of a longer seat in the public councils of this country, one of its supporters and placing in his stead a man who is supposed unfriendly to that species of revenue—They indeed nobly and successfully exercised right of election, which certainly is the most proper and efficacious mode of address.

That man must have passed through life without much reflection who does not know that in other countries as well as our own, aristocracy has ever been disposed to proclaim every real or imaginary delinquency on the part of the people a reason for depriving them of their rights, and for strengthening the arm of government. In Europe, we find, the present diabolical combination leagued against the rights of man have endeavored to promulgate the abominable doctrine that the swinish multitude are unequal to the task of governing themselves by reason of their deficiency in virtue and knowledge. Hence they claim a right to subjugate their fellow-creatures, and to compel them to relinquish those invaluable privileges which they derived from the deity. Some of our temporary rulers seemed to have adopted the same righteous policy. They too are striving to propagate an opinion that public measures ought only to be discussed by public characters. What! Shall the servants of the people who derive their political consequence from the people and who, at their pleasure, may be stripped of all authority if found to abuse it, dispute the right of their employers to discuss their public proceedings? Do they imagine that all knowledge, public spirit and virtue are exclusively confined to themselves? Is it already an offence of the deepest dye to meet and consult on matters which respect our freedom and happiness? Should this be the case, our future prospects must be deplorable indeed! The liberty of the press, that luminary of the mind, as emphatically expressed may be next proscribed: for such is the nature of despotism that having made some encroachments upon the liberties of the people, its rapacious jaws are constantly extended to swallow every vestige of freedom. If we are thus, without a shadow of reason or justice, to be filched of our rights—if we are not permitted to detect and expose the iniquity of public men and measures—if it be deemed a heresy to question the infallibility of the rulers of our land, in the name of God to what purpose did we struggle thro' and maintain a seven years war against a corrupt court, unless to submit to be "hewers of wood and drawers of water" at home, for surely foreign domination is not more grievous than domestic.

In this view of the subject fellow-citizens, it may be proper to inquire, whether you are prepared to relinquish those invaluable privileges obtained at the expense of so much blood, and recognized by our constitution? Whether you are disposed to bend the knee to Baal? We trust and hope you will spurn at the idea. Let us then exercise the right of peaceably meeting for the purpose of considering public affairs—to pass strictures upon any proceedings which are not congenial with freedom—and to propose such measures as in our opinion, may advance the general weel. Let us combat with Herculean strength the fashionable tenet of some among us that the people have no right to be informed of the actions and proceedings of government. Nothing, surely, presents a stronger barrier against the encroachments of tyranny than a free public discussion—by this means the attention is roused—the sources of intelligence are multiplied and truth is developed.

Where then is the propriety of questioning this important privilege? Good rulers will not shrink from public inquiry, because it is to their honor and advantage to encourage free disquisitions. It is to the policy only of a corrupt administration to suppress all animadversions on their conduct, and to persecute the authors of them. If the laws of our country are the echo of the sentiments of the people is it not of importance that those sentiments should be *generally* known? How can they be better understood than by a free discussion, publication and communication of them by means of political societies? And so long as they conduct their deliberations with prudence and moderation, they merit attention.

Among other rights secured to the people by the constitution is the right of election. This, Fellow-Citizens, is certainly one of the most important. Political societies by combining the attention and exertions of the people to this great object, add much to the preservation of liberty. Aristocracy will, as heretofore, preach up the excellency of our Constitution—its balances and checks against tyranny. Let not this however, lull us into a fatal security or divert us from the great objects of our duty. Let us keep in mind that supiness with regard to public concerns is the direct road to slavery, while vigilance and jealousy are the safeguards of liberty.

We sincerely hope that wisdom and harmony may attend all the deliberations in your laudable and patriotic society, and that those institutions may be the means, as we doubt not, of securing and perpetuating equal liberty to the most remote posterity. . . .

Jay's Treaty and Washington's Farewell

John Jay's nomination as minister plenipotentiary to Britain was confirmed by the Senate on 19 April 1794. He arrived in England in June and negotiated against a background of British military successes in the West Indies and the Whiskey Rebellion at home. On 19 November he concluded a treaty that addressed most of the issues which had divided the two nations since the end of the Revolutionary War. Britain agreed to evacuate its forts in the American Northwest, which she had continued to occupy in violation of the Treaty of Peace, and—if America agreed to cease its carrying trade in staples such as cotton, sugar, and molasses—to admit small American vessels to direct trade with the British West Indies. In exchange, the United States agreed to abandon its traditional insistence that the neutral flag protected enemy goods being carried by neutral vessels, to accept a narrower definition of contraband of war, and to grant Britain most-favored-nation status in its ports. Disputes over boundaries, American claims for illegal seizures, and demands by British creditors for American payment of prewar debts were referred to joint commissions. Disagreements over loyalist claims against the states, American claims for slaves carried away by the British at the end of the war, and American objections to British impressment of sailors from American vessels were left unresolved.

The terms of the Treaty of Amity and Commerce were sufficiently unattractive that Washington kept it secret until a special meeting of the Senate could assemble. On 24 June 1795, the Senate (in which debates were secret and unrecorded) ratified it without a vote to spare—and only after rejecting the provisions concerning the trade with the West Indies. Public meetings around the country, which had been protesting the treaty ever since the news of its terms had begun to leak, appealed to Washington to refuse to sign. Even when he signed it anyway, many Republicans remained determined to defeat it in the House of Representatives by refusing the appropriations necessary to establish the joint commissions and carry it into effect.

ALEXANDER JAMES DALLAS

"Features of Mr. Jay's Treaty"

18 July–7 August 1795

Several newspaper series, many of which were reprinted in other papers and also published separately as pamphlets or collected by Matthew Carey in a work called the *American Remembrancer,* condemned the treaty with Britain in great detail. Among the best known were the sixteen essays of "Cato" (Robert R. Livingston), which appeared originally in the *New York Argus* between 15 July and 30 September 1795, Tench Coxe's "Examination of the Pending Treaty with Britain," and the following five-part examination, published originally in the *American Daily Advertiser,* by the state secretary of Pennsylvania.

I. *The origin and progress of the negotiation for the treaty are not calculated to excite confidence.*

1. The administration of our government have, seemingly at least, manifested a policy favorable to Great Britain and adverse to France.

2. But the House of Representatives of Congress, impressed with the general ill conduct of Great Britain towards America, were adopting measures of a mild, though retaliating, nature to obtain redress and indemnification. The injuries complained of were, principally,—1st, the detention of the western posts; 2dly, the delay in compensating for the Negroes carried off at the close of the war; and 3dly, the spoliations committed on our commerce. The remedies proposed were, principally,—1st, the commercial regulations of Mr. Madison; 2dly, the non-intercourse proposition of Mr. Clarke; 3dly, the sequestration motion of Mr. Dayton; 4thly, an embargo; and 5thly, military preparation.

3. Every plan of the legislature was, however, suspended, or rather annihilated, by the interposition of the

executive authority; and Mr. Jay, the Chief Justice of the United States, was taken from his judicial seat to negotiate with Great Britain. . . .

4. The political dogmas of Mr. Jay are well known; his predilection in relation to France and Great Britain has not been disguised, and even on the topic of American complaints, his reports, while in the office of Secretary for Foreign Affairs, and his adjudications while in the office of Chief Justice, were not calculated to point him out as the single citizen of America fitted for the service in which he was employed. . . . Mr. Jay was driven from the ground of an injured to the ground of an aggressing party; he made atonement for imaginary wrongs before he was allowed justice for real ones; he converted the *resentments* of the American citizens (under the impressions of which he was avowedly sent to England) into *amity and concord;* and seems to have been so anxious to rivet a commercial chain about the neck of America that he even forgot, or disregarded, a principal item of her own produce (cotton) in order to make a sweeping sacrifice to the insatiable appetite of his maritime antagonist. . . .

5. The treaty being sent here for ratification, the President and the Senate pursue the mysterious plan in which it was negotiated. It has been intimated that, till the meeting of the Senate, the instrument was not communicated even to the most confidential officers of the government; and the first resolution taken by the Senate was to stop the lips and ears of its members against every possibility of giving or receiving information. . . .

6. But still the treaty remains *unratified;* for, unless the British government shall assent to suspend the obnoxious twelfth article (in favor of which, however, many *patriotic* members declared their readiness to vote), the whole is destroyed by the terms of the ratification; and if the British government shall agree to add an article allowing the suspension, the whole must return for the reconsideration of the Senate. . . .

II. *Nothing is settled by the treaty.*

1. The western posts are *to be given up.*

2. The northern boundary of the United States is *to be amicably settled.*

3. The river meant by St. Croix River in the treaty is *to be settled.*

4. The payment for spoliations is *to be adjusted and made.*

5. The ultimate regulation of the West India trade is to depend on a negotiation *to be made* in the course of two years after the termination of the existing war.

6. The question of neutral bottoms making neutral goods is *to be considered* at the same time.

7. The articles that may be deemed contraband are *to be settled* at the same time.

8. The equalization of duties laid by the contracting parties on one another is *to be hereafter treated of.* . . .

III. *The treaty contains a colorable, but no real, reciprocity.*

1. The second article provides for the surrender of the western posts in June, 1796; but it stipulates that, in the mean time, the citizens of the United States shall not settle within the precincts and jurisdiction of those posts; that the British settlers there shall hold and enjoy all their property of every kind, real and personal; and that when the posts are surrendered, such settlers shall have an election either to remain British subjects or to become American citizens. Query—Were not the western posts and all their precincts and jurisdiction, the absolute property of the United States by the treaty of peace? Query—What equivalent is given for this cession of the territory of the United States to a foreign power? Query—How far do the precincts and jurisdiction of the posts extend? . . .

2. The third article stipulates that the two contracting parties may frequent the ports of *either party* on the eastern banks of the Mississippi. Query—What ports has Great Britain on the eastern banks of the Mississippi?

3. The third article likewise opens an amicable intercourse on the lakes; but excludes us from their seaports and the limits of the Hudson's Bay Company . . . while Great Britain is in fact admitted to all the advantages of which our Atlantic rivers are susceptible.

4. The sixth and seventh articles provide for satisfying every demand which Great Britain has been able, at any time, to make against the United States (the payment of the British debts due before the war, and the indemnification for vessels captured within our territorial jurisdiction); but the provision made for the American claims upon Great Britain is not equally explicit or efficient in its terms, nor is it coextensive with the object. Query—Why is the demand for the Negroes carried off by the British troops suppressed, waived, or abandoned? The preamble to the treaty recites an intention to *terminate the differences*

between the nations: was not the affair of the Negroes a difference between the nations? and how has it been terminated?

5. The ninth article stipulates that the subjects of Great Britain and the citizens of the United States, respectively, who now hold lands within the territories of either nation, shall hold the lands in the same manner as natives do. Query—What is the relative proportion of lands so held? Query—The effect to revive the claims of British subjects who, either as traitors or aliens, have forfeited their property within the respective States? . . .

6. The tenth article declares that neither party shall sequester or confiscate the debts or property in the funds, etc. belonging to the citizens of the other in case of a war or of national differences. Great Britain has fleets and armies: America has none. Query—Does not this, supported by other provisions, which forbid our changing the commercial situation of Great Britain, or imposing higher duties on her than on other nations, deprive the United States of their best means of retaliation and coercion? Query—Is it not taking from America her only weapon of defense; but from Great Britain the least of two weapons which she possesses? . . .

7. The twelfth article opens to our vessels, not exceeding seventy tons, an intercourse with the British West India Islands during the present war and for two years after; but it prohibits our exporting from the United States molasses, sugar, cocoa, coffee, or cotton to any part of the world, whether those articles are brought from British, French, or Spanish islands, or even raised (as cotton is) within our own territory. . . .

IV. *The treaty is an instrument of party.*

1. The discussions during the session of congress in which Mr. Jay's mission was projected evinced the existence of two parties upon the question,—whether it was more our interest to be allied with the republic of France than with the monarchy of Great Britain. Query—Does not the general complexion of the treaty decide the question in favor of the alliance with Great Britain? . . .

2. The measures proposed by one party to retaliate the injuries offered by Great Britain to our territorial, commercial, and political rights were opposed by the other, precisely as the treaty opposes them. For instance: (1) Mr. Madison projects a regulation of our commerce with Great Britain by which the hostile spirit of that nation might be controlled on the footing of its interest.

The treaty legitimizes the opposition which was given to the measure in Congress by declaring, in article fifteen, "that no other or higher duties shall be paid by the ships or merchandise of the one party in the ports of the other than such as are paid by the like vessels or merchandise of all other nations; nor shall any other or higher duty be imposed in one country on the importation of any articles of the growth, produce, or manufactures of the other than are, or shall be, payable on the importation of the like articles of the growth, etc. of any foreign country." (2) Mr. Clarke proposed to manifest and enforce the public resentment by prohibiting all intercourse between the two nations. The treaty destroys the very right to attempt that species of national denunciation by declaring, in the same article, that "no prohibition shall be imposed on the exportation or importation of any articles to or from the territories of the two parties, respectively, which shall not equally extend to all other nations." (3) But Mr. Dayton moves, and the House of Representatives supports his motion, for the sequestration of British debts, etc., to insure a fund for paying the spoliations committed on our trade. The treaty . . . despoils the government of this important instrument to coerce a powerful yet interested adversary into acts of justice. . . . (4) It has, likewise, been thought by some politicians that the energies of our executive department require every aid that can be given to them in order more effectually to resist and control the popular branches of the government. Hence we find the treaty-making power employed in that service; and Congress cannot exercise a legislative discretion on the prohibited points (though it did not participate in making the cession of its authority) without a declaration of war against Great Britain. George the Third enjoys by the treaty a more complete negative to bind us as states than he ever claimed over us as colonies.

V. *The treaty is a violation of the general principles of neutrality and is in collision with the positive previous engagements which subsist between America and France.*

1. It is a general principle of the law of nations that during the existence of a war neutral powers shall not, by favor or by treaty, so alter the situation of one of the belligerent parties as to enable him more advantageously to prosecute hostilities against his adversary. If, likewise, a neutral power shall refuse or evade treating with one of the parties, but eagerly enter into a treaty with the other, it is a partiality that amounts to a breach of neutrality. . . .

2. That we have, on the one hand, evaded the overtures of a treaty with France, and on the other hand, solicited a treaty from Great Britain, are facts public and notorious. Let us inquire, then, what Great Britain has gained on the occasion, to enable her more advantageously to prosecute her hostilities against France.

(1) *Great Britain has gained time.* As nothing is settled by the treaty, she has it in her power to turn all the chances of the war in her favor, and, in the interim, being relieved from the odium and embarrassment of adding America to her enemies, the current of her operations against France is undivided and will of course flow with greater vigor and certainty. . . .

(2) *Great Britain gains supplies for her West India colonies;* and *that* for a period almost limited to the continuance of the war, under circumstances which incapacitate her from furnishing the colonial supplies herself; and, indeed, compel her to invite the aid of all nations in furnishing provisions for her own domestic support. The supplies may be carried to the islands either in *American* bottoms *not exceeding seventy tons,* or in *British* bottoms of *any tonnage.* . . .

(5) *The admission of Great Britain to all the commercial advantages of the most favored nation and the restraints imposed upon our legislative independence,* as stated in the *party feature* of the treaty, are proofs of predilection and partiality in the American government which cannot fail to improve the resources of Great Britain and to impair the interests as well as the attachments of France.

(6) *The assent to the seizure of all provision ships,* and that, in effect, upon any pretext, at a period when Great Britain is distressed for provisions as well as France, and when the system of *subduing by famine* has been adopted by the former against the latter nation, is clearly changing our position as an independent republic in a manner detrimental to our original ally. . . .

(7) *Great Britain has gained the right of preventing our citizens from being volunteers in the armies or ships of France.* This is not simply the grant of a new right to Great Britain, but is, at the same time, a positive deprivation of a benefit hitherto enjoyed by France. Neither the laws of nations, nor our municipal constitution and laws, prohibited our citizens from *going to another country* and *there,* either for the sake of honor, reward, or instruction, serving in a foreign navy or army. . . .

3. But it is time to advert to *the cases of collision* between the two treaties; and these are of such a nature as to produce a violation of the spirit, though not a positive violation of the words, of the previous engagements that subsist between France and America,—they are causes of offense, and clash in the highest degree. . . .

(2) By our treaty with France, and, indeed, with several other nations, *it is expressly stipulated that free vessels* shall *make free goods.* . . . While France adheres to her treaty, by permitting *British goods* to be protected by American bottoms, is it honest, honorable, or consistent on our part *to enter voluntarily into a compact with the enemies of France* for permitting them to take *French goods* out of our vessels? We may not be able *to prevent,* but ought we to *agree* to the proceeding? Let the question be repeated—Does not such an *express agreement* clash with our express, as well as implied, obligations to France?

(3) By enumerating as contraband articles in the treaty with Great Britain certain articles which are declared free in the treaty with France, *we may, consistently with the latter, supply Great Britain; but, consistently with the former, we cannot supply France.* . . .

VI. *The treaty with Great Britain is calculated to injure the United States in the friendship and favor of other foreign nations.*

1. That the friendship and favor of France will be affected by the formation of so heterogeneous an alliance with her most implacable enemy cannot be doubted, if we reason upon any scale applicable to the policy of nations or the passions of man. From that republic, therefore, if not an explicit renunciation of all connection with the United States, we may at least expect an alteration of conduct; and, finding the success which has flowed from the hostile treatment that Great Britain has shown towards us, she may be at length tempted to endeavor at *extorting from fear* what she has not been able to obtain *from affection.* . . .

VII. *The treaty with Great Britain is impolitic and pernicious in respect to the domestic interests and happiness of the United States.*

1. If it is true, and incontrovertibly it is true, that the *interest* and *happiness* of America consist, as our patriotic President, in his letter to Lord *Buchan,* declares, "in being little heard of in the great world of politics; in having nothing to do in the political intrigues or the squabbles of European nations; but, on the contrary, in exchanging commodities, and living in peace and amity with all the inhabitants of the earth, and in doing justice to and in

receiving it from every power we are connected with"; it is likewise manifest that all the wisdom and energy of those who administer our government should be constantly and sedulously employed to preserve or to attain for the United States that enviable rank among nations. To *refrain from forming hasty and unequal alliances,* to let commerce flow in its own natural channels, to afford every man, whether alien or citizen, a remedy for every wrong, and to resist, on the first appearance, every violation of our national rights and independence, are the means best adapted to the end which we contemplate.

VIII. *The British treaty and the Constitution of the United States are at war with each other.* . . .

The second section of the second article of the Constitution says that "the President shall have power, by and with the advice and consent of the Senate, to make treaties, provided two-thirds of the senators present concur."

To the exercise of this power no immediate qualification or restriction is attached; but must we, therefore, suppose that the jurisdiction of the President and Senate, like the jurisdiction ascribed to the British Parliament, is omnipotent? . . .

Whenever the President and two-thirds of the Senate shall be desirous to counteract the conduct of the House of Representatives; whenever they may wish to enforce a particular point of legislation; or whenever they shall be disposed to circumscribe the power of a succeeding Congress—a treaty with a foreign nation, nay, a talk with a savage tribe, affords the ready and effectual instrument for accomplishing their views, since the treaty or the talk will constitute the supreme law of the land. . . .

By the Constitution, Congress is empowered to regulate commerce with foreign nations.

By the treaty, the commerce of the United States, not only directly with Great Britain, but incidentally with *every* foreign nation, is regulated. . . .

Can a power so given to one department be divested by implication in order to amplify and invigorate another power given in general terms to another department? . . .

Such, upon the whole, are "THE FEATURES OF MR. JAY'S TREATY." . . . If it shall, in any degree, serve the purposes of truth, by leading, through the medium of a candid investigation, *to a fair, honorable, and patriotic decision,* the design with which it was written will be completely accomplished, *whether* RATIFICATION *OR* REJECTION *is the result.*

Antitreaty Memorials
Memorial of the Citizens of Philadelphia
July 1795

This petition to the president, published in Dunlap and Claypoole's *American Daily Advertiser* on 28 July 1795, was typical of those requesting Washington to refuse his consent.

That your memorialists, sincerely and affectionately attached to you from a sense of the important services which you have rendered to the United States and a conviction of the purity of the motives that will forever regulate your public administration, do, on an occasion in which they feel themselves deeply interested, address you as a friend and patriot: as a friend who will never take offense at what is well intended and as a patriot who will never reject what may be converted to the good of your country.

That your memorialists entertain a proper respect for your constitutional authority; and, whatever may be the issue of the present momentous question, they will faithfully acquiesce in the regular exercise of the delegated powers of the government; but they trust that in the formation of a compact which is to operate upon them and upon their posterity in their most important internal as well as external relations, which, in effect, admits another government to control the legislative functions of the union, and which, if found upon experience to be detrimental, can only be repealed by soliciting the assent or provoking the hostilities of a foreign power, you will not deem it improper or officious in them thus anxiously, but respectfully, to present a solemn testimonial of their public opinion, feelings, and interest. . . .

The treaty is objected to,

1st. Because it does not provide for a fair and effectual settlement of the differences that previously subsisted between the United States and Great Britain. . . .

2. Because, by the treaty, the federal government accedes to restraints upon the American commerce and navigations, internal as well as external, that embrace no principle of real reciprocity and are inconsistent with the rights and destructive to the interests of an independent nation. . . .

3. Because the treaty is destructive to the domestic independence and prosperity of the United States. . . .

4. Because the treaty surrenders certain inherent powers of an independent government, which are essential in the circumstances of the United States to their safety and defense . . . inasmuch as the right of sequestration, the right of regulating commerce in favor of a friendly and against a rival power, and the right of suspending a commercial intercourse with an inimical nation are voluntarily abandoned.

5. Because the treaty is an infraction of the rights of friendship, gratitude, and alliance which the Republic of France may justly claim from the United States, and deprives the United States of the most powerful means to secure the good will and good offices of other nations— inasmuch as it alters, during a war, the relative situation of the different nations advantageously to Great Britain and prejudicially to the French Republic; inasmuch as it is in manifest collision with several articles of the American treaty with France; and inasmuch as it grants to Great Britain certain high, dangerous, and exclusive privileges.

And your memorialists, having thus upon general ground concisely but explicitly avowed their wishes and opinions, and forbearing a minute specification of the many other objections that occur, conclude with an assurance that, by refusing to ratify the projected treaty, you will, according to their best information and judgment, at once evince an exalted attachment to the principles of the Constitution of the United States and an undiminished zeal to advance the prosperity and happiness of your constituents.

Petition to the General Assembly of the Commonwealth of Virginia

12 October 1795

Widely reprinted after its initial appearance in Richmond and Fredericksburg papers, this petition was drafted by James Madison after Washington had signed the treaty and responded sharply to a critical petition from Boston. Madison assumed at this point that the Senate's rejection of Article XII of the treaty, if acquiesced in by the British, would require that it be submitted to the Senate again for final approval.

THE PRESIDENT of the UNITED STATES in his letter to the Selectmen of Boston, dated 28th of July, 1795, copies whereof have since been transmitted to similar meetings of the people in other parts of the United States, having, as it is conceived, virtually refused to view the representations of the people as a source of information worthy of his consideration in deliberating upon the propriety of ratifying or rejecting the late treaty between Great Britain and the United States, . . . and having, by these proceedings, rendered all further representations and applications to him upon the subject absurd and nugatory, . . . the people should boldly exercise their right of addressing their objections to all other constituted authorities within the United States who possess any agency relative to this highly interesting subject.

Upon this principle, the following PETITION to the GENERAL ASSEMBLY of VIRGINIA, in virtue of their constitutional right of appointing Senators for this state to the Congress of the United States, is submitted to the independent citizens thereof. . . .

Through these means one more effort may be made by a declaration of the public sentiment to prevent the final ratification and ultimate energy of an instrument which is deemed fatal to the interests, the happiness, and perhaps finally to the liberty and independence of the United States.

12 October 1795

To the General Assembly of the Commonwealth of Virginia.

The Memorial and Petition of the subscribers thereof respectfully showeth, that they have seen and maturely considered the treaty lately negotiated with Great Britain and conditionally ratified by the President of the United States.

That they infer from the nature of the condition annexed to the ratification that the said treaty ought to receive and must again receive the sanction of the constituted authorities before it can be finally binding on the United States. . . .

That in the present stage of the transaction they deem it their right and their duty to pursue every constitutional and proper mode of urging those objections to the treaty which in their judgment require to be entirely removed before it ought to be finally established.

That under this conviction, they submit the following observations to the consideration of the General Assembly.

I. . . . The execution of the Treaty of Peace equally by both ought to have been provided for. Yet, whilst the

United States are to comply in the most ample manner with the article unfulfilled by them, and to make compensation for whatever losses may have accrued from their delay, Great Britain is released altogether from one of the articles unfulfilled by her and is not obliged to make the smallest compensation for the damages which have accrued from her delay in fulfilling the other. . . .

II. Without remarking the inexplicit provision for redressing past spoliations and vexations, no sufficient precautions are taken against them in future. On the contrary, by omitting to provide for the respect due to sea letters, passports, and certificates, and for other customary safeguards to neutral vessels, "a general search warrant" (in the strong but just language of our fellow-citizens of Charleston) is granted against the American navigation. Examples of such provisions were to be found in our other treaties, as well as in the treaties of other nations. And it is matter of just surprise that they should have no place in a treaty with Great Britain, whose conduct on the seas so particularly suggested and enforced every guard to our rights that could be reasonably insisted on.

By omitting to provide against the arbitrary seizure and imprisonment of American seamen, that valuable class of citizens remains exposed to all the outrages and our commerce to all the interruptions hitherto experienced from that cause.

By expressly admitting that provisions are to be held contraband in cases other than when bound to an invested place, and impliedly admitting that such cases exist at present, not only a retrospective sanction may be given to proceedings against which an indemnification is claimed, but an apparent license is granted to fresh and more rapacious depredations on our lawful commerce; and facts seem to show that such is to be the fruit of this impolitic concession. It is conceived that the pretext set up by Great Britain of besieging and starving whole nations, and the doctrine grounded thereon of a right to intercept the customary trade of neutral nations, in articles not contraband, ought never to have been admitted into a treaty of the United States—Because 1. It is a general outrage on humanity and an attack on the useful intercourse of nations. 2. It appears that the doctrine was denied by the executive in the discussions with Mr. Hammond, the British minister, and that demands of compensation founded on that denial are now depending. 3. As provisions constitute not less than two-thirds of our exports,

and Great Britain is nearly half her time at war, an admission of the doctrine sacrifices in a correspondent degree the intrinsic value of our country. 4. After public denial of the doctrine, to admit it in the midst of the present war by a formal treaty would have but too much of the effect as well as the appearance of voluntarily concurring in the scheme of distressing a nation whose friendly relations to the United States, as well as the struggles for freedom in which it is engaged, give a title to every good office which is permitted by a just regard to our own interest and not strictly forbidden by the duties of neutrality. 5. It is no plea for the measure to hold it up as an alternative to the disgrace of being involuntarily treated in the same manner, without a faculty to redress ourselves. The disgrace of being plundered with impunity against our consent being under no circumstances so great as the disgrace of consenting to be plundered with impunity. By annexing to the implements of war enumerated as contraband the articles of ship timber, tar, or rosin, copper in sheets, sails, hemp and cordage, our neutral rights and national interests are still further *narrowed*. These articles were excluded from the contraband list by the United States when they were themselves in a state of war. (See ordinance relating to captures in fourth of December, 1781.) Their other treaties expressly declare them not to be contraband.

British Treaties have done the same, nor as is believed, do the treaties of any nation in Europe producing these articles for exportation allow them to be subjects of confiscation. The stipulation was the less to be admitted as the reciprocity assumed by it is a mere cover for the violation of that principle, most of the articles in question being among the exports of the United States, whilst all of them are among the imports of Great Britain.

By expressly stipulating with Great Britain against the freedom of enemy's property in neutral bottoms, the progress towards a complete and formal establishment of a principle in the law of nations so favorable to the general interest and security of commerce receives all the check the United States could give to it. Reason and experience have long taught the propriety of considering free ships as giving freedom to their cargoes. The several great maritime nations of Europe have not only established, at different times, by their treaties with each other, but on a solemn occasion jointly declared it to be the law of nations, by a specific compact, of which the United States entered their entire approbation (see their act of the 5th of October, 1780).

Great Britain alone dissented. But she herself, in a variety of prior treaties and in a treaty with France since, has acceded to the principle. Under these circumstances, the United States, of all nations, ought to be the last to combine in a retrograde effort on this subject, as being more than any other interested in extending and establishing the commercial rights of neutral nations. Their situation particularly fits them to be carriers for the great nations of Europe during their wars; and both their situation and the genius of their government and people promise them a greater share of peace and neutrality than can be expected by any other nation. The relation of the United States by a treaty on this point to the enemies of Great Britain was another reason for avoiding this stipulation. Whilst British goods, in American vessels, are protected against French and Dutch captures, it was enough to leave French and Dutch goods in American vessels to the ordinary course of judicial determination without a voluntary, a positive, and invidious provision for condemning them. It has not been overlooked that a clause in the treaty proposes to renew at some future period the discussion of the principle now settled; but the question is then to be not only in what, but *whether in any cases,* neutral vessels shall protect enemies' property; and it is to be discussed at the same time, not whether *in any, but in what cases,* provisions and other articles not bound to invested places may be treated as contraband. So that when the principle is in favor of the United States, the principle itself is to be the subject of discussion; when the principle is in favor of Great Britain, the application of it only is to be the subject of discussion.

III. Whenever the law of nations has been a topic for consideration, the result of the treaty accommodates Great Britain in relation to one or both of the republics at war with her, as well as in the abandonment of the rights and interests of the United States.

Thus American vessels bound to Great Britain are protected by sea papers against French and Dutch searches; but when bound to France or Holland, are left exposed to British searches without regard to such papers.

American provisions in American vessels bound to the enemies of Great Britain are left by treaty to the seizure and use of Great Britain; but provisions, whether American or not, in American vessels, cannot be touched by the enemies of Great Britain.

British property in American vessels is not subject to French or Dutch confiscation—French or Dutch property in American vessels is subjected to British confiscation. Articles of shipbuilding bound to the enemies of Great Britain for the equipment of vessels of trade only are contraband—bound to Great Britain for the equipment of vessels of war, are not contraband.

American citizens entering as volunteers in the service of France or Holland are punishable; but American volunteers joining the arms of Great Britain against France or Holland are not punishable.

British ships of war and privateers, with their prizes, made on citizens of Holland, may freely enter and depart the ports of the United States; but Dutch ships of war, and privateers with their prizes, made on subjects of Great Britain, are to receive no shelter or refuge in the ports of the United States. This advantage in war is given to Great Britain, not by treaty prior to an existing war, but by a treaty made in the midst of war, and expressly stipulating against a like article of treaty with the other party for equalizing the advantage.

The article prohibiting confiscations and sequestrations is unequal between Great Britain and the United States: American citizens have little if any interest in private or bank stock, or private debts, within Great Britain. So where much would be in the power of the United States and little in the power of Great Britain, the power is interdicted: Where more is in the power of Great Britain than of the United States, the power is unconfined. Another remark is applicable—when the modern usage of nations is in favor of Great Britain, the modern usage is the rule of the treaty; but when the modern usage is in favor of the United States, the modern usage is rejected as a rule for the treaty.

IV. The footing on which the treaty places the subject of commerce is liable to insuperable objections.

I. The nature of our exports and imports, compared with those of other countries and particularly of Great Britain, has been thought by the legislature of the United States to justify certain differences in the tonnage and other duties in favor of American bottoms, and the advantage possessed by Great Britain in her superior capital was thought at the same time to require such countervailing encouragements. Experience has shown the solidity of both these considerations. The American navigation has in a good degree been protected against the advantage on the side of British capital, and has increased in proportion; whilst the nature of our exports, being generally necessaries or raw materials, and our imports, consisting mostly of British manufactures, has restrained the disposition of Great Britain to counteract the protecting duties afforded to our navigation. If the treaty is carried into effect, this protection is relinquished and Congress are prohibited from substituting any other. Then the British capital, having no longer the present inducement to make use of American bottoms, may be expected, in whatever hands operating, to give the preference to British bottoms.

2. The provisions of the treaty which relate to the West-Indies, where the nature of our exports and imports gives a commanding energy to our just pretensions, instead of alleviating the general evil, are a detail of particular humiliations and sacrifices. Nor will a remedy by any means be found in a revision of that part alone in the treaty. On the contrary, if Great Britain should accede to the proposition of the Senate and the treaty be finally established without that part of it, but in all its other parts, she will in that event be able to exclude American bottoms altogether from that channel of intercourse and to regulate the whole trade with the West-Indies in the manner heretofore complained of, whilst the United States will be completely dispossessed of the right and the means of counteracting the monopoly, unless they submit to a universal infraction of their trade, not excepting with nations whose regulations may be reciprocal and satisfactory.

3. The treaty, not content with these injuries to the United States in their commerce with Great Britain, provides in the XV article against the improvement or preservation of their commerce with other nations by any beneficial treaties that may be attainable. The general rule of the United States in their treaties, founded on the example of other nations, has been that where a nation was to have the privileges of the most favored nations, it shall be admitted gratuitously to such privileges only as may be gratuitously granted, but shall pay for privileges not gratuitously granted the compensation paid by others; this prudent and equitable qualification of the footing of the most favored nation was particularly requisite in a treaty with Great Britain, whose commercial system in relation to other countries being matured and settled, is not likely to be varied by grants of new privileges that might result to the United States. It was particularly requisite at the present juncture, also, when an advantageous revision of the treaty with France is said to be favored by that Republic; when a treaty with Spain is actually in negotiation; and when treaties with other nations whose commerce is important to the United States cannot be out of contemplation.

The proposed treaty, nevertheless, puts Great Britain in all respects gratuitously on the footing of the nations most favored, even as to future privileges, for which the most valuable considerations may be given; so that it is not only out of the power of the United States to grant any peculiar privileges to any other nation, as an equivalent for peculiar advantages in commerce or navigation granted to the United States, but every nation desiring to treat on this subject with the United States is reduced to the alternative either of declining the treaty altogether or of including Great Britain gratuitously in all the privileges it purchases for itself. An article of this import is the greatest obstruction next to an absolute prohibition that could have been thrown in the way of other treaties; and that it was insidiously meant by Great Britain to be such is rendered the less doubtful by the kindred features of the treaty.

4. The President and Senate by ratifying this treaty usurp the powers of regulating commerce, of making rules with respect to aliens, of establishing tribunals of justice, and of defining piracy. . . .

It can be no apology for the commercial disadvantages that better terms could not be obtained. If proper terms could not be obtained at that time, commercial articles which were no wise essentially connected with the objects of the embassy ought to have waited for a more favorable season. Nor is a better apology to be drawn from our other treaties. These not only avoid many of the sacrifices in the new treaty; but the chief of them were the guarantees or the auxiliaries of our independence; and in that view, would have been an equivalent for greater commercial concessions than were insisted on.

V. A treaty thus unequal in its conditions, thus derogating from our national rights, thus insidious in some of its objects, and thus alarming in its operation to the dearest interest of the United States in their commerce and navigation, is, in its present form, unworthy the voluntary acceptance of an independent people, and is happily not dictated to them by the circumstances in which a kind providence has placed them. A treaty thus incompatible with our Constitution, thus unequal in its conditions, thus derogating from our national rights, thus insidious in some of its objects, and thus alarming in all its operation, is not only unworthy of the voluntary acceptance of an independent and happy people, but is an abject sacrifice which ought to have been rejected with disdain in the most humiliating and adverse circumstances. It is sincerely believed that such a treaty would not have been listened to at any former period, even when Great Britain was most powerful, at her ease, and the United States most feeble, without the respectability they now enjoy. To pretend that however objectionable the instrument may be, it ought to be considered as the only escape from a hostile resentment of Great Britain, which would evidently be as impolitic as it would be unjust on her part, is an artifice too contemptible to answer its purpose. . . . To do justice to all nations, to obtain it from them by every peaceable effort, in preference to war; and to confide in this policy for avoiding that extremity or for meeting it with firmness under the blessing of Heaven, when it may be forced upon us, is the only course of which the United States can never have reason to repent.

The petitioners, relying on the wisdom and patriotism of the General Assembly, pray that the objections to the treaty comprised in these observations may be taken into their serious consideration; and that such measures towards a remedy may be pursued as may be judged most conformable to the nature of the case and most consistent with constitutional principles.

ALEXANDER HAMILTON

The "Camillus" Essays

22 July 1795–9 January 1796

During the fall of 1795 and into the winter, public opinion began to shift quite markedly behind the treaty. Not least among the reasons was the appearance of capable defenses of its terms by "Curtius" (Noah Webster) and others. Incomparably the best of these defenses were the thirty-eight essays of "Camillus," which were published originally in two New York newspapers, the *Argus* and the *Herald,* and reprinted widely around the country before appearing also as a pamphlet. Hamilton wrote twenty-eight of these essays, Rufus King the rest.

"The Defence, No. 1"

22 July 1795

It was to have been foreseen that the treaty which Mr. Jay was charged to negotiate with Great Britain, whenever it should appear, would have to contend with many perverse dispositions and some honest prejudices. That there was no measure in which the government could engage so little likely to be viewed according to its intrinsic merits—so very likely to encounter misconception, jealousy, and unreasonable dislike. For this many reasons may be assigned. . . .

It was known, that the resentment produced by our revolution war with Great Britain had never been entirely extinguished, and that recent injuries had rekindled the flame with additional violence. It was a natural consequence of this that many should be disinclined to any amicable arrangement with Great Britain and that many others should be prepared to acquiesce only in a treaty which should present advantages of so striking and preponderant a kind as it was not reasonable to expect could be obtained, unless the United States were in a condition to give the law to Great Britain. . . .

It was not to be mistaken that an enthusiasm for France and her revolution throughout all its wonderful vicissitudes has continued to possess the minds of the great body of the people of this country, and it was to be inferred that this sentiment would predispose to a jealousy of any agreement or treaty with her most persevering competitor—a jealousy so excessive as would give the fullest hope to insidious arts to perplex and mislead the public opinion. It was well understood that a numerous party among us, though disavowing the design, because the avowal would defeat it, have been steadily endeavoring to make the United States a party in the present European war, by advocating all those measures which would widen the breach between us and Great Britain and by resisting all those which could tend to close it; and it was morally certain that this party would eagerly improve every circumstance which could serve to render the treaty odious and to frustrate it, as the most effectual road to their favorite goal.

It was also known beforehand that personal and party rivalships of the most active kind would assail whatever treaty might be made, to disgrace, if possible, its organ.

There are three persons prominent in the public eye as the successor of the actual President of the United States in the event of his retreat from the station: Mr. Adams, Mr. Jay, Mr. Jefferson.

No one has forgotten the systematic pains which have been taken to impair the well earned popularity of the first gentleman. Mr. Jay too has been repeatedly the object of attacks with the same view. His friends as well as his enemies anticipated that he could make no treaty which would not furnish weapons against him—and it were to have been ignorant of the indefatigable malice of his adversaries to have doubted that they would be seized with eagerness and wielded with dexterity. . . .

From the combined operation of these different causes, it would have been a vain expectation that the treaty would be generally contemplated with candor and moderation, or that reason would regulate the first impressions concerning it. It was certain, on the contrary, that however unexceptionable its true character might be, it would have to fight its way through a mass of unreasonable opposition; and that time, examination and reflection would be requisite to fix the public opinion on a true basis. It was certain that it would become the instrument of a systematic effort against the national government and its administration: a decided engine of party to advance its own views at the hazard of the public peace and prosperity. . . .

At Boston it was published one day, and the next a town meeting was convened to condemn it, without ever being read; without any serious discussion, sentence was pronounced against it. . . .

The intelligence of this event had no sooner reached New York than the leaders of the clubs were seen haranguing in every corner of the city to stir up our citizens into an imitation of the example of the meeting at Boston. An invitation to meet at the City Hall quickly followed, not to consider or discuss the merits of the treaty, but to unite with the meeting at Boston to address the president against its ratification. . . .

In vain did a respectable meeting of the merchants endeavor, by their advice, to moderate the violence of these views and to promote a spirit favorable to a fair discussion of the treaty; in vain did a respectable body of citizens of every description attend for that purpose. The leaders of the clubs resisted all discussion, and their followers, by their clamors and vociferations, rendered it impracticable, notwithstanding the wish of a manifest majority of the citizens convened upon the occasion. . . .

It cannot be doubted that the real motive to the opposition was the fear of a discussion; the desire of excluding light; the adherence to a plan of surprise and deception. Nor need we desire any fuller proof of that spirit of party, which has stimulated the opposition to the treaty than is to be found in the circumstances of that opposition.

To every man who is not an enemy to the national government, who is not a prejudiced partisan, who is capable of comprehending the argument and passionate enough to attend to it with impartiality, I flatter myself I shall be able to demonstrate satisfactorily in the course of some succeeding papers—

1. That the treaty adjusts in a reasonable manner the points in controversy between the United States and Great Britain, as well those depending on the inexecution of the treaty of peace as those growing out of the present European war.

2. That it makes no improper concessions to Great Britain, no sacrifices on the part of the United States.

3. That it secures to the United States equivalents for what they grant.

4. That it lays upon them no restrictions which are incompatible with their honor or their interest.

5. That in the articles which respect war, it conforms to the laws of nations.

6. That it violates no treaty with, nor duty toward, any foreign power.

7. That compared with our other commercial treaties, it is upon the whole entitled to a preference.

8. That it contains concessions of advantages by Great Britain to the United States which no other nation has obtained from the same power.

9. That it gives to her no superiority of advantages over other nations with whom we have treaties.

10. That interests of primary importance to our general welfare are promoted by it.

11. That the too probable result of a refusal to ratify is war, or what would be still worse, a disgraceful passiveness under violations of our rights, unredressed and unadjusted; and consequently, that it is the true interest of the United States that the treaty should go into effect. . . .

"The Defence, No. 2"

25 July 1795

. . . All must remember the very critical posture of this country at the time that mission was resolved upon. A recent violation of our rights too flagrant and too injurious to be submitted to had filled every American breast with indignation and every prudent man with alarm and disquietude. A few hoped, and the great body of the community feared, that war was inevitable.

In this crisis two sets of opinions prevailed; one looked to measures which were to have a compulsory effect upon Great Britain—the sequestration of British debts and the cutting off of intercourse wholly or partially between the two countries—the other to *vigorous preparation* for war and *one more effort* of negotiation by a solemn mission to avert it.

That the latter was the best opinion no truly sensible man can doubt, and it may be boldly affirmed that the event has entirely justified it.

If measures of coercion and reprisal had taken place, war in all human probability would have followed.

National pride is generally a very intractable thing. In the councils of no country does it act with greater force than in those of Great Britain. Whatever it might have been in her power to yield to negotiation, she could have yielded nothing to compulsion, without self-degradation and without the sacrifice of that political consequence which, at all times very important to a nation, was peculiarly so to her at the juncture in question. It must be remembered too that from the relations in which the two countries have stood to each other it must have cost more to the pride of Great Britain to have received the law from us than from any other power.

When one nation has cause of complaint against another, the course marked out by practice, the opinion of writers, and the principles of humanity, the object being to avoid war, is to precede reprisals of any kind by a demand of reparation. To begin with reprisals is to meet on the ground of war and puts the other party in a condition not to be able to recede without humiliation.

Had this course been pursued by us it would not only have rendered war morally certain, but it would have united the British nation in the vigorous support of their government in the prosecution of that war, while on our parts we should have been quickly distracted and divided. The calamities of war would have brought the most ardent to their senses and placed them among the first in reproaching the government with precipitation, rashness, and folly; for not having taken every chance by pacific means to avoid so great an evil. . . .

Few nations can have stronger inducements than the U States to cultivate peace. Their infant state in general—

their want of a marine in particular to protect their commerce—would render war in an extreme degree a calamity. It would not only arrest our present rapid progress to strength and prosperity, but would probably throw us back into a state of debility and impoverishment from which it would require years to emerge. Our trade, navigation, and mercantile capital would be essentially destroyed. Spain being an associate with Great Britain, a general Indian war would probably have desolated the whole extent of our frontier. Our exports obstructed, agriculture would have seriously languished. All other branches of industry must have proportionally suffered. Our public debt, instead of a gradual diminution, must have sustained a great augmentation and drawn with it a large increase of taxes and burdens on this people.

But this perhaps was not the worst to be apprehended. It was to be feared that the war would be conducted in a spirit which would render it more than ordinarily calamitous. There are too many proofs that a considerable party among us is deeply infected with those horrid principles of Jacobinism which, proceeding from one excess to another, have made France a theater of blood and which notwithstanding the most vigorous efforts of the national representation to suppress it keeps the destinies of France to this moment suspended by a thread. It was too probable that the direction of the war if commenced would have fallen into the hands of men of this description. The consequences of this even in imagination are such as to make any virtuous man shudder.

It was therefore in a peculiar manner the duty of the Government to take all possible chances for avoiding war. The plan adopted was the only one which could claim this advantage. . . .

It cannot escape an attentive observer that the language which in the first instance condemned the mission of an envoy extraordinary to Great Britain, and which now condemns the treaty negotiated by him, seems to consider the U States as among the first rate powers of the world in point of strength and resource and proposes to them a conduct predicated upon that condition.

To underrate our just importance would be a degrading error. To overrate it may lead to dangerous mistakes.

A very powerful state may frequently hazard a high and haughty tone with good policy, but a weak state can scarcely ever do it without imprudence. The last is yet our character, though we are the embryo of a great empire.

It is therefore better suited to our situation to measure each step with the utmost caution; to hazard as little as possible; in the cases in which we are injured to blend moderation with firmness; and to brandish the weapons of hostility only when it is apparent that the use of them is unavoidable.

It is not to be inferred from this that we are to crouch to any power on earth or tamely to suffer our rights to be violated. A nation which is capable of this meanness will quickly have no rights to protect, no honor to defend.

But the true inference is that we ought not lightly to seek or provoke a resort to arms; that in the differences between us and other nations we ought carefully to avoid measures which tend to widen the breach; and that we should scrupulously abstain from whatever may be construed into reprisals 'till after the fruitless employment of all amicable means has reduced it to a certainty that there is no alternative and ought then only to endanger the necessity of that resort.

If we can avoid war for ten or twelve years more, we shall then have acquired a maturity which will make it no more than a common calamity and will authorize us on our national discussions to take a higher and more imposing tone.

This is a consideration of the greatest weight to determine us to exert all our prudence and address to keep out of war as long as it shall be possible to defer to a state of manhood a struggle to which infancy is ill-adapted. This is the most effectual way to disappoint the enemies of our welfare; to pursue a contrary conduct may be to play into their hands and to gratify their wishes. If there be a foreign power which sees with envy or ill will our growing prosperity, that power must discern that our infancy is the time for clipping our wings. We ought to be wise enough to see that this is not the time for trying our strength.

Should we be able to escape the storm which at this juncture agitates Europe, our disputes with Great Britain terminated, we may hope to postpone war to a distant period. This at least will greatly diminish the chances of it. For then there will remain only one power with whom we have any embarrassing discussion. I allude to Spain and the question of the Mississippi; and there is reason to hope that this question by the natural progress of things and perseverance in an amicable course will finally be arranged to our satisfaction without the necessity of the *dernier* resort.

The allusion to this case suggests one or two important reflections. How unwise was it to invite or facilitate a quarrel with Great Britain at a moment when she and Spain were engaged in a common cause, both of them having besides controverted points with the U States! How wise will it be to adjust our differences with the most formidable of those two powers and to have only to contest with one of them.

This policy is so obvious that it requires an extraordinary degree of infatuation not to be sensible of it, and not to view with favor any measure which tends to so important a result.

This cursory review of the motives which may be supposed to have governed our public councils in the mission to Great Britain serves not only to vindicate the measures then pursued but to warn us against a prejudiced judgment of the result which may in the end defeat the salutary purposes of those measures.

I proceed to observe summarily that the objects of the mission, contrary to what has been asserted, have been substantially obtained. What were these? They were principally—

I. to adjust the matters of controversy concerning the inexecution of the Treaty of Peace and especially to obtain restitution of our Western posts.

II. to obtain reparation for the captives and spoliations of our property in the course of the existing war.

Both these objects have been provided for, and it will be shown when we come to comment upon the articles which make the provision in each case, that it is a reasonable one, as good a one as ought to have been expected—as good a one as there is any prospect of obtaining hereafter: one which it is consistent with our honor to accept and which our interest bids us to close with.

The provisions with regard to commerce were incidental and auxiliary—some provisions on this subject were of importance to fix for a time the basis on which the commerce of the two countries was to be carried on, that the merchants of each might know what they had to depend upon—that sources of collision on this head might be temporarily stilled if not permanently extinguished—that an essay might be made of some plan conciliating as far as possible the opinions and prejudices of both parties—and laying perhaps the foundation of further and more extensive arrangements. Without something of this kind, there would be constant danger of the tranquillity of the two countries being disturbed by commercial conflicts. . . .

"The Defence, No. 18"

6 October 1795

It is provided by the tenth article of the treaty that "Neither Debts due from individuals of the one Nation to Individuals of the other, nor shares nor monies, which they may have in the public funds, or in the public or private banks, shall ever in any event of war or national differences be sequestered or confiscated, it being unjust and impolitic that debts and engagements contracted and made by individuals having confidence in each other and in their respective Governments should ever be destroyed or impaired by national authority on account of National Differences and Discontents."

The virulence with which this article has been attacked cannot fail to excite very painful sensations in every mind duly impressed with the sanctity of public faith and with the importance of national credit and character, at the same time that it furnishes the most cogent reasons to desire that the preservation of peace may obviate the pretext and the temptation to sully the honor and wound the interests of the country by a measure which the truly enlightened of every nation would condemn.

I acknowledge without reserve that in proportion to the vehemence of the opposition against this part of the treaty is the satisfaction I derive from its existence; as an obstacle the more to the perpetration of a thing which in my opinion, besides deeply injuring our real and permanent interest, would cover us with ignominy. No powers of language at my command can express the abhorrence I feel at the idea of violating the property of individuals which in an authorized intercourse in time of peace has been confided to the faith of our government and laws on account of controversies between nation and nation. In my view every moral and every political sentiment unite to consign it to execration.

Neither will I dissemble that the dread of the effects of the spirit which patronizes that idea has ever been with me one of the most persuasive arguments for a pacific policy on the part of the U States. Serious as the evil of war has appeared at the present stage of our affairs the manner in which it was to be apprehended it might be carried on was still more formidable than the thing itself. It was to be feared that in the fermentation of certain wild opinions, those wise, just, and temperate maxims which will forever constitute the true security and felicity of a state would be overruled and that a war upon credit, eventually upon property and upon the general principles of public order, might aggravate and embitter the ordinary calamities of foreign war. The confiscation of debts due to the enemy might have been the first step of this destructive process. From one violation of justice to another the passage is easy. Invasions of right still more fatal to credit might have followed, and this by extinguishing the resources which that could have afforded might have paved the way to more comprehensive and more enormous depredations for a substitute. Terrible examples were before us, and there were too many not sufficiently remote from a disposition to admire and imitate them. . . .

Even in a revolutionary war, a war of liberty against usurpation, our national councils were never provoked or tempted to depart so widely from the path of rectitude by every man who, though careful not to exaggerate for rash and extravagant projects, can nevertheless fairly estimate the real resources of the country for meeting dangers which prudence cannot avert.

Such a man will never endure the base doctrine that our security is to depend on the tricks of a swindler. He will look for it in the courage and constancy of a free, brave, and virtuous people—in the riches of a fertile soil—an extended and progressive industry—in the wisdom and energy of a well constituted and well administered government—in the resources of a solid, if well supported, national credit—in the armies which if requisite could be raised—in the means of maritime annoyance which if necessary we could organize and with which we could inflict deep wounds on the commerce of a hostile nation. He will indulge an animating consciousness that while our situation is not such as to justify our courting imprudent enterprises, neither is it such as to oblige us in any event to stoop to dishonorable means of security or to substitute a crooked and piratical policy for the manly energies of fair and open war. . . .

"The Defence, No. 37"

6 January 1796

It shall now be shown, that the objections to the treaty founded on its pretended interference with the powers of Congress tend to render the power of making treaties in a very great degree if not altogether nominal. This will be best seen by an enumeration of the cases of pretended interference.

I. The power of Congress to lay taxes is said to be impaired by those stipulations which prevent the laying of duties on particular articles, which also prevent the laying of higher or other duties on British commodities than on the commodities of other countries, and which restrict the power of increasing the difference of duties on British tonnage and on goods imported in British bottoms.

II. The power of Congress to regulate trade is said to be impaired by the same restrictions respecting duties, inasmuch as they are intended and operate as regulations of trade, by the stipulations against prohibitions in certain cases, and in general by all the rights, privileges, immunities, and restrictions in trade which are contained in the treaty, all which are so many regulations of commerce, which are said to encroach upon the legislative authority. . . .

The absurdity of the alleged interferences will fully appear by showing how they would operate upon the several kinds of treaties usual among nations. These may be classed under three principal heads: 1. Treaties of Commerce 2. Treaties of Alliance 3. Treaties of Peace.

Treaties of commerce are of course excluded, for every treaty of commerce is a system of rules devised to regulate and govern the trade between contracting nations, invading directly the *exclusive* power of regulating trade which is attributed to Congress.

Treaties of alliance whether defensive or offensive are equally excluded, and this on two grounds— 1. because it is their immediate object to define a case or cases in which one nation shall take part with another in war, contrary, in the sense of the objection, to that clause of the Constitution which gives to Congress the power of declaring war, and, 2. because the succors stipulated, in whatever form they may be, must involve an expenditure of money—not to say that it is common to stipulate succors in money either in the first instance or by way of alternative. . . .

Treaties of peace are also excluded or at the least are so narrowed as to be in the greatest number of cases impracticable. The most common conditions of these treaties are restitutions or cessions of territory on one side or on the other, frequently, on both sides, regulations of boundary, restitutions and confirmations of property—pecuniary indemnifications for injuries or expenses. It will probably not be easy to find a precedent of a treaty of peace which does not contain one or more of these provisions as the basis of the cessation of hostilities, and they are all of them naturally to be looked for in an agreement which is to put an end to the state of war between conflicting nations. Yet they are all precluded by the objections which have been enumerated. . . .

It follows that if the objections which are taken to the treaty on the point of constitutionality are valid, the President with the advice and consent of the Senate can make neither a treaty of commerce nor alliance and, rarely if at all, a treaty of peace. It is probable that on a minute analysis there is scarcely any species of treaty which would not clash in some particular with the principle of those objections; and thus, as was before observed, the power to make treaties granted in such comprehensive and indefinite terms and guarded with so much precaution would become essentially nugatory.

This is so obviously against the principles of sound construction, it at the same time exposes the government to so much impotence in one great branch of political power, in opposition to a main intent of the Constitution, and it tends so directly to frustrate one principal object of the institution of a general government—the convenient management of our external concerns—that it cannot but be rejected by every discerning man who will examine and pronounce with sincerity.

It is against the principles of sound construction, because these teach us that every instrument is so to be interpreted that all the parts may if possible consist with each other and have effect. But the construction which is combated would cause the legislative power to destroy the power of making treaties. Moreover, if the power of the executive department be inadequate to the making of the several kinds of treaties which have been mentioned, there is then no power in the government to make them; for there is not a syllable in the Constitution which authorizes either the legislative or judiciary department to make a treaty with a foreign nation. And our Constitution would then exhibit the ridiculous spectacle of a government without a power to make treaties with foreign nations: a result as inadmissible as it is absurd, since in fact our Constitution grants the power of making treaties in the most explicit and ample terms to the President with the advice and consent of the Senate. . . .

"The Defence, No. 38"

9 January 1796

The manner in which the power of treaty as it exists in the Constitution was understood by the Convention in framing it and by the people in adopting it is the point next to be considered.

As to the sense of the Convention, the secrecy with which their deliberations were conducted does not permit any formal proof of the opinions and views which prevailed in digesting the power of treaty. But from the *best opportunity of knowing the fact,* I aver that it was understood *by all* to be the intent of the provision to give to that power the most ample latitude to render it competent to all the stipulations which the exigencies of national affairs might require—competent to the making of treaties of alliance, treaties of commerce, treaties of peace and every other species of convention usual among nations and competent in the course of its exercise to control and bind the legislative power of Congress. And it was emphatically for this reason that it was so carefully guarded, the cooperation of two thirds of the Senate with the President being required to make a treaty. I appeal for this with confidence to every member of the Convention—particularly to those in the two houses of Congress. Two of these are in the House of Representatives, Mr. Madison and Mr. Baldwin. It is expected by the adversaries of the treaty that these gentlemen will in their places obstruct its execution. However this may be, I feel a confidence that neither of them will deny the assertion I have made. To suppose them capable of such a denial were to suppose them utterly regardless of truth. . . .

As to the sense of the community in the adoption of the Constitution, this can only be ascertained from two sources, the writings for and against the Constitution and the debates in the several state conventions.

I possess not at this moment materials for an investigation which would enable me to present the evidence they afford. But I refer to them, with confidence, for proof of the fact that the organization of the power of treaty in the Constitution was attacked and defended with an admission on both sides of its being of the character which I have assigned to it. Its great extent and importance—its effect to control by its stipulations the legislative authority were mutually taken for granted—and, upon this basis, it was insisted by way of objection that there were not adequate guards for the safe exercise of so vast a power, that there ought to have been reservations of certain rights, a better disposition of the power to impeach, and a participation, general or special, of the House of Representatives. The reply to these objections, acknowledging the delicacy and magnitude of the power, was directed to show

that its organization was a proper one and that it was sufficiently guarded. . . .

House Debates on Implementing Jay's Treaty
1796

On 2 March 1796, with the Republicans in Congress determined to deny the appropriations necessary to carry the treaty into effect, Edward Livingston of New York moved to ask the president to deliver the instructions, correspondence, and other documents related to the treaty. The long debate occasioned by Federalist complaints that the House had no discretionary power over whether a treaty would go into effect was one of the most important constitutional arguments of the decade, climaxed by Washington's refusal of the House request.

8 March

Mr. Smith (of South Carolina) said that he had listened attentively to the reasons advanced in favor of this resolution and that he had heard nothing to convince him of its propriety. The President and Senate have, by the Constitution, the power of making treaties, and the House have no agency in them, except to make laws necessary to carry them into operation; he considered the House as bound, in common with their fellow-citizens, to do everything in their power to carry them into full execution. He recognized but one exception to this rule, and that was when the instrument was clearly unconstitutional. . . .

They have no right to investigate the merits of the Treaty; it is the law of the land, and they are bound to carry it into effect unless they intended to resist the constituted authorities. . . .

He was surprised that gentlemen who displayed such zeal for the Constitution should support a proposition, the tendency of which went indirectly to break down the constitutional limits between the executive and legislative departments. The Constitution had assigned to the executive the business of negotiation with foreign powers; this House can claim no right by the Constitution to interfere in such negotiations; every movement of the kind must be considered as an attempt to usurp powers not delegated, and will be resisted by the executive; for a concession would be a surrender of the powers specially delegated to him and a violation of his trust. . . .

Mr. Gallatin would state his opinion that the House had a *right* to ask for the papers proposed to be called for, because their cooperation and sanction was necessary to carry the treaty into full effect, to render it a binding instrument, and to make it, properly speaking, a law of the land; because they had a full discretion either to give or to refuse that cooperation; because they must be guided, in the exercise of that discretion, by the merits and expediency of the treaty itself, and therefore had a *right* to ask for every information which could assist them in deciding that question. . . .

A treaty is unconstitutional if it provides for doing such things, the doing of which is forbidden by the Constitution; but if a treaty embraces objects within the sphere of the general powers delegated to the federal government, but which have been exclusively and specially granted to a particular branch of government, say to the legislative department, such a treaty, though not unconstitutional, does not become the law of the land until it has obtained the sanction of that branch. In this case, and to this end, the legislature have a right to demand the documents relative to the negotiation of the treaty, because that treaty operates on objects specially delegated to the legislature. He turned to the Constitution. It says that the President shall have the power to make treaties, by and with the advice and consent of two-thirds of the Senate. It does not say what treaties. If the clause be taken by itself, then it grants an authority altogether undefined. But the gentlemen quote another clause of the Constitution, where it is said that the Constitution and the laws made in pursuance thereof, and all treaties, are the supreme law of the land; and thence, they insist that treaties made by the President and Senate are the supreme law of the land, and that the power of making treaties is undefined and unlimited. He proceeded to controvert this opinion, and contended that it was limited by other parts of the Constitution.

That general power of making treaties, *undefined* as it is by the clause which grants it, may either be expressly *limited* by some other positive clauses of the Constitution, or it may be *checked* by some powers vested in other branches of the government, which, although not diminishing, may control the treaty-making power. Mr. G. was of opinion that both positions would be supported by the Constitution; that the specific legislative powers delegated to Congress were limitations of the undefined power of making treaties vested in the President and Senate, and that the general power of granting money, also vested in Congress, would at all events be used, if necessary, as a check upon, and as controlling the exercise of, the powers claimed by the President and Senate. . . .

To what, he asked, would a contrary doctrine lead? If the power of making treaties is to reside in the President and Senate unlimitedly: in other words, if, in the exercise of this power, the President and Senate are to be restrained by no other branch of the government, the President and Senate may absorb all legislative power—the executive has, then, nothing to do but to substitute a foreign nation for the House of Representatives, and they may legislate to any extent. If the treaty-making power is unlimited and undefined, it may extend to every object of legislation. Under it money may be borrowed, as well as commerce regulated; and why not money appropriated? For, arguing as the gentlemen do, they might say the Constitution says that no money shall be drawn from the Treasury but in consequence of appropriations made by law. But treaties, whatever provision they may contain, are law; appropriations, therefore, may be made by treaties.

To the construction he had given to this part of the Constitution, no such formidable objections could be raised. He did not claim for the House a power of making treaties, but a check upon the treaty-making power—a mere negative power; whilst those who are in favor of a different construction advocate a positive and unlimited power.

Since this is the striking difference between the doctrine held by the friends and by the opposers of the present motion, why, added Mr. G., with some warmth, are the first endeavored to be stigmatized as rebellious, disorganizers, as traitors against the Constitution? Do they claim a dangerous active power? No, they only claim the right of checking the exercise of a general power when clashing with the special powers expressly vested in Congress by the Constitution.

He should not say that the treaty is unconstitutional, but he would say that it was not the supreme law of the land until it received the sanction of the legislature. He turned to the Constitution. That instrument declares that the Constitution, and laws made in pursuance thereof, and treaties made under the authority of the United States, shall be the supreme law of the land. The words are, "under the authority of the United States," not signed and ratified by the President: so that a treaty clashing in any of its provisions with the express powers of Congress, until it has so far obtained the sanction of Congress, is not a treaty made under the authority of the United States. . . .

But if, as it was said, the powers specifically delegated to the House are not to operate as a limitation of the general powers granted to the President and Senate; if these powers are contended to be as unlimited as they are undefined, then the necessity of a check must strike as doubly necessary. The power of granting money should be exercised as a check on the treaty-making power. The more limited the treaty-making power is contended to be, the more dangerous it is, and the more should the House consider the power of originating grants of money exclusively vested in them as a precious deposit.

He maintained, that the treaty with Great Britain, or any other in similar circumstances, was not, until the necessary appropriations were made, and until the existing laws that stood in its way were repealed, and the requisite laws enacted, the supreme law of the land. Existing laws declare that goods shall not be imported by land into the United States, except in certain districts; the third article of the treaty allows a general importation; the laws declare that foreign vessels trading with us shall pay an additional ten per cent upon the duties paid by our own vessels, the same article again interferes here; in other particulars, also, but these are sufficient to illustrate. Now, if the doctrine of gentlemen be sanctioned, and the House have no discretion left to use on the treaty, but are bound thereby, specific and explicit clauses in the Constitution notwithstanding, the power of granting money becomes nugatory, and a treaty, made by the Executive, may repeal a law. If a treaty can repeal a law, then the act of the President and Senate can repeal the act of the three branches; and although all legislative powers be vested in Congress by the Constitution, yet Congress are controlled by two of its branches; those clauses of the Constitution vesting the legislative powers in Congress are annihilated, and the President and Senate, by substituting a foreign nation for the House of Representatives, assume, in fact, an unlimited legislative power; since, under color of making treaties, they may repeal laws and may enact laws.

If this doctrine is sanctioned; if it is allowed that treaties may regulate appropriations and repeal existing laws, and the House, by rejecting the present resolution, declare that they give up all control, all right to the exercise of discre-

tion, it is tantamount to saying that they abandon their share in legislation, and that they consent the whole power should be concentered in the other branches. He did not believe such a doctrine could be countenanced by the House. If gentlemen should insist upon maintaining this doctrine, should deny the free agency of the House and their right to judge of the expediency of carrying the treaty into effect, the friends to the independence of the House will be driven to the necessity to reject the treaty, whether good or bad, to assert the contested right. If the gentlemen abandoned this ground, then the policy of the measure could be weighed on fair ground and the treaty carried into effect, if reconcilable to the interests of the United States. . . .

Mr. Madison said that the direct proposition before the House had been so absorbed by the incidental question which had grown out of it, concerning the constitutional authority of Congress in the case of treaties, that he should confine his present observations to the latter.

On some points there could be no difference of opinion; and there need not, consequently, be any discussion. All are agreed that the sovereignty resides in the people; that the Constitution, as the expression of their will, is the guide and the rule to the government; that the distribution of powers made by the Constitution ought to be sacredly observed by the respective departments; that the House of Representatives ought to be equally careful to avoid encroachments on the authority given to other departments and to guard their own authority against encroachments from the other departments: These principles are as evident as they are vital and essential to our political system.

The true question, therefore, before the Committee, was not whether the will of the people expressed in the Constitution was to be obeyed; but how that will was to be understood; in what manner it had actually divided the powers delegated to the government; and what construction would best reconcile the several parts of the instrument with each other and be most consistent with its general spirit and object.

On comparing the several passages in the Constitution which had been already cited to the Committee, it appeared that if taken literally and without limit, they must necessarily clash with each other. Certain powers to regulate commerce, to declare war, to raise armies, to borrow money, etc., etc., are first specifically vested in

Congress. The power of making treaties, which may relate to the same subjects, is afterwards vested in the President and two thirds of the Senate. And it is declared in another place that the Constitution and the laws of the U. States made in pursuance thereof, and treaties made or to be made under the authority of the U. States shall be the supreme law of the land: and the judges in every state shall be bound thereby, anything in the Constitution or laws of any state to the contrary notwithstanding.

The term *supreme,* as applied to treaties, evidently meant a supremacy over the state constitutions and laws, and not over the Constitution and laws of the U. States. And it was observable that the judicial authority and the existing laws alone of the states fell within the supremacy expressly enjoined. The injunction was not extended to the legislative authority of the states or to laws requisite to be passed by the states for giving effect to treaties; and it might be a problem worthy of the consideration, though not needing the decision of the Committee, in what manner the requisite provisions were to be obtained from the states.

It was to be regretted, he observed, that on a question of such magnitude as the present there should be any apparent inconsistency or inexplicitness in the Constitution that could leave room for different constructions. As the case however had happened, all that could be done was to examine the different constructions with accuracy and fairness, according to the rules established therefor, and to adhere to that which should be found most rational, consistent, and satisfactory. . . .

It was an important, and appeared to him to be a decisive, view of the subject that, if the treaty-power alone could perform any one act for which the authority of Congress is required by the Constitution, it may perform every act for which the authority of that part of the government is required. Congress have power to regulate trade, to declare war, to raise armies, to levy, borrow, and appropriate money, etc. If by treaty, therefore, as paramount to the legislative power, the President and Senate can regulate trade; they can also declare war; they can raise armies to carry on war; and they can procure money to support armies. These powers, however different in their nature or importance, are on the same footing in the Constitution and must share the same fate. . . .

The Constitution of the U. States is a Constitution of limitations and checks. The powers given up by the people

for the purposes of government had been divided into two great classes. One of these formed the state governments, and the other the federal government. The powers of the government had been further divided into three great departments; and the legislative department again subdivided into two independent branches. Around each of these portions of power were seen, also, exceptions and qualifications, as additional guards against the abuses to which power is liable. With a view to this policy of the Constitution, it could not be unreasonable, if the clauses under discussion were thought doubtful, to lean towards a construction that would limit and control the treaty-making power, rather than towards one that would make it omnipotent.

He came next to the . . . construction which left with the President and Senate the power of making treaties, but required at the same time the legislative sanction and cooperation in those cases where the Constitution had given express and specific powers to the legislature. It was to be presumed that in all such cases, the legislature would exercise its authority with discretion, allowing due weight to the reasons which led to the treaty and to the circumstance of the existence of the treaty. Still, however, this House in its legislative capacity, must exercise its reason; it must deliberate; for deliberation is implied in legislation. If it *must* carry all treaties into effect, it would no longer exercise a legislative power: it would be the mere instrument of the will of another department and would have no will of its own. Where the Constitution contains a specific and peremptory injunction on Congress to do a particular act, Congress must of course do the act, because the Constitution, which is paramount over all the departments, has *expressly taken away* the legislative discretion of Congress. The case is essentially different where the act of one department of government interferes with a power expressly vested in another and nowhere expressly taken away. Here the latter power must be exercised according to its nature; and if it be a legislative power, it must be exercised with that deliberation and discretion which is essential to the nature of legislative power.

It was said yesterday that a treaty was paramount to all other acts of government, because all power resided in the people, and the President and Senate, in making a treaty, being the constitutional organs of the people for that purpose, a treaty when made was the act of the people. The argument was as strong the other way. Congress are as much the organs of the people, in making laws, as the President and Senate can be in making treaties; and laws, when made, are as much the acts of the people as any acts whatever can be. . . .

No construction, he said, might be perfectly free from difficulties. That which he had espoused was subject to the least; as it gave signification to every part of the Constitution, was most consistent with its general spirit, and was most likely in practice to promote the great object of it, the public good. The construction which made the treaty power in a manner omnipotent he thought utterly inadmissible in a Constitution marked throughout with limitations and checks. . . .

11 March
Mr. Sedgwick said that he considered it in principle, and in its consequences, as the most important question which had ever been debated in this House. It was no less than whether this House should, by construction and implication, extend its controlling influence to subjects which were expressly, and he thought exclusively, delegated by the people to another department of the government. We had heretofore been warned emphatically against seizing on power by construction and implication. He had known no instance in which the caution that warning enforced deserved more attention than on the present occasion. . . .

He, in his conscience, believed that if the Constitution could operate the benefits its original institution intended—that if the government should be rendered adequate to the protection of liberty and the security of the people, it must be by keeping the several departments distinct and within their prescribed limits. Hence, that man would give as good evidence of Republicanism, of virtue, of sincere love of country, who should defend the executive in the exercise of his constitutional rights as the man who should contend for any other department of government. If either should usurp the appropriate powers of another, anarchy, confusion, or despotism, must ensue: the functions of the usurping power would not be legitimate, but their exercise despotism. If the power of controlling treaties was not in the House, the same spirit which might usurp it might also declare the existence of the House perpetual and fill the vacancies as they should occur. The merits of the present question, it seemed to be agreed, depended on this right; it was of infinite importance, therefore, to decide it justly. . . .

It was not now to be inquired whether the power of treating was wisely deposited, although he was inclined to believe it could not be entrusted to safer hands. It was sufficient that those who had the right, the citizens of America, had declared their will, which we were bound to respect, because we had sworn to support it, and because we were their deputies. . . .

Gentlemen had spoken of the subject as if the members of this House were the only representatives of the people, as their only protectors against the usurpations and oppressions of the other departments of the government. Who then, he asked, were the Senators? Were they unfeeling tyrants, whose interests were separated from and opposed to those of the people? No. Did they possess hereditary powers and honors? No. Who, as contemplated by the Constitution, were they? The most enlightened and the most virtuous of our citizens. What was the source from whence they derived their elevation? From the confidence of the people and the free choice of their electors. Who were those electors? Not an ignorant herd, who could be cajoled, flattered, and deceived—not even the body of enlightened American citizens; but their legislators, men to whom the real characters of the candidates would be known. They did not possess their seats in consequence of influence obtained by cajoling and deceit, practiced in obscure corners, where the means of detection were difficult if not impracticable; but they were selected from the most conspicuous theaters, where their characters could be viewed under every aspect and by those most capable of distinguishing the true from the false. For what purposes were they elected? To represent the most essential interests of their country; as the guardians of the sovereignty of the states, the happiness of the people, and their liberties. Who, as contemplated by the Constitution, was the President? The man elected, by means intended to exclude the operation of faction and ambition, as the one best entitled to public confidence and esteem. And was no confidence to be reposed in such characters, thus elected? Might it not, to say no more, be at least doubtful whether the treating power might not be as safely entrusted in such hands exclusively as with the participation and under the control of the more numerous branch of the legislature, elected in small districts, assailed by party and faction, and exposed to foreign influence and intrigue? Whatever merits this, as an original question, might possess, the people had decided their will. To the President and Senate they had given powers to make treaties; they had given no such powers to the House.

The original question (the call for papers) had now resolved itself into another, which alone had become the subject of discussion, to wit: whether a treaty made by the President and Senate was, although it embraced objects specifically delegated to Congress by the Constitution, a compact completely binding on the nation and Congress, so as to repeal any law which stood in its way, so as to oblige Congress (without leaving them any discretion except that of breaking a binding compact) to pass any law the enacting of which was necessary to fulfill a condition of the treaty, so as forever afterwards to restrain the legislative discretion of Congress upon the subjects regulated by the treaty; or, in other words, whether, when the President and Senate had, by treaty, agreed with another nation that a certain act should be done on our part, the doing of which was vested in and depended solely on the will of Congress, Congress lost the freedom of their will, the discretion of acting or refusing to act, and were bound to do the act thus agreed on by the treaty?

An assertion repeatedly made by the opposers of the motion that their doctrine rested on the letter of the Constitution, whilst that of those who contended for the powers of the House was grounded only on construction and implication, had not the least foundation. The clauses which vest certain specific legislative powers in Congress are positive, and, indeed, far better defined than that which gives the power of making treaties to the President and Senate; nor does the clause which declares laws and treaties the supreme law of the land decide in favor of either and say which shall be paramount. And yet some gentlemen had argued as if they meant to attend exclusively to one part of the Constitution, without noticing the other; the consequence was that many of their arguments applied with equal force in support of the opposite doctrine. Thus, when they said that there was no part of the Constitution which declared that the legislature had power to make a treaty; that, had it been intended to except legislative objects out of the general treaty-making power, an express proviso for that purpose should have been added to the clause which gives the power of making treaties; and that Congress, when making laws, were bound to obey the will of the people, as expressed by their agents the President and Senate; it might, with equal strength of argument, be replied that there was no part of the Constitution

which declared that the President and Senate had power to make laws; that if it had been intended to except out of and to limit the legislative powers of Congress by the treaty-making power, an express proviso for that purpose should have been added to the clause which gives the legislative powers; and that the President and Senate, when making treaties, were bound to obey the will of the people as expressed by their agents, Congress. . . .

On 24 March, the resolution calling for the papers passed by a margin of 62 to 37.

30 March

The following message was received from the President in answer to the resolution of the House:

Gentlemen of the House of Representatives:

With the utmost attention I have considered your resolution of the 24th instant, requesting me to lay before your House a copy of the instructions to the Minister of the United States who negotiated the Treaty with the King of Great Britain, together with the correspondence and other documents relative to that treaty, excepting such of the said papers as any existing negotiation may render improper to be disclosed. . . .

I trust that no part of my conduct has ever indicated a disposition to withhold any information which the Constitution has enjoined upon the President, as a duty, to give, or which could be required of him by either House of Congress as a right; and, with truth, I affirm, that it has been, as it will continue to be, while I have the honor to preside in the Government, my constant endeavor to harmonize with the other branches thereof, so far as the trust delegated to me by the people of the United States and my sense of the obligation it imposes, to "preserve, protect, and defend the Constitution," will permit.

The nature of foreign negotiations requires caution; and their success must often depend on secrecy; and even when brought to a conclusion, a full disclosure of all the measures, demands, or eventual concessions which may have been proposed or contemplated would be extremely impolitic: for this might have a pernicious influence on future negotiations; or produce immediate inconveniences, perhaps danger and mischief, in relation to other powers. The necessity of such caution and secrecy was one cogent reason for vesting the power of making treaties in the

President with the advice and consent of the Senate; the principle on which the body was formed confining it to a small number of members. To admit, then, a right in the House of Representatives to demand, and to have, as a matter of course, all the papers respecting a negotiation with a foreign power would be to establish a dangerous precedent.

It does not occur that the inspection of the papers asked for can be relative to any purpose under the cognizance of the House of Representatives, except that of an impeachment, which the resolution has not expressed. I repeat, that I have no disposition to withhold any information which the duty of my station will permit, or the public good shall require, to be disclosed; and, in fact, all the papers affecting the negotiation with Great Britain were laid before the Senate when the treaty itself was communicated for their consideration and advice.

The course which the debate has taken on the resolution of the House leads to some observations on the mode of making treaties under the Constitution of the United States.

Having been a member of the General Convention, and knowing the principles on which the Constitution was formed, I have ever entertained but one opinion on this subject, and from the first establishment of the government to this moment, my conduct has exemplified that opinion, that the power of making treaties is exclusively vested in the President, by and with the advice and consent of the Senate, provided two-thirds of the Senators present concur; and that every treaty so made, and promulgated, thenceforward becomes the law of the land. It is thus that the treaty-making power has been understood by foreign nations, and in all the treaties made with them, *we* have declared, and *they* have believed, that when ratified by the President, with the advice and consent of the Senate, they become obligatory. In this construction of the Constitution every House of Representatives has heretofore acquiesced, and until the present time not a doubt or suspicion has appeared to my knowledge that this construction was not the true one. Nay, they have more than acquiesced; for until now, without controverting the obligation of such treaties, they have made all the requisite provisions for carrying them into effect.

There is also reason to believe that this construction agrees with the opinions entertained by the state conventions, when they were deliberating on the Constitution, especially by those who objected to it because there was not required in commercial treaties the consent of two-thirds of the whole number of the members of the Senate, instead of two-thirds of the Senators present, and because, in treaties respecting territorial and certain other rights and claims, the concurrence of three-fourths of the whole number of the members of both Houses respectively was not made necessary.

It is a fact declared by the General Convention and universally understood that the Constitution of the United States was the result of a spirit of amity and mutual concession. And it is well known that, under this influence, the smaller states were admitted to an equal representation in the Senate with the larger States; and that this branch of the government was invested with great powers; for, on the equal participation of those powers, the sovereignty and political safety of the smaller states were deemed essentially to depend.

If other proofs than these, and the plain letter of the Constitution itself, be necessary to ascertain the point under consideration, they may be found in the Journals of the General Convention, which I have deposited in the office of the Department of State. In those Journals it will appear that a proposition was made, "that no treaty should be binding on the United States which was not ratified by a law," and that the proposition was explicitly rejected.

As, therefore, it is perfectly clear to my understanding, that the assent of the House of Representatives is not necessary to the validity of the treaty; as the Treaty with Great Britain exhibits in itself all the objects requiring legislative provision, and on these the papers called for can throw no light; and as it is essential to the due administration of the government that the boundaries fixed by the Constitution between the different departments should be preserved — a just regard to the Constitution and to the duty of my office, under all the circumstances of this case, forbid a compliance with your request.

G. WASHINGTON

Mr. Blount brought forward the following resolutions:

"*Resolved*, That, it being declared by the second section of the second article of the Constitution, 'that the President shall have power, by and with the advice of the Senate, to make treaties, provided two-thirds of the Senate present concur,' the House of Representatives do not claim any agency in making treaties; but, that when a treaty stipulates regulations on any of the subjects submitted by the

Constitution to the power of Congress, it must depend, for its execution, as to such stipulations, on a law or laws to be passed by Congress. And it is the Constitutional right and duty of the House of Representatives, in all such cases, to deliberate on the expediency or inexpediency of carrying such treaty into effect, and to determine and act thereon, as, in their judgment, may be most conducive to the public good.

"*Resolved,* That it is not necessary to the propriety of any application from this House to the Executive, for any information desired by them, and which may relate to any Constitutional functions of the House, that the purpose for which such information may be wanted, or to which the same may be applied, should be stated in the application."

6 April

Mr. Madison rose and spoke as follows: . . . When the bill for establishing a national bank was under consideration, he had opposed it as not warranted by the Constitution, and incidentally remarked that his impression might be stronger as he remembered that in the convention, a motion was made and negatived for giving Congress a power to grant charters of incorporation. This slight reference to the convention, he said, was animadverted on by several in the course of the debate, and particularly by a gentleman from Massachusetts, who had himself been a member of the convention, and whose remarks were not unworthy the attention of the committee. Here Mr. M. read a paragraph in Mr. Gerry's speech, from the *Gazette of the United States,* p. 814, protesting in strong terms against arguments drawn from that source.

Mr. M. said he did not believe a single instance could be cited in which the sense of the convention had been required or admitted as material in any constitutional question. In the case of the bank, the committee had seen how a glance at that authority had been treated in this House. When the question on the suability of the states was depending on the supreme court, he asked whether it had ever been understood that the members of the bench who had been members of the convention were called on for the meaning of the convention of that very important point, although no constitutional question would be presumed more susceptible of elucidation from that source.

He then adverted to that part of the message which contained an extract from the journal of the convention,

showing that a proposition "that no treaty should be binding on the United States, which was not ratified by law," was explicitly rejected. . . . What did this abstract vote amount to? Did it condemn the doctrine of the majority? So far from it that, as he understood their doctrine, they must have voted as the convention did: For they do not contend that *no* treaty shall be operative without a law to sanction it; on the contrary they admit that *some* treaties will operate without this sanction; and that it is no further applicable in any case than where legislative objects are embraced by treaties. The term *ratify* also deserved some attention, for although of loose signification in general, it had a technical meaning different from the agency claimed by the House on the subject of treaties.

But, after all, whatever veneration might be entertained for the body of men who formed our Constitution, the sense of that body could never be regarded as the oracular guide in the expounding the Constitution. As the instrument came from them, it was nothing more than the draught of a plan, nothing but a dead letter, until life and validity were breathed into it, by the voice of the people, speaking throughout the several state conventions. If we were to look, therefore, for the meaning of the instrument, beyond the face of the instrument, we must look for it not in the general convention which proposed, but in the state conventions which accepted and ratified the constitution. To these also the message had referred, and it would be proper to follow it.

The debates of the conventions in three states, Pennsylvania, Virginia, and N. Carolina, had been before introduced into the discussion of this subject, and were he believed the only publications of the sort which contained any lights with respect to it. He would not fatigue the committee with a repetition of the passages then read to them. He would only appeal to the committee to decide whether it did not appear from a candid and collected view of the debates in those conventions, and particularly in that of Virginia, that the treaty-making power was a limited power; and that the powers in our Constitution, on this subject, bore an analogy to the powers on the same subject in the government of G. Britain.

The amendments proposed by the several conventions were better authority and would be found on a general view to favor the sense of the Constitution which had prevailed in this House. . . . He would not undertake to say that the particular amendment referred to in the message by which two states required that "no commercial treaty should be ratified without the consent of two thirds of *the whole number* of Senators; and that no territorial rights &c. should be ceded without the consent of *three fourths* of the members of both houses" was digested with an accurate attention to the whole subject. On the other hand it was no proof that those particular conventions in annexing these guards to the treaty power understood it as different from that espoused by the majority of the House. They might consider Congress as having the power contended for over treaties stipulating on legislative subjects and still very consistently wish for the amendment they proposed. . . .

But said Mr. M. it will be proper to attend to other amendments proposed by the ratifying conventions, which may throw light on their opinions and intentions on the subject in question. He then read from the Declaration of Rights proposed by Virginia to be prefixed to the Constitution, the 7th article as follows:

"That *all* power of suspending laws, or the execution of laws by *any* authority without the consent of the *Representatives* of the people in the *Legislature,* is injurious to their rights, and ought not to be exercised."

The convention of North Carolina, as he showed, had laid down the same principle in the same words. And it was to be observed that in both conventions, the article was under the head of a DECLARATION OF RIGHTS, "asserting and securing from encroachment the essential and inalienable rights of the people" according to the language of the Virginia convention; and "asserting and securing from encroachment the great principles of civil and religious liberty, and the inalienable rights of the people" as expressed by the convention of North Carolina. It must follow that these two conventions considered it as a fundamental and inviolable and universal principle in free governments that no power could supercede a law without the consent of the Representatives of the people in the legislature.

In the Maryland convention also, it was among the amendments proposed, though he believed not decided on, "that no power of suspending laws, or the execution of laws, unless derived from the Legislature, ought to be exercised or allowed."

The convention of North Carolina had further explained themselves on this point by their 23rd amendment proposed to the Constitution, in the following words, "That no treaties which shall be directly opposed to the existing laws of the United States in Congress assembled, shall be valid until such laws shall be repealed, or made conformable to such treaty; nor shall any treaty be valid which is contradictory to the Constitution of the United States." . . .

It was with great reluctance, he said, that he should touch on the third topic, the alledged interest of the smaller states in the present question. He was the more unwilling to enter into this delicate part of the discussion as he happened to be from a state which was in one of the extremes in point of size. He should limit himself therefore to two observations. The first was, that if the spirit of amity and mutual concession from which the Constitution resulted was to be consulted on expounding it, that construction ought to be favored which would preserve the mutual control between the Senate and the House of Representatives, rather than that which gave powers to the Senate not controllable by and paramount over those of the House of Representatives, whilst the House of Representatives could in no instance exercise their powers without the participation and control of the Senate. The second observation was that whatever jealousy might have unhappily prevailed between the smaller and larger states, as they had most weight in one or other branch of the government, it was a fact, for which he appealed to the journals of the old Congress from its birth to its dissolution, and to those of the Congress under the present government, that in no instance would it appear from the yeas and nays that a question had been decided by a division of the votes according to the size of the states. He considered this truth as worthy of the most pleasing and consoling reflection, and as one that ought to have the most conciliating and happy influence on the temper of all the states.

A fourth argument in the message was drawn from the manner by which the treaty power had been understood in both parties in the negotiations with foreign powers. "In all the treaties made *we* have declared and *they* have believed, &c." By *we* he remarked, was to be understood the executive alone who had made the declaration, and in no respect, the House of Representatives. It was certainly to be regretted as had often been expressed that different branches of the government should disagree in the construction of their powers; but when this could not be avoided, each branch must judge for itself; and the judgment of the executive could in this case be no more an authority overruling the judgment of the House than the judgment of the House could be an authority overruling that of the executive. It was also to be regretted that any foreign nation should at any time proceed under a misconception of the meaning of our Constitution. But no principle was better established in the law of nations, as well as in common reason, than that one nation is not to be the interpreter of the constitution of another. Each nation must adjust the forms and operation of its own government: and all others are bound to understand them accordingly. It had before been remarked, and it would be proper to repeat here, that of all nations Great Britain would be least likely to object to this principle, because the construction given to our government was particularly exemplified in her own.

In the fifth and last place, he had to take notice of the suggestion that every House of Representatives had concurred in the construction of the treaty power now maintained by the executive; from which it followed that the House could not now consistently act under a different construction. On this point it might be sufficient to remark that this was the first instance in which a foreign treaty had been made since the establishment of the Constitution; and that this was the first time the treaty-making power had come under formal and accurate discussion. Precedents, therefore, would readily be seen to lose much of their weight. But whether the precedents found in the proceedings preparatory to the Algerine treaty or in the provisions relative to the Indian treaties were inconsistent with the right which had been contended for in behalf of the House, he should leave to be decided by the committee. A view of these precedents had been pretty fully presented to them by a gentleman from New York (Mr. Livingston) with all the observations which the subject seemed to require.

On the whole, it appeared that the rights of the House on two great constitutional points had been denied by a high authority in the message before the committee. This message was entered on the journals of the House. If nothing was entered in opposition thereto, it would be inferred that the reasons in the message had changed the opinion of the House, and that their claims on those great points were relinquished. It was proper therefore that the questions brought fairly before the committee in the propositions of the gentleman (Mr. Blount) from North Carolina should be examined and formally decided. If the reasoning of the message should be deemed satisfactory, it would be the duty of this branch of the government to reject the propositions, and thus accede to the doctrines asserted by the executive: If on the other hand this reasoning should not be satisfactory, it would be equally the duty of the House, in some such firm, but very decent terms, as are proposed, to enter their opinions on record. In either way, the meaning of the Constitution would be established as far as depends on a vote of the House of Representatives.

Although the resolution reaffirming the House's right to call for the papers passed by a margin of 57 to 35, Washington continued to withhold them. Debate then turned to the merits of the treaty. Little could be added that had not been hackneyed in the press, but the proceedings concluded with one of the most famous speeches of the decade, rendered all the more effective because the speaker, pale and garbed in black, rose from his sickbed to give it. Anticipating its delivery, many senators were in the gallery; and, according to John Adams, there were many tears. On the following morning, 29 April, Frederick Muhlenberg of Pennsylvania, who was in the chair of the committee of the whole, cast a tie-breaking vote for carrying the treaty into effect.

Only excerpts are provided from a speech in which the representative from Massachusetts proved strong enough to hold forth for an hour and a half.

28 April

Mr. Fisher-Ames rose and addressed the Chair as follows:

Mr. Chairman: I entertain the hope, perhaps a rash one, that my strength will hold me out to speak a few minutes. . . .

It would be strange that a subject which has roused in turn all the passions of the country should be discussed without the interference of any of our own. We are men and, therefore, not exempt from those passions; as citizens and representatives, we feel the interest that must excite them. The hazard of great interests cannot fail to agitate strong passions; we are not disinterested, it is impossible we should be dispassionate. The warmth of such feelings may becloud the judgment and, for a time, pervert the understanding; but the public sensibility and our own has sharpened the spirit of inquiry and given an animation to the debate. The public attention has been quickened to mark the progress of the discussion, and its judgment, often hasty and erroneous on first impressions, has become solid and enlightened at last. Our result will, I hope, on that account, be the safer and more mature, as well as more accordant with that of the nation. The only constant agents in political affairs are the passions of men—shall we complain of our nature? Shall we say that man ought to have been made otherwise? It is right already, because He from whom we derive our nature ordained it so, and because thus made and thus acting, the cause of truth and the public good is the more surely promoted.

But an attempt has been made to produce an influence of a nature more stubborn and more unfriendly to truth. It is very unfairly pretended that the constitutional right of this House is at stake, and to be asserted and preserved only by a vote in the negative. We hear it said that this is a struggle for liberty, a manly resistance against the design to nullify this assembly and to make it a cipher in the government. That the President and Senate, the numerous meetings in the cities, and the influence of the general alarm of the country are the agents and instruments of a scheme of coercion and terror, to force the treaty down our throats, though we loathe it, and in spite of the clearest convictions of duty and conscience.

It is necessary to pause here and inquire whether suggestions of this kind be not unfair in their very texture and fabric, and pernicious in all their influences? They oppose an obstacle in the path of inquiry, not simply discouraging, but absolutely insurmountable. They will not yield to argument; for, as they were not reasoned up, they cannot be reasoned down. They are higher than a Chinese wall in truth's way, and built of materials that are indestructible. While this remains, it is in vain to argue; it is in vain to say to this mountain, be thou cast into the sea. . . .

The self-love of an individual is not warmer in its sense or more constant in its action than what is called in French *l'esprit de corps,* or the self-love of an assembly; that jealous affection which a body of men is always found to bear towards its own prerogatives and power. I will not condemn this passion. . . . [T]his very spirit is a guardian instinct that watches over the life of this assembly. It cherishes the principle of self-preservation; and without its existence, and its existence with all the strength we see it possess, the privileges of the representatives of the people, and immediately the liberties of the people, would not be guarded, as they are, with a vigilance that never sleeps and an unrelaxing constancy and courage.

If the consequences most unfairly attributed to the vote in the affirmative were not chimerical and worse, for they are deceptive, I should think it a reproach to be found even moderate in my zeal to assert the constitutional powers of this assembly; and whenever they shall be in real danger, the present occasion affords proof that there will be no want of advocates and champions. . . .

. . . This, incredible and extravagant as it may seem, is asserted. . . . [T]he President and Senate are to make national bargains, and this House has nothing to do in making them. But bad bargains do not bind this House and, of inevitable consequence, do not bind the nation. When a national bargain, called a treaty, is made, its binding force does not depend upon the making, but upon our opinion that it is good. As our opinion on the matter can be known and declared only by ourselves, when sitting in our legislative capacity, the treaty, though ratified and, as we choose to term it, made, is hung up in suspense till our sense is ascertained. We condemn the bargain and it falls, though, as we say, our faith does not. We approve a bargain as expedient and it stands firm and binds the nation. Yet, even in this latter case, its force is plainly not derived from the ratification by the treaty-making power, but from our approbation. Who will trace these inferences and pretend that we may have no share, according to the argument, in the treaty-making power? These opinions, nevertheless, have been advocated with infinite zeal and perseverance. Is it possible that any man can be hardy enough to avow them and their ridiculous consequences? . . .

If we choose to observe it with good faith, our course is obvious. Whatever is stipulated to be done by the nation must be complied with. Our agency, if it should be requisite, cannot be properly refused. And I do not see why it is not as obligatory a rule of conduct for the legislature as for the courts of law. . . .

Shall we break the treaty?

The treaty is bad, fatally bad, is the cry. It sacrifices the interest, the honor, the independence of the United States, and the faith of our engagements to France. If we listen to the clamor of party intemperance, the evils are of a number not to be counted and of a nature not to be borne, even in idea. The language of passion and exaggeration may silence that of sober reason in other places, it has not done it here. The question here is whether the treaty be really so very fatal as to oblige the nation to break its faith? I admit that such a treaty ought not to be executed. I admit that self-preservation is the first law of society as well as of individuals. It would, perhaps, be deemed an abuse of terms to call that a treaty which violates such a principle. . . .

But I lay down two rules which ought to guide us in this case. The treaty must appear to be bad, not merely in the petty details, but in its character, principle, and mass. And, in the next place, this ought to be ascertained by the decided and general concurrence of the enlightened public. . . .

[But] what do those mean who say that our honor was forfeited by treating at all, and especially by such a treaty? Justice, the laws and practice of nations, a just regard for peace as a duty to mankind and known wish of our citizens, as well as that self-respect which required it of the nation to act with dignity and moderation—all these forbid an appeal to arms before we had tried the effect of negotiation. The honor of the United States was saved, not forfeited, by treating. The treaty itself, by its stipulations for the posts, for indemnity, and for a due observance of our neutral rights, has justly raised the character of the nation. Never did the name of America appear in Europe with more luster than upon the event of ratifying this instrument. The fact is of a nature to overcome all contradiction. . . .

I proceed to the second proposition which I have stated as indispensably requisite to a refusal of the performance of the treaty. Will the state of public opinion justify the deed? . . .

Who, I would inquire, is hardy enough to pretend that the public voice demands the violation of the treaty? The evidence of the sense of the great mass of the nation is often equivocal. But when was it ever manifested with more energy and precision than at the present moment? The voice of the people is raised against the measure of refusing the appropriations. . . . Is the treaty ruinous to our commerce? What has blinded the eyes of the merchants and traders? Surely they are not enemies to trade or ignorant of their own interests. Their sense is not so liable to be mistaken as that of a nation, and they are almost unanimous. . . .

The consequences of refusing to make provision for the treaty are not all to be foreseen. By rejecting, vast interests are committed to the sport of the winds, chance becomes the arbiter of events, and it is forbidden to human foresight to count their number or measure their extent.

Before we resolve to leap into this abyss, so dark and so profound, it becomes us to pause and reflect upon such of the dangers as are obvious and inevitable. . . .

. . . Five millions of dollars, and probably more, on the score of spoliations committed on our commerce, depend upon the treaty. The treaty offers the only prospect of indemnity. . . . Will you interpose and frustrate that hope, leaving to many families nothing but beggary and despair? . . .

The refusal of the posts (inevitable if we reject the treaty) is a measure too decisive in its nature to be neutral in its consequences. From great causes we are to look for great effects. A plain and obvious one will be, the price of the Western lands will fall. Settlers will not choose to fix their habitation on a field of battle. . . .

On this theme, my emotions are unutterable. If I could find words for them—if my powers bore any proportion to my zeal—I would swell my voice to such a note of remonstrance it should reach every log house beyond the mountains. I would say to the inhabitants, Wake from your false security! Your cruel dangers—your more cruel apprehensions—are soon to be renewed; the wounds, yet unhealed, are to be torn open again. In the daytime, your path through the woods will be ambushed; the darkness of midnight will glitter with the blaze of your dwellings. You are a father: the blood of your sons shall fatten your cornfield! You are a mother: the war whoop shall wake the sleep of the cradle! . . .

By rejecting the posts, we light the savage fires—we bind the victims. This day we undertake to render account to the widows and orphans whom our decision will make; to the wretches that will be roasted at the stake; to our country; and I do not deem it too serious to say, to conscience and to God. . . .

. . . The voice of humanity issues from the shade of their wilderness. It exclaims that, while one hand is held up to reject this treaty, the other grasps a tomahawk. It summons our imagination to the scenes that will open. It is no great effort of the imagination to conceive that events so near are already begun. I can fancy that I listen to the yells of savage vengeance and the shrieks of torture. Already they seem to sigh in the west wind; already they mingle with every echo from the mountains. . . .

Look again at this state of things. On the seacoast, vast losses uncompensated. On the frontier, Indian war, actual encroachment on our territory. Everywhere discontent; resentments ten-fold more fierce because they will be impotent and humbled; national discord and abasement. . . .

I rose to speak under impressions that I would have resisted if I could. Those who see me will believe that the reduced state of my health has unfitted me, almost equally, for much exertion of body or mind. . . . Sinking, as I really am, under a sense of weakness, I imagined the very desire of speaking was extinguished by the persuasion that I had nothing to say. Yet, when I come to the moment of deciding the vote, I start back with dread from the edge of the pit into which we are plunging. In my view, even the minutes I have spent in expostulation have their value, because they protract the crisis and the short period in which alone we may resolve to escape it.

I have thus been led by my feelings to speak more at length than I had intended; yet I have, perhaps, as little personal interest in the event as anyone here. There is, I believe, no member who will not think his chance to be a witness of the consequences greater than mine. If, however, the vote should pass to reject and a spirit should rise, as it will, with the public disorders, to make confusion worse confounded, even I, slender and almost broken as my hold upon life is, may outlive the government and Constitution of my country.

Washington's Farewell Address
19 September 1796

In the aftermath of the national argument over the British treaty, during his final year in office, Washington's virtual immunity from partisan attacks could no longer protect him. Several Republican publicists mounted a deliberate campaign to destroy his reputation. In these circumstances, the famous Farewell Address was partly a partisan statement.

Friends and Fellow-Citizens: The period for a new election of a citizen to administer the executive government of the United States being not far distant, and the time actually arrived when your thoughts must be employed in designating the person who is to be clothed with that important trust, it appears to me proper, especially as it may conduce to a more distinct expression of the public voice, that I should now apprise you of the resolution

I have formed to decline being considered among the number of those out of whom a choice is to be made.

I beg you, at the same time, to do me the justice to be assured that this resolution has not been taken without a strict regard to all the considerations appertaining to the relation which binds a dutiful citizen to his country, and that, in withdrawing the tender of service which silence in my situation might imply, I am influenced by no diminution of zeal for your future interest, no deficiency of grateful respect for your past kindness; but am supported by a full conviction that the step is compatible with both.

The acceptance of, and continuance hitherto in, the office to which your suffrages have twice called me have been a uniform sacrifice of inclination to the opinion of duty, and to a deference for what appeared to be your desire. I constantly hoped that it would have been much earlier in my power, consistently with motives which I was not at liberty to disregard, to return to that retirement from which I had been reluctantly drawn. The strength of my inclination to do this, previous to the last election, had even led to the preparation of an address to declare it to you; but mature reflection on the then perplexed and critical posture of our affairs with foreign nations, and the unanimous advice of persons entitled to my confidence, impelled me to abandon the idea.

I rejoice that the state of your concerns, external as well as internal, no longer renders the pursuit of inclination incompatible with the sentiment of duty or propriety; and am persuaded, whatever partiality may be retained for my services, that in the present circumstances of our country, you will not disapprove my determination to retire.

In looking forward to the moment which is intended to terminate the career of my public life, my feelings do not permit me to suspend the deep acknowledgment of that debt of gratitude which I owe to my beloved country for the many honors it has conferred upon me; still more for the stedfast confidence with which it has supported me; and for the opportunities I have thence enjoyed of manifesting my inviolable attachment, by services faithful and persevering, though in usefulness unequal to my zeal. If benefits have resulted to our country from these services, let it always be remembered to your praise, and as an instructive example in our annals, that, under circumstances in which the passions agitated in every direction were liable to mislead, amidst appearances sometimes dubious, vicissitudes of fortune often discouraging, in situations in which not infrequently want of success has countenanced the spirit of criticism, the constancy of your support was the essential prop of the efforts, and a guarantee of the plans by which they were effected. Profoundly penetrated with this idea, I shall carry it with me to my grave, as a strong incitement to unceasing vows that Heaven may continue to you the choicest tokens of its beneficence; that your Union and brotherly affection may be perpetual; that the free constitution, which is the work of your hands, may be sacredly maintained; that its administration in every department may be stamped with wisdom and virtue; that, in fine, the happiness of the people of these states, under the auspices of liberty, may be made complete, by so careful a preservation and so prudent a use of this blessing as will acquire to them the glory of recommending it to the applause, the affection, and adoption of every nation which is yet a stranger to it.

Here, perhaps, I ought to stop. But a solicitude for your welfare, which cannot end but with my life, and the apprehension of danger natural to that solicitude, urge me on an occasion like the present to offer to your solemn contemplation, and to recommend to your frequent review, some sentiments which are the result of much reflection, of no inconsiderable observation, and which appear to me all important to the permanency of your felicity as a people. These will be offered to you with the more freedom as you can only see in them the disinterested warnings of a parting friend, who can possibly have no personal motive to bias his counsel. Nor can I forget, as an encouragement to it, your indulgent reception of my sentiments on a former and not dissimilar occasion.

Interwoven as is the love of liberty with every ligament of your hearts, no recommendation of mine is necessary to fortify or confirm the attachment.

The unity of government which constitutes you one people is also now dear to you. It is justly so, for it is a main pillar in the edifice of your real independence, the support of your tranquility at home, your peace abroad, of your safety, of your prosperity, of that very liberty which you so highly prize. But as it is easy to foresee that from different causes and from different quarters, much pains will be taken, many artifices employed, to weaken in your minds the conviction of this truth; as this is the point in your political fortress against which the batteries of internal and external enemies will be most constantly and actively (though often covertly and

insidiously) directed, it is of infinite moment that you should properly estimate the immense value of your national Union to your collective and individual happiness; that you should cherish a cordial, habitual and immovable attachment to it; accustoming yourselves to think and speak of it as of the Palladium of your political safety and prosperity; watching for its preservation with jealous anxiety; discountenancing whatever may suggest even a suspicion that it can in any event be abandoned, and indignantly frowning upon the first dawning of every attempt to alienate any portion of our country from the rest, or to enfeeble the sacred ties which now link together the various parts.

For this you have every inducement of sympathy and interest. Citizens by birth or choice of a common country, that country has a right to concentrate your affections. The name of American, which belongs to you, in your national capacity, must always exalt the just price of patriotism, more than any appellation derived from local discriminations. With slight shades of difference, you have the same religion, manners, habits, and political principles. You have in a common cause fought and triumphed together. The independence and liberty you possess are the work of joint councils and joint efforts; of common dangers, sufferings, and successes.

But these considerations, however powerfully they address themselves to your sensibility, are greatly outweighed by those which apply more immediately to your interest. Here every portion of our country finds the most commanding motives for carefully guarding and preserving the Union of the whole.

The *North,* in an unrestrained intercourse with the *South,* protected by the equal laws of a common government, finds in the productions of the latter great additional resources of maritime and commercial enterprise and precious materials of manufacturing industry. The *South,* in the same intercourse, benefiting by the agency of the *North,* sees its agriculture grow and its commerce expand. Turning partly into its own channels the seamen of the *North,* it finds its particular navigation invigorated; and while it contributes, in different ways, to nourish and increase the general mass of the national navigation, it looks forward to the protection of the maritime strength to which itself is unequally adapted. The *East,* in a like intercourse with the *West,* already finds, and in the progressive improvement of interior communications by land and water, will more and more find a valuable vent for the commodities which it brings from abroad or manufactures at home. The *West* derives from the *East* supplies requisite to its growth and comfort, and what is perhaps of still greater consequence, it must of necessity owe the secure enjoyment of indispensable outlets for its own productions to the weight, influence, and the future maritime strength of the Atlantic side of the Union, directed by an indissoluble community of interest as *one nation.* Any other tenure by which the *West* can hold this essential advantage, whether derived from its own separate strength or from an apostate and unnatural connection with any foreign power, must be intrinsically precarious.

While, then, every part of our country thus feels an immediate and particular interest in Union, all the parts combined cannot fail to find in the united mass of means and efforts greater strength, greater resource, proportionately greater security from external danger, a less frequent interruption of their peace by foreign nations; and, what is of inestimable value! they must derive from Union an exemption from those broils and wars between themselves which so frequently afflict neighboring countries not tied together by the same government; which their own rivalships alone would be sufficient to produce, but which opposite foreign alliances, attachments, and intrigues would stimulate and embitter. Hence likewise they will avoid the necessity of those overgrown military establishments which under any form of government are inauspicious to liberty, and which are to be regarded as particularly hostile to Republican Liberty: In this sense it is that your Union ought to be considered as a main prop of your liberty, and that the love of the one ought to endear to you the preservation of the other.

These considerations speak a persuasive language to every reflecting and virtuous mind, and exhibit the continuance of the Union as a primary object of patriotic desire. Is there a doubt whether a common government can embrace so large a sphere? Let experience solve it. To listen to mere speculation in such a case were criminal. We are authorized to hope that a proper organization of the whole, with the auxiliary agency of governments for the respective subdivisions, will afford a happy issue to the experiment. 'Tis well worth a fair and full experiment. With such powerful and obvious motives to Union, affecting all parts of our country, while experience shall not have demonstrated its impracticability, there will always be reason to distrust the patriotism of those who in any quarter may endeavor to weaken its bands.

In contemplating the causes which may disturb our Union, it occurs as matter of serious concern that any ground should have been furnished for characterizing parties by *geographical* discriminations: *Northern* and *Southern; Atlantic* and *Western;* whence designing men may endeavor to excite a belief that there is a real difference of local interests and views. One of the expedients of party to acquire influence within particular districts is to misrepresent the opinions and aims of other districts. You cannot shield yourselves too much against the jealousies and heart burnings which spring from these misrepresentations. They tend to render alien to each other those who ought to be bound together by fraternal affection. The inhabitants of our Western country have lately had a useful lesson on this head. They have seen, in the negotiation by the Executive and in the unanimous ratification by the Senate, of the treaty with Spain, and in the universal satisfaction at that event throughout the United States, a decisive proof how unfounded were the suspicions propagated among them of a policy in the general government and in the Atlantic states unfriendly to their interests in regard to the Mississippi. They have been witnesses to the formation of two treaties, that with G. Britain and that with Spain, which secure to them everything they could desire in respect to our foreign relations towards confirming their prosperity. Will it not be their wisdom to rely for the preservation of these advantages on the Union by which they were procured? Will they not henceforth be deaf to those advisers, if such there are, who would sever them from their brethren and connect them with aliens?

To the efficacy and permanency of Your Union, a government for the whole is indispensable. No alliances however strict between the parts can be an adequate substitute. They must inevitably experience the infractions and interruptions which all alliances in all times have experienced. Sensible of this momentous truth, you have improved upon your first essay by the adoption of a Constitution of Government better calculated than your former for an intimate Union, and for the efficacious management of your common concerns. This government, the offspring of our own choice uninfluenced and unawed, adopted upon full investigation and mature deliberation, completely free in its principles, in the distribution of its powers uniting security with energy, and containing within itself a provision for its own amendment, has a just claim to your confidence and your support. Respect for its authority, compliance with its laws, acquiescence in its measures, are duties enjoined by the fundamental maxims of true liberty. The basis of our political systems is the right of the people to make and to alter their Constitutions of Government. But the Constitution which at any time exists, 'till changed by an explicit and authentic act of the whole people, is sacredly obligatory upon all. The very idea of the power and the right of the people to establish government presupposes the duty of every individual to obey the established government.

All obstructions to the execution of the laws, all combinations and associations, under whatever plausible character, with the real design to direct, control, counteract, or awe the regular deliberation and action of the constituted authorities are destructive of this fundamental principle and of fatal tendency. They serve to organize faction, to give it an artificial and extraordinary force; to put in the place of the delegated will of the nation the will of the party; often a small but artful and enterprising minority of the community; and, according to the alternate triumphs of different parties, to make the public administration the mirror of the ill concerted and incongruous projects of faction, rather than the organ of consistent and wholesome plans digested by common councils and modified by mutual interests. However combinations or associations of the above description may now and then answer popular ends, they are likely, in the course of time and things, to become potent engines by which cunning, ambitious, and unprincipled men will be enabled to subvert the power of the people, and to usurp for themselves the reins of government; destroying afterwards the very engines which have lifted them to unjust dominion.

Towards the preservation of your government and the permanency of your present happy state, it is requisite, not only that you steadily discountenance irregular oppositions to its acknowledged authority, but also that you resist with care the spirit of innovation upon its principles however specious the pretexts. One method of assault may be to effect, in the forms of the Constitution, alterations which will impair the energy of the system, and thus to undermine what cannot be directly overthrown. In all the changes to which you may be invited, remember that time and habit are at least as necessary to fix the true character of governments as of other human institutions; that experience is the surest standard by which to test the real tendency of the existing Constitution of a country; that facility in changes upon the credit of mere hypotheses and

opinion exposes to perpetual change, from the endless variety of hypotheses and opinion: and remember, especially, that for the efficient management of your common interests, in a country so extensive as ours, a government of as much vigor as is consistent with the perfect security of liberty is indispensable. Liberty itself will find in such a government, with powers properly distributed and adjusted, its surest guardian. It is indeed little else than a name where the government is too feeble to withstand the enterprises of faction, to confine each member of the society within the limits prescribed by the laws, and to maintain all in the secure and tranquil enjoyment of the rights of person and property.

I have already intimated to you the danger of parties in the state, with particular reference to the founding of them on geographical discriminations. Let me now take a more comprehensive view and warn you in the most solemn manner against the baneful effects of the spirit of party, generally.

This spirit, unfortunately, is inseparable from our nature, having its root in the strongest passions of the human mind. It exists under different shapes in all governments, more or less stifled, controlled, or repressed; but in those of the popular form it is seen in its greatest rankness and is truly their worst enemy.

The alternate domination of one faction over another, sharpened by the spirit of revenge natural to party dissension, which in different ages and countries has perpetuated the most horrid enormities, is itself a frightful despotism. But this leads at length to a more formal and permanent despotism. The disorders and miseries which result gradually incline the minds of men to seek security and repose in the absolute power of an individual: and sooner or later the chief of some prevailing faction more able or more fortunate than his competitors turns this disposition to the purposes of his own elevation on the ruins of public liberty.

Without looking forward to an extremity of this kind (which nevertheless ought not to be entirely out of sight) the common and continual mischiefs of the spirit of party are sufficient to make it the interest and the duty of a wise people to discourage and restrain it.

It serves always to distract the public councils and enfeeble the public administration. It agitates the community with ill founded jealousies and false alarms, kindles the animosity of one part against another, foments occasionally riot and insurrection. It opens the door to foreign influence and corruption, which find a facilitated access to the government itself through the channels of party passions. Thus the policy and the will of one country are subjected to the policy and will of another.

There is an opinion that parties in free countries are useful checks upon the administration of the government and serve to keep alive the spirit of liberty. This within certain limits is probably true, and in governments of a monarchical cast patriotism may look with indulgence, if not with favor, upon the spirit of party. But in those of the popular character, in governments purely elective, it is a spirit not to be encouraged. From their natural tendency, it is certain there will always be enough of that spirit for every salutary purpose. And there being constant danger of excess, the effort ought to be, by force of public opinion, to mitigate and assuage it. A fire not to be quenched, it demands a uniform vigilance to prevent its bursting into a flame, lest, instead of warming, it should consume.

Of all the dispositions and habits which lead to political prosperity, religion and morality are indispensable supports. In vain would that man claim the tribute of patriotism who should labor to subvert these great pillars of human happiness, these firmest props of the duties of men and citizens. The mere politician, equally with the pious man, ought to respect and to cherish them. A volume could not trace all their connections with private and public felicity. Let it simply be asked where is the security for property, for reputation, for life, if the sense of religious obligation desert the oaths which are the instruments of investigation in courts of justice? And let us with caution indulge the supposition that morality can be maintained without religion. Whatever may be conceded to the influence of refined education on minds of peculiar structure, reason and experience both forbid us to expect that national morality can prevail in exclusion of religious principle.

'Tis substantially true that virtue or morality is a necessary spring of popular government. The rule indeed extends with more or less force to every species of free government. Who that is a sincere friend to it can look with indifference upon attempts to shake the foundation of the fabric.

Promote then as an object of primary importance institutions for the general diffusion of knowledge. In proportion as the structure of a government gives force to public opinion, it is essential that public opinion should be enlightened.

As a very important source of strength and security, cherish public credit. One method of preserving it is to use it as sparingly as possible: avoiding occasions of expense by cultivating peace, but remembering also that timely disbursements to prepare for danger frequently prevent much greater disbursements to repel it; avoiding likewise the accumulation of debt, not only by shunning occasions of expense, but vigorous exertions in time of peace to discharge the debts which unavoidable wars may have occasioned, not ungenerously throwing upon posterity the burden which we ourselves ought to bear. The execution of these maxims belongs to your representatives, but it is necessary that public opinion should cooperate. To facilitate to them the performance of their duty, it is essential that you should practically bear in mind that, towards the payment of debts, there must be revenue; that to have revenue there must be taxes; that no taxes can be devised which are not more or less inconvenient and unpleasant; that the intrinsic embarrassment inseparable from the selection of the proper objects (which is always a choice of difficulties) ought to be a decisive motive for a candid construction of the conduct of the government in making it, and for a spirit of acquiescence in the measures for obtaining revenue which the public exigencies may at any time dictate.

Observe good faith and justice towards all nations. Cultivate peace and harmony with all. Religion and morality enjoin this conduct; and can it be that good policy does not equally enjoin it? It will be worthy of a free, enlightened, and, at no distant period, a great nation, to give to mankind the magnanimous and too novel example of a people always guided by an exalted justice and benevolence. Who can doubt that in the course of time and things the fruits of such a plan would richly repay any temporary advantages which might be lost by a steady adherence to it? Can it be that Providence has not connected the permanent felicity of a nation with its virtue? The experiment, at least, is recommended by every sentiment which ennobles human nature. Alas! is it rendered impossible by its vices?

In the execution of such a plan nothing is more essential than that permanent, inveterate antipathies against particular nations and passionate attachments for others should be excluded; and that in place of them just and amicable feelings towards all should be cultivated. The nation which indulges towards another an habitual hatred, or an habitual fondness, is in some degree a slave. It is a slave to its animosity or to its affection, either of which is sufficient to lead it astray from its duty and its interest. Antipathy in one nation against another disposes each more readily to offer insult and injury, to lay hold of slight causes of umbrage, and to be haughty and intractable when accidental or trifling occasions of dispute occur. Hence frequent collisions, obstinate, envenomed, and bloody contests. The nation, prompted by ill will and resentment, sometimes impels to war the government, contrary to the best calculations of policy. The government sometimes participates in the national propensity and adopts through passion what reason would reject; at other times, it makes the animosity of the nation subservient to projects of hostility instigated by pride, ambition, and other sinister and pernicious motives. The peace often, sometimes perhaps the liberty, of nations has been the victim.

So likewise, a passionate attachment of one nation for another produces a variety of evils. Sympathy for the favorite nation, facilitating the illusion of an imaginary common interest, in cases where no real common interest exists, and infusing into one the enmities of the other, betrays the former into a participation in the quarrels and wars of the latter, without adequate inducement or justification: It leads also to concessions to the favorite nation of privileges denied to others, which is apt doubly to injure the nation making the concessions; by unnecessarily parting with what ought to have been retained and by exciting jealousy, ill will, and a disposition to retaliate in the parties from whom equal privileges are withheld: And it gives to ambitious, corrupted, or deluded citizens (who devote themselves to the favorite nation) facility to betray or sacrifice the interests of their own country without odium, sometimes even with popularity; gilding with the appearances of a virtuous sense of obligation a commendable deference for public opinion or a laudable zeal for public good, the base or foolish compliances of ambition, corruption, or infatuation.

As avenues to foreign influence in innumerable ways, such attachments are particularly alarming to the truly enlightened and independent patriot. How many opportunities do they afford to tamper with domestic factions, to practice the arts of seduction, to mislead public opinion, to influence or awe the public councils? Such an attachment of a small or weak towards a great and powerful nation dooms the former to be the satellite of the latter.

Against the insidious wiles of foreign influence (I conjure you to believe me fellow citizens), the jealousy of a free people ought to be *constantly* awake; since history and experience prove that foreign influence is one of the most

baneful foes of republican government. But that jealousy to be useful must be impartial; else it becomes the instrument of the very influence to be avoided, instead of a defense against it. Excessive partiality for one foreign nation and excessive dislike of another cause those whom they actuate to see danger only on one side, and serve to veil and even second the arts of influence on the other. Real patriots, who may resist the intrigues of the favorite, are liable to become suspected and odious; while its tools and dupes usurp the applause and confidence of the people, to surrender their interests.

The great rule of conduct for us in regard to foreign nations is, in extending our commercial relations, to have with them as little *political* connection as possible. So far as we have already formed engagements let them be fulfilled, with perfect good faith. Here let us stop.

Europe has a set of primary interests which to us have none or a very remote relation. Hence she must be engaged in frequent controversies, the causes of which are essentially foreign to our concerns. Hence, therefore, it must be unwise in us to implicate ourselves, by artificial ties, in the ordinary vicissitudes of her politics or the ordinary combinations and collisions of her friendships or enmities.

Our detached and distant situation invites and enables us to pursue a different course. If we remain one people, under an efficient government, the period is not far off when we may defy material injury from external annoyance; when we may take such an attitude as will cause the neutrality we may at any time resolve upon to be scrupulously respected; when belligerent nations, under the impossibility of making acquisitions upon us, will not lightly hazard the giving us provocation; when we may choose peace or war as our interest guided by our justice shall counsel.

Why forego the advantages of so peculiar a situation? Why quit our own to stand upon foreign ground? Why, by interweaving our destiny with that of any part of Europe, entangle our peace and prosperity in the toils of European ambition, rivalship, interest, humor or caprice?

'Tis our true policy to steer clear of permanent alliances with any portion of the foreign world. So far, I mean, as we are now at liberty to do it, for let me not be understood as capable of patronizing infidelity to existing engagements (I hold the maxim no less applicable to public than to private affairs that honesty is always the best policy). I repeat it, therefore, let those engagements be observed in their genuine sense. But in my opinion, it is unnecessary and would be unwise to extend them.

Taking care always to keep ourselves, by suitable establishments, on a respectably defensive posture, we may safely trust to temporary alliances for extraordinary emergencies.

Harmony, liberal intercourse with all nations, are recommended by policy, humanity and interest. But even our commercial policy should hold an equal and impartial hand: neither seeking nor granting exclusive favors or preferences; consulting the natural course of things; diffusing and diversifying by gentle means the streams of commerce, but forcing nothing; establishing with powers so disposed, in order to give to trade a stable course, to define the rights of our merchants, and to enable the government to support them, conventional rules of intercourse, the best that present circumstances and mutual opinion will permit, but temporary, and liable to be from time to time abandoned or varied as experience and circumstances shall dictate; constantly keeping in view that 'tis folly in one nation to look for disinterested favors from another; that it must pay with a portion of its independence for whatever it may accept under that character; that, by such acceptance, it may place itself in the condition of having given equivalents for nominal favors and yet of being reproached with ingratitude for not giving more. There can be no greater error than to expect or calculate upon real favors from nation to nation. 'Tis an illusion which experience must cure, which a just pride ought to discard.

In offering to you, my countrymen, these counsels of an old and affectionate friend, I dare not hope they will make the strong and lasting impression I could wish; that they will control the usual current of the passions or prevent our nation from running the course which has hitherto marked the destiny of nations. But if I may even flatter myself that they may be productive of some partial benefit, some occasional good; that they may now and then recur to moderate the fury of party spirit, to warn against the mischiefs of foreign intrigue, to guard against the impostures of pretended patriotism; this hope will be a full recompense for the solicitude for your welfare by which they have been dictated.

PART 4

Liberty and Order

John Adams defeated Thomas Jefferson in the presidential election of 1796 by a margin of three electoral votes (and Jefferson became vice president under the terms of the Constitution at that time). Washington had left his successor with a crisis. Damaged and offended by Jay's Treaty, the French Directory announced that France would treat American ships "in the same manner as they suffer the English to treat them." Seizures followed, and the new administration responded to the crisis much as Washington had responded to the crisis with England in 1794. As Congress increased appropriations for national defense, Adams sent two envoys to join with Charles C. Pinckney, whom the French had refused to accept as minister, to negotiate a resolution. The negotiations failed when unofficial agents of the French foreign minister—referred to in American dispatches as X, Y, and Z—demanded a bribe for Talleyrand, a large American loan to the Republic, and an apology for remarks in Adams's address to Congress before negotiations could begin.

In April 1798, goaded by Republicans in Congress, who could not believe administration statements that negotiations had failed, Adams released the papers revealing the XYZ Affair. Patriotic fury swept the country, swelling into a widespread fear of treasonable plots between the French and their domestic admirers. On the crest of this hysteria, the Federalists in Congress launched a limited naval war with France and seized the opportunity to attack their domestic opponents. Over the next two years, the Quasi-War and the Federalists' Alien and Sedition Acts would be the focus of party debates.

The Black Cockade Fever

Philadelphia, 1798

The letters of several national figures capture something of the atmosphere in Philadelphia, in the country, and in the president's own house during the spring and summer of 1798.

Abigail Adams to Her Sister

7 April 1798

My Dear Sister:

The Senate on Thursday voted to have the dispatches from our envoys made public. . . . If the communications should have the happy effect which present appearances lead me to hope, that of uniting the people of our country, I shall not regret that they were called for. Out of apprehension what might prove the result of such communications to our envoys, if they still remain in Paris, the President forbore to communicate them and in his message was as explicit as was necessary for those who reposed confidence in him. But such lies and falsehoods were continually circulated, and base and incendiary letters sent to the house addressed to him, that I really have been alarmed for his personal safety, tho I have never before expressed it. With this temper in a city like this, materials for a mob might be brought together in 10 minutes.

Abigail Adams to Her Sister

22 April 1798

My Dear Sister:

. . . Addresses from the Merchants, Traders & Underwriters have been presented and signed by more than 500 of men of the greatest property here in this city, highly approving the measures of the executive. A similar one from the Grand Jurors, one from York Town, and yesterday, one from the Mayor, Aldermen & common counsel of the city, a very firm and manly address. Others are coming from New York, from Baltimore, and I presume Boston will be no longer behind than time to consult upon the measure. They must in this way show the haughty tyrants that we are not that divided people we have appeared to be; their vile emissaries make all our trouble, and all our difficulty.

Abigail Adams to Her Sister

26 April 1798

My Dear Sister:

I enclose to you a National Song ["Hail Columbia"] composed by [Joseph] Hopkinson. French tunes have for a long time usurped an uncontrolled sway. Since the change in the public opinion respecting France, the people began to lose the relish for them, and what had been harmony now becomes discord. Accordingly there had been for several evenings at the theater something like disorder, one party crying out for the President's March and Yankee Doodle, whilst Ça Ira was vociferated from the other. It was hissed off repeatedly. The managers were blamed. Their excuse was that they had not any words to the President's March—Mr. Hopkinson accordingly composed these to the tune. Last evening they were sung for the first time. I had a great curiosity to see for myself the effect. I got Mr. Otis to take a box and silently went off with Mr. and Mrs. Otis, Mr. and Mrs. Buck to the play, where I had only once been this winter. . . . Mr. Fox came upon the stage, to sing the song. He was welcomed by applause. The house was very full, and at every chorus, the most unbounded applause ensued. In short it was enough to stun one. They had the song repeated—After this Rossina was acted. When Fox came upon the [stage] after the curtain dropped to announce the piece for Friday, they called again for the song, and made him repeat it to the fourth time. And the last time, the whole audience broke forth in the chorus whilst the thunder from their hands was incessant, and at the close they rose, gave 3 Huzzas that you might have heard a mile—My head aches in consequence of it. . . . There have been six different addresses presented from this city alone; all expressive of the approbation of the measures of the executive. Yet daringly do the vile incendiaries keep up in Bache's paper the most wicked and base, violent & calumniating abuse. . . . But nothing will have an effect until Congress passes a Sedition Bill, which I presume they will do before they rise.

Abigail Adams to Her Sister

10 May 1798

My Dear Sister:

. . . The young men of the city as I wrote you on Monday to the amount of near eleven hundred came at 12 o'clock in procession two and two. There were assembled upon the occasion it is said ten thousand persons. . . . In great order & decorum the young men with each a black cockade marched through the multitude and all of them entered the house preceded by their committee. When a young gentleman by the name of Hare, a nephew of Mrs. Bingham's, read the address, the President received them in his Levee Room dressed in his uniform, and as usual upon such occasions, read his answer to them, after which they all retired. The multitude gave three cheers and followed them to the State House Yard, where the answer to the address was again read by the chairman of the committee, with acclamations. They then closed the scene by singing the new song, which at 12 o'clock at night was sung by them under our windows, they having dined together or rather a part of them. This scene burnt in the hearts of some Jacobins and they determined either to terrify or bully the young men out of their patriotism. Bache published some saucy pieces the young men resented, and he would have felt the effects of their resentment if some cooler heads had not interposed. Yesterday [the day of Public Humiliation, Fasting, and Prayer] was observed with much solemnity. The meeting houses & churches were filled. About four o'clock as is usual the State House Yard, which is used for a walk, was very full of the inhabitants, when about 30 fellows, some with snow balls in their hats & some with tri-colored cockades, entered and attempted to seize upon the hats of the young men to tear out their cockades. A scuffle ensued when the young men became conquerors, and some of these tri-colored cockades were trampled in the dust. One fellow was taken and committed to jail, but this was sufficient to alarm the inhabitants, and there were everywhere large collections of people. The Light Horse were called out & patrolled the streets all night. A guard was placed before this house tho, through the whole of the proceeding and amidst all the collection, the President's name was not once mentioned, nor any one grievance complained of, but a foreign attempt to try their strength & to awe the inhabitants if possible was no doubt at the bottom. Congress are upon an Alien Bill. This Bache is cursing & abusing daily. If that fellow & all is not suppressed, we shall come to a civil war. I hope the Gen'll Court of our state will take the subject up & if they have not a strong Sedition Bill, make one. . . .

Alexander Hamilton to George Washington

19 May 1798

My Dear Sir,

At the present dangerous crisis of public affairs, I make no apology for troubling you with a political letter. Your impressions of our situation, I am persuaded, are not different from mine. There is certainly great probability that we may have to enter into a very serious struggle with France, and it is more and more evident that the powerful faction which has for years opposed the government is determined to go every length with France. I am sincere in declaring my full conviction, as the result of a long course of observation, that they are ready to *new model* our constitution under the *influence* or *coercion* of France—to form with her a perpetual alliance *offensive* and *defensive*—and to give her a monopoly of our trade by *peculiar* and *exclusive* privileges. This would be in substance, whatever it might be in name, to make this country a province of France. Neither do I doubt that her standard displayed in this country would be directly or indirectly seconded by them in pursuance of the project I have mentioned.

It is painful and alarming to remark that the opposition faction assumes so much a geographical complexion. As yet from the south of Maryland nothing has been heard but accents of disapprobation of our government and approbation of or apology for France. This is a most portentous symptom & demands every human effort to change it.

In such a state of public affairs it is impossible not to look up to you and to wish that your influence could in some proper mode be brought into direct action. Among the ideas which have passed through my mind for this purpose, I have asked myself whether it might not be expedient for you to make a circuit through Virginia and North Carolina under some pretense of health, etc. This would call forth addresses, public dinners, etc. which would give you an opportunity of expressing sentiments in answers, toasts, etc. which would throw the weight of your character into the scale of the government and revive an enthusiasm for your person that may be turned into the right channel. . . .

You ought to be aware, My Dear Sir, that in the event of an open rupture with France, the public voice will again call you to command the armies of your country; and though all who are attached to you will, from attachment as well as public considerations, deplore an occasion which should once more tear you from that repose to which you have so good a right, yet it is the opinion of all those with whom I converse that you will be compelled to make the sacrifice. All your past labor may demand, to give it efficacy, this further, this very great sacrifice.

Thomas Jefferson to John Taylor

4 June 1798

Mr. New showed me your letter on the subject of the patent, which gave me an opportunity of observing what you said as to the effect with you of public proceedings, and that it was not unusual now to estimate the separate mass of Virginia and N. Carolina with a view to their separate existence. It is true that we are completely under the saddle of Massachusetts & Connecticut, and that they ride us very hard, cruelly insulting our feelings as well as exhausting our strength and substance. Their natural friends, the three other eastern states, join them from a sort of family pride, and they have the art to divide certain other parts of the Union so as to make use of them to govern the whole. This is not new. It is the old practice of despots to use a part of the people to keep the rest in order, and those who have once got an ascendency and possessed themselves of all the resources of the nation, their revenues and offices, have immense means for retaining their advantages. But our present situation is not a natural one. The body of our countrymen is substantially republican through every part of the Union. It was the irresistible

influence & popularity of General Washington, played off by the cunning of Hamilton, which turned the government over to anti-republican hands, or turned the republican members chosen by the people into anti-republicans. He delivered it over to his successor in this state, and very untoward events, since improved with great artifice, have produced on the public mind the impression we see; but still, I repeat it, this is not the natural state. Time alone would bring round an order of things more correspondent to the sentiments of our constituents; but are there not events impending which will do it within a few months? The invasion of England, the public and authentic avowal of sentiments hostile to the leading principles of our Constitution, the prospect of a war in which we shall stand alone, land tax, stamp tax, increase of public debt, etc. Be this as it may, in every free & deliberating society there must, from the nature of man, be opposite parties & violent dissensions & discords; and one of these, for the most part, must prevail over the other for a longer or shorter time. Perhaps this party division is necessary to induce each to watch & relate to the people the proceedings of the other. But if, on a temporary superiority of the one party, the other is to resort to a scission of the Union, no federal government can ever exist. If to rid ourselves of the present rule of Massachusetts & Connecticut, we break the Union, will the evil stop there? Suppose the N. England States alone cut off, will our natures be changed? Are we not men still to the south of that, & with all the passions of men? Immediately we shall see a Pennsylvania & a Virginia party arise in the residuary confederacy, and the public mind will be distracted with the same party spirit. What a game, too, will the one party have in their hands by eternally threatening the other that unless they do so & so, they will join their Northern neighbors. If we reduce our Union to Virginia & N. Carolina, immediately the conflict will be established between the representatives of these two states, and they will end by breaking into their simple units. Seeing, therefore, that an association of men who will not quarrel with one another is a thing which never yet existed, from the greatest confederacy of nations down to a town meeting or a vestry, seeing that we must have somebody to quarrel with, I had rather keep our New England associates for that purpose than to see our bickerings transferred to others. They are circumscribed within such narrow limits, & their population so full, that their numbers will ever be the minority, and they are marked, like the Jews, with such a peculiarity of character as to constitute from that circumstance the natural division of our parties. A little patience and we shall see the reign of witches pass over, their spells dissolve, and the people, recovering their true sight, restore their government to its true principles. It is true that in the meantime we are suffering deeply in spirit and incurring the horrors of a war and long oppressions of enormous public debt. But who can say what would be the evils of a scission, and when & where they would end? Better keep together as we are, haul off from Europe as soon as we can, & from all attachments to any portions of it. And if we feel their power just sufficiently to hoop us together, it will be the happiest situation in which we can exist. If the game runs sometimes against us at home, we must have patience till luck turns, & then we shall have an opportunity of winning back the *principles* we have lost, for this is a game where principles are the stake. Better luck, therefore, to us all; and health, happiness, & friendly salutations to yourself. Adieu.

Addresses to the President, with His Replies
April–August 1798

Through the spring and summer of 1798, as Congress moved to authorize a quasi-war with France, addresses praising the administration poured into Philadelphia, where many were reprinted in the papers. Adams's replies did much to fan the patriotic fever, to further popular suspicion of the friends of France, and thus to lay the groundwork for repressive legislation.

Address of the Mayor, Aldermen, and Citizens of Philadelphia to the President of the United States
April 1798

At a moment when dangers threaten the peace and prosperity of the United States, when foreign violence and rapine have deeply wounded our national honor and injured our lawful commerce, it is presumed the mayor, aldermen, and citizens of the city of Philadelphia will not be unwelcome when they come forward to assure you of their perfect approbation of your administration and their entire confidence in your wisdom, integrity, and patriotism. While we admire the prudence and moderation with which our government has received the unprovoked aggressions of France and the sincerity and equity of your endeavors to conciliate her friendship, we feel the independent pride of Americans in your dignity and firmness. As we are satisfied that nothing has been wanting on your part to preserve to us the blessings of peace and safety, we prepare to meet with fortitude the consequences that may follow the failure of your exertions. Confident that our government has been just and impartial in her dealings with all nations, and grateful for the happiness we have enjoyed under it in the days of tranquility, we do not hesitate to promise it our utmost assistance in the time of difficulty and need. Presiding over the councils of your country in a most eventful crisis, we hope and trust you will find a fixed and energetic support in the people of America.—Permit us to congratulate you on the prospects of unanimity that now presents itself to the hopes of every American, and on the spirit of independent patriotism that is rapidly rising into active exertion—and to offer a sincere prayer that while you continue to serve your country with wisdom and fidelity, you may never find her ungrateful.

Answer
. . . At a time when all the old republics of Europe are crumbling into dust, and others forming whose destinies are dubious; when the monarchies of the old world are, some of them, fallen, and others are trembling to their foundations; when our own infant republic has scarcely had time to cement its strength or decide its own practicable form; when these agitations of the human species have affected our people, and produced a spirit of party which scruples not to go all lengths of profligacy, falsehood, and malignity in defaming our government; your approbation and confidence are to me a great consolation. Under your immediate observation and inspection the principal operations of the government are directed; and to you, both characters and conduct must be intimately known.

I am but one of the American people, and my fate and fortunes must be decided with theirs. As far as the forces of nature may remain to me, I will not be wanting in my duties to them, nor will I harbor a suspicion that they will fail to afford me all necessary aid and support.

While with the greatest pleasure I reciprocate your congratulations "on the prospect of unanimity that now presents itself to the hopes of every American, and on that spirit of patriotism and independence that is rising into active exertion" in opposition to seduction, domination, and rapine, I offer a sincere prayer that the citizens of Philadelphia may persevere in the virtuous course, maintain the honorable character of their ancestors, and be protected from every calamity physical, moral, and political.

Address of the Young Men of the City of Philadelphia, the District of Southwark, and the Northern Liberties

May 1798

Sir,

At a period so interesting to the United States, permit us to believe that an address from the youth of Philadelphia, anxious to preserve the honor and independence of their country, will not be unwelcome to their chief magistrate.

Actuated by the same principles on which our forefathers achieved their Independence, the recent attempts of a foreign power to derogate from the dignity and rights of our country awaken our liveliest sensibility and our strongest indignation.

The executive of the United States, filled with a spirit of friendship towards the whole world, has resorted to every just and honorable means of conciliating the affections of the French Republic, who have received their propositions of peace with determined hostility and contempt, have wounded our national independence by insulting its representatives, and calumniated the honor and virtue of our citizens by insinuating that we were a divided, insubordinate people.

The youth of the American nation will claim some share of the difficulty, danger, and glory of its defense; and although we do not hold ourselves competent to form an opinion respecting the tendency of every measure, yet we have no hesitation in declaring that we place the most entire confidence in your wisdom, integrity, and patriotism; that we regard our liberty and independence as the richest portion given to us by our ancestors; that we perceive no difference between the illegal and oppressive measures of one government and the insolent attempts now made to usurp our rights by another; that as our ancestors have magnanimously resisted the encroachments of the one, we will no less vigorously oppose the attacks of the other; that at the call of our country we will assemble with promptitude, obey the orders of the constituted authorities with alacrity, and on every occasion act with all the exertion of which we are capable; and for this we pledge ourselves to you, to our country, and to the world.

Answer
7 May 1798

Gentlemen,

Nothing of the kind could be more welcome to me than this address from the ingenuous youth of Philadelphia in their virtuous anxiety to preserve the honor and independence of their country.

For a long course of years, my amiable young friends, before the birth of the oldest of you, I was called to act with your fathers in concerting measures the most disagreeable and dangerous, not from a desire of innovation, not from discontent with the government under which we were born and bred, but to preserve the honor of our country and vindicate the immemorial liberties of our ancestors. In pursuit of these measures, it became, not an object of predilection and choice, but of indispensable necessity to assert our independence, which, with many difficulties and much suffering, was at length secured. I have long flattered myself that I might be gathered to the ashes of my fathers leaving unimpaired and unassailed the liberties so dearly purchased; and that I should never be summoned a second time to act in such scenes of anxiety, perplexity, and danger as war of any kind always exhibits. If my good fortune should not correspond with my earnest wishes and I should be obliged to act with you, as with your ancestors, in defense of the honor and independence of our country, I sincerely wish that none of you may ever have your constancy of mind and strength of body put to so severe a trial as to be compelled, again, in your advanced age to the contemplation and near prospect of any war of offense or defense.

It would neither be consistent with my character nor yours, on this occasion, to read lessons to gentlemen of your education, conduct, and character; if, however, I might be indulged the privilege of a father, I should with the tenderest affection recommend to your serious and constant consideration that science and morals are the great pillars on which this country has been raised to its present population, opulence, and prosperity, and that these alone can advance, support, and preserve it.

Without wishing to damp the ardor of curiosity or influence the freedom of inquiry, I will hazard a prediction that, after the most industrious and impartial researches, the longest liver of you all will find no principles, institutions, or systems of education more fit in general to be transmitted to your posterity than those you have received from your ancestors.

No prospect or spectacle could excite a stronger sensibility in my bosom than this which now presents itself before me. I wish you all the pure joys, the sanguine hopes, and bright prospects which are decent at your age, and that your lives may be long, honorable, and prosperous in the constant practice of benevolence to men and reverence to the divinity, in a country preserving in liberty and increasing in virtue, power, and glory.

The sentiments of this address, everywhere expressed in language as chaste and modest as it is elegant and masterly, which would do honor to the youth of any country, have raised a monument to your fame more durable than brass or marble. The youth of all America must exult in this early sample, at the seat of government, of their talents, genius, and virtues.

America and the world will look to our youth as one of our firmest bulwarks. The generous claim which you now present of sharing in the difficulty, danger, and glory of our defense is to me and to your country a sure and pleasing pledge that your birthrights will never be ignobly bartered or surrendered, but that you will in your turn transmit to future generations the fair inheritance obtained by the unconquerable spirit of your fathers.

Address of the Officers and Soldiers of the Chester Light Infantry Company of Volunteers in the County of Delaware and State of Pennsylvania

25 August 1798

Sir,

In the present eventful crisis of public affairs, we beg leave to approach you with affection and confidence: With affection because we believe its constituted authorities have done all that could be done, consistent with national honor and independence, to preserve peace. Believing with you that "a free republic is the best of governments and the greatest blessing to which mortals can aspire," it is our fixed determination to give it every support in our power, and we trust that under chiefs who have hitherto so ably conducted our country to independence, there will be no doubt of maintaining it against a foe who has left no arts untried to rob us of it. Averse to war, both as Americans and Christians, we should have been happy to have spent our lives in the enjoyment of peace, but when peace is to be the price of national degradation, and the enjoyment of it, if so purchased, wholly insecure, we have no hesitation in choosing the alternative with a confident reliance on that Providence which on more than one occasion has manifestly interfered for the safety and happiness of the American people.

Under these impressions we offer our best services to our country and beg you to accept of this tender of them, with an assurance that as soon as circumstances require it we are ready to take the field. In the presence of the "God of Armies," we make the offer and pledge ourselves to fulfill it.

Accept, Sir, our best wishes for your happiness; may you have the felicity of seeing our country permanently placed in that situation of peace and independence which your ardent patriotism and unwearied exertions in the cause of genuine freedom lead us to suppose is the prime wish of your heart.

Answer
17 September 1798

Gentlemen,

The affection and confidence expressed in your obliging address of the twenty-fifth of August is very satisfactory to me. Although there is no truth of which I am more fully convinced than this, which you approve, that "a free republic is the best government and the greatest blessing to which mortals can aspire," it is too apparent from history and experience that such a government has always too many enemies, both within and without, to be ever secure for any long period of time without a constant preparation and readiness for war. Such a government has always within itself its worst enemies in those who are most clamorous and boisterous in its praise.

The Sedition Act

14 July 1798

French and Irish immigrants usually sympathized with revolutionary France in its war with Britain and voted for Republican opponents of what they perceived as the pro-British policies of the Federalist administrations. On 18 June 1798, Congress passed a new Naturalization Act, extending from five to fourteen years the period of residence required for naturalization. On 25 June, it followed with the Alien Act, which gave the president power to summarily deport any alien whose residence he considered dangerous to the United States. (A nonpartisan Alien Enemies Act, passed on 6 July, authorized the president, in the event of a declared war, to arrest, imprison, or deport the citizens of an enemy power.) Within Congress and without, Republicans would insist that the Alien Act unconstitutionally deprived alien friends of a right to a judicial determination of their fates. Even sharper protests would greet the Sedition Act, which was aimed squarely at American citizens who criticized federal officials and programs.

Section 1. *Be it enacted* . . . That if any persons shall unlawfully combine or conspire together with intent to oppose any measure or measures of the government of the United States, which are or shall be directed by proper authority, or to impede the operation of any law of the United States, or to intimidate or prevent any person holding a place or office in or under the government of the United States from undertaking, performing, or executing his trust or duty; and if any person or persons, with intent as aforesaid, shall counsel, advise, or attempt to procure any insurrection, riot, unlawful assembly, or combination, whether such conspiracy, threatening, counsel, advice, or attempt shall have the proposed effect or not, he or they shall be deemed guilty of a high misdemeanor, and on conviction before any court of the United States having jurisdiction thereof, shall be punished by a fine not exceeding five thousand dollars, and by imprisonment during a term not less than six months nor exceeding five years; and further, at the discretion of the court, may be holden to find sureties for his good behavior in such sum and for such time as the said court may direct.

Section 2. That if any person shall write, print, utter, or publish, or shall cause or procure to be written, printed, uttered or published, or shall knowingly and willingly assist or aid in writing, printing, uttering or publishing any false, scandalous and malicious writing or writings against the government of the United States, or either house of the Congress of the United States, or the President of the United States, with intent to defame the said government, or either house of the said Congress, or the said President, or to bring them, or either of them, into contempt or disrepute; or to excite against them, or either or any of them, the hatred of the good people of the United States, or to stir up sedition within the United States, or to excite any unlawful combinations therein, for opposing or resisting any law of the United States, or any act of the President of the United States, done in pursuance of any such law or of the powers in him vested by the Constitution of the United States, or to resist, oppose, or defeat any such law or act, or to aid, encourage or abet any hostile designs of any foreign nation against the United States, their people or government, then such person, being thereof convicted before any court of the United States having jurisdiction thereof, shall be punished by a fine not exceeding two thousand dollars, and by imprisonment not exceeding two years.

Section 3. That if any person shall be prosecuted under this act for the writing or publishing any libel aforesaid, it shall be lawful for the defendant, upon the trial of the cause, to give in evidence in his defense, the truth of the matter contained in the publication charged as a libel. And the jury who shall try the cause shall have a right to determine the law and the fact, under the direction of the court, as in other cases.

Section 4. That this act shall continue to be in force until March 3, 1801, and no longer. . . .

Popular Protest

The Sedition Act was not a laughing matter. It was enforced by a partisan judiciary and a vigilant, High-Federalist secretary of state—all the more rigorously, in fact, once the crisis with France began to ease. Under its provisions or under the common law of seditious libel, all of the most important Republican newspapers in the country and several of the party's most influential pamphleteers felt the sting of prosecutions. The *Argus* and the *Time Piece,* the only Republican newspapers in New York City, were driven out of business. Men were prosecuted under the Sedition Act for offenses as diverse and as trivial as erecting a liberty pole, advocating the act's repeal, and expressing a drunken wish that cannon firing a salute were shooting at the president's "arse." Benjamin Franklin Bache, the grandson of Benjamin Franklin, whose Philadelphia paper, the *General-Advertiser,* had added the title *Aurora* to its masthead and replaced the *National Gazette* as the leading opposition newspaper when the latter went out of business in 1793, was another of its victims. William Duane, the assistant who succeeded Bache at the *Aurora* after the latter died in the yellow fever epidemic of 1798, was harried by common law proceedings. Neither ever relented in his condemnations of the Federalist regime, starting with this squib:

"Advertisement Extraordinary!!!"
(Philadelphia) *Aurora*

14 July 1798

Orator Mum takes this *very orderly* method of announcing to his fellow citizens that a THINKING CLUB will be established in a few days at the sign of the *Muzzle* in *Gag* Street. The first subject for cogitation will be:

"Ought a Free People to obey laws which violate the constitution they have sworn to support?"

N.B. No member will be permitted to think longer than fifteen minutes.

The Kentucky and Virginia Resolutions

With the Federalists in control of all three branches of the federal government, Jefferson and Madison decided to arouse the states for a counterattack on the repressive legislation of the summer. Jefferson gave a draft of legislative resolutions to John Breckinridge of Kentucky. Madison drafted a second set, which he would give to Virginia's John Taylor. Breckinridge or his fellow Kentucky legislators softened Jefferson's resolutions considerably before they passed the state house of representatives on 10 November 1798, replacing his suggestion that the rightful remedy for federal usurpations was a "nullification" of such acts by each state acting on its own with a declaration that unconstitutional acts were "void and of no force" and a call for the other states to join Kentucky in "requesting their repeal." The authorship of both sets of resolutions was a closely guarded secret until 1809, when Taylor mentioned Madison in print, and Jefferson's draft of the Kentucky Resolutions would not become public until later still. The two sets of resolutions nevertheless proved hugely controversial at the time, and during the succeeding generation, their elucidation of a compact theory of the Constitution and a doctrine of state interposition against unconstitutional federal laws would become a groundwork for the doctrines of nullification and secession.

THOMAS JEFFERSON

Draft of the Kentucky Resolutions
October 1798

1. *Resolved,* That the several States composing the United States of America, are not united on the principle of unlimited submission to their General Government; but that, by a compact under the style and title of a Constitution for the United States, and of amendments thereto, they constituted a general Government for special purposes,—delegated to that government certain definite powers, reserving, each State to itself, the residuary mass of right to their own self-government; and that whensoever the General Government assumes undelegated powers, its acts are unauthoritative, void, and of no force; that to this compact each State acceded as a State, and is an integral party, its co-States forming, as to itself, the other party: that the government created by this compact was not made the exclusive or final judge of the extent of the powers delegated to itself; since that would have made its discretion, and not the Constitution, the measure of its powers; but that, as in all other cases of compact among powers having no common judge, each party has an equal right to judge for itself, as well of infractions as of the mode and measure of redress.

2. *Resolved,* That the Constitution of the United States, having delegated to Congress a power to punish treason, counterfeiting the securities and current coin of the United States, piracies, and felonies committed on the high seas, and offenses against the law of nations, and no other crimes whatsoever; and it being true as a general principle, and one of the amendments to the Constitution having also declared, that "the powers not delegated to the States, are reserved to the States respectively, or to the people," therefore the act of Congress, passed on the 14th day of July, 1798, and entitled "An Act in addition to the act entitled An Act for the punishment of certain crimes against the United States," as also the act passed by them on the __ day of June, 1798, entitled "An Act to punish frauds committed on the bank of the United States," (and all their other acts which assume to create, define, or punish crimes, other than those so enumerated in the Constitution), are altogether void, and of no force; and that the power to create, define, and punish such other crimes is reserved, and, of right, appertains solely and exclusively to the respective States, each within its own territory.

3. *Resolved,* That it is true as a general principle, and is also expressly declared by one of the amendments to the Constitution, that "the powers not delegated to the United States by the Constitution, nor prohibited by it to the States, are reserved to the States respectively, or to the people"; and that no power over the freedom of religion, freedom of speech, or freedom of the press being delegated

to the United States by the Constitution, nor prohibited by it to the States, all lawful powers respecting the same did of right remain, and were reserved to the States or the people: that thus was manifested their determination to retain to themselves the right of judging how far the licentiousness of speech and of the press may be abridged without lessening their useful freedom, and how far those abuses which cannot be separated from their use should be tolerated, rather than the use be destroyed. And thus also they guarded against all abridgment by the United States of the freedom of religious opinions and exercises, and retained to themselves the right of protecting the same, as this State, by a law passed on the general demand of its citizens, had already protected them from all human restraint or interference. And that in addition to this general principle and express declaration, another and more special provision has been made by one of the amendments to the Constitution, which expressly declares, that "Congress shall make no law respecting an establishment of religion, or prohibiting the free exercise thereof, or abridging the freedom of speech or of the press": thereby guarding in the same sentence, and under the same words, the freedom of religion, of speech, and of the press: insomuch, that whatever violated either, throws down the sanctuary which covers the others, and that libels, falsehood, and defamation, equally with heresy and false religion, are withheld from the cognizance of federal tribunals. That, therefore, the act of Congress of the United States, passed on the 14th day of July, 1798, entitled "An Act in addition to the act entitled An Act for the punishment of certain crimes against the United States," which does abridge the freedom of the press, is not law, but is altogether void, and of no force.

4. *Resolved,* That alien friends are under the jurisdiction and protection of the laws of the State wherein they are: that no power over them has been delegated to the United States, nor prohibited to the individual States, distinct from their power over citizens. And it being true as a general principle, and one of the amendments to the Constitution having also declared, that "the powers not delegated to the United States by the Constitution, nor prohibited by it to the States, are reserved to the States respectively, or to the people," the act of the Congress of the United States, passed on the __ day of July, 1798, entitled "An Act concerning aliens," which assumes powers over alien friends, not delegated by the Constitution, is not law, but is altogether void, and of no force.

5. *Resolved,* That in addition to the general principle, as well as the express declaration, that powers not delegated are reserved, another and more special provision, inserted in the Constitution from abundant caution, has declared that "the migration or importation of such persons as any of the States now existing shall think proper to admit, shall not be prohibited by the Congress prior to the year 1808;" that this commonwealth does admit the migration of alien friends, described as the subject of the said act concerning aliens: that a provision against prohibiting their migration, is a provision against all acts equivalent thereto, or it would be nugatory: that to remove them when migrated, is equivalent to a prohibition of their migration, and is, therefore, contrary to the said provision of the Constitution, and void.

6. *Resolved,* That the imprisonment of a person under the protection of the laws of this commonwealth, on his failure to obey the simple *order* of the President to depart out of the United States, as is undertaken by said act entitled "An Act concerning aliens," is contrary to the Constitution, one amendment to which has provided that "no person shall be deprived of liberty without due process of law"; and that another having provided that "in all criminal prosecutions the accused shall enjoy the right to public trial by an impartial jury, to be informed of the nature and cause of the accusation, to be confronted with the witnesses against him, to have compulsory process for obtaining witnesses in his favor, and to have the assistance of counsel for his defense," the same act, undertaking to authorize the President to remove a person out of the United States, who is under the protection of the law, on his own suspicion, without accusation, without jury, without public trial, without confrontation of the witnesses against him, without hearing witnesses in his favor, without defense, without counsel, is contrary to the provision also of the Constitution, is therefore not law, but utterly void, and of no force: that transferring the power of judging any person, who is under the protection of the laws, from the courts to the President of the United States, as is undertaken by the same act concerning aliens, is against the article of the Constitution which provides that "the judicial power of the United States shall be vested in courts, the judges of which shall hold their offices during good behavior"; and the said act is void for that reason also. And it is further to be noted, that this transfer of judiciary power is to that magistrate of the General Government who already possesses all the Executive, and a negative on all legislative powers.

7. *Resolved,* That the construction applied by the General Government (as is evidenced by sundry of their proceedings) to those parts of the Constitution of the United States which delegate to Congress a power "to lay and collect taxes, duties, imports, and excises, to pay the debts, and provide for the common defense and general welfare of the United States," and "to make all laws which shall be necessary and proper for carrying into execution the powers vested by the Constitution in the government of the United States, or in any department or officer thereof," goes to the destruction of all limits prescribed to their power by the Constitution: that words meant by the instrument to be subsidiary only to the execution of limited powers, ought not to be so construed as themselves to give unlimited powers, nor a part to be so taken as to destroy the whole residue of that instrument: that the proceedings of the General Government under color of these articles, will be a fit and necessary subject of revisal and correction, at a time of greater tranquillity, while those specified in the preceding resolutions call for immediate redress.

8th. *Resolved,* That a committee of conference and correspondence be appointed, who shall have in charge to communicate the preceding resolutions to the legislatures of the several States; to assure them that this commonwealth continues in the same esteem of their friendship and union which it has manifested from that moment at which a common danger first suggested a common union: that it considers union, for specified national purposes, and particularly to those specified in their late federal compact, to be friendly to the peace, happiness and prosperity of all the States: that faithful to that compact, according to the plain intent and meaning in which it was understood and acceded to by the several parties, it is sincerely anxious for its preservation: that it does also believe, that to take from the States all the powers of self-government and transfer them to a general and consolidated government, without regard to the special delegations and reservations solemnly agreed to in that compact, is not for the peace, happiness or prosperity of these States; and that therefore this commonwealth is determined, as it doubts not its co-States are, to submit to undelegated, and consequently unlimited powers in no man or body of men on earth: that in cases of an abuse of the delegated powers, the members of the General Government, being chosen by the people, a change by the people would be the constitutional remedy; but, where powers are assumed which have not been delegated, a nullification of the act is the rightful remedy: that every State has a natural right in cases not within the compact, (casus non foederis), to nullify of their own authority all assumptions of power by others within their limits: that without this right, they would be under the dominion, absolute and unlimited, of whosoever might exercise this right of judgment for them: that nevertheless, this commonwealth, from motives of regard and respect for its co-States, has wished to communicate with them on the subject: that with them alone it is proper to communicate, they alone being parties to the compact, and solely authorized to judge in the last resort of the powers exercised under it, Congress being not a party, but merely the creature of the compact, and subject as to its assumptions of power to the final judgment of those by whom, and for whose use itself and its powers were all created and modified: that if the acts before specified should stand, these conclusions would flow from them; that the General Government may place any act they think proper on the list of crimes, punish it themselves whether enumerated or not enumerated by the Constitution as cognizable by them: that they may transfer its cognizance to the President, or any other person, who may himself be the accuser, counsel, judge and jury, whose *suspicions* may be the evidence, his *order* the sentence, his *officer* the executioner, and his breast the sole record of the transaction: that a very numerous and valuable description of the inhabitants of these States being, by this precedent, reduced, as outlaws, to the absolute dominion of one man, and the barrier of the Constitution thus swept away from us all, no rampart now remains against the passions and the powers of a majority in Congress to protect from a like exportation, or other more grievous punishment, the minority of the same body, the legislatures, judges, governors, and counsellors of the States, nor their other peaceable inhabitants, who may venture to reclaim the constitutional rights and liberties of the States and people, or who for other causes, good or bad, may be obnoxious to the views, or marked by the suspicions of the President, or be thought dangerous to his or their election, or other interests, public or personal: that the friendless alien has indeed been selected as the safest subject of a first experiment; but the citizen will soon follow, or rather, has already followed, for already has a sedition act marked him as its prey: that these and successive acts of the same character, unless arrested at the threshold, necessarily drive these States into revolution and blood, and will furnish new calumnies against republican government, and new pretexts for those who wish it to be believed that man cannot be governed but by a rod of iron: that it would be a dangerous delusion were a confidence in the men of our choice to silence our fears for the safety of our rights: that confidence is everywhere the parent of despotism—free government is founded in jealousy, and not in confidence; it is jealousy and not confidence which prescribes limited constitutions to bind down those whom we are obliged to trust with power: that our Constitution has accordingly fixed the limits to which, and no further, our confidence may go; and let the honest advocate of confidence read the alien and sedition acts, and say if the Constitution has not been wise in fixing limits to the government it created, and whether we should be wise in destroying those limits. Let him say what the government is, if it be not a tyranny, which the men of our choice have conferred on our President, and the President of our choice has assented to, and accepted over the friendly strangers to whom the mild spirit of our country and its laws have pledged hospitality and protection: that the men of our choice have more respected the bare *suspicions* of the President, than the solid right of innocence, the claims of justification, the sacred force of truth, and the forms and substance of law and justice. In questions of power, then, let no more be heard of confidence in man, but bind him down from mischief by the chains of the Constitution. That this commonwealth does therefore call on its co-States for an expression of their sentiments on the acts concerning aliens, and for the punishment of certain crimes herein before specified, plainly declaring whether these acts are or are not authorized by the federal compact. And it doubts not that their sense will be so announced as to prove their attachment unaltered to limited government, whether general or particular. And that the rights and liberties of their co-States will be exposed to no dangers by remaining embarked in a common bottom with their own. That they will concur with this commonwealth in considering the said acts as so palpably against the Constitution as to amount to an undisguised declaration that compact is not meant to be the measure of the powers of the General Government, but that it will proceed in the exercise over these States, of all powers whatsoever: that they will view this as seizing the rights of the States, and consolidating them in the hands of the General Government, with a power assumed to bind the States, not merely as the cases made federal (casus foederis), but in all cases whatsoever, by laws made, not with their consent, but by others against their consent: that this would

be to surrender the form of government we have chosen, and live under one deriving its powers from its own will, and not from our authority; and that the co-States, recurring to their natural right in cases not made federal, will concur in declaring these acts void, and of no force, and will each take measures of its own for providing that neither these acts, nor any others of the General Government not plainly and intentionally authorized by the Constitution, shall be exercised within their respective territories.

9th. *Resolved,* That the said committee be authorized to communicate by writing or personal conferences, at any times or places whatever, with any person or persons who may be appointed by any one or more co-States to correspond or confer with them; and that they lay their proceedings before the next session of Assembly.

JAMES MADISON

The Virginia Resolutions
21 December 1798

In the House of Delegates

Resolved, that the General Assembly of Virginia doth unequivocally express a firm resolution to maintain and defend the constitution of the United States, and the Constitution of this state, against every aggression, either foreign or domestic, and that they will support the government of the United States in all measures warranted by the former.

That this Assembly most solemnly declares a warm attachment to the Union of the States, to maintain which, it pledges all its powers; and that for this end, it is their duty, to watch over and oppose every infraction of those principles, which constitute the only basis of that union, because a faithful observance of them, can alone secure its existence, and the public happiness.

That this Assembly doth explicitly and peremptorily declare, that it views the powers of the federal government, as resulting from the compact to which the states are parties; as limited by the plain sense and intention of the instrument constituting that compact; as no farther valid than they are authorized by the grants enumerated in that compact, and that in case of a deliberate, palpable and dangerous exercise of other powers not granted by the said compact, the states who are parties thereto have the right, and are in duty bound, to interpose for arresting the progress of the evil, and for maintaining within their respective limits, the authorities, rights and liberties appertaining to them.

That the General Assembly doth also express its deep regret that a spirit has in sundry instances, been manifested by the federal government, to enlarge its powers by forced constructions of the constitutional charter which defines them; and that indications have appeared of a design to expound certain general phrases (which having been copied from the very limited grant of powers in the former articles of confederation were the less liable to be misconstrued) so as to destroy the meaning and effect of the particular enumeration, which necessarily explains and limits the general phrases; and so as to consolidate the states by degrees into one sovereignty, the obvious tendency and inevitable consequence of which would be, to transform the present republican system of the United States, into an absolute, or at best a mixed monarchy.

That the General Assembly doth particularly protest against the palpable and alarming infractions of the constitution, in the two late cases of the "alien and sedition acts," passed at the last session of Congress; the first of which exercises a power no where delegated to the federal government; and which by uniting legislative and judicial powers, to those of executive, subverts the general principles of free government, as well as the particular organization and positive provisions of the federal constitution: and the other of which acts, exercises in like manner a power not delegated by the constitution, but on the contrary expressly and positively forbidden by one of the amendments thereto; a power which more than any other ought to produce universal alarm, because it is levelled against that right of freely examining public characters and measures, and of free communication among the people thereon, which has ever been justly deemed, the only effectual guardian of every other right.

That this State having by its convention which ratified the federal constitution, expressly declared, "that among other essential rights, the liberty of conscience and of the press cannot be cancelled, abridged, restrained or modified by any authority of the United States" and from its extreme anxiety to guard these rights from every possible attack of sophistry or ambition, having with other states recommended an amendment for that purpose, which amendment was in due time annexed to the Constitution, it would mark a

reproachful inconsistency and criminal degeneracy, if an indifference were now shown to the most palpable violation of one of the rights thus declared and secured, and to the establishment of a precedent which may be fatal to the other.

That the good people of this Commonwealth having ever felt and continuing to feel the most sincere affection for their brethren of the other states, the truest anxiety for establishing and perpetuating the union of all, and the most scrupulous fidelity to that Constitution which is the pledge of mutual friendship, and the instrument of mutual happiness, the General Assembly doth solemnly appeal to the like dispositions of the other States, in confidence that they will concur with this Commonwealth in declaring, as it does hereby declare, that the acts aforesaid are unconstitutional, and that the necessary and proper measures will be taken by each, for cooperating with this State in maintaining unimpaired the authorities, rights, and liberties, reserved to the States respectively, or to the people.

That the Governor be desired to transmit a copy of the foregoing resolutions to the Executive authority of each of the other States, with a request, that the same may be communicated to the Legislature thereof.

And that a copy be furnished to each of the Senators and Representatives, representing this State in the Congress of the United States.

State Replies to the Resolutions

Ten of the fourteen other states responded to Kentucky and/or Virginia, in every case condemning state interference in the federal sphere. The resolutions of Rhode Island and New Hampshire were representative in content and tone.

The State of Rhode Island and Providence Plantations to Virginia

February 1799

Certain resolutions of the Legislature of Virginia, passed on the 21st of December last, being communicated to the Assembly,—

1. *Resolved*, That, in the opinion of this legislature, the second section of the third article of the Constitution of the United States, in these words, to wit—"The judicial power shall extend to all cases arising under the laws of the

United States"—vests in the federal courts, exclusively, and in the Supreme Court of the United States, ultimately, the authority of deciding on the constitutionality of any act or law of the Congress of the United States.

2. *Resolved,* That for any state legislature to assume that authority would be—

1st. Blending together legislative and judicial powers;

2nd. Hazarding an interruption of the peace of the states by civil discord, in case of a diversity of opinions among the state legislatures; each state having, in that case, no resort for vindicating its own opinions but the strength of its own arm;

3rd. Submitting most important questions of law to less competent tribunals; and,

4th. An infraction of the Constitution of the United States, expressed in plain terms.

3. *Resolved,* That although, for the above reasons, this legislature, in their public capacity, do not feel themselves authorized to consider and decide on the constitutionality of the Sedition and Alien Laws (so called), yet they are called upon by the exigency of this occasion to declare that, in their private opinions, these laws are within the powers delegated to Congress, and promotive of the welfare of the United States.

4. *Resolved,* That the governor communicate these resolutions to the supreme executive of the state of Virginia and at the same time express to him that this legislature cannot contemplate, without extreme concern and regret, the many evil and fatal consequences which may flow from the very unwarrantable resolutions aforesaid. . . .

New Hampshire Resolution on the Virginia and Kentucky Resolutions

15 June 1799

The legislature of New Hampshire, having taken into consideration certain resolutions of the General Assembly of Virginia, dated December 21, 1798; also certain resolutions of the legislature of Kentucky, of the 10th of November 1798—

Resolved, That the legislature of New Hampshire unequivocally express a firm resolution to maintain and defend the Constitution of the United States, and the constitution of this state, against every aggression, either foreign or domestic, and that they will support the government of the United States in all measures warranted by the former.

That the state legislatures are not the proper tribunals to determine the constitutionality of the laws of the general government; that the duty of such decision is properly and exclusively confided to the judicial department.

That if the legislature of New Hampshire, for mere speculative purposes, were to express an opinion on the acts of the general government commonly called "the Alien and Sedition Bills," that opinion would unreservedly be that those acts are constitutional and, in the present critical situation of our country, highly expedient.

That the constitutionality and expediency of the acts aforesaid have been very ably advocated and clearly demonstrated by many citizens of the United States, more especially by the minority of the General Assembly of Virginia. The legislature of New Hampshire, therefore, deem it unnecessary, by any train of arguments, to attempt further illustration of the propositions, the truth of which, it is confidently believed, at this day, is very generally seen and acknowledged.

Congressional Report Defending the Alien and Sedition Laws

21 February 1799

The committee to whom were referred the memorials of sundry inhabitants . . . , complaining of the act entitled "An act concerning aliens," and other late acts of Congress, submit the following report:

It is the professed object of these petitions to solicit a repeal of two acts passed during the last session of Congress, the one "An act concerning aliens," the other "An act in addition to an act for the punishment of certain crimes against the United States," on the ground of their being unconstitutional, oppressive, and impolitic.

The committee cannot, however, forbear to notice that the principal measures hitherto adopted for repelling the aggressions and insults of France have not escaped animadversion.

Complaints are particularly directed against the laws providing for a navy; for augmenting the army; authorizing a provisional army and corps of volunteers; for laying a duty on stamped vellum, parchment, and paper; assessing and collecting direct taxes; and authorizing loans for the public service.

With these topics of complaint, in some of the petitions, are intermingled invectives against the policy of the government from an early period and insinuations derogatory to the character of the legislature and of the administration. . . .

The act concerning aliens and the act in addition to the act entitled an act for the punishment of certain crimes shall be first considered.

Their *constitutionality* is impeached. It is contended that Congress have no power to pass a law for removing aliens.

To this it is answered that the asylum given by a nation to foreigners is mere matter of favor, resumable at the public will. On this point abundant authorities might be adduced, but the common practice of nations attests the principle.

The right of removing aliens, as an incident to the power of war and peace, according to the theory of the Constitution, belongs to the government of the United States. By the fourth section of the fourth article of the Constitution, Congress is required to protect each state from invasion, and is vested by the eighth section of the fifth article with power to make all laws which shall be proper to carry into effect all powers vested by the Constitution in the government of the United States or in any department or officer thereof; and to remove from the country, in times of hostility, dangerous aliens, who may be employed in preparing the way for invasion, is a measure necessary for the purpose of preventing invasion and, of course, a measure that Congress is empowered to adopt. . . .

This law is said to violate that part of the Constitution which provides that the trial of all crimes, except in cases of impeachment, shall be by jury; whereas this act invests the President with power to send away aliens on his own suspicion, and thus to inflict punishment without trial by jury.

It is answered, in the first place, that the Constitution was made for citizens, not for aliens, who of consequence have no rights under it, but remain in the country and enjoy the benefit of the laws, not as matter of right, but merely as matter of favor and permission; which favor and permission may be withdrawn whenever the government charged with the general welfare shall judge their further continuance dangerous.

It is answered, in the second place, that the provisions in the Constitution relative to presentment and trial of offenses by juries, do not apply to the revocation of an asylum given to aliens. Those provisions solely respect crimes, and the alien may be removed without having committed any offense, merely from motives of policy or security. The citizen, being a member of society, has a right to remain in the country, of which he cannot be disfranchised, except for offenses first ascertained on presentment and trial by jury.

It is answered, thirdly, that the removal of aliens, though it may be inconvenient to them, cannot be considered as a punishment inflicted for an offense, but, as before remarked, merely the removal from motives of general safety of an indulgence which there is danger of their abusing, and which we are in no manner bound to grant or continue.

The "Act in addition to an act entitled an act for the punishment of certain crimes against the United States," commonly called the "sedition act," contains provisions of a two-fold nature: first, against seditious acts; and, second, against libelous and seditious writings. The first have never been complained of, nor has any objection been made to its validity. The objection applies solely to the second; and on the ground, in the first place, that Congress have no power by the Constitution to pass any act for punishing libels, no such power being expressly given; and all powers not given to Congress being reserved to the states, respectively, or the people thereof.

To this objection it is answered that a law to punish false, scandalous, and malicious writings against the government, with intent to stir up sedition, is a law necessary for carrying into effect the power vested by the Constitution in the government of the United States and in the departments and officers thereof, and, consequently, such a law as Congress may pass; because the direct tendency of such writings is to obstruct the acts of the government by exciting opposition to them, to endanger its existence, by rendering it odious and contemptible in the eyes of the people, and to produce seditious combinations against the laws, the power to punish which has never been questioned; because it would be manifestly absurd to suppose that a government might punish sedition and yet be void of power to prevent it by punishing those acts which plainly and necessarily lead to it; and because, under the general power to make all laws proper and necessary for carrying into effect the powers vested by the Constitution in the government of the United States, Congress has passed many laws for which no express provision can be found in the Constitution, and the constitutionality of which has never been questioned; such as the first section of the act now under consideration, for punishing seditious combinations; the act passed during the present session for punishing persons who, without authority from the government, shall carry on any correspondence relative to foreign affairs with any foreign government; the act for the punishment of certain crimes against the United States, which defines and punishes misprision of treason; the tenth and twelfth sections, which declare the punishment of accessories to piracy, and of persons who shall confederate to become pirates themselves, or to induce others to become so; the fifteenth section, which inflicts a penalty on those who steal or falsify the record of any court of the United States; the eighteenth and twenty-first sections, which provide for the punishment of persons committing perjury in any court of the United States, or attempting to bribe any of their judges; the twenty-second section, which punishes those who obstruct or resist the process of any court of the United States; and the twenty-third, against rescuing offenders who have been convicted of any capital offense before those courts; provisions, none of which are expressly authorized, but which have been considered as constitutional because they are necessary and proper for carrying into effect certain powers expressly given to Congress.

It is objected to this act, in the second place, that it is expressly contrary to that part of the Constitution which declares that "Congress shall make no law respecting an establishment of religion, or prohibiting the free exercise thereof, or abridging the liberty of the press." The act in question is said to be an abridgment of the liberty of the press and therefore unconstitutional.

To this it is answered, in the first place, that the liberty of the press consists, not in a license for every man to publish what he pleases, without being liable to punishment if he should abuse this license to the injury of others, but in a permission to publish, without previous restraint, whatever he may think proper, being answerable to the public and individuals for any abuse of this permission to their prejudice; in like manner as the liberty of speech does not authorize a man to speak malicious slanders against his neighbor, nor the liberty of action justify him in going by violence into another man's house, or in assaulting any person whom he may meet in the streets. In the several states the liberty of the press has always been understood in this manner, and no other; and the constitution of every state which has been

framed and adopted since the Declaration of Independence asserts "the liberty of the press;" while in several, if not all, their laws provide for the punishment of libellous publications, which would be a manifest absurdity and contradiction if the liberty of the press meant to publish any and every thing without being amenable to the laws for the abuse of this license. According to this just, legal, and universally admitted definition of "the liberty of the press," a law to restrain its licentiousness in publishing false, scandalous, and malicious libels against the government, cannot be considered as an "abridgment" of its "liberty."

It is answered, in the second place, that the liberty of the press did never extend, according to the laws of any state, or of the United States, or of England, from whence our laws are derived, to the publication of false, scandalous, and malicious writings against the government, written or published with intent to do mischief, such publications being unlawful and punishable in every state; from whence it follows, undeniably, that a law to punish seditious and malicious publications is not an abridgment of the "liberty of the press"; for it would be a manifest absurdity to say that a man's liberty was abridged by punishing him for doing that which he never had a liberty to do.

It is answered, thirdly, that the act in question cannot be unconstitutional because it makes nothing penal that was not penal before, and gives no new powers to the court, but is merely declaratory of the common law and useful for rendering that law more generally known and more easily understood. This cannot be denied if it be admitted, as it must be, that false, scandalous, and malicious libels against the government of the country, published with intent to do mischief, are punishable by the common law; for, by the second section of the third article of the Constitution, the judicial power of the United States is expressly extended to all offenses arising under the Constitution. By the Constitution, the government of the United States is established, for many important objects, *as the government of the country;* and libels against that government, therefore, are offenses arising under the Constitution, and consequently are punishable at common law by the courts of the United States. The act, indeed, is so far from having *extended* the law and the power of the court, that it has abridged both and has enlarged instead of abridging the "liberty of the press"; for, at common law, libels against the government might be punished with fine and imprisonment at the discretion of the court, whereas the act limits the fine to two thousand dollars and the imprisonment to two years; and it also allows the party accused to give the *truth* in evidence for his justification, which, by the common law, was expressly forbidden.

And lastly, it is answered that had the Constitution intended to prohibit Congress from legislating at all on the subject of the press, which is the construction whereon the objections to this law are founded, it would have used the same expressions as in that part of the clause which relates to religion and religious tests; whereas the words are wholly different: "Congress," says the Constitution [First Amendment], "shall make no law *respecting* an establishment of religion, or *prohibiting* the free exercise thereof or *abridging* the freedom of speech, or the press." Here it is manifest that the Constitution intended to prohibit Congress from legislating at all on the subject of *religious establishments,* and the prohibition is made in the most express terms. Had the same intention prevailed respecting the press, the same expressions would have been used, and Congress would have been "prohibited from passing any law *respecting* the press." They are not, however, "prohibited" from legislating at all on the subject, but merely from *abridging* the liberty of the press. It is evident they may legislate respecting the press, may pass laws for its regulation, and to punish those who pervert it into an engine of mischief, provided those laws do not "abridge" its "liberty." Its *liberty,* according to the well-known and universally admitted definition, consists in permission to publish, without previous restraint upon the press, but subject to punishment afterwards for improper publications. A law, therefore, to impose previous restraint upon the press, and not one to inflict punishment on wicked and malicious publications, would be a law to abridge the liberty of the press, and, as such, unconstitutional.

The foregoing reasoning is submitted as vindicating the validity of the laws in question.

Although the committee believe that each of the measures adopted by Congress during the last session is susceptible of an analytical justification on the principles of the Constitution and national policy, yet they prefer to rest their vindication on the true ground of considering them as parts of a general system of defense, adapted to a crisis of extraordinary difficulty and danger.

It cannot be denied that the power to declare war, to raise and support armies, to provide and maintain a navy, to suppress insurrections, and repel invasions, and also the power to defray the necessary expense by loans or taxes, is vested in Congress. Unfortunately for the present generation of mankind, a contest has arisen and rages with unabated ferocity, which has desolated the fairest portions of Europe and shaken the fabric of society through the civilized world. From the nature and effects of this contest, as developed in the experience of nations, melancholy inferences must be drawn, that it is unsusceptible of the restraints which have either designated the objects, limited the duration, or mitigated the horrors of national contentions. In the internal history of France, and in the conduct of her forces and partisans in the countries which have fallen under her power, the public councils of our country were required to discern the dangers which threatened the United States, and to guard not only against the usual consequences of war, but also against the effects of an unprecedented combination to establish new principles of social action on the subversion of religion, morality, law, and government. Will it be said that the raising of a small army and an eventual provision for drawing into the public service a considerable proportion of the whole force of the country was, in such a crisis, unwise or improvident?

If such should be the assertion, let it be candidly considered whether some of our fertile and flourishing states did not, six months since, present as alluring objects for the gratification of ambition or cupidity as the inhospitable climate of Egypt. What then appeared to be the comparative difficulties between invading America and subverting the British power in the East Indies? If this was a professed, not real object of the enterprise, let it be asked if the Sultan of the Ottoman empire was not really the friend of France at the time when his unsuspecting dependencies were invaded; and whether the United States were not, at the same time, loaded with insults and assailed with hostility? If, however, it is asserted that the system of France is hostile only to despotic or monarchical governments, and that our security arises from the form of our Constitution, let Switzerland, first divided and disarmed by perfidious seductions, now agonized by relentless power, illustrate the consequences of similar credulity. Is it necessary at this time to vindicate the naval armament? Rather may not the inquiry be boldly made, whether the guardians of the public weal would not have deserved and received the reproaches of every patriotic American if a contemptible naval force had been longer permitted to intercept our necessary supplies, destroy our principal source of revenue, and seize, at the entrance of our harbors and rivers, the products of our industry destined to our foreign markets? If such injuries were at all to be repelled, is not the restriction which confined captures by our ships solely to armed vessels of France a sufficient proof of our moderation?

If, therefore, naval and military preparations were necessary, a provision of funds to defray the consequent expenses was of course indispensable; a review of all the measures that have been adopted since the establishment of the government will prove that Congress have not been unmindful of the wishes of the American people to avoid an accumulation of the public debt; and the success which has attended these measures affords conclusive evidence of the sincerity of their intentions. But to purchase sufficient quantities of military supplies to establish a navy and provide for all the contingencies of an army without recourse to new taxes and loans, was impracticable; both measures were, in fact, adopted. In devising a mode of taxation, the convenience and ease of the least wealthy class of the people were consulted as much as possible; and, although the expenses of assessment have furnished a topic of complaint, it is found that the allowances are barely sufficient to ensure the execution of the law, even aided as they are by the disinterested and patriotic exertions of worthy citizens; besides, it ought to be remembered that the expenses of organizing a new system should not, on any principle, be regarded as a permanent burden on the public.

In authorizing a loan of money, Congress have not been inattentive to prevent a permanent debt; in this particular, also, the public opinion and interest have been consulted. On considering the law, as well as the manner in which it is proposed to be carried into execution, the committee are well satisfied in finding any excess in the immediate charge upon the revenue is likely to be compensated by the facility of redemption which is secured to the government.

The alien and sedition acts, so called, form a part, and in the opinion of the committee an essential part, in these precautionary and protective measures adopted for our security.

France appears to have an organized system of conduct towards foreign nations to bring them within the sphere and under the dominion of her influence and control. It has been unremittingly pursued under all the changes of her internal polity. Her means are in wonderful coincidence with her ends: among these, and not least successful, is the direction and employment of the active and versatile talents of her citizens abroad as emissaries and spies. With

a numerous body of French citizens and other foreigners, and admonished by the passing scenes in other countries as well as by aspects in our own, knowing they had the power, and believing it to be their duty, Congress passed the law respecting aliens, directing the *dangerous* and *suspected* to be removed and leaving to the *inoffensive* and *peaceable* a safe asylum.

The principles of the sedition law, so called, are among the most ancient principles of our governments. They have been engrafted into statutes, or practiced upon as maxims of the common law, according as occasion required. They were often and justly applied in the revolutionary war. Is it not strange that now they should first be denounced as oppressive, when they have long been recognized in the jurisprudence of these States?

The necessity that dictated these acts, in the opinion of the committee, still exists.

So eccentric are the movements of the French government that we can form no opinion of their future designs towards our country. They may recede from the tone of menace and insolence to employ the arts of seduction, before they astonish us with their ultimate designs. Our safety consists in the wisdom of the public councils, a cooperation, on the part of the people with the government, by supporting the measures provided for repelling aggressions, and an obedience to the social laws.

After a particular and general review of the whole subject referred to their consideration, the committee see no ground for rescinding these acts of the legislature. The complaints preferred by some of the petitioners may be fairly attributed to a diversity of sentiment naturally to be expected among a people of various habits and education, widely dispersed over an extensive country; the innocent misconceptions of the American people will, however, yield to reflection and argument, and from *them* no danger is to be apprehended.

In such of the petitions as are conceived in a style of vehement and acrimonious remonstrance, the committee perceive too plain indications of the principles of that exotic system which convulses the civilized world. With this system, however organized, the public councils cannot safely parley or temporize, whether it assumes the guise of patriotism to mislead the affections of the people; whether it be employed in forming projects of local and eccentric ambition, or shall appear in the more generous form of open hostility, it ought to be regarded as the bane of public as well as private tranquillity and order.

Those to whom the management of public affairs is now confided cannot be justified in yielding any established principles of law or government to the suggestions of modern theory; their duty requires them to respect the lessons of experience and transmit to posterity the civil and religious privileges which are the birthright of our country, and which it was the great object of our happy Constitution to secure and perpetuate.

Impressed with these sentiments, the committee beg leave to report the following resolutions:

Resolved, that it is inexpedient to repeal the act passed the last session, entitled "An act concerning aliens."

Resolved, That it is inexpedient to repeal the act passed the last session, entitled "An act in addition to the act entitled 'An act for the punishment of certain crimes against the United States.'"

Resolved, That it is inexpedient to repeal any of the laws respecting the navy, military establishment, or revenue of the United States.

JAMES MADISON

The Report of 1800

Although he had retired from national office in 1797, Madison stood for reelection to the Virginia House of Delegates in 1799 in order to defend the resolutions of 1798 against the criticisms of the other states. His Report of 1800, dated 7 January, is lengthy, but it is also one of the most important documents of the 1790s. It not only refined the doctrines of 1798, it would also prove a classic defense of First Amendment freedoms.

Whatever room might be found in the proceedings of some of the states who have disapproved of the resolutions of the General Assembly of this commonwealth, passed on the 21st day of December, 1798, for painful remarks on the spirit and manner of those proceedings, it appears to the committee most consistent with the duty as well as dignity of the General Assembly to hasten an oblivion of every circumstance which might be construed into a diminution of mutual respect, confidence, and affection among the members of the union.

The committee have deemed it a more useful task to revise with a critical eye the resolutions which have met

with this disapprobation; to examine fully the several objections and arguments which have appeared against them; and to inquire, whether there be any errors of fact, of principle, or of reasoning which the candor of the General Assembly ought to acknowledge and correct. . . .

The third resolution is in the words following:

That this Assembly doth explicitly and peremptorily declare that it views the powers of the Federal Government as resulting from the compact to which the states are parties, as limited by the plain sense and intention of the instrument constituting that compact; as no farther valid than they are authorized by the grants enumerated in that compact; and that in case of a deliberate, palpable and dangerous exercise of other powers, not granted by the said compact, the states who are parties thereto have the right, and are in duty bound, to interpose for arresting the progress of the evil and for maintaining within their respective limits the authorities, rights and liberties appertaining to them.

On this resolution, the committee have bestowed all the attention which its importance merits: They have scanned it not merely with a strict, but with a severe eye; and they feel confidence in pronouncing that in its just and fair construction, it is unexceptionably true in its several positions, as well as constitutional and conclusive in its inferences.

The resolution declares, *first,* that "it views the powers of the Federal Government as resulting from the compact to which the states are parties," in other words, that the federal powers are derived from the Constitution, and that the Constitution is a compact to which the states are parties. . . .

. . . The committee satisfy themselves here with briefly remarking that in all the co-temporary discussions and comments which the Constitution underwent, it was constantly justified and recommended on the ground that the powers not given to the government were withheld from it; and that if any doubt could have existed on this subject, under the original text of the Constitution, it is removed as far as words could remove it by the [tenth] amendment, now a part of the Constitution, which expressly declares "that the powers not delegated to the United States, by the Constitution, nor prohibited by it to the states, are reserved to the states respectively, or to the people."

The other position involved in this branch of the resolution, namely, "that the states are parties to the Constitution or compact," is in the judgment of the committee equally free from objection. It is indeed true that the term "States" is sometimes used in a vague sense, and sometimes in different senses, according to the subject to which it is applied. Thus it sometimes means the separate sections of territory occupied by the political societies within each; sometimes the particular governments established by those societies; sometimes those societies as organized into those particular governments; and lastly, it means the people composing those political societies in their highest sovereign capacity. Although it might be wished that the perfection of language admitted less diversity in the signification of the same words, yet little inconveniency is produced by it where the true sense can be collected with certainty from the different applications. In the present instance, whatever different constructions of the term "States" in the resolution may have been entertained, all will at least concur in that last mentioned; because in that sense the Constitution was submitted to the "States": In that sense the "States" ratified it; and in that sense of the term "States," they are consequently parties to the pact from which the powers of the Federal Government result.

The next position is that the General Assembly views the powers of the Federal Government "as limited by the plain sense and intention of the instrument constituting that compact," and "as no farther valid than they are authorized by the grants therein enumerated." It does not seem possible that any just objection can lie against either of these clauses. The first amounts merely to a declaration that the compact ought to have the interpretation plainly intended by the parties to it; the other, to a declaration that it ought to have the execution and effect intended by them. If the powers granted be valid, it is solely because they are granted; and if the granted powers are valid because granted, all other powers not granted must not be valid.

The resolution, having taken this view of the federal compact, proceeds to infer "that in case of a deliberate, palpable, and dangerous exercise of other powers not granted by the said compact, the states who are parties thereto have the right, and are in duty bound, to interpose for arresting the progress of the evil and for maintaining within their respective limits the authorities, rights and liberties appertaining to them."

It appears to your committee to be a plain principle, founded in common sense, illustrated by common practice, and essential to the nature of compacts, that where resort can be had to no tribunal superior to the authority of the parties, the parties themselves must be the rightful judges in the last resort whether the bargain made has been pursued or violated. The Constitution of the United States was formed by the sanction of the states, given by each in its sovereign capacity. It adds to the stability and dignity as well as to the authority of the Constitution that it rests on this legitimate and solid foundation. The states then being the parties to the constitutional compact, and in their sovereign capacity, it follows of necessity that there can be no tribunal above their authority to decide in the last resort whether the compact made by them be violated; and consequently that as the parties to it, they must themselves decide in the last resort such questions as may be of sufficient magnitude to require their interposition.

It does not follow, however, that because the states as sovereign parties to their constitutional compact must ultimately decide whether it has been violated, that such a decision ought to be interposed either in a hasty manner or on doubtful and inferior occasions. Even in the case of ordinary conventions between different nations, where, by the strict rule of interpretation, a breach of a part may be deemed a breach of the whole, every part being deemed a condition of every other part and of the whole, it is always laid down that the breach must be both wilful and material to justify an application of the rule. But in the case of an intimate and constitutional union, like that of the United States, it is evident that the interposition of the parties in their sovereign capacity can be called for by occasions only deeply and essentially affecting the vital principles of their political system.

The resolution has accordingly guarded against any misapprehension of its object by expressly requiring for such as interposition "the case of a *deliberate, palpable* and *dangerous* breach of the Constitution, by the exercise of *powers not granted* by it." It must be a case, not of a light and transient nature, but of a nature *dangerous* to the great purposes for which the Constitution was established. It must be a case, moreover, not obscure or doubtful in its construction, but plain and *palpable*. Lastly, it must be a case not resulting from a partial consideration or hasty determination, but a case stamped with a final consideration and *deliberate* adherence. It is not necessary, because the resolution does not require, that the question should be discussed how far the exercise of any particular power ungranted by the Constitution would justify the interposition of the parties to it. As cases might easily be stated which none would contend ought to fall within that description, cases, on the other hand, might, with equal ease, be stated, so flagrant and so fatal as to unite every opinion in placing them within the description.

But the resolution has done more than guard against misconstruction by expressly referring to cases of a *deliberate, palpable,* and *dangerous* nature. It specifies the object of the interposition which it contemplates to be solely that of arresting the progress of the *evil* of usurpation and of maintaining the authorities, rights and liberties appertaining to the states, as parties to the Constitution.

From this view of the resolution, it would seem inconceivable that it can incur any just disapprobation from those who, laying aside all momentary impressions and recollecting the genuine source and object of the federal constitution, shall candidly and accurately interpret the meaning of the General Assembly. If the deliberate exercise of dangerous powers, palpably withheld by the Constitution, could not justify the parties to it in interposing even so far as to arrest the progress of the evil, and thereby to preserve the Constitution itself as well as to provide for the safety of the parties to it, there would be an end to all relief from usurped power, and a direct subversion of the rights specified or recognized under all the state constitutions, as well as a plain denial of the fundamental principle on which our independence itself was declared.

But it is objected that the judicial authority is to be regarded as the sole expositor of the Constitution in the last resort; and it may be asked for what reason the declaration by the General Assembly, supposing it to be theoretically true, could be required at the present day and in so solemn a manner.

On this objection it might be observed, *first,* that there may be instances of usurped power which the forms of the Constitution would never draw within the control of the judicial department; secondly, that if the decision of the judiciary be raised above the authority of the sovereign parties to the Constitution, the decisions of the other departments, not carried by the forms of the Constitution before the judiciary, must be equally authoritative and final with the decisions of that department. But the proper answer to the objection is, that the resolution of the General Assembly relates to those great and extraordinary cases in which all the forms of the Constitution may prove ineffectual against infractions dangerous to the essential rights of the parties to it. The resolution supposes that dangerous powers not delegated may not only be usurped and executed by the other departments, but that the judicial

department also may exercise or sanction dangerous powers beyond the grant of the Constitution; and consequently that the ultimate right of the parties to the Constitution to judge whether the compact has been dangerously violated must extend to violations by one delegated authority as well as by another, by the judiciary as well as by the executive or the legislature.

However true therefore it may be that the judicial department is, in all questions submitted to it by the forms of the Constitution, to decide in the last resort, this resort must necessarily be deemed the last in relation to the authorities of the other departments of the government; not in relation to the rights of the parties to the constitutional compact, from which the judicial as well as the other departments hold their delegated trusts. On any other hypothesis, the delegation of judicial power would annul the authority delegating it; and the concurrence of this department with the others in usurped powers might subvert forever, and beyond the possible reach of any rightful remedy, the very Constitution which all were instituted to preserve.

The truth declared in the resolution being established, the expediency of making the declaration at the present day may safely be left to the temperate consideration and candid judgment of the American public. It will be remembered that a frequent recurrence to fundamental principles is solemnly enjoined by most of the state constitutions, and particularly by our own, as a necessary safeguard against the danger of degeneracy to which republics are liable, as well as other governments, though in a less degree than others. And a fair comparison of the political doctrines not unfrequent at the present day with those which characterized the epoch of our Revolution, and which form the basis of our republican constitutions, will best determine whether the declaratory recurrence here made to those principles ought to be viewed as unseasonable and improper or as a vigilant discharge of an important duty. The authority of constitutions over governments, and of the sovereignty of the people over constitutions, are truths which are at all times necessary to be kept in mind; and at no time perhaps more necessary than at the present.

The fourth resolution stands as follows:—

That the General Assembly doth also express its deep regret that a spirit has in sundry instances been manifested by the Federal Government to enlarge its powers by forced constructions of the constitutional charter which defines them; and that indications have appeared of a design to expound certain general phrases (which, having been copied from the very limited grant of powers in the former Articles of Confederation were the less liable to be misconstrued) so as to destroy the meaning and effect of the particular enumeration which necessarily explains and limits the general phrases; and so as to consolidate the states by degrees into one sovereignty, the obvious tendency and inevitable result of which would be to transform the present republican system of the United States into an absolute, or at best a mixed monarchy.

The *first* question to be considered is whether a spirit has in sundry instances been manifested by the Federal Government to enlarge its powers by forced constructions of the constitutional charter.

The General Assembly having declared their opinion merely by regreting in general terms that forced constructions for enlarging the federal powers have taken place, it does not appear to the committee necessary to go into a specification of every instance to which the resolution may allude. The Alien and Sedition Acts being particularly named in a succeeding resolution are of course to be understood as included in the allusion. Omitting others which have less occupied public attention, or been less extensively regarded as unconstitutional, the resolution may be presumed to refer particularly to the bank law, which from the circumstances of its passage as well as the latitude of construction on which it is founded, strikes the attention with singular force; and the carriage tax, distinguished also by circumstances in its history having a similar tendency. Those instances alone, if resulting from forced construction and calculated to enlarge the powers of the Federal Government, as the committee cannot but conceive to be the case, sufficiently warrant this part of the resolution. The committee have not thought it incumbent on them to extend their attention to laws which have been objected to rather as varying the constitutional distribution of powers in the Federal Government than as an absolute enlargement of them; because instances of this sort, however important in their principles and tendencies, do not appear to fall strictly within the text under review.

The other questions presenting themselves are—
1. Whether indications have appeared of a design to expound certain general phrases copied from the "Articles of Confederation" so as to destroy the effect of the particular enumeration explaining and limiting their meaning.
2. Whether this exposition would by degrees consolidate the states into one sovereignty.   3. Whether the tendency and result of this consolidation would be to transform the republican system of the United States into a monarchy.

1. The general phrases here meant must be those "of providing for the common defense and general welfare."

In the "Articles of Confederation," the phrases are used as follows, in article VIII. "All charges of war, and all other expenses that shall be incurred *for the common defense and general welfare*, and allowed by the United States in Congress assembled, shall be defrayed out of a common treasury.". . .

In the existing Constitution, they make the following part of section 8. "The Congress shall have power, to lay and collect taxes, duties, imposts and excises to pay the debts, and provide for the common defense and general welfare of the United States."

This similarity in the use of these phrases in the two great federal charters might well be considered as rendering their meaning less liable to be misconstrued in the latter; because it will scarcely be said that in the former they were ever understood to be either a general grant of power or to authorize the requisition or application of money by the old Congress to the common defense and general welfare except in the cases afterwards enumerated which explained and limited their meaning; and if such was the limited meaning attached to these phrases in the very instrument revised and remodelled by the present Constitution, it can never be supposed that when copied into this Constitution, a different meaning ought to be attached to them.

That notwithstanding this remarkable security against misconstruction, a design has been indicated to expound these phrases in the Constitution so as to destroy the effect of the particular enumeration of powers by which it explains and limits them, must have fallen under the observation of those who have attended to the course of public transactions. Not to multiply proofs on this subject, it will suffice to refer to the debates of the federal legislature in which arguments have on different occasions been drawn with apparent effect from these phrases in their indefinite meaning.

To these indications might be added, without looking farther, the official report on manufactures by the late Secretary of the Treasury, made on the 5th of December, 1791; and the report of a committee of Congress in January 1797 on the promotion of agriculture. In the first of these it is expressly contended to belong "to the discretion of the national legislature to pronounce upon the objects which concern the *general welfare* and for which, under that description, an appropriation of money is requisite and proper. And there seems to be no room for a doubt that whatever concerns the general interests of LEARNING, of AGRICULTURE, of MANUFACTURES, and of COMMERCE are within the sphere of the national councils, *as far as regards an application of money.*" The latter report assumes the same latitude of power in the national councils and applies it to the encouragement of agriculture, by means of a society to be established at the seat of government. Although neither of these reports may have received the sanction of a law carrying it into effect, yet, on the other hand, the extraordinary doctrine contained in both has passed without the slightest positive mark of disapprobation from the authority to which it was addressed.

Now, whether the phrases in question be construed to authorize every measure relating to the common defense and general welfare, as contended by some, or every measure only in which there might be an application of money, as suggested by the caution of others, the effect must substantially be the same, in destroying the import and force of the particular enumeration of powers which follow these general phrases in the Constitution. For it is evident that there is not a single power whatever which may not have some reference to the common defense or the general welfare, nor a power of any magnitude which in its exercise does not involve or admit an application of money. The government therefore which possesses power in either one or other of these extents is a government without the limitations formed by a particular enumeration of powers; and consequently the meaning and effect of this particular enumeration is destroyed by the exposition given to these general phrases.

This conclusion will not be affected by an attempt to qualify the power over the "general welfare" by referring it to cases where the *general welfare* is beyond the reach of *separate* provisions by the *individual states;* and leaving to these their jurisdictions in cases to which their separate provisions may be competent. For as the authority of the individual states must in all cases be incompetent to general regulations operating through the whole, the authority of the United States would be extended to every object relating to the general welfare which might by any possibility be provided for by the general authority. This

qualifying construction therefore would have little, if any, tendency to circumscribe the power claimed under the latitude of the terms "general welfare."

The true and fair construction of this expression, both in the original and existing federal compacts, appears to the committee too obvious to be mistaken. In both, the Congress is authorized to provide money for the common defense and *general welfare.* In both is subjoined to this authority an enumeration of the cases to which their powers shall extend. Money cannot be applied to the *general welfare* otherwise than by an application of it to some *particular* measure conducive to the general welfare. Whenever, therefore, money has been raised by the general authority, and is to be applied to a particular measure, a question arises whether the particular measure be within the enumerated authorities vested in Congress. If it be, the money requisite for it may be applied to it; if it be not, no such application can be made. This fair and obvious interpretation coincides with, and is enforced by, the clause in the Constitution which declares that "no money shall be drawn from the treasury, but in consequence of appropriations by law." An appropriation of money to the general welfare would be deemed rather a mockery than an observance of this constitutional injunction.

2. Whether the exposition of the general phrases here combated would not, by degrees, consolidate the states into one sovereignty, is a question concerning which the committee can perceive little room for difference of opinion. To consolidate the states into one sovereignty, nothing more can be wanted than to supercede their respective sovereignties in the cases reserved to them by extending the sovereignty of the United States to all cases of the "general welfare," that is to say, to *all cases whatever.*

3. That the obvious tendency and inevitable result of a consolidation of the states into one sovereignty would be to transform the republican system of the United States into a monarchy is a point which seems to have been sufficiently decided by the general sentiment of America. In almost every instance of discussion relating to the consolidation in question, its certain tendency to pave the way to monarchy seems not to have been contested. The prospect of such a consolidation has formed the only topic of controversy. It would be unnecessary, therefore, for the committee to dwell long on the reasons which support the position of the General Assembly. It may not be improper however to remark two consequences evidently flowing from an

extension of the federal powers to every subject falling within the idea of the "general welfare."

One consequence must be to enlarge the sphere of discretion allotted to the executive magistrate. Even within the legislative limits properly defined by the Constitution, the difficulty of accommodating legal regulations to a country so great in extent, and so various in its circumstances, has been much felt; and has led to occasional investments of power in the executive which involve perhaps as large a portion of discretion as can be deemed consistent with the nature of the executive trust. In proportion as the objects of legislative care might be multiplied, would the time allowed for each be diminished, and the difficulty of providing uniform and particular regulations for all be increased. From these sources would necessarily ensue a greater latitude to the agency of that department which is always in existence, and which could best mold regulations of a general nature so as to suit them to the diversity of particular situations. And it is in this latitude, as a supplement to the deficiency of the laws, that the degree of executive prerogative materially consists.

The other consequence would be that of an excessive augmentation of the offices, honors, and emoluments depending on the executive will. Add to the present legitimate stock all those of every description which a consolidation of the states would take from them and turn over to the Federal Government, and the patronage of the executive would necessarily be as much swelled in this case as its prerogative would be in the other.

This disproportionate increase of prerogative and patronage must, evidently, either enable the chief magistrate of the union, by quiet means, to secure his reelection from time to time, and finally to regulate the succession as he might please; or, by giving so transcendent an importance to the office, would render the elections to it so violent and corrupt that the public voice itself might call for an hereditary in place of an elective succession. Whichever of these events might follow, the transformation of the republican system of the United States into a monarchy, anticipated by the General Assembly from a consolidation of the states into one sovereignty, would be equally accomplished; and whether it would be into a mixed or an absolute monarchy might depend on too many contingencies to admit of any certain foresight.

The resolution next in order is contained in the following terms:

That the General Assembly doth particularly protest against the palpable and alarming infractions of the Constitution in the two late cases of the "Alien and Sedition Acts," passed at the last session of Congress; the first of which exercises a power nowhere delegated to the Federal Government, and which by uniting legislative and judicial powers to those of executive, subverts the general principles of a free government, as well as the particular organization and positive provisions of the federal constitution; and the other of which acts exercises in like manner a power not delegated by the Constitution, but on the contrary, expressly and positively forbidden by one of the amendments thereto; a power which, more than any other, ought to produce universal alarm, because it is leveled against that right of freely examining public characters and measures, and of free communication among the people thereon, which has ever been justly deemed the only effectual guardian of every other right. . . .

All [the] principles of the only preventive justice known to American jurisprudence are violated by the Alien Act. The ground of suspicion is to be judged of, not by any judicial authority, but by the executive magistrate alone; no oath or affirmation is required; if the suspicion be held reasonable by the President, he may order the suspected alien to depart the territory of the United States without the opportunity of avoiding the sentence by finding pledges for his future good conduct; as the President may limit the time of departure as he pleases, the benefit of the writ of habeas corpus may be suspended with respect to the party, although the Constitution ordains that it shall not be suspended unless when the public safety may require it in case of rebellion or invasion, neither of which existed at the passage of the act: And the party being, under the sentence of the President, either removed from the United States, or being punished by imprisonment or disqualification ever to become a citizen on conviction of not obeying the order of removal, he cannot be discharged from the proceedings against him and restored to the benefits of his former situation, although the *highest judicial authority* should see the most sufficient cause for it. . . .

One argument offered in justification of this power exercised over aliens is that the admission of them into the country being of favor not of right, the favor is at all times revocable. . . .

But it cannot be a true inference that because the admission of an alien is a favor, the favor may be revoked at pleasure. A grant of land to an individual may be of favor not of right; but the moment the grant is made, the favor becomes a right, and must be forfeited before it can be taken away. To pardon a malefactor may be a favor, but the pardon is not, on that account, the less irrevocable. To admit an alien to naturalization is as much a favor as to admit him to reside in the country, yet it cannot be pretended that a person naturalized can be deprived of the benefit, any more than a native citizen can be disfranchised.

Again it is said that aliens not being parties to the Constitution, the rights and privileges which it secures cannot be at all claimed by them.

To this reasoning also, it might be answered that, although aliens are not parties to the Constitution, it does not follow that the Constitution has vested in Congress an absolute power over them. The parties to the Constitution may have granted, or retained, or modified the power over aliens without regard to that particular consideration.

But a more direct reply is that it does not follow, because aliens are not parties to the Constitution as citizens are parties to it, that whilst they actually conform to it, they have no right to its protection. Aliens are not more parties to the laws than they are parties to the Constitution; yet it will not be disputed that, as they owe on one hand a temporary obedience, they are entitled in return to their protection and advantage. . . .

The *second* object against which the resolution protests is the Sedition Act.

Of this act it is affirmed: 1. That it exercises in like manner a power not delegated by the Constitution. 2d. That the power, on the contrary, is expressly and positively forbidden by one of the amendments to the Constitution. 3d. That this is a power which more than any other ought to produce universal alarm because it is leveled against that right of freely examining public characters and measures, and of free communication thereon, which has ever been justly deemed the only effectual guardian of every other right.

I. That it exercises a power not delegated by the Constitution.

Here, again, it will be proper to recollect that the Federal Government being composed of powers specifically granted, with a reservation of all others to the states or to the people, the positive authority under which the Sedition Act could be passed must be produced by those who assert its constitutionality. In what part of the Constitution then is this authority to be found?

Several attempts have been made to answer this question, which will be examined in their order. The committee will begin with one which has filled them with equal astonishment and apprehension; and which, they cannot but persuade themselves, must have the same effect on all who will consider it with coolness and impartiality, and with a reverence for our Constitution in the true character in which it issued from the sovereign authority of the people. The committee refer to the doctrine lately advanced as a sanction to the Sedition Act: "that the common or unwritten law," a law of vast extent and complexity, and embracing almost every possible subject of legislation, both civil and criminal, "makes a part of the law of these states, in their united and national capacity." . . .

Prior to the Revolution, it is certain that the common law under different limitations made a part of the colonial codes. But whether it be understood that the original colonists brought the law with them or made it their law by adoption, it is equally certain that it was the separate law of each colony within its respective limits, and was unknown to them as a law pervading and operating through the whole, as one society.

It could not possibly be otherwise. The common law was not the same in any two of the colonies; in some, the modifications were materially and extensively different. There was no common legislature by which a common will could be expressed in the form of a law; nor any common magistracy by which such a law could be carried into practice. The will of each colony alone and separately had its organs for these purposes.

This stage of our political history furnishes no foothold for the patrons of this new doctrine.

Did, then, the principle or operation of the great event which made the colonies independent states imply or introduce the common law as a law of the union?

The fundamental principle of the revolution was that the colonies were co-ordinate members with each other, and with Great-Britain, of an Empire united by a common Executive Sovereign, but not united by any common Legislative Sovereign. The legislative power was maintained to be as complete in each American Parliament as in the British Parliament. And the royal prerogative was in force in each colony by virtue of its acknowledging the King for its executive magistrate, as it was in Great-Britain by virtue of a like acknowledgment there. A denial of these principles by Great-Britain, and the assertion of them by America, produced the revolution. . . .

Such being the ground of our revolution, no support nor color can be drawn from it for the doctrine that the common law is binding on these states as one society. The doctrine, on the contrary, is evidently repugnant to the fundamental principle of the revolution.

The Articles of Confederation are the next source of information on this subject.

In the interval between the commencement of the revolution and the final ratification of these Articles, the nature and extent of the union was determined by the circumstances of the crisis rather than by any accurate delineation of the general authority. It will not be alledged that the "common law" could have had any legitimate birth as a law of the United States during that state of things. If it came as such into existence at all, the charter of confederation must have been its parent.

Here again, however, its pretensions are absolutely destitute of foundation. This instrument does not contain a sentence or syllable that can be tortured into a countenance of the idea that the parties to it were with respect to the objects of the common law to form one community. No such law is named or implied, or alluded to, as being in force, or as brought into force by that compact. No provision is made by which such a law could be carried into operation; whilst on the other hand, every such inference or pretext is absolutely precluded by article 2d, which declares "that each state retains its sovereignty, freedom and independence, and every power, jurisdiction and right, which is not by this confederation expressly delegated to the United States, in Congress assembled." . . .

Is this exclusion revoked, and the common law introduced as a national law, by the present Constitution of the United States? This is the final question to be examined.

It is readily admitted that particular parts of the common law may have a sanction from the Constitution, so far as they are necessarily comprehended in the technical phrases which express the powers delegated to the government; and so far, also, as such other parts may be adopted as necessary and proper for carrying into execution the powers expressly delegated. But the question does not relate to either of these portions of the common law. It relates to the common law beyond these limitations.

The only part of the Constitution which seems to have been relied on in this case is the 2d sect. of art. III. "The judicial power shall extend to all cases, *in law and equity,* arising *under this Constitution,* the laws of the United States, and treaties made or which shall be made under their authority."

It has been asked what cases distinct from those arising under the laws and treaties of the United States can arise under the Constitution other than those arising under the common law; and it is inferred that the common law is accordingly adopted or recognized by the Constitution.

Never perhaps was so broad a construction applied to a text so clearly unsusceptible of it. . . . Rather than resort to a construction affecting so essentially the whole character of the government, it would perhaps be more rational to consider the expression as a mere pleonasm or inadvertence. But it is not necessary to decide on such a dilemma. The expression is fully satisfied, and its accuracy justified, by two descriptions of cases to which the judicial authority is extended, and neither of which implies that the common law is the law of the United States. One of these descriptions comprehends the cases growing out of the restrictions on the legislative power of the states. For example, it is provided that "no state shall emit bills of credit," or "make any thing but gold and silver coin a tender in payment of debts." Should this prohibition be violated, and a suit *between citizens of the same state* be the consequence, this would be a case arising under the Constitution before the judicial power of the United States. A second description comprehends suits between citizens and foreigners, or citizens of different states, to be decided according to the state or foreign laws; but submitted by the Constitution to the judicial power of the United States; the judicial power being, in several instances, extended beyond the legislative power of the United States. . . .

To this explanation of the text, the following observations may be added.

The expression, cases in law and equity, is manifestly confined to cases of a civil nature; and would exclude cases of criminal jurisdiction. Criminal cases in law and equity would be a language unknown to the law. . . .

It is further to be considered, that even if this part of the Constitution could be strained into an application to every common law case, criminal as well as civil, it could have no effect in justifying the Sedition Act; which is an exercise of legislative, and not of judicial power: and it is the judicial power only of which the extent is defined in this part of the Constitution. . . .

In aid of these objections, the difficulties and confusion inseparable from a constructive introduction of the common law would afford powerful reasons against it.

Is it to be the common law with or without the British statutes?

If without the statutory amendments, the vices of the code would be insupportable.

If with these amendments, what period is to be fixed for limiting the British authority over our laws?

Is it to be the date of the eldest or the youngest of the colonies?

Or are the dates to be thrown together and a medium deduced?

Or is our independence to be taken for the date?

Is, again, regard to be had to the various changes in the common law made by the local codes of America?

Is regard to be had to such changes, subsequent, as well as prior, to the establishment of the Constitution?

Is regard to be had to future as well as past changes?

Is law to be different in every state, as differently modified by its code; or are the modifications of any particular state to be applied to all?

And on the latter supposition, which among the state codes would form the standard?

Questions of this sort might be multiplied with as much ease as there would be difficulty in answering them.

The consequences flowing from the proposed construction furnish other objections equally conclusive. . . .

If it be understood that the common law is established by the Constitution, it follows that no part of the law can be altered by the legislature; such of the statutes already passed as may be repugnant thereto would be nullified, particularly the "Sedition Act" itself which boasts of being a melioration of the common law; and the whole code with all its incongruities, barbarisms, and bloody maxims would be inviolably saddled on the good people of the United States.

Should this consequence be rejected, and the common law be held, like other laws, liable to revision and alteration by the authority of Congress, it then follows that the authority of Congress is co-extensive with the objects of common law; that is to say, with every object of legislation: For to every such object does some branch or other of the common law extend. The authority of Congress would therefore be no longer under the limitations marked out in the Constitution. They would be authorized to legislate in all cases whatsoever. . . .

The consequence of admitting the common law as the law of the United States on the authority of the individual states is as obvious as it would be fatal. As this law relates to every subject of legislation, and would be paramount to the constitutions and laws of the states, the admission of it would overwhelm the residuary sovereignty of the states and by one constructive operation new model the whole political fabric of the country.

From the review thus taken of the situation of the American colonies prior to their independence; of the effect of this event on their situation; of the nature and import of the Articles of Confederation; of the true meaning of the passage in the existing Constitution from which the common law has been deduced; of the difficulties and uncertainties incident to the doctrine; and of its vast consequences in extending the powers of the Federal Government and in superceding the authorities of the state governments; the committee feel the utmost confidence in concluding that the common law never was, nor by any fair construction, ever can be, deemed a law for the American people as one community; and they indulge the strongest expectation that the same conclusion will finally be drawn by all candid and accurate inquirers into the subject. It is indeed distressing to reflect that it ever should have been made a question whether the Constitution, on the whole face of which is seen so much labor to enumerate and define the several objects of federal power, could intend to introduce in the lump, in an indirect manner, and by a forced construction of a few phrases, the vast and multifarious jurisdiction involved in the common law; a law filling so many ample volumes; a law overspreading the entire field of legislation; and a law that would sap the foundation of the Constitution as a system of limited and specified powers. A severer reproach could not in the opinion of the committee be thrown on the Constitution, on those who framed, or on those who established it, than such a supposition would throw on them.

The argument then drawn from the common law, on the ground of its being adopted or recognized by the Constitution, being inapplicable to the Sedition Act, the committee will proceed to examine the other arguments which have been founded on the Constitution.

They will waste but little time on the attempt to cover the act by the preamble to the Constitution; it being contrary to every acknowledged rule of construction to set up this part of an instrument in opposition to the plain meaning expressed in the body of the instrument. A preamble usually contains the general motives or reasons for the particular regulations or measures which follow it; and is always understood to be explained and limited by them. In the present instance, a contrary interpretation would have the inadmissible effect of rendering nugatory or improper every part of the Constitution which succeeds the preamble.

The paragraph in art. I, sect. 8, which contains the power to lay and collect taxes, duties, imposts, and excises, to pay the debts, and provide for the common defense and general welfare, having been already examined, will also require no particular attention in this place. It will have been seen that in its fair and consistent meaning, it cannot enlarge the enumerated powers vested in Congress.

The part of the Constitution which seems most to be recurred to in defense of the "Sedition Act," is the last clause of the above section, empowering Congress "to make all laws which shall be necessary and proper for carrying into execution the foregoing powers, and all other powers vested by this Constitution in the government of the United States, or in any department or officer thereof."

The plain import of this clause is that Congress shall have all the incidental or instrumental powers necessary and proper for carrying into execution all the express powers; whether they be vested in the government of the United States more collectively or in the several departments or officers thereof. It is not a grant of new powers to Congress, but merely a declaration, for the removal of all uncertainty, that the means of carrying into execution those otherwise granted are included in the grant.

Whenever, therefore, a question arises concerning the constitutionality of a particular power, the first question is whether the power be expressed in the Constitution. If it be, the question is decided. If it be not expressed, the next inquiry must be whether it is properly an incident to an express power, and necessary to its execution. If it be, it may be exercised by Congress. If it be not, Congress cannot exercise it.

Let the question be asked, then, whether the power over the press exercised in the "Sedition Act" be found among the powers expressly vested in the Congress? This is not pretended.

Is there any express power for executing which it is a necessary and proper power?

The power which has been selected, as least remote, in answer to this question, is that of "suppressing insurrec-

tions"; which is said to imply a power to *prevent* insurrections, by punishing whatever may *lead* or *tend* to them. But it surely cannot, with the least plausibility, be said that a regulation of the press and a punishment of libels are exercises of a power to suppress insurrections. The most that could be said would be that the punishment of libels, if it had the tendency ascribed to it, might prevent the occasion of passing or executing laws necessary and proper for the suppression of insurrections.

Has the Federal Government no power, then, to prevent as well as to punish resistance to the laws?

They have the power which the Constitution deemed most proper in their hands for the purpose. The Congress has power, before it happens, to pass laws for punishing it; and the Executive and Judiciary have power to enforce those laws when it does happen.

It must be recollected by many, and could be shown to the satisfaction of all, that the construction here put on the terms "necessary and proper" is precisely the construction which prevailed during the discussions and ratifications of the Constitution. It may be added, and cannot too often be repeated, that it is a construction absolutely necessary to maintain their consistency with the peculiar character of the government, as possessed of particular and defined powers only; not of the general and indefinite powers vested in ordinary governments. For if the power to *suppress insurrections* includes a power to *punish libels;* or if the power to *punish* includes a power to *prevent,* by all means that may have that *tendency;* such is the relation and influence among the most remote subjects of legislation that a power over a very few would carry with it a power over all. And it must be wholly immaterial whether unlimited powers be exercised under the name of unlimited powers or be exercised under the name of unlimited means of carrying into execution limited powers.

This branch of the subject will be closed with a reflection which must have weight with all; but more especially with those who place peculiar reliance on the judicial exposition of the Constitution as the bulwark provided against undue extensions of the legislative power. If it be understood that the powers implied in the specified powers have an immediate and appropriate relation to them, as means necessary and proper for carrying them into execution, questions on the constitutionality of laws passed for this purpose will be of a nature sufficiently precise and determinate for judicial cognizance and control. If, on the other hand, Congress are not limited in the choice of means by any such appropriate relation of them to the specified powers; but may employ all such means as they may deem fitted to *prevent* as well as to *punish* crimes subjected to their authority; such as may have a *tendency* only to *promote* an object for which they are authorized to provide; every one must perceive that questions relating to means of this sort must be questions of mere policy and expediency; on which legislative discretion alone can decide, and from which the judicial interposition and control are completely excluded.

II. The next point which the resolution requires to be proved is that the power over the press exercised by the Sedition Act is positively forbidden by one of the amendments to the Constitution.

The amendment stands in these words—"Congress shall make no law respecting an establishment of religion, or prohibiting the free exercise thereof, *or abridging the freedom of speech or of the press;* or the right of the people peaceably to assemble, and to petition the government for a redress of grievances."

In the attempts to vindicate the "Sedition Act" it has been contended, 1. That the "freedom of the press" is to be determined by the meaning of these terms in the common law. 2. That the article supposes the power over the press to be in Congress, and prohibits them only from *abridging* the freedom allowed to it by the common law.

Although it will be shown, in examining the second of these positions, that the amendment is a denial to Congress of all power over the press; it may not be useless to make the following observations on the first of them. . . .

The freedom of the press under the common law is, in the defenses of the Sedition Act, made to consist in an exemption from all *previous* restraint on printed publications, by persons authorized to inspect and prohibit them. It appears to the committee that this idea of the freedom of the press can never be admitted to be the American idea of it: since a law inflicting penalties on printed publications would have a similar effect with a law authorizing a previous restraint on them. It would seem a mockery to say that no law should be passed preventing publications from being made, but that laws might be passed for punishing them in case they should be made.

The essential difference between the British government and the American constitutions will place this subject in the clearest light.

In the British government, the danger of encroachments on the rights of the people is understood to be con-fined to the executive magistrate. The representatives of the people in the legislature are not only exempt themselves from distrust, but are considered as sufficient guardians of the rights of their constituents against the danger from the executive. Hence it is a principle that the parliament is unlimited in its power; or in their own language, is omnipotent. Hence, too, all the ramparts for protecting the rights of the people, such as their magna charta, their bill of rights, etc. are not reared against the parliament, but against the royal prerogative. They are merely legislative precautions against executive usurpations. Under such a government as this, an exemption of the press from previous restraint by licensers appointed by the king is all the freedom that can be secured to it.

In the United States, the case is altogether different. The people, not the government, possess the absolute sovereignty. The legislature, no less than the executive, is under limitations of power. Encroachments are regarded as possible from the one as well as from the other. Hence in the United States, the great and essential rights of the people are secured against legislative as well as against executive ambition. They are secured, not by laws paramount to prerogative; but by constitutions paramount to laws. This security of the freedom of the press requires that it should be exempt, not only from previous restraint by the executive, as in Great Britain; but from legislative restraint also; and this exemption, to be effectual, must be an exemption, not only from the previous inspection of licensers, but from the subsequent penalty of laws.

The state of the press, therefore, under the common law, cannot in this point of view, be the standard of its freedom in the United States.

But there is another view under which it may be necessary to consider this subject. It may be alledged that although the security for the freedom of the press be different in Great Britain and in this country; being a legal security only in the former, and a constitutional security in the latter; and although there may be a further difference in an extension of the freedom of the press, here, beyond an exemption from previous restraint to an exemption from subsequent penalties also; yet that the actual legal freedom of the press, under the common law, must determine the degree of freedom which is meant by the terms and which is constitutionally secured against both previous and subsequent restraints.

The committee are not unaware of the difficulty of all general questions which may turn on the proper boundary between the liberty and licentiousness of the press. They will leave it therefore for consideration only how far the difference between the nature of the British government and the nature of the American governments, and the practice under the latter, may show the degree of rigor in the former to be inapplicable to, and not obligatory in, the latter.

The nature of governments elective, limited, and responsible in all their branches may well be supposed to require a greater freedom of animadversion than might be tolerated by the genius of such a government as that of Great Britain. In the latter, it is a maxim that the king, a hereditary, not a responsible magistrate, can do no wrong; and that the legislature, which in two-thirds of its composition is also hereditary, not responsible, can do what it pleases. In the United States, the executive magistrates are not held to be infallible, nor the legislatures to be omnipotent; and both being elective, are both responsible. Is it not natural and necessary under such different circumstances that a different degree of freedom in the use of the press should be contemplated?

Is not such an inference favored by what is observable in Great Britain itself? Notwithstanding the general doctrine of the common law on the subject of the press, and the occasional punishment of those who use it with a freedom offensive to the government; it is well known that with respect to the responsible members of the government, where the reasons operating here become applicable there; the freedom exercised by the press, and protected by the public opinion, far exceeds the limits prescribed by the ordinary rules of law. The ministry, who are responsible to impeachment, are at all times animadverted on by the press, with peculiar freedom; and during the elections for the House of Commons, the other responsible part of the government, the press is employed with as little reserve towards the candidates.

The practice in America must be entitled to much more respect. In every state, probably, in the union, the press has exerted a freedom in canvassing the merits and measures of public men, of every description, which has not been confined to the strict limits of the common law. On this footing, the freedom of the press has stood; on this footing it yet stands. And it will not be a breach either of truth or of candor to say that no persons or presses are in the habit of more unrestrained animadversions on the proceedings and functionaries of the state governments than the persons and presses most zealous in vindicating the act of Congress for punishing similar animadversions on the government of the United States.

The last remark will not be understood as claiming for the state governments an immunity greater than they have heretofore enjoyed. Some degree of abuse is inseparable from the proper use of every thing; and in no instance is this more true than in that of the press. It has accordingly been decided by the practice of the states that it is better to leave a few of its noxious branches to their luxuriant growth than, by pruning them away, to injure the vigor of those yielding the proper fruits. And can the wisdom of this policy be doubted by any who reflect that to the press alone, checkered as it is with abuses, the world is indebted for all the triumphs which have been gained by reason and humanity over error and oppression; who reflect that to the same beneficent source, the United States owe much of the lights which conducted them to the rank of a free and independent nation; and which have improved their political system into a shape so auspicious to their happiness. Had "Sedition Acts," forbidding every publication that might bring the constituted agents into contempt or disrepute, or that might excite the hatred of the people against the authors of unjust or pernicious measures, been uniformly enforced against the press; might not the United States have been languishing at this day under the infirmities of a sick confederation? Might they not possibly be miserable colonies, groaning under a foreign yoke?

To these observations one fact will be added which demonstrates that the common law cannot be admitted as the *universal* expositor of American terms which may be the same with those contained in that law. The freedom of conscience and of religion are found in the same instruments which assert the freedom of the press. It will never be admitted that the meaning of the former, in the common law of England, is to limit their meaning in the United States.

Whatever weight may be allowed to these considerations, the committee do not, however, by any means, intend to rest the question on them. They contend that the article of amendment, instead of supposing in Congress a power that might be exercised over the press, provided its freedom be not abridged, was meant as a positive denial to Congress of any power whatever on the subject.

To demonstrate that this was the true object of the article, it will be sufficient to recall the circumstances which led to it, and to refer to the explanation accompanying the article.

When the Constitution was under the discussions

which preceded its ratification, it is well known that great apprehensions were expressed by many lest the omission of some positive exception from the powers delegated of certain rights, and of the freedom of the press particularly, might expose them to the danger of being drawn by construction within some of the powers vested in Congress; more especially of the power to make all laws necessary and proper for carrying their other powers into execution. In reply to this objection, it was invariably urged to be a fundamental and characteristic principle of the Constitution; that all powers not given by it were reserved; that no powers were given beyond those enumerated in the Constitution and such as were fairly incident to them; that the power over the rights in question, and particularly over the press, was neither among the enumerated powers nor incident to any of them; and consequently that an exercise of any such power would be a manifest usurpation. It is painful to remark how much the arguments now employed in behalf of the Sedition Act are at variance with the reasoning which then justified the Constitution, and invited its ratification.

From this posture of the subject resulted the interesting question in so many of the conventions whether the doubts and dangers ascribed to the Constitution should be removed by any amendments previous to the ratification, or be postponed, in confidence that as far as they might be proper, they would be introduced in the form provided by the Constitution. The latter course was adopted; and in most of the states, the ratifications were followed by propositions and instructions for rendering the Constitution more explicit and more safe to the rights not meant to be delegated by it. Among those rights, the freedom of the press, in most instances, is particularly and emphatically mentioned. The firm and very pointed manner in which it is asserted in the proceedings of the convention of this state will be hereafter seen.

In pursuance of the wishes thus expressed, the first Congress that assembled under the Constitution proposed certain amendments which have since, by the necessary ratifications, been made a part of it; among which amendments is the article containing, among other prohibitions on the Congress, an express declaration that they should make no law abridging the freedom of the press.

Without tracing farther the evidence on this subject, it would seem scarcely possible to doubt that no power whatever over the press was supposed to be delegated by the Constitution as it originally stood; and that the amendment was intended as a positive and absolute reservation of it.

But the evidence is still stronger. The proposition of amendments made by Congress is introduced in the following terms: *"The Conventions of a number of the states having at the time of their adopting the Constitution, expressed a desire, in order to prevent misconstructions or abuse of its powers, that further declaratory and restrictive clauses should be added; and as extending the ground of public confidence in the government, will best ensure the beneficent ends of its institution."*

Here is the most satisfactory and authentic proof that the several amendments proposed were to be considered as either declaratory or restrictive; and whether the one or the other, as corresponding with the desire expressed by a number of the states, and as extending the ground of public confidence in the government.

Under any other construction of the amendment relating to the press than that it declared the press to be wholly exempt from the power of Congress, the amendment could neither be said to correspond with the desire expressed by a number of the states, nor be calculated to extend the ground of public confidence in the government.

Nay more; the construction employed to justify the "Sedition Act" would exhibit a phenomenon without a parallel in the political world. It would exhibit a number of respectable states as denying first that any power over the press was delegated by the Constitution; as proposing next, that an amendment to it should explicitly declare that no such power was delegated; and finally, as concurring in an amendment actually recognizing or delegating such a power.

Is then the Federal Government, it will be asked, destitute of every authority for restraining the licentiousness of the press, and for shielding itself against the libellous attacks which may be made on those who administer it?

The Constitution alone can answer this question. If no such power be expressly delegated, and it be not both necessary and proper to carry into execution an express power; above all, if it be expressly forbidden by a declaratory amendment to the Constitution, the answer must be that the Federal Government is destitute of all such authority.

And might it not be asked in turn, whether it is not more probable, under all the circumstances which have been reviewed, that the authority should be withheld by the Constitution than that it should be left to a vague and violent construction: whilst so much pains were bestowed in enumerating other powers, and so many less important powers are included in the enumeration.

Might it not be likewise asked, whether the anxious circumspection which dictated so many *peculiar* limitations on the general authority would be unlikely to exempt the press altogether from that authority? The peculiar magnitude of some of the powers necessarily committed to the Federal Government; the peculiar duration required for the functions of some of its departments; the peculiar distance of the seat of its proceedings from the great body of its constituents; and the peculiar difficulty of circulating an adequate knowledge of them through any other channel; will not these considerations, some or other of which produced other exceptions from the powers of ordinary governments, all together, account for the policy of binding the hand of the Federal Government from touching the channel which alone can give efficacy to its responsibility to its constituents; and of leaving those who administer it to a remedy for injured reputations under the same laws and in the same tribunals which protect their lives, their liberties, and their properties.

But the question does not turn either on the wisdom of the Constitution or on the policy which gave rise to its particular organization. It turns on the actual meaning of the instrument; by which it has appeared that a power over the press is clearly excluded from the number of powers delegated to the Federal Government.

III. And in the opinion of the committee well may it be said, as the resolution concludes with saying, that the unconstitutional power exercised over the press by the "Sedition Act" ought "more than any other, to produce universal alarm; because it is leveled against that right of freely examining public characters and measures, and of free communication among the people thereon, which has ever been justly deemed the only effectual guardian of every other right."

Without scrutinizing minutely into all the provisions of the "Sedition Act" it will be sufficient to cite so much of section 2. as follows: "And be it further enacted, that if any person shall write, print, utter or publish, or shall cause or procure to be written, printed, uttered or published, or shall knowingly and willingly assist or aid in writing, printing, uttering or publishing any false, scandalous, and malicious writing or writings against the government of the United States, or either house of the Congress of the United States, or the President of the United States, *with*

an intent to defame the said government, or either house of the said Congress, or the President, or to bring them, or either of them, into contempt or disrepute; or to excite against them, or either, or any of them, the hatred of the good people of the United States, etc. then such person being thereof convicted before any court of the United States, having jurisdiction thereof, shall be punished by a fine not exceeding two thousand dollars, and by imprisonment not exceeding two years."

On this part of the act the following observations present themselves.

1. The Constitution supposes that the President, the Congress, and each of its houses, may not discharge their trusts, either from defect of judgment or other causes. Hence, they are all made responsible to their constituents at the returning periods of election; and the President, who is singly entrusted with very great powers, is, as a further guard, subjected to an intermediate impeachment.

2. Should it happen, as the Constitution supposes it may happen, that either of these branches of the government may not have duly discharged its trust; it is natural and proper that, according to the cause and degree of their faults, they should be brought into contempt or disrepute, and incur the hatred of the people.

3. Whether it has, in any case, happened that the proceedings of either or all of those branches evinces such a violation of duty as to justify a contempt, a disrepute or hatred among the people, can only be determined by a free examination thereof, and a free communication among the people thereon.

4. Whenever it may have actually happened that proceedings of this sort are chargeable on all or either of the branches of the government, it is the duty as well as right of intelligent and faithful citizens to discuss and promulge them freely, as well to control them by the censorship of the public opinion as to promote a remedy according to the rules of the Constitution. And it cannot be avoided that those who are to apply the remedy must feel, in some degree, a contempt or hatred against the transgressing party.

5. As the act was passed on July 14, 1798, and is to be in force until March 3, 1801, it was of course that during its continuance, two elections of the entire House of Representatives, an election of a part of the Senate, and an election of a President were to take place.

6. That consequently, during all these elections, intended by the Constitution to preserve the purity or to

purge the faults of the administration, the great remedial rights of the people were to be exercised, and the responsibility of their public agents to be screened, under the penalties of this act.

May it not be asked of every intelligent friend to the liberties of his country whether, the power exercised in such an act as this ought not to produce great and universal alarm? Whether a rigid execution of such an act, in time past, would not have repressed that information and communication among the people which is indispensable to the just exercise of their electoral rights? And whether such an act, if made perpetual and enforced with rigor, would not, in time to come, either destroy our free system of government or prepare a convulsion that might prove equally fatal to it.

In answer to such questions, it has been pleaded that the writings and publications forbidden by the act are those only which are false and malicious, and intended to defame; and merit is claimed for the privilege allowed to authors to justify, by proving the truth of their publications, and for the limitations to which the sentence of fine and imprisonment is subjected.

To those who concurred in the act under the extraordinary belief that the option lay between the passing of such an act and leaving in force the common law of libels, which punishes truth equally with falsehood, and submits the fine and imprisonment to the indefinite discretion of the court, the merit of good intentions ought surely not to be refused. A like merit may perhaps be due for the discontinuance of the *corporal punishment* which the common law also leaves to the discretion of the court. This merit of *intention,* however, would have been greater, if the several mitigations had not been limited to so short a period; and the apparent inconsistency would have been avoided between justifying the act at one time by contrasting it with the rigors of the common law otherwise in force; and at another time by appealing to the nature of the crisis as requiring the temporary rigor exerted by the act.

But whatever may have been the meritorious intentions of all or any who contributed to the Sedition Act; a very few reflections will prove that its baneful tendency is little diminished by the privilege of giving in evidence the truth of the matter contained in political writings.

In the first place, where simple and naked facts alone are in question, there is sufficient difficulty in some cases, and sufficient trouble and vexation in all, of meeting a prosecution from the government with the full and formal proof necessary in a court of law.

But in the next place, it must be obvious to the plainest minds that opinions, and inferences, and conjectural observations are not only in many cases inseparable from the facts, but may often be more the objects of the prosecution than the facts themselves; or may even be altogether abstracted from particular facts; and that opinions and inferences and conjectural observations cannot be subjects of that kind of proof which appertains to facts before a court of law.

Again, it is no less obvious that the *intent* to defame or bring into contempt or disrepute or hatred, which is made a condition of the offense created by the act, cannot prevent its pernicious influence on the freedom of the press. For omitting the inquiry how far the malice of the intent is an inference of the law from the mere publication, it is manifestly impossible to punish the intent to bring those who administer the government into disrepute or contempt without striking at the right of freely discussing public characters and measures: because those who engage in such discussions must expect and *intend* to excite these unfavorable sentiments so far as they may be thought to be deserved. To prohibit therefore the intent to excite those unfavorable sentiments against those who administer the government, is equivalent to a prohibition of the actual excitement of them; and to prohibit the actual excitement of them, is equivalent to a prohibition of discussions having that tendency and effect; which, again, is equivalent to a protection of those who administer the government if they should at any time deserve the contempt or hatred of the people against being exposed to it by free animadversions on their characters and conduct. Nor can there be a doubt, if those in public trust be shielded by penal laws from such strictures of the press as may expose them to contempt or disrepute or hatred, where they may deserve it, that in exact proportion as they may deserve to be exposed will be the certainty and criminality of the intent to expose them, and the vigilance of prosecuting and punishing it; nor a doubt that a government thus entrenched in penal statutes against the just and natural effects of a culpable administration will easily evade the responsibility which is essential to a faithful discharge of its duty.

Let it be recollected, lastly, that the right of electing the members of the government constitutes more particularly the essence of a free and responsible government. The value and efficacy of this right depends on the knowledge of the comparative merits and demerits of the candidates for public trust; and on the equal freedom, consequently, of examining and discussing these merits and demerits of the candidates respectively. It has been seen that a number of important elections will take place whilst the act is in force; although it should not be continued beyond the term to which it is limited. Should there happen, then, as is extremely probable in relation to some or other of the branches of the government, to be competitions between those who are and those who are not members of the government; what will be the situations of the competitors? Not equal; because the characters of the former will be covered by the "Sedition Act" from animadversions exposing them to disrepute among the people; whilst the latter may be exposed to the contempt and hatred of the people without a violation of the act. What will be the situation of the people? Not free; because they will be compelled to make their election between competitors whose pretensions they are not permitted by the act equally to examine, to discuss, and to ascertain. And from both these situations, will not those in power derive an undue advantage for continuing themselves in it; which by impairing the right of election, endangers the blessings of the government founded on it.

It is with justice, therefore, that the General Assembly hath affirmed in the resolution as well that the right of freely examining public characters and measures, and of free communication thereon, is the only effectual guardian of every other right; as that this particular right is leveled at by the power exercised in the "Sedition Act.". . .

The act of ratification by Virginia . . . stands in the ensuing form.

We, the Delegates of the people of Virginia, duly elected in pursuance of a recommendation from the General Assembly, and now met in Convention, having fully and freely investigated and discussed the proceedings of the federal convention, and being prepared as well as the most mature deliberation hath enabled us, to decide thereon; DO, in the name and in behalf of the people of Virginia, declare and make known, that the powers granted under the Constitution, being derived from the people of the United States, may be resumed by them whensoever the same shall be perverted to their injury or oppression; and that every power not granted thereby remains with them and at their will. That therefore, no right of any denomination can be cancelled, abridged, restrained or modified, by the Congress, by the Senate or House of Representatives acting in any capacity, by the President, or any department or officer of the

United States, except in those instances in which power is given by the Constitution for those purposes; and, that among other essential rights, the liberty of conscience and of the press, cannot be cancelled, abridged, restrained or modified by any authority of the United States.

Here is an express and solemn declaration by the convention of the state that they ratified the Constitution in the sense that no right of any denomination can be cancelled, abridged, restrained or modified by the government of the United States or any part of it, except in those instances in which power is given by the Constitution; and in the sense particularly, "that among other essential rights, the liberty of conscience and freedom of the press cannot be cancelled, abridged, restrained or modified, by any authority of the United States."

Words could not well express in a fuller or more forcible manner the understanding of the convention that the liberty of conscience and the freedom of the press were *equally* and *completely* exempted from all authority whatever of the United States.

Under an anxiety to guard more effectually these rights against every possible danger, the convention, after ratifying the Constitution, proceeded to prefix to certain amendments proposed by them a declaration of rights, in which are two articles providing, the one for the liberty of conscience, the other for the freedom of speech and of the press.

Similar recommendations having proceeded from a number of other states, and Congress, as has been seen, having in consequence thereof, and with a view to extend the ground of public confidence, proposed among other declaratory and restrictive clauses, a clause expressly securing the liberty of conscience and of the press; and Virginia having concurred in the ratifications which made them a part of the Constitution; it will remain with a candid public to decide whether it would not mark an inconsistency and degeneracy if an indifference were now shown to a palpable violation of one of those rights, the freedom of the press; and to a precedent therein, which may be fatal to the other, the free exercise of religion. . . .

It has been said that it belongs to the judiciary of the United States, and not to the state legislatures, to declare the meaning of the Federal Constitution.

But a declaration that proceedings of the Federal Government are not warranted by the Constitution is a novelty neither among the citizens nor among the legislatures of the states; nor are the citizens or the legislature of Virginia singular in the example of it.

Nor can the declarations of either, whether affirming or denying the constitutionality of measures of the Federal Government; or whether made before or after judicial decisions thereon, be deemed, in any point of view, an assumption of the office of the judge. The declarations in such cases are expressions of opinion, unaccompanied with any other effect than what they may produce on opinion, by exciting reflection. The expositions of the judiciary, on the other hand, are carried into immediate effect by force. The former may lead to a change in the legislative expression of the general will; possibly to a change in the opinion of the judiciary: the latter enforces the general will whilst that will and that opinion continue unchanged.

And if there be no impropriety in declaring the unconstitutionality of proceedings in the Federal Government, where can be the impropriety of communicating the declaration to other states and inviting their concurrence in a like declaration? What is allowable for one must be allowable for all; and a free communication among the states, where the Constitution imposes no restraint, is as allowable among the state governments as among other public bodies or private citizens. This consideration derives a weight that cannot be denied to it from the relation of the state legislatures to the federal legislature, as the immediate constituents of one of its branches.

The legislatures of the states have a right, also, to originate amendments to the Constitution, by a concurrence of two thirds of the whole number, in applications to Congress for the purpose. When new states are to be formed by a junction of two or more states, or parts of states, the legislatures of the states concerned are, as well as Congress, to concur in the measure. The states have a right, also, to enter into agreements or compacts with the consent of Congress. In all such cases, a communication among them results from the object which is common to them.

It is lastly to be seen, whether the confidence expressed by the resolution that the *necessary and proper measures* would be taken by the other states for cooperating with Virginia in maintaining the rights reserved to the states, or to the people, be in any degree liable to the objections which have been raised against it.

If it be liable to objection, it must be because either the object or the means are objectionable.

The object being to maintain what the Constitution has ordained is in itself a laudable object.

The means are expressed in the terms "the necessary and proper measures." A proper object was to be pursued, by means both necessary and proper.

To find an objection, then, it must be shown that some meaning was annexed to these general terms which was not proper; and for this purpose, either that the means used by the General Assembly were an example of improper means, or that there were no proper means to which the terms could refer.

In the example given by the state of declaring the Alien and Sedition Acts to be unconstitutional, and of communicating the declaration to the other states, no trace of improper means has appeared. And if the other states had concurred in making a like declaration, supported too by the numerous applications flowing immediately from the people, it can scarcely be doubted that these simple means would have been as sufficient as they are unexceptionable.

It is no less certain that other means might have been employed, which are strictly within the limits of the Constitution. The legislatures of the states might have made a direct representation to Congress, with a view to obtain a rescinding of the two offensive acts; or they might have represented to their respective senators in Congress their wish that two thirds thereof would propose an explanatory amendment to the Constitution; or two thirds of themselves, if such had been their option, might, by an application to Congress, have obtained a convention for the same object.

These several means, though not equally eligible in themselves, nor probably to the states, were all constitutionally open for consideration. And if the General Assembly, after declaring the two acts to be unconstitutional, the first and most obvious proceeding on the subject, did not undertake to point out to the other states a choice among the farther measures that might become necessary and proper, the reserve will not be misconstrued by liberal minds into any culpable imputation.

These observations appear to form a satisfactory reply to every objection which is not founded on a misconception of the terms employed in the resolutions. There is one other, however, which may be of too much importance not to be added. It cannot be forgotten that among the arguments addressed to those who apprehended danger to liberty from the establishment of the general government over so great a country, the appeal was emphatically made to the intermediate existence of the state governments between the people and that government, to the vigilance with which they would descry the first symptoms of usurpation, and to the promptitude with which they would sound the alarm to the public. This argument was probably not without its effect; and if it was a proper one, then, to recommend the establishment of the constitution; it must be a proper one now, to assist in its interpretation.

The only part of the two concluding resolutions that remains to be noticed is the repetition in the first of that warm affection to the union and its members and of that scrupulous fidelity to the Constitution which have been invariably felt by the people of this state. As the proceedings were introduced with these sentiments, they could not be more properly closed than in the same manner. Should there be any so far misled as to call in question the sincerity of these professions, whatever regret may be excited by the error, the General Assembly cannot descend into a discussion of it. Those who have listened to the suggestion can only be left to their own recollection of the part which this state has borne in the establishment of our national independence; in the establishment of our national constitution; and in maintaining under it the authority and laws of the union, without a single exception of internal resistance or commotion. By recurring to these facts, they will be able to convince themselves that the representatives of the people of Virginia must be above the necessity of opposing any other shield to attacks on their national patriotism than their own consciousness and the justice of an enlightened public; who will perceive in the resolutions themselves the strongest evidence of attachment both to the Constitution and to the union, since it is only by maintaining the different governments and departments within their respective limits that the blessings of either can be perpetuated. The extensive view of the subject thus taken by the committee has led them to report to the house, as the result of the whole, the following resolution.

Resolved, That the General Assembly, having carefully and respectfully attended to the proceedings of a number of the states, in answer to their resolutions of December 21, 1798, and having accurately and fully re-examined and reconsidered the latter, find it to be their indispensable duty to adhere to the same, as founded in truth, as consonant with the Constitution, and as conducive to its preservation; and more especially to be their duty, to renew, as they do hereby renew, their protest against "the Alien and Sedition Acts," as palpable and alarming infractions of the Constitution.

PART 5

The Jeffersonian Ascendancy: Domestic Policy, 1801–1808

Thomas Jefferson defeated John Adams in the presidential election of 1800, 73 electoral votes to 65. Indeed, in an impressive display of party unity (and an instructive revelation of a notable flaw in the Constitution as originally written), every Republican elector in the country cast one vote for Jefferson and one for the party's vice-presidential candidate, Aaron Burr, whose triumph over Hamilton in the legislative elections in New York City had carried that state, and the election, for the Jeffersonians. The electoral tie threw the final selection of the president into the lame-duck House of Representatives, where the Federalists controlled enough states to prevent a decision. With some of them hoping that they could get better terms from Burr than from Jefferson, perhaps even that a deadlock would compel a choice of a president in another way, the defeated party stubbornly blocked a decision through 35 ballots. Burr, however, declined to play this game (though he also damaged himself irreparably with the Virginians by doing nothing to rule himself completely out); and on the thirty-sixth ballot, James A. Bayard, the lone representative from Delaware, brought the dangerous impasse to an end.

Adams's defeat in 1800 was far from overwhelming. The people had about as indirect a voice as they have ever had in a presidential election. In ten of the sixteen states, the legislatures kept the choice of the presidential electors in their own hands. The switch of a few hundred votes in the assembly elections in New York or of fewer than that in the legislature of South Carolina would have reversed the outcome. Adams had broken sharply with the Hamiltonian wing of his party and moved decisively toward peace with France. Although the split within his party probably contributed to his defeat, it may also have strengthened his popular appeal.

But if the president was not, by any means, decisively repudiated at the polls, his party certainly was. The Federalists lost more than twenty seats in the House of Representatives and, for the first time, control of the Senate as well. Having captured a House majority of 65 to 41 for the incoming Seventh Congress, the Republicans were well positioned to insist upon a new national course. And months before the Seventh Congress met, Jefferson established guidelines that his own and Madison's administrations would adhere to through the coming sixteen years.

The Jeffersonian Program

THOMAS JEFFERSON

The First Inaugural Address

4 March 1801

Friends and Fellow-Citizens,

Called upon to undertake the duties of the first executive office of our country, I avail myself of the presence of that portion of my fellow-citizens which is here assembled to express my grateful thanks for the favor with which they have been pleased to look toward me, to declare a sincere consciousness that the task is above my talents, and that I approach it with those anxious and awful presentiments which the greatness of the charge and the weakness of my powers so justly inspire. A rising nation, spread over a wide and fruitful land, traversing all the seas with the rich productions of their industry, engaged in commerce with nations who feel power and forget right, advancing rapidly to destinies beyond the reach of mortal eye—when I contemplate these transcendent objects, and see the honor, the happiness, and the hopes of this beloved country committed to the issue and the auspices of this day, I shrink from the contemplation, and humble myself before the magnitude of the undertaking. Utterly, indeed, should I despair did not the presence of many whom I here see remind me that in the other high authorities provided by our Constitution I shall find resources of wisdom, of virtue, and of zeal on which to rely under all difficulties. To you, then, gentlemen, who are charged with the sovereign functions of legislation, and to those associated with you, I look with encouragement for that guidance and support which may enable us to steer with safety the vessel in which we are all embarked amidst the conflicting elements of a troubled world.

During the contest of opinion through which we have passed the animation of discussions and of exertions has sometimes worn an aspect which might impose on strangers unused to think freely and to speak and to write what they think; but this being now decided by the voice of the nation, announced according to the rules of the Constitution, all will, of course, arrange themselves under the will of the law, and unite in common efforts for the common good. All, too, will bear in mind this sacred principle, that though the will of the majority is in all cases to prevail, that will to be rightful must be reasonable; that the minority possess their equal rights, which equal law must protect, and to violate would be oppression. Let us, then, fellow-citizens, unite with one heart and one mind. Let us restore to social intercourse that harmony and affection without which liberty and even life itself are but dreary things. And let us reflect that, having banished from our land that religious intolerance under which mankind so long bled and suffered, we have yet gained little if we countenance a political intolerance as despotic, as wicked, and capable of as bitter and bloody persecutions. During the throes and convulsions of the ancient world, during the agonizing spasms of infuriated man, seeking through blood and slaughter his long-lost liberty, it was not wonderful that the agitation of the billows should reach even this distant and peaceful shore; that this should be more felt and feared by some and less by others, and should divide opinions as to measures of safety. But every difference of opinion is not a difference of principle. We have called by different names brethren of the same principle. We are all Republicans, we are all Federalists. If there be any among us who would wish to dissolve this Union or to change its republican form, let them stand undisturbed as monuments of the safety with which error of opinion may be tolerated where reason is left free to combat it. I know, indeed, that some honest men fear that a republican government cannot be strong, that this Government is not strong enough; but would the honest patriot, in the full tide of successful experiment, abandon a government which has so far kept us free and firm on the theoretic and visionary fear that this Government, the world's best hope, may by possibility want energy to preserve itself? I trust not. I believe this, on the contrary, the strongest Government on earth. I believe it the only one where every man, at the call of the law, would fly to the standard of the law, and would meet invasions of the public order as his own personal concern. Sometimes it is said that man cannot be trusted with the government of himself. Can he, then, be trusted with the government of others? Or have we found angels in the forms of kings to govern him? Let history answer this question.

Let us, then, with courage and confidence pursue our own Federal and Republican principles, our attachment to union and representative government. Kindly separated by nature and a wide ocean from the exterminating havoc of one quarter of the globe; too high-minded to endure the degradations of the others; possessing a chosen country, with room enough for our descendants to the thousandth and thousandth generation, entertaining a due sense of our equal right to the use of our own faculties, to the acquisitions of our own industry, to honor and confidence from our fellow-citizens, resulting not from birth, but from our actions and their sense of them; enlightened by a benign religion, professed, indeed, and practiced in various forms, yet all of them inculcating honesty, truth, temperance, gratitude, and the love of man; acknowledging and adoring an overruling Providence, which by all its dispensations proves that it delights in the happiness of man here and his greater happiness hereafter—with all these blessings, what more is necessary to make us a happy and a prosperous people? Still one thing more, fellow-citizens— a wise and frugal Government, which shall restrain men from injuring one another, shall leave them otherwise free to regulate their own pursuits of industry and improvement, and shall not take from the mouth of labor the bread it has earned. This is the sum of good government, and this is necessary to close the circle of our felicities.

About to enter, fellow-citizens, on the exercise of duties which comprehend everything dear and valuable to you, it is proper you should understand what I deem the essential principles of our government, and consequently those which ought to shape its administration. I will compress them within the narrowest compass they will bear, stating the general principle, but not all its limitations. Equal and exact justice to all men, of whatever state or persuasion, religious or political; peace, commerce, and honest friendship with all nations, entangling alliances with none; the support of the state governments in all their rights, as the most competent administrations for our domestic concerns and the surest bulwarks against antirepublican tendencies; the preservation of the General Government in its whole constitutional vigor, as the sheet anchor of our peace at home and safety abroad; a jealous care of the right of election by the people—a mild and safe corrective of abuses which are lopped by the sword of revolution where peaceable remedies are unprovided; absolute acquiescence in the decisions of the majority, the vital principle of republics, from which is no appeal but to force, the vital principle and immediate parent of despotism; a well-disciplined militia, our best reliance in peace and for the first moments of war till regulars may relieve them; the supremacy of the civil over the military authority; economy in the public expense, that labor may be lightly burthened; the honest payment of our debts and sacred preservation of the public faith; encouragement of agriculture, and of commerce as its handmaid; the diffusion of information and arraignment of all abuses at the bar of the public reason; freedom of religion; freedom of the press, and freedom of person under the protection of the habeas corpus, and trial by juries impartially selected. These principles form the bright constellation which has gone before us and guided our steps through an age of revolution and reformation. The wisdom of our sages and blood of our heroes have been devoted to their attainment. They should be the creed of our political faith, the text of civic instruction, the touchstone by which to try the services of those we trust; and should we wander from them in moments of error or of alarm, let us hasten to retrace our steps and to regain the road which alone leads to peace, liberty, and safety.

I repair, then, fellow-citizens, to the post you have assigned me. With experience enough in subordinate offices to have seen the difficulties of this the greatest of all, I have learnt to expect that it will rarely fall to the lot of imperfect man to retire from this station with the reputation and the favor which bring him into it. Without pretensions to that high confidence you reposed in our first and greatest revolutionary character, whose preeminent services had entitled him to the first place in his country's love and destined for him the fairest page in the volume of faithful history, I ask so much confidence only as may give firmness and effect to the legal administration of your affairs, I shall often go wrong through defect of judgment. When right, I shall often be thought wrong by those whose positions will not command a view of the whole ground. I ask your indulgence for my own errors, which will never be intentional, and your support against the errors of others, who may condemn what they would not if seen in all its parts. The approbation implied by your suffrage is a great consolation to me for the past, and my future solicitude will be to retain the good opinion of those who have bestowed it in advance, to conciliate that of others by doing them all the good in my power, and to be instrumental to the happiness and freedom of all.

Relying, then, on the patronage of your good will, I advance with obedience to the work, ready to retire from it whenever you become sensible how much better choice it is in your power to make. And may that Infinite Power which rules the destinies of the universe lead our councils to what is best, and give them a favorable issue for your peace and prosperity.

THOMAS JEFFERSON

First Annual Message

8 December 1801

FELLOW CITIZENS OF THE SENATE AND HOUSE
OF REPRESENTATIVES:

It is a circumstance of sincere gratification to me that on meeting the great council of our nation, I am able to announce to them, on the grounds of reasonable certainty, that the wars and troubles which have for so many years afflicted our sister nations have at length come to an end, and that the communications of peace and commerce are once more opening among them. While we devoutly return thanks to the beneficent Being who has been pleased to breathe into them the spirit of conciliation and forgiveness, we are bound with peculiar gratitude to be thankful to him that our own peace has been preserved through so perilous a season, and ourselves permitted quietly to cultivate the earth and to practice and improve those arts which tend to increase our comforts. The assurances, indeed, of friendly disposition, received from all the powers with whom we have principal relations, had inspired a confidence that our peace with them would not have been disturbed. But a cessation of the irregularities which had affected the commerce of neutral nations, and of the irritations and injuries produced by them, cannot but add to this confidence; and strengthens, at the same time, the hope that wrongs committed on offending friends, under a pressure of circumstances, will now be reviewed with candor and will be considered as founding just claims of retribution for the past and new assurances for the future.

Among our Indian neighbors, also, a spirit of peace and friendship [is] generally prevailing and I am happy to inform you that the continued efforts to introduce among them the implements and the practice of husbandry and of the household arts, have not been without success; that they are becoming more and more sensible of the superiority of this dependence for clothing and subsistence over the precarious resources of hunting and fishing; and already we are able to announce that instead of that constant diminution of their numbers, produced by their wars and their wants, some of them begin to experience an increase of population.

To this state of general peace with which we have been blessed, one only exception exists. Tripoli, the least considerable of the Barbary States, had come forward with demands unfounded either in right or in compact and had permitted itself to denounce war on our failure to comply before a given day. The style of the demand admitted but one answer. I sent a small squadron of frigates into the Mediterranean, with assurances to that power of our sincere desire to remain in peace, but with orders to protect our commerce against the threatened attack. The measure was seasonable and salutary. The bey had already declared war in form. His cruisers were out. Two had arrived at Gibraltar. Our commerce in the Mediterranean was blockaded and that of the Atlantic in peril. The arrival of our squadron dispelled the danger. One of the Tripolitan cruisers having fallen in with and engaged the small schooner Enterprise, commanded by Lieutenant Sterett, which had gone as a tender to our larger vessels, was captured after a heavy slaughter of her men, without the loss of a single one on our part. The bravery exhibited by our citizens on that element will, I trust, be a testimony to the world that it is not the want of that virtue which makes us seek their peace, but a conscientious desire to direct the energies of our nation to the multiplication of the human race and not to its destruction. Unauthorized by the constitution, without the sanction of Congress, to go out beyond the line of defense, the vessel being disabled from committing further hostilities, was liberated with its crew. The legislature will doubtless consider whether, by authorizing measures of offense also, they will place our force on an equal footing with that of its adversaries.

I communicate all material information on this subject, that in the exercise of the important function confided by the Constitution to the legislature exclusively, their judgment may form itself on a knowledge and consideration of every circumstance of weight. . . .

I lay before you the result of the census lately taken of our inhabitants, to a conformity with which we are to reduce the ensuing rates of representation and taxation. You will perceive that the increase of numbers during the last ten years, proceeding in geometrical ratio, promises a duplication in little more than twenty-two years. We contemplate this rapid growth, and the prospect it holds up to us, not with a view to the injuries it may enable us to do to others in some future day, but to the settlement of the extensive country still remaining vacant within our limits, to the multiplications of men susceptible of happiness, educated in the love of order, habituated to self-government, and valu[ing] its blessings above all price.

Other circumstances, combined with the increase of numbers, have produced an augmentation of revenue arising from consumption in a ratio far beyond that of population alone, and . . . there is reasonable ground of confidence that we may now safely dispense with all the internal taxes, comprehending excises, stamps, auctions, licenses, carriages, and refined sugars, to which the postage on newspapers may be added, to facilitate the progress of information, and that the remaining sources of revenue will be sufficient to provide for the support of government, to pay the interest on the public debts, and to discharge the principals in shorter periods than the laws or the general expectations had contemplated. War, indeed, and untoward events, may change this prospect of things and call for expenses which the imposts could not meet; but sound principles will not justify our taxing the industry of our fellow citizens to accumulate treasure for wars to happen we know not when, and which might not perhaps happen but from the temptations offered by that treasure.

These views, however, of reducing our burdens are formed on the expectation that a sensible, and at the same time a salutary reduction may take place in our habitual expenditures. For this purpose, those of the civil government, the army, and navy will need revisal.

When we consider that this government is charged with the external and mutual relations only of these states; that the states themselves have principal care of our persons, our property, and our reputation, constituting the great field of human concerns, we may well doubt whether our organization is not too complicated, too expensive; whether offices or officers have not been multiplied unnecessarily, and sometimes injuriously to the service they were meant to promote. . . . Among those who are dependent on executive discretion, I have begun the reduction of what was deemed necessary. The expenses of diplomatic agency have been considerably diminished. The inspectors of internal revenue who were found to obstruct the accountability of the institution, have been discontinued. Several agencies created by executive authority, on salaries fixed by that also, have been suppressed, and should suggest the expediency of regulating that power by law so as to subject its exercises to legislative inspection and sanction. Other reformations of the same kind will be pursued with that caution which is requisite in removing useless things, not to injure what is retained. But the great mass of public offices is established by law and, therefore, by law alone can be abolished. Should the legislature think it expedient to pass this roll in review and try all its parts by the test of public utility, they may be assured of every aid and light which executive information can yield. Considering the general tendency to multiply offices and dependencies, and to increase expense to the ultimate term of burden which the citizen can bear, it behooves us to avail ourselves of every occasion which presents itself for taking off the surcharge; that it may never be seen here that, after leaving to labor the smallest portion of its earnings on which it can subsist, government shall itself consume the residue of what it was instituted to guard.

In our care, too, of the public contributions entrusted to our direction, it would be prudent to multiply barriers against their dissipation by appropriating specific sums to every specific purpose susceptible of definition; by disallowing applications of money varying from the appropriation in object or transcending it in amount; by reducing the undefined field of contingencies and thereby circumscribing discretionary powers over money; and by bringing back to a single department all accountabilities for money where the examination may be prompt, efficacious, and uniform.

An account of the receipts and expenditures of the last year, as prepared by the secretary of the treasury, will as usual be laid before you. The success which has attended the late sales of the public lands shows that with attention they may be made an important source of receipt. Among the payments, those made in discharge of the principal and interest of the national debt will show that the public faith has been exactly maintained. To these will be added an estimate of appropriations necessary for the ensuing year. This last will of course be effected by such modifications of the systems of expense as you shall think proper to adopt.

A statement has been formed by the secretary of war, on mature consideration, of all the posts and stations where garrisons will be expedient and of the number of men requisite for each garrison. The whole amount is considerably short of the present military establishment. For the surplus no particular use can be pointed out. For defense against invasion, their number is as nothing; nor is it conceived needful or safe that a standing army should be kept up in time of peace for that purpose. Uncertain as we must ever be of the particular point in our circumference where an enemy may choose to invade us, the only force which can be ready at every point and competent to oppose them is the body of neighboring citizens as formed into a militia. On these, collected from the parts most convenient, in numbers proportioned to the invading foe, it is best to rely, not only to meet the first attack, but if it threatens to be permanent, to maintain the defense until regulars may be engaged to relieve them. These considerations render it important that we should at every session continue to amend the defects which from time to time show themselves in the laws for regulating the militia until they are sufficiently perfect. Nor should we now or at any time separate until we can say we have done everything for the militia which we could do were an enemy at our door.

The provisions of military stores on hand will be laid before you, that you may judge of the additions still requisite.

With respect to the extent to which our naval preparations should be carried, some difference of opinion may be expected to appear; but just attention to the circumstances of every part of the Union will doubtless reconcile all. A small force will probably continue to be wanted for actual service in the Mediterranean. Whatever annual sum beyond that you may think proper to appropriate to naval preparations would perhaps be better employed in providing those articles which may be kept without waste or consumption, and be in readiness when any exigence calls them into use. . . .

Agriculture, manufactures, commerce, and navigation, the four pillars of our prosperity, are the most thriving when left most free to individual enterprise. Protection from casual embarrassments, however, may sometimes be seasonably interposed. If in the course of your observations or inquiries they should appear to need any aid within the limits of our constitutional powers, your sense of their importance is a sufficient assurance they will occupy your attention. We cannot, indeed, but all feel an anxious solicitude for the difficulties under which our carrying trade will soon be placed. How far it can be relieved, otherwise than by time, is a subject of important consideration.

The judiciary system of the United States, and especially that portion of it recently erected, will of course present itself to the contemplation of Congress; and that they may be able to judge of the proportion which the institution bears to the business it has to perform, I have caused to be procured from the several States, and now lay before Congress, an exact statement of all the causes decided since the first establishment of the courts and of those which were depending when additional courts and judges were brought in to their aid.

And while on the judiciary organization, it will be worthy your consideration whether the protection of the inestimable institution of juries has been extended to all the cases involving the security of our persons and property. Their impartial selection also being essential to their value, we ought further to consider whether that is sufficiently secured in those states where they are named by a marshal depending on executive will or designated by the court or by officers dependent on them.

I cannot omit recommending a revisal of the laws on the subject of naturalization. Considering the ordinary chances of human life, a denial of citizenship under a residence of fourteen years is a denial to a great proportion of those who ask it, and controls a policy pursued from their first settlement by many of these states and still believed of consequence to their prosperity. And shall we refuse the unhappy fugitives from distress that hospitality which the savages of the wilderness extended to our fathers arriving in this land? Shall oppressed humanity find no asylum on this globe? The constitution, indeed, has wisely provided that, for admission to certain offices of important trust, a residence shall be required sufficient to develop character and design. But might not the general character and capabilities of a citizen be safely communicated to every one manifesting a *bona fide* purpose of embarking his life and fortunes permanently with us? with restrictions, perhaps, to guard against the fraudulent usurpation of our flag; an abuse which brings so much embarrassment and loss on the genuine citizen, and so much danger to the nation of being involved in war, that no endeavor should be spared to detect and suppress it.

These, fellow citizens, are the matters respecting the state of the nation, which I have thought of importance to be submitted to your consideration at this time. Some others of less moment, or not yet ready for communication, will be the subject of separate messages. I am happy in this opportunity of committing the arduous affairs of our government to the collected wisdom of the Union. Nothing shall be wanting on my part to inform, as far as in my power, the legislative judgment, nor to carry that judgment into faithful execution. The prudence and temperance of your discussions will promote, within your own walls, that conciliation which so much befriends national conclusion; and by its example will encourage among our constituents that progress of opinion which is tending to unite them in object and in will. That all should be satisfied with any one order of things is not to be expected, but I indulge the pleasing persuasion that the great body of our citizens will cordially concur in honest and disinterested efforts, which have for their object to preserve the general and state governments in their constitutional form and equilibrium; to maintain peace abroad and order and obedience to the laws at home; to establish principles and practices of administration favorable to the security of liberty and prosperity, and to reduce expenses to what is necessary for the useful purposes of government.

The Jeffersonian Vision

As he entered the campaign of 1800 and, again, as the Congress began to act on the suggestions of his message of December 1801, the president sketched his program and intentions in letters to his friends. For years, he was to prove remarkably successful in keeping his party behind him. But there were dissidents on both of his extremes.

Letters of the President

1799–1802

To Elbridge Gerry

26 January 1799

. . . I shall make to you a profession of my political faith, in confidence that you will consider every future imputation on me of a contrary complexion as bearing on its front the mark of falsehood & calumny.

I do then, with sincere zeal, wish an inviolable preservation of our present federal constitution according to the true sense in which it was adopted by the states, that in which it was advocated by its friends, & not that which its enemies apprehended, who therefore became its enemies; and I am opposed to the monarchising its features by the forms of its administration, with a view to conciliate a first transition to a President & Senate for life, & from that to a hereditary tenure of these offices, & thus to worm out the elective principle. I am for preserving to the states the powers not yielded by them to the Union, & to the legislature of the Union its constitutional share in the division of powers; and I am not for transferring all the powers of the states to the general government, & all those of that government to the executive branch. I am for a government rigorously frugal & simple, applying all the possible savings of the public revenue to the discharge of the national debt; and not for a multiplication of officers & salaries merely to make partisans, & for increasing, by every device the public debt, on the principle of its being a public blessing. I am for relying, for internal defense, on our militia solely, till actual invasion, and for such a naval force only as may protect our coasts and harbors from such depredations as we have experienced; and not for a standing army in time of peace, which may overawe the public sentiment; nor for a navy, which, by its own expenses and the eternal wars in which it will implicate us, will grind us with public burthens, & sink us under them. I am for free commerce with all nations; political connection with none; & little or no diplomatic establishment. And I am not for linking ourselves by new treaties with the quarrels of Europe; entering that field of slaughter to preserve their balance, or joining in the confederacy of kings to war against the principles of liberty. I am for freedom of religion, & against all maneuvers to bring about a legal ascendancy of one sect over another: for freedom of the press, & against all violations of the constitution to silence by force & not by reason the complaints or criticisms, just or unjust, of our citizens against the conduct of their agents. And I am for encouraging the progress of science in all its branches; and not for raising a hue and cry against the sacred name of philosophy; for awing the human mind by stories of rawhead & bloody bones to a distrust of its own vision, & to repose implicitly on that of others; to go backwards instead of forwards to look for improvement; to believe that government, religion, morality, & every other science were in the highest perfection in ages of the darkest ignorance, and that nothing can ever be devised more perfect than what was established by our forefathers. To these I will add, that I was a sincere well-wisher to the success of the French Revolution, and still wish it may end in the establishment of a free & well-ordered republic; but I have not been insensible under the atrocious depredations they have committed on our commerce. The first object of my heart is my own country. In that is embarked my family, my fortune, & my own existence. I have not one farthing of interest, nor one fiber of attachment out of it, nor a single motive of preference of any one nation to another, but in proportion as they are more or less friendly to us. But though deeply feeling the injuries of France, I did not think war the surest means of redressing them. I did believe, that a mission sincerely disposed to preserve peace, would obtain for us a peaceable & honorable settlement & retribution; and I appeal to you to say, whether this might not have been obtained, if either of your colleagues had been of the same sentiment with yourself.

These, my friend, are my principles; they are unquestionably the principles of the great body of our fellow citizens, and I know there is not one of them which is not yours also. In truth, we never differed but on one ground, the funding system; and as, from the moment of its being adopted by the constituted authorities, I became religiously principled in the sacred discharge of it to the uttermost farthing, we are united now even on that single ground of difference.

To P. S. Dupont de Nemours

18 January 1802

Dear Sir,—It is rare I can indulge myself in the luxury of philosophy. Your letters give me a few of those delicious moments. Placed as you are in a great commercial town, with little opportunity of discovering the dispositions of the country portions of our citizens, I do not wonder at your doubts whether they will generally and sincerely concur in the sentiments and measures developed in my message of the 7th Jany. But from 40 years of intimate conversation with the agricultural inhabitants of my country, I can pronounce them as different from those of the cities, as those of any two nations known. The sentiments of the former can in no degree be inferred from those of the latter. You have spoken a profound truth in these words, "Il y a dans les etats unis un bon sens silencieux, un esprit de justice froide, qui lorqu'il est question d'emettre un *vote* comme les bavardages de ceux qui font les habiles." A plain country farmer has written lately a pamphlet on our public affairs. His testimony of the sense of the country is the best which can be produced of the justness of your observation. His words are "The tongue of man is not his whole body. So, in this case, the noisy part of the community was not all the body politic. During the career of fury and contention (in 1800), the sedate, grave part of the people were still; hearing all and judging for themselves what method to take, when the constitutional time of action should come, the exercise of the right of suffrage." The majority of the present legislature are in unison with the agricultural part of our citizens, and you

will see that there is nothing in the message to which they do not accord. Some things may perhaps be left undone from motives of compromise for a time, and not to alarm by too sudden a reformation, but with a view to be resumed at another time. I am perfectly satisfied the effect of the proceedings of this session of congress will be to consolidate the great body of well meaning citizens together, whether federal or republican, heretofore called. I do not mean to include royalists or priests. Their opposition is immovable. But they will be vox et preterea nihil, leaders without followers. I am satisfied that within one year from this time were an election to take place between two candidates merely republican and federal, where no personal opposition existed against either, the federal candidate would not get the vote of a single elector in the U.S. I must here again appeal to the testimony of my farmer, who says "The great body of the people are one in sentiment. If the federal party and the republican party, should each of them choose a convention to frame a constitution of government or a code of laws, there would be no radical difference in the results of the two conventions." This is most true. The body of our people, tho' divided for a short time by an artificial panic, and called by different names, have ever had the same object in view, to wit, the maintenance of a federal, republican government, and have never ceased to be all federalists, all republicans: still excepting the noisy band of royalists inhabiting cities chiefly, and priests both of city and country. When I say that in an election between a republican and federal candidate, free from personal objection, the former would probably get every vote, I must not be understood as placing myself in that view. It was my destiny to come to the government when it had for several years been committed to a particular political sect, to the absolute and entire exclusion of those who were in sentiment with the body of the nation. I found the country entirely in the enemy's hands. It was necessary to dislodge some of them. Out of many thousands of officers in the U.S. 9 only have been removed for political principle, and 12 for delinquencies chiefly pecuniary. The whole herd have squealed out, as if all their throats were cut. These acts of justice few as they have been, have raised great personal objections to me, of which a new character would be [faded]. When this government was first established, it was possible to have kept it going on true principles, but the contracted, English, half-lettered ideas of Hamilton destroyed that hope in the bud. We can pay off his debt in 15 years; but we can never get rid of his financial system. It mortifies me to be strengthening principles which I deem radically vicious, but this vice is entailed on us by the first error. In other parts of our government I hope we shall be able by degrees to introduce sound principles and make them habitual. What is practicable must often control what is pure theory; and the habits of the governed determine in a great degree what is practicable. Hence the same original principles, modified in practice according to the different habits of different nations, present governments of very different aspects. The same principles reduced to forms of practice accommodated to our habits, and put into forms accommodated to the habits of the French nation would present governments very unlike each other. I have no doubt but that a great man, thoroughly knowing the habits of France, might so accommodate to them the principles of free government as to enable them to live free. But in the hands of those who have not this coup d'oeil, many unsuccessful experiments I fear are yet to be tried before they will settle down in freedom and tranquility. I applaud therefore your determination to remain here, tho' for yourself and the adults of your family the dissimilitude of our manners and the difference of tongue will be sources of real unhappiness. Yet less so than the horrors and dangers which France would present to you, and as to those of your family still in infancy, they will be formed to the circumstances of the country, and will, I doubt not, be happier here than they could have been in Europe under any circumstances. Be so good as to make my respectful salutations acceptable to Made. Dupont, and all of your family and to be assured yourself of my constant and affectionate esteem.

EDMUND PENDLETON

"The Danger Not Over"

5 October 1801

Reprinted by the *Aurora* on 28 October from the Richmond *Examiner* of 20 October and picked up from there by other papers, this essay by one of Virginia's most venerable revolutionaries and jurists insisted that a change of men, without a change of measures, would not correct the problems of the

1790s. Appearing just before the meeting of the first Republican Congress, it outlined a program of radical reforms grounded on ideas and assumptions that would eventually flower into an Old Republican opposition to the more moderate course of Jefferson's and Madison's administrations.

Although one of my age [*eighty*] can have little to hope, and less to fear, from forms of government, . . . and possibly may be charged with intermeddling where he has no interest whenever he utters opinions concerning social regulations; yet I feel impelled by an anxious desire to promote the happiness of my country to submit to the public consideration some reflections on our present political state.

It is far from my intention to damp the public joy occasioned by the late changes of our public agents or to disturb the calm which already presages the most beneficial consequences; on the contrary, I consider this event as having arrested a train of measures which were gradually conducting us towards ruin.

These changes will be a matter of tenfold congratulation if we make the proper use of them: If, instead of negligently reposing upon that wisdom and integrity which have already softened even political malice, we seize an opportunity to erect new barriers against folly, fraud, and ambition; and to explain such parts of the Constitution as have been already, or may be, interpreted contrary to the intention of those who adopted it.

This proposition does not argue a want of proper confidence in our present Chief Magistrate, but the contrary. It can be no censure to believe that he has a nobler destiny to fulfil, than that of making his contemporary countrymen happy for a few years, and that the rare event of such a character at the head of a nation imposes on Us the sacred duty of seizing the propitious opportunity to do all in our power to perpetuate that happiness. As to that species of confidence which would extinguish free inquiry and popular watchfulness, it is never desired by *patriotism* nor ought to be yielded by *freemen*.

In pursuit of our purpose, we ought to keep in mind certain principles which are believed to be sound; to enquire whether they have been violated under the Constitution; and then consider how a repetition of those violations may be prevented—As thus:

1. Government is instituted for the good of the community and not to gratify avarice or ambition; therefore,

unnecessary increase of debt—appointment of useless officers such as stationary ministers to foreign courts with which we have little connection and sixteen additional judges at a time when the business of the federal courts had greatly diminished—and engaging us in a war abroad for the sake of advancing party projects at home, are abuses in government.

2. The chief good derivable from government is *civil liberty;* and if government is so constructed as to enable its administration to assail that liberty with the several weapons heretofore most fatal to it, the structure is defective: of this sort, standing armies, fleets, severe penal laws, war, and a multitude of civil officers, are universally admitted to be; and if our government can, with ease and impunity, array those forces against social liberty, the Constitution is defective.

3. Peace is undoubtedly that state which proposes to society the best chance for the continuance of freedom and happiness, and the situation of America is such as to expose her to fewer occasions for war than any other nation, whilst it also disables her from gaining anything by war. But if, by indirect means, the executive can involve us in war not declared by the legislature; if a treaty may be made which will incidentally produce a war, and the legislature are bound to pass all laws necessary to give it full effect; or if the judiciary may determine a war to exist altho' the legislature hath refused to declare it; then the Constitution is defective, since it admits constructions which pawn our freedom and happiness upon the security of executive patriotism, which is inconsistent with republican principles.

4. Union is certainly the basis of our political prosperity, and this can only be preserved by confining, with precision, the federal government to the exercise of powers clearly required by the general interest or respecting foreign nations and the state governments to objects of a local nature; because the states exhibit such varieties of character and interests that a consolidated general government would be in a perpetual conflict with state interests, from its want of local knowledge or from a prevalence of local prejudice or interest, so as certainly to produce civil war and disunion. If, then, the distinct provinces of the general and state governments are not clearly defined; if the former may assail the latter by penalties and by absorbing all subjects of taxation, if a system leading to consolidation may be formed or pursued, and if, instead of leaving it to the

respective states to encourage their agriculture or manufactures as their local interest may dictate, the general government may by bounties or protecting duties tax the one to promote the other, then the Constitution has not sufficiently provided for the continuance of the union by securing the rights of the state governments and local interests.

5. It is necessary for the preservation of republican government that the legislative, executive, and judiciary powers should be kept separate and distinct from each other, so that no man or body of men shall be authorized to exercise more than one of them at the same time. The Constitution, therefore, in consigning to the federal senate a participation in the powers of each department, violates this important principle and tends to create in that body a dangerous aristocracy. And

6. An essential principle of representative government is that it be influenced by the will of the people, which will can never be expressed if such representatives are corrupted or influenced by hopes of office. If this hope may multiply offices and extend patronage, if the president may nominate to valuable offices members of the legislature who shall please him and displease the people by increasing his power and patronage, if he may be tempted to use this power and patronage for securing his reelection, and if he may even bestow lucrative diplomas upon judges whilst they are receiving liberal salaries paid as the price of their independence and purity, then a risk exists lest the legislature should legislate, the judges decide, and the senator concur in nominations with an eye to those offices, and lest the president may appoint with a view to his reelection; and thus may at length appear the phenomenon of a government republican in form without possessing a single chaste organ for expressing the public will.

Many of these observations were foreseen when the Constitution was ratified by those who voted for its adoption, but waived then because of the vast importance of the union, which a rejection might have placed in hazard, of the provision made for amendments as trial should discover defects, and the hope that in the meantime the instrument, with all its defects, might produce social happiness if a proper tone was given to the government by the several agents in its operation. But since experience has evinced that much mischief may be done under an unwise administration and that even the most valuable parts of the Constitution may be evaded or violated, we count no longer to rest our security upon the vain hope which depends on the rectitude of fallible men in successive administrations. But now that the union is as firmly established by the general opinion of the citizens as we can ever hope to be, it behoves us to bring forward amendments which may fix it upon principles capable of restraining human passions.

Having, I trust, shown the utility and necessity of such efforts at this time, I will venture to submit to the consideration of my fellow citizens, with great humility and deference, whether it would not be advisable to have the Constitution amended.

1. By rendering a president ineligible for the next turn and transferring from him to the legislature the appointment of the judges and stationary foreign ministers, making the stipends of the latter to be no longer discretionary in the president.

2. By depriving the senate of all executive power and shortening their term of service, or subjecting its members to removal by their constituents.

3. By rendering members of the legislature and the judges whilst in office [and] for a limited time thereafter incapable of taking any other office whatsoever (the offices of president and vice-president excepted) and subjecting the judges to removal by the concurring vote of both houses of Congress.

4. By forming some check upon the abuse of *public credit*, which, tho' in some instances useful, like fleets and armies, may, like those, be carried to extremes dangerous to liberty and inconsistent with economical government.

5. By instituting a fair mode of impaneling juries.

6. By declaring that no treaty with a foreign nation, so far as it may relate to peace or war, to the expenditure of public money, or to commercial regulations, shall be law until ratified by the legislature, the interval between such treaty and the next meeting of Congress excepted, so far as it may not relate to the grant of money.

7. By defining prohibited powers so explicitly as to defy the wiles of construction. If nothing more should be gained, it will be a great acquisition clearly to interdict laws relating to the freedom of speech, of the press, and of religion, to declare that the common law of England or of any other foreign country in criminal cases shall not be considered as a law of the United States, and that treason shall be confined to the cases stated in the Constitution, so as not to be extended further by law or construction or by using other terms such as sedition, etc.—and

8. By marking out with more precision the distinct powers of the *general* and *state* governments.

In the Virginia Bill of Rights is expressed this inestimable sentiment: "That no free government, or the blessing of liberty, can be preserved to any people but by a firm adherence to justice, moderation, temperance, frugality, and virtue; and by frequent recurrence to fundamental principles." A sentiment produced, no doubt, by the experience of this melancholy truth, "That of men advanced to power, more are inclined to destroy *liberty*, than to defend it; there is of course a continual effort for its destruction, which ought to be met by correspondent efforts for its preservation."

These principles and propositions are most respectfully submitted to my fellow citizens with this observation: "That it is only when great and good men are at the head of a nation that the people can expect to succeed in forming such barriers to counteract recent encroachments on their rights; and whenever a nation is so supine as to suffer such an opportunity to be lost, they will soon feel that THE DANGER WAS NOT OVER."

FISHER AMES

"Falkland," No. 2
6 February 1801

In the aftermath of his famous speech on Jay's Treaty, Ames, who had been suffering from pneumonia and perhaps from tuberculosis for much of the session, declined to stand for reelection. Although a brief term on the governor's council in Massachusetts would be his only later office, he wrote numerous essays condemning Jeffersonian pandering to the people. This one appeared in the *Palladium* a month before Jefferson's inauguration.

. . . The jacobins and anarchists . . . will act at first, and until they have brought things into the confusion that democrats ever do, . . . according to the forms of the Constitution. The legal powers of a president are not too great, and unless a majority in Congress should cooperate in the abuse of them, we have more to apprehend immediately from their neglect. The executive department will probably be suffered to droop in imbecility and to struggle with embarrassments. The men who have hitherto opposed order have not understood nor respected its principles, and it is expected they will more frequently obstruct than enforce them. The Secretary of the Treasury will be treated as a head clerk—his reports and plans will not be asked for nor tolerated, much less adopted. No department of power will be allowed to be safe except that of the House of Representatives—nor that in opposition to a rabble. What if the pipe should get choked up through which the funding system is nourished, what is that to the people?

If, merely by neglect, the work of destruction, though sure, should appear to be too slow and they should be impatient to hasten it by projects of innovation, there must be a majority in Congress. At present, the Senate of the United States is disposed to stand as a barrier against the democratic flood, the very office for which it was erected. Accordingly, we see that the imported patriots of Pennsylvania are already armed to assail the senate of that state as a useless and dangerous branch of government. The like attempt will be made against the Senate of the United States. Indeed, Virginia proposed, some years ago, so to amend that branch that it should become in future a tool in the hands of faction, not a defense against it. All barriers against the licentiousness of democracy will be called usurpations on the *people*—meaning always the vile, and ignorant, and needy—and be rendered odious in order to be broken down. Demagogues found their influence on the popular passions—they are certainly sincere, therefore, when they execrate senates and courts, and Sedition Laws, and all other impediments to the current of those passions. They pretend to be the friends of liberty, but all demagogues are the rivals and the enemies of free government. The most conspicuous of the new men are demagogues. New York and Pennsylvania were subjected to such influence, and Virginia was trained and disciplined according to its tactics. Hence their victory.

The leading men of the ruling party will certainly endeavor to support and exercise their power in the way that they gained it, by soothing the meanest of the vulgar prejudices and exciting and assuming the direction of their passions. Things that are to be destroyed must be made unpopular, and whatever is popular in Virginia must be attempted. What is popular then? Is credit—is finance—is impost or excise, or the carriage tax, or the stamp act, or the compulsory payment of debts, is trade, and especially trade with the British dominions, popular among those lazy feudal barons? But regulations and restrictions on the commerce of other states, projects and visionary schemes to make France rich and to starve British manufactures, projects of finance to pay debts by discrimination, pretending to give to original holders what we do not owe and denying to purchasing holders what we do. Projects to administer the government without departments, without banks, and without compulsion have been popular, and we are to expect they will be resumed. Impracticable theories will be recommended and if possible established by law, because they are not British, and because they *seem* to be philosophy.

It is very much to be apprehended that the next House of Representatives in Congress will be hurried away by a democratic impulse. If the majority should be great, they will feel incited to execute the most extravagant of their plans, for which they have long sought the opportunity, conscious that this may not last long and that they may never enjoy another. What will they do? is the question. It has been already hinted, as one equally momentous, what will they not neglect to do? Waiving that consideration, however, for the present, it is material to inquire into the state of their inclinations and of their power; in other words, what they will desire and what they will be able to do.

They will desire to reduce their darling theories to practice. There is in the democratic sect, which will be the prevailing one, a fanaticism that disdains argument and is mad with zeal to make converts; a presumption that disdains experience and is blind to difficulties. . . . The people are deemed to be perfect in their intelligence and all rulers corrupted by their power. The will or the caprice or, if that could be, the vice of the people, whether regularly and distinctly known or only guessed at, is a law paramount to all laws, not excepting those of public faith and honor, of God and virtue. Hence the instructions of a representative bind him more than the constitution or his oath, his duty or conscience. With all democrats, the state of nature is still assumed as existing, each man being a sovereign invested with power which he has delegated to his representative in Congress as his ambassador, but no man is a subject even of the laws. The very name subject stinks of slavery and is disdainfully disclaimed in the gazettes of the democrats.

There is no temperate man of sense who will take the trouble to examine these gazettes for the last twelve years, who will say that any sensible or safe system of administration could be extracted from them. He will pronounce with decision that their principles are absolutely chimerical and impracticable. It is observable that the machine of our government has moved with a great deal of friction and a very feeble and intermitting momentum. Sensible men have seriously dreaded that it would stop or drop to pieces. The government has not been obeyed in the back country. It has not dared to enforce obedience nor to punish rebellion. Yet the democrats have professed unfeignedly to fear this nerveless government, that could not stand up, but was ever to be held up, as a necromancer whose magic would bind the people in chains of slavery; a giant whose colossal tread would crush them into the earth. Accordingly, for twelve years there is no measure now a law that they did not obstruct in its passage; and not one of any importance that is a law that they originated. Mr. Madison's abortive commercial resolutions were projected and urged against the opinion of every well-informed merchant in the United States. There is no other plan or system that has even been so much as proposed by the democratic party in Congress. It has been their sufficient employment to *oppose* all business but to do none. It has even been avowed as a salutary principle of duty thus to check the proneness of our government to extremes unfavorable to the liberty of the people. That our farmers may at once comprehend the usefulness and good sense of this democratic principle of opposing, let them apply a like rule in their own business. Instead of trying to make it easier to do, what would they think of schemes to make it harder? What would they say if, while two of their laborers were getting a load of hay, a third should *think it his duty* to pitch it off? Would they like to have their axle-trees made square or eight-sided, in order that the wagon wheels might not turn so fast, and perhaps not turn at all? For it is not the fault of this party that the wheels of the government have not stood still.

In a word, the fundamental principle of the democratic system is to consider *their own power* as liberty and all other power, even that ordained by the Constitution, as despotism.

Accordingly, we may expect that they will feel neither affection nor reverence for the Senate nor the departments, nor even for their democratic president, except as the head of their party, but not as president. They will profess to obey the popular prejudices and passions and rely on their cooperation to sustain their power. Of course, it will be a

system of demagogy. Let it be repeated, the power gained by flattering the prejudices of the whisky, the treaty, the French, the house tax and the stamp act and sedition act mobs, and mob-meetings, must be supported as it was obtained. It is hostile to law, order, property, and government, in feeling, principle, tendency, and object.

This is the general description of the party. The detail of the measures that they will probably pursue is only a matter of conjecture. But the most fearful conjecture is corroborated by the analogy of the party here with the principles and examples of France. If they should exercise power, now they are in, with the same spirit that they have opposed while they were out, revolution and confusion have no terrors that would deter, no extremes that would stop them. Is there one principal head of legislation on which their ideas have been temperate, rational, and salutary? On the contrary, is there one on which they have not avowed and urged the wildest and most disorganizing theories of their own, and like objections to the systems devised by others? Banks, credit, finance, revenue, commerce, manufactures, fisheries, army, and navy are subjects that have afforded so many classes of absurdities. *Within,* they would restore chaos by the jumble of committees, instead of the heads of departments.—*Without,* they would court the curse of a French alliance, while they inconsistently affect to separate America from Europe and its politics. They have tried on all momentous questions to interpret the Constitution to mean nothing and to pervert it with amendments that would make it mean less—and worse.

What, then, are we to expect from such men but the execution of their systems? But will they be able to do it?

There will be impediments. Let us examine their nature. It is not the nature of democracy to stop short of extremes, and least of all in the delirium of newly acquired power. The Senate of the United States will be truly republican and a barrier against licentiousness. Such will be its disposition. But its firmness will much depend on the energy of the true federal republicans dispersed through the nation. We are to expect every method of intimidation will be used by the jacobins, as in Pennsylvania, to bend the Senate from virtue. Finding, as they will find, that these men will not change their principles, they will raise a clamor in all the federal states to change the men. This, however, will take time that is precious, because it is short—for such the reign of democracy will be. In Massachusetts we have had experience of the noble firmness of our senate when they saved the state from Shays, perhaps the union from civil war and confusion.

The judiciary is another rampart against the foes of all right. There is no question of the virtue of the judges. But when jacobin juries have to determine on great contested cases, we have seen enough to make us dread their perversion of the law. The best things, when misapplied, are the worst. Jacobin verdicts for damages might prove proscriptions and confiscations to the federalists.

There will also be a spirited and able minority in Congress, who will expose the bad principles and tendencies of the democratic measures. There public opinion will discern a center of light and heat. The old republican prin-

ciples, the wise and tried measures and institutions of the federal administrations, will there have skillful advocates and bold champions. It cannot be that such champions will not be strongly reinforced from the sound and enlightened part of the public. New England is not democratic, and many who now think the system of the party delightful in prospect will abhor it in the trial. It cannot be tried without shaking New England to its center. All its interests and systems and even its institutions, political and religious, are such as are detested by the democrats, because they are the strong entrenchments of an enemy. Expect, then, to see them often mined and at last battered in breach.

Repeal of the Judiciary Act of 1801

On 27 February 1801, after the resolution of the electoral tie between Jefferson and Burr, the lame-duck Sixth Congress passed a new Judiciary Act. Federalists had long insisted that the old act of 1789 was inadequate to the nation's needs, leaving the United States with too few circuit courts and requiring Supreme Court justices to ride circuit. The new law created sixteen circuit courts, increased the number of federal marshals, clerks, and attorneys, and reduced the Supreme Court from six Justices to five. Jefferson was convinced that the act of 1801 was a Federalist ploy to pack the courts with partisans of the defeated party, and, indeed, it was said that John Adams was signing commissions for the new positions until midnight on inauguration day. Repeal of the act was a leading recommendation of Jefferson's First Annual Message. In the course of the congressional debates, members of both parties also reviewed the struggle of the past ten years.

Congressional Proceedings

The Senate
Friday, 8 January 1802

Agreeably to the order of the day, the Senate proceeded to the consideration of the motion made on the 6th instant, to wit:

> That the act of Congress passed on the 13th day of February, 1801, entitled "An act to provide for the more convenient organization of the Courts of the United States," ought to be repealed.

Mr. Breckinridge then rose and addressed the President, as follows:

It will be expected of me, I presume, sir, as I introduced the resolution now under consideration, to assign my reasons for wishing a repeal of this law. This I shall do; and shall endeavor to show,

1. That the law is unnecessary and improper, and was so at its passage; and

2. That the courts and judges created by it can and ought to be abolished.

1st. That the act under consideration was unnecessary and improper is, to my mind, no difficult task to prove.

No increase of courts or judges could be necessary or justifiable unless the existing courts and judges were incompetent to the prompt and proper discharge of the duties consigned to them. To hold out a show of litigation, when in fact little exists, must be impolitic; and to multiply expensive systems and create hosts of expensive officers, without having experienced an actual necessity for them, must be a wanton waste of the public treasure.

The [executive] document before us shows that, at the passage of this act, the existing courts, not only from their number, but from the suits depending before them, were fully competent to a speedy decision of those suits. It shows that on the 15th day of June last, there were depending in all the circuit courts (that of Maryland only excepted, whose docket we have not been furnished with) one thousand five hundred and thirty-nine suits. It shows that eight thousand two hundred and seventy-six suits of every description have come before those courts in ten years and upwards. From this it appears that the annual average amount of suits has been about eight hundred.

But sundry contingent things have conspired to swell the circuit court dockets. In Maryland, Virginia, and in all the Southern and Southwestern States, a great number of suits have been brought by British creditors; this species of controversy is nearly at an end.

In Pennsylvania, the docket has been swelled by prosecutions in consequence of the Western insurrection, by the disturbances in Bucks and Northampton Counties; and by the Sedition Act. These I find amount in that state to two hundred and forty suits. . . .

In most of the states there have been prosecutions under the Sedition Act. This source of litigation is, I trust, forever dried up. And, lastly, in *all* the states a number of suits have arisen under the excise law; which source of controversy will, I hope, before this session terminates, be also dried up.

But this same document discloses another important fact; which is, that notwithstanding all these untoward and temporary sources of federal adjudication, the suits in those courts are *decreasing;* for, from the dockets exhibited (except Kentucky and Tennessee, whose suits are summed up in the aggregate) it appears that in 1799 there were one thousand two hundred and seventy-four and in 1800 there were six hundred and eighty-seven suits commenced; showing a decrease of five hundred and eighty-seven suits.

Could it be necessary then to *increase* courts when suits were *decreasing*? Could it be necessary to multiply judges when their duties were diminishing? And will I not be justified, therefore, in affirming that the law was unnecessary and that Congress acted under a mistaken impression when they multiplied courts and judges at a time when litigation was actually decreasing?

But, sir, the decrease of business goes a small way in fixing my opinion on this subject. I am inclined to think that, so far from there having been a necessity at this time for an increase of courts and judges, that the time never will arrive when America will stand in need of thirty-eight federal judges. Look, sir, at your Constitution, and see the judicial power there consigned to federal courts, and seriously ask yourself, can there be fairly extracted from those powers subjects of litigation sufficient for six supreme and thirty-two inferior court judges? To me it appears impossible. . . .

I will now inquire into the power of Congress to put down these additional courts and judges.

First, as to the courts, Congress are empowered by the Constitution "from time to time, to ordain and establish inferior courts." The act now under consideration is a legislative construction of this clause in the Constitution, that Congress may abolish as well as create these judicial officers; because it does expressly, in the twenty-seventh section of the act, abolish the then existing inferior courts for the purpose of making way for the present. This construction, I contend, is correct; but it is equally pertinent to my object, whether it be or be not. If it be correct, then the present inferior courts may be abolished as constitutionally as the last; if it be not, then the law for abolishing the former courts and establishing the present was unconstitutional and consequently repealable.

But independent of this legislative construction, on which I do not found my opinion, nor mean to rely my argument, there is little doubt indeed, in my mind, as to the power of Congress on this law. The first section of the third article vests the judicial power of the United States in one Supreme Court and such inferior courts as Congress

may, from time to time, ordain and establish. By this clause Congress *may,* from time to time, establish inferior courts; but it is clearly a discretionary power, and they *may not* establish them. . . . It would, therefore, in my opinion, be a perversion, not only of language, but of intellect, to say, that although Congress may, from time to time, establish inferior courts, yet, when established, that they shall not be abolished by a subsequent Congress possessing equal powers. It would be a paradox in legislation.

2d. As to the judges. . . . [T]he Constitution affords the proper checks to secure their honesty and independence in office. It declares they shall not be removed from office during good behavior; nor their salaries diminished during their continuance in office. From this it results that a judge, after his appointment, is totally out of the power of the President and his salary secured against legislative diminution during his continuance in office. . . .

But because the Constitution declares that a judge shall hold his office during good behavior, can it be tortured to mean that he shall hold his office after it is abolished? Can it mean that his tenure should be limited by behaving well in an office which did not exist? Can it mean that an office may exist although its duties are extinct? Can it mean, in short, that the shadow, to wit, the judge, can remain, when the substance, to wit, the office, is removed? It must have intended all these absurdities or it must admit a construction which will avoid them. . . .

. . . It is a principle of our Constitution, as well as of common honesty, that no man shall receive public money but in consideration of public services. Sinecure offices, therefore, are not permitted by our laws or Constitution. . . .

Upon the whole, sir, as all courts under any free government must be created with an eye to the administration of justice only; and not with any regard to the advancement or emolument of individual men; as we have undeniable evidence before us that the creation of the courts now under consideration was totally unnecessary; and as no government can, I apprehend, seriously deny that this Legislature has a right to repeal a law enacted by a preceding one, we will, in any event, discharge our duty by repealing this law; and thereby doing all in our power to correct the evil. . . .

Mr. Morris, of New York.—Mr. President, I am so very unfortunate that the arguments in favor of the motion have confirmed my opinion that the law to which it refers ought not to be repealed. The honorable mover has rested his proposition on two grounds:

1st. That the Judiciary Law passed last session is unnecessary; and

2dly. That we have a right to repeal it and ought to exercise that right.

The numerical mode of argument made use of to establish his first point is perfectly novel, and commands my tribute of admiration. This is the first time I ever heard the utility of the courts of justice estimated by the number of suits carried before them. . . .

The expense arising under this law, that it is proposed to repeal, amounts to thirty thousand dollars, exclusive of fifteen thousand dollars estimated for contingent expenses, making, together, forty-five thousand dollars. But let us not stint that allowance; throw in a few thousand more, and let the whole be stated at fifty thousand; apportion this sum among the people of the United States, according to the census lately taken, and you will find that each individual will pay just one cent. And for this insignificant saving of a cent a man, we are called upon to give up all that is valuable to a nation. . . .

Gentlemen say, recur to the ancient system. What is the ancient system? Six judges of the Supreme Court to ride the circuit of America twice a year and sit twice a year at the seat of government. . . . Cast an eye over the extent of our country, and a moment's consideration will show that the First Magistrate, in selecting a character for the bench, must seek less the learning of a judge than the agility of a post-boy. . . . I have been told by men of eminence on the bench, that they could not hold their offices under the old arrangement.

What is the present system? You have added to the old judges seven district and sixteen circuit judges. What will be the effect of the desired repeal? Will it not be a declaration to the remaining judges that they hold their offices subject to your will and pleasure? And what will be the result of this? It will be that the check established by the Constitution, wished for by the people, and necessary in every contemplation of common sense, is destroyed. . . . Did the people of America vest all powers in the Legislature? No; they had vested in the judges a check intended to be efficient—a check of the first necessity, to prevent an invasion of the Constitution by unconstitutional laws—a

check which might prevent any faction from intimidating or annihilating the tribunals themselves.

On this ground, said Mr. Morris, I stand to arrest the victory meditated over the Constitution of my country; a victory meditated by those who wish to prostrate that Constitution for the furtherance of their own ambitious views. Not of him who had recommended this measure, nor of those who now urge it; for, on his uprightness and their uprightness, I have the fullest reliance; but of those in the back-ground who have further and higher objects. These troops that protect the outworks are to be first dismissed. Those posts which present the strongest barriers are first to be taken, and then the Constitution becomes an easy prey. . . .

Tuesday, 12 January 1802

Mr. Tracy, of Connecticut.—Feeble as I am, I have thought it my duty to offer my sentiments on this subject. Owing to severity of indisposition I have not been in my place, nor have I heard any of the discussion. This circumstance will be my apology, if, in the remarks I shall make, repetitions shall occur on the one hand and apparent inattention to arguments on the other. . . .

Soon after the first law was enacted, as early as the year 1793, and I believe sooner, complaints were made of the system of circuit courts. . . . Experience taught us that some alteration in the system was requisite. It will be recollected that the judges had to travel over this extensive country twice in each year and to encounter the extremes of both heat and cold. Of this they complained; but this was not all; the business was not done. . . .

I take it to be a sound rule, adopted by all wise and deliberate bodies, not to repeal an existing law until experiment shall have discovered errors or unless there is a vice so apparent on the face of the law as that justice shall require an immediate destruction of it. Has there been time to gain information by experiment? No man will pretend this as a justification of the repeal; for the little time the law has been in force, so far as I have obtained any knowledge upon the subject, it has gained credit. . . .

Is this system so very vicious, that it deserves nothing but abhorrence and destruction? It costs us a little more than thirty thousand dollars, and by it the number of circuit judges is increased to sixteen; and by it likewise is contemplated reducing the number of supreme judges to five, when it can constitutionally be done. . . .

But there is another objection to the repeal of the judiciary law, which in my mind is conclusive: I mean the letter and spirit of the Constitution.

In the formation of every government in which the people have a share in its administration, some established and indisputable principles must be adopted. In our government, the formation of a Legislative, Executive, and Judiciary power is one of the incontrovertible principles; and that each should be independent of the other, so far as human frailty will permit, is equally incontrovertible. Will it be expected, that I should quote Sidney, De Lolme, Montesquieu, and a host of elementary writers to prove this assertion? There is probably no conflict of opinion upon this subject. When we look into our Constitution of government, we shall find, in every part of it, a close and undeviating attention to this principle. Our particular form is singular in its requirements, that full force and operation be given to this all important principle. Our powers are limited, many acts of sovereignty are prohibited to the national government and retained by the states, and many restraints are imposed upon state sovereignty. If either, by accident or design, should exceed its powers, there is the utmost necessity that some timely checks, equal to every exigency, should be interposed. The Judiciary is established by the Constitution for that valuable purpose. . . .

. . . The great object of the independence of the Judiciary must here have reference not only to our Executive, but our Legislature. The Legislature with us is the fountain of power. No person will say that the judges of the Supreme Court can be removed, unless by impeachment and conviction of misbehavior; but the judges of the inferior courts, as soon as ordained and established, are placed upon precisely the same grounds of independence with the judges of the Supreme Court. Congress may take their own time to ordain and establish, but the instant that is done, all the rights of independence attach to them.

If this reasoning is correct, can you repeal a law establishing an inferior court under the Constitution? Will it be said that although you cannot remove the judge from office, yet you can remove his office from him? Is murder prohibited, and may you shut a man up and deprive him of sustenance till he dies, and this not be denominated murder? The danger in our Government is, and always will be, that the Legislative body will become restive and perhaps unintentionally break down the barriers of our Constitution. It is incidental to man, and a part of our imperfections, to believe that power may be safely lodged in our hands. We have the wealth of the nation at command and are invested with almost irresistible strength; the judiciary has neither force nor wealth to protect itself. That we can, with propriety, modify our judiciary system so that we always leave the judges independent is a correct and reasonable position; but if we can, by repealing a law, remove them, they are in the worst state of dependence. . . .

I am strongly impressed with the magnitude of this subject; perhaps the whims of a sick man's fancy have too much possessed me to view it correctly; but, sir, I apprehend the repeal of this law will involve in it the total destruction of our Constitution. It is supported by three independent pillars: the Legislative, Executive, and Judiciary; and if any rude hand should pluck either of them away, the beautiful fabric must tumble into ruins. The Judiciary is the center pillar, and a support to each by checking both; on the one side is the sword and on the other is the wealth of the nation; and it has no inherent capacity to defend itself. . . .

This Constitution is an invaluable inheritance; if we make inroads upon it and destroy it, no matter with what intentions, it cannot be replaced; we shall never have another. . . .

The House of Representatives
Thursday, 18 February 1802

Mr. Giles said that . . . it must be obvious to the most common observer that, from the commencement of the Government of the United States, and perhaps before it, a difference of opinion existed among the citizens. . . . On one side, it was contended that in the organization of the Constitution a due apportionment of authority had not been made among the several departments; that the legislature was too powerful for the executive department; and to create and preserve a proper equipoise, it was necessary to infuse in the executive department, by legislation, all artificial powers compatible with the Constitution, upon which the most diffusive construction was given; or, in other words, to place in executive hands all the patronage it was possible to create, for the purpose of protecting the President against the full force of his constitutional responsibility to the people. On the other side, it was contended that the doctrine of patronage was repugnant to the opinions and feelings of the people; that it was unnecessary, expensive, and oppressive; and that the highest energy the government could possess would flow from the confidence of the mass of the people, founded upon their own sense of their common interests. Hence, what is called party in the United States grew up from a division of opinion respecting these two great characteristic principles. . . . A variety of circumstances existed in the United States at the commencement of the government, and a great number of favorable incidents continued afterwards to arise, which gave the patronage system the preponderancy during the first three presidential terms of election; notwithstanding it was evident that the system was adopted and pursued in direct hostility to the feelings and opinions of a great portion of the American people. The government was ushered into operation under a vast excitement of federal fervor, flowing from its recent triumph on the question of adopting the Constitution. At that time a considerable debt was afloat in the United States, which had grown out of the Revolutionary War. This debt was of two kinds: the debt proper of the United States, or engagements made by the United States in their federal capacity; the other, the state debts, or engagements entered into by the respective states for the support of the common cause.

The favorers of the patronage system readily availed themselves of these materials for erecting a moneyed interest; gave to it a stability, or qualified perpetuity, and calculated upon its certain support in all their measures of irresponsibility.

This was done not only by funding the debt proper of the United States, but by assuming the payment of the state debts and funding them also; and it is believed, extending the assumption beyond the actual engagements of the states. Hence the Federal axiom, that a public debt is a public blessing. Shortly after this event, an Indian war sprang up—he would not say by what means—in consequence of which an army was added to the list of patronage. The Algerines commenced a predatory war upon the commerce of the United States, and thence a navy formed a new item of patronage. Taxes became necessary to meet the expenses of this system, and an arrangement of internal taxes, an excise, &c., still swelled the list of patronage. But the circumstance which most favored this system was the breaking out of a tremendous and unprecedented war in those countries of Europe with which the United States

had the most intimate relations. The feelings and sympathies of the people of the United States were so strongly attracted by the tremendous scenes existing there that they considered their own internal concerns in a secondary point of view. After a variable conduct had been pursued by the United States in relation to these events, the depredations committed upon commerce and the excitements produced thereby enabled the Administration to indulge themselves in a more decisive course, and they at once pushed forward the people to the X, Y, Z of their political alphabet, before they had well learned and understood the A, B, C of the principles of the Administration.

Armies and navies were raised, and a variety of other schemes of expense were adopted, which placed the Administration in the embarrassing predicament either to violate their faith with their public creditors or to resort to new taxes. The latter alternative was preferred, accompanied with other strong coercive measures to enforce obedience. A land tax was laid for two millions of dollars. This measure awakened the people to a sense of their situation; and shook to the foundation all those federal ramparts which had been planned with so much ingenuity and erected around the executive with so much expense and labor. Another circumstance peculiarly favorable to the advocates of executive patronage was that, during the two first presidential terms, the Chief Executive Magistrate possessed a greater degree of popularity and the confidence of the people than ever was or perhaps will ever be again attached to the person occupying that dignified station. The general disquietude which manifested itself in consequence of these enterprising measures, in the year 1800, induced the Federal party to apprehend that they had pushed their principles too far, and they began to entertain doubts of the result of the presidential election, which was approaching. In this state of things, it was natural for them to look out for some department of the government in which they could entrench themselves in the event of an unsuccessful issue in the election and continue to support those favorite principles of irresponsibility which they could never consent to abandon.

The Judiciary department, of course, presented itself as best fitted for their object, not only because it was already filled with men who had manifested the most indecorous zeal in favor of their principles, but because they held their offices by indefinite tenures and of course were further removed from any responsibility to the people than either of the other departments. Accordingly, on the 11th of March 1800, a bill for the more convenient organization of the courts of the United States was presented to the House of Representatives. This bill appears to have had for its objects, First, the gradual demolition of the state courts, by increasing the number and extending the jurisdiction of the federal courts. Second, to afford additional protection to the principles of the then existing Administration by creating a new corps of judges of concurring political opinions. . . . At the next session, after the result of the late election was ascertained, the bill, after having undergone some considerable alterations, was passed into the law now under discussion. This law, it is now said, is inviolable and irrepealable. It is said, the independence of the judge will be thereby immolated. . . . We are now called upon to rally round the Constitution as the ark of our political safety. Gentlemen, discarding all generalizing expressions and the spirit of the instrument, tie down all construction to the strict letter of the Constitution. He said, it gave him great pleasure to meet gentlemen on this ground; and the more so, because he had long been in the habit of hearing very different language from the same gentlemen. He had long been in the habit of hearing the same gentlemen speak of the expressions of "the common defense and the general welfare" as the only valuable part of the Constitution; that they were sufficient to obliterate all specifications and limitations of power. . . . But, he said, as if it was always the unfortunate destiny of these gentlemen to be upon extremes, they have now got round to the opposite extreme point of the political compass, and even beyond it. For, he said, they not only tie down all construction to the letter of the instrument, but they tell us that they see and call upon us also to see written therein, in large capital characters, "the independence of judges"; which, to the extent they carry the meaning of the term, is neither to be found in the letter or spirit of that instrument, or in any other political establishment, he believed, under the sun. . . .

Friday, 19 February 1802

Mr. Bayard.—Mr. Chairman, I must be allowed to express my surprise at the course pursued by the honorable gentleman from Virginia (Mr. Giles) in the remarks which he has made on the subject before us. . . . Every effort has been made to revive the animosities of the House and inflame the passions of the nation. . . . That there may be a few individuals having a preference for monarchy is not improbable; but will the gentleman from Virginia, or any

other gentleman, affirm in his place that there is a party in the country who wish to establish monarchy? Insinuations of this sort belong not to the Legislature of the Union. Their place is an election ground or an alehouse. Within these walls they are lost; abroad, they have an effect, and I fear are still capable of abusing the popular credulity.

We were next told of the parties which have existed, divided by the opposite views of promoting executive power and guarding the rights of the people. . . .

I know that this is the distinction of party which some gentlemen have been anxious to establish; but this is not the ground on which we divide. I am satisfied with the constitutional powers of the executive and never wished nor attempted to increase them; and I do not believe that gentlemen on the other side of the House ever had a serious apprehension of danger from an increase of executive authority. No, sir, our views as to the powers which do and ought to belong to the general and state governments are the true sources of our divisions. I cooperate with the party to which I am attached because I believe their true object and end is an honest and efficient support of the general government in the exercise of the legitimate powers of the Constitution. . . .

He represents the government as seizing the first moment which presented itself to create a dependent moneyed interest, ever devoted to its views. What are we to understand by this remark of the gentleman? Does he mean to say that Congress did wrong in funding the public debt? Does he mean to say that the price of our liberty and independence ought not to have been paid? Is he bold enough to denounce this measure as one of the Federal victims marked for destruction? Is it the design to tell us that its day has not yet come, but is approaching; and that the funding system is to add to the pile of Federal ruins? Do I hear the gentleman say we will reduce the Army to a shadow; we will give the Navy to the worms; the Mint, which presented the people with the emblems of their liberty and of their sovereignty, we will abolish; the revenue shall depend upon the winds and waves; the judges shall be made our creatures; and the great work shall be crowned and consecrated by relieving the country from an odious and oppressive public debt? These steps, I presume, are to be taken in progression. The gentleman will pause at each, and feel the public pulse. As the fever increases he will proceed, and the moment of delirium will be seized to finish the great work of destruction. . . .

After, Mr. Chairman, the honorable member had

exhausted one quiver of arrows against the late executive, he opened another, equally poisoned, against the judiciary. He has told us, sir, that when the power of the government was rapidly passing from Federal hands—after we had heard the thundering voice of the people which dismissed us from their service—we erected a judiciary which we expected would afford us the shelter of an inviolable sanctuary. The gentleman is deceived. We knew better, sir, the characters who were to succeed us, and we knew that nothing was sacred in the eyes of infidels. No, sir, I never had a thought that anything belonging to the Federal Government was holy in the eyes of those gentlemen. I could never, therefore, imagine that a sanctuary could be built up which would not be violated. I believe these gentlemen regard public opinion, because their power depends upon it; but I believe they respect no existing establishment of the government; and if public opinion could be brought to support them, I have no doubt they would annihilate the whole. I shall at present only say further, on this head, that we thought the reorganization of the judicial system a useful measure, and we considered it as a duty to employ the remnant of our power to the best advantage of our country. . . .

I know, sir, that some have said, and perhaps not a few have believed, that the new system was introduced not so much with a view to its improvement of the old, as to the places which it provided for the friends of the administration. This is a calumny so notoriously false, and so humble, as not to require nor to deserve an answer upon this floor. It cannot be supposed that the paltry object of providing for sixteen unknown men could have ever offered an inducement to a great party basely to violate their duty, meanly to sacrifice their character, and foolishly to forego all future hopes.

. . . I have heard much said about the additional courts created by the act of last session. I perceive them spoken of in the President's Message. In the face of this high authority, I undertake to state, that no additional court was established by that law. Under the former system there was one Supreme Court, and there is but one now. There were seventeen district courts, and there are no more now. There was a circuit court held in each district, and such is the case at present. Some of the district judges are directed to hold their courts at new places, but there is still in each district but one district court. What, sir, has been done? The unnatural alliance between the supreme and district courts has been severed, but the jurisdiction of both these courts remains untouched. The power of authority of neither of them has been augmented or diminished. The jurisdiction of the circuit court has been extended to the cognizance of debts of four hundred dollars, and this is the only material change in the power of that court. The chief operation of the late law is a new organization of the circuit courts. To avoid the evils of the former plan, it became necessary to create a new corps of judges. It was considered that the Supreme Court ought to be stationary, and to have no connection with the judges over whose sentences they had an appellate jurisdiction. . . .

The Supreme Court has been rendered stationary. Men of age, of learning, and of experience are now capable of holding a seat on the bench; they have time to mature their opinions in causes on which they are called to decide, and they have leisure to devote to their books and to augment their store of knowledge. It was our hope, by the present establishment of the court, to render it the future pride, and honor, and safety of the nation. It is this tribunal which must stamp abroad the judicial character of our country. It is here that ambassadors and foreign agents resort for justice; and it belongs to this high court to decide finally, not only on controversies of unlimited value between individuals and on the more important collision of state pretensions, but also upon the validity of the laws of the states and of this government. Will it be contended that such great trusts ought to be reposed in feeble or incapable hands? . . .

Let us next consider, sir, the present state of the circuit courts.

There are six courts, which sit in twenty-two districts; each court visits at least three districts, some four. The courts are now composed of three judges of equal power and dignity. Standing on equal ground, their opinions will be independent and firm. Their number is the best for consultation, and they are exempt from the inconvenience of an equal division of opinion. But what I value most, and what was designed to remedy the great defect of the former system, is the identity which the court maintains. Each district has now always the same court. Each district will hereafter have a system of practice and uniformity of decision. The judges of each circuit will now study, and learn, and retain the laws and practice of their respective districts. It never was intended, nor is it practicable, that the same rule of property or of proceeding should prevail from New Hampshire to Georgia. The old courts were enjoined to obey the laws of the respective states. Those laws fluctuate with the will of the state legislatures, and no other uniformity could ever be expected but in the construction of the Constitution and statutes of the United States. This uniformity is still preserved by the control of the Supreme Court over the courts of the circuits. Under the present establishment, a rational system of jurisprudence will arise. The practice and local laws of the different districts may vary, but in the same district they will be uniform. The practice of each district will suggest improvements to the others, the progressive adoption of which will in time assimilate the systems of the several districts. . . .

[Mr. Bayard here stated, that he . . . observed that the common hour of adjournment had gone by, and that he should sit down in order to allow the Committee to rise, if they thought proper; and that he should beg leave to be heard the following day upon the second point. After some conversation, the Committee rose, reported—and the House adjourned.]

Saturday, 20 February 1802

The House again resolved itself into a Committee of the Whole on the bill sent from the Senate, entitled "An act to repeal certain acts respecting the organization of the Courts of the United States, and for other purposes."

Mr. Bayard.—. . . I have considered it as conceded, upon all hands, that the legislature have not the power of removing a judge from his office; but it is contended only that the office may be taken from the judge. Sir, it is a principle in law, which ought, and I apprehend does, hold more strongly in politics, that what is prohibited from being done directly is restrained from being done indirectly. Is there any difference, but in words, between taking the office from a judge and removing a judge from the office? Do you not indirectly accomplish the end which you admit is prohibited? I will not say that it is the sole intention of the supporters of the bill before us to remove the circuit judges from their offices, but I will say that they establish a precedent which will enable worse men than themselves to make use of the legislative power for that purpose upon any occasion. If it be constitutional to vacate the office, and in that way to dismiss the judge, can there be a question as to the power to re-create the office and fill it with another man? Repeal to-day the bill of the last session, and the circuit judges are no longer in office. To-morrow, rescind the repealing act (and no one will doubt the right to do it), and no effect is produced but the removal of the judges. . . .

It was once thought by gentlemen who now deny the principle, that the safety of the citizen and of the states rested upon the power of the judges to declare an unconstitutional law void. How vain is a paper restriction if it confers neither power nor right! Of what importance is it to say, Congress are prohibited from doing certain acts, if no legitimate authority exists in the country to decide whether an act done is a prohibited act? . . .

If, said Mr. B., you mean to have a Constitution, you must discover a power to which the acknowledged right is attached of pronouncing the invalidity of the acts of the legislature which contravene the instrument. Does the power reside in the states? Has the legislature of a state a right to declare an act of Congress void? This would be erring upon the opposite extreme. It would be placing the general government at the feet of the state governments. It would be allowing one member of the Union to control all the rest. It would inevitably lead to civil dissension and a dissolution of the general government. Will it be pretended that the state courts have the exclusive right of deciding upon the validity of our laws? I admit that they have the right to declare an act of Congress void. But this right they enjoy in practice, and it ever essentially must exist, subject to the revision and control of the courts of the United States. If the state courts definitively possessed the right of declaring the invalidity of the laws of this Government, it would bring us in subjection to the states. The judges of those courts, being bound by the laws of the state, if a state declared an act of Congress unconstitutional, the law of the state would oblige its courts to determine the law invalid. This principle would also destroy the uniformity of obligation upon all the states, which should attend every law of the government. If a law were declared void in one state, it would exempt the citizens of that state from its operation, whilst obedience was yielded to it in the other states. I go further, and say, if the states or state courts had a final power of annulling the acts of this government, its miserable and precarious existence would not be worth the trouble of a moment to preserve. It would endure but a short time, as a subject of derision, and, wasting into an empty shadow, would quickly vanish from our sight. . . .

Let me now suppose that in our frame of government the judges are a check upon the legislature; that the Constitution is deposited in their keeping. Will you say afterwards that their existence depends upon the legislature? That the body whom they are to check had the power to destroy them? . . . Can any thing be more absurd than to admit that the judges are a check upon the legislature, and yet to contend that they exist at the will of the legislature? A check must necessarily imply a power commensurate to its end. The political body designed to check another must be independent of it, otherwise there can be no check. What check can there be when the power designed to be checked can annihilate the body which is to restrain it?

I go further, Mr. Chairman, and take a still stronger ground. . . . If you pass the bill upon your table the judges have a constitutional right to declare it void. I hope they will have courage to exercise that right; and if, sir, I am called upon to take my side, standing acquitted in my conscience and before my God of all motives but the support of the Constitution of my country, I shall not tremble at the consequences.

The Constitution may have its enemies, but I know that it has also its friends. I beg gentlemen to pause before they take this rash step. There are many, very many, who believe, if you strike this blow, you inflict a mortal wound on the Constitution. There are many now willing to spill their blood to defend that Constitution. Are gentlemen disposed to risk the consequences? . . . Will they risk civil dissension, will they hazard the welfare, will they jeopardize the peace of the country, to save a paltry sum of money—less than thirty thousand dollars?

. . . Sir, the morals of your people, the peace of the country, the stability of the government, rest upon the maintenance of the independence of the judiciary. It is not of half the importance in England that the judges should be independent of the Crown, as it is with us that they should be independent of the legislature. Am I asked, would you render the judges superior to the legislature? I answer, no, but co-ordinate. Would you render them independent of the legislature? I answer, yes, independent of every power on earth, while they behave themselves well. The essential interests, the permanent welfare of society, require this independence. . . .

Friday, 26 February 1802

Mr. Nicholson.—. . . Sir, when I am told that the party advocating this repeal have grown out of the party originally opposed to the Constitution, and are now about to prostrate it, I feel more than I am willing to express; but when gentlemen talk about parties in this country, permit me to turn their attention to an earlier period of our political history, to that period when our liberties and independence were at stake, and when every nerve was strong to resist the encroachments of tyranny. At this time where were many of that gentleman's political friends? Upon examination it will be found that many of them basely deserted their country in her distress and were openly fighting in the ranks of her enemies. In the list of my political friends, none such are to be found, for we do not require their support. But I can look about me, upon my right hand and upon my left, and can see men, even upon this floor, advocating the present bill, who bore the burden of the Revolutionary war, who drew their swords to establish the independence we now enjoy, and who will not hesitate to draw them again if those threats are carried into execution which have been recently thrown out against the Constitution. I know men too, equally distinguished for their talents and their virtues, friendly to this repeal, who signed the Constitution as members of the General Convention, who used every effort to promote its adoption, and who, I have no doubt, are ready to defend it to the last moment. There are men likewise, and gentlemen dare not contradict me, who refused their signatures to the Constitution as members of the General Convention, and who opposed it in every stage of its adoption, but were afterwards received into favor and were high in the confidence of the former administration. Which of these two descriptions of persons are most likely to cherish the Constitution, I cheerfully leave to the American people to decide. . . .

The gentleman from North Carolina, who opened the debate, . . . commenced an unwarrantable attack upon a majority of the House by declaring that on the seventh of December the same spirit of innovation had entered these walls which had laid waste the fairest portions of Europe; that it was now about to tear down all the valuable institutions which had been erected by former administrations and even to destroy the Constitution itself. Did gentlemen imagine that such observations were to pass unnoticed? Did they suppose that we would sit tamely down under an imputation at once so heavy and so groundless? Was it not natural that we should go back and look into the nature and origin of those measures which had been denominated the fairest institutions and which the gentleman had particularized as the debt, the taxes, the judiciary, and the mint? Yes, sir, the gentleman from Virginia did take a view of these fair institutions, and did show, whatever might have been the motives of their authors, that their inevitable tendency was to strengthen the power of the executive.

It is this undue influence of the executive power of the government that we wish to reduce; it is this influence that we wish to confine within its proper limits, in order to prevent the government from taking that course which most republican governments have heretofore taken; to prevent it from arriving at that goal where the spirit of republicanism is lost and monarchy commences. . . .

When we attempt to correct these errors, let us not be told that we are about to prostrate the Constitution. The Constitution is as dear to us as to our adversaries, and we will go as far to support it. It is by repairing the breaches that we mean to save it and to set it on a firm and lasting foundation, that shall resist the attacks of its enemies and defy the encroachments of ambition. We are yet a young nation and must learn wisdom from the experience of others. By avoiding the course which other nations have steered, we shall avoid likewise their catastrophe. Public debts, standing armies, and heavy taxes have converted the English nation into a mere machine to be used at the pleasure of the crown. . . . It is true we have had no riot act, but we have had a Sedition Act, calculated to secure the conduct of the executive from free and full investigation; we have had an army, and still have a small one, securing to the executive an immensity of patronage; and we have a large national debt, for the payment of the principal and interest of which it is necessary to collect "yearly millions," by means of a cloud of officers spread over the face of the country. By repealing a part of the taxes from which a part of this money has been raised, we not only lessen the burdens of the people, but we likewise discharge a large portion of those officers who are appointed by the executive and who add greatly to his influence.

This debt, which now hangs as a dead weight about us, had been called the price of our independence, and has been spoken of as a debt due to the "war-worn soldier," which we assumed and funded to alleviate his sufferings. This position I cannot assent to. When the veteran soldier returned from the fatigues and hardships of the war, to enjoy domestic comfort, he brought with him, as an evidence of the service he had rendered, nothing but his certificates and his wounds. They were, indeed, honorable testimonials; the latter he felt would remain with him while life lasted, and the former he left with the hope that, one day or other, his country would be in a situation to pay him; but the hard hand of poverty pressed upon him, and stern necessity compelled him to part with them for a pit-

tance. The rich and cunning speculator, who had sheltered himself from the storm, now came out to prey upon his distress, and, for two shillings and sixpence in the pound, he purchased this poor reward of toil and hardship. When you were about to make provision for the payment of this debt, you were called on, loudly called on, by the voice of humanity, by the spirit of justice, to make a discrimination in favor of the soldier. He asked you to give to the speculator what the speculator had advanced, but to give the balance to the poor, though valiant soldier, who had faithfully earned it in the frozen regions of Canada or the burning sands of South Carolina; you regarded him not; to his tale of distress you turned a deaf ear; his services and his sufferings were forgotten; the cold and hunger he had endured, the blood he had spilt, were no longer remembered; you cast him upon the unfeeling world, a miserable dependent upon charity for subsistence. Let not then the gentleman from Delaware call this debt the price of our independence or a compensation to the war-worn soldier. To him it was a poor compensation indeed. Its effect was to intrench yourselves around by rich speculators, whose interest and influence you secured, and who would be ready to support you in any measures, provided you would insure them the payment of the interest on that debt, which was funded for their benefit, but which was created at the hazard and expense of a brave and meritorious soldiery. From motives of a shameful policy you enabled the proud speculator to roll along in his gilded chariot, while the hardy veteran, who had fought and bled for your liberties, was left to toil for his support or to beg his bread from door to door.

But this debt, iniquitous as we deem the manner of its settlement, we mean to discharge; but we mean not to perpetuate it; it is no part of our political creed that "a public debt is a public blessing." We will, I trust, make ample provision for its final redemption; and when in a few days a proposition shall be submitted for the annual appropriation of seven millions and three hundred thousand dollars to this object, I challenge gentlemen on the other side of the House, who express so much anxiety about public faith, to be as forward in support of this measure as I shall be. We will then show to the American nation who are most inclined to support the public credit, whether those who are desirous of paying the debt or those who are anxious for its perpetuation.

The member from Delaware told us that the gentleman

from Virginia (Mr. Giles), after exhausting one quiver, had unlocked another and discharged it upon the judges. . . . But why all this uneasiness about dismissals from office? Have the friends of gentlemen heretofore been so eager in their pursuit of the loaves and fishes that they are now unwilling to surrender them? Have they enjoyed them with such peculiar delight that they now murmur at the exercise of the constitutional right which the President possesses of displacing from office all those whom he thinks unfit for the duties and of putting in those who, in his opinion, are better qualified? Surely when gentlemen are so strenuously contending for the constitutional rights of the judiciary, they ought not to murmur at the exercise of a constitutional right by the executive. Nor do I think they can with any propriety complain when it is recollected that, although the President had the power of disposing of all offices, yet he has left by far the larger proportion in the possession of men who are personally and politically his enemies. From the great discontent expressed on the subject of removals, it might seem that the judges themselves were rather the objects of general solicitude than the system of constitutional privileges of the judiciary.

This judiciary, however, the gentleman from Delaware has said, in that same spirit of Christian meekness which appears to have characterized him throughout, he never considered a sanctuary, because he knew that nothing was sacred in the eyes of infidels. May I be permitted to ask what the honorable gentleman means by infidels? . . . If, sir, an unqualified aversion to the high-fashioned opinion that a public debt is a public blessing; if a total unbelief in the propriety of laying heavy and oppressive taxes to pay a useless and expensive army; if the strongest reprobation or every law calculated to restrain the liberty of the press and thereby prevent the nation from inquiring into its own concerns; if the entire rejection of the odious principle that the reins of government are to be placed in the hands of a set of men who are independent of and beyond the control of the people, afford any evidence of infidelity, then do I avow myself as much an infidel as any man living. . . .

Mr. N. sat down; the Committee rose, and the House adjourned.

Saturday, 27 February 1802

The House again resolved itself into a Committee on the bill sent from the Senate, entitled "An act of repeal certain acts respecting the organization of the Courts of the United States, and for other purposes."

Mr. Nicholson (in continuation) offered his acknowledgments to the Committee for consenting to hear him again today. . . .

. . . We say that we have the same right to repeal the law establishing inferior courts that we have to repeal the law establishing post offices and post roads, laying taxes, or raising armies. This right would not be denied but for the construction given to that part of the Constitution which declares that "the judges both of the supreme and inferior courts shall hold their offices during good behavior." The arguments of gentlemen generally have been directed against a position that we never meant to contend for: against the right to remove the judges in any other manner than by impeachment. This right we have never insisted on. . . . Our doctrine is that every Congress has a right to repeal any law passed by its predecessors, except in cases where the Constitution imposes a prohibition. . . .

. . . The independence of the three branches of government has, in my opinion, been much talked of without being fairly defined or correctly understood. The powers of our government are distributed under three different heads, and are committed to the different departments. The legislative power extends to the enacting, revising, amending, or repealing all laws, as the various interests of the nation may require. The judiciary power consists in an authority to apply those laws to the various controversies which may arise between man and man, or between the government and its citizens, and to pronounce sentence agreeably to the dictates of their judgment and consciences. After the judicial decree, it then becomes the business of the executive to carry it into effect according to its true intent, and conformably to the laws of the land. In all governments where they have the semblance of freedom, the great *desideratum* has been to keep these three branches so entirely separate and distinct as that the powers of neither should be exercised by the other; or, in other words, that the legislative powers should never be exercised by the executive or the judiciary, that the judicial powers should not be exercised by the legislative or executive, and that the executive powers should not be exercised by the legislature or judiciary. But there is no government on the face of the earth, whose history I am acquainted with, in which a total and entire independence has been established. In England the judiciary hold their offices at the will of Parliament. In the States of Vermont, Massachusetts, Connecticut, Rhode Island, New Jersey, Pennsylvania, Delaware, Maryland, and Georgia, the judges are either elected by the legislature for a limited time, or are subject to removal by them; in New York, some of the judges are in the same situation; in New Hampshire, the legislature are authorized to limit the duration of their commissions, and, I believe, are in the habit of doing so; and in Maryland, Virginia, North Carolina, South Carolina, and Georgia, the executive is absolutely dependent on the legislature for his continuance in office, being annually or biennially elected. In Tennessee, and in most, perhaps all of the others, both the judiciary and the executive are dependent on the legislature for the amount and payment of their salaries. Yet, sir, in all these states, where we find no such idea of independence as is now contended for, there has been no confusion, no disorder. The people are happy and contented, and I venture to affirm, are more free than the inhabitants of any other part of the globe. They are happy, because none can oppress them; they are free, because they have a control over their public agents. But if the public agents of the federal government are to be set above the nation and are to be invested with the arbitrary and uncontrolled powers which some gentlemen insist on, who can say where they will stop, or what bounds shall be prescribed to them? Man is fond of power, is continually grasping after it, and is never satisfied. He is not, therefore, to be trusted. Unlimited confidence is the bane of a free government. Those who would retain their freedom, must likewise retain power over agents, or they will be driven to destruction. I have been taught to believe, that the power is never so safe as in the hands of those for whose benefit it is to be employed. I consider it in their hands when it is delegated to representatives freely chosen by themselves for a short period, and immediately responsible to them for its use. "Power in the people has been well compared to light in the sun; native, original, inherent, and not to be controlled by human means." But power, when once surrendered to independent rulers, instantly becomes a despot, and arms itself with whips and chains. While the people retain it in their own hands, it exalts the character of a nation, and is at once their pride and their security; if they surrender it to others, it becomes restless and active, until it debases the human character, and enslaves the human mind; it is never satisfied until it finally tramples upon

all human rights. It is against this surrender of power that I contend; it is this vital principle of the Constitution that I never will yield. The people are the fountain of all power; they are the source from which every branch of this government springs, and never shall any act of mine place one branch beyond their control. . . .

Editorials on the Repeal

"A Friend of the Constitution" [William Cranch], No. 1

Washington Federalist

7 December 1801

. . . [If a provision creating a dependent judiciary] had stolen into the Constitution, offered to the states for their acceptance, we need only examine the several governments they have framed for themselves to determine what would have been its fate. We cannot doubt but that so pernicious a principle would have been universally execrated; the opponents of the Constitution would throughout our continent have taken this strong ground:—from every quarter of the nation, the danger to which liberty would have been exposed from an enslaved judiciary, would have resounded in our ears: and not all the necessity, nor all the other excellencies of that instrument, could have saved it from rejection. For this I appeal to the opinions then entertained by those who acted either in the general or state conventions, and conjure them by the sacred flame of patriotism which then glowed in their bosoms, and which cannot yet be entirely extinguished to examine well the causes which have changed their opinions, before they yield to that change.

If at any time before the late revolution in men (I hope not fatally in measure) the abstract proposition, unapplied to particular characters, of creating a dependent judiciary, had been made to the people of America, who would have been found to have supported it? Who would not with all his powers have reprobated a doctrine so fraught with baneful consequences, so surcharged with danger to the dearest rights of man? If the first or second administration could have so deviated from their principles as to have countenanced such a measure, how would it have been received by those who, under a third administration, are themselves its patrons? Let their efforts to agitate the public mind on the mission of Mr. Jay answer this question.

What can have produced this ominous change? The very men who then affected to tremble for the independence of the judiciary, because a judge might be bribed by being appointed to a temporary employment without emolument, who affected to tremble for the constitution because a judge entered on the performance of duties he was not forbidden to discharge; now boldly and openly support a measure which totally prostrates that independence, by making the office dependent on the will of the legislature, and at the same time inflicts a vital wound on the constitution, which explicitly declares the tenure of the judicial office to be *during good behavior.*

These things require the serious consideration, not only of the wise and good, but of all those who, from any motives whatever, wish to perpetuate to themselves and their posterity, the blessings of civil liberty.

The subject shall be more closely examined in a succeeding number.

"A Friend of the Constitution" [William Cranch], No. 5

Washington Federalist

12 December 1801

. . . To the judicial department in every society is committed the important power of deciding between the government and individuals, and between different individuals having claims on each other. The dearest interests of man, life, liberty, reputation, and property, often depend on the integrity and talents of the judge. All important as is this department to the happiness and safety of individuals, it is from its structure much exposed to invasion from the other departments and but little capable of defending itself from the attacks which insatiate ambition, wearing the public good as a mask, will make upon it. It wields not the sword, nor does it hold the purse. It stands aloof from both. What is still more decisive, its purity, its decorum of station, requires a total abstinence from the use of those means by which popular favor is to be obtained. In a government constituted like that of the United States, popularity is a real power, and those who hold it will always be found too mighty for such as they may choose to attack. It will be forever arranged on the side of those whom the people elect, and their very election evinces that they possess it. Whenever then the representatives of the people enter into a contest with the judges, power is all on one side, and the issue will seldom be favorable to the weaker party. The judiciary can only expect support from the considerate and patriotic, who see, when yet at a distance, the evils to result necessarily from measures to which numbers may be impelled by their present passions.

The judiciary then not only possesses not that force which will enable it to encroach on others to aggrandize itself or to enlarge its own sphere, but is not even able to protect itself in the possession of those rights which are conferred upon it for the benefit of the people. Incapable of acting offensively, its real and only character is that of a shield for the protection of innocence, a tribunal for the faithful execution and exposition of the law. This character it will retain unless it be made subservient to the views of one of the other departments of government. Thus debased, it becomes in the hands of the executive or legislature one of the most terrible instruments of oppression with which man has ever been scourged. "Were the power of judging," says the justly celebrated Montesquieu, "joined with the legislative, the life and liberty of the subject would be exposed to arbitrary control, for the judge would then be the legislator. Were it joined to the executive power, the judge might behave with all the violence of an oppressor."

Impressed with the force of these eternal truths, the wise and good of America, the enlightened friends of civil liberty and of human happiness, have fought to separate the judiciary from, and to render it independent of, the executive and legislative powers. They have used all the means they possessed to render this independence secure and permanent, for they have laid its foundation in the Constitution of their country. Before we tear up this foundation, and tumble into ruins the fair edifice erected on it, let us pause for a moment and examine the motives which led to its formation.

In all governments created by consent, the essential objects to be obtained are security from external force and protection from internal violence. In arming government with powers adequate to these objects, the possibility of their being turned upon individuals ought never to be forgotten. It is the province of wisdom so to modify them as not to impair their energies when directed to the purposes for which they were given, and yet to render them impotent if employed in the hateful task of individual oppression. The best security yet discovered, is found in the principle that no man shall be condemned, no pains or penalties incurred, but in conformity with laws previously enacted and rendered public.

But the acknowledgment of this principle would be of no avail without its practical use. To obtain this, the laws must be applied with integrity and discernment to the cases which occur. If the same passions which direct the prosecution dictate its decision, innocence will cease to afford protection, and condemnation will certainly follow arraignment. It is therefore indispensable to individual safety that the tribunal which decides should, as far as possible, be a stranger to the passions and feelings which accuse: that it should be actuated by neither hope nor fear: that it should feel no interest in the event and should be under the influence of no motive which might seduce it from the correct line of duty and of law.

It is not in prosecutions instituted by the government only that such a tribunal is necessary. In civil actions between man and man it is not less essential. Justice may sometimes be unpopular, and the powerful may sometimes be wrong. What shall then protect the weak? What shall shield prosecuted virtue? What but purity in the judgment seat and exemption from those prejudices and dispositions which for a time obscure right and tempt to error?

The principle which could alone preserve this purity was believed to have been discovered. It was to remove all those irresistable temptations to a deviation from rectitude which interest will create by rendering the judges truly independent—by making the tenure of their office *during good behavior.* . . . It was supposed that men thus independent would, in a sense of duty, find motives sufficiently strong to support them in an upright administration of justice against the influence of those who govern or the still more powerful influence of popular favor. If this expectation should sometimes be disappointed, it must yet be acknowledged that the principle affords the fairest prospect to be furnished by human means of obtaining a good so all important to the felicity of man. . . .

Nor is a dependence of the judges on the legislature in republican governments less fatal to the rights of individuals than a dependence on the executive in those which are monarchical. Let the dependence exist, and its consequence will be an improper and injurious subserviency to the will of the superior. Legislative is as heavy as executive oppression and is the more to be dreaded as it cannot be checked by public opinion, for public opinion is generally with it. When public opinion changes, the governing party changes also, and the persecuted become the persecutors. The instrument of persecution, an enslaved judiciary, is ready for any hand bold and strong enough to seize it. . . .

The government of a party continuing for a great length of time the majority, and consequently in power, may gradually soften and assume the appearance of the nation. But where the division is nearly equal, the struggle incessant, and success alternate, all the angry passions of the human mind are in perpetual exercise. The new majority brings with it into power a keen recollection of injuries supposed, if not real, and is entirely disposed to retort them. Vile calumny, exclusion from social rights, proscriptions, and banishments have, in democracies where the ruling party acts without the check of an independent judiciary, been the bitter fruits of this temper. The best safeguard against evils so serious, and it is to be feared, so certain, is a tribunal beyond the reach of these passions, without the judgment of which punishment cannot be inflicted. How is this tribunal to be obtained but by rendering independent those who compose it? Is it to be expected that if in this war of angry passions, an irritated majority in Congress should pursue with unjust vengeance an obnoxious individual, judges dependent on that majority for their continuance in office will constitute a barrier which shall check its resentments? If in any influence the virtue of the judge should induce him to prefer his duty to his interest, his exertions would be of no avail. He would immediately become the victim of his integrity: by repealing a law or by some other means he would be removed from office and a successor appointed, inflamed with all the passions which burn in the bosoms of the majority.

In private actions too the same prejudices would prevail. An influential member of the majority in Congress could not be in the wrong should his cause be referred to a man whose political existence may depend on the breath of that member. . . .

In controversies between an individual of the majority and minority, the case of the impotent and unpopular suitor would be hopeless. His demonstrations of his right would avail him nothing before a judge whose continuance in office might depend on pronouncing a decision against him. . . .

Will you then, my fellow citizens, for the paltry gratification of wreaking vengeance on a party so grossly calumniated and which no longer governs, destroy the Constitution of your country and deprive yourselves of the security resulting from independent judges? Will you establish a principle which must place in the hands of the predominant party for the time being the persons and the property of those who are divided from them by shades of opinion? which will subject the weak to the powerful and convert the seat of justice into a tribunal where influence, not law, must rule? Will you render a judiciary which being constitutionally independent is now a safe and steady check to the encroachments of power and the persecutions of party, a mere instrument of vengeance in the hands of the tyrants of the day? Will you make the judges what a late ministerial writer, whose calumnies have attracted some attention, has very untruly stated them to be already: a body of men "under the dominance of political and personal prejudice, habitually employed in preparing or executing political vengeance"?

Patriotism, public virtue, a regard for your own safety and happiness, a just national pride, and respect for that Constitution on which your national character depends, and which many of you have solemnly sworn to support—all forbid it.

"Serious Considerations Addressed to All Serious Federalists," No. 3

(Washington) *National Intelligencer*

1 December 1802

. . . What have the republican administration done?

They have restored the old and long established mode of administering justice, with a very few improvements—that mode which had been devised by a Federal lawyer of great eminence, Oliver Ellsworth, whose reputed talent and integrity had rapidly carried him, under Federal auspices, through the successive great offices of Senator of the United States, Chief Justice of the United States, and Minister Plenipotentiary to France; that mode which had been the offspring of a mind replete with deep experience derived from the enjoyment of many years of practical engagement—instead of one, the hasty creation of two young men, deeply involved in the contentions of party animosity and acknowledged, on all hands, to be more intent on political aggrandizement than on any other end.

This restoration of the old system has been pronounced unconstitutional. But the charge would never have been made but from party animosity, from the hope of gaining party advantage by working on the prejudices of the people. The measure has been demonstrated in abstract argument to be constitutional. But what, to the plain strong sense of an unprejudiced mind, shows it to be so in the most irrefragable manner is the undisputed exercise of the same power, under like circumstances, by most of the states in the Union. Cases precisely analogous are to be found in the statute books of Massachusetts, Pennsylvania, Maryland, and Virginia, which occurred before the rage of party passions, and which therefore furnish the *strongest possible attestation* to the constitutionality of the power.

Whatever doubt, therefore, may be entertained of the expediency of this measure, none ought to be entertained of its constitutionality.

But, granting that there exists such doubts, is there to be no end of political controversy upon every disputed point? Are not the constituted authorities to decide? Have they not decided? Does not the decision express unequivocally the opinions of the nation? Can a doubt be entertained of this when it is considered that the law embraced the sanction of the President, himself the representative of the whole nation; of the Senate, the representatives of the states; and of nearly two-thirds of the House of Representatives, the representatives of the people? The majority have spoken in the audible language of a law, and the minority must obey. Such is the nature of our government. It is the only despotic feature it contains.

This important subject then stands thus. The Republicans have restored, with but little variation, what the Federalists formed. Ought not both sides, ought not the nation, to be satisfied with this? . . .

The Impeachment of Samuel Chase, 1804–1805

Republican attacks on the Federalist judiciary culminated in the impeachment, trial, and narrow acquittal of Supreme Court Justice Samuel Chase. John Randolph of Roanoke, currently a floor leader for the Jeffersonians but later perhaps the most acerbic Old Republican critic of Jefferson's and Madison's administrations, managed the impeachment for the House, assisted by Joseph Nicholson, the Republican stalwart from Maryland. Robert Goodloe Harper of Maryland and Caesar Rodney of Delaware, both former Federalist congressmen, defended Chase. James Thomson Callender, who figured prominently in the House indictment, was probably the most scurrilous Republican pamphleteer of the later 1790s. In 1802, however, Callender had turned against Thomas Jefferson, whom he accused of having several children by his slave Sally Hemings.

Articles of Impeachment

30 November 1804

ARTICLE 1.   That, unmindful of the solemn duties of his office, and contrary to the sacred obligation by which he stood bound to discharge them "faithfully and impartially, and without respect to persons," the said Samuel Chase, on the trial of John Fries, charged with treason, before the circuit court of the United States, held for the district of Pennsylvania, in the city of Philadelphia, during the months of April and May, one thousand eight hundred, whereat the said Samuel Chase presided, did, in his judicial capacity, conduct himself in a manner highly arbitrary, oppressive, and unjust. . . .

ART. 2.   That, prompted by a similar spirit of persecution and injustice, at a circuit court of the United States, held at Richmond, in the month of May, one thousand eight hundred, for the district of Virginia, whereat the said Samuel Chase presided, and before which a certain James Thomson Callender was arraigned for a libel on John Adams, then President of the United States, the said Samuel Chase, with intent to oppress and procure the conviction of the said Callender, did overrule the objection of John Basset,

one of the jury, who wished to be excused from serving on the said trial because he had made up his mind as to the publication from which the words charged to be libellous in the indictment were extracted; and the said Basset was accordingly sworn and did serve on the said jury, by whose verdict the prisoner was subsequently convicted.

ART. 3.   That, with intent to oppress and procure the conviction of the prisoner, the evidence of John Taylor, a material witness on behalf of the aforesaid Callender, was not permitted by the said Samuel Chase to be given in, on pretense that the said witness could not prove the truth of the whole of one of the charges contained in the indictment, although the said charge embraced more than one fact.

ART. 4.   That the conduct of the said Samuel Chase was marked, during the whole course of the said trial, by manifest injustice, partiality, and intemperance. . . .

ART. 5.   . . . The said Samuel Chase did, at the court aforesaid, award a capias against the body of the said James Thomson Callender, indicted for an offense not capital, whereupon the said Callender was arrested and committed to close custody, contrary to law in that case made and provided.

ART. 6.   And whereas it is provided by the 34th section of . . . "An act to establish the judicial courts of the United States," that the laws of the several states, except where the Constitution, treaties, or statutes of the United States shall otherwise require or provide, shall be regarded as the rules of decision in trials at common law in the courts of the United States, in cases where they apply; and whereas, by the laws of Virginia, it is provided that, in cases not capital, the offender shall not be held to answer any presentment of a grand jury until the court next succeeding that during which such presentment shall have been made, yet the said Samuel Chase, with intent to oppress and procure the conviction of the said James Thomson Callender, did, at the court aforesaid, rule and adjudge the said Callender to trial, during the term at which he, the said Callender, was presented and indicted, contrary to law in that case made and provided.

ART. 7.   That, at a circuit court of the United States for the district of Delaware, held at Newcastle in the month of June, one thousand eight hundred, whereat the said Samuel Chase presided, the said Samuel Chase, disregarding the duties of his office, did descend from the dignity of a judge, and stoop to the level of an informer, by refusing to discharge the grand jury, although entreated by several of the said jury so to do; and after the said grand jury had regularly declared, through their foreman, that they had found no bills of indictment, nor had any presentments to make, by observing to the said grand jury, that he, the said Samuel Chase, understood "that a highly seditious temper had manifested itself in the state of Delaware, among a certain class of people, particularly in Newcastle County, and more especially in the town of Wilmington, where lived a most seditious printer, unrestrained by any principle of virtue, and regardless of social order—that the name of this printer was"—but checking himself, as if sensible of the indecorum he was committing, added, "that it might be assuming too much to mention the name of this person, but it becomes your duty, gentlemen, to inquire diligently into this matter," or words to that effect; and that, with intention to procure the prosecution of the printer in question, the said Samuel Chase did, moreover, authoritatively enjoin on the District Attorney of the United States the necessity of procuring a file of the papers to which he alluded (and which were understood to be those published under the title of "Mirror of the Times and General Advertiser") and, by a strict examination of them, to find some passage which might furnish the ground-work of a prosecution against the printer of the said paper; thereby degrading his high judicial functions, and tending to impair the public confidence in, and respect for, the tribunals of justice, so essential to the general welfare.

ART. 8.   And whereas mutual respect and confidence between the Government of the United States and those of the individual states, and between the people and those governments respectively, are highly conducive to that public harmony without which there can be no public happiness, yet the said Samuel Chase, disregarding the duties and dignity of his judicial character, did, at a circuit court for the district of Maryland held at Baltimore in the month of May, one thousand eight hundred and three, pervert his official right and duty to address the grand jury then and there assembled on the matters coming within the province of the said jury, for the purpose of delivering to the said grand jury an intemperate and inflammatory political harangue, with intent to excite the fears and resentment of the said grand jury and of the good people of Maryland against their state government and constitution, a conduct highly censurable in any, but peculiarly indecent and unbecoming, in a Judge of the Supreme Court of the United States; and moreover that the said Samuel Chase, then and there, under pretense of exercising his judicial right to address the said grand jury, as aforesaid, did, in a manner highly unwarrantable, endeavor to excite the odium of the said grand jury and of the good people of Maryland, against the Government of the United States, by delivering opinions, which, even if the judicial authority were competent to their expression on a suitable occasion and in a proper manner, were at that time, and as delivered by him, highly indecent, extra-judicial, and tending to prostitute the high judicial character with which he was invested to the low purpose of an electioneering partisan.

And the House of Representatives, by protestation, saving to themselves the liberty of exhibiting, at any time hereafter, any farther articles, or other accusation, or impeachment, against the said Samuel Chase, and also of replying to his answers which he shall make unto the said articles, or any of them, and of offering proof to all and every the aforesaid articles, and to all and every other articles, impeachment, or accusation which shall be exhibited by them as the case shall require, do demand that the said Samuel Chase may be put to answer the said crimes and misdemeanors, and that such proceedings, examinations, trials, and judgments, may be thereupon had and given as are agreeable to law and justice. . . .

Proceedings in the Senate
February 1805

Address of John Randolph
9 February 1805

I ask this honorable Court whether the prostitution of the bench of justice to the purposes of a hustings is to be tolerated? We have nothing to do with the politics of the *man*. Let him speak, and write, and publish, as he pleases. This is his right in common with his fellow citizens. The press is free. If he must electioneer and abuse the government under which he lives, I know no law to prevent or punish him, provided he seeks the wonted theaters for his exhibition. But shall a judge declaim on these topics from his seat of office? Shall he not put off the political partisan when he ascends the tribune? Or shall we have the pure stream of public justice polluted with the venom of party virulence? In short, does it follow that a judge carries all the rights of a private citizen with him upon the bench, and that he may there do every act which, as a freeman, he may do elsewhere, without being questioned for his conduct?

But, sir, we are told that this high Court [the Senate] is not a court of errors and appeals, but a Court of Impeachment, and that however incorrectly the respondent may have conducted himself, proof must be adduced of criminal intent, or wilful error, to constitute guilt. . . . Even the respondent admits that there are acts of a nature so flagrant that guilt must be inferred from them, if the party be of sound mind. But this concession is qualified by the monstrous pretension that an act to be impeachable must be indictable. Where? In the federal courts? There, not even robbery and murder are indictable, except in a few places under our executive jurisdiction. It is not an indictable offense under the laws of the United States for a judge to go on the bench in a state of intoxication — it may not be in all the state courts; and it is indictable nowhere for him to omit to do his duty, to refuse to hold a court. But who can doubt that both are impeachable offenses and ought to subject the offender to removal from office? . . .

Mr. President, it appears to me that one great distinction remains yet to be taken. A distinction between a judge zealous to punish and repress crimes generally and a judge anxious only to enforce a particular law, whereby he may recommend himself to power or to his party. It is this hideous feature of the respondent's judicial character on which I would fix your attention. We do not charge him with a general zeal in the discharge of his high office, but with an indecent zeal, in particular cases, for laws of doubtful and suspicious aspect. It is only in cases of constructive treason and libel that this zeal breaks out. Through the whole tenor of his judicial conduct runs the spirit of party. . . .

The Testimony

The Managers proceeded to the examination of witnesses in support of the prosecution. . . .

19 February 1805
Gunning Bedford, sworn.

Mr. Harper.   Please to state to the court whether you were present in your judicial character at a circuit court held at Wilmington in 1800, and relate the circumstances which occurred?

A.   I attended that court on the 27th of June. Judge Chase presided. I arrived in the morning about half an hour before Judge Chase. We went into court about eleven o'clock. The grand jury was called and empaneled. The judge delivered a charge; they retired to their box; after an absence of not more than an hour they returned to the bar. They were asked by the judge whether they had any bills or presentments to make to the court. They said they had none. The court called on the attorney of the district to say whether there was any business likely to be brought forward. He replied that there was none. Some of the grand jury then expressed a wish to be discharged. Judge Chase said it was unusual for the court to discharge the grand jury so early in the session; it is not the practice in any circuit court in which I have sat. He turned round to me and said, Mr. Bedford, what is your usual practice? I said it depended upon circumstances and on the business before the court; that when the court was satisfied there was nothing to detain them they were discharged. Judge Chase then turned to the jury and observed, "But, gentlemen of the jury. I am informed that there is conducted in this state (but I am only *informed*) a seditious newspaper, the editor of which is in the practice of libeling and abusing the government. His name is _____, but perhaps I may do injustice to the man by mentioning his name. Have you, gentlemen of the jury, ever turned your attention to the subject?" It was answered, no. "But, resumed the judge, it is your duty to attend to things of this kind. I have given you in charge the Sedition Act, among other things. If there is anything in what is suggested to you, it is your duty to inquire into it." He added, "It is high time that this seditious printer should be corrected; you know that the prosperity and happiness of the country depend upon it." He then turned to the attorney of the district and said, Mr. Attorney, can you find a file of those papers?

He answered that he did not know. A person in court offered to procure a file. The attorney then said, as a file was found, he would look it over. Can you, said the judge, look it over and examine it by tomorrow at ten o'clock. Mr. Attorney said he would. Judge Chase then turned to the grand jury and said, gentlemen, you must attend tomorrow at ten o'clock. Other business was gone into, and the court adjourned about two o'clock.

On my way to Judge Chase's lodgings, I said to him, my friend, I believe you know not where you are; the people of this country are very much opposed to the Sedition Law and will not be pleased with what you said. Judge Chase clapped his hand on my shoulders and replied, "my dear Bedford, no matter where we are, or among whom we are, we must do our duty."

The next day we went into court about ten o'clock. The grand jury went to their chamber, and I believe Mr. Read returned with them into court. They were asked if they had anything to offer to the court; and the attorney was called on again to state whether he had found anything in the file of a seditious nature. He had a file of the paper before him, and he said he had found nothing that was a proper subject for the notice of the jury, unless a piece relating to Judge Chase himself. The judge answered, take no notice of that, my shoulders are broad, and they are able to bear it; but where there is a violation of a positive law of the United States it is necessary to notice it.

Mr. Harper. Did Judge Chase say nothing about a seditious temper in the town of Wilmington in Newcastle county?

A. I do not recollect that he did. The subject has occupied my attention since I saw Mr. Read's testimony given to the committee of inquiry of the House of Representatives; and I have not been able to trace in my mind any recollection of the kind. What I said to the judge shows that I did not hear such remarks. Another circumstance strengthened my conviction that no such remarks fell from him. There was a publication in the Mirror, on the fourth of July, giving an account of the proceedings of the court; in which many circumstances that occurred appeared to me to be highly exaggerated; and yet in that publication no such remarks are ascribed to the judge.

Mr. Harper. Was there anything authoritative or commanding in the language of Judge Chase to the attorney of the district; or was what he said in the nature of a request?

A. It was a request, made in the usual style of a request.

Mr. Harper. Was the business conducted with apparent good humor?

A. It appeared so to me.

Mr. Harper. From what source did the printer obtain his statement of the proceedings of the court?

A. The printer stated that he had it from a person in court.

Mr. Randolph. Was the title of the paper mentioned at this time?

A. I think not. I believe I suggested the title when inquiry was made as to the procuring a file.

Mr. Rodney. In what manner did the judge address the grand jury?

A. In his usual manner of speaking; but without passion.

Mr. Rodney. Do you recollect whether on the second day there was not an unusual concourse of people in court?

A. I believe there was.

Mr. Rodney. Did not Judge Chase ask whether there were not two printers in town?

A. I believe he did ask that question. . . .

Mr. Nicholson. You are not certain whether Judge Chase cited the title of the paper?

A. I am not certain.

Mr. Nicholson. What induced you to consider what he said as applicable to the Mirror?

A. We had two papers printed in Wilmington, one of which was federal, and the other, the Mirror, democratic.

Mr. Rodney. Do you recollect whether it is the general practice in Delaware to discharge the grand jury the same day they are empanelled?

A. I believe it is the general practice.

Mr. Randolph. Do you recollect whether the judge, when speaking of the printer, said, "and one of them, if report does not much belie him, is a seditious printer and must be taken notice of. I consider it a part of my duty, and it shall or must be noticed. And it is your duty, Mr. Attorney, to examine minutely and unremittingly into affairs of this nature; the times, sir, require that this seditious spirit, which pervades too many of our presses, should be discouraged and repressed."

A. I have no recollection of such words. . . .

Archibald Hamilton, sworn.

Mr. Harper.   Please to inform the court whether you were present at a circuit court for Delaware in 1800?

A.   I recollect that I was present on the 27th of June. I arrived about ten o'clock, at which time Judge Chase was not there. Some time after, the court was formed, the grand jury was sworn, and Judge Chase delivered a charge. Having retired for about an hour, the grand jury returned to the bar. Judge Chase asked them if they had any bills or presentments to make. Their reply was that they had not. Judge Chase then asked the Attorney of the District if he had no business to lay before them. He said he had not. The jury requested to be discharged. Judge Chase said it was not usual to discharge them so early, some business might occur during the course of the day. He told them he had been informed that there was a printer who was guilty of libelling the Government of the United States; his name is_____; here he stopped and said, "perhaps I may commit myself, and do injustice to the man. Have you not two printers?" The attorney said there were. Well, said Judge Chase, cannot you find a file of the papers of the one I allude to? Mr. Read said he did not take the papers or that he had not a file. Some person then observed that a file could be got at Mr. Crow's. Judge Chase asked the attorney if he could examine the papers by the next morning. Mr. Read said that, under the directions of the court, he conceived it to be his duty, and he would do it.

On the second day the same questions, whether they had found any bills, were put to the grand jury. They answered that they had not. Mr. Chase asked the Attorney of the District if he had found anything in the papers that required the interposition of the jury. He said that he had found nothing which in his opinion came within the Sedition Law; but there was a paragraph against his honor. Judge Chase said that was not what he alluded to. He was abused from one end of the continent to the other; but his shoulders were broad enough to bear it.

Mr. Harper.   Did the judge say anything of a seditious temper in that State?

A.   I do not recollect any such expressions.

Mr. Harper.   Were you in the court the whole time?

A.   I was.

Mr. Harper.   How were you situated?

A.   I was directly under Judge Chase, and nothing could fall from him without my hearing it.

Mr. Rodney.   Do you recollect whether he mentioned the name of the paper?

A.   I do not recollect that he did.

Mr. Rodney.   What was the manner of the judge?

A.   I saw nothing unusual.

Mr. Rodney.   Do you recollect whether his manner made any impression at the bar?

A.   On nobody but the printer.

Mr. Rodney.   Do you recollect that the District Attorney said he conceived it his duty to inquire into matter of the kind he alluded to?

A.   I do. . . .

Gunning Bedford, called.

Mr. Rodney.   Did Judge Chase, in a conversation with you, subsequent to the discharge of the grand jury, complain that he could not get a person indicted in Delaware for sedition, though he could in Virginia.

Mr. Bedford.   I have no distinct recollection of that kind. I have some indistinct recollection that in a small circle of friends, though not to me personally, he said some such thing in a jocular way.

William H. Winder, sworn.

Mr. Harper.   I will ask you whether you were in the circuit court of the United States, held at Baltimore, in May, 1803?

Mr. Winder.   I was present at that court when it was opened and the jury empaneled, and I heard Judge Chase deliver his charge. After delivering the general and usual charge to the grand jury, he said he begged leave to detain them a few minutes while he made some general reflections on the situation of public affairs. He commenced by laying down some abstract opinions, stating that that Government was the most free and happy that was the best administered; that a republic might be in slavery and a monarchy free. He also drew some distinctions with regard to the doctrine of equal rights, and said that the idea of perfect equality of rights, more particularly such as had been broached in France, was fanciful and untrue; that the only doctrine contended for with propriety was the equal protection of all classes from oppression. He commented on the repeal of the judiciary system of the United States and remarked that it had a tendency to weaken the judiciary and to render it dependent. He then adverted to the laws of Maryland respecting the judiciary, as tending to the same effect. One was a law for the repeal of the county court system. He also alluded to the depending law for the abolition of two of the courts of Maryland. He said something of the toil and labor and patriotism of those who had raised the fair fabric (constitution of Maryland) and said that he saw with regret some of their sons now employed in destroying it. He also said that the tendency of the general suffrage law was highly injurious, as, under it, a man was admitted to full political rights, who might be here today and gone tomorrow.

This is the amount of my recollection; and I think I have stated the language of the judge in as strong terms as he himself used. Since I was summoned as a witness I have never seen the charge of the judge, or that published in the National Intelligencer, or by Mr. Montgomery. I conclude that it was most proper not to avail myself of those publications. My impressions, therefore, are altogether unassisted by them.

Mr. Harper.   Did you attend carefully to the charge?

A.   I did. I am sure no part of it escaped me.

Mr. Harper.   Did Judge Chase appear to read it from a paper?

A.   I so took it. Occasionally he raised his eyes, but not longer than I should imagine a person would who was familiarly acquainted with what he was reading.

Mr. Harper.   Did you hear him use any of those expressions deposed by one of the witnesses—that the Administration was feeble and inadequate to the discharge of its duties, and that their object was to preserve power unfairly acquired. Did he use any such words?

A.   To my best belief, he did not. . . .

Mr. Harper.   Did the judge use any arguments against pending measures?

A.   Certainly.

Mr. Harper.   Did he mention the present Administration?

A.   I believe not. If he had, it would have struck my mind very forcibly. . . .

Mr. Nicholson.   Did Judge Chase say anything of the motives of the members of the Legislature of Maryland?

A.   He did, according to my impression.

Mr. Nicholson.   What were the motives he ascribed to them?

A.   As I understood him, the motive he ascribed to them was to get rid of the judges, and not the system.

Mr. Nicholson.   He did certainly, then, allude to the motives of the members of the Assembly of Maryland?

A.   I think he did. If he did not, that was the impression produced on my mind by what he said.

Mr. Nicholson.   Do you recollect whether Judge Chase did at the close of his charge recommend to the members of the grand jury to return home and prevent certain laws from being passed?

A.   I think that was the result which he drew from what he had previously said.

James Winchester, sworn.

Mr. Harper.   Please, sir, to state to this court your recollection respecting a charge delivered by Judge Chase in the circuit court of Maryland in May, 1803?

Mr. Winchester.   As already stated, that court sat in May, 1803, in a room in Evans's tavern. The court and gentlemen of the bar sat round several dining tables. I sat on the left of Judge Chase, and the jury were on his right. He addressed a charge to them, the beginning of which was in the usual style of such addresses. He then commenced what has been called the political part of the charge, with some general observations on the nature of government. He afterwards adverted to two measures of the Legislature of Maryland; the first related to an alteration of the Constitution on the subject of suffrage; the other contemplated an alteration in the judiciary. He commented on the injurious tendency of the principle of universal suffrage, and deprecated the evil effects it was likely to have. Incidental to these remarks, he adverted to the repeal of the judiciary law of the United States. I say incidental, for my impression was that his object was to show the dangerous consequences that would result to the people of Maryland from a repeal of their judiciary system, and to show that as the act of Congress had inflicted a violent blow on the independence of the federal judiciary, it was more necessary for the State of Maryland to preserve their judiciary perfectly independent. I was very attentive to the charge for several reasons. I regretted it as imprudent. I felt convinced that it would be complained of; and I am very confident from my recollection, and from the publications respecting it, which I afterwards perused, that all the political observations of the judge related to the State of Maryland. . . .

Mr. Harper.   Did you hear any expressions applied to the present Administration, or was the Administration mentioned at all?

A.   My impression is very strong that neither the present Administration was mentioned or the views or designs of any member of it in any manner whatever. I am confident of this, because if such remarks had been uttered, they would have made a strong impression on my mind.

Mr. Harper.   Did you ever hear the judge allude to such topics in his charges?

A.   I never heard Judge Chase in any of his charges reflect on any Administration. I have heard a great many charges of his containing political matter, and they have been all rather calculated to support the existing Administration.

Mr. Harper.   Have you heard any since 1800?

A.   I recollect no particular charge delivered by him since that time.

Mr. Harper.   Was the general tenor of his charges since and before 1800 calculated to support the laws?

A.   I think there has been this difference. Those delivered before 1800 called on the jury to support the measures of the government as wise and upright; since that period he has made no allusion to the measures of the Administration.

Mr. Harper.   But his general practice has been to recommend to them the observance of law and the support of government?

A.   He generally addressed the jury on the necessity of obeying the laws; that has been the tenor of his charges at all times. . . .

Mr. Nicholson.   I will ask you whether Judge Chase recommended to the jury, on their return home, to use their exertions to prevent the adoption of a depending law?

A.   I do not know whether the recommendation came from the judge in language and terms. I rather think it flowed as an inference from what he had said. . . .

Exhibit Number Eight, Referred to in Judge Chase's Answer

Copy of the conclusion of a charge delivered and read from the original manuscript at a circuit court of the United States, holden in the city of Baltimore, on Monday the second day of May, 1803, by Samuel Chase, one of the judges of the Supreme Court of the United States.

Before you retire, gentlemen, to your chamber to consider such matters as may be brought before you, I will take the liberty to make a few observations, which I hope you will receive as flowing only from my regard to the welfare and prosperity of our common country. . . .

The purposes of civil society are best answered by those governments where the public safety, happiness, and prosperity are best formed, whatever may be the constitution and form of government; but the history of mankind (in ancient and modern times) informs us "that a monarchy may be free, and that a republic may be a tyranny." The true test of liberty is in the practical enjoyment of protection to the person and the property of the citizen from all injury. Where the same laws govern the whole society without any distinction and there is no power to dispense with the execution of the laws; where justice is impartially and speedily administered and the poorest man in the community may obtain redress against the most wealthy and powerful, and riches afford no protection to violence; and where the person and property of every man are secure from insult and injury; in that country the people are free. This is our present situation. Where law is uncertain, partial, or arbitrary; where justice is not impartially administered to all; where property is insecure and the person is liable to insult and violence without redress by law, the people are *not free,* whatever may be their form of government. To this situation I greatly fear we are fast approaching!

You know, gentlemen, that our state and national institutions were framed to secure to every member of the society equal liberty and equal rights; but the late alteration of the federal judiciary by the abolition of the office of the sixteen circuit judges, and the recent change in our state constitution by the establishing of universal suffrage, and the further alteration that is contemplated in our state judiciary (if adopted) will, in my judgment, take away all security for property and personal liberty. The independence of the national judiciary is already shaken to its foundation, and the virtue of the people alone can restore it. The independence of the judges of this state will be entirely destroyed, if the bill for the abolition of the two supreme courts should be ratified by the next General Assembly. The change of the state constitution, by allowing universal suffrage, will, in my opinion, certainly and rapidly destroy all protection to property and all security to personal liberty; and our republican constitution will sink into a mobocracy, the worst of all possible governments.

I can only lament that the main pillar of our state constitution has already been thrown down by the establishment of universal suffrage. By this shock alone the whole building totters to its base and will crumble into ruins before many years elapse, unless it be restored to its original state. If the independency of your state judges, which your bill of rights wisely declares "to be essential to the impartial administration of justice, and the great security to the rights and liberties of the people," shall be taken away by the ratification of the bill passed for that purpose, it will precipitate the destruction of your whole state constitution, and there will be nothing left in it worthy the care or support of freemen.

I cannot but remember the great and patriotic characters by whom your state constitution was framed. I cannot but recollect that attempts were then made in favor of universal suffrage and to render the judges dependent upon the legislature. You may believe that the gentlemen who framed your constitution possessed the full confidence of the people of Maryland, and that they were esteemed for their talents and patriotism, and for their public and private virtues. You must have heard that many of them held the highest civil and military stations, and that they, at every risk and danger, assisted to obtain and establish your independence. Their names are enrolled on the journals of the First Congress and may be seen in the proceedings of the Convention that framed our form of government. With great concern I observe that the sons of some of these characters have united to pull down the beautiful fabric of wisdom and republicanism that their fathers erected!

The declarations respecting the natural rights of man, which originated from the claim of the British Parliament to make laws to bind America in all cases whatsoever; the publications since that period of visionary and theoretical writers, asserting that men in a state of society are entitled to exercise rights which they possessed in a state of nature; and the modern doctrines by our late reformers, that all men in a state of society are entitled to enjoy equal liberty and equal rights, have brought this mighty mischief upon us; and I fear that it will rapidly progress, until peace and order, freedom and property, shall be destroyed. Our people are taught as a political creed that men living under an established government are, nevertheless, entitled to exercise certain rights which they possessed in a state of nature; and also, that every member of this government is entitled to enjoy an equality of liberty and rights.

I have long since subscribed to the opinion that there could be no rights of man in a state of nature previous to the institution of society; and that liberty, properly speaking, could not exist in a state of nature. I do not believe that any number of men ever existed together in a state of nature without some head, leader, or chief, whose advice they followed and whose precepts they obeyed. I really consider a state of nature as a creature of the imagination only, although great names give a sanction to a contrary opinion. The great object for which men establish any form of government is to obtain security to their persons and property from violence; destroy the security to either, and you tear up society by the roots. It appears to me that the institution of government is really no sacrifice made, as some writers contend, to natural liberty, for I think that previous to the formation of some species of government, a state of liberty could not exist. It seems to me that personal *liberty* and *rights* can only be acquired by becoming a member of a community, which gives the protection of the whole to every individual. Without this protection it would, in my opinion, be impracticable to enjoy personal liberty or rights. From hence I conclude that liberty and rights (and also property) must spring out of civil society, and must be forever subject to the modification of particular governments. I hold the position clear and safe that all the rights of man can be derived only from the *conventions* of society, and may with propriety be called social rights. I cheerfully subscribe to the doctrine of equal liberty and equal rights, if properly explained. I understand by equality of liberty and rights only this, that every citizen, without respect to property or station, should enjoy an equal share of civil liberty, an equal protection from the laws, and an equal security for his person and property. Any other interpretation of these terms is, in my judgment, destructive of all government and all laws. If I am substantially correct in these sentiments, it is unnecessary to make any application of them, and I will only ask two questions. Will justice be impartially administered by judges dependent on the legislature for their continuance in office, and also for their support? Will liberty or property be protected or secured by laws made by representatives chosen by electors, who have no property in, a common interest with, or attachment to the community?

ALBERT GALLATIN

Report on Internal Improvements

4 April 1808

Subordinating much else to the speedy retirement of the public debt, the Republicans could anticipate a Treasury surplus before the end of Jefferson's second term. The third member of the great triumvirate at the head of the administration offered a plan for its use.

The Secretary of the Treasury, in obedience to the resolution of the Senate of the 2d March, 1807, respectfully submits the following report on roads and canals:

The general utility of artificial roads and canals is at this time so universally admitted as hardly to require any additional proofs. . . . Advantages have become so obvious that in countries possessed of a large capital, where property is sufficiently secure to induce individuals to lay out that capital on permanent undertakings, and where a compact population creates an extensive commercial intercourse within short distances, those improvements may often, in ordinary cases, be left to individual exertion, without any direct aid from government.

There are, however, some circumstances which, whilst they render the facility of communication throughout the United States an object of primary importance, naturally check the application of private capital and enterprise to improvements on a large scale.

The price of labor is not considered as a formidable obstacle, because whatever it may be, it equally affects the expense of transportation, which is saved by the improvement, and that of effecting the improvement itself. The want of practical knowledge is no longer felt; and the occasional influence of mistaken local interests, in sometimes thwarting or giving an improper direction to public improvements, arises from the nature of man and is common to all countries. The great demand for capital in the United States and the extent of territory compared with the population are, it is believed, the true causes which prevent new undertakings and render those already accomplished less profitable than had been expected.

1. Notwithstanding the great increase of capital during the last fifteen years, the objects for which it is required continue to be more numerous and its application is generally more profitable than in Europe. A small portion therefore is applied to objects which offer only the prospect of remote and moderate profit. And it also happens that a less sum being subscribed at first than is actually requisite for completing the work, this proceeds slowly; the capital applied remains unproductive for a much longer time than was necessary, and the interest accruing during that period becomes, in fact, an injurious addition to the real expense of the undertaking.

2. The present population of the United States, compared with the extent of territory over which it is spread, does not, except in the vicinity of the seaports, admit that extensive commercial intercourse within short distances which, in England and some other countries, forms the principal support of artificial roads and canals. With a few exceptions, canals particularly cannot, in America, be undertaken with a view solely to the intercourse between the two extremes of and along the intermediate ground which they occupy. It is necessary, in order to be productive, that the canal should open a communication with a natural extensive navigation which will flow through that new channel. It follows that whenever that navigation requires to be improved, or when it might at some distance be connected by another canal to another navigation, the first canal will remain comparatively unproductive until the other improvements are effected, until the other canal is also completed. Thus the intended canal between the Chesapeake and Delaware will be deprived of the additional benefit arising from the intercourse between New York and the Chesapeake until an inland navigation shall have been opened between the Delaware and New York. Thus the expensive canals completed around the falls

of Potomac will become more and more productive in proportion to the improvement, first, of the navigation of the upper branches of the river, and then of its communication with the Western waters. Some works already executed are unprofitable; many more remain unattempted, because their ultimate productiveness depends on other improvements too extensive or too distant to be embraced by the same individuals.

The General Government can alone remove these obstacles.

With resources amply sufficient for the completion of every practicable improvement, it will always supply the capital wanted for any work which it may undertake as fast as the work itself can progress; avoiding thereby the ruinous loss of interest on a dormant capital and reducing the real expense to its lowest rate.

With these resources, and embracing the whole Union, it will complete on any given line all the improvements, however distant, which may be necessary to render the whole productive and eminently beneficial.

The early and efficient aid of the Federal Government is recommended by still more important considerations. The inconveniences, complaints, and perhaps dangers which may result from a vast extent of territory can not otherwise be radically removed or prevented than by opening speedy and easy communications through all its parts. Good roads and canals will shorten distances, facilitate commercial and personal intercourse, and unite, by a still more intimate community of interests, the most remote quarters of the United States. No other single operation within the power of government can more effectually tend to strengthen and perpetuate that Union which secures external independence, domestic peace, and internal liberty.

With that view of the subject the facts respecting canals, which have been collected in pursuance of the resolution of the Senate, have been arranged under the following heads: . . .

I. From north to south, in a direction parallel to the seacoast.
   1. Canals opening an inland navigation for sea vessels from Massachusetts to North Carolina, being more than two-thirds of the Atlantic seacoast of the United States, and across all the principal capes, Cape Fear excepted, $3,000,000
   2. A great turnpike road from Maine to Georgia along the whole extent of the Atlantic Seacoast, $4,800,000
   $7,800,000

II. From east to west, forming communications across the mountains between the Atlantic and western rivers.
   1. Improvement of the navigation of four great Atlantic rivers, including canals parallel to them, $1,500,000
   2. Four first-rate turnpike roads from those rivers across the mountains, to the four corresponding western rivers, $2,800,000
   3. Canal around the falls of the Ohio, $300,000
   4. Improvement of roads to Detroit, St. Louis and New Orleans, $200,000
   $4,800,000

III. In a northern and northwestwardly direction, forming inland navigations between the Atlantic seacoast and the Great Lakes and the St. Lawrence.
   1. Inland navigation between the North River and Lake Champlain, $800,000
   2. Great inland navigation opened the whole way by canals from the North River to Lake Ontario, $2,200,000
   3. Canal around the falls and rapids of Niagara, opening a sloop navigation from Lake Ontario to the upper lakes as far as the extremities of Lake Michigan, $1,000,000
   $4,000,000

Making, together, $16,600,000

IV. The great geographical features of the country have been solely adhered to in pointing out those lines of communication; and these appear to embrace all the great interests of the Union and to be calculated to diffuse and increase the national wealth in a very general way, by opening an intercourse between the remotest extremes of the United States. Yet it must necessarily result from an adherence to that principle that those parts of the Atlantic States through which the great western and northwest communications will be carried must, in addition to the general advantages in which they will participate, receive from those communications greater local and immediate benefits than the Eastern and perhaps Southern States. As the expense must be defrayed from the general funds of the Union, justice, and perhaps policy not less than justice, seems to require that a number of local improvements sufficient to equalize the advantages should also be undertaken in those states, parts of states, or districts which are less immediately interested in those inland communications. Arithmetical precision cannot, indeed, be attained in objects of that kind; nor would an apportionment of the moneys applied according to the population of each state be either just or practicable, since roads and particularly canals are often of greater utility to the states which they unite than to those through which they pass. But a sufficient number of local improvements, consisting either of roads or canals may, without any material difficulty, be selected, so as to do substantial justice and give general satisfaction. Without pretending to suggest what would be the additional sum necessary for that object, it will, for the sake of round numbers, be estimated at $ 3,400,000

Which, added to the sum estimated
for general improvements, $ 16,600,000

Would make an aggregate of $20,000,000

An annual appropriation of two millions of dollars would accomplish all those great objects in ten years and may, without inconvenience, be supplied in time of peace by the existing revenues and resources of the United States. This may be exemplified in several ways.

The annual appropriation on account of the principal and interest of the public debt has, during the last six years, amounted to eight millions of dollars. After the present year or, at furthest, after the ensuing year, the sum which, on account of the irredeemable nature of the remaining debt, may be applied to that object cannot, in any one year, exceed four million six hundred thousand dollars;

leaving, therefore, from that source alone, an annual surplus of three million four hundred thousand dollars applicable to any other object.

From the 1st January, 1801 to the 1st January, 1809, a period of eight years, the United States shall have discharged about thirty-four millions of the principal of the old debt, or deducting the Louisiana debt incurred during the same period and not yet discharged, about twenty-three millions of dollars. They may, with equal facility, apply, in a period of ten years, a sum of twenty millions of dollars to internal improvements.

The annual permanent revenue of the United States, calculated on a state of general peace and on the most moderate estimate, was, in a report made to Congress on the 6th day of December, 1806, computed for the years 1809, 1815, at fourteen millions of dollars. The annual expenses on the peace establishment, and including the four million six hundred thousand dollars on account of the debt, and four hundred thousand dollars for contingencies, do not exceed eight millions and a half, leaving an annual surplus of five millions and a half of dollars. To provide for the protection and defense of the country is undoubtedly the object to which the resources of the United States must, in the first instance, be applied, and to the exclusion of all others, if the times shall require it. But it is believed that, in times of peace, and to such period only are these remarks applicable, the surplus will be amply sufficient to defray the expenses of all the preparatory measures of a permanent nature which prudence may suggest, and to pay the sum destined for internal improvements. Three millions annually applied during the same period of ten years would arm every man in the United States, fill the public arsenals and magazines, erect every battery and fortification which could be manned, and even, if thought eligible, build a navy. That the whole surplus would be inadequate to the support of any considerable increase of the land or naval force kept in actual service in time of peace will be readily admitted. But such a system is not contemplated; if ever adopted, the objects of this report must probably be abandoned; for it has not heretofore been found an easy task for any Government to indulge in that species of expense, which, leaving no trace behind it, adds nothing to the real strength of the country, and, at the same time, to provide for either its permanent defense or improvement.

It must not be omitted that the facility of communications constitutes, particularly in the United States, an important branch of national defense. Their extensive territory opposes a powerful obstacle to the progress of an enemy; but, on the other hand, the number of regular forces which may be raised, necessarily limited by the population, will, for many years, be inconsiderable when compared with that extent of territory. That defect cannot otherwise be supplied than by those great national improvements which will afford the means of a rapid concentration of that regular force and of a formidable body of militia on any given point.

Amongst the resources of the Union, there is one which, from its nature, seems more particularly applicable to internal improvements. Exclusively of Louisiana, the General Government possesses, in trust for the people of the United States, about one hundred millions of acres fit for cultivation, north of the River Ohio, and near fifty millions south of the State of Tennessee. For the disposition of these lands a plan has been adopted, calculated to enable every industrious citizen to become a freeholder, to secure indisputable titles to the purchasers, to obtain a national revenue, and, above all, to suppress monopoly. Its success has surpassed that of every former attempt and exceeded the expectations of its authors. But a higher price than had usually been paid for waste lands by the first inhabitants of the frontier became an unavoidable ingredient of a system intended for general benefit and was necessary in order to prevent the public lands being engrossed by individuals possessing greater wealth, activity, and local advantages. It is believed that nothing could be more gratifying to the purchasers and to the inhabitants of the Western States generally, or better calculated to remove popular objections and to defeat insidious efforts, than the application of the proceeds of the sales to improvements conferring general advantages on the nation and an immediate benefit on the purchasers and inhabitants themselves. It may be added that the United States, considered merely as owners of the soil, are also deeply interested in the opening of those communications which must necessarily enhance the value of their property. Thus the opening an inland navigation from tidewater to the great lakes would immediately give to the great body of lands bordering on those lakes as great value as if they were situated at the distance of one hundred miles by land from the seacoast. And if the proceeds of the first ten millions of acres which may be sold were applied to such improvements, the United States would be amply repaid in the sale of the other ninety millions.

The annual appropriation of two millions of dollars drawn from the general revenues of the Union, which has been suggested, could operate to its full extent only in times of peace and under prosperous circumstances. The application of the proceeds of the sales of the public lands, might, perhaps, be made permanent until it had amounted to a certain sum and until the most important improvements had been effected. The fund created by those improvements, the expense of which has been estimated at twenty millions of dollars, would afterwards become itself a perpetual resource for further improvements. Although some of those first communications should not become immediately productive; and although the same liberal policy which dictated the measure would consider them less as objects of revenue to government than of increased wealth and general convenience to the nation, yet they would all, sooner or later, acquire, as productive property, their par value. Whenever that had taken place in relation to any of them, the stock might be sold to individuals or companies and the proceeds applied to a new improvement. And by persevering in that plan, a succession of improvements would be effected until every portion of the United States should enjoy all the advantages of inland navigation and improved roads of which it was susceptible. To effect that great object, a disbursement of twenty millions of dollars, applied with more or less rapidity, according to the circumstances of the United States, would be amply sufficient.

The manner in which the public moneys may be applied to such objects remains to be considered.

It is evident that the United States cannot, under the Constitution, open any road or canal without the consent of the state through which such road or canal must pass. In order, therefore, to remove every impediment to a national plan of internal improvements, an amendment to the Constitution was suggested by the executive when the subject was recommended to the consideration of Congress. Until this be obtained, the assent of the state being necessary for each improvement, the modifications under which that assent may be given will necessarily control the manner of applying the money. It may be, however, observed that in relation to the specific improvements which have been suggested, there is hardly any which is not either already authorized by the states respectively or so immediately beneficial to them as to render it highly probable that no material difficulty will be experienced in that respect.

The moneys may be applied in two different manners. The United States may, with the assent of the states, undertake some of the works at their sole expense, or they may subscribe a certain number of shares of the stock of companies incorporated for the purpose. Loans might also, in some instances, be made to such companies. The first mode would, perhaps, by effectual controlling local interests, give the most proper general direction to the work. Its details would probably be executed on a more economical plan by private companies. Both modes may, perhaps, be blended together so as to obtain the advantages pertaining to each. But the modifications of which the plan is susceptible must vary according to the nature of the work and of the charters, and seem to belong to that class of details which are not the immediate subject of consideration.

At present the only work undertaken by the United States at their sole expense, and to which the assent of the states has been obtained, is the road from Cumberland to Brownsville; an appropriation may, for that purpose, be made at any time. In relation to all other works, the United States having nothing at this time in their power but to assist those already authorized, either by loans or by becoming stockholders; and the last mode appears the most eligible. The only companies incorporated for effecting some of the improvements considered in this report as of national and first-rate importance, which have applied for such assistance, are the Chesapeake and Delaware Canal, the Susquehannah Canal, and the Dismal Swamp companies; and authority might be given to subscribe a certain number of shares to each on condition that the plan of the work to be executed should be approved by the General Government. A subscription to the Ohio Canal, to the Pittsburg Road, and perhaps to some other objects not fully ascertained, is also practicable at this time. As an important basis of the general system, an immediate authority might also be given to take the surveys and levels of the routes of the most important roads and canals which are contemplated: a work always useful, and by which the practicability and expense of the undertakings would be ascertained with much more correctness than in this report. . . .

PART 6

Jeffersonian Foreign Policy

The Louisiana Purchase

France had ceded Louisiana to Spain in 1762, but Napoleon envisioned a rebuilding of the French empire in North America. At his insistence, Spain returned the province by the Treaty of Madrid, 21 March 1801.

News of the retrocession provoked intense alarm in the United States. Some of the Federalists in Congress urged an immediate recourse to force. But lacking both the means and the desire to initiate a conflict with France, Jefferson instead instructed Robert R. Livingston, the U.S. minister to France, to attempt to purchase a tract of land on the lower Mississippi, which could become an American port, or to obtain a guarantee of free navigation of the river with a right of deposit for American goods. On 12 January 1803, not long after the Spanish intendant at New Orleans (without instructions from his government) interdicted the American right of deposit at New Orleans, provoking more Federalist calls for a resort to force, the president nominated James Monroe as minister plenipotentiary to France. Monroe would join Livingston under instructions to offer up to $10 million for the purchase of New Orleans and West Florida. Two million dollars had already been appropriated by Congress.

Even before Monroe arrived in France, Napoleon had abandoned his dream of a new American empire. A French army was hopelessly ensnarled in a slave revolt in Haiti, and Napoleon was beginning to prepare for a resumption of the war with Britain, in which event he would not be able to protect any of his North American possessions. On 11 April 1803, Foreign Minister Talleyrand offered Livingston the whole of Louisiana. Livingston and Monroe quickly decided to exceed their instructions and, on 2 May, signed a treaty. For roughly $15 million, the ministers acquired some 828,000 square miles of land between the Mississippi and the Rockies, doubling the national territory of the United States. The greatest coup of Jefferson's administration, the Louisiana Purchase was nevertheless not free from problems. It was not entirely clear whether the boundaries of the province included West Florida, as Jefferson and his successor would both maintain. Moreover, the Constitution made no provision for the purchase of foreign territory and its eventual incorporation into the American Union, and the Jeffersonian Republicans had always insisted on a strict interpretation of the Constitution.

Despite his reservations, Jefferson decided not to urge a constitutional amendment. The Senate ratified the treaty on 20 October by a vote of 24 to 7. On 20 December the United States took possession of New Orleans, and on 27 October 1812, after years of arguments with the Spanish and a local revolt led by American inhabitants, President Madison simply issued a proclamation insisting on American possession of West Florida from the Mississippi to the Perdido Rivers and ordering its military occupation. On 14 May 1812, Congress incorporated this area into the Mississippi Territory.

Thomas Jefferson to Robert R. Livingston
18 April 1802

. . . The cession of Louisiana and the Floridas by Spain to France works most sorely on the U.S. On this subject the Secretary of State has written to you fully. Yet I cannot forbear recurring to it personally, so deep is the impression it makes in my mind. It completely reverses all the political relations of the U.S. and will form a new epoch in our political course. Of all nations of any consideration France is the one which hitherto has offered the fewest points on which we could have any conflict of right and the most points of a communion of interests. From these causes we have ever looked to her as our *natural friend,* as one with which we never could have an occasion of difference. Her growth therefore we viewed as our own, her misfortunes ours. There is on the globe one single spot, the possessor of which is our natural and habitual enemy. It is New Orleans, through which the produce of three-eighths of our territory must pass to market, and from its fertility it will ere long yield more than half of our whole produce and contain more than half our inhabitants. France placing herself in that door assumes to us the attitude of defiance. Spain might have retained it quietly for years. Her pacific dispositions, her feeble state, would induce her to increase our facilities there, so that her possession of the place would be hardly felt by us, and it would not perhaps be very long before some circumstance might arise which might make the cession of it to us the price of something of more worth to her. Not so can it ever be in the hands of France. The impetuosity of her temper, the energy and restlessness of her character, placed in a point of eternal friction with us, and our character, which, though quiet and loving peace and the pursuit of wealth, is high-minded, despising wealth in competition with insult or injury, enterprising and energetic as any nation on earth, these circumstances render it impossible that France and the U.S. can continue long friends when they meet in so irritable a position. They as well as we must be blind if they do not see this; and we must be very improvident if we do not begin to make arrangements on that hypothesis. The day that France takes possession of N. Orleans fixes the sentence which is to restrain her forever within her low water mark. It seals the union of two nations who in conjunction can maintain exclusive possession of the ocean. From that moment we must marry ourselves to the British fleet and nation. We must turn all our attentions to a maritime force, for which our resources place us on very high grounds: and having formed and cemented together a power which may render reinforcement of her settlements here impossible to France, make the first cannon which shall be fired in Europe the signal for tearing up any settlement she may have made, and for holding the two continents of America in sequestration for the common purposes of the united British and American nations. This is not a state of things we seek or desire. It is one which this measure, if adopted by France, forces on us, as necessarily as any other cause, by the laws of nature, brings on its necessary effect. It is not from a fear of France that we deprecate this measure proposed by her. For however greater her force is than ours compared in the abstract, it is nothing in comparison of ours when to be exerted on our soil. But it is from a sincere love of peace and a firm persuasion that, bound to France by the interests and the strong sympathies still existing in the minds of our citizens and holding relative positions which ensure their continuance, we are secure of a long course of peace. Whereas the change of friends which will be rendered necessary if France changes that position embarks us necessarily as a belligerent power in the first war of Europe. In that case France will have held possession of New Orleans during the interval of a peace, long or short, at the end of which

it will be wrested from her. Will this short-lived possession have been an equivalent to her for the transfer of such a weight into the scale of her enemy? Will not the amalgamation of a young, thriving nation continue to that enemy the health and force which are at present so evidently on the decline? And will a few years possession of N. Orleans add equally to the strength of France? She may say she needs Louisiana for the supply of her West Indies. She does not need it in time of peace. And in war she could not depend on them because they would be so easily intercepted. I should suppose that all these considerations might in some proper form be brought into view of the government of France. Tho' stated by us, it ought not to give offense; because we do not bring them forward as a menace, but as consequences not controllable by us, but inevitable from the course of things. We mention them not as things which we desire by any means, but as things we deprecate; and we beseech a friend to look forward and to prevent them for our common interests.

If France considers Louisiana, however, as indispensable for her views, she might perhaps be willing to look about for arrangements which might reconcile it to our interest. If anything could do this it would be the ceding to us the island of New Orleans and the Floridas. This would certainly in a great degree remove the causes of jarring and irritation between us, and perhaps for such a length of time as might produce other means of making the measure permanently conciliatory to our interests and friendships. It would at any rate relieve us from the necessity of taking immediate measures for countervailing such an operation by arrangements in another quarter. Still we should consider N. Orleans and the Floridas as equivalent for the risk of a quarrel with France produced by her vicinage. I have no doubt you have urged these considerations on every proper occasion with the government where you are. They are such as must have effect if you can find the means of producing thorough reflection on them by that government. The idea here is that the troops sent to St. Domingo were to proceed to Louisiana after finishing their work in that island. If this were the arrangement, it will give you time to return again and again to the charge, for the conquest of St. Domingo will not be a short work. It will take considerable time to wear down a great number of soldiers. Every eye in the U.S. is now fixed on this affair of Louisiana. Perhaps nothing since the revolutionary war has produced more uneasy sensations through the body of the nation. Notwithstanding temporary bickerings have taken place with France, she has still a strong hold on the affections of our citizens generally. I have thought it not amiss, by way of supplement to the letters of the Secretary of State, to write you this private one to impress you with the importance we affix to this transaction. I pray you to cherish Dupont. He has the best dispositions for the continuance of friendship between the two nations, and perhaps you may be able to make a good use of him. Accept assurance of my affectionate esteem and high consideration.

Thomas Jefferson to John C. Breckinridge

12 August 1803

The enclosed letter, tho' directed to you, was intended to me also, and was left open with a request that when perused, I would forward it to you. It gives me occasion to write a word to you on the subject of Louisiana, which being a new one, an interchange of sentiments may produce correct ideas before we are to act on them.

Our information as to the country is very incomplete; we have taken measures to obtain it in full as to the settled part, which I hope to receive in time for Congress. The boundaries, . . . will be a subject of negotiation with Spain, and if, as soon as she is at war, we push them strongly with one hand, holding out a price in the other, we shall certainly obtain the Floridas, and all in good time. In the meanwhile, without waiting for permission, we shall enter into the exercise of the natural right we have always insisted on with Spain, to wit, that of a nation holding the upper part of streams having a right of innocent passage thro' them to the ocean. We shall prepare her to see us practice on this, & she will not oppose it by force.

Objections are raising to the Eastward against the vast extent of our boundaries, and propositions are made to exchange Louisiana, or a part of it, for the Floridas. But, as I have said, we shall get the Floridas without, and I would not give one inch of the waters of the Mississippi to any nation, because I see in a light very important to our peace the exclusive right to its navigation & the admission of no nation into it but, as into the Potomac or Delaware, with our consent & under our police. These Federalists see in this acquisition the formation of a new confederacy, embracing all the waters of the Mississippi on both sides of it, and a separation of its Eastern waters from us. These combinations depend on so many circumstances which we cannot foresee that I place little reliance on them. We have seldom seen neighborhood produce affection among nations. The reverse is almost the universal truth. Besides, if it should become the great interest of those nations to separate from this, if their happiness should depend on it so strongly as to induce them to go through that convulsion, why should the Atlantic States dread it? But especially why should we, their present inhabitants, take side in such a question? When I view the Atlantic States procuring for those on the eastern waters of the Mississippi friendly instead of hostile neighbors on its western waters, I do not view it as an Englishman would the procuring future blessings for the French nation, with whom he has no relations of blood or affection. The future inhabitants of the Atlantic & Mississippi States will be our sons. We leave them in distinct but bordering establishments. We think we see their happiness in their union, & we wish it. Events may prove it otherwise; and if they see their interest in separation, why should we take side with our Atlantic rather than our Mississippi descendants? It is the elder and the younger son differing. God bless them both, & keep them in union, if it be for their good, but separate them, if it be better. The inhabited part of Louisiana, from Point Coupé to the sea, will of course be immediately a territorial government, and soon a state. But above that, the best use we can make of the country for some time will be to give establishments in it to the Indians on the east side of the Mississippi in exchange for their present country, and open land offices in the last, & thus make this acquisition the means of filling up the eastern side, instead of drawing off its population. When we shall be full on this side, we may lay off a range of states on the western bank from the head to the mouth, & so, range after range, advancing compactly as we multiply.

This treaty must of course be laid before both Houses, because both have important functions to exercise respecting it. They, I presume, will see their duty to their country in ratifying & paying for it, so as to secure a good which would otherwise probably be never again in their power. But I suppose they must then appeal to *the nation* for an additional article to the Constitution, approving & confirming an act which the nation had not previously authorized. The Constitution has made no provision for our holding foreign territory, still less for incorporating foreign nations into our Union. The Executive in seizing the fugitive occurrence which so much advances the good of their country, have done an act beyond the Constitution. The Legislature in casting behind them metaphysical subtleties and risking themselves like faithful servants, must ratify & pay for it, and throw themselves on their country for doing for them unauthorized what we know they would have done for themselves had they been in a situation to do it. It is the case of a guardian investing the money of his ward in purchasing an important adjacent territory; & saying to him when of age, I did this for your good; I pretend to no right to bind you: you may disavow me, and I must get out of the scrape as I can: I thought it my duty to risk myself for you. But we shall not be disavowed by the nation, and their act of indemnity will confirm & not weaken the Constitution, by more strongly marking out its lines. . . .

Thomas Jefferson to Wilson Cary Nicholas

7 September 1803

. . . I enclose you a letter from Monroe on the subject of the late treaty. You will observe a hint in it to do without delay what we are bound to do. There is reason, in the opinion of our ministers, to believe that if the thing were to do over again, it could not be obtained, and that if we give the least opening, they will declare the treaty void. A warning amounting to that has been given to them and an unusual kind of letter written by their minister to our Secretary of State, direct. Whatever Congress shall think it necessary to do should be done with as little debate as possible, and particularly so far as respects the constitutional difficulty. I am aware of the force of the observations you make on the power given by the Constitution to Congress to admit new states into the Union, without restraining the subject to the territory then constituting the U.S. But when I consider that the limits of the U.S. are precisely fixed by the treaty of 1783, that the Constitution expressly declares itself to be made for the U.S., I cannot help believing the intention was to permit Congress to admit into the Union new states which should be formed out of the territory for which, and under whose authority alone, they were then acting. I do not believe it was meant that they might receive England, Ireland, Holland, etc. into it, which would be the case on

your construction. When an instrument admits two constructions, the one safe, the other dangerous, the one precise, the other indefinite, I prefer that which is safe and precise. I had rather ask an enlargement of power from the nation, where it is found necessary, than to assume it by a construction which would make our powers boundless. Our peculiar security is in possession of a written Constitution. Let us not make it a blank paper by construction. I say the same as to the opinion of those who consider the grant of the treaty-making power as boundless. If it is, then we have no Constitution. If it has bounds, they can be no others than the definitions of the powers which that instrument gives. It specifies and delineates the operations permitted to the federal government, and gives all the powers necessary to carry these into execution. Whatever of these enumerated objects is proper for a law, Congress may make the law; whatever is proper to be executed by way of a treaty, the President and Senate may enter into the treaty; whatever is to be done by a judicial sentence, the judges may pass the sentence. Nothing is more likely than that their enumeration of powers is defective. This is the ordinary case of all human works. Let us go on then perfecting it, by adding, by way of amendment to the Constitution, those powers which time and trial show are still wanting. . . . I confess, then, I think it important in the present case to set an example against broad construction by appealing for new power to the people. If, however, our friends shall think differently, certainly I shall acquiesce with satisfaction, confiding that the good sense of our country will correct the evil of construction when it shall produce ill effects. . . .

[ALEXANDER HAMILTON]

"Purchase of Louisiana"

New York Evening Post

5 July 1803

At length the business of New Orleans has terminated favorably to this country. Instead of being obliged to rely any longer on the force of treaties for a place of deposit, the jurisdiction of the territory is now transferred to our hands and in future the navigation of the Mississippi will be ours unmolested. This, it will be allowed, is an important acquisition, not, indeed, as territory, but as being essential to the peace and prosperity of our Western country, and as opening a free and valuable market to our commercial states. This purchase has been made during the period of Mr. Jefferson's presidency and will, doubtless, give éclat to his administration. Every man, however, possessed of the least candor and reflection will readily acknowledge that the acquisition has been solely owing to a fortuitous concurrence of unforseen and unexpected circumstances and not to any wise or vigorous measures on the part of the American government.

As soon as we experienced from Spain a direct infraction of an important article of our treaty, in withholding the deposit of New Orleans, it afforded us justifiable cause of war, and authorized immediate hostilities. Sound policy unquestionably demanded of us to begin with a prompt, bold and vigorous resistance against the injustice: to seize the object at once; and having this *vantage ground,* should we have thought it advisable to terminate hostilities by a purchase, we might then have done it on almost our own terms. This course, however, was not adopted, and we were about to experience the fruits of our folly when another nation has found it her interest to place the French Government in a situation substantially as favorable to our views and interests as those recommended by the Federal party here, excepting indeed that we should probably have obtained the same object on better terms.

On the part of France the short interval of peace had been wasted in repeated and fruitless efforts to subjugate St. Domingo; and those means which were originally destined to the colonization of Louisiana had been gradually exhausted by the unexpected difficulties of this ill-starred enterprise.

To the deadly climate of St. Domingo and to the courage and obstinate resistance made by its black inhabitants are we indebted for the obstacles which delayed the colonization of Louisiana till the auspicious moment when a rupture between England and France gave a new turn to the projects of the latter, and destroyed at once all her schemes as to this favorite object of her ambition.

It was made known to Bonaparte that among the first objects of England would be the seizure of New Orleans and that preparations were even then in a state of forwardness for that purpose. The First Consul could not doubt that if an English fleet was sent thither, the place must fall without resistance; it was obvious, therefore, that it would be in every shape preferable that it should be placed in the possession of a neutral power; and when, besides, some millions of money, of which he was extremely in want, were offered him to part with what he could no longer hold it affords a moral certainty that it was to an accidental state of circumstances, and not to wise plans, that this cession, at this time, has been owing. We shall venture to add that neither of the ministers through whose instrumentality it was effected will ever deny this, or even pretend that previous to the time when a rupture was believed to be inevitable, there was the smallest chance of inducing the First Consul, with his ambitious and aggrandizing views, to commute the territory for any sum of money in their power to offer. The real truth is, Bonaparte found himself absolutely compelled by situation to relinquish his darling plan of colonizing the banks of the Mississippi, and thus have the Government of the United States, by the unforeseen operation of events, gained what the feebleness and pusillanimity of its miserable system of measures could never have acquired. Let us then, with all due humility, acknowledge this as another of those signal instances of the kind interpositions of an over-ruling Providence, which we more especially experienced during our revolutionary war, & by which we have more than once been saved from the consequences of our errors and perverseness.

We are certainly not disposed to lessen the importance of this acquisition to the country, but it is proper that the public should be correctly informed of its real value and extent as well as of the terms on which it has been acquired. We perceive by the newspapers that various & very vague opinions are entertained; and we shall therefore venture to state our ideas with some precision as to the territory; but until the instrument of cession itself is published, we do not think it prudent to say much as to the conditions on which it has been obtained.

Prior to the treaty of Paris, 1763, France claimed the country on both sides of the river under the name of Louisiana, and it was her encroachments on the rear of the British Colonies which gave rise to the war of 1755. By the conclusion of the treaty of 1763, the limits of the colonies of Great Britain and France were clearly and permanently fixed; and it is from that and subsequent treaties that we are to ascertain what territory is really comprehended under the name of Louisiana. France ceded to Great Britain all the country east and southeast of a line drawn along the middle of the Mississippi from its source to the Iberville, and from thence along that river and the Lakes Maurepas and Pontchartrain to the sea; France retaining the country lying west of the river, besides the town and Island of New Orleans on the east side. This she soon after ceded to Spain, who acquiring also the Floridas by the treaty of 1783, France was entirely shut out from the continent of North America. Spain, at the instance of Bonaparte, ceded to him Louisiana, including the Town and Island (as it is commonly called) of New Orleans. Bonaparte has now ceded the same tract of country, and this only, to the United States. The whole of East and West Florida, lying south of Georgia and of the Mississippi Territory, and extending to the Gulf of Mexico, still remains to Spain, who will continue, therefore, to occupy, as formerly, the country along the southern frontier of the United States, and the east bank of the river from the Iberville to the American line.

Those disposed to magnify its value will say that this western region is important as keeping off a troublesome neighbor and leaving us in the quiet possession of the Mississippi. Undoubtedly this has some force, but on the other hand it may be said that the acquisition of New Orleans is perfectly adequate to every purpose; for whoever is in possession of that has the uncontroled command of the river. Again, it may be said, and this probably is the most favorable point of view in which it can be placed, that although not valuable to the United States for settlement, it is so to Spain, and will become more so, and therefore at some distant period will form an object which we may barter with her for the Floridas, obviously of far greater value to us than all the immense, undefined region west of the river.

It has been usual for the American writers on this subject to include the Floridas in their ideas of Louisiana, as the French formerly did, and the acquisition has derived no inconsiderable portion of its value and importance with the public from this view of it. It may, however, be relied on, that no part of the Floridas, not a foot of land on the east of the Mississippi, excepting New Orleans, falls within the present cession. As to the unbounded region west of the Mississippi, it is, with the exception of a very few settlements of Spaniards and Frenchmen bordering on the banks of the river, a wilderness through which wander numerous tribes of Indians. And when we consider the present extent of the United States, and that not one sixteenth part of its territory is yet under occupation, the advantage of the acquisition, as it relates to actual settlement, appears too distant and remote to strike the mind of a sober politician

with much force. This, therefore, can only rest in speculation for many years, if not centuries to come, and consequently will not perhaps be allowed very great weight in the account by the majority of readers. But it may be added that should our own citizens, more enterprising than wise, become desirous of settling this country and emigrate thither, it must not only be attended with all the injuries of a too widely dispersed population, but by adding to the great weight of the western part of our territory, must hasten the dismemberment of a large portion of our country or a dissolution of the Government. On the whole, we think it may with candor be said that, whether the possession at this time of any territory west of the river Mississippi will be advantageous, is at best extremely problematical. For ourselves, we are very much inclined to the opinion that, after all, it is the Island of New Orleans, by which the command of a free navigation of the Mississippi is secured, that gives to this interesting cession its greatest value, and will render it in every view of immense benefit to our country. By this cession we hereafter shall hold within our own grasp what we have heretofore enjoyed only by the uncertain tenure of a treaty, which might be broken at the pleasure of another, and (governed as we now are) with perfect impunity. Provided therefore we have not purchased it too dear, there is all the reason for exultation which the friends of the administration display, and which all Americans may be allowed to feel.

As to the pecuniary value of the bargain; we know not enough of the particulars to pronounce upon it. It is understood generally that we are to assume *debts* of France to our own citizens not exceeding four millions of dollars; and that for the remainder, being a very large sum, 6 per cent stock to be created and payment made in that. But should it contain no conditions or stipulations on our part, no "tangling alliances" of all things to be dreaded, we shall be very much inclined to regard it in a favorable point of view though it should turn out to be what may be called a costly purchase. . . .

The Island of New Orleans is in length about 150 miles; its breadth varies from 10 to 30 miles. Most of it is a marshy swamp, periodically inundated by the river. The town of New Orleans, situated about 105 miles from the mouth of the river, contains near 1300 houses and about 8000 inhabitants, chiefly Spanish and French. It is defended from the overflowings of the river by an embankment, or *leveé,* which extends near 50 miles.

The rights of the present proprietors of real estate in New Orleans and Louisiana, whether acquired by descent or by purchase, will, of course, remain undisturbed. How they are to be governed is another question; whether as a colony or to be formed into an integral part of the United States is a subject which will claim consideration hereafter. The probable consequences of the cession and the ultimate effect it is likely to produce on the political state of our country will furnish abundant matter of speculation to the American statesman.

Federalist Alarm

The discontents of northeastern Federalists with the Louisiana purchase are captured in these letters. Rufus King, a Massachusetts native and member of the Constitutional Convention, had gone on to become a senator from New York and ambassador to Britain; in 1816, he would be the last Federalist candidate for president. Timothy Pickering, the High-Federalist secretary of state dismissed by John Adams in 1800, was now a senator from Massachusetts.

Rufus King to Timothy Pickering (?)

4 November 1803

Congress may admit new states, but can the Executive by treaty admit them, or, what is equivalent, enter into engagements binding Congress to do so? As by the Louisiana Treaty, the ceded territory must be formed into states & admitted into the Union, is it understood that Congress can annex any condition to their admission? If not, as slavery is authorized & exists in Louisiana, and the treaty engages to protect the property of the inhabitants, will not the present inequality arising from the representation of slaves be increased?

As the provision of the Constitution on this subject may be regarded as one of its greatest blemishes, it would be with reluctance that one could consent to its being extended to the Louisiana states; and provided any act of Congress or of the several states should be deemed requisite to give validity to the stipulation of the treaty on this subject, ought not an effort to be made to limit the representation to the free inhabitants only? Had it been foreseen that we could raise revenue to the extent we have done from indirect taxes, the representation of slaves would never have been admitted; but going upon the maxim that taxation and representation are inseparable, and that the Genl. Govt. must resort to direct taxes, the states in which slavery does not exist were injudiciously led to concede to this unreasonable provision of the Constitution. On account of the effect upon the public opinion produced by alterations of the fundamental laws of a country, we should hesitate in proposing what may appear to be beneficial; but I know no one alteration of the Constitution of the U.S. which I would so readily propose as to confine representation and taxation to the free inhabitants. . . .

Timothy Pickering to Rufus King

3 March 1804

As long ago as the 4th of November last, you were so obliging as to notice my letter concerning Louisiana. The ruling party do not *now* pretend that the Louisianians are *Citizens* of the U. States. They do not venture to say—they have never said—that the government had a constitutional power to incorporate that new & immense country into the Union; yet they will not give themselves the trouble to alter the Constitution for that purpose. It appears very evident that in a few years, when their power shall be more confirmed and the implicit obedience of the people has been habitual, they will erect states in that territory and incorporate them into the Union. . . . It is further evident that the Constitution will henceforward be only a convenient instrument, to be shaped, by construction, into any form that will best promote the views of the operators. In the name of the Constitution they will commit every arbitrary act which their projects may require; or they will alter it to suit their purposes. I begin to think it would be better if we had none. The leaders of the populace wanting the sanction of a constitutional power might then be more cautious in their measures. . . .

Timothy Pickering to Rufus King

4 March 1804

I must request you to consider this as a continuation of my letter yesterday.

I am disgusted with the men who now rule us and with their measures. At some manifestations of their malignancy

I am shocked. The coward wretch at the head, while, like a Parisian revolutionary monster, prating about humanity, could feel an infernal pleasure in the utter destruction of his opponents. We have too long witnessed his general turpitude—his cruel removals of faithful officers and the substitution of corruption and baseness for integrity and worth. We have now before the Senate a nomination of Meriweather Jones of Richmond, editor of the *Examiner,* a paper devoted to Jefferson and Jacobinism; and he is now to be rewarded. Mr. Hopkins, Commissioner of Loans, a man of property and integrity, is to give room to this Jones. The Commissioner may have at once in his hands thirty thousand dollars, to pay the public creditors in Virginia. He is required by law to give bond only in a sum of from five to ten thousand dollars; and Jones' character is so notoriously bad that we have satisfactory evidence he could not now get credit at any store in Richmond for a suit of clothes! Yet I am far from thinking if this evidence were laid before the Senate that his nomination will be rejected! I am therefore ready to say "come out from among them and be separate." Corruption is the object and instrument of the Chief and the tendency of his administration, for the purpose of maintaining himself in power & for the accomplishment of his infidel and visionary schemes. The corrupt portion of the people are the agents of his misrule; corruption is the recommendation to office; and many of some pretensions to character, but too feeble to resist temptation, become apostates. Virtue and worth are his enemies, and therefore he would overwhelm them.

The collision of democrats in your state promised some amendment. The administration of your government cannot possibly be worse. The Federalists here in general anxiously desire the election of Mr. Burr to the chair of New York; for they despair of a present ascendancy of the Federal party. Mr. Burr alone, we think, can break your democratic phalanx, and we anticipate much good from his success. Were New York detached (as under his administration it would be) from the Virginia influence, the whole Union should be benefited. Jefferson would then be forced to observe some caution and forbearance in his measures. And if a *separation* should be deemed proper, the five New England States, New York, and New Jersey would naturally be united. Among those seven states there is a sufficient congeniality of character to authorize the expectation of practicable harmony and a permanent union; New York the center. Without a

separation, can those states ever rid themselves of Negro Presidents and Negro Congresses and regain their just weight in the political balance? At this moment the slaves of the middle and southern states have fifteen representatives in Congress; and they will appoint 15 Electors of the next President & Vice President; and the number of slaves is continually increasing. You know this evil. But will the slave states ever renounce this advantage? As population is *in fact* no rule of taxation, the Negro representation ought to be given up. If refused, it would be a strong ground of separation; tho' perhaps an earlier occasion may occur to declare it. How many Indian wars, excited by the avidity of the western and southern states of Indian lands, shall we have to encounter? And who will pay the millions to support them? The Atlantic States. Yet the first moment we ourselves need assistance and call on the western states for taxes, they will declare off, or at any rate refuse to obey the call. Kentucky effectually resisted the collection of the excise; and of the $37,000 direct tax assessed upon her so many years ago, she has paid only $4,000, & probably will never pay the residue. In the mean time we are maintaining their representatives in Congress for governing us, who surely can much better govern ourselves. Whenever the western states detach themselves they will take Louisiana with them. In thirty years, the white population in the western states will equal that of the 13 States when they declared themselves independent of G. Britain. On the Census of 1790, Kentucky was entitled to *two* Representatives; under that of 1800 she sends *six*.

The facility with which we have seen an essential change in the Constitution proposed and generally adopted will perhaps remove your scruples about proposing what you intimate respecting Negro representation. But I begin to doubt whether that or any other change we could propose, with a chance of adoption, would be worth the breath, paper, and ink which would be expended in the acquisition. Some think Congress will rise in 15 or 20 days. . . .*

* I do not know *one reflecting* [New Englander] who is not anxious for the GREAT EVENT at which I have glanced. They fear, *they dread* the effects of the corruption so rapidly extending; and that if a decision be long delayed, it will be in vain to attempt it. If there be no improper delay, we have not any doubt but that the *great measure* be taken without the smallest hazard to private property or the public funds; the revenues of the Northern States being equal to their portion of the public debt. Leaving that for Louisiana on those who incurred it.

A Republican Response

"Desultory Reflections on the Aspect of Politics in Relation to the Western People," by "Phocion" (Essay #1)

Kentucky Gazette and General Advertiser

27 September 1803

It is notorious that the people of the United States are at this time divided into two parties, the one attached to the administration of Mr. Jefferson and the other hostile to the man, his principles and his conduct. That whatever policy the former recommends or pursues is assailed by the latter with a violence unknown to any period of our history.

The motives which prompt them on to this opposition and the opposition itself must be worth an examination.

To do this successfully, we must examine into the characters of those composing the party.

One description of them appear to have attached themselves to the administrations which successively governed the United States prior to the year 1801, and upon the same principles the same class of men would attach themselves to any administration, in any age or country. I allude to those enemies to our Revolution from fear, those political fortune hunters that abound in every country, and to those who will abandon any party or enter into the service of any administration from motives of interest and reward.

A second class of them may consist of those who, acting from principle and prejudice, are yet respectable by their motives; and acting from mistaken views are entitled to all that charity which religion inculcates and sanctions.

In the former are to be found the leaders, who, whether their conduct is consistent or not, always find in the latter the instruments and tools adapted to every exigency and every occasion. Honest men are not infrequently victims or agents to the designing, and we should, therefore, ascribe the conduct of the latter to the imperfection of our nature. Nevertheless, their conduct, in its consequences, is equally dangerous to society, from whatever motives it may proceed; since if the blow is aimed, it must be immaterial to the sufferer whether from the mistaken, honest, or designing character. . . .

This abuse of power and influence led a number of enlightened and independent characters to an opposition which enlightened the public mind and finally placed Mr. Jefferson in the presidency.

After this event it was to be expected that a people which complained of abuses in every department of government would insist upon their removal; and that Mr. Jefferson would remove their authors from power.

The people directed it; Mr. Jefferson obeyed.

Then commenced a systematic opposition to his measures. No proposition was made, or act done, but what was immediately opposed. All the attempts of the opposition were directed to one end—the embarrassment of the executive. . . .

Consistency of principle and conduct they did not regard, provided they had consistency of opposition.

Such was their conduct during two sessions of Congress.

But one subject during the session of last Congress engrossed most of their attention, and in which they made exertions worthy a better cause. We allude to the measures which they proposed and opposed relative to the occlusion of the port of Orleans.

At that period they enlarged upon the misfortunes which would flow from the French colonization of Louisiana. Our wealth would be torn from us; the commerce of the western people ruined by the monopoly & exaction of the Frenchmen; the value of our western property lessened by the encouragement they would give to migration; our citizens enticed from their present habitations to become the instrument of French ambition and intrigue; our union dissolved by the machinations and intrigues of their officers; our independence endangered and our whole country fall a prey to the ambition of the consul. The attempt to secure our rights by negotiation was the child of a weak old man; the result of a disordered imagination. Whilst Monroe and Livingston were negotiating, the consul would seize this important territory himself. The period of action would be lost. The loss of blood in the old world were nothing when compared with the advantages of possessing ourselves of the whole country. But all these advantages would be lost by a weak, pusillanimous administration, ignorant of the true interest and right of the country, without capacity to comprehend or firmness to enforce them.

But the country has become ours without the effusion of blood, without entering upon a war, the expenses of which would have been incalculable, without incurring the dislike of powers whose commerce is most important to us, because they are the consumers of our produce; and it appears the act which secured these advantages is to be opposed because it is the act of Mr. Jefferson and the people.

A writer in an eastern paper says fifteen millions is too great a price for Louisiana, a country nearly as large as the United States, and upon which the western people must depend for their commercial importance. Last winter the party were for involving the union in a war, not to secure the country but to embarrass the executive. The western people, more reasonable, required security only, with less expense and risk.

Had war taken place as they desired, more than fifteen millions must have been expended on the operations of a single year.

The country must have been retained and the expense increased to retain it. If to all this we add the immense losses of our citizens engaged in commerce and the expenses of convoys to our merchantmen, how will the calculation then hold? Not to mention the loss of blood, the heartburning of the people of France, the eternalizing of their prejudices and rancor, by an attack upon them for the unprovoked aggression of a petty officer of another, before a demand of reparation had been made, conformable to the conduct of all civilized nations. Not to notice the advantages which other commercial states would obtain over us whilst our commerce to France, Spain, Italy, Holland, and their colonies should be interrupted, & the disadvantages we must have labored under at its revival. Whilst we were suffering all the inconveniences of war, others would be gaining at our expense, without an attempt on our part being made to ward off the evils or to obtain a peaceable remedy. Thus have nations ever been the sport of ambitious statesmen, devouring each other, and permitting states inimical to both to enrich themselves by their common quarrels. Why should we engage in war? Why should we abandon the road which has led us on with unexampled rapidity to the summit of wealth, distinction and power? We have profited by the misfortunes of others without the imputation of a crime, and we have profited to no purpose if we abandon our advantages in the moment of passion. . . .

Senate Debates on the Louisiana Purchase

2–3 November 1803

Despite constitutional objections by several of the Federalists in Congress, the treaty of cession itself was pushed through the Senate quickly by a vote of 24 to 7 on 27 October 1803. The Spanish, however, were still in possession of New Orleans, and Spain was known to object. On 2 November, Senator Samuel White of Delaware moved to postpone a bill creating a fund to pay for the purchase until it was clear that France could actually deliver. Most of the many issues raised by the purchase entered again into the debate on White's motion.

Wednesday, 2 November 1803
Samuel White

. . . I wish not to be understood as predicting that the French will not cede to us the actual and quiet possession of the territory. I hope to God they may, for possession of it we must have—I mean of New Orleans, and of such other positions on the Mississippi as may be necessary to secure to us forever the complete and uninterrupted navigation of that river. This I have ever been in favor of; I think it essential to the peace of the United States and to the prosperity of our Western country. But as to Louisiana, this new, immense, unbounded world, if it should ever be incorporated into this Union, which I have no idea can be done but by altering the Constitution, I believe it will be the greatest curse that could at present befall us; it may be productive of innumerable evils, and especially of one that I fear even to look upon. Gentlemen on all sides, with very few exceptions, agree that the settlement of this country will be highly injurious and dangerous to the United States; but as to what has been suggested of removing the Creeks and other nations of Indians from the eastern to the western banks of the Mississippi, and of making the fertile regions of Louisiana a howling wilderness never to be trodden by the foot of civilized man, it is impracticable. . . . You had as well pretend to inhibit the fish from swimming in the sea as to prevent the population of that country after its sovereignty shall become ours. To every man acquainted with the adventurous, roving, and enterprising temper of our people, and with the manner in which our Western country has been settled, such an idea must be chimerical. The inducements will be so strong that it will be impossible to restrain our citizens from crossing the river. Louisiana must and will become settled, if we hold it, and with the very population that would otherwise occupy part of our present territory. Thus our citizens will be removed to the immense distance of two or three thousand miles from the capital of the Union, where they will scarcely ever feel the rays of the General Government; their affections will become alienated; they will gradually begin to view us as strangers; they will form other commercial connections, and our interests will become distinct.

These, with other causes that human wisdom may not now foresee, will in time effect a separation, and I fear our bounds will be fixed nearer to our houses than the waters of the Mississippi. We have already territory enough, and when I contemplate the evils that may arise to these States from this intended incorporation of Louisiana into the Union, I would rather see it given to France, to Spain, or to any other nation of the earth, upon the mere condition that no citizen of the United States should ever settle within its limits, than to see the territory sold for a hundred millions of dollars, and we retain the sovereignty. But however dangerous the possession of Louisiana might prove to us, I do not presume to say that the retention of it would not have been very convenient to France, and we know that at the time of the mission of Mr. Monroe, our administration had never thought of the purchase of Louisiana, and that nothing short of the fullest conviction of the part of the First Consul that he was on the very eve of a war with England, that this being the most defenseless point of his possessions, if such they could be called, was the one at which the British would first strike, and that it must inevitably fall into their hands, could ever have induced his pride and ambition to make the sale. He judged wisely that he had better sell it for as much as he could get than lose it entirely. And I do say that under existing circumstances, even supposing that this extent of territory was a desirable acquisition, fifteen millions of dollars was a most enormous sum to give. Our Commissioners were negotiating in Paris—they must have known the relative situation of France and England—they must have known at the moment that a war was unavoidable between the two countries, and they knew the pecuniary necessities of France and the naval power of Great Britain. These imperious circumstances should have been turned to our advantage, and if we were to purchase, should have

lessened the consideration. Viewing, Mr. President, this subject in any point of light—either as it regards the territory purchased, the high consideration to be given, the contract itself, or any of the circumstances attending it, I see no necessity for precipitating the passage of this bill; and if this motion for postponement should fail, and the question of the final passage of the bill be taken now, I shall certainly vote against it.

Thursday, 3 November
James Jackson

. . . The delay of the passage of the bill before you may have the most fatal consequences; and if, as some gentlemen have hinted on former occasions, the French are sick of their bargain, will give them an opportunity to break it altogether, or create such jealousies between the two nations as may render the ceded territory and its inhabitants of little value to us. In my opinion, policy, as well as justice, requires that we should comply with the stipulations on our part, promptly and with good faith, and leave no opening for complaint with the other party. We shall then stand justified in the eyes of the world and to ourselves, not only to take, but keep possession of this immense country, let what nation will oppose it.

But the honorable gentleman (Mr. Wells) has said that the French have no title, and, having no title herself, we can derive none from her. Is not, I ask, the King of Spain's proclamation declaring the cession of Louisiana to France and his orders to his governor and officers to deliver it to France, a title? Do nations give any other? . . . The King of Spain's proclamation fully satisfies me on that head, and I hope and believe he will be more prudent than in existing circumstances to involve himself in war with us. The English nation, after the handsome letter of Lord Hawkesbury to our Minister, Mr. King, expressing the approval of His Britannic Majesty of the treaty, cannot, in decency, interfere; and Bonaparte is bound in honor and good faith to protect us in the possession of that country; disgrace would cover him and his nation if he took any part against us. Whom, then, should we have to contend with? With the bayonets of the intrepid French grenadiers, as the honorable gentleman from Delaware, last session, told us, or with the enervated, degraded, and emaciated Spaniards? Shall we be told now that we are no match for these emaciated beings? Last session we were impressed with the necessity of taking immediate possession of the island of New Orleans in the face of two nations, and now we entertain doubts if we can combat the weakest of those powers; and we are further told we are going to sacrifice the immense sum of fifteen millions of dollars and have to go to war with Spain for the country afterwards; when, last session, war was to take place at all events and no costs were equal to the object. Gentlemen seem to be displeased because we have procured it peaceably and at probably ten times less expense than it would have cost us had we taken forcible possession of New Orleans alone, which, I am persuaded, would have involved us in a war which would have saddled us with a debt of from one to two hundred millions, and perhaps have lost New Orleans and the right of deposit after all. I again repeat, sir, that I do not believe that Spain will venture war with the United States. I believe she dare not; if she does, she will pay the costs. The Floridas will be immediately ours; they will almost take themselves. The inhabitants pant for the blessings of your equal and wise government; they ardently long to become a part of the United States. . . . With two or three squadrons of dragoons and the same number of companies of infantry, not a doubt ought to exist of the total conquest of East Florida by an officer of tolerable talents. Exclusive, however, of the loss of the Floridas, to use the language of a late member of Congress, the road to Mexico is now open to us, which, if Spain acts in an amicable way, I wish may, and hope will, be shut as respects the United States forever. For these reasons, I think, sir, Spain will avoid a war, in which she has nothing to gain and everything to lose. . . . The bill is as carefully worded as possible; for the money is not to be paid until after Louisiana shall be placed in our possession.

Sir, it has been observed by a gentleman in debate yesterday (Mr. White) that Louisiana would become a grievance to us, and that we might as well attempt to prevent fish from swimming in water as to prevent our citizens from going across the Mississippi. The honorable gentleman is not so well acquainted with the frontier citizens as I am. . . . The citizens of the state I represent, scattered along an Indian frontier of from three to four hundred miles, have been restrained, except with one solitary instance, by two or three companies of infantry and a handful of dragoons, from crossing over artificial lines and water-courses, sometimes dry, into the Indian country,

after their own cattle, which no human prudence could prevent from crossing to a finer and more luxuriant range, and this too at a time when the feelings of Georgians were alive to the injuries they had received by the New York Treaty with the Creek Indians, which took Tallassee county from them after even three Commissioners appointed by the United States had reported to the President that it was *bona fide* the property of Georgia and sold under as fair a contract as could be formed by a civilized with an uncivilized society. If the Georgians, under these circumstances, were restrained from going on their ground, cannot means be devised to prevent citizens crossing into Louisiana? The frontier people are not the people they are represented; they will listen to reason and respect the laws of their country; it cannot be their wish, it is not their interest to go to Louisiana or see it settled for years to come; the settlement of it at present would part father and son, brother and brother, and friend and friend, and lessen the value of their lands beyond all calculation. If Spain acts an amicable part, I have no doubt myself but the Southern tribes of Indians can be persuaded to go there; it will be advantageous for themselves; they are now hemmed in on every side; their chance of game decreasing daily; plows and looms, whatever may be said, have no charms for them; they want a wider field for the chase, and Louisiana presents it. Spain may, in such case, discard her fears for her Mexican dominions, for half a century at least; and we should fill up the space the Indians removed from with settlers from Europe, and thus preserve the density of population within the original states. . . . In a century, sir, we shall be well populated and prepared to extend our settlements, and that world of itself will present itself to our approaches, and instead of the description given of it by the honorable gentleman, of making it a howling wilderness, where no civilized foot shall ever tread, if we could return at the proper period we would find it the seat of science and civilization.

Mr. President, in whatever shape I view this bill, I conceive it all-important that it should pass without a moment's delay. We have a bargain now in our power which, once missed, we never shall have again. Let us close our part of the contract by the passage of this bill, let us leave no opportunity for any power to charge us with a want of good faith; and having executed our stipulations in good faith we can appeal to God for the justice of our cause; and I trust that, confiding in that justice, there is virtue, patriotism, and courage sufficient in the American nation, not only to take possession of Louisiana, but to keep that possession against the encroachments or attacks of any Power of earth. . . .

John Breckinridge

observed that he little expected a proceeding so much out of order would have been attempted as a re-discussion of the merits of the treaty on the passage of this bill; but as the gentlemen in the opposition had urged it, he would, exhausted as the subject was, claim the indulgence of the Senate in replying to some of their remarks.

No gentleman, continued he, has yet ventured to deny that it is incumbent on the United States to secure to the citizens of the western waters the uninterrupted use of the Mississippi. Under this impression of duty, what has been the conduct of the General Government, and particularly of the gentlemen now in the opposition, for the last eight months? When the right of deposit was violated by a Spanish officer without authority from his government, these gentlemen considered our national honor so deeply implicated, and the rights of the western people so wantonly violated, that no atonement or redress was admissible except through the medium of the bayonet. Negotiation was scouted at. It was deemed pusillanimous and was said to exhibit a want of fellow-feeling for the Western people and a disregard to their essential rights. Fortunately for their country, the counsel of these gentlemen was rejected, and their war measures negatived. The so much scouted process of negotiation was, however, persisted in, and instead of restoring the right of deposit and securing more effectually for the future our right to navigate the Mississippi, the Mississippi itself was acquired, and everything which appertained to it. I did suppose that those gentlemen who, at the last session, so strongly urged war measures for the attainment of this object, upon an avowal that it was too important to trust to the tardy and less effectual process of negotiation, would have stood foremost in carrying the treaty into effect and that the peaceful mode by which it was acquired would not lessen with them the importance of the acquisition. But it seems to me, sir, that the opinions of a certain portion of the United States with respect to this ill-fated Mississippi have varied as often as the fashions. [Here Mr. B. made some remarks on the attempts which were made in the old Congress, and which had

nearly proved successful, to cede this river to Spain for twenty-five years.] But, I trust, continued he, these opinions, schemes, and projects will forever be silenced and crushed by the vote which we are this evening about to pass. . . .

As to the enormity of price, I would ask that gentleman, would his mode of acquiring it through fifty thousand men have cost nothing? Is he so confident of this as to be able to pronounce positively that the price is enormous? Does he make no calculation on the hazard attending this conflict? Is he sure the God of battles was enlisted on his side? Were France and Spain, under the auspices of Bonaparte, contemptible adversaries? Good as the cause was, and great as my confidence is in the courage of my countrymen, sure I am that I shall never regret, as the gentleman seems to do, that the experiment was not made. I am not in the habit Mr. President, on this floor, of panegyrizing those who administer the government of this country. Their good works are their best panegyrists, and of these my fellow-citizens are as competent to judge as I am; but if my opinion were of any consequence, I should be free to declare that this transaction, from its commencement to its close, not only as to the mode in which it was pursued, but as to the object achieved, is one of the most splendid which the annals of any nation can produce. To acquire an empire of perhaps half the extent of the one we possessed from the most powerful and warlike nation on earth, without bloodshed, without the oppression of a single individual, without in the least embarrassing the ordinary operations of your finances, and all this through the peaceful forms of negotiation, and in despite too of the opposition of a considerable portion of the community, is an achievement of which the archives of the predecessors, at least, of those now in office, cannot furnish a parallel.

The same gentleman has told us that this acquisition will, from its extent, soon prove destructive to the Confederacy.

This, continued Mr. B., is an old and hackneyed doctrine; that a republic ought not to be too extensive. But the gentleman has assumed two facts, and then reasoned from them. First, that the extent is too great; and secondly, that the country will be soon populated. I would ask, sir, what is his standard extent for a Republic? How does he come at that standard? Our boundary is already extensive. Would his standard extent be violated by including the island of Orleans and the Floridas? I presume not, as all parties seem to think their acquisition, in part or in whole, essential. Why not then acquire territory on the west as well as on the east side of the Mississippi? Is the Goddess of Liberty restrained by water courses? Is she governed by geographical limits? Is her dominion on this continent confined to the east side of the Mississippi? So far from believing in the doctrine that a republic ought to be confined within narrow limits, I believe, on the contrary, that the more extensive its dominion the more safe and more durable it will be. In proportion to the number of hands you entrust the precious blessings of a free government to, in the same proportion do you multiply the chances for their preservation. I entertain, therefore, no fears for the Confederacy on account of its extent. The American people too well know the art of governing and of being governed to become the victims of party factions or of domestic tyranny. . . .

But is the immediate population of that country, even admitting its extent were too great, a necessary consequence? Cannot the General Government restrain the population within such bounds as may be judged proper? Will gentlemen say that this is impracticable? Let us not then, sir, assume to ourselves so much wisdom and foresight in attempting to decide upon things which properly belong to those who are to succeed us. It is enough for us to make the acquisition: the time and manner of disposing of it must be left to posterity. If they do not improve the means of national prosperity and greatness which we have placed in their hands, the fault or the folly will lie with them. But nothing so remote is more clear to me than that this acquisition will tend to strengthen the Confederacy. It is evident, as this country had passed out of the hands of Spain, that whether it remained with France or should be acquired by England, its population would have been attempted. Such is the policy of all nations but Spain. From whence would that population come? Certainly not from Europe. It would come almost exclusively from the United States. The question, then, would simply be, "Is the Confederacy more in danger from Louisiana when colonized by American people under American jurisdiction than when populated by Americans under the control of some foreign, powerful, and rival nation?" Or, in other words, whether it would be safer for the United States to populate this country when and how she pleased or permit some foreign nation to do it at her expense?

The gentlemen from Delaware and Massachusetts both contend that the third article of the treaty is unconstitutional and our consent to its ratification a nullity, because the United States cannot acquire foreign territory. I am really at a loss how to understand gentlemen. They admit, if I do understand them, that the acquisition of a part at least of this country is essential to the United States and must be made. That this acquisition must extend to the soil; and to use the words of their resolutions last session, "that it is not consistent with the dignity of the Union to hold a right so important by a tenure so uncertain." How, I ask, is this "certain tenure" to be acquired but by conquest or a purchase of the soil? Did not gentlemen intend, when they urged its seizure, that the United States, if successful, should hold it in absolute sovereignty? Were any constitutional difficulties then in the way? And will they now be so good as to point out that part of the Constitution which authorizes us to acquire territory by conquest, but forbids us to acquire it by treaty? But if gentlemen are not satisfied with any of the expositions which have been given of the third article of the treaty, is there not one way, at least, by which this territory can be held? Cannot the Constitution be so amended (if it should be necessary) as to embrace this territory? If the authority to acquire foreign territory be not included in the treaty-making power, it remains with the people; and in that way all the doubts and difficulties of gentlemen may be completely removed; and that, too, without affording France the smallest ground of exception to the literal execution on our part of that article of the treaty. . . .

The Embargo

Thomas Jefferson entered office shortly after the Peace of Amiens (1801–1803) inaugurated the only interval of peace in a quarter century of war between the great European powers. During his initial term, the Republican administration could concentrate on its domestic agenda. In 1805, however, Admiral Lord Nelson destroyed the French fleet at the battle of Trafalgar, and Napoleon's great victory at Austerlitz demolished the continental coalition of Great Britain's allies. France and Britain—the tiger and the shark—then turned to economic warfare, and the commercial problems of the 1790s returned with redoubled force. Both powers resumed seizures of neutral vessels trading with the West Indian possessions of the other; Britain attempted to enforce a general blockade of Napoleonic Europe; Napoleon responded with his Continental system, which sought to exclude British merchants from much of Europe; and in 1807, Britain replied to that with Orders in Council providing for the seizure of any neutral vessel trading with ports from which her own ships were excluded unless that vessel had paid a fee in a British port. Napoleon's Milan Decree, in turn, promised to seize any vessel that did submit to a British search or pay a duty in a British port. Finally, on 22 June, near the mouth of the Chesapeake Bay, the British frigate *Leopard* fired upon the American warship *Chesapeake,* forced her to submit to search, and pressed four sailors, alleged to be deserters, into British service. Against a background of considerable sentiment for war, Jefferson issued a proclamation ordering British warships to leave American waters and, when Congress met, recommended a complete embargo on the country's foreign trade. The Republicans had long maintained that the United States possessed a more effective weapon in her trade than in the ordinary instruments of force. The great embargo was to test this theory.

An Act Laying an Embargo on All Ships and Vessels in the Ports and Harbors of the United States

22 December 1807

Be it enacted by the Senate and House of Representatives of the United States of America, in Congress assembled, That an embargo be and hereby is laid on all ships and vessels in the ports and places within the limits or jurisdiction of the United States, cleared or not cleared, bound to any foreign port or place; and that no clearance be furnished to any ship or vessel bound to such foreign port or place except vessels under the immediate direction of the President of the United States; and that the President be authorized to give such instructions to the officers of the revenue and of the navy and revenue cutters of the United States as shall appear best adapted for carrying the same into full effect. . . .

Sec. 2. *And be it further enacted,* That during the continuance of this act, no registered or sea-letter vessel having on board goods, wares, and merchandise shall be allowed to depart from one port of the United States to another within the same unless the master, owner, consignee, or factor of such vessel shall first give bond with one or more sureties to the Collector of the district from which she is bound to depart in a sum of double the value of the vessel and cargo, that the said goods, wares and merchandise shall be relanded in some port of the United States, dangers of the seas excepted. . . .

Editorials on the Embargo

Washington's *National Intelligencer,* which often spoke for the administration, offered a fuller explanation and defense of the embargo than the administration itself would ever do. Among the many condemnations, Timothy Pickering's stands out.

"Embargo"

National Intelligencer

23 December 1807

This is a strong measure proceeding from the energy of the public councils, appealing to the patriotism of their constituents, and is of all measures the one peculiarly adapted to the crisis. The honest judgment of all parties has anticipated and called for it.

The measure could no longer, in fact, be delayed without sacrificing the vital interests of the nation.

Great Britain [violating neutral rights] furnished an occasion which was seized by the French government for the decree of November 1806, interdicting commerce with G. Britain, which was adopted by the allies of France, particularly by Spain, in her decree of February 1807.

The decree of November was followed by the retaliating British order of January 1807, making war on all neutral trade usually carried on from the ports of one enemy to those of another.

France, again seconded by Spain and other allies, is retaliating on this order by new constructions extending their decrees to all trade from British territories or in British articles.

And it is clear that, if not already done, G. Britain meditates further retaliations, most probably an interdict of all trade by this country (now the only neutral one) with the enemies of G. Britain, that is to say with the whole commercial world.

To these destructive operations against our commerce is to be added the late proclamation of G. Britain on the subject of seamen. . . . With respect to seamen on board merchant vessels, the proclamation has made it the *duty* of all her sea officers to search for and seize all such as they may call British natives, whether wanted or not for the service of their respective ships. From the proportion of American citizens heretofore taken under the name of British seamen may be calculated the number of victims to be added by this formal sanction to the claim of British officers and the conversion of that claim into a *duty*.

Thus the ocean presents a field . . . where no harvest is to be reaped but that of danger, of spoliation, and of disgrace.

Under such circumstances the best to be done is what has been done: a dignified retirement within ourselves; a watchful preservation of our resources; and a demonstration to the world that we possess a virtue and a patriotism which can take any shape that will best suit the occasion.

It is singularly fortunate that an embargo, whilst it guards our essential resources, will have the collateral effect of making it the interest of all nations to change the system which has driven our commerce from the ocean.

Great Britain will feel it in her manufactures, in the loss of naval stores, and above all in the supplies essential to her colonies, to the number of which she is adding by new conquests.

France will feel it in the loss of all those colonial luxuries which she has hitherto received through our neutral commerce; and her colonies will at once be cut off from the sale of their productions and the source of their supplies.

Spain will feel it more, perhaps, than any, in the failure of imported food, not making enough within herself, and in her populous and important colonies which depend wholly on us for the supply of their daily wants.

It is a happy consideration also attending this measure that, although it will have these effects, salutary it may be hoped, on the policy of the great contending nations, it affords neither of them the slightest ground for complaint. The embargo violates the rights of none. Its object is to secure ourselves. It is a measure of precaution, not of aggression. It is resorted to by all nations when their great interests require it. . . .

But may not the embargo bring on war from some of the nations affected by it? Certainly not, if war be not predetermined on against us. Being a measure of peace and precaution; being universal and therefore impartial; extending in reality as well as ostensibly to all nations, there is not a shadow of pretext to make it a cause of war. . . .

All that remains, then, for a people confiding in their government is to rally round the measure which that government has adopted for their good, and to secure its just effect by patiently and proudly submitting to every inconvenience which such a measure necessarily carries with it.

Friday, 25 December

A rapid view was taken in our last paper of the nature and effects of the Embargo. . . . For a time it will materially reduce the price of our produce and enhance that of many foreign commodities. . . . There will [be] occasion for much fortitude, perhaps for great patience.

Is the state of our affairs such as requires this sacrifice? Might not a resort to milder measures do as well? We confidently answer no. . . .

A crisis has arrived that calls for some decided step. The national spirit is up. That spirit is invaluable. In case of a war it is to lead us to conquest. . . . In our solemn appeal to the world, it is to silence forever the idle hope that flatters itself with the phantom, either that we are a divided people or that our republican institutions have not energy enough to defend us, much less to inflict serious injury on our enemies. . . .

The people having shown their spirit, the season has arrived for the government to sustain, second, and direct it. To delay any longer to do this would be to jeopardize its existence. The crisis not requiring war, still hoping if not expecting peace, an embargo is the next best measure for maintaining the national tone. It will arm the nation. It will do more. It will arm the executive government. It is an unequivocal and efficient expression of confidence in the executive and gives the President a new weapon of negotiation—we say *weapon* of negotiation, for, in the present state of the world, even negotiation has ceased to be pacific. Without being backed by force it is an empty sound.

The embargo furnishes this weapon. The sword is not drawn from the scabbard, but it may be drawn at a moment's warning. By it, every member of the community will be sensibly impressed with the solemnity of the crisis and will be prepared for events. The public will be impatient for a decision of the great interests depending. All will be anxious for a restoration of their ordinary pursuits. Our negotiator will be armed with the public sensibility. . . .

We believe it will be a popular measure with all classes. We are certain that the farmer, the planter, and the mechanic will approve it from the security it offers to the public interests; and if the merchants be as honest and enlightened as we trust they are, they will perceive the indissoluble connection between their solid and permanent prosperity and the general welfare.

Alarming Information: A Letter from the Hon. Timothy Pickering, a Senator of the United States from the State of Massachusetts, exhibiting to his constituents, a view of the imminent danger of an UNNECESSARY and RUINOUS WAR, addressed to His Excellency JAMES SULLIVAN, Governor of said State

Connecticut Courant

23 March 1808

The EMBARGO demands the first notice. For perhaps no act of the national government has ever produced so much solicitude or spread such universal alarm. Because all naturally conclude that a measure pregnant with incalculable mischief to all classes of our fellow citizens would not have been proposed by the President and adopted by Congress but for causes deeply affecting the interests and safety of the nation. It must have been under the influence of this opinion that the legislative bodies of some states have expressed their approbation of the Embargo, whether explicitly or by implication. . . .

In the Senate, . . . papers were referred to a committee. The committee quickly reported a bill for laying an Embargo, agreeably to the President's proposal. This was read a first, a second, and a third time, and passed; and all in the short compass of about four hours! A little time was repeatedly asked to obtain further information, and to consider a measure of such moment, of such universal concern; but these requests were denied. We were hurried into the passage of the bill, as if there was danger of its being rejected if we were allowed time to obtain further information and deliberately consider the subject. . . . In truth, the measure appeared to me then, as it still does, and as it appears to the public, without a sufficient motive, without a legitimate object. Hence the general inquiry—"For what is the Embargo laid?" And I challenge any man not in the secrets of the Executive to tell. I know, Sir, that the President said that the papers aforementioned "showed that great and increasing dangers threatened our vessels, our seamen, and our merchandise:" but I also know that they exhibited *no new dangers; none* of which our merchants and seamen had not been well apprised. . . . The great numbers of vessels loading or loaded and prepared for sea; the exertions everywhere made, on the first rumor of the Embargo, to dispatch them, demonstrate the President's dangers to be *imaginary*—to have been *assumed*. . . .

It is true that considerable numbers of vessels were collected in our ports, and many held in suspense, not, however, from any new dangers which *appeared;* but from the mysterious conduct of our affairs after the attack on the Chesapeake; and from the painful apprehensions that the course the President was pursuing would terminate in war. The *National Intelligencer* (usually considered as the Executive newspaper) gave the alarm; and it was echoed through the United States. War, probable or inevitable war, was the constant theme of the newspapers and of the conversations, as was reported, of persons supposed to be best informed of Executive designs. Yet amid this din of war, no adequate preparations were seen making to meet it. . . . No well informed man doubted that the British

Government would make suitable reparation for the attack on the Chesapeake.... And it is now well known that such reparation might have been promptly obtained in London had the President's instructions to Mr. Monroe been compatible with such an adjustment. He was required not to negotiate on this single, transient act (which when once adjusted was forever settled) but in connection with another claim of long standing and, to say the least, of doubtful right, to wit, the exemption from impressment of *British* seamen found on board American *merchant* vessels. To remedy the evil arising from its exercise, by which our own citizens were sometimes impressed, the attention of our government, under every administration, had been earnestly engaged; but no predictable plan has yet been contrived, while no man who regards the truth will question the disposition of the British Government to adopt any arrangement that will secure to Great Britain the services of *her own subjects.* And now, when the unexampled situation of that country (left alone to maintain the conflict with France and her numerous dependent states—left alone to withstand the power which menaces the liberties of the world) rendered the aid of all her subjects more than ever needful, there was no reasonable ground to expect that she would yield the right to take them when found on board the merchant vessels of any nation. Thus to insist on her yielding this point and inseparably to connect it with the affair of the Chesapeake was tantamount to a determination not to negotiate at all.

I write, Sir, with freedom; for the times are too perilous to allow those who are placed in high and responsible situations to be silent or reserved. The peace and safety of our country are suspended on a thread. The course we have seen pursued leads on to a war—to a war with Great Britain—a war absolutely without necessity—a war which whether disastrous or successful, must bring misery and ruin to the United States: *misery* by the destruction of our navigation and commerce (perhaps also of our fairest seaport towns and cities), the loss of markets for our produce, the want of foreign goods and manufactures, and the other evils incident to a state of war; and *ruin,* by the loss of our liberty and independence. For if with the aid of our arms Great Britain were subdued—from that moment (though flattered perhaps with the name of *allies*) we should become the *Provinces of France.* This is a result so obvious, that I must crave your pardon for noticing it. Some advocates of Executive measures admit it. They acknowledge that the navy of Britain is our shield against the overwhelming power of France—Why then do they persist in a course of conduct tending to a rupture with Great Britain?—Will it be believed that it is principally, or solely, to procure inviolability to the *merchant flag* of the United States? In other words, to protect all seamen, *British subjects,* as well as our own citizens, on board our merchant vessels? It is a fact that this has been *made* the greatest obstacle to an amicable settlement with Great Britain. Yet (I repeat it) it is perfectly well known that she desires to obtain *only her own subjects;* and that American citizens, impressed by mistake, are delivered up on duly authenticated proof. The evil we complain of arises from the impossibility of always distinguishing the persons of two nations who a few years since were one people, who exhibit the same manners, speak the same language, and possess similar features. But seeing that we seldom hear complaints in the great *navigating states,* how happens there to be such extreme sympathy for American seamen at *Washington?* ...

Can gentlemen of known *hostility* to foreign commerce *in our own vessels*—who are even willing to *annihilate it* (and such there are)—can these gentlemen plead the cause of our *seamen* because they really wish to *protect* them? Can those desire to *protect* our seamen who, by laying an unnecessary embargo, expose them by thousands to *starve* or *beg?* ... But for the Embargo, thousands depending on the ordinary operations of commerce would now be employed. Even under the restraints of the orders of the British Government, retaliating the French imperial decree, very large portions of the world remain open to the commerce of the United States. We may yet pursue our trade with the British dominions in every part of the globe; with Africa, with China, and with the colonies of France, Spain, and Holland. And let me ask, whether in the midst of a profound peace, when the powers of Europe possessing colonies would, as formerly, confine the trade with them to their own bottoms, or admit us, as foreigners, only under great limitations, we could enjoy a commerce much more extensive than is practicable at the moment, if the Embargo were not in the way? Why then should it be continued? Why rather was it ever laid? ... Has the French Emperor declared that he will have no neutrals? Has he declared that *our ports,* like those of his vassal states in Europe, *be shut against British commerce?* Is the Embargo a *substitute,* a *milder form* of compliance, with that harsh demand, which if exhibited in its naked and insulting aspect, the American spirit might yet resent! . . .

I am alarmed, Sir, at this perilous state of things; I cannot repress my suspicions, or forbear thus to exhibit to you the grounds on which they rest. . . . I declare to you that I have no confidence in the wisdom or correctness of our public measures; that our country is in imminent danger; that it is essential to the public safety that the blind confidence in our rulers should cease; that the state legislatures should know the facts and reasons on which important general laws are founded; *and especially that those states whose farms are on the ocean, and whose harvests are gathered in every sea, should immediately and seriously consider how to preserve them.*

Are our thousands of ships and vessels to rot in our harbors? Are our sixty thousand seamen and fishermen to be deprived of employment and, with their families, reduced to want and beggary? Are our hundreds of thousands of farmers to be compelled to suffer their millions in surplus produce to perish on their hands; that the President may make an experiment on *our* patience and fortitude and on the towering pride, the boundless ambition, and unyielding perseverance of the Conqueror of Europe? Sir, I have reason to believe that the President contemplates the continuance of the Embargo until the French Emperor repeals his decrees violating as well his treaty with the United States as every neutral right; and until Britain thereupon recalls her retaliating orders! By that time we may have neither ships nor seamen; and that is precisely the point to which some men wish to reduce us. . . .

Notwithstanding the well-founded complaints of some individuals and the murmurs of others; notwithstanding the frequent executive declarations of maritime aggressions committed by Great Britain; notwithstanding the outrageous decrees of France and Spain and the wanton spoliations practiced and executed by their cruisers and tribunals, of which we sometimes hear a faint whisper, the commerce of the United States has hitherto prospered beyond all example. Our citizens have accumulated wealth; and the public revenue, annually increasing, has been the President's annual boast.

These facts demonstrate that although Great Britain, with her thousand ships of war, could have destroyed our commerce, she has really done it no essential injury; and

that the other belligerents, heretofore restrained by some regard to national law and limited by the small number of their cruisers, have not inflicted upon it any deep wound. Yet in this full tide of success, our commerce is suddenly arrested; an alarm of war is raised; fearful apprehensions are excited; the merchants, in particular, thrown into a state of consternation, are advised, by a voluntary embargo, to keep their vessels at home. . . . For myself, Sir, I must declare the opinion that no *free* country was ever before so causelessly, and so blindly, thrown from the height of prosperity and plunged into a state of dreadful anxiety and suffering. . . .

Resistance, Enforcement, and Repeal

Embargoes were a tested and conventional method of protecting merchant shipping when it was under threat, especially as preliminaries to war. One of thirty days had been imposed in 1794 during the crisis preceding Jay's Treaty, another after the Leopard-Chesapeake confrontation. The act of 1807 passed the Senate (meeting in secret session) within four or five hours of the president's message recommending it by a vote of 22 to 6. The House also met in secret session, and we are told only that there was a warm debate before an amendment limiting the measure to a period of sixty days was defeated 82 to 46. Thus, the act contained no limitation of time; and it seems clear that Jefferson and Madison, although they never thoroughly explained it to the country, were planning to employ an indefinite embargo as a weapon of economic coercion and an alternative to war, proceeding from their long-standing assumption that all the advantages in a commercial confrontation would lie on the American side.

Despite real hardships, much of the country supported the embargo. But Albert Gallatin, the always-faithful secretary of the treasury, warned Jefferson from the beginning against a long-term experiment with economic warfare. And, indeed, especially in New England, resistance was fierce. Evasion, both on the seas and in the overland trade to Canada, was an increasing problem. The administration answered with ever more stringent enforcement measures, including the employment of the army and state militias. In the end, nevertheless, Congress rebelled; and in his last days in office, on 1 March 1809, Jefferson reluctantly signed legislation replacing the complete embargo with a measure confining nonintercourse to trade with Britain and France and promising repeal of that if either country ceased its violations of neutral rights.

Albert Gallatin to Jefferson

18 December 1807

. . . I also think that an embargo for a limited time will be preferable in itself and less objectionable in Congress. In every point of view—privations, sufferings, revenue, effect on the enemy, politics at home, etc.—I prefer war to a permanent embargo. Governmental prohibitions do always more mischief than had been calculated; and it is not without much hesitation that a statesman should hazard to regulate the concerns of individuals, as if he could do it better than themselves. The measure being of a doubtful policy and hastily adopted on the first view of our foreign intelligence, I think that we had better recommend it with modifications and, at first, for such a limited time as will afford us all time for reconsideration and, if we think proper, for an alteration in our course without appearing to retract. As to the hope that it may have an effect on the negotiation with Mr. Rose or induce England to treat us better, I think it entirely groundless.

Jefferson to Jacob Crowninshield, Secretary of the Navy

16 July 1808

Complaints multiply upon us of evasions of the embargo laws, by fraud and force. These come from Newport, Portland, Machias, Nantucket, Martha's Vineyard, etc., etc. As I do consider the severe enforcement of the embargo to be of an importance not to be measured by money for our future government as well as present objects, I think it will be advisable that during this summer all the gunboats actually manned and in commission should be distributed through as many ports and bays as may be necessary to assist the embargo. On this subject I will pray you to confer with Mr. Gallatin, who will call on you on his passage through Baltimore, and to communicate with him hereafter, *directly,* without the delay of consulting me, and generally to aid this object with such means of your department as are consistent with its situation. . . .

Gallatin to Jefferson

29 July 1808

I sent yesterday to the Secretary of the Navy, and he will transmit to you, a letter from General Dearborn and another from General Lincoln showing the violations of the embargo. . . .

With those difficulties we must struggle as well as we can this summer; but I am perfectly satisfied that if the embargo must be persisted in any longer, two principles must necessarily be adopted in order to make it sufficient: 1st, that not a single vessel shall be permitted to move without the special permission of the executive; 2nd, that the collectors be invested with the general power of seizing property anywhere and taking the rudders or otherwise effectually preventing the departure of any vessel in harbor, though ostensibly intended to remain there, and that without being liable to personal suits. I am sensible that such arbitrary powers are equally dangerous and odious. But a restrictive measure of the nature of the embargo applied to a nation under such circumstances as the United States cannot be enforced without the assistance of means as strong as the measure itself. To that legal authority to prevent, seize, and detain must be added a sufficient physical force to carry it into effect; and although I believe that in our seaports little difficulty would be encountered, we must have a little army along the Lakes and British lines generally. . . . For the Federalists having at least prevented the embargo from becoming a measure generally popular, and the people being distracted by the complexity of the subject, orders of council, decrees, embargoes, and wanting a single object which might rouse their patriotism and unite their passions and affections, selfishness has assumed the reins in several quarters, and the people are now there altogether against the law. . . .

That in the present situation of the world every effort should be attempted to preserve the peace of this nation cannot be doubted. But if the criminal party-rage of Federalists and Tories shall have so far succeeded as to defeat our endeavors to obtain that object by the only measure that could possibly have effected it, we must submit and prepare for war. . . . I have not time to write correctly or even with sufficient perspicuity; but you will guess at my meaning where it is not sufficiently clear.

I mean generally to express an opinion founded on the experience of this summer that Congress must either invest the executive with the most arbitrary powers and sufficient force to carry the embargo into effect, or give it up altogether. And in this last case I must confess that unless a change takes place in the measures of the European powers, I see no alternative but war. But with whom? This is a tremendous question if tested only by policy; and so extraordinary is our situation that it is equally difficult to decide it on the ground of justice, the only one by which I wish the United States to be governed. At all events, I think it the duty of the Executive to contemplate that result as probable, and to be prepared accordingly. . . .

Jefferson to Henry Dearborn, Secretary of War

9 August 1808

Yours of July 27th is received. It confirms the accounts we receive from others that the infractions of the embargo in Maine and Massachusetts are open. I have removed Pope, of New Bedford, for worse than negligence. The collector of Sullivan is on the totter. The Tories of Boston openly threaten insurrection if their importation of flour is stopped. The next post will stop it. I fear your governor is not up to the tone of these parricides, and I hope, on the first symptom of an open opposition of the law by force, you will fly to the scene and aid in suppressing any commotion. . . .

Elisha Tracy (of Norwich, Conn.) to Jefferson

15 September 1808

. . . A few weeks since a Reverend D. D. from the state of Massachusetts, and then standing in the desk of the house where I usually attend divine worship, after describing the administration of the general government in colors suited to his imagination, declared that we ought no longer to *confederate in such a confederation.* This was the first time I had heard the sentiment avowed before a public assembly, tho I had for about four years perceived the leading Federalists cautiously beating the pulse of the people to the tune

of separation. The great body of the people, even Federalist, are still opposed to such a step, and did they but fully see its object, they would execrate its advocates; but they are impelled forward by the great phalanx of the *pulpit,* the *bar,* and the monied interest of New England. The headquarters of this spirit is to be found in the town of Boston, and there is not a doubt to my mind that the object of getting town meetings to express sentiments respecting the Embargo is not to effect its removal, but with a view of increasing discontents and wanton calumnies and . . . to work up such a state of irritation as will furnish them with a favorable opportunity to boldly avow their objects. . . .

Jefferson to Mr. Letue

8 November 1808

While the opposition to the late laws of embargo has in one quarter amounted almost to rebellion and treason, it is pleasing to know that all the rest of the nation has approved of the proceedings of the constituted authorities. The steady union which you mention of our fellow citizens of South Carolina is entirely in their character. They have never failed in fidelity to their country and the republican spirit of its constitution. Never before was that union more needed or more salutary than under our present crisis. I enclose you my message to both houses of Congress, this moment delivered. You will see that we have to choose between the alternatives of embargo and war; there is indeed one and only one other, that is submission and tribute. For all the Federal propositions for trading to the places permitted by the edicts of the belligerents, result in fact in submission. . . . I do not believe, however, that our fellow citizens . . . will concur with those to the east in this parricide purpose, any more than in the disorganizing conduct which has disgraced the latter. . . .

Resolutions of the Connecticut General Assembly

23 February 1809

Resolved, that to preserve the Union and support the Constitution of the United States, it becomes the duty of the legislatures of the states, in such a crisis of affairs, vigilantly to watch over and vigorously to maintain the powers not delegated to the United States but reserved to the states respectively, or to the people, and that a due regard to this duty will not permit this Assembly to assist or concur in giving effect to the . . . unconstitutional act passed to enforce the embargo.

Resolved, that this Assembly highly approve of the conduct of his Excellency, the Governor, in declining to designate persons to carry into effect, by the aid of *military power,* the act of the United States enforcing the embargo. . . .

Resolved, that persons holding executive office under this state are restrained by the duties which they owe this state from affording any official aid or cooperation in the execution of the act aforesaid; and that his Excellency the Governor be requested, as commander in chief of the military force of this state, to cause those resolutions to be published in general orders; and that the secretary of this state be, and he is hereby, directed to transmit copies of the same to the several sheriffs and town clerks.

Resolved, that his Excellency the Governor be requested to communicate the foregoing resolution to the President of the United States with an assurance that this Assembly regret that they are thus obliged under a paramount sense of public duty to assert the unquestionable right of this state to abstain from any agency in the execution of measures which are unconstitutional and despotic.

Resolved, that this Assembly accord in sentiment with the Senate and House of Representatives of the Commonwealth of Massachusetts that it is expedient to effect certain alterations in the Constitution of the United States and will zealously cooperate with that Commonwealth and any other of the states in all legal and constitutional measures for procuring such amendments . . . as shall be judged necessary to obtain more effectual protection and defense for commerce, and to give to the commercial states their fair and just consideration in the union and for affording permanent security as well as present relief from the oppressive measures under which they now suffer.

Resolved, that his Excellency the Governor be requested to transmit copies of the foregoing resolution to the President of the Senate and Speaker of the House of Representatives in the Commonwealth of Massachusetts, and to the legislatures of such of our sister states as manifest a disposition to concur in restoring to commerce its former activity and preventing

the repetition of measures which have a tendency, not only to destroy it, but to dissolve the union, which ought to be inviolate.

John Adams to Benjamin Rush
27 September 1808

. . . I believe, with you, "a republican government," while the people have the virtues, talents, and love of country necessary to support it, "the best possible government to promote the interest, dignity, and happiness of man." But you know that commerce, luxury, and avarice have destroyed every republican government. England and France have tried the experiment, and neither of them could preserve it for twelve years. It might be said with truth that they could not preserve it for a moment, for the commonwealth of England, from 1640 to 1660, was in reality a succession of monarchies under Pym, Hampden, Fairfax, and Cromwell, and the republic of France was a similar monarchy under Mirabeau, Brissot, Danton, Robespierre, and a succession of others like them, down to Napoleon, the Emperor. The mercenary spirit of commerce has recently destroyed the republics of Holland, Switzerland, and Venice. Not one of these republics, however, dared at any time to trust the people with any elections whatever, much less with the election of first magistrates. In all those countries, the monster venality would instantly have appeared and swallowed at once all security of liberty, property, fame, and life. . . .

Americans, I fondly hope and candidly believe, are not yet arrived at the age of Demosthenes or Cicero. If we can preserve our union entire, we may preserve our republic; but if the union is broken, we become petty principalities, little better than the feudatories, one of France and the other of England.

If I could lay an embargo or pass a new importation law against corruption and foreign influence, I would not make it a temporary, but a perpetual law, and I would not repeal it, though it should raise a clamor as loud as my gag-law, or your grog-law, or Mr. Jefferson's embargo. The majorities in the five states of New England, though small, are all on one side. New York has fortified the same party with half a dozen members, and anxious are the expectations from New Jersey, Pennsylvania, and Maryland. There is a body of the same party in every other state.

The Union, I fear, is in some danger. Nor is the danger of foreign war much diminished. An alliance between England and Spain is a new aspect of planets towards us. Surrounded by land on the east, north, west, and south by the territories of two such powers, and blockaded by sea by two such navies as the English and Spanish, without a friend or ally by sea or land, we may have all our republican virtues put to a trial.

I am weary of conjectures, but not in despair.

John Adams to J. B. Varnum

26 December 1808

. . . Ever since my return from Europe, where I had resided ten years and could not be fully informed of the state of affairs in my own country, I have been constantly anxious and alarmed at the intemperance of party spirit and the unbounded license of our presses. In the same view I could not but lament some things which have lately passed in public bodies. To instance, at Dedham and Topsfield, and last of all in the resolutions of our Massachusetts legislature. Upon principle, I see no right in our Senate and House to dictate, nor to advise, nor to request our representatives in Congress. The right of the people to instruct their representatives is very dear to them and will never be disputed by me. But this is a very different thing from an interference of a state legislature. Congress must be "the cloud by day and the pillar of fire by night" to conduct this nation, and if their eyes are to be diverted by wandering light, accidentally springing up in every direction, we shall never get through the wilderness.

I have not been inattentive to the course of our public affairs and agree with Congress in their resolutions to resist the decrees, edicts, and orders of France and England; but I think the king's proclamation for the impressment of seamen on board our merchant ships has not been distinctly enough reprobated. It is the most groundless pretension of all. Retired as I am, conversing with very few of any party, out of the secret of affairs, collecting information only from public papers and pamphlets, many links in the great chain of deliberations, actions, and events may have escaped me. You will easily believe that an excessive diffidence in my own opinions has not been the sin that has most easily beset me. I must nevertheless confess to you that in all the intricate combinations of our affairs to which I have ever been a witness, I never found myself so much at a loss to form a judgment of what the nation ought to do or what part I ought to act. No man, then, I hope, will have more confidence in the solidity of any thing I may suggest than I have myself.

I revere the upright and enlightened general sense of our American nation. It is nevertheless capable, like all other nations, of general prejudices and national errors. Among these, I know not whether there is any more remarkable than that opinion so universal that it is in our power to bring foreign nations to our terms by withholding our commerce. When the executive and legislative authority of any nation, especially in the old governments and great powers of Europe, have adopted measures upon deliberation and published them to the world, they cannot recede without a deep humiliation and disgrace, in the eyes of their own subjects as well as all Europe. They will therefore obstinately adhere to them at the expense even of great sacrifices and in defiance of great dangers. In 1774, Congress appeared almost unanimously sanguine that a non-importation and a non-consumption association would procure an immediate repeal of acts of parliament and royal orders. I went heartily along with the rest in all these measures, because I knew that the sense of the nation, the public opinion in all the colonies, required them, and I did not see that they could do harm. But I had no confidence in their success in anything but uniting the American people. I expressed this opinion freely to some of my friends, particularly to Mr. Henry of Virginia and to Major Hawley of Massachusetts. These two, and these only, agreed with me in opinion that we must fight, after all. We found by experience that a war of eight years, in addition to all our resolutions, was necessary, and the aid of France, Spain, and Holland, too, before our purposes could be accomplished. Do we presume that we can excite insurrection, rebellion, and a revolution in England? Even a revolution would be of no benefit to us. A republican government in England would be more hostile to us than the monarchy is. The resources of that country are so great, their merchants, capitalists, and principal manufacturers are so rich, that they can employ their manufacturers and store their productions for a long time, perhaps longer than we can or will bear to hoard ours. In 1794, upon these principles and for these reasons, I thought it my duty to decide, in Senate, against Mr. Madison's resolutions, as they were called, and I have seen no reason to alter my opinion since. I own I was sorry when the late non-importation law passed. When a war with England was seriously apprehended in 1794, I approved of an embargo as a temporary measure to preserve our seamen and property, but not with any expectation that it would influence England. I thought the embargo which was laid a year ago a wise and prudent measure for the same reason, namely to preserve our seamen and as much of our property as we could get in, but not with the faintest hope that it would influence the British Councils. At the same time I confidently expected that it would be raised in a few months. I have not censured any of these measures, because I knew the fond attachment of the nation to them; but I think the nation must soon be convinced that they will not answer their expectations. The embargo and the non-intercourse laws, I think, ought not to last long. They will lay such a foundation of disaffection to the national government as will give great uneasiness to Mr. Jefferson's successor and produce such distractions and confusions as I shudder to think of. The naval and military force to carry them into execution would maintain a war.

Are you then for war, you will ask. I will answer you candidly. I think a war would be a less evil than a rigorous enforcement of the embargo and non-intercourse. But we have no necessity to declare war against England or France, or both. We may raise the embargo, repeal the non-intercourse, authorize our merchants to arm their vessels, give them special letters of marque to defend themselves against all unlawful aggressors and take and burn or destroy all vessels, or make prize of them as enemies, that shall attack them. In the meantime apply all our resources to build frigates, some in every principal seaport. . . . I never was fond of the plan of building line of battle ships. Our policy is not to fight squadrons at sea, but to have fast-sailing frigates to scour the seas and make impression on the enemy's commerce; and in this way we can do great things. Our great seaports and most exposed frontier places ought not to be neglected in their fortifications; but I cannot see for what purpose a hundred thousand militia are called out, nor why we should have so large an army at present. The revenues applied to these uses would be better appropriated to building frigates. We may depend upon it, we shall never be respected by foreign powers until they see that we are sensible of the great resources which the Almighty in his benevolent providence has put into our hands. No nation under the sun has better materials, architects, or mariners for a respectable maritime power. I have no doubt but our people, when they see a necessity, will cheerfully pay the taxes necessary for their defense and to support their union, independence, and national honor. When our merchants are armed, if they are taken, they cannot blame the government; if they fight well and captivate their enemies, they will acquire glory and encouragement at home, and England or France may determine for themselves whether they will declare war. I believe neither will do it, because each will be afraid of our joining the other. If either should, in my opinion, the other will rescind; but if we should have both to fight, it would not be long before one or the other would be willing to make peace, and I see not much difference between fighting both and fighting England alone. My heart is with the Spanish patriots, and I should be glad to assist them as far as our commerce can supply them.

I conclude with acknowledging that we have received greater injuries from England than from France, abominable as both have been. I conclude that whatever the government determines, I shall support as far as my small voice extends.

The War of 1812

Although he seems to have believed that war was the only honorable alternative to the embargo, Jefferson declined to provide any firm guidance to Congress during his last weeks in office. Madison, who was as much an architect of the policy of commercial coercion as Jefferson himself, but even more inclined toward diffidence in the executive's relationships with Congress, inherited the same set of troubles. Through the next several years, Congress and the administration struggled constantly to find a means by which the economic weapon could be used without damaging the United States more than it did the warring European powers. In 1809, the administration reached an agreement with British minister David Erskine and reopened trade with Britain, but Britain disavowed the arrangement; nonintercourse was once again imposed. In 1810, Macon's Bill Number 2 (named after congressman Nathaniel Macon of North Carolina) ended nonintercourse, but provided that it was to be reimposed against either of the European powers if the other ceased its violations of neutral rights without a comparable response. On 2 November 1810, believing that Napoleon had rescinded his decrees so far as they applied to American shipping, Madison proclaimed that nonintercourse would go into effect again unless Great Britain followed suit. On 11 March 1811, Congress sanctioned its reimposition. With Britain still refusing to rescind its orders and the governor of Canada providing aid and encouragement to Tecumseh and the Prophet, Shawnee brothers who were at the head of an Indian confederacy which was at war with the United States in the Northwest, several new and vigorous members of the Twelfth Congress, which met in November 1811, favored war. Madison had probably already made the same decision.

Madison's War Message

2 June 1812

I communicate to Congress certain documents, being a continuation of those heretofore laid before them on the subject of our affairs with Great Britain.

Without going back beyond the renewal in 1803 of the war in which Great Britain is engaged, and omitting unrepaired wrongs of inferior magnitude, the conduct of her government presents a series of acts hostile to the United States as an independent and neutral nation.

British cruisers have been in the continued practice of violating the American flag on the great highway of nations and of seizing and carrying off persons sailing under it, not in the exercise of a belligerent right founded on the law of nations against an enemy, but of a municipal prerogative over British subjects. . . . Could the seizure of British subjects in such cases be regarded as within the exercise of a belligerent right, the acknowledged laws of war, which forbid an article of captured property to be adjudged without a regular investigation before a competent tribunal, would imperiously demand the fairest trial where the sacred rights of persons were at issue. In place of such a trial these rights are subjected to the will of every petty commander.

The practice, hence, is so far from affecting British subjects alone that, under the pretext of searching for these, thousands of American citizens, under the safeguard of public law and of their national flag, have been torn from their country and from everything dear to them; have been dragged on board ships of war of a foreign nation and exposed, under the severities of their discipline, to be exiled to the most distant and deadly climes, to risk their lives in the battles of their oppressors, and to be the melancholy instruments of taking away those of their own brethren.

Against this crying enormity, which Great Britain would be so prompt to avenge if committed against herself, the United States have in vain exhausted remonstrances and expostulations, and that no proof might be wanting of their conciliatory dispositions, and no pretext left for a continuance of the practice, the British Government was formally assured of the readiness of the United States to enter into arrangements such as could not be rejected if the recovery of British subjects were the real and the sole object. The communication passed without effect.

British cruisers have been in the practice also of violating the rights and the peace of our coasts. They hover over and harass our entering and departing commerce. To the most insulting pretensions they have added the most lawless proceedings in our very harbors, and have wantonly spilt American blood within the sanctuary of our territorial jurisdiction. The principles and rules enforced by that nation, when a neutral nation, against armed vessels of belligerents hovering near her coasts and disturbing her commerce are well known. When called on, nevertheless, by the United States to punish the greater offenses committed by her own vessels, her government has bestowed on their commanders additional marks of honor and confidence.

Under pretended blockades, without the presence of an adequate force and sometimes without the practicability of applying one, our commerce has been plundered in every sea, the great staples of our country have been cut off from their legitimate markets, and a destructive blow aimed at our agricultural and maritime interests. In aggravation of these predatory measures they have been considered as in force from the dates of their notification, a retrospective effect being thus added, as has been done in other important cases, to the unlawfulness of the course pursued. And to render the outrage the more signal these mock blockades have been reiterated and enforced in the face of official communications from the British government declaring as the true definition of a legal blockade "that particular ports must be actually invested and previous warning given to vessels bound to them not to enter."

Not content with these occasional expedients for laying waste our neutral trade, the cabinet of Britain resorted at length to the sweeping system of blockades, under the name of Orders in Council, which has been molded and managed as might best suit its political views, its commercial jealousies, or the avidity of British cruisers.

To our remonstrances against the complicated and transcendent injustice of this innovation the first reply was that the orders were reluctantly adopted by Great Britain as a necessary retaliation on decrees of her enemy proclaiming a general blockage of the British Isles at a time when the naval force of that enemy dared not issue from his own ports. She was reminded without effect that her own prior blockades, unsupported by an adequate naval force actually applied and continued, were a bar to this plea; that executed edicts against millions of our property could not be retaliation on edicts confessedly impossible to be executed; that retaliation, to be just, should fall on the party setting the guilty example, not on an innocent party which was not even chargeable with an acquiescence in it.

When deprived of this flimsy veil for a prohibition of our trade with her enemy by the repeal of his prohibition of our trade with Great Britain, her cabinet, instead of a corresponding repeal or a practical discontinuance of its orders, formally avowed a determination to persist in them against the United States until the markets of her enemy should be laid open to British products, thus asserting an obligation on a neutral power to require one belligerent to encourage by its internal regulations the trade of another belligerent, contradicting her own practice toward all nations, in peace as well as in war, and betraying the insincerity of those professions which inculcated a belief that, having resorted to her orders with regret, she was anxious to find an occasion for putting an end to them.

Abandoning still more all respect for the neutral rights of the United States and for its own consistency, the British government now demands as prerequisites to a repeal of its orders as they relate to the United States that a formality should be observed in the repeal of the French decrees nowise necessary to their termination nor exemplified by British usage, and that the French repeal, besides including that portion of the decrees which operates within a territorial jurisdiction, as well as that which operates on the high seas, against the commerce of the United States should not be a single and special repeal in relation to the United States, but should be extended to whatever other neutral nations unconnected with them may be affected by those decrees. And as an additional insult, they are called on for a formal disavowal of conditions and pretensions advanced by the French government for which the United States are so far from having made themselves responsible that, in official explanations which have been published to the world, and in a correspondence of the American minister at London with the British minister for foreign affairs such a responsibility was explicitly and emphatically disclaimed.

It has become, indeed, sufficiently certain that the commerce of the United States is to be sacrificed, not as interfering with the belligerent rights of Great Britain; not as supplying the wants of her enemies, which she herself supplies; but as interfering with the monopoly which she covets for her own commerce and navigation. She carries on a war against the lawful commerce of a friend that she may the better carry on a commerce with an enemy—a commerce polluted by the forgeries and perjuries which are for the most part the only passports by which it can succeed.

Anxious to make every experiment short of the last resort of injured nations, the United States have withheld from Great Britain, under successive modifications, the benefits of a free intercourse with their market, the loss of which could not but outweigh the profits accruing from her restrictions of our commerce with other nations. And to entitle these experiments to the more favorable consideration they were so framed as to enable her to place her adversary under the exclusive operation of them. To these appeals her government has been equally inflexible, as if willing to make sacrifices of every sort rather than yield to the claims of justice or renounce the errors of a false pride. Nay, so far were the attempts carried to overcome the attachment of the British cabinet to its unjust edicts that it received every encouragement within the competency of the executive branch of our government to expect that a repeal of them would be followed by a war between the United States and France, unless the French edicts should also be repealed. Even this communication, although silencing forever the plea of a disposition in the United States to acquiesce in those edicts, originally the sole plea for them, received no attention.

If no other proof existed of a predetermination of the British Government against a repeal of its orders, it might be found in the correspondence of the minister plenipotentiary of the United States at London and the British secretary for foreign affairs in 1810, on the question whether the blockade of May, 1806, was considered as in force or as not in force. It had been ascertained that the French Government, which urged this blockade as the ground of its Berlin decree, was willing in the event of its removal to repeal that decree, which, being followed by alternate repeals of the other offensive edicts, might abolish the whole system on both sides. This inviting opportunity for accomplishing an object so important to the United States, and professed so often to be the desire of both the belligerents, was made known to the British government. As that government admits that an actual application of an adequate force is necessary to the existence of a legal blockade, and it was notorious that if such a force had ever been applied its long discontinuance had

annulled the blockade in question, there could be no sufficient objection on the part of Great Britain to a formal revocation of it, and no imaginable objection to a declaration of the fact that the blockade did not exist. The declaration would have been consistent with her avowed principles of blockade, and would have enabled the United States to demand from France the pledged repeal of her decrees, either with success, in which case the way would have been opened for a general repeal of the belligerent edicts, or without success, in which case the United States would have been justified in turning their measures exclusively against France. The British Government would, however, neither rescind the blockade nor declare its nonexistence, nor permit its nonexistence to be inferred and affirmed by the American plenipotentiary. On the contrary, by representing the blockade to be comprehended in the orders in council, the United States were compelled so to regard it in their subsequent proceedings.

There was a period when a favorable change in the policy of the British cabinet was justly considered as established. The minister plenipotentiary of His Britannic Majesty here proposed an adjustment of the differences more immediately endangering the harmony of the two countries. The proposition was accepted with the promptitude and cordiality corresponding with the invariable professions of this government. A foundation appeared to be laid for a sincere and lasting reconciliation. The prospect, however, quickly vanished. The whole proceeding was disavowed by the British government without any explanations which could at that time repress the belief that the disavowal proceeded from a spirit of hostility to the commercial rights and prosperity of the United States; and it has since come into proof that at the very moment when the public minister was holding the language of friendship and inspiring confidence in the sincerity of the negotiation with which he was charged, a secret agent of his government was employed in intrigues having for their object a subversion of our government and a dismemberment of our happy union.

In reviewing the conduct of Great Britain toward the United States our attention is necessarily drawn to the warfare just renewed by the savages on one of our extensive frontiers—a warfare which is known to spare neither age nor sex and to be distinguished by features peculiarly shocking to humanity. It is difficult to account for the activity and combinations which have for some time been developing themselves among tribes in constant intercourse with British traders and garrisons without connecting their hostility with that influence and without recollecting the authenticated examples of such interpositions heretofore furnished by the officers and agents of that government.

Such is the spectacle of injuries and indignities which have been heaped on our country, and such the crisis which its unexampled forbearance and conciliatory efforts have not been able to avert. It might at least have been expected that an enlightened nation, if less urged by moral obligations or invited by friendly dispositions on the part of the United States, would have found in its true interest alone a sufficient motive to respect their rights and their tranquillity on the high seas; that an enlarged policy would have favored that free and general circulation of commerce in which the British nation is at all times interested, and which in times of war is the best alleviation of its calamities to herself as well as to other belligerents; and more especially that the British cabinet would not, for the sake of a precarious and surreptitious intercourse with hostile markets, have persevered in a course of measures which necessarily put at hazard the invaluable market of a great and growing country, disposed to cultivate the mutual advantages of an active commerce.

Other counsels have prevailed. Our moderation and conciliation have had no other effect than to encourage perseverance and to enlarge pretensions. We behold our seafaring citizens still the daily victims of lawless violence, committed on the great common and highway of nations, even within sight of the country which owes them protection. We behold our vessels, freighted with the products of our soil and industry, or returning with the honest proceeds of them, wrested from their lawful destinations, confiscated by prize courts no longer the organs of public law but the instruments of arbitrary edicts, and their unfortunate crews dispersed and lost, or forced or inveigled in British ports into British fleets, whilst arguments are employed in support of these aggressions which have no foundation but in a principle equally supporting a claim to regulate our external commerce in all cases whatsoever.

We behold, in fine, on the side of Great Britain a state of war against the United States, and on the side of the United States a state of peace toward Great Britain.

Whether the United States shall continue passive under these progressive usurpations and these accumulating wrongs, or, opposing force to force in defense of their national rights, shall commit a just cause into the hands of the Almighty Disposer of Events, avoiding all connections which might entangle it in the contest or views of other powers, and preserving a constant readiness to concur in an honorable reestablishment of peace and friendship, is a solemn question which the Constitution wisely confides to the legislative department of the Government. In recommending it to their early deliberations I am happy in the assurance that the decision will be worthy the enlightened and patriotic councils of a virtuous, a free, and a powerful nation.

Having presented this view of the relations of the United States with Great Britain and of the solemn alternative growing out of them, I proceed to remark that the communications last made to Congress on the subject of our relations with France will have shown that since the revocation of her decrees, as they violated the neutral rights of the United States, her government has authorized illegal captures by its privateers and public ships, and that other outrages have been practiced on our vessels and our citizens. It will have been seen also that no indemnity had been provided or satisfactorily pledged for the extensive spoliations committed under the violent and retrospective orders of the French government against the property of our citizens seized within the jurisdiction of France. I abstain at this time from recommending to the consideration of Congress definitive measures with respect to that nation, in the expectation that the result of unclosed discussions between our minister plenipotentiary at Paris and the French government will speedily enable Congress to decide with greater advantage on the course due to the rights, the interests, and the honor of our country.

Samuel Taggart, Speech Opposing the War

24 June 1812

Most of the Federalists in Congress, including twenty of the thirty delegates from New England, voted against the war. Among them was congressman Samuel Taggart of Massachusetts. Congress made the decision for war in closed session, and Taggart decided not to deliver the speech he had prepared, but it was published in the *Alexandria Gazette* on 24 June and then in the *Annals of Congress.*

I consider the question now before the House as the most important of any on which I have been called upon to decide since I have been honored with a seat in this House, whether it can be considered in relation to its principles or consequences. It is no less than whether I will give my vote to change the peaceful habits of the people of the United States for the attitude of war and the din of arms, and familiarize our citizens with blood and slaughter. . . . I cannot contemplate my country as on the verge of a war, especially of a war which to me appears both unnecessary and impolitic in the outset, and which will probably prove disastrous in the issue, a war, which, in my view, goes to put not only the lives and property of our most valuable citizens, but also our liberty and independence itself, at hazard, without experiencing the most painful sensations. Believing, as I most conscientiously do, that a war, at this time, would jeopardize the best, the most vital interests, of the country which gave me birth and in which is contained all that I hold near and dear in life, I have, so far as depended upon my vote, uniformly opposed every measure which I believed had a direct tendency to lead to war. . . .

. . . I wish it to be kept in view, that I have no intention, neither do I entertain a wish, to vindicate the Orders in Council. Every neutral, and especially every American, must view the principles contained in these orders as injurious to his rights. . . . I shall barely consider the Orders in Council on the footing in which we have placed the subject in dispute by the law of the first of May, 1810, in which the Congress of the United States declares, that in case either Great Britain or France shall, before the first day of March next, so revoke or modify her edicts that they shall cease to violate the neutral commerce of the United States, and the other does not, in three months thereafter, revoke and modify in like manner, certain enumerated sections of the former non-intercourse law of 1809 shall be revived. . . . I have always doubted whether a repeal in the proper and literal sense of the term, or whether anything like a substantial or even a virtual repeal has taken place.

Sir, if there had been ever anything like a formal explicit act of the French Government, officially communicated, declaring these decrees repealed; if this supposed repeal had been communicated to the ordinary tribunals of justice in France, and they had received directions to act accordingly; if these ordinary tribunals had declined to take cognizance of cases of capture and condemnation under these decrees, for the express reason that they no longer existed; if similar orders had been given to the commanders of French cruisers on the high seas; but more especially if the effects of these decrees had ceased, and American commerce was now no longer subject to vexation or to capture and condemnation under their operation, this would have afforded such evidence of their repeal as would have been satisfactory to my mind, and it is such evidence as the nature of the case required and was reasonably to be expected. We would then have to complain of no other infringement of our rights on the ocean only what arose from the Orders in Council, and we might with propriety insist upon their repeal, on the grounds which we have set up. . . .

I do not urge these observations with a view either to justify or palliate the Orders in Council, but merely to show that, on the foundation on which we have chosen to place the controversy by our law of May 1st, 1810, they are no cause either of war or of non-importation. France has never in good faith complied with the proposal held out by the United States in that law. . . . I shall not at present attempt to take a comparative view of the degree of injury and vexation which we receive in our lawful commerce from the decrees and orders. I will admit that the orders have been more vexatious, and more rigorously carried into effect, during the last twelve or eighteen months, and that captures under them have been both more numerous and more valuable than for the same space of time previous to that period. One cause of this may be found in the attitude which we have assumed. So long as we placed both the belligerents upon an equal footing, the Orders in Council were not very rigorously carried into effect. By our non-importation law we have departed from our neutral ground and have no longer considered the different belligerents as on an equal footing. The consequence has been that the Orders in Council have been more rigorously carried into effect on the part of Great Britain. And since the additional hostile attitude assumed during the present session of Congress has been known in Great Britain, I understand, from the public prints, that orders have been given for their still more rigid execution. Unless she saw fit to rescind them, this was naturally to be expected.

In proportion as we assume a more hostile attitude towards her and show a disposition to embrace her enemy in the arms of friendship and affection, it was to be expected that she would either relax and accede to our demands or adhere more rigorously to her own system. She has chosen the latter.

As it respects the impressment of seamen, this is a delicate and a difficult subject, and if it is ever adjusted to mutual satisfaction it must be by war; and whenever there is mutually a disposition to accommodate, it will be found necessary to concede something on both sides. With respect to the practice of impressments generally, as it respects the citizens or subjects of the country adopting that method of manning her ships, it may be, and doubtless is, in many instances, attended with circumstances of real hardship. The practice may be oppressive, but it is founded upon a principle which is adopted and more or less practiced upon by every nation, i.e. that the nation has a right, either in one shape or another, to compel the services of its citizens or subjects in time of war. The practice of drafting militiamen into actual service, which is authorized by our laws, the conscription of France for the purpose of recruiting her armies, and the impressment of seamen to man a navy, are all greater or less extensions of the same principle. It is vain to contend against the principle itself, since we have sanctioned it by our laws and daily practice upon it, however hardly we may think of some of the particular modes in which it is applied. I feel satisfaction, however, in the reflection that it has never had the sanction of my vote. The principle then being admitted, the only ground of complaint is the irregular application of it to Americans. Great Britain does not claim, she never has claimed the right of impressing American citizens. She claims the right of reclaiming her own subjects, even although they should be found on board of American vessels. And in the assertion of that claim, many irregularities have without doubt been committed by her officers, on account of the similarity of language, manners, and habits. American citizens have been frequently mistaken for British subjects; but I do not know of any instance in which a real American has been reclaimed, where sufficient testimony of his being an American has been adduced, in which his liberation has been refused. No person would, I presume, wish to involve this country in a war for the sake of protecting deserters, either from British vessels or the British service, who may choose to shelter themselves on board of our ships, allured by the prospects of gain. No, sir, we do not want their services. They are a real injury to the America seamen, both by taking their bread from them and exposing them to additional perils of impressment on the high seas. But it is a fact which can easily be substantiated, and will not be disputed by any one having a competent knowledge of the subject, that thousands of men of that description have been and still are employed on board our ships, and have been by some means furnished with all the usual documents of American seamen. Could an efficient plan be devised to prevent men of this description from assuming the garb, personating the character, and claiming the privileges of Americans, I presume the difficulties which occur in settling the question about impressments might be easily surmounted. But so long as such a large number of foreign seamen are employed on board our vessels, and so long as American protections for these foreigners can be obtained with such facility, and are mere matters of bargain and sale, and English, Scotch, and Irish sailors are furnished with them, I pretend not to say by what means, indiscriminately with American citizens, it will be difficult to adjust that subject by treaty, it will be impossible to settle it by war. Only let us adopt a plan whereby a discrimination can be made, and the controversy may be amicably settled. But to say that the flag of every merchant ship shall protect every foreigner who may choose to take refuge on board of it, is the same as to say that we will have no accommodation on the subject, because it is a point which, it is well known, never can be conceded. There is another description of citizens about which there may be some difficulty, I mean naturalized foreigners. These, however, are few in number, it being rarely found that seamen take the benefit of our naturalization laws. There are still some. It is I believe a truth that neither Great Britain nor any other European nation admits of expatriation, and that the United States both admit the expatriation of their own citizens and, on terms sufficiently liberal, naturalizes foreigners. But we cannot expect, with any color of reason, that our naturalization laws will make any alteration in the policy of foreign nations, any more than the European doctrine of perpetual allegiance will influence us. Both are municipal regulations, which can be executed only in the respective territories of the parties and make no part of the law of nations, which is alone binding on the high seas. And every nation claims a right to the services of all its citizens or subjects in time of war. If the United States protect these naturalized foreigners in all the rights and privileges of American citizens, so long as they choose to continue among us, it is a protection sufficiently ample and as much as they can reasonably claim from the government. As long as they continue in the quiet pursuits of civil life on shore, they are in no danger of being remanded back into the service of the country they have abandoned. But when they chose to abandon the land for the ocean, and place themselves in a situation in which it is entirely optional with them whether they return or not, or whether they continue or renounce their allegiance, to attempt to afford protection to them in this situation, at the risk of a war, is to extend to them the privileges of citizenship much farther than they have a right either to expect or claim. If our protections were thus limited to the proper subjects, it would be easy to render them sufficient. This would narrow down the difficulty in adjusting the affairs of impressments and would greatly diminish the numbers of supposed impressed Americans, which are said to be contained in these floating hells, as they have been called. They would be found to be comparatively few, probably not so many hundreds as they have been estimated at thousands, the obstacles in the way of their release would be removed, and impressments probably prevented in future. None of these objects will be obtained by war, but rather by grasping at too much, we will fail of obtaining what we have a right to demand. I do not make these observations with a view to excuse the practice of impressments as generally conducted. But when we are insisting on this as one cause of war, it is proper to view the subject as it is and not through a magnifying mirror which represents every object as being tenfold larger than the life.

I shall say no more of the causes of war as they respect the aggressions of foreign nations. I must now beg the attention of the House for a few minutes to an inquiry, what there is in the present situation of the United States which so imperiously calls for this war. It is said to be necessary to go to war for the purpose of securing our commercial rights, of opening a way for obtaining the best market for our produce, and in order to avenge the insults which have been offered to our flag. But what is there in the present situation of the United States which we could reasonably expect would be ameliorated by war? In a situation of the world which is perhaps without a parallel in the annals of history, it would be strange, indeed, if the

United States did not suffer some inconveniences, especially in their mercantile connections and speculations. In a war which has been unequaled for the changes which it has effected in ancient existing establishments and for innovations in the ancient laws and usages of nations, it would be equally wonderful if, in every particular, the rights of neutrals were scrupulously respected. But, upon the whole, we have reaped greater advantages and suffered fewer inconveniences from the existing state of things than it was natural to expect. During a considerable part of the time in which so large and fair a portion of Europe has been desolated by the calamities of war, our commerce has flourished to a degree surpassing the most sanguine calculations. Our merchants have been enriched beyond any former example. Our agriculture has been greatly extended, the wilderness has blossomed like a rose, and cities and villages have sprung up, almost, as it were, by the force of magic. It is true that this tide of prosperity has received a check. The aggression and encroachments of foreign nations have set bounds to our mercantile speculations; heavy losses have been sustained by the merchant; and the cotton planter of the South and West can no longer reap those enormous profits, those immense golden harvests, from that species of agriculture which he did a few years ago. But if the shackles which we have placed upon commerce by our own restrictive system were completely done away and the enterprise of the merchant was left free to explore new channels, it is probable that it would at this moment be more extensive and more gainful than in times of profound peace in Europe. During the operation of the war a much greater proportion of the commerce of the world was thrown into the hands of the Americans than in times less turbulent would have fallen to their share. . . .

. . . What is the particular achievement to be accomplished by this armament. . . . Canada must be ours; and this is to be the sovereign balm, the universal panacea, which is to heal all the wounds we have received either in our honor, interest, or reputation. This is to be the boon which is to indemnify us for all past losses on the ocean, secure the liberty of the seas hereafter, protect our seamen from impressments, and remunerate us for all the blood and treasure which is to be expended in the present war. Our rights on the ocean have been assailed, and, however inconsistent it may seem to go as far as possible from the ocean to seek redress, yet this would appear to be the policy. We are to seek it, it seems, by fighting the Indians on the Wabash or at Tippecanoe, or the Canadians at Fort Malden, at Little York, at Kingston, at Montreal, and at Quebec. . . . I shall say nothing of either the morality or the humanity, or of the reverse of both, which will be displayed in attacking an inoffensive neighbor and endeavoring to overwhelm a country which has done us no wrong with a superior military force alone. The conquest of Canada has been represented to be so easy as to be little more than a party of pleasure. We have, it has been said, nothing to do but to march an army into the country and display the standard of the United States, and the Canadians will immediately flock to it and place themselves under our protection. They have been represented as ripe for revolt, panting for emancipation from a tyrannical government, and longing to enjoy the sweets of liberty under the fostering hand of the United States. On taking a different view of their situation, it has been suggested that, if they should not be disposed to hail us on our arrival as brothers, come to emancipate and not to subdue them, that they are a debased race of poltroons, incapable of making anything like a stand in their own defense, that the mere sight of an army of the United States would immediately put an end to all thoughts of resistance; that we had little else to do only to march, and that in the course of a few weeks one of our valiant commanders, when writing a dispatch to the President of the United States, might adopt the phraseology of Julius Caesar: *Veni, Vidi, Vici.* This subject deserves a moment's consideration. To presume on the disaffection or treasonable practices of the inhabitants for facilitating the conquest will probably be to reckon without our host. The Canadians have no cause of disaffection with the British government. They have ever been treated with indulgence. They enjoy all that security and happiness, in their connection with Great Britain, that they could reasonably expect in any situation. Lands can be acquired by the industrious settlers at an easy rate, I believe for little more than the office fees for issuing patents, which may amount to three to four cents per acre. They have few or no taxes to pay. I believe none, only a trifle for the repairs of highways. They have a good market for their surplus produce, unhampered with embargoes or commercial restrictions of any kind, and are equally secure both in person and property, both in their civil and religious rights, with the citizens of the United States. What have they, therefore, to gain by a connection with the United States? Would it be any advantage to them to have the price of vacant lands raised from a sum barely sufficient to pay office fees, say three or four dollars one hundred acres, to two dollars per acre? Have we any other boon to hold out to them which can ameliorate their condition? It cannot be pretended. Why, then, should they desire a revolution? They want nothing of us, only not to molest them, and to buy and sell on terms of mutual reciprocity. We, therefore, ought to calculate on every man in Canada as an enemy, or if he is not hostile at the moment of the commencement of the expedition, an invasion of the country will soon make him so, and when an enemy is in the heart of a country, ready to attack our homes and houses, it will inspire even a poltroon with courage. . . .

But, let us admit, for the sake of argument, that Canada is at length conquered, and everything settled in that quarter—*Cui bono?* For whose benefit is the capture of Canada? What advantages are we likely to reap from the conquest? Will it secure the liberty of the seas or compel Great Britain to rescind her Orders in Council? Did we ever know an instance in which Great Britain gave up a favorite measure for the sake of saving a foreign possession, perhaps of very little value to her? Will the advantages to be derived from the conquest of Canada be an equivalent for the loss and damage we may sustain in other quarters? What is Great Britain to be about all the time that we are wresting Canada out of her possession? Is it consistent with the vigor with which she usually acts to stand by and tamely look on? Either she will attempt a vigorous defense of Canada or she will not. If she does, some of the difficulties of the enterprise have been stated. If she does not, it will be that she may be the better able to inflict a severe blow in some other quarter. Admitting war to be sincerely intended, no course could be devised more inconsistent with the maxims of sound policy than that which appears to be pursuing by the United States. . . .

Henry Clay, Speech Supporting the War

9 January 1813

Among the newly elected members of the Twelfth Congress, none was more conspicuous than the representative from Kentucky, whose prompt election as Speaker of the House proved the beginning of a long and distinguished career. One of the most vigorous "War Hawks," Clay delivered this defense of the war during a debate on a bill to enlist additional troops.

. . . The war was declared because Great Britain arrogated to herself the pretension of regulating our foreign trade under the delusive name of retaliatory orders in council, a pretension by which she undertook to proclaim to American enterprise—"Thus far shalt thou go, and no farther"—Orders which she refused to revoke after the alleged cause of their enactment had ceased; because she persisted in the practice of impressing American seamen; because she had instigated the Indians to commit hostilities against us; and because she refused indemnity for her past injuries upon our commerce. I throw out of the question other wrongs. The war in fact was announced, on our part, to meet the war which she was waging on her part. So undeniable were the causes of the war—so powerfully did they address themselves to the feelings of the whole American people—that when the bill was pending before this House, gentlemen in the opposition, although provoked to debate, would not, or could not, utter one syllable against it. It is true they wrapped themselves up in sullen silence, pretending that they did not choose to debate such a question in secret session. Whilst speaking of the proceedings on that occasion, I beg to be permitted to advert to another fact that transpired, an important fact, material for the nation to know, and which I have often regretted had not been spread upon our journals. My honorable colleague (Mr. M'Kee) moved, in committee of the whole, to comprehend France in the war; and when the question was taken upon the proposition, there appeared but ten votes in support of it, of whom seven belonged to this side of the House and three only to the other!

It is said that we were inveigled into the war by the perfidy of France; and that had she furnished the document in time, which was first published in England in May last, it would have been prevented. I will concede to gentlemen every thing they ask about the injustice of France towards this country. I wish to God that our ability was equal to our disposition to make her feel the sense we entertain of that injustice. The manner of the publication of the paper in question was undoubtedly extremely exceptionable. But I maintain that, had it made its appearance earlier, it would not have had the effect supposed; and the proof lies in the unequivocal declarations of the British government. I will trouble you, sir, with going no further back than to the letters of the British minister addressed to the Secretary of State, just before the expiration of his diplomatic functions. It will be recollected by the committee that he exhibited to this government a dispatch from Lord Castlereagh in which the principle was distinctly avowed that to produce the effect of the repeal of the Orders in Council, the French decrees must be absolutely and entirely revoked as to all the world, and not as to America alone. . . . Thus, sir, you see that the British government would not be content with a repeal of the French decrees as to us only. . . . All the world knows that the repeal of the Orders in Council resulted from the inquiry, reluctantly acceded to by the ministry, into the effect upon their manufacturing establishments of our non-importation law, or to the warlike attitude assumed by this government, or to both. But it is said that the Orders in Council are done away, no matter from what cause; and that having been the sole motive for declaring the war, the relations of peace ought to be restored. This brings me into an examination of the grounds for continuing the war.

I am far from acknowledging that, had the Orders in Council been repealed, as they have been, before the war was declared, the declaration would have been prevented. In a body so numerous as this is, from which the declaration emanated, it is impossible to say with any degree of certainty what would have been the effect of such a repeal. Each member must answer for himself. I have no hesitation, then, in saying that I have always considered the impressment of American seamen as much the most serious aggression. But, sir, how have those orders at last been repealed? Great Britain, it is true, has intimated a willingness to suspend their practical operation, but she still arrogates to herself the right to revive them upon certain contingencies, of which she constitutes herself the sole judge. She waives the temporary use of the rod, but she suspends it in terrorem over our heads. Supposing it was conceded to gentlemen that such a repeal of the Orders in Council as took place on the 23rd of June last, exceptionable as it is being known before the war, would have prevented the war, does it follow that it ought to induce us to lay down our arms without the redress of any other injury? Does it follow, in all cases, that that which would have prevented the war in the first instance should terminate the war? By no means. It requires a great struggle for a nation, prone to peace as this is, to burst through its habits and encounter the difficulties of war. Such a nation ought but seldom to go to war. When it does, it should be for clear and essential rights alone, and it should firmly resolve to extort, at all hazards, their recognition. The war of the revolution is an example of a war began for one object and prosecuted for another. It was waged, in its commencement, against the right asserted by the parent country to tax the colonies. Then no one thought of absolute independence. The idea of independence was repelled. But the British government would have relinquished the principle of taxation. The founders of our liberties saw, however, that there was no security short of independence, and they achieved our independence. When nations are engaged in war, those rights in controversy which are not acknowledged by the Treaty of Peace are abandoned. And who is prepared to say that American seamen shall be surrendered, the victims to the British principle of impressment? And, sir, what is this principle? She contends that she has a right to the services of her own subjects; that, in the exercise of this right, she may lawfully impress them, even although she finds them in our vessels, upon the high seas, without her jurisdiction. Now, I deny that she has any right, without her jurisdiction, to come on board our vessels upon the high seas for any other purpose but in pursuit of enemies, or their goods, or goods contraband of war. But she further contends that her subjects cannot renounce their allegiance to her and contract a new obligation to other sovereigns. I do not mean to go into the general question of the right [of] expatriation. If, as is contended, all nations deny it, all nations at the same time admit and practice the right of naturalization. G. Britain herself does. Great Britain, in the very case of foreign seamen, imposes, perhaps, fewer restraints upon naturalization than any other nation. Then, if subjects cannot break their original allegiance, they may, according to universal usage, contract a new allegiance. What is the effect of this double obligation? Undoubtedly, that the sovereign having the possession of the subject would have the right to the services of the subject. If he return within the jurisdiction of his primitive sovereign, he may resume his right to his services, of which the subject by his own act could not divest himself. But his primitive sovereign can have no right to go in quest of him out of his own jurisdiction into the jurisdiction of another sovereign, or upon the high seas, where there exists either no jurisdiction or it belongs to the nation owning the ship navigating them. But, sir, this discussion is altogether useless. It is not to the British principle, objectionable as it is, that we are alone to look;—it is to her practice—no matter what guise she puts on. It is in vain to assert the inviolability of the obligation of allegiance. It is in vain to set up the plea of necessity and to allege that she cannot exist without the impression of HER seamen. The naked truth is, she comes, by her press-gangs, on board of our vessels, seizes OUR native seamen as well as naturalized, and drags them into her service. . . .

. . . If there be a description of rights which, more than any other, should unite all parties in all quarters of the Union, it is unquestionably the rights of the person. No matter what his vocation, whether he seeks subsistence amidst the dangers of the deep, or draws it from the bowels of the earth, or from the humblest occupations of mechanic life, whenever the sacred rights of an American freeman are assailed, all hearts ought to unite and every arm should be braced to vindicate his cause.

The gentleman from Delaware sees in Canada no object worthy of conquest. According to him, it is a cold, sterile, and inhospitable region. And yet, such are the allurements which it offers, that the same gentleman apprehends that, if it be annexed to the United States, already too much weakened by an extension of territory, the people of New England will rush over the line and depopulate that section of the Union! That gentleman considers it honest to hold Canada as a kind of hostage, to regard it as a sort of bond, for the good behavior of the enemy. But he will not enforce the bond. The actual conquest of that country would, according to him, make no impression upon the enemy, and yet the very apprehension only of such a conquest would at all times have a powerful operation upon him! Other gentlemen consider the invasion of that country as wicked and unjustifiable. Its inhabitants are represented as unoffending, connected with those of the bordering states by a thousand tender ties, interchanging acts of kindness and all the offices of good neighborhood; Canada, said Mr. C., innocent! Canada unoffending! It is not in Canada that the tomahawk of the savage has been molded into its death-like form? From Canadian magazines, Malden and others, that those supplies have been issued which nourish and sustain the Indian hostilities? Supplies which have enabled the savage hordes to butcher the garrison of Chicago and to commit other horrible murders? Was it not by the joint cooperation of Canadians and Indians that a remote American fort, Michilimackinac, was fallen upon and reduced, in ignorance of a state of war? But, sir, how soon have the opposition changed. When administration was striving, by the operation of peaceful measures, to bring Great Britain back to a sense of justice, they were for old-fashioned war. And now that they have got old-fashioned war, their sensibilities are cruelly shocked, and all their sympathies are lavished upon the harmless inhabitants of the adjoining provinces. What does a state of war present? The united energies of one people arrayed against the combined energies of another—a conflict in which each party aims to inflict all the injury it can, by sea and land, upon the territories, property, and citizens of the other, subject only to the rules of mitigated war practiced by civilized nations. The gentlemen would not touch the continental provinces of the enemy, nor, I presume, for the same reason, her possessions in the West Indies. The same humane spirit would spare the seamen and soldiers of the enemy. The sacred person of his majesty must not be attacked, for the learned gentlemen, on the other side, are quite familiar with the maxim that the king can do no wrong. Indeed, sir, I know of no person on whom we may make war, upon the principles of the honorable gentlemen, but Mr. Stephen, the celebrated author of the Orders in Council, or the Board of Admiralty, who authorize and regulate the practice of impressment!

The disasters of the war admonish us, we are told, of the necessity of terminating the contest. If our achievements upon the land have been less splendid than those of our intrepid seamen, it is not because the American soldier is less brave. On the one element organization, discipline, and a thorough knowledge of their duties exist on the part of the officers and their men. On the other, almost every thing is yet to be acquired. We have however the consolation that our country abounds with the richest materials and that in no instance when engaged in an action have our arms been tarnished. At Brownstown and at Queenstown the valor of veterans was displayed and acts of the noblest heroism were performed. It is true, that the disgrace of Detroit remains to be wiped off. That is a subject on which I cannot trust my feelings, it is not fitting I should speak. But this much I will say, it was an event which no human foresight could have anticipated, and for which administration cannot be justly censured. It was the parent of all the misfortunes we have experienced on land.

But for it the Indian war would have been in a great measure prevented or terminated; the ascendency on Lake Erie acquired, and the war pushed perhaps to Montreal. With the exception of that event, the war, even upon the land, has been attended by a series of the most brilliant exploits, which, whatever interest they may inspire on this side of the mountains, have given the greatest pleasure on the other. . . .

It is alleged that the elections in England are in favor of the ministry and that those in this country are against the war. If in such a cause (saying nothing of the impurity of their elections) the people of that country have rallied around their government, it affords a salutary lesson to the people here, who at all hazards ought to support theirs, struggling as it is to maintain our just rights. But the people here have not been false to themselves; a great majority approve the war, as is evinced by the recent re-election of the chief magistrate. Suppose it were even true that an entire section of the Union were opposed to the war, that section being a minority, is the will of the majority to be relinquished? In that section the real strength of the opposition had been greatly exaggerated. Vermont has, by two successive expressions of her opinion, approved the declaration of war. In New Hampshire, parties are so nearly equipoised that out of 30 or 35 thousand votes, those who approved and are for supporting it lost the election by only 1,000 or 1,500 votes. In Massachusetts alone have they obtained any considerable accession. If we come to New York, we shall find that other and local causes have influenced her elections.

What cause, Mr. Chairman, which existed for declaring the war has been removed? We sought indemnity for the past and security for the future. The Orders in Council are suspended, not revoked; no compensation for spoliations; Indian hostilities, which were before secretly instigated, now openly encouraged; and the practice of impressment unremittingly persevered in and insisted upon. Yet administration has given the strongest demonstrations of its love of peace. On the 29th June, less than ten days after the declaration of war, the Secretary of State writes to Mr. Russell, authorizing him to agree to an armistice upon two conditions only, and what are they? That the Orders in Council should be repealed and the practice of impressing American seamen cease, those already impressed being released. . . . In return, the enemy is offered a prohibition of the employment of his seamen in our service, thus removing entirely all pretext for the practice of impressment. The very proposition which the gentleman from Connecticut (Mr. Pitkin) contends ought to be made has been made. How are these pacific advances met by the other party? Rejected as absolutely inadmissible, . . . An honorable peace is attainable only by an efficient war. My plan would be to call out the ample resources of the country, give them a judicious direction, prosecute the war with the utmost vigor, strike wherever we can reach the enemy, at sea or on land, and negotiate the terms of a peace at Quebec or Halifax. We are told that England is a proud and lofty nation, that disdaining to wait for danger, meets it half way. Haughty as she is, we *once* triumphed over her, and if we do not listen to the councils of timidity and despair we shall again prevail. In such a cause, with the aid of Providence, we must come out crowned with success; but if we fail, let us fail like men, lash ourselves to our gallant tars, and expire together in one common struggle, fighting for *"seamen's rights and free trade."*

Report and Resolutions of the Hartford Convention

4 January 1815

Alienated by years of Republican experiments with commercial coercion, much of New England resented and resisted the war. Disaffection included legislative addresses condemning the war and discouraging volunteering, refusal by the governors of Massachusetts and Connecticut to permit their militias to be used outside their states, trading with the enemy, and, in December 1814, the convocation at Hartford, Connecticut, of a convention to consider the section's grievances against the course of federal affairs. Listing these, the meeting's resolutions proceeded to demand a lengthy set of constitutional amendments.

First.—A deliberate and extensive system for effecting a combination among certain states, by exciting local jealousies and ambition, so as to secure to popular leaders in one section of the Union the control of public affairs in perpetual succession. To which primary object most other characteristics of the system may be reconciled.

Secondly.—The political intolerance displayed and avowed in excluding from office men of unexceptionable merit for want of adherence to the executive creed.

Thirdly.—The infraction of the judiciary authority and rights, by depriving judges of their offices in violation of the constitution.

Fourthly.—The abolition of existing taxes requisite to prepare the country for those changes to which nations are always exposed, with a view to the acquisition of popular favor.

Fifthly.—The influence of patronage in the distribution of offices, which in these states has been almost invariably made among men the least entitled to such distinction, and who have sold themselves as ready instruments for distracting public opinion and encouraging administration to hold in contempt the wishes and remonstrances of a people thus apparently divided.

Sixthly.—The admission of new states into the Union, formed at pleasure in the western region, has destroyed the balance of power which existed among the original states and deeply affected their interest.

Seventhly.—The easy admission of naturalized foreigners to places of trust, honor, or profit, operating as an inducement to the malcontent subjects of the old world to come to these states in quest of executive patronage and to repay it by an abject devotion to executive measures.

Eighthly.—Hostility to Great Britain and partiality to the late government of France, adopted as coincident with popular prejudice and subservient to the main object, party power. Connected with these must be ranked erroneous and distorted estimates of the power and resources of those nations, of the probable results of their controversies, and of our political relations to them respectively.

Lastly and principally.—A visionary and superficial theory in regard to commerce, accompanied by a real hatred but a feigned regard to its interests, and a ruinous perseverance in efforts to render it an instrument of coercion and war.

But it is not conceivable that the obliquity of any administration could, in so short a period, have so nearly consummated the work of national ruin, unless favored by defects in the Constitution.

To enumerate all the improvements of which that instrument is susceptible and to propose such amendments as might render it in all respects perfect, would be a task which this convention has not thought proper to assume. They have confined their attention to such as experience has demonstrated to be essential, and even among these, some are considered entitled to a more serious attention than others. They are suggested without any intentional disrespect to other states and are meant to be such as all shall find an interest in promoting. Their object is to strengthen, and if possible to perpetuate, the union of the states, by removing the grounds of existing jealousies and providing for a fair and equal representation and a limitation of powers, which have been misused. . . .

THEREFORE RESOLVED,

That it be and hereby is recommended to the legislatures of the several states represented in this Convention to adopt all such measures as may be necessary effectually to protect the citizens of said states from the operation and effects of all acts which have been or may be passed by the Congress of the United States which shall contain provisions subjecting the militia or other citizens to forcible drafts, conscriptions, or impressments, not authorized by the Constitution of the United States.

Resolved, That it be and hereby is recommended to the said legislatures to authorize an immediate and earnest application to be made to the government of the United States, requesting their consent to some arrangement whereby the said states may, separately or in concert, be empowered to assume upon themselves the defense of their territory against the enemy; and a reasonable portion of the taxes collected within said states may be paid into the respective treasuries thereof, and appropriated to the payment of the balance due said states and to the future defense of the same. The amount so paid into the said treasuries to be credited and the disbursements made as aforesaid to be charged to the United States.

Resolved, That it be, and hereby is, recommended to the legislatures of the aforesaid states to pass laws (where it has not already been done) authorizing the governors or commanders-in-chief of their militia to make detachments from the same or to form voluntary corps, as shall be most convenient and conformable to their constitutions, and to cause the same to be well armed, equipped, and disciplined, and held in readiness for service; and upon the request of the governor of either of the other states to employ the whole of such detachment or corps, as well as the regular forces of the state, or such part thereof as may be required and can be spared consistently with the safety of the state, in assisting the state, making such request to repel any invasion thereof which shall be made or attempted by the public enemy.

Resolved, That the following amendments of the Constitution of the United States be recommended to the states represented as aforesaid, to be proposed by them for adoption by the state legislatures and in such cases as may be deemed expedient by a convention chosen by the people of each state.

And it is further recommended that the said states shall persevere in their efforts to obtain such amendments until the same shall be effected.

First. Representatives and direct taxes shall be apportioned among the several states which may be included within this Union according to their respective numbers of free persons, including those bound to serve for a term of years, and excluding Indians not taxed, and all other persons.

Second. No new state shall be admitted into the Union by Congress in virtue of the power granted by the Constitution without the concurrence of two thirds of both houses.

Third. Congress shall not have power to lay any embargo on the ships or vessels of the citizens of the United States, in the ports or harbors thereof, for more than sixty days.

Fourth. Congress shall not have power, without the concurrence of two thirds of both houses, to interdict the commercial intercourse between the United States and any foreign nation or the dependencies thereof.

Fifth. Congress shall not make or declare war or authorize acts of hostility against any foreign nation without the concurrence of two thirds of both houses, except such acts of hostility be in defense of the territories of the United States when actually invaded.

Sixth. No person who shall hereafter be naturalized shall be eligible as a member of the Senate or House of Representatives of the United States, nor capable of holding any civil office under the authority of the United States.

Seventh. The same person shall not be elected president of the United States a second time; nor shall the president be elected from the same state two terms in succession.

Resolved, That if the application of these states to the government of the United States, recommended in a foregoing resolution, should be unsuccessful and peace should not be concluded, and the defense of these states should be neglected, as it has since the commencement of the war, it will, in the opinion of this convention, be expedient for the legislatures of the several states to appoint delegates to another convention, to meet at Boston . . . with such powers and instructions as the exigency of a crisis so momentous may require.

PART 7

The End of an Era

In spite of New England's resistance—and very mixed success on the battlefields in most of the campaigns—the War of 1812 was brought to a conclusion without significant concessions by either side. Indeed, an interesting succession of events allowed Americans to feel that they had won. News of Andrew Jackson's smashing victory in the battle of New Orleans (8 January 1815) reached the East shortly before the news of the Treaty of Ghent, which had in fact been signed in Belgium on Christmas Eve, 1814, two weeks before the battle was fought. Commissioners carrying the report of the Hartford Convention reached the capital just in time for the celebration of the news from New Orleans, and the attempt to extort constitutional amendments under pressure of war damaged the reputation of the Federalist party beyond repair. Within four years, for practical purposes, the Republicans were the only party left. Moreover, the lessons from the war and from the years of unsuccessful efforts to coerce the European powers encouraged a considerable revision of Republican ideas. In his final year in office, Madison would recommend, and Congress would approve, a program going very far toward marking the conclusion of the first party war.

Madison's Seventh Annual Message

5 December 1815

FELLOW CITIZENS OF THE SENATE AND OF THE HOUSE OF REPRESENTATIVES

. . . The treaty of peace with Great Britain has been succeeded by a convention on the subject of commerce concluded by the plenipotentiaries of the two countries. In this result a disposition is manifested on the part of that nation corresponding with the disposition of the United States, which it may be hoped will be improved into liberal arrangements on other subjects on which the parties have mutual interests, or which might endanger their future harmony. Congress will decide on the expediency of promoting such a sequel by giving effect to the measure of confining the American navigation to American seamen— a measure which, at the same time that it might have that conciliatory tendency, would have the further advantage of increasing the independence of our navigation and the resources for our maritime defense.

In conformity with the articles in the Treaty of Ghent relating to the Indians, as well as with a view to the tranquillity of our western and northwestern frontiers, measures were taken to establish an immediate peace with the several tribes who had been engaged in hostilities against the United States. Such of them as were invited to Detroit acceded readily to a renewal of the former treaties of friendship. Of the other tribes who were invited to a station on the Mississippi the greater number have also accepted the peace offered to them. The residue, consisting of the more distant tribes or parts of tribes, remain to be brought over by further explanations, or by such other measures as may be adapted to the dispositions they may finally disclose. . . .

Although the embarrassments arising from the want of a uniform national currency have not been diminished since the adjournment of Congress, great satisfaction has been derived in contemplating the revival of the public credit and the efficiency of the public resources. . . .

. . . It is true that the improved condition of the public revenue will not only afford the means of maintaining the faith of the government with its creditors inviolate, and of prosecuting successfully the measures of the most liberal policy, but will also justify an immediate alleviation of the burdens imposed by the necessities of the war. It is, however, essential to every modification of the finances that the benefits of a uniform national currency should be restored to the community. The absence of the precious metals will, it is believed, be a temporary evil, but until they can again be rendered the general medium of exchange it devolves on the wisdom of Congress to provide a substitute which shall equally engage the confidence and accommodate the wants of the citizens throughout the Union. If the operation of the state banks cannot produce this result, the probable operation of a national bank will merit consideration; and if neither of these expedients be deemed effectual it may become necessary to ascertain the terms upon which the notes of the government (no longer required as an instrument of credit) shall be issued upon motives of general policy as a common medium of circulation.

Notwithstanding the security for future repose which the United States ought to find in their love of peace and their constant respect for the rights of other nations, the character of the times particularly inculcates the lesson that, whether to prevent or repel danger, we ought not to be unprepared for it. This consideration will sufficiently recommend to Congress a liberal provision for the immediate extension and gradual completion of the works of defense, both fixed and floating, on our maritime frontier, and an adequate provision for guarding our inland frontier against dangers to which certain portions of it may continue to be exposed.

As an improvement in our military establishment, it will deserve the consideration of Congress whether a corps of invalids might not be so organized and employed as at once to aid in the support of meritorious individuals excluded by age or infirmities from the existing establishment, and to procure to the public the benefit of their stationary services and of their exemplary discipline. I recommend also an enlargement of the Military Academy already established, and the establishment of others in other sections of the Union; and I cannot press too much on the attention of Congress such a classification and organization of the militia as will most effectually render it the safeguard of a free state. If the experience has shown in the recent splendid achievements of militia the value of this resource for the public defense, it has shown also the importance of that skill in the use of arms and that familiarity with the essential rules of discipline which cannot be expected from the regulations now in force. With this subject is intimately connected the necessity of accommodating the laws in every respect to the great object of enabling the political authority of the Union to employ promptly and effectually the physical power of the Union in the cases designated by the Constitution.

The signal services which have been rendered by our Navy and the capacities it has developed for successful cooperation in the national defense will give to that portion of the public force its full value in the eyes of Congress, at an epoch which calls for the constant vigilance of all governments. To preserve the ships now in a sound state, to complete those already contemplated, to provide amply the imperishable materials for prompt augmentations, and to improve the existing arrangements into more advantageous establishments for the construction, the repairs, and the security of vessels of war is dictated by the soundest policy.

In adjusting the duties on imports to the object of revenue the influence of the tariff on manufactures will necessarily present itself for consideration. However wise the theory may be which leaves to the sagacity and interest of individuals the application of their industry and resources, there are in this as in other cases exceptions to the general rule. Besides the condition which the theory itself implies of a reciprocal adoption by other nations, experience teaches that so many circumstances must concur in introducing and maturing manufacturing establishments, especially of the more complicated kinds, that a country may remain long without them, although sufficiently advanced and in some respects even peculiarly fitted for carrying them on with success. Under circumstances giving a powerful impulse to manufacturing industry, it has made among us a progress and exhibited an efficiency which justify the belief that with a protection not more than is

due to the enterprising citizens whose interests are now at stake it will become at an early day not only safe against occasional competitions from abroad, but a source of domestic wealth and even of external commerce. In selecting the branches more especially entitled to the public patronage a preference is obviously claimed by such as will relieve the United States from a dependence on foreign supplies, ever subject to casual failures, for articles necessary for the public defense or connected with the primary wants of individuals. It will be an additional recommendation of particular manufactures where the materials for them are extensively drawn from our agriculture and consequently impart and insure to that great fund of national prosperity and independence an encouragement which cannot fail to be rewarded.

Among the means of advancing the public interest the occasion is a proper one for recalling the attention of Congress to the great importance of establishing throughout our country the roads and canals which can best be executed under the national authority. No objects within the circle of political economy so richly repay the expense bestowed on them, there are none the utility of which is more universally ascertained and acknowledged; none that do more honor to the governments whose wise and enlarged patriotism duly appreciates them. Nor is there any country which presents a field where nature invites more the art of man to complete her own work for his accommodation and benefit. These considerations are strengthened, moreover, by the political effect of these facilities for intercommunication in bringing and binding more closely together the various parts of our extended confederacy. Whilst the states individually, with a laudable enterprise and emulation, avail themselves of their local advantages by new roads, by navigable canals, and by improving the streams susceptible of navigation, the General Government is the more urged to similar undertakings, requiring a national jurisdiction and national means, by the prospect of thus systematically completing so inestimable a work; and it is a happy reflection that any defect of constitutional authority which may be encountered can be supplied in a mode which the Constitution itself has providently pointed out.

The present is a favorable season also for bringing again into view the establishment of a national seminary of learning within the District of Columbia, and with means drawn from the property therein, subject to the authority of the General Government. Such an institution claims the patronage of Congress as a monument of their solicitude for the advancement of knowledge, without which the blessings of liberty cannot be fully enjoyed or long preserved; as a model instructive in the formation of other seminaries; as a nursery of enlightened preceptors; and as a central resort of youth and genius from every part of their country, diffusing on their return examples of those national feelings, those liberal sentiments, and those congenial manners which contribute cement to our Union and strength to the great political fabric of which that is the foundation.

In closing this communication I ought not to repress a sensibility, in which you will unite, to the happy lot of our country and to the goodness of a superintending Providence, to which we are indebted for it. Whilst other portions of mankind are laboring under the distresses of war or struggling with adversity in other forms, the United States are in the tranquil enjoyment of prosperous and honorable peace. In reviewing the scenes through which it has been attained we can rejoice in the proofs given that our political institutions, founded in human rights and framed for their preservation, are equal to the severest trials of war, as well as adapted to the ordinary periods of repose. As fruits of this experience and of the reputation acquired by the American arms on the land and on the water, the nation finds itself possessed of a growing respect abroad and of a just confidence in itself, which are among the best pledges for its peaceful career. Under other aspects of our country the strongest features of its flourishing condition are seen in a population rapidly increasing on a territory as productive as it is extensive; in a general industry and fertile ingenuity which find their ample rewards; and in an affluent revenue which admits a reduction of the public burdens without withdrawing the means of sustaining the public credit, of gradually discharging the public debt, of providing for the necessary defensive and precautionary establishments, and of patronizing in every authorized mode undertakings conducive to the aggregate wealth and individual comfort of our citizens.

It remains for the guardians of the public welfare to persevere in that justice and good will toward other nations which invite a return of these sentiments toward the United States; to cherish institutions which guarantee their safety and their liberties, civil and religious; and to combine with a liberal system of foreign commerce an improvement of the national advantages and a protection and extension of the independent resources of our highly favored and happy country.

In all measures having such objects my faithful cooperation will be afforded.

Madison's Veto of the Internal Improvements Bill

3 March 1817

Among the recommendations of December 1815, few were clearer than initiation of a program to support internal improvements, which Jefferson's and Madison's administrations had had in mind since Gallatin prepared his great report of 1808. In his last days in office, nevertheless, Madison left a vivid reminder that the measures of 1815 were hardly a surrender to the Federalists' ideas.

To the House of Representatives of the United States

Having considered the bill this day presented to me entitled "An act to set apart and pledge certain funds for internal improvements," and which sets apart and pledges funds "for constructing roads and canals, and improving the navigation of water courses, in order to facilitate, promote, and give security to internal commerce among the several states, and to render more easy and less expensive the means and provisions for the common defense," I am constrained by the insuperable difficulty I feel in reconciling the bill with the Constitution of the United States to return it with that objection to the House of Representatives, in which it originated.

The legislative powers vested in Congress are specified and enumerated in the eighth section of the first article of the Constitution, and it does not appear that the power proposed to be exercised by the bill is among the enumerated powers, or that it falls by any just interpretation within the power to make laws necessary and proper for carrying into execution those or other powers vested by the Constitution in the Government of the United States.

"The power to regulate commerce among the several states" cannot include a power to construct roads and canals and to improve the navigation of water courses in order to facilitate, promote, and secure such a commerce without a latitude of construction departing from the ordinary import of the terms strengthened by the known inconveniences which doubtless led to the grant of this remedial power to Congress.

To refer the power in question to the clause "to provide for the common defense and general welfare" would be contrary to the established and consistent rules of interpretation, as rendering the special and careful enumeration of powers which follow the clause nugatory and improper. Such a view of the Constitution would have the effect of giving to Congress a general power of legislation instead of the defined and limited one hitherto understood to belong to them, the terms "common defense and general welfare" embracing every object and act within the purview of a legislative trust. It would have the effect of subjecting both the Constitution and laws of the several states in all cases not specifically exempted to be superseded by laws of Congress, it being expressly declared "that the Constitution of the United States and laws made in pursuance thereof shall be the supreme law of the land, and the judges of every state shall be bound thereby, anything in the constitution or laws of any state to the contrary notwithstanding." Such a view of the Constitution, finally, would have the effect of excluding the judicial authority of the United States from its participation in guarding the boundary between the legislative powers of the general and the state governments, inasmuch as questions relating to the general welfare, being questions of policy and expediency, are unsusceptible of judicial cognizance and decision.

A restriction of the power "to provide for the common defense and general welfare" to cases which are to be provided for by the expenditure of money would still leave within the legislative power of Congress all the great and most important measures of government, money being the ordinary and necessary means of carrying them into execution.

If a general power to construct roads and canals and to improve the navigation of water courses, with the train of powers incident thereto, be not possessed by Congress, the assent of the states in the mode provided in the bill cannot confer the power. The only cases in which the consent and cession of particular states can extend the power of Congress are those specified and provided for in the Constitution.

I am not unaware of the great importance of roads and canals and the improved navigation of water courses, and that a power in the national legislature to provide for them might be exercised with signal advantage to the general prosperity. But seeing that such a power is not expressly given by the Constitution, and believing that it cannot be deduced from any part of it without an inadmissible latitude of construction and a reliance on insufficient precedents; believing also that the permanent success of the Constitution depends on a definite partition of powers between the general and the state governments, and that no adequate landmarks would be left by the constructive extension of the powers of Congress as proposed in the bill, I have no option but to withhold my signature from it, and to cherishing the hope that its beneficial objects may be attained by a resort for the necessary powers to the same wisdom and virtue in the nation which established the Constitution in its actual form and providently marked out in the instrument itself a safe and practicable mode of improving it as experience might suggest.

In Retrospect

Alexander Hamilton was mortally wounded on 11 July 1804, in a duel with Aaron Burr. The disruption in 1791 of the friendship between John Adams and Thomas Jefferson was not repaired until early in 1812, thanks in great part to the determination of Dr. Benjamin Rush to bring about a reconciliation between his two old friends and fellow signers of the Declaration. After Rush's intercession, Adams wrote to Jefferson that he believed the two of them ought not to die before they had explained themselves to one another. A rich correspondence ensued and continued until their deaths, both of them on 4 July 1826, the fiftieth anniversary of Independence. These famous letters were occupied more with philosophical matters than with the great events in which the two had been allies and opponents. From time to time, however, Adams insisted on bringing the subject back to their collaborations and collisions. Jefferson usually resisted the reopening of old debates, but Jefferson's other correspondence suggests that he never changed his mind about the issues that had been at stake or about the dangers of the constitutional interpretations promulgated by the Marshall court. Those issues were still on his mind when Jefferson and Madison said their last farewells.

The Adams-Jefferson Correspondence

John Adams to Thomas Jefferson

13 July 1813

The first time that you and I differed in opinion on any material question was after your arrival from Europe; and that point was the French Revolution.

You was well persuaded in your own mind that the nation would succeed in establishing a free republican government; I was as well persuaded, in mine, that a project of such a government over five and twenty millions of people, when four and twenty millions and five hundred thousands of them could neither write nor read, was as unnatural, irrational, and impracticable as it would be over the elephants, lions, tigers, panthers, wolves, and bears in the Royal Managerie at Versailles.

. . . When Lafayette harangued you and me and John Quincy Adams through a whole evening in your hotel in the cul de sac at Paris and developed the plans then in operation to reform France, though I was as silent as you was, . . . I was astonished at the grossness of his ignorance of government and history, as I had been for years before at that of Turgot, Rochefaucault, Condorcet, and Franklin. This gross Ideology of them all first suggested to me the thought and the inclination which I afterwards hinted to you in London of writing something upon aristocracy. I was restrained for years by many fearful considerations. . . . I should make enemies of all the French Patriots, the Dutch Patriots, the English Republicans, Dissenters, Reformers, call them what you will; and, what came nearer home to my bosom than all the rest, I knew I should give offense to many if not all of my best friends in America and very probably destroy all the little popularity I ever had in a country where popularity had more omnipotence than the British Parliament assumed. . . .

But when the French Assembly of Notables met and I saw that Turgot's "Government in one center and that center the nation"—a sentence as mysterious or as contradictory as the Athanasian Creed—was about to take place; and when I saw that Shays's Rebellion was breaking out in Massachusetts; and when I saw that even my obscure name was often quoted in France as an advocate for simple democracy; when I saw that the sympathies in America had caught the French flame: I was determined to wash my own hands as clean as I could of all this foulness. I had then strong forebodings that I was sacrificing all the honors and emoluments of this life; and so it has happened, but not in so great a degree as I apprehended.

In truth, my *Defence of the Constitutions* and "Discourses on Davila" laid the foundation of that immense unpopularity which fell like the Tower of Siloam upon me.

Your steady defense of democratical principles and your invariable favorable opinion of the French Revolution laid the foundation of your unbounded popularity.

Sic transit gloria mundi. . . .

Adams to Jefferson

30 June 1813

. . . You never felt the terrorism of Shays's Rebellion in Massachusetts. I believe you never felt the terrorism of Gallatin's Insurrection in Pennsylvania. . . . You certainly never felt the terrorism excited by Genet in 1793, when ten thousand people in the streets of Philadelphia, day after day, threatened to drag Washington out of his house and effect a revolution in the government, or compel it to declare war in favor of the French Revolution and against England. The coolest and the firmest minds, even among the Quakers in Philadelphia, have given their opinions to me that nothing but the yellow fever . . . could have saved the United States from a total revolution of government. I have no doubt you was fast asleep in philosophical tranquility when ten thousand people, and perhaps many more, were parading the streets of Philadelphia on the evening of my Fast Day [25 April 1799]; when Governor Mifflin himself thought it his duty to order a patrol of horse and foot to preserve the peace; when Market Street was as full as men could stand by one another, and even before my door; when some of my domestics, in frenzy, determined to sacrifice their lives in my defense; when all were ready to make a desperate sally among the multitude and others were with difficulty and danger dragged back by the others; when I myself judged it prudent and necessary to order chests of arms from the War Office to be brought through bylanes and back doors, determined to defend my house at the expense of my life and the lives of the few, very few, domestics and friends within it. What think you of terrorism, Mr. Jefferson?

Adams to Jefferson

13 November 1815

. . . The Eighteenth Century, notwithstanding all its errors and vices, has been, of all that are past, the most honorable to human nature. Knowledge and virtues were increased and diffused, arts, sciences useful to men, ameliorating their condition, were improved, more than in any former equal period.

But what are we to say now? Is the Nineteenth Century to be a contrast to the Eighteenth? Is it to extinguish all the lights of its predecessor? . . . The proceedings of the allies and their Congress at Vienna, the accounts from Spain, France, etc. . . . indicate which way the wind blows. The priests are at their old work again. The Protestants are denounced and another St. Bartholomew's Day threatened.

Jefferson to Adams

11 January 1816

I agree with you . . . on the 18th century. It certainly witnessed the sciences and arts, manners and morals, advanced to a higher degree than the world had ever before seen. . . . How then has it happened that these nations, France especially and England, so great, so dignified, so distinguished by science and the arts, plunged at once into all the depths of human enormity, threw off suddenly and openly all the restraints of morality, all sensation to character, and unblushingly avowed and acted on the principle that power was right? . . . Was it from the terror of monarchs alarmed at the light returning on them from the West and kindling a volcano under their thrones? Was it a combination to extinguish that light and to bring back, as their best auxiliaries, those enumerated by you: the Sorbonne, the Inquisition, the Index Expurgatorius, and the Knights of Loyola? Whatever it was, the close of the century saw the moral world thrown back again to the age of the Borgias, to the point from which it had departed 300 years before. . . . Your prophecies . . . proved truer than mine; and yet fell short of the fact. . . . But altho' your prophecy has proved true so far, I hope it does not preclude a better final result. That same light from our West seems to have spread and illuminated the very engines employed to extinguish it. It has given them a glimmering of their rights and their power. The idea of representative government has taken root and growth among them. Their masters feel it and are saving themselves by timely offers of this modification of their own powers. Belgium, Prussia, Poland, Lombardy, etc. are now offered a representative organization: illusive probably at first, but it will grow into power in the end. . . . Even France will yet attain representative government . . . altho' rivers of blood may yet flow between them and their object.

Thomas Jefferson to Justice William Johnson

12 June 1823

. . . I learn . . . with great pleasure that you have resolved on continuing your history of parties. Our opponents are far ahead of us in preparations for placing their cause favorably before posterity. Yet I hope even from some of them [for] the escape of precious truths, in angry explosions or effusions of vanity, which will betray the genuine monarchism of their principles. They do not themselves believe what they endeavor to inculcate: that we were an opposition party, not on principle, but merely seeking for office. The fact is, that at the formation of our government, many had formed their political opinions on European writings and practices, believing the experience of old countries, and especially of England, abusive as it was, to be a safer guide than mere theory. The doctrines of Europe were that men in numerous associations cannot be restrained within the limits of order and justice but by forces physical and moral, wielded over them by authorities independent of their will. Hence their organization of kings, hereditary nobles, and priests. Still further to constrain the brute force of the people, they deem it necessary to keep them down by hard labor, poverty, and ignorance, and to take from them, as from bees, so much of their earnings as that unremitting labor shall be necessary to obtain a sufficient surplus barely to sustain a scanty and miserable life. And these earnings they apply to maintain their privileged orders in splendor and idleness, to fascinate the eyes of the people and excite in them a humble adoration and submission, as to an order of superior beings. Although few among us had gone all these lengths of opinion, yet many had advanced, some more, some less, on the way. And in the convention which formed our government, they endeavored to draw the cords of power as tight as they could obtain them, to lessen the dependence of the general functionaries on their constituents, to subject to them those of the states, and to weaken their

means of maintaining the steady equilibrium which the majority of the convention had deemed salutary for both branches, general and local. To recover, therefore, in practice, the powers which the nation had refused, and to warp to their own wishes those actually given, was the steady object of the federal party. Ours, on the contrary, was to maintain the will of the majority of the convention and of the people themselves. We believed, with them, that man was a rational animal, endowed by nature with rights and with an innate sense of justice; and that he could be restrained from wrong and protected in right by moderate powers confided to persons of his own choice and held to their duties by dependence on his own will. We believed that the complicated organization of kings, nobles, and priests was not the wisest nor best to effect the happiness of associated man; that wisdom and virtue were not hereditary; that the trappings of such a machinery consumed by their expense those earnings of industry they were meant to protect, and, by the inequalities they produced, exposed liberty to sufferance. We believed that men enjoying in ease and security the full fruits of their own industry, enlisted by all their interests on the side of law and order, habituated to think for themselves and to follow their reason as their guide, would be more easily and safely governed than with minds nourished in error and vitiated and debased, as in Europe, by ignorance, indigence, and oppression. The cherishment of the people, then, was our principle, the fear and distrust of them that of the other party. Composed, as we were, of the landed and laboring interests of the country, we could not be less anxious for a government of law and order than were the inhabitants of the cities, the strongholds of federalism. And whether our efforts to save the principles and form of our Constitution have not been salutary, let the present republican freedom, order, and prosperity of our country determine. History may distort truth, and will distort it for a time, by the superior efforts at justification of those who are conscious of needing it most. Nor will the opening scenes of our present government be seen in their true aspect until the letters of the day, now held in private hoards, shall be broken up and laid open to public view. What a treasure will be found in General Washington's cabinet when it shall pass into the hands of as candid a friend to truth as he was himself! When no longer, like Caesar's notes and memorandums in the hands of Anthony, it shall be open to the high priests of Federalism only, and garbled to say so much and no more as suits their views! . . .

The original objects of the Federalists were, 1st, to warp our government more to the form and principles of monarchy, and, 2d, to weaken the barriers of the state governments as coordinate powers. In the first they have been so completely foiled by the universal spirit of the nation that they have abandoned the enterprise, shrunk from the odium of their old appellation, taken to themselves a participation of ours, and under the pseudo-republican mask are now aiming at their second object and, strengthened by unsuspecting or apostate recruits from our ranks, are advancing fast towards an ascendancy. I have been blamed for saying that a prevalence of the doctrines of consolidation would one day call for reformation or *revolution*. I answer by asking if a single state of the union would have agreed to the Constitution had it given all powers to the general government? If the whole opposition to it did not proceed from the jealousy and fear of every state of being subjected to the other states in matters merely its own? And if there is any reason to believe the states more disposed now than then to acquiesce in this general surrender of all their rights and powers to a consolidated government, one and undivided? . . .

Republican Farewells

Jefferson to Madison

17 February 1826

. . . The friendship which has subsisted between us, now half a century, and the harmony of our political principles and pursuits, have been sources of constant happiness to me through that long period. And if I remove beyond the reach of attention to the University, or beyond the bourne of life itself, as I soon must, it is a comfort to leave that institution under your care. . . . It has also been a great solace to me to believe that you are engaged in vindicating to posterity the course we have pursued for preserving to them, *in all their purity,* the blessings of self-government, which we had assisted, too, in acquiring for them. If ever the earth has beheld a system of administration conducted with a single and steadfast eye to the general interest and happiness of those committed to it, one which, protected by truth, can never know reproach, it is that to which our lives have been devoted. To myself you have been a pillar of support through life. Take care of me when dead, and be assured I shall leave with you my last affections.

Madison to Jefferson

24 February 1826

You cannot look back to the long period of our private friendship and political harmony with more affecting recollections than I do. If they are a source of pleasure to you, what ought they not to be to me? We cannot be deprived of the happy consciousness of the pure devotion to the public good with which we discharged the trusts committed to us. And I indulge a confidence that sufficient evidence will find its way to another generation to insure, after we are gone, whatever of justice may be withheld whilst we are here. The political horizon is already yielding, in your case at least, the surest auguries of it. Wishing and hoping that you may yet live to increase the debt which our country owes you, and to witness the increasing gratitude which alone can pay it, I offer you the fullest return of affectionate assurances.

Bibliography

More authoritative texts of the documents printed in the collection may be found in the following sources:

Adams, Charles Francis, ed. *The Works of John Adams*. 10 vols. Boston: Little, Brown, 1850–1856.

Adams, Henry, ed. *The Writings of Albert Gallatin*. Philadelphia: J. B. Lippincott, 1870.

Allen, W. B., ed. *The Works of Fisher Ames, as Published by Seth Ames*. 2 vols. Indianapolis: Liberty Fund, 1983.

Banning, Lance, ed. *Jefferson and Madison: Three Conversations from the Founding*. Madison, Wisc.: Madison House, 1995.

Boyd, Julian P., et al., eds. *The Papers of Thomas Jefferson*. Princeton: Princeton University Press, 1950–.

Cappon, Lester J., ed. *The Adams-Jefferson Letters: The Complete Correspondence between Thomas Jefferson and Abigail and John Adams*. 2 vols. Chapel Hill: University of North Carolina Press, 1959.

Commager, Henry Steele, and Milton Cantor, eds. *Documents of American History*. 2 vols. Englewood Cliffs, N.J.: Prentice Hall, 1988.

Cunningham, Noble E., Jr., ed. *The Early Republic, 1789–1828*. New York: Harper and Row, 1968.

Dallas, George Mifflin. *Life and Writings of Alexander James Dallas*. Philadelphia: J. B. Lippincott, 1871.

Depauw, Linda Grant, et al., eds. *Documentary History of the First Federal Congress of the United States of America, March 4, 1789–March 3, 1791*. Baltimore: Johns Hopkins University Press, 1972–.

Elliot, Jonathan, ed. *The Debates in the Several State Conventions on the Adoption of the Federal Constitution*. 5 vols. Washington, D.C.: Government Printing Office, 1834–1856.

Foner, Philip S., ed. *The Democratic-Republican Societies, 1790–1800: A Documentary Sourcebook of Constitutions, Declarations, Addresses, Resolutions, and Toasts*. Westport, Conn.: Greenwood Press, 1972.

Gales, Joseph, comp. *The Debates and Proceedings in the Congress of the United States*. 42 vols. Washington, D.C.: Gales and Seaton, 1834–1856. Commonly referred to as *Annals of Congress*.

Hutchinson, William T., et al., eds. *The Papers of James Madison*. Chicago and Charlottesville: University of Chicago Press and University Press of Virginia, 1962–.

Jensen, Merrill, et al., eds. *The Documentary History of the Ratification of the Constitution*. Madison: State Historical Society of Wisconsin, 1976–.

King, Charles R., ed. *The Life and Correspondence of Rufus King*. 6 vols. New York: G. P. Putnam's Sons, 1894–1900.

Kohn, Richard H., ed. "Judge Alexander Addison on the Origin and History of the Whiskey Rebellion." In *The Whiskey Rebellion: Past and Present Perspectives*, edited by Steven R. Boyd. Westport, Conn.: Greenwood Press, 1985.

Letters of Abigail Adams to Her Husband. Boston: Little, Brown, 1886.

Marsh, Philip M., ed. *A Freneau Sampler*. New York: Scarecrow Press, 1963.

Meyers, Marvin, ed. *The Mind of the Founder: Sources of the Political Thought of James Madison*. Rev. ed. Hanover, N.H.: University Press of New England, 1981.

Mitchell, Stewart, ed. *New Letters of Abigail Adams, 1788–1801*. Boston: Houghton Mifflin, 1947.

Peterson, Merrill D., ed. *Thomas Jefferson: Writings*. New York: Literary Classics of the United States, 1984.

Smith, James Morton, ed. *The Republic of Letters: The Correspondence Between Thomas Jefferson and James Madison 1776–1826*. 3 vols. New York: W. W. Norton, 1995.

Storing, Herbert J., ed. *The Complete Anti-federalist*. Chicago: University of Chicago Press, 1981.

Syrett, Harold C., and Jacob E. Cooke, eds. *The Papers of Alexander Hamilton*. 26 vols. New York: Columbia University Press, 1961–1979.

Veit, Helen E., Kenneth R. Bowling, and Charlene Banks Bickford, eds. *Creating the Bill of Rights: The Documentary Record from the First Federal Congress*. Baltimore: Johns Hopkins University Press, 1991.

Index

Adams, Abigail, 225–26

Adams, John: Alien and Sedition Acts (*see* Alien and Sedition Acts); Callender arraigned for libel on, 292; defeat by Jefferson for presidency, 262; *Defence of the Constitution,* 353; "Discourses on Davila," 102, 112, 134, 353; the Embargo, 328–30; Jay's Treaty, 197; Jefferson, reconciliation with, 352–54; judicial commissions, 277; titles, 42; vice presidency of, 19–20, 111, 131; XYZ affair, 224, 228–30

Adams, John Quincy, 352

Addison, Alexander, 173–76

admiralty and maritime law: commerce and manufactures, 88; constitutional amendments, 12, 16; Great Britain's navigation laws, 88, 156, 158–59; impressment of seamen by foreign powers, 188, 194, 321, 322, 324, 329–31, 336, 339–42, 347; Jay's Treaty, 188; navy, 242–43, 267, 281, 282, 325, 330, 348; sailor, life of, 105–6; seizure of American vessels, 153–68, 224, 242, 321

agriculture. *See* landed property and agricultural interests

alcohol: taxes and duties on, 15, 92; whiskey excise tax and Whiskey Rebellion, 169, 172, 173–79, 180, 275, 277, 353

Alexandria Gazette, 335

Algiers and Algerine pirates, 164, 281

alienage, 77, 79

Alien and Sedition Acts, 224, 231, 286; Ames's Federalist position on, 274, 275; anticipation of, 225, 228; and Chase, Samuel, impeachment of, 294–96; congressional report in defense of, 238–43; constitutionality of, 233–60; judicial cases resulting from, 277; Kentucky Resolution, 233–36; Madison's Report of 1800, 243–60; prosecutions under, 232; protests of, 232–60; Sedition Act of 1798, text of, 231; state resolutions and replies, 233–38

amendments to Constitution: circular letter from New York ratification convention, 17; congressional proceedings regarding, 21–33; the Embargo, Resolutions of Connecticut General Assembly on, 328; federalist opposition to, 34–35; Hartford Convention, 342–43, 346; implication or broad construction, amendment preferable to, 310; Madison on, 18–21; New York ratification document proposing, 12–17; popular instruction of representatives, 36–38; Virginia state convention proposal, 10–12. *See also* Bill of Rights

American Daily Advertiser: Dallas on Jay's Treaty, 188–92; Philadelphia Memorial on Jay's Treaty, 192–93

American Indians. *See* Indians

American Remembrancer (Matthew Carey), 188

American Revolution, fundamental principles of, 249–50

Ames, Fisher, 41, 110–11, 182–83, 212–15, 273–76

Amiens, Peace of, 321

Annals of Congress, 335

annual messages, presidential: Jefferson's first annual message, 265–68; Madison's seventh annual message, 347–49

Anthony, Mark, 354

anti-Federalists: amendment of Constitution/Bill of Rights, 19, 20, 21, 34, 35, 36; Ames, Fisher, 110–11; commerce and manufacture, 91; national assumption of state debts, 66; nature of government, 3–9; parties, division of government into, 123–24; popular societies, 170, 186. *See also* Republicans

appeals, 16

appropriations: Jay's Treaty, 188; Jefferson's first annual message, 266–67; Louisiana Purchase, 316–20; public roads and canals, 300–304

aristocracy and nobility, 4–5, 24, 103, 111–15, 171, 173, 181, 186–87

arms, right to keep and bear, 11, 13

army. *See* military; standing army

Articles of Confederation, 246, 250, 251

assembly, right of, 11, 14, 171, 182

associations and combinations. *See* party politics; popular societies

assumption of state debts by federal government, 44, 48–51, 64–65, 126–27, 181

Attorney General, 44

authority. *See* power and authority

Bache, Benjamin Franklin, 133, 226, 232

Bacon, Francis, 136

bail, 11, 13

Baldwin, Abraham, 203

bank, national. *See* national bank

bankruptcy laws, 16

Barbary States, 265–66, 267

Barlow, Joel, 134

Bartlett, Judge Josiah, 20

Bassett, Richard, 20

Bayard, John, 282–85

Beccaria, Cesare, Marquis, 4, 5

Bedford, Gunning, 294–96

Belgium, 346, 347, 353

Bill of Rights: congressional proceedings regarding, 21–33; Federalist opposition to, 34–35; Jefferson's support for, 132–33; need for, 6–9; New York and Virginia amendments proposing, 10–11, 12–14

Bingham, Mrs., 226

black cockades, 226

blockades and War of 1812, 332, 333

Blount, William, 209–10, 212

Bonaparte, Napoléon, 307, 311, 321, 328, 331

borrowing money by government. *See* national debt

Boston: *Columbian Centinel,* 172–73; the Embargo, 327; *Independent Chronicle,* 67; Jay's Treaty, selectmen's petition regarding, 193, 198

Boudinot, Elias, 56

Bourne, B., 181

Brackenridge, Henry, 173

Bradford, David, 174

Breckinridge, John C., 233, 277–78, 309–10, 319–20

Brissot, Jacques-Pierre, 328

Britain. *See* Great Britain

"Brutus" essays, 6–9

Buchan, John, Lord, 191

Burke, Aedanus, 22, 37, 39

Burke, Edmund, 102

Burlamaqui, Jean-Jacques, 146

Burr, Aaron, 130, 262, 277, 314, 352

Caesar, 130, 338, 354

"Ça Ira" (song), 225

Callender, James Thomson, 292

Canada, 286, 325, 337–38, 340–41

canals and roads, public. *See* internal improvements bill

capital, effect of national bank on, 70, 71

capitation tax, 15

Carey, Matthew, 188

Carrington, Edward, 66–67, 115–20

Carroll, Charles, 117

Castlereagh, Robert Stewart, Lord, 339

Cataline, 130

Catholic Church, 353

Cato, 130

"Cato" (Robert R. Livingston), 188

censure by legislature, 179–87

census, 266, 279

certificates of public debt. *See* national debt

Chase, Samuel, impeachment of, 292: articles of impeachment, 292–93; charge delivered by Judge Chase, 297–99; Randolph, John, address of, 293–94; Senate proceedings, 293–99; testimony, 294–98

checks and balances, 104, 187. *See also* separation of powers

Chesapeake (vessel), 321, 324

Chester Light Infantry Company of Volunteers, County of Delaware, Pennsylvania, 230

China, 89, 324

Cicero, 328

Cincinnati Society, 173, 179

citizenship: Jefferson's first annual message regarding, 267–68; requirements for, 15, 231, 267–68, 342, 343

civil government. *See* federal government

classes of persons, 4, 5, 105–6

Clinton, George, 17, 20

Clymer, George, 36, 41

cockades, black vs. tri-color, 226

coins. *See* currency

colonialism, 154–55

combinations and associations. *See* party politics; popular societies

commerce and manufacture: agriculture vs. internal commerce and manufacture, 88–89, 94–95, 99–100, 105–6; amendment of Constitution/Bill of Rights, 5, 11–12; Ames' Federalist position, 274; discrimination, commercial, 88, 90, 91–94, 132, 153–68, 188, 190, 198–200; diversification of industry, 96–97, 99; duties and tariffs, 348; the Embargo (*see* the Embargo, *under* "E"); fashion, effects of, 106–7; free trade, 88, 90; Hamilton's Report on Manufactures, 94–101, 102, 132; Hartford Convention, 342, 343; interior commerce and native manufacture, encouragement of, 88, 94–101; interstate commerce clause, 78, 85–86, 90–91, 101, 158, 163, 165, 350; Jefferson on, 88–89, 93–94, 119, 264; Louisiana Purchase, 307, 311, 315, 316, 319; Madison on, 88–94, 119; Mississippi River, American trade on, 173, 175, 189, 217, 310, 319; national bank, 70; postwar depression, concerns raised by, 88; property, right to acquire, 107–8; public roads and canals, 300–304; republican governments destroyed by, 328; retaliation and discrimination, 88, 90, 91–94, 132, 153–68, 188, 190, 198–200; seizure of American vessels, 153–68, 224, 242, 321; state debts, federal assumption of, 68; War of 1812, 332–34, 337, 339–43. *See also* foreign commerce, imports, and exports

commerce clause, 78, 85–86, 90–91, 101, 158, 163, 165, 350

common defense and general welfare: Alien and Sedition Acts,

Genet, Edmond, 141, 142, 169, 172–73, 181, 354

George III, 190

Georgia, 20, 110, 283, 288, 301, 312, 318

Gerry, Elbridge, 29–30, 32–33, 36, 210, 269–70

Ghent, Treaty of, 346, 347

Giles, William Branch, 108–9, 179–80, 280–82

Goodhue, Benjamin, 22

government office. *See* federal government, employees, and officials

grain trade, 157

grand jury, 13, 292–96

Grayson, William, 20, 35

Great Britain: Adams on republican governments, 328; amendments to Constitution/Bill of Rights, 4, 26, 35, 46; American political opinions formed on, 353; Ames's Federalist position, 274; commercial retaliation and discrimination, 88, 90, 91–94, 132, 153–68, 188, 190, 198–200; common law, 249–52; eighteenth and nineteenth centuries, Adams and Jefferson on, 353; foreign affairs and war, control over, 149; foreign trade with, 157, 159–62; France, war with, 141, 307, 311, 317, 321–30; Ghent, Treaty of, 346, 347; Hamilton on Jefferson and Madison's womanish antipathy to, 118–19, 132; impressment of American seamen, 188, 194, 321, 322, 324, 329, 331, 336, 339–42, 347; Judiciary Act of 1801, debates on repeal of, 286, 288; legislative vs. monarchical power, 249, 254; Louisiana Purchase, approval of, 317; national bank, 70, 71, 73, 75, 82; national debt, 50, 55, 65, 67, 127, 286; navigation laws, effect of, 88, 156, 158–59; Orders in Council, 321, 322, 335, 339, 341; seizures of American vessels by, 153–68. *See also* the Embargo, *under "E"*; Jay's Treaty; War of 1812

Great Lakes, 189, 301

Greenleaf, Thomas, 6

habeas corpus, 13, 15, 248, 264, 292

"Hail Columbia," 225

Haiti (St. Domingo), slave revolt in, 307, 308, 311

Hamilton, Alexander: advantages of national bank, notes on, 70–73; anti-Republican government, blamed by Jefferson for, 227; attacked by Madison and Jefferson, 102–8, 115–21, 126–31, 136–38, 227, 270; attacks on Madison and Jefferson, 115–21, 126–31; Carrington, Edward, letter to, 115–20; Constitution, ability of persons to create, 2; constitutionality of national bank, 80–86; death of, 352; defeated by Burr in New York City legislative elections, 262; financial stability and public funding plans, 44; First Report on Public Credit (national debt), 45–49; Jay's Treaty, "Camillus" essays in support of, 197–203; liberty, viewed as danger to, 108, 111, 118, 125, 129–30, 131–32, 135; Louisiana Purchase, 310–13; Re-

port on Manufactures, 94–101, 102, 132; Republican system, support for, 120; Second Report on Public Credit (national bank), 70; seizure of American vessels during French Revolution, 153; state debts, federal assumption of, 64–65, 68; war or neutrality, views on power to declare, 141, 142–45; Washington, letters to, 126–31; Whiskey Rebellion, 169, 173; XYZ affair, letter to Washington regarding, 226–27

Hamilton, Archibald, 296

Hamilton, John C., 153

Hammond, George, 194

Hampden, John, 328

Hancock, John, 10, 133

Hand, General Edward, 125

happiness, 271

Harper, Robert Goodloe, 292, 294–98

Hartford Convention, 342–43, 346

Hartley, Thomas, 36

Hawkesbury, Lord, 317

Hawley, Major, 329

Hemmings, Sally, 292

Henry, Patrick, 19, 20, 35, 66, 68, 110, 329

hereditary classes, 4–5, 24, 103, 111–15, 171, 173, 181, 186–87

History of the Insurrection of the Four Western Counties of Pennsylvania (William Findley), 173

Hogendorp, G. K. van, 89

Holland, 55, 71, 127, 159, 160, 195, 324, 328, 329

Hopkinson, John, 225

House of Representatives: amendments and Bill of Rights, proceedings as to, 21–33; Ames's Federalist position, 274; Chase, Samuel, impeachment of, 293; constituency of representative, 34–35; election of representative, 16–17; Embargo Act of 1807, 325; Federalist loss of seats in, 262; First Report on Public Credit, debates on, 49–64; import and tonnage duties, Madison's proposals regarding, 91–94; Jay's Treaty, debates on, 203–15; Judiciary Act of 1801, proceedings on repeal of, 280–88; Madison's predictions regarding, 20; popular instruction of representatives, 36–38; popular societies, proceedings related to Washington's denunciation of, 179–85; proportionate representation, 11, 14–15; reapportionment and enlargement, 108–9; seizure of American vessels during French Revolution, speeches on, 153–62; titles, debate on, 38–42

Hudson's Bay Company, 189

husbandry. *See* landed property and agricultural interests

immigration to the United States, 67, 96, 231, 234, 267–68. *See also* naturalization of foreigners

impeachment of Samuel Chase. *See* Chase, Samuel, impeachment of impeachment tribunals, amendments to Constitution regarding, 12, 16

implication, doctrine of, 75, 81–82, 310

imports. *See* foreign commerce, imports, and exports

impressment of seamen by foreign powers, 188, 194, 321, 322, 324, 329–31, 336, 339–42, 347

inalienability of certain rights, 7, 10, 13

inaugural addresses: Jefferson's first inaugural address, 263–65; Washington's first inaugural address, 21, 38

Incidents of the Insurrection in the Western Parts of Pennsylvania (Henry Brackenridge), 173

incorporation: national bank, 73–77, 80–86; public roads and canals, companies constructing, 304

Index Expurgatorius, 353

Indians: Ghent, Treaty of, 347; Jefferson's first annual message, 265; Louisiana Purchase, 309, 314, 316, 318; representation and taxation, 343; standing army, 281; War of 1812, 331, 333–34, 338, 339, 340–42, 347; wars with, 281, 314, 331, 333–34, 338, 339, 340–42; Western resentment of federal failure to control, 173

industry. *See* commerce and manufacture

inheritance and descents, 78, 79

innocence, presumption of, 236, 289, 290

Inquisition, 353

inspectors of internal revenue, 266

internal improvements bill (public roads and canals): constitutionality of, 350–51; Gallatin's report, 300–304; Madison's veto, 350–51

interstate commerce clause, 78, 85–86, 90–91, 101, 158, 163, 165, 350

invalids, corps of, 347–48

Ireland, 174, 231

Jackson, Andrew, 346

Jackson, James, 21–22, 29, 32, 36, 40–41, 50–53, 317–19

Jacobins, 170, 172, 226, 273, 275, 276, 314

Jamaica, 162

Jay, John, 153, 188, 189, 197–98. *See also* Jay's Treaty

Jay's Treaty, 153, 188, 273; Boston selectmen, petition of, 193, 198; "Camillus" essays (Alexander Hamilton), 197–203; constitutionality of agreement, 192, 201–15; Dallas's summary of features of, 188–92; embargo prior to, 325; French outrage at, 224; House debates on, 203–15; Madison on, 193–97, 203, 205–7, 210–12; opposition to, 188–97, 203–15; Philadelphia, Memorial of the Citizens of, 192–93; popular societies, 198; support for, 197–215; Virginia General Assembly, Petition to, 193–97; Washington on, 188, 208–9, 212

Jefferson, Thomas: Adams, loss of election to, 224; Adams, reconciliation with, 352–54; Alien and Sedition Acts, Kentucky Resolution regarding, 233–36; attacked by Hamilton, 115–21, 126–31, 126–31; attacks on Hamilton and Federalists, 102, 121–26, 131–36, 227, 270; commerce and manufacture, 88–89, 93–94, 119; commercial retaliation and discrimination, 88, 90, 93–94, 153, 155; domestic policy as president (*see* Jeffersonian domestic policy); Embargo letters, 326–27; foreign policy as president (*see* Jeffersonian foreign policy); France, ambassador to, 88, 92, 118, 121–22; French Revolution, views on, 141, 145, 153, 263, 265, 269; Hemmings, Sally, 292; Johnson, Justice William, letter to, 354–55; Madison's letters to (*see* Jefferson, Thomas, Madison's letters to); national bank, views on, 77–80, 125; national debt, views on, 123–24, 125–26, 132–33; *Notes on the State of Virginia*, 88–89; party politics, 262, 263–64, 270; presidency, desire for, 119, 197; presidency of (*see* Jeffersonian presidency); retirement plans, 121, 134–35; science, progress of, 269; state debts, national assumption of, 64–65, 68; State Department appointment, 44; titles, 94; University of Virginia, 355; Washington, memoranda on conversations with and letters to, 121–26, 131–36; XYZ affair, letter to John Taylor regarding, 227–28

Jefferson, Thomas, Madison's letters to: amendments to Constitution/Bill of Rights, 19–20; commerce and manufacture, 89–90, 92–93; final correspondence, 355; national bank and speculative excess, 86–87; titles, debate on, 41–42

Jeffersonian domestic policy, 262; Ames's attack on, 273–76; first annual message, 265–68, 277; first inaugural address, 263–65; Gallatin's Treasury Report on public roads and canals, 300–304; government officials, removal of, 266–67, 270, 278, 280–81, 286, 314, 315; impeachment of Samuel Chase (*see* Chase, Samuel, impeachment of); Judiciary Act (*see* Judiciary Act of 1801, repeal of); letters from Jefferson outlining, 269–71; Pendleton's Old Republican position versus, 271–73

Jeffersonian foreign policy: the Embargo (*see also* the Embargo, *under* "E"); first annual message, 265–66; first inaugural address, 264; Louisiana Purchase (*see also* Louisiana Purchase); neutrality, 264, 265, 269; War of 1812, 331 (*see also* War of 1812)

Jeffersonian presidency: Ames's attack on, 273–76; desire for presidency, 119, 197; election defeating Adams, 262; first annual message, 265–68, 277; first election, 262; first inaugural address, 263–65; Judiciary Act (*see* Judiciary Act of 1801, repeal of); letters from Jefferson outlining vision of, 269–71; Old Republican opposition to, 271–73, 292; Pickering's attack on, 314. *See also* Jeffersonian domestic policy; Jeffersonian foreign policy

Jeffersonian Republicans. *See* Republicans

Jews, 227

Johnson, William (Justice), 354–55

Johnson, William Samuel (Connecticut delegate), 20

Jones, Merriweather, 314

Jones, Walter, 65–66

judicial power: Alien and Sedition Acts as intruding on, 234, 245, 248, 250, 252; amendments to Constitution regarding, 12, 14, 16; Ames's Federalist position, 276; constitutionality of federal laws, 238, 259; foreign affairs, 142–43; Jefferson's first annual message, 267, 277, 283; Louisiana Purchase, constitutional issues raised by, 310; Pendleton's Old Republican position on appointment of judges, 272; political/partisan opinions, delivery of, 293, 294, 296–99; salaries/compensation of judges, 12, 16; Supreme Court, 12, 14, 16, 277, 279, 280, 283, 352. *See also* separation of powers

Judiciary Act of 1789, 44

Judiciary Act of 1801, repeal of, 267, 277: Chase, Samuel, impeachment of, 297, 298–99; editorials on, 288–91; executive power, 281, 282, 286, 287, 289; expense of extra judges, 279; House proceedings, 280–88; independence of judges, 278, 279, 280, 282, 285, 287–91, 298–99; Jefferson's first annual message, 267, 277, 283; legislative power of judicial establishment and removal, 278, 279, 280, 284–85, 289, 342; number of cases requiring prosecution, 277–78, 279; party politics in enactment and repeal, role of, 277, 280–83, 285–87, 291; Senate proceedings, 277–80; separation of powers, 280, 284–85, 287–88

Julius Caesar, 130, 338, 354

juries: grand jury, 13, 292–96; trial by jury, 10, 12, 13, 234, 239, 264, 267, 273, 292

justice and fairness: Jefferson's first inaugural address, 264; national debt instruments, discrimination between holders of, 59–60, 61, 62, 65, 162

Kentucky, 127, 173, 175, 233–36, 278, 314

Kentucky Gazette and General Advertiser, 315–16

King, Rufus, 117, 197, 313–14, 317

Knights of Loyola, 353

Knox, Henry, 44, 119

Lafayette, Marie Jean Paul Joseph Roche Yves Gilbert du Motier, Marquis de, 352

landed property and agricultural interests: internal commerce and manufacture versus, 88–89, 94–95, 99–100, 105–6; Jefferson on, 264, 270; national debt, 46, 68; sale of public lands, 266–67, 303; surplus, stimulating demand for, 97–98; virtuous nature of agricultural life, 88–89, 90, 105–6

land, redistribution of, 89, 90

Langdon, John, 20

Laurence, John, 58–59

laws, right of recourse to, 10–11

Lee, Henry ("Light Horse Harry"), 66, 68, 169, 173–76

Lee, Richard Bland, 38

Lee, Richard Henry, 3, 20, 35, 42, 64

legislative power: Alien and Sedition Acts, 249, 252; censure of legal actions, 179–87; corruption of legislature by government actions, 125–26, 127–30, 131–33, 136, 172; foreign affairs and power to declare war or neutrality in war, 142–52; Jay's Treaty, constitutionality of agreement, 192, 201–15; Jefferson on, 268, 269; Judiciary Act of 1801, repeal of, 278, 279, 280, 284–85, 289; Louisiana Purchase, constitutional issues raised by, 310; national bank, constitutionality of, 74–75, 79; Pendleton's Old Republican position, 273; veto power of executive, 77, 80, 350–51; war, power to make declarations of, 15, 142–52, 165, 167–68, 172, 334, 343. *See also* Congress; separation of powers

Leopard (vessel), 321

Letters from the Federal Farmer, 3–6

Leyden Gazette, 133

libel, slander, and defamation, 231, 234, 239–41, 257, 292, 296

liberty and freedom, xiii; Ames's Federalist position, 274; Bill of Rights intended to assure, 23, 24–29; charters of liberty, Madison on, 103–4; Chase, Samuel, 298–99; federal power, threat of, 260; French Revolution as war between liberty and despotism, 142, 168; government versus, 6–9, 23, 24–29, 103, 118; Hamilton viewed as danger to, 108, 111, 118, 125, 129–30, 131–32, 135; independent judiciary, 288, 289–91; Pendleton's Old Republican position, 273; popular societies, aims of, 169–73, 180, 183, 186–87; regular government, connection to, 185; Republicans known as friends of liberty, xiii; right of, 6, 10; state debts, federal assumption of, 68. *See also* rights; *specific liberties and freedoms*

"Light Horse Harry" Lee, 66, 68, 169, 173–76

Lincoln, General Benjamin, 326

liquor: taxes and duties on, 15, 92; whiskey excise tax and Whiskey Rebellion, 169, 172, 173–79, 180, 275, 277, 353

Livermore, Samuel, 31–32, 52

Livingston, Robert R., 188, 212, 307–309, 315

loans, public. *See* national debt

Locke, Edmund, 136, 147

Lombardy, 353

Louisiana Purchase, 307; constitutional issues raised by, 307, 309–10, 313, 316, 320; Federalists on, 307, 310–14; Hamilton on, 310–13; history and geography of, 311–12; Indians, 309, 314, 316, 318; Jefferson's letters on, 307–10; monetary value, 307, 312; payment for, bill allowing, 316–20; public roads and canals, 302, 303; Republicans on, 315–16; Senate debates, 307, 316–20; settlement of territory, concerns regarding, 309, 310, 312, 314, 316–20; West Florida, 307

Louis XVI, execution of, 141

loyalist claims against the states, 188, 190

policies believed by Jefferson to undermine, 122; eighteenth and nineteenth centuries, Adams and Jefferson on, 353; excise taxes as leading to corruption of, 172; necessity for political prosperity, 219; speculative excess, 86–87, 127–28

Morris, Robert, 20, 65, 278–79

mortmain, 77, 79

most-favored-nation status, 188, 191

Napoléon, 307, 311, 321, 328, 331

national bank, 44, 70, 102, 114, 162; constitutionality of, 70, 73–86, 210; duration of charter, 71, 72, 73; Hamilton's notes on advantages of, 70–73; Hamilton's opinion as to constitutionality of, 80–86; Hamilton to Edward Carrington on Madison and Jefferson's views on, 118, 119; Jefferson's views on, 77–80, 125; legislators as holders of private stock in, 128–29; location of, 71–72, 73; Madison's speech on bank bill, 73–77; national debt, 72, 73; speculative excess, Madison's letter to Jefferson on, 86–87; uniform national currency, 347

national debt, 44; advantages of, 45–46; Ames's Federalist position, 274; borrowing money, government power of, 15, 74, 78, 85, 86; Congressional Report on Alien and Sedition Acts, 242–43; constitutionality of, 109; corruption of legislature by, 125–26, 127–30, 131–33, 136, 172; discrimination between original holders and present possessors, 46–48, 52–64; European system, 50, 66; excise law and taxes, 66, 68, 126, 127; foreign creditors, 46, 50, 52, 62, 63; Great Britain, 50, 55, 65, 67, 127; Hamilton's defense to Washington of, 126–30; Hamilton's First Report on Public Credit, 45–49; Hamilton's letter to Edward Carrington on Madison and Jefferson's views on, 116–19; House debates on First Report on Public Credit, 49–64; Jefferson's views on, 123–24, 125–26, 132–33, 264, 266, 267, 271; Judiciary Act of 1801, 281, 282, 285, 286–87; Louisiana Purchase, 314; Madison's seventh annual message, 347; national bank, 72, 73; opposition outside Congress to funding plans, 65–69; Pendleton's Old Republican position, 273; public opinion as to, 181; republican attacks on, 108–9, 110–11, 112–14, 162–63; sinking fund, 51–52; states, national assumption of unpaid debts of, 44, 48–51, 64–65, 126–27, 181; surplus replacing, plan for public roads and canals, 300–304; Washington's Farewell Address, 219

National Gazette: Freneau's "Rules for Changing a Limited Republican Government into an Unlimited Hereditary One," 111–15; Hamilton's attack on, 115, 117, 118, 131; Jefferson's defense of, 125, 132–34; Madison's essays, 102–8, 136–38

National Intelligencer, 291, 321–23

national newspapers, 86, 102, 120–21, 133. *See also Gazette of the United States; National Gazette*

national songs, 226–27

Native Americans. *See* Indians

naturalization of foreigners: Hartford Convention, 342, 343; Jefferson's first annual message regarding, 267–68; Naturalization Act, 231; War of 1812 and expatriation of naturalized foreigners, 336–37, 340

natural rights. *See* rights

naval law. *See* admiralty and maritime law

navigation: canals and roads, public, 300–304, 350–51; commercial (*see* commerce and manufacture); laws of (*see* admiralty and maritime law)

navy, 242–43, 267, 281, 282, 325, 330, 348

Nelson, Horatio, Admiral Lord, 321

Netherlands, 55, 71, 127, 159, 160, 195, 324, 328, 329

neutrality: French Revolution, 141–52; Jay's Treaty, 188, 190–91, 195; Jeffersonian foreign policy, 264, 265, 269; War of 1812, 331, 332, 335. *See also* the Embargo, *under "E"*

Neville, John, 173, 175, 177

Newark Gazette, 171–72

Newark (New Jersey), Republican Society of, 171–72

New Hampshire, 20, 238, 283, 288, 341

New Jersey, 19, 20, 127, 169, 178, 288, 314, 328

New Orleans. *See* Louisiana Purchase

New Orleans, battle of, 346

newspapers, national, 86, 102, 120–21, 133. *See also Gazette of the United States; National Gazette*

Newton, Isaac, 136

New York *Argus,* 188, 197, 232

New York Daily Gazette, 169

New York *Herald,* 197

New York Journal, 169

New York (state): constitutional amendments and ratifications, 2, 3, 6, 12–17, 18; demagogy in, 274; elections of 1800, 262; the Embargo, 328; Judiciary Act of 1801, repeal of, 288; Louisiana Purchase, 314; national debt, 127; public roads and canals, 300; seizure of American vessels, 158

New York Times, 232

Nicholas, Wilson Cary, 180–81, 310

Nicholson, Joseph, 285–88, 292, 295, 297, 298

nineteenth vs. eighteenth century, Adams and Jefferson on, 353

nobility and aristocracy, 4–5, 24, 103, 111–15, 171, 173, 181, 186–87

North Carolina, 2, 18, 23, 35, 110, 173, 210–11, 227, 288, 301

north vs. south: amendment of Constitution, 19; commerce and manufacture, 91, 100–101; Federalist vs. Republican viewpoints, 110–11, 113, 124, 136; national debt, 66; Washington's Farewell Address, 216–17; XYZ affair, 227–28. *See also* union/disunion

Notes on the State of Virginia (Thomas Jefferson), 88–89

nullification (constitutionality of federal laws, state power to determine), 233, 235, 238, 259, 284, 328, 329

Ohio River, 301
Old Republicans, 271–73, 292
old republics of Europe, death of, 228
order: Adams, John, 352–53; Ames's Federalist position on, 273–76; Chase, Samuel, 298–99; Federalists known as friends of order, xiii; Jefferson's first inaugural address, 264; terrorism, 353
Orders in Council, 321, 322, 335, 339, 341
Otis, Harrison Gray, 225

"Pacificus" articles, *Gazette of the United States*, 142–45
Page, John, 24, 36, 38, 41
Paine, Thomas, 102, 131, 134
Palladium, 273
paper money, 70, 71, 73, 122, 123, 179. *See also* currency
paper speculation. *See* stock
Paris, Treaty of, 311
Parker, Josiah, 38, 40
party politics: Adams on intemperance of, 329; Chase, Samuel, impeachment of, 293, 294, 296–99; division of American political leaders into parties, xiii, 44, 102, 120–21, 123–24; French Revolution, position on, 141; Jay's Treaty, 190, 197; Jefferson on, 263–64, 354–55; Johnson, Justice William, composing history of, 354; Judiciary Act of 1801, enactment and repeal of, 277, 280–83, 285–87, 291; Louisiana Purchase, 315; Madison on, 104, 137–38; opposition party, Ames on existence of, 111; War of 1812, effect on parties of, 346; Washington's Farewell Address, 215, 217–19. *See also* Federalists; Republicans
patents, 227
patriotic societies. *See* popular societies
patriotism: Alien and Sedition Acts, opposition to, 260; Chase, Samuel, 299; the Embargo, 321, 326; independent judiciary, 288, 291; Jay's Treaty, 188–92, 217, 219; Jefferson's first inaugural address, 263–64; Louisiana Purchase, 318; popular societies, views on, 170, 172, 186–87; XYZ affair and, 224, 225, 226, 228–30
patronage, doctrine of, 280–81, 286, 342
Paterson, William, 20
pay. *See* salaries
peace, American love of, 340, 347
Peace of Amiens, 321
Pendleton, Edmund, 271–73
Pennsylvania: Constitution, amendment and ratification of, 18, 19, 20; the Embargo, 328; Federalist vs. Republican principles, 274, 275; Jay's Treaty, 210; Judiciary Act of 1801, repeal of, 277, 288, 291; national debt, 127; Pittsburgh, 173, 175; popular societies, 169–70, 172, 178; whiskey excise tax and Whiskey Rebellion, 169, 172, 173–79, 180, 275, 277, 353; XYZ affair, 225–30. *See also* Philadelphia

people, power invested in and derived from, xiii; amendments to Constitution/Bill of Rights, 10, 13, 16; common good, government instituted for, 6, 10, 289–90; government power turned on the people, 289–90; Jefferson's first inaugural address, 264; legislature, censure by, 179, 184; Madison in *National Gazette* on, 104, 137–38; national bank, constitutionality of, 78, 81, 83; Pendleton's Old Republican position, 271–73; popular instruction of representatives, 36–38, 329; popular societies, aims of, 169, 182, 184, 187; regular government, support of, 185; retention of rights not expressly delegated, 78, 81, 83, 184, 235, 328; separation of powers, 104, 105
Philadelphia: Adams's Fast Day (1799), 353; *Aurora*, 232, 271; Democratic Society of Pennsylvania (Philadelphia), 169–70, 172, 186–87; *General Advertiser*, 141–42, 232; Jay's Treaty, Memorial of the Citizens of Philadelphia regarding, 192–93; XYZ affair, 225–30
"Phocion," 315–16
Pickering, Timothy, 313–14, 321, 323–25
Pinckney, Charles C., 135, 164, 224
Pintard, Lewis, 133
piracy, 164, 233, 240, 265–66, 267, 281
Pitkin, Timothy, 341
Pittsburgh, 173, 175
Pitt, William, 166
Poland, 353
political intolerance, 263
political parties. *See* party politics
poll (capitation) tax, 15
Pope, John, 327
popular self-governance. *See* people, power invested in and derived from
popular societies: condemnations and defenses of, 169–73, 174–86; Democratic Society of Pennsylvania (Philadelphia), 169–70, 172, 186–87; Democratic Society of Wythe County, Virginia, 171–72; House of Representatives proceedings, 179–85; Jay's Treaty, 198; Madison's defense of, 169, 179, 183–86; Republican Society of Newark (New Jersey), 171–72; Washington's condemnation of, 169, 174–79; whiskey excise tax resistance and Whiskey Rebellion, connected to, 172, 177, 184, 185, 186
populousness of country, 89–90, 92, 300, 314, 349
Portugal, 159, 160
post office, 44, 49, 121, 287
power and authority: despotic governments, 3, 24, 103, 142, 187, 236, 263, 264, 296, 298; government's tendency to take on, 6–9, 23, 24–29, 103, 288, 289–90. *See also* executive power; judicial power; legislative power; people, power invested in and derived from; separation of powers
presidency: citizenship requirements, 15, 343; commander in chief, 148, 167, 178; election of, 14; Jay's Treaty, constitution-

ality of, 192, 201–15; Jefferson's desire for, 119; Madison's predictions regarding, 19; term limits, 12; titles, House of Representatives debate on, 38–42; veto power, 77, 80, 350–51. *See also* executive power; *individual presidents*

"President's March" (song), 225

press, freedom of: Adams on unbounded license of presses, 329; Alien and Sedition Acts, 231, 234, 239–41, 243, 253–60; Chase, Samuel, impeachment of, 293–96; constitutional amendment, ratification, and Bill of Rights, 11, 13, 30, 36; Jefferson on, 264, 269; Judiciary Act of 1801, debates on repeal of, 287; popular societies, 172, 187

private interest in place of public duty, 125–26, 127–30, 131–33, 136

private juntos or factions, fear of, 4–6

professional classes, 106

property: Ames, Fisher, 110, 111; Madison on, 107–8; public lands and property, 15, 266–67, 303; redistribution of land, 89, 90. *See also* landed property and agricultural interests

the Prophet, 331

Prussia, 353

publication of government proceedings, 11, 15

public debt. *See* national debt

public emoluments or privileges, entitlement to, 10, 109, 278, 280–81, 286

public lands and property: legislation regarding, 15; sale of public lands, 266–67, 303

public office. *See* federal government

Publicola, 134

public opinion and governmental power. *See* people, power invested in and derived from

public roads and canals. *See* internal improvements bill

Pym, John, 328

Quakers, 66, 353

quasi-war with France. *See* XYZ affair

Randolph, Beverley (Governor of Virginia), 19

Randolph, Edmund, 44

Randolph, John, 292–95

Reed, George, 20

Reflections on the Revolution in France (Edmund Burke), 102

religion, freedom of: Alien and Sedition Acts, 107, 233, 234, 240, 241; arms, exemption to bearing, 11; constitutional amendments and Bill of Rights, 11, 13, 30, 36; Jefferson on, 263, 269, 353; Madison on property rights and, 107; political prosperity, necessity of religion to, 219; separation of church and state, 11

representative government: adequacy of number of representatives, 3–6, 34–35; Indians, 343; Jefferson on spread of idea of, 353–54; slaves, counting, 314, 343

Representatives. *See* House of Representatives

Republicans: Adams, John, 329; Ames, Fisher, 109–10, 273–76; characterization by Madison, 137–38; commerce and manufacture, 89–92; commercial retaliation and discrimination, 89–92, 153, 162–68, 198–200; consolidation of states into one government, 102; Constitution, 5; the Embargo, 321; Freneau's "Rules for Changing a Limited Republican Government into an Unlimited Hereditary One," 111–15; friends of liberty, known as, xiii; Giles on reapportionment and enlargement of House, 108–9; Hamilton blamed by Jefferson for losses of, 227; Hamilton on, 115; Hartford Convention opposing practices of, 342–43; immigrant vote, 231; Jay's Treaty, opposition to, 188; Jefferson on, 115, 120–21, 123–24, 263–64, 270, 354–55; Louisiana Purchase, 315–16; *National Gazette* essays, 102–8; Old Republicans, 271–73, 292; popular societies, defense of, 169; seizure of American vessels, 153, 162–68; self-characterization of, 123–24, 137–38; war, accused of desiring, 164–68; War of 1812, effect on party of, 346; Whiskey Rebellion, condemnation of, 169; XYZ affair, 224. *See also* anti-Federalists; Jefferson, Thomas; Madison, James

republican societies. *See* popular societies

republican system, Hamilton's support for, 120

retaliation, commercial, 88, 90, 91–94, 132, 153–68, 188, 190, 198–200

revenue. *See* economic policies; taxes and taxation

Rhode Island, 2, 6, 18, 35, 237–38, 288

Richmond *Examiner,* 271

rights: anti-Federalist fears regarding failure of Constitution to express, 6–9; Chase, Samuel, impeachment of, 296, 298–99; government authority and surrender of, 6–9, 23, 24–29, 103, 118; inalienability, 7, 10, 13; popular societies, aims of, 169, 187. *See also* Bill of Rights; states' rights

The Rights of Man (Thomas Paine), 102, 131

Rittenhouse, William, 134

roads and canals, public. *See* internal improvements bill

Robespierre, Maximilien-François-Marie-Isidore de, 328

Rochefaucault, François, 352

Rodney, Caesar, 292, 295, 296

Roman Catholic Church, 353

Rome and Roman law, 4, 82

"Rossina," 225

Rush, Dr. Benjamin, 65, 67, 328–29, 352

Russia, 159

sailors. *See* seamen

St. Clair, General Arthur, 184

tional bank, 78, 84; nullification (constitutionality of federal laws, state power to determine), 233, 235, 238, 259, 284, 328, 329; Pendleton's Old Republican position, 272, 273; retention of rights not expressly delegated, 78, 81, 83, 184, 235, 328

St. Clair, General Arthur, 184

St. Domingo (Haiti), slave revolt in, 307, 308, 311

Sterett, Lieutenant Andrew, 265

St. Lawrence River, 301

stock: morality and virtue, effect on, 86–87, 127–28; national bank (*see* national bank); public debt instruments (*see* national debt); public roads and canals, 304; speculative excess, Madison's letter to Jefferson on, 86–87

Stone, Michael Jenifer, 37

Strong, Caleb, 20

Sullivan, James, 323, 327

Supreme Court, 12, 14, 16, 277, 279, 280, 283, 352

surplus revenue, plan for use of, 300–304

suspension of laws, 10, 13

Sweden, 160

Switzerland, 328

Talleyrand[-Périgord], Charles-Maurice de, 307

taxes and taxation: amendments to Constitution/Bill of Rights, 11, 14, 15; constitutional power to lay and collect excises, 175; Freneau's "Rules for Changing a Limited Republican Government into an Unlimited Hereditary One," 113, 114; Great Britain, 162; Hartford Convention, 342, 343; interstate commerce clause, 101; Jefferson's first annual message, 266; Judiciary Act of 1801, debates on repeal of, 281, 285, 286, 287; national bank, 70, 74, 75, 78, 79, 85, 86; national debt, 66, 68, 126, 127; property rights, 108; slaves counted for purposes of, 314, 343; whiskey excise (*see* whiskey excise tax and Whiskey Rebellion)

Taylor, John, 227–28, 233, 292

technological development, 96–97

Tecumseh, 331

Tennessee, 278

term limits and terms of office, 12, 14, 15, 273

terrorism, 353

thought, freedom of. *See* speech and thought, freedom of

titles: Freneau's "Rules for Changing a Limited Republican Government into an Unlimited Hereditary One," 112; House of Representatives debate on, 38–42; Jefferson on, 94

tobacco trade, 157

Tories, 130, 170, 171

Tracy, Elisha, 180, 279–80, 327

trade. *See* commerce and manufacture

Trafalgar, battle of, 321

transportation over public roads and canals, 300–304, 350–51

treason, 16, 169, 233, 240, 292

Treasury Department, 44, 119, 122, 131

treaties: French treaty of alliance of 1778, 141; Ghent, Treaty of, 346, 347; Jay's Treaty (*see* Jay's Treaty); Jefferson on avoidance of, 269; Madrid, Treaty of, 307; Paris, Treaty of, 311; Senate participation in making of, 144, 146; Spain, treaty with, 217

trial by jury, 10, 12, 13, 234, 239, 264, 267, 273, 292

tribunes, Rome, 4

tri-colored cockades, 226

Tripoli, 265–66, 267

Trumbell, Jonathan, Jr., 39

Tucker, Thomas Tudor, 36, 38–39

Turberville, George Lee, 67

Turgot, Anne-Robert-Jacques, 352

union/disunion: Alien and Sedition Acts, 233, 235, 236, 237, 260; the Embargo, 327, 328–29; Federalist vs. Republican viewpoints, 111; Hartford Convention, 342–43; Jefferson's first inaugural address, 263–64; Louisiana Purchase, 314; national debt, 66; Pendleton's Old Republican position, 272; Washington's Farewell Address, 216–17; XYZ affair, 227–28. *See also* north vs. south

unitary or consolidated central government, concerns regarding, 3–6, 102–3, 247

United Kingdom. *See* Great Britain

United Netherlands, 55, 71, 127, 159, 160, 195, 324, 328, 329

universal suffrage, 297–99

University of Virginia, 355

unreasonable searches and seizures, 11, 13–14

van Hogendorp, G. K., 89

Varnum, J. B., 329

Vattel, Emmerich de, 146

Venice, 328

Vermont, 288, 341

veterans of American Revolution, 286

veto power, 77, 80, 350–51

vice president: Adams, John, 19–20, 111, 131; Burr, Aaron, 262; citizenship requirements, 15; election of, 14; Madison's predictions regarding, 19–20

Virginia: Alien and Sedition Acts, resolution regarding, 236–37, 243–60; Ames's Federalist position, 274; Bill of Rights, 273; Chase, Samuel, impeachment of, 296; Constitution, amendments, and Bill of Rights, 2, 10–12, 18, 20, 21; disunion, talk of, 227–28; foreign commerce, regulation of, 158, 163, 165, 210, 211; grand jury, 292; Hamilton's suggestion that Washington make a circuit through, 227; judiciary, 288, 291; national assumption of state debts, 68–69; national debt, excise law regarding, 127; New York, influence over, 314; *Notes on the State of Virginia* (Thomas Jefferson), 88–89;

pride of, 110; Report of 1800, 243–60; Richmond *Examiner,* 271; Whiskey Rebellion, militia sent against, 169, 174, 178

virtue. *See* morality and virtue

wages. *See* salaries

war: Alien Enemies Act, 231; American Revolution, fundamental principles of, 249–50; declarations of, power to make, 15, 142–52, 165, 167–68, 172, 334, 343; the Embargo, effect of, 321–30; French Revolution (*see* French Revolution); Indian wars, 281, 314, 331, 333–34, 338, 339, 340–42; Jay's Treaty as means of avoiding, 198–200; Jefferson on, 265, 266, 269–70; neutrality (*see* neutrality); peace, American love of, 340, 347; Pendleton's Old Republican position, 272; Republicans accused of desiring, 164–68, 198–200; Shays's Rebellion, 110, 276, 352, 353; War of 1812 (*see* War of 1812); Whiskey Rebellion, 169, 172, 173–79, 180, 254, 275, 277. *See also* military; militia

War Department, 44, 122, 131

War of 1812, 331, 346; Adams's prediction of, 329–30; Canada, 337–38, 340–41; Clay's speech supporting war, 338–42; commerce, interference with, 332–33, 334, 337, 339, 341, 342, 343; the Embargo and, 331; expatriation of naturalized foreigners, 336–37, 340; Federalists, 334; France, 331, 333, 334, 335, 339; Ghent, Treaty of, 346, 347; Hartford Convention on grievances regarding, 342–43, 346; impressment of seamen by foreign powers, 331, 336, 339–42; Indians, 331, 333–34, 338, 339, 340–42; Madison's war message to Congress, 331–34; Orders in Council, 321, 322, 335, 339, 341; Taggart's speech opposing war, 334–38

Washington Federalist, 288–91

Washington, George: additional term, urged to serve, 121, 124–25; administration divided under, 121–38; constitutional amendment, ratification, and Bill of Rights, 18–19, 21, 38, 42; Farewell Address, 215–21; first address to first session of first federal Congress, 2; first inaugural address, 21, 38; French neutrality, 141; Hamilton's letters to, 126–31; Jay's Treaty, 188, 208–9, 212; Jefferson's first inaugural address, 264; Jefferson's memoranda on conversations with and letters to, 121–26, 131–36; Knox, opinion of, 119; Madison's letters to, 18–19; national bank, 70, 77, 86; popular societies, condemnation of, 169; records and documents of, Jefferson on value to be found in, 354; seizure of American vessels, 153; titles, 38, 42; veneration of, 110, 167–68, 181, 183, 184, 185, 215, 227, 281; Whiskey Rebellion, proclamations on, 169, 173, 175, 176–79; XYZ affair, letter from Hamilton regarding, 226–27

wealth, distribution of, 108–9

Wealth of Nations (Adam Smith), 73

Webster, Noah, 34–35, 197

Wells, William Hill, 317

West and East Floridas, 307, 309, 312, 318

western expedition, 119

western posts of Great Britain, 188, 189, 200

Western Territory, 51, 84, 173, 175, 217

West Indies trade: commercial retaliation and discrimination, 88, 91, 92, 93; the Embargo, 321; Great Britain's legislative power over, 104; Jay's Treaty, 88, 189, 190, 196; Louisiana Purchase, 308; neutrality in French Revolution, 141; seizure of American vessels by Great Britain, 153–68; War of 1812, 341

Whigs, 130, 170

whiskey excise tax and Whiskey Rebellion, 169, 172, 173–79, 180, 275, 277, 353

White, Alexander, 23, 64

White, Samuel, 316–17, 318

Winder, William H., 296–97

Wolfius, 146

Wythe County, Virginia, Democratic Society of, 171–72

XYZ affair, 224; Congressional Report on Alien and Sedition Acts, 241–243; Judiciary Act of 1801, repeal of, 281; letters regarding, 225–28; presidential addresses regarding, 226, 228–30

"Yankee Doodle," 225

Yates, Robert, 6

yellow fever, 353

youth, addresses from and to, 229–30